ISBN 978-1-330-24821-8
PIBN 10000368

Forgotten Books is a registered trademark of FB &c Ltd.
Copyright © 2017 FB &c Ltd.
FB &c Ltd, Dalton House, 60 Windsor Avenue, London, SW19 2RR.
Company number 08720141. Registered in England and Wales.

For support please visit www.forgottenbooks.com

ANCIENT EGYPT

and The East

1920.–1923   PART I.

CONTENTS.

EDITOR, PROF. FLINDERS PETRIE, F.R.S., F.B.A.

395524

5. 8. 41

YEARLY, 7s. POST FREE.   QUARTERLY PART, 2s.

MACMILLAN AND CO.,
LONDON AND NEW YORK;
AND
EGYPTIAN RESEARCH ACCOUNT,
BOSTON.

ANCIENT EGYPT.   Net price of each number from booksellers is 2s.

Subscriptions for the four quarterly parts, prepaid, post free, 7s., are received by Hon. Sec. "Ancient Egypt" (H. Flinders Petrie), University College, Gower Street, London, W.C. 1.

Books for review, papers offered for insertion, or news, should be addressed:—
Editor of "Ancient Egypt,"
University College, Gower Street, London, W.C. 1.

Subscriptions, received in the United States by:—
Rev. Dr. Winslow, 525, Beacon Street, Boston.

PL. I. GOLD NECKLET ABOUT A.D. 540. SCALE 1/2.

ANCIENT EGYPT.

THE RETURN TO RESEARCH.

At last it is justifiable again for writers to meet their friends in these pages. Our perils as a nation are by no means over, but they do not need to be met by every kind of energy that was required two years ago, to save our civilisation from the flood of destruction. Great have been the changes since the peace of the world was broken. In Egypt the main actors are gone : Sir Gaston Maspero, his son Jean Maspero, the indefatigable Legrain, worn out prematurely, and the ever-useful Barsanti. With the passing of these the face of affairs is changed. On the English side other losses are felt : Sir Armand Ruffer, Horace Thompson, James Dixon, and K. T. Frost, were all victims of the war, to the loss of Egyptology ; and at home the early death of Prof. Leonard King has left history and archaeology crippled.

The necessary inspection of sites in Syria and Palestine was carried out by two former workers of the British School in Egypt, Capt. Mackay and Capt. Engelbach, under the orders of Field-Marshal Sir Edmund Allenby. This was the first step towards preservation, and their reports give details of the work and restrictions necessary on each site.

The latest School of Archaeology is that for Jerusalem, founded by a joint committee of the Palestine Exploration Fund and the British Academy. Prof. Garstang has actively organised it, Capt. Mackay will be Chief Inspector of Sites, and probably another of our former excavators will be Librarian and Registrar.

The British School in Egypt, with a large staff, hopes to have as full a season of excavation as in the past. In the United States a new basis of work has been started as the Oriental Institute of the University of Chicago, under the efficient management of Prof. Breasted. In his recent address he takes his stand on the importance of all kinds of evidence for history, and places philology in its true position as an interpreter of some evidence of historic times, but only thus touching a brief part of man's past. The whole evidences of the past are to be the care of the new Oriental Institute, which thus comes in line with what has always been the system of the British School in Egypt.

With much regret it is found that the present costs of production, being about doubled, must make some difference to the issue of this Journal. At the present time it is unreasonable to expect anyone to pay more to meet the cost, and therefore some reduction in pages and illustration is necessary. So soon as our readers will expand the circulation to its former extent, the previous scale of issue will be resumed. The summarising of what has been published abroad during the war is the prime requirement to place readers in touch with present conditions. The reviews will therefore be fully carried on in this and following numbers.

NILE BOATS AND OTHER MATTERS.

WE have been told many times how unchanging is the East, and undoubtedly at the root of things there is but little change ; but the statement must be taken with considerable reserve. In many directions things go on in Egypt even as they did in the times of the Pharaohs, in others fresh fashions are eagerly sought after, fresh methods succeed one another with considerable rapidity.

We have but to compare the appearance of Cairo to-day, with its aspect as shown to us in the drawings of David Roberts, Prisse d'Avennes, and others, to see that, except in the eastern quarters of the city where some of the older streets are yet untouched, the changes are radical.

Glass windows have chased away the beautiful Mushrabiya; the picturesque open shop front is dying in all directions ; nor does the change stop here.

The old style of costume so pleasant to see, so well suited to the climate, so easy to keep clean, has almost disappeared. The Egyptian of all classes is now ashamed to admit that he belongs to this wonderful old country ; he will not appear in the old style ; he must ape the ugly, inconvenient and dirty European coat, trousers, starched collars and uncomfortable hat.

The changes have of late become so rapid, that photographs of street scenes taken but twenty years since, show a crowd quite differently dressed from that which we see to-day.

To give some particulars of changes in the region of fashion and clothes. Within the last twenty-four years I have observed considerable variation to take place in, for example, the material of which the qallabiah, the universal garb of the fellaheen must be made. This convenient and comely garment, of cotton, was usually dyed either of a light blue tint or of a blue so dark as to pass for black. The native term for the light blue tint is "labany." "Laban" is the Arabic for milk. We may suppose that the Egyptian saw in the colour of the blue dye something suggesting the colour of milk, but I venture on this speculation not without fear.

The cotton was usually dyed locally. It took but a few months to make a change. That mean looking stuff glazed calico was introduced ; in this material all new qallabiahs must be made: the shining surface, which soon wore off, immensely pleasing the purchaser.

In the course of a few years there came another change, which spread through the country as quickly as the preceding had done.

Although the shape of the garment was retained, fashion decreed that the stuff of which it must be made must be of a material so " dressed " on its surface as, when it was new, to look not unlike silk.

Head-gear also underwent a variation. The soft and charming white of the turban ('*Emma*) was voted old fashioned, next time it was washed its colour was sadly changed by an overdose of " washing blue " ; indeed all white garments were, and are, spoiled by this nasty stuff. Another thing. It is the mark of distinction in these days to wear boots or shoes, no matter how burst, split or disreputable they may be. Socks, or the relics of them, are very essential to a complete effect.

Cast-off European clothes have had a deplorable influence, especially since the war began. The King's livery is everywhere dragged in the mire.

Egypt does not possess a long list of native musical instruments, but the list has now been increased by one. The Scotch bagpipes have been enthusiastically welcomed by the native population, and are on sale in Cairo.

We now come to sailing boats, especially those of small size.

The old latine rig is passing away ; the lugger takes its place ; just as many years since the latine sail displaced the horizontal yard and square sail.

Before we touch upon the build of the boats we may be permitted to say a few words on the rig.

There is not any need in this Journal to do more than refer to the numerous sculptured representations and models of ancient Nile boats, which show us the square sail stretched between upper and lower horizontal yards.

At what period did this type of sail disappear ?

The earliest observation which I have been able to find, by a European writer, relating to types of rig, is by De Lannoy. *A Survey of Egypt and Syria undertaken in the Year 1422 by Sir Gilbert de Lannoy, Knt., from a manuscript in the Bodleian Library at Oxford*, by the Rev. John Webb, M.A., F.S.A. (*Archaeologia*, XXI, 281)

De Lannoy states :—

" Item. Y'a sur ceste rivière tout du pay's du soudan une si tres grosse quantité de barkes alaut de lun a lautre en marchandise qui s'appellent germes[1] les aucunes et le plus avoiles latine et les autres voiles quares."

Perhaps some reader of this paper may know of a writer more ancient than de Lannoy from whom we may gather some statement about the rig of boats on the Nile, but it is the habit of most travellers to leave such details out of account, overlooking the fact that what is commonplace to-day, becomes more or less of ancient history in a very few years.

My search has been for illustrated books, as in them I felt I should find my best chance of information. The earliest book I have met with is Pocock— *A Description of the East and some other Countries.* Vol. the first. " Observations on Egypt," by Richard Pocock, LL.D., F.R.S. London, 1743."

On Pl. VIII is a representation of a boat with three masts, the mainmast a little the tallest. Across this, part of the way up, swings a yard. From the way it is canted one may suppose that the yard carried a triangular and not a square sail. The other masts are without yards or indications of sails.

Pocock does not give any other representation of a boat.

On p. 69 he tells us as follows : " The large boats called marshes, such as we embarked on, have a mast about the middle, and another towards the prow." We are not much the wiser for this as he tells us nothing about the sails. The next book I know of is by Norden, a Dane, who was sent out by the French Government in 1737. He died at Paris in 1742.

---

[1] This name for a cargo boat was in use in the time of Curzon, 1838. See *Monasteries of the Levant,* p. 18, 3rd Edition, 1850.

The book (I quote from the second edition, Paris, Didot, 1795, in three volumes) is well supplied with engraved views, in which the Nile is frequently depicted with many boats thereon. There is always difficulty in estimating the value of the evidence given by engraved plates. In many, if not most, cases the travellers knew but little how to draw ; this is notably the case with regard to Pocock. The traveller had, at any rate, seen the objects. The engraver, on the other hand, had no knowledge whatever of the original ; but he did his best to " invest with artistic merit " the clumsy handiwork of the author.

Scenes in Egypt were tricked out with European adornments. Uncertain indeed may be the value, as evidence, of an engraving that has been thus produced, and yet it may be better than nothing or than the foggy smears which are now so usually printed as photographs.

In the case of the engravings in Norden's book we find the Nile dotted with boats of an extremely European rig. Many boats carry the latine sails, but on the same plates, as for example Pls. XXXVI, LII, LIII, LXXII, etc., we find boats of a considerable size with a very tall mainmast carrying two square sails, one above the other, on horizontal yards ; a mizenmast with one square sail and a bowsprit with a horizontal yard and a sail on it. As we look through the plates we come to that numbered CXXXVI—a view of Philae (also called Heiff). On this plate we see the horizontal yard and square sail, also the horizontal yard on the bowsprit. It seems very improbable that a boat with such a heavy top rig was hauled, standing, up the cataract. All further plates of places in Nubia south of Philae show boats with latine sails.

· Are we to conclude from what is above stated that there were square rigged boats in use on the Nile and at a date as late as Norden so far up the river as the First Cataract, or may we assume that the engraver had enlivened Norden's drawings with a marine type of square rigged boat which was not really to be seen in Egypt ?

In 1780 C. S. Sonnini brought to a conclusion certain travels in Egypt which he undertook at the instance of the French Government. An illustrated translation of his travels was published in England in 1800. Boats are to be seen in several of the engravings in this book, always with latine sails.

Then follows Denou, who accompanied the French expedition, and published a book of travels. This was issued several years before the monumental *Description de l'Égypte* appeared. Denon was a draughtsman by no means dependent on the engraver. Not a single horizontal yard is seen in the engravings in his book. This type of yard seems completely to have disappeared by the year 1798, the date at which, with the years 1799 and 1800, the materials for the *Description de l'Égypte* were being collected by the French savants.

It is easy to observe that in many engravings in this great work some very indifferent drawings have been largely " made up " by the engravers, but however that may be, square rigged boats are not represented.

If we consult Gau (published in 1822), a book in which are beautiful and scrupulously careful engravings, evidently prepared under the author's eye from admirable drawings, very few boats are seen, none of them square rigged.

Few men were more observant than Edward William Lane, who in the year 1826 ascended the Nile to the Second Cataract, and afterwards published that delightful book *Manners and Customs of the Modern Egyptians.* In Chapter XIV, " Industries," he refers to the navigation of the Nile, and tells us that the boats have two large triangular sails.

Many of Lane's drawings are preserved at the British Museum, amongst them those made during his voyage up the Nile. I admit that I have not studied them with a view to the methods of rigging boats, but am disposed to believe that had there been horizontal yards depicted, my attention would have been arrested.

On the exterior of the little temple of Rameses II which lies in the desert east of the great walls at El-Kab may be seen, perfectly well-preserved, incised drawings of boats with horizontal yards.

I am not able to recall any other place where I have found this type of rig depicted as a mere rough drawing. It is evidently an ancient piece of work. Scratchings of boats with latine rig are sufficiently common, but they are undoubtedly more modern than the drawing first described.

Mr. Quibell tells me that at the monastery of S. Jeremias at Saqqara he found a rude painting of a ship with three masts and horizontal yards. This painting he attributes to the sixth century A.D.

Sir Gardiner Wilkinson gives a drawing of a sailing boat which he names " cangia." This was evidently a near relation to the dahabeah of to-day with its latine rig.[1]

I am much indebted to my friend Mr. G. Walter Grabham, of the Sudan Geological Service, for notes he has collected during his extensive travels on the Blue and White Niles,—notes as careful as they are accurate, and relating to the types and names of the types of boats he has found in these distant places. Of the " gyassa," which we see so commonly on the Nile as far as Halfa, built with ribs and planked, he says : " Of this type of Egyptian cargo boat few are seen higher up the river than Berber, most of them apparently belong to the Government. The type is essentially exotic." It is probable that these boats are the relics of the Gordon expedition, 1884.

He then speaks of the ' naggr,' the common type of native-built boat, ribless and with a width of beam often approximating to half its length. The bottom curved, the sides continuing the same curve. These boats range in size from small feluccas to large craft, such as can carry 500 ardebs.

" The naggr type of boat was evidently in use in the times of the old Government, as shown by pictures in the later books of travel, but I have been unable to find pictures or descriptions of any boats in the early books at my disposal. With the establishment of the Egyptian *régime* the need for river carriage must have increased, and we know that travellers and goods generally came by boat from Berber to Khartum.

" It was only after 1840 that traffic arose on the White Nile. At present (1917) we find the largest boat owners at Omdurman, and their craft are sailed up either the White Nile or the Blue, according to season and demand.

" Kawa and Shawal are important centres on the White Nile from which boats ply up the river. Considerable numbers are to be seen as far as the mouth of the Sobat, and a few penetrate the lower part of the Zeraf. The ' sunt ' wood of which the naggr is made, grows on sandy soil in damp situations. On the White Nile sunt is not met with beyond Kosti, but on the Blue it is found as far up as Roseires, and that is the limit of navigation. It also grows near the river north of Khartum. At present the main centre of boat building is certainly

---

[1] Manners and customs of the ancient Egyptians. New edition by Sam. Birch, Vol. II, Murray, 1878.

Omdurman, and, for this purpose, the wood is chiefly obtained from the large forests between Dueim and Kosti.

" The naggrs are Arab-owned craft, and are the only kind of boats used by the inhabitants for carrying merchandise.

" The Nilotic negroid tribes use canoes for ferry and fishing purposes. The Shilluk on the White Nile possess rather large built canoes which are put together somewhat after the style of the naggr, but by means of rope. They have a rising bow and stern like the gondola, and a V-shaped section, save that the point of the V is cut off leaving a narrow flat bottom.

" These built canoes are only met with on the White Nile ; not on the swift waters of the Bahr el-Jebel. The Shilluks also make use of the hollowed tree-trunk, which is almost the only type found amongst the Dinkas, Bari, Madi, Alur, etc., who inhabit the river banks as far as Lake Albert."

Mr. Grabham calls my attention to a book by Legh, *Legh's Journey in Egypt*, second edition, 1817. He was travelling on the Nile in 1812-13 and remarks that there are three kinds of boats used in the navigation of the Nile. He hires a " maish " at Rosetta to convey him up the river (p. 15). This boat is large enough to take Legh, Smelt and their servants, also three British officers. They were nine days from Rosetta to Cairo.

Legh also mentions a " djerm " (p. 14). This has two masts, but not a cabin ; it is chiefly used for the conveyance of merchandise.

He also refers to the " cangia," which he describes as having but one mast, but from eight to fourteen oars and two cabins.

Mr. Grabham tells me that he heard the term " maish " used by the Reis for the capacious barge attached to the steamer side on his journey to Roseires. None of the boats here referred to, bear square sails.

Must we not conclude that several centuries back the square sail began to yield to the triangular ?

At the present day we see evidences of an important change. About twelve years ago a few private sailing boats made their appearance in Cairo, lugger rigged and provided with a centre board. Some were soon to be seen at Aswân. In the secluded regions of Wadi Halfa a similar type of boat and rig appeared. The type was found where groups of British officials were stationed. The " lines " of the boats were quite different from those of the clumsy craft which then, and now, are produced and reproduced, as they probably have been for centuries by native hands. The new type was by the natives called " London," which we may take as a compliment. At Aswân there has grown up quite a profitable business in building boats on these improved lines, with centre boards and lugger rig. None of these boats are of sunt. All are with ribs. The old " felucca " has in many parts of the river almost given place, for light work, to the new " London " ; the improvement is so manifest that even the conservative Egyptian bows before it and adopts it. So far as I have been able to observe no boat carrying cargo has yet been built in the new mode. Having raised the question, but failed to trace the time or manner of disappearance of the old square rig, let us go back to a type of boat still built and very largely used, but which belongs to remote ages of antiquity ; a boat nearly as primitive as that described by Herodotus, if not in many essentials the same.

This type of boat is called a " naggr."

We see but few specimens of the class until we have ascended the Nile as far as Asyût, but from that place southward it is met with very frequently and in the Sudan is far more common than boats of any other type. It may be known by its exceedingly ancient appearance, its rotundity and clumsiness of form, the slowness of progress, the absence of ribs in its construction, and the fact that it is never tarred or painted, the wood soon acquires a silver grey tone which adds very much to the appearance of age.

A more unmanageable, primitive contrivance than the naggr, except it moves right before the wind, cannot be imagined. As an example, I have, in Sudan, been half an hour crossing the stream with a favourable N.W. wind to a spot but a little above the starting point. I have been four hours getting back and yet the current was with us and the ever-blowing N.W. wind by no means violent.

Before describing how the naggr is built I will give a few words to the two most ancient boats that now exist in Egypt, to be seen in the Museum at Cairo. It will be appreciated that the naggr is a very direct descendant of the boats of the XIIth dynasty. These boats were found at Dahshûr by M. de Morgan during his excavations in 1894-5.[1]

The boats, on their arrival at the Museum (then at Giza), were a good deal repaired, and like so many repairs carried on then and now in that institution they incline very much in the direction of skilful forgeries.

It is indeed most important in a museum that any object standing in need of repair should be so treated that the student can tell at a glance what is original and what is new. No register exists telling us what was the actual condition of the objects we are considering, when they were found, or what has been done to them by way of repairs.

When these ancient boats were in the Museum at Giza I made some careful notes (in 1894); they had then but just arrived and were in a good light. At Cairo they are unfortunately very much in the dark. It is now exceedingly difficult to distinguish new pieces of wood from the original. The hopes I had entertained (in 1916) of correcting my studies of 1894 have come to little. The passage of twenty-two years has made a considerable difference in the colour and surface of the inserted pieces, which now approximate pretty closely to the colour of the old.

The two boats are so nearly alike in all respects that it is sufficient to describe one of them.

As the section shows, Fig. 1, they are built entirely without ribs.

The two boats are described in the official catalogue, but the measured drawings which accompany the description have been so reduced in the printing as to lose much of their value.

Certain of the terms made use of in the description are, no doubt, correct in the United States, but the words have not similar values in England. It is unfortunate that this is so, or that equivalents are not given by Dr. Reisner, than whom a more patient and painstaking archaeologist cannot be found. We will, however, go back to more ancient times than those of the Museum Catalogue, and see what evidence we can find from tomb drawings.

In Lepsius' *Denkmäler*, II, 126, is found a drawing from the tomb of Khnum-hetep. In this the building of a boat is shown in progress. Fig. 2.

We see clearly that the sides are made of short pieces of wood, set together, breaking joint (like bricks), as described by Herodotus. At least one of the

---

[1] Fouilles à Dahchour, Mars–Juin, 1894. By J. de Morgan. Vienne, 1895.

workmen is shown standing inside the boat. If this boat had been built with an inner frame of vertical ribs we should have seen them standing up above the planks, and to them we should have seen the workmen attaching the outside skin of planks ; but nothing of this sort is visible. The planks are shown one lying above the other exactly as in the Museum boats, or as, in building a naggr, we see done at this day. One workman holds an adze. Others have hatchets. The

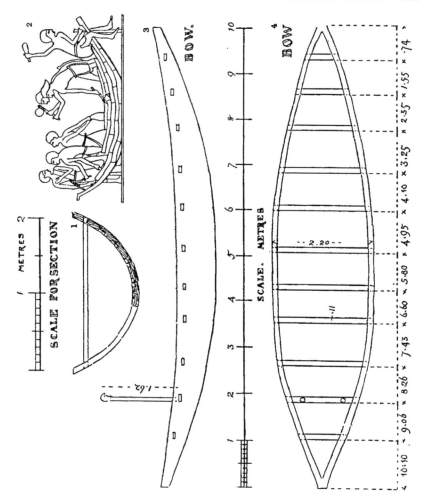

implements bulbous at the end are mallets ; the way in which they are held suggests that use.

The tomb of Khnumhetep is of the reign of Senusert II, so that we have before us a well-developed picture of boat-building in the XIIth dynasty.

As the very unwieldy Catalogues of the Cairo Museum are not often to be met with, I will venture to give a short, but by no means as complete, a description of the boats, as Dr. Reisner has done. I also give measured drawings ; a plan with a longitudinal elevation and transverse section. (Figs. 1, 3, 4.)   The transverse section, Fig. 1, shows clearly how the boat is built up of planks, and without a keel.   The two boats are not exactly of the same dimensions, the planks forming the hull of the larger boat average 9 cm. in thickness ; the planks of the smaller, 7 cm.

The planks vary both in length and in width, but are wide as compared with those we should use to-day in building boats of the size of those in the Museum.

The middle bottom plank which takes the place of the keel is 25 cm. in width,[1] those immediately adjoining are of the same width.   The total length of the boat is 10·10 m.

We now come to consider the method of construction.

The planks vary a good deal in their length.   In all cases the sides and ends of the planks butt against each other without any· overlap.   See the section Fig. 1, and the drawing from Beni Hasan, Fig. 2.   The boats are, in fact, as we call the method to-day " carvel built."   The Beni Hasan drawing indicates very well the Egyptian peculiarity that the sides of the planks are not parallel one to the other, but undulate according to the configuration of the grain of the natural wood.   A lower plank having been set in the place the plank which rests upon it has its lower side cut into undulations to fit.   In masonry likewise the irregular thickness of courses was adjusted by letting one into another.

The boat builders never placed vertical butting joints one over the other, and with good reason, for there not being any internal ribs the stability of the hull rests entirely on the success with which they accomplished their aim of making a continuous skin, each part supporting and supported by the parts adjoining.

---

[1] Why, in the Museum Catalogue, the middle plank is called a " beam " is hard to say.

SOMERS CLARKE.

(To be continued.)

THE TREASURE OF ANTINOE.

SOME ten years ago a hoard of personal ornaments was found in Upper Egypt ; the more likely report is that they were in the ruin of a monastery at Antinoe. That city was undoubtedly a wealthy centre of foreign influence, and a monastery was the safest place during the Arab invasion, which closely followed on the making of this group ; so the probabilities are in favour of this report. For the present, at all events, the name of the Treasure of Antinoe is the best that we can give to this hoard. It suffered the fate of most finds of valuables in the present state of the law ; it was violently broken up among the finders, they sold it surreptitiously to dealers, it was bought up in scattered lots by private collectors, and it is now separated in London, Berlin, Detroit and the Pierpont Morgan collection. The archaeological value of the hoard has been much weakened by the admixture of objects from other sources, so that there is no certainty as to what was found together.

Under these disastrous results of Government control, which destroys more than it preserves, the best course was to have the material all published together. Thanks to the labour of the late Prof. Walter Dennison of Swarthmore College, Pennsylvania, this was successfully done ; but most unhappily his death in 1917 frustrated his seeing the issue of his work. It is a sad loss for archaeology, that a man who might have done much to develop our knowledge, was cut off at the age of forty-eight. The volume on *A Gold Treasure of the Late-Roman Period in Egypt* (85 pp., 54 plates, 57 figures, Macmillan, $2.50) is his best memorial, and will give his name immortality on the shelves of museums and scholars. Besides the full illustration, sometimes on an enlarged scale, of all the objects of the hoard, many similar pieces already known are also illustrated to serve for comparison. The author generously gave permission for reproducing the main results in *Ancient Egypt*.

Before describing the objects that probably belong together, we may note what should be excluded. The greater part of the articles are dated by coins to the time between Justinian and Mauricius Tiberius, the latter half of the sixth century, or else are of similar work and age. Dr. Dennison agrees that two necklaces (8, 9) are from another source, probably of the second and early in the third century, and he puts as possibly earlier a pair of spiral serpent bracelets (24, 25), which seem obviously of the first century, or earlier still. With these we may set aside a pair of armlets (21, 22), the shell pattern on which is probably of the second century (see the necklace and gold ring in *Heliopolis*, XXXIX), also a pair of bracelets with a wavy vine stem for the elastic circle (32, 33), which can hardly be dated after the third century. After excluding these we can only say of the remaining bulk that there is nothing against their having been buried together before the sack in the Arab invasion of 641.

The whole hoard contained, then, two necklets with groups of coins attached, three gold coins set in linked framing, five necklaces or collars, a long chain for the body, six pairs and one odd bracelet, a small cross and a crystal figure. The

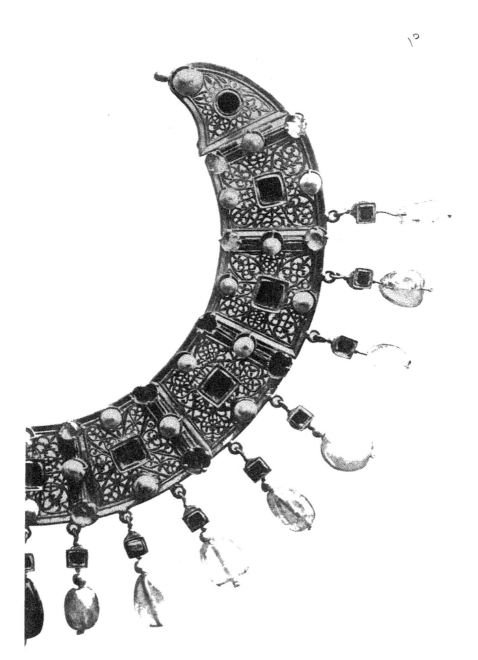

PL II. HALF OF GOLD COLLAR OF LINKED PLATES. FULL SIZE

absolute dating by the attached coins is only in the two necklets and the linked coins. In these three cases, the earliest date for the making of the jewellery is under Justinian (528–556) for one necklet and the coins, and under Mauricius (582–602) for the other necklet, which is obviously of later and more debased work. As it is unlikely that such wealth of gold would be displayed after the Arab conquest of 641, the limits of date are fairly close. To this we refer later.

The finest object for display is the great necklet (Pl. I here) with fourteen inserted coins from Theodosius to Justinian, a pendant medallion of Theodosius, and a barbaric imitation of a gold coin of Valentinian III as a centre piece. This taste for making imitations of coins for ornament is very familiar in the North of Europe (see Montelius, *Civilisation of Sweden*, Fig. 134, copy of Theodosius; Worsaae, *Pre-History of the North*, Figs. 6–16). Some other features are also alike in Northern work and Romano-Egyptian, as the crystal fibulae and garnet inlays, and large discs of ornament on necklets. These are northern in origin, and probably all this class of ornament was brought into Egyptian use by the bands of northern troops in the Roman garrisons.

A fellow necklet, copied from the previous about fifty years later, has coins ranging from Justinian to Mauricius, and therefore after 582. The middle piece is a struck medallion more intelligently made than the previous imitation of a coin, as it has a rational Greek inscription, " Lord, succour the wearer," alike on both sides. The pendant, however, seems to have been an entirely independent work, converted to a pectoral, and too large for the necklet. It has on one side the Annunciation, and on the other the Conversion of water into wine ; the style is distinctly early Christian rather than classical.

A pleasing detail in these pectorals, which seems to be post-classical, is the filling up of spaces with the small three-petal flowers, like arrow-head or water plantain (see Fig. 22 here).

The three linked solidi of Justinian have borders cast around the coins, apparently by *cire perdue ;* inscriptions were then punched on a band of the border. These are Greek, and read " For He shall give His angels charge over thee " ; next, " to keep thee in all thy ways " ; thirdly, "Emmanuel which, being interpreted, is God with us." These, as well as the medallion in the pectoral, are therefore prophylactic charms, to protect the wearer.

The necklaces are very varied. No. 10 is of small balls linked together, with fifteen crosses each of four pearl and sapphire beads. No. 11 of eight lengths of woven wire chain alternating with beads, and a large circular openwork pendant, with four interior circles forming a cross. No. 12 has alternate stones with the ugly late device of beads threaded on a wire around ; but the other alternatives are six-leaved rosettes in circles, of the fresh geometrical style which arose on the ruins of classical work. No. 13 is a common form of wire links with beads, and a row of bead dangles. No. 14 is a remarkable wide collar, passing round three quarters of the neck, of eleven open-work gold plates hinged together, with seventeen sapphire pendants (see Pl. II). The plates are in pairs, on opposite sides, there being six different designs. The patterns are good, descended from Greek palmetto and foliage, but the whole effect is far too stiff and awkward for wearing.

The large body chain is very unusual, and the most satisfactory and original design in the whole hoard (see Pl. III). It consists of two large open-work discs, one worn on the chest, the other on the back, as shown on terracotta figures. These were joined by a chain of small discs over each shoulder, and a chain round each side, twenty-three small discs in each chain. There are only two patterns for the discs, but the whole effect is varied, and the two designs look quite distinct, yet harmonious. The use of such a body chain was probably to retain ample flowing robes near the body, and prevent the garment bagging out awkwardly.

There are three pairs of earrings, all of which have long dangles of beads, a style probably coming from the North with the barbaric invasions.

Two pairs of bracelets have elaborately pierced openwork discs. These are ingenious in design, reminding us of the marble-work screens of San Clemente, or the rather later ones of Saint Mark's. All of this style seems to be the result of the northern introduction of wicker-work screens, which belonged to nomadic life. Another pair of bracelets, or rather armlets, are made of hollow hexagonal tube, notched to imitate banding, and with two imitations of aurei of Honorius at the fastening. A single bracelet is of twisted wire pattern, with a fulsome bezel of thirteen set stones.

This gold work from Egypt, and other examples that Prof. Dennison has published for comparison, supply a good basis for dating details of ornament. The employment of gold coins set in later framings serves to give an anterior limit of date for the work, and it is unlikely that the posterior limit is more than two or three generations later. The mixture of coins of various ages in the large breast ornaments shows how far such material precedes the ornamental setting. In one group, Pl. VIII, the coins are—two of Theodosius I, two of Theodosius II, five of Anthemius, one of Basilicus, and four of Justinian, or between about A.D. 390 and 530. In another group, Pl. XIV, there is one of Justinian, five of Justin II, one of Tiberius II, six of Mauricius, or between about A.D. 550 and 600. Thus, in one case, half the coins are within sixty years, in the other case half are of the last two reigns, or a very few years. Thus on the average the age of coins when used was less than half a century. This gives ground for dating jewellery by single coins to within half a century in most cases.

The elements of the ornament are here separated, and classed by their motives (Figs. 1–22). Thus the degradation of design is shown, and this will help in dating other jewellery. The dates placed after the emperor's name are the earliest to which the work would be reasonably assigned, allowing a few years for coins to circulate into the provinces. The date of the ornament is therefore to be taken as probably within fifty years after the dates here given. Different dates are given for Nos. 6 and 19, according to the age of the head of Justinian on the coin.

The foliage work of Nos. 1, 2 and 3 is obviously like that of the first century architecture debased, such as on the great Altar of Peace. This foliage work is familiar on the sculpture of the Severan age. No. 3 seems to be the back of an openwork design like No. 2 ; but, judging from the photograph, Nos. 1 and 2 are of wirework on a sheet-metal basis. In No. 4, perhaps a generation later, the foliage work has lost its tradition and become irregular and senseless. The revival of openwork about A.D. 600, No. 5, was on an entirely different system, cut out of a continuous sheet instead of being built up of soldered wire.

The foliage, or running vine, pattern in Nos. 6 and 7 is made of detached curved wires soldered on to a sheet-metal basis. In A.D. 530 they still had a binding put across to hide the junction ; but by 600 A.D. the separate wires are stuck down, detached and unashamed. The old sense of structure was lost, but this may have been due to a workman below the average of his generation. Small neat scrolls, to fill up spaces, are also of Justinian (No. 8).

The row of pelta-shaped objects which form a border under Caracalla

(Nos. 9 and 10), seem to have originated a favourite device of the sixth century. On No. 10 the dotted lines are placed to suggest how the designer came to regard the pattern, and from this to make it in wirework, with a pile of globules up the middle to stiffen it, as in Nos. 11 and 12. It was simplified, as wire on a sheet-metal basis (No. 13), under Focas (Univ. Coll.), and this element is common on earrings and small work of that age.

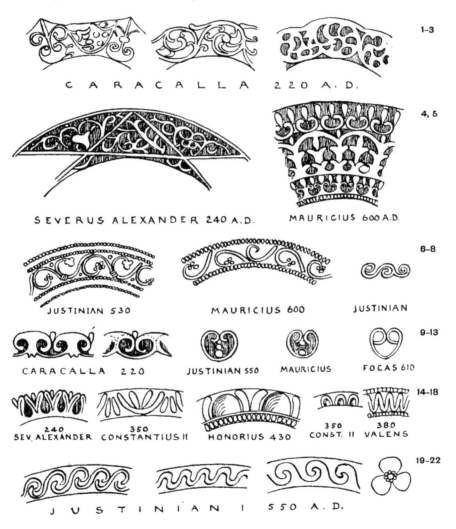

A border of flowers, No. 14, was copied very formally under Alexander. By the time of Constantius II the flower forms are scarcely recognisable (No. 15). Under Honorius the flower is reduced to two lobes, with a concave hollow between; this might, perhaps, be a degradation of the Greek dart-and-egg. Similar concave hollows in a row are used for a border (No. 17) under Constantius II, and are modified to a zigzag line pattern (No. 18) under Valens.

The continuous scroll was carelessly made in several modifications all at the same time ; in fact, on small work it is difficult to settle which form is used, as it varies so much according to the lighting. In No. 19 the scrolls are clear, in No. 20 they become a running line, in No. 21 they form a series of pendant curls. The little flower, No. 22, was a favourite and graceful mode of covering up junctions and filling small spaces of ground.

Whenever it may be possible to put together all the dated examples of jewellery, and to analyse the different elements, we shall be able to recover more of the stages of change in the various patterns. This will serve later to fix the greater part of jewellery which has no self-evident dating.

A curious figure in rock crystal, nearly four inches high, is supposed to have come from the hoard. It is a female figure, dressed in chiton and peplos swathing the whole person : round her neck is a high band. The aspect is Christian rather than classic. It is on a silver gilt base that has been broken from a larger object. This obviously is not an empress or a person of pretensions. The meek aspect, almost deferential, rather suggests it is intended for a saint, so it might have been the crowning figure of a reliquary. The rage for relics in the fourth to the sixth century would make it quite likely that a reliquary might be hidden along with other treasures in the seventh century.

The fate of all valuable antiquities under the present law is a melancholy one. The Egyptian Government claims to have seized two great groups of silver work at Zagazig, though even from these some pieces went astray. But the present hoard of Antinoe, the great group of gold medallions from Abukir, the large gold hawk from Dendereh, the great find of a royal burial of the XVIIIth dynasty with much gold work, and innumerable lesser discoveries, have all been lost to the Government, and many lost to all knowledge by being melted up, owing to the fear of Government claims. This suicidal policy, which is a loss of values to the Government, is also an irreparable loss to archaeology. If the Government would give local values for everything, such as a dealer pays, the whole would be secured at a small part of the full European value. The confidence of the people should be gained by a liberal payment for everything that is declared at once, and seizure should be the penalty for concealment and not declaring any discoveries. If the Government had to pay out £10,000 in a year they would make a large profit on the result ; the more they paid the larger the gain, which would otherwise fall to the dealers. Let us hope that Palestine and Mesopotamia will not be mismanaged in the shortsighted way that prevails under the English and the Egyptian laws.

W. M. FLINDERS PETRIE.

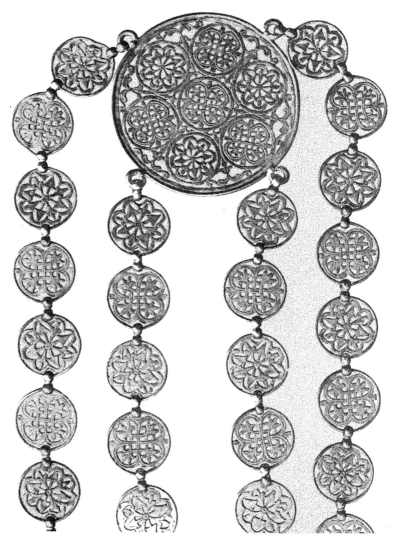

PL. III. GOLD BODY-CHAIN OF 2 LARGE AND 92 SMALL DISCS. SCALE 5/6.

THE FIRST MACE-HEAD OF HIERAKONPOLIS.

THE great carved mace-heads of Hierakonpolis have been the subject of much careful study, especially in the case of the second and third, which are now in the Ashmolean Museum, Oxford. The first has received less attention, owing to its damaged condition. It is broken into several pieces, but though a great deal has been preserved, the surface of the stone is corroded in many places, and flakes have split off, so that much of the sculpture is irretrievably lost. The sculpture thus left falls into three groups, of which two are on the largest fragment.

1. The first group represents the king who wears the crown of Lower Egypt and is wrapped in a cloak or shawl ; one hand appears to project, and to hold a whip. He is beardless and is seated on a throne, but the sculpture is so worn away that only the square box-like lines of the back of the throne are visible. The figure is placed under a curved canopy supported at the front by two slender shafts ; on each shaft there is an ornament immediately under the canopy, and each shaft terminates in a sharp point. Both the canopy and the figure of the king are of the same type as on the second mace. It is interesting to note that on the maces the king when wearing the crown of Lower Egypt is represented as being smaller, both actually and in proportion, than when wearing the White Crown. On the third mace-head the Scorpion King is considerably larger than the figures among whom he stands ; while on the first and second maces the figure of the king is actually smaller than the others ; this is markedly the case in the mace-head under discussion. This disproportion in size is against the usual rule of Egyptian art, which makes the principal person larger than the other figures in a scene. A possible explanation is that these are representations of the king's statue, and not of the king himself. As the figure is placed under a canopy of the type of the early shrines, and is dressed in the close-wrapped garment peculiar to Osiris, it may represent the dead and deified king to whom his people are paying homage.

2. On the same fragment as the king's figure, but removed from it by a wide space, originally sculptured and now blank, is a figure of a pig-tailed man. Only the back of the head and the back of one leg are visible, the rest being utterly destroyed. Immediately above the head is a curved rope, and above that again is an object of which so little remains that it is impossible even to guess at what it was intended to represent. Behind the rope and almost touching it is a rect-angular object, apparently the ground or base of other figures or objects ; these would be on a level with the king's face. The figure stands on another peculiar and indeterminate object ; the angle of the leg suggests that the man is running or dancing. Two points in this figure are noticeable : the first is the pigtail, which I will discuss below ; the second is the size. It is the largest figure on any of the maces ; and if the canon of Egyptian art held good at that early period this should be the principal personage in the scene. Taken together with the object on which he stands, and the object above his head, he fills the whole height of the mace-head. The size of this figure should be compared with the bearers of offerings, and especially with the king.

3. Three or four fragments joined together give part of a scene of bearers of

offerings. These fragments come from the middle and lower part of one side of the mace, but unfortunately do not join the main piece anywhere. The scene is divided horizontally into two registers, in each of which there are the remains of three figures. In the upper register, one leg and arm only remain of the first man ; he is dressed apparently in a short kilt and carries a fox-skin (?) in his hand. The second and third figures have skirts to the middle of the calf, the skirt being ornamented either with patterns or with rope-work   There are indications of some object suspended from the hand of the third figure.

In the lower register, there is practically nothing remaining of the first figure except the back of the head and the plaited pigtail. The second man is, however, almost complete. He wears a short beard, apparently fastened to the hair, which is arranged in a heavy mass at the back of the neck while the upper part is plaited into a short pigtail. His dress consists of a short kilt from the waist to above the knee, fastened at the waist with a narrow band ; down the front is an ornamented piece which may perhaps be a piece of pleated cloth such as occurs on the loin-cloths of the late Old Kingdom. In his right hand he holds a barrel-shaped vase of the type of the second Prehistoric Period, a form which approximates very closely to the heart-sign of the later hieroglyphs. The left arm with the fist clenched is raised above the head. The legs and feet are bare, and one knee is raised as though in the act of dancing. The third man differs from the second only in attitude ; in his right hand he holds a fox skin (?) already conventionalised in form, the left arm hangs at his side. The right knee is raised above the level of the waist as if in an active dance. Again these figures are all considerably larger than the king. Below their feet is a curved line, apparently a rope.

Pigtailed figures are rare in Egypt, and even among those known two types of pig-tails are discernible. The first type is when the hair is gathered into a thick twist or plait just above or below the nape of the neck (*Hierakonpolis*, I, Pl. XI, *Abydos*, II, Pl. IV). In these cases the hair covers the curve of the back of the head and neck. In the second type, the pigtail starts at the crown of the head, as amongst the Chinese, and is apparently plaited with some stiffening material as it falls quite clear of the head and neck. When the hair is dressed in this fashion it is sometimes all gathered into the plait as in Figs. 2 and 7, leaving the nape bare, this may perhaps be caused by shaving the back of the head under the plait ; in other cases, as in Figs. 3 and 8, the hair falls in a heavy mass under the pigtail, which is plaited only from the hair of the upper part of the head. Pigtails of any sort appear to occur only in the beginning of the historic period, and at no other time. The only exception is perhaps the *nms* headdress of the king (Fig. 9), where, however, the pigtail is obviously made of cloth and not of hair.

From the comparative size of the figures, it is evident that they were of more importance than the king. The type of face is not that of the aborigines as, shown in the slate palettes. Not only is the hair differently dressed but these people are clothed, sometimes in a short kilt, sometimes in a long robe, whereas the aborigines are either very scantily clothed or quite nude. The long-robed people are never represented as prisoners : on the contrary, the battlefield palette shows a captive aborigine being driven forward by a person whose garment reaches to his ankles. The short kilt and the artificial beard suggest the royal costume, so also perhaps does the pigtail. If then, the royal figure is that of the dead and deified king, are these the competitors for the throne ?

Thothmes III

Prof. Newberry has pointed out that this is probably the meaning of the scene on the mace-head of Narmer, and that it is there complicated by the presence of the heiress to the throne, by marriage with whom the successful candidate legitimised his claim. Another possibility may be kept in mind, that the piece with the king (1, 2) did not belong to the same mace-head as piece 3.

M. A. Murray.

B

AN EARLY PORTRAIT.

AMONG the antiquities in the New York Historical Society's collection there are some so unusual that Mrs. Grant Williams has kindly allowed us to reproduce them here. These and many other objects have been published by her in the *Quarterly Bulletin* of the New York Historical Society in the last two years. A very remarkable portrait head is that of Smenkhu-ptah, who had the "good name" of Atu-shep-er-onkh. His tomb is known at Saqqarah, from which the sculptures have come : it is dated to the end of the Vth or early in the VIth dynasty. The type is so far from that of the usual Egyptian that we have more certainty in its being a careful portrait. The detail of the profile differs from the usual type in the sharp brow, the pointed nose, the long upper lip, the sharp edges of the mouth, and the retreating chin. The form of the nose is closely like that of the wife of Ka-aper ; but the heavy, morose, face is not like any other.

A remarkable coffin-box in the same collection has in it two wooden ushabtis, one wrapped, and a roll of inscribed linen, probably part of the Book of the Dead. These, and a scarab, being all bedded in pitch, are not modern insertions. The style of the ushabtis is of the early XIXth dynasty ; the name is unusual, Sebaur. The burial of two ushabtis in a coffin descends from the belief of the XVIIIth dynasty, when the ushabti was a figure of the deceased person. Yet this burial must be just after that time, as one of these is an overseer with whip, and the other is plain, showing that the serf idea of the XIXth dynasty had by this time come in.

W. M. F. P.

GEORGES LEGRAIN.

THE following notes upon the really remarkable work carried out by the late Georges Legrain at Karnak, are offered as a tribute to his memory. Unless there be set forth a description with some amount of detail, it is difficult for his ungrudging labours to be at all estimated. Let us consider what was the condition of the immense agglomeration of ruins of which he was put in charge in 1894.

Quite twenty years before that time Mariette had removed great masses of earth, with the object of general investigation, and the recovery of the buried plan. A plan was afterwards published, and if it has proved very incorrect in many respects, that is hardly to be wondered at. The undertaking was one greater than Mariette, over-burdened as he was, had either time or means to carry through.

M. Jacques de Morgan was appointed Director-General of Antiquities in 1893. He decided that a systematic investigation of Karnak should be made ; and in 1894 he nominated Georges Legrain to preside over that work. Legrain then made a programme of what to do and how to do it, which has proved really remarkable for its foresightedness. He did not approach the subject only from the side of the excavator, and of one who had to repair and maintain as he went

PORTRAIT OF SMENKHU-PTAH. VTH DYNASTY.

COFFIN-BOX WITH USHABTIS.

along. He realised the impossibility of one man seeing through to the end so
immense an undertaking. He saw that he must thoroughly register the progress
of the works and the objects found, so that his notes and observations could
be taken up by those who followed, and thereby the history of this prodigious
place could be properly built up. He viewed Karnak as a vast historical monument. He set to work so to arrange the system for tabulating the immense series
of inscriptions and sculptures, that a complete record of the whole group of
temples could be published.

Legrain was but twenty-six years of age when he was appointed. His
methods have proved perfectly sound after twenty-three years' progress.

The works went on increasing very greatly in volume and in interest.

From an engineering point of view the risks were often great, but such was
the forethought and care taken, there was, I believe, never an accident, although
there were workers by the hundred, and immense blocks of stone to be moved,
taken down and reinstated, some of them weighing more than 25 tons apiece.

M. Maspero, succeeding De Morgan, was unhappily very unsympathetic
with Legrain. Here lay in fact the " opposition and difficulties " referred to in
the short notice of Legrain already published, ANCIENT EGYPT, 1917, p. 142. But
Maspero is dead and cannot defend himself. It would therefore be undesirable
to say more. What is past is past.

It is a thing not a little to be deplored that of all the work that has been done
at Karnak since the year 1894, of all the remarkable discoveries that have been
made, no consistent or scientific account has ever been published.

There exist a few notes and records buried in the *Annales du Service des
Antiquités*. These, a few pages at a time, are scattered about in the aforesaid
Annales extending from the year 1900 to 1914. If we wish to study a plan of
Karnak we must turn to that published by Mariette as long since as 1875, and now
completely out of date.

We must not suppose that the Department of Antiquities had been idle
all this time. Portly volumes on Saqqarah, Lower Nubia, Les Temples Immergés
de la Nubie, with many plans, photographs and much documentary evidence,
had been published—the materials for several volumes on Karnak were at hand,
but Karnak was kept in the shade.

The reader must be left to draw his own conclusions upon this curious state of
things above mentioned.

SOMERS CLARKE.

REVIEWS.

—•—

The Empire of the Amorites.—ALBERT A. CLAY. Sm. 4to. 192 pp. (Yale University Press.) Milford, London, 1919.

As to the term "empire" for the dominion of the Amorites, different opinions may be felt, but a mere question of a term must not hinder our acceptance of the facts. The broad position is that Semite names are as early as Sumerian in Babylonia, and that the fertile Syro-Babylonian region was far more likely to be the home of a race than Arabia, which is a semi-desert : it is, therefore, likely that the Semite centre was in Northern Syria rather than in Arabia.

As to the prominence of Semites in early Babylonia, more than a hundred thousand personal names are known, and in the early part of this material many of the rulers' names are Semitic, and the names of the antediluvian kings in Berossos are Semitic. Further, the elements in these early names, Abu, Akhu, Ammi, are Western Semitic rather than Arabian. Another evidence is from the figures of the Sumerian gods who are hairy and bearded, as Semites, and not like the shaven Sumerians, pointing to the Sumerians having taken over the earlier Semitic gods of the land. So far as opinions go, Brünnow thought the Semites to be the original Euphrateans and the Sumerians to be invaders : Meyer holds that the Semites were there before the Sumerians settled in South Babylonia and drove the Semites northward. Jastrow says " The mixture of Sumerians and Semites was so pronounced, even in the oldest period revealed by the documents at our command, that a differentiation between the Semitic and non-Semitic ideas in the conceptions formed of the gods is not generally possible."

That this Semitic influence belonged to Syria and not to Arabia is shown by the elements of the names, stated above, and by the name Abram, or Abraham, which is not found in Arabian inscriptions, but is known in the Euphratean tablets. The Cappadocian tablets are naturally North Semitic in names and gods, and not Arabian. The view that successive waves of emigration had flowed from Arabia is discussed. The distinction should be drawn, however, between movements of people from a half-desert land as it dries up, and movements because of a pressure of population in a fertile land. The desert land will have but few people to pour out, they will be hardy but not strong, they will scarcely overcome a full population in a fertile land. The Islamic conquest of Egypt was by only 12,000 or 20,000 men ; they succeeded not because they were strong, but because Egypt and the Roman provinces generally were miserably weak, drained by taxation for centuries, harried by the Persian war, and preferring liberty under Arabs to taxation under Romans. This success must not be taken as a type of all emigrants from Arabia. Dr. Clay well maintains that the reason of the civilisation being more primitive in Arabia than in other Semitic lands, does not imply that Arabia was the source, but that it was isolated as a backwater, and so retained early ideas and forms less changed than in lands subject to other influences.

The question of the Khabiri is noticed, with the fairly conclusive fact that at Boghaz-koi there is a list of gods called the "Gods of the Khabiri." The conclusion is that they cannot be Hebrews, but were related to the Hittites, if not Aramaeans. We' may also notice that in the Amarna letters the Khabiri invade Damascus and Ashtaroth, that is, they move east of Jordan, opposite to Galilee. It seems at least possible, therefore, that they were at some time east of Judaea, and gave the name to the mountains of 'Abarim. If the *cheth* of Khabiri may represent the initial *ayin* of Hebrew, it may equally represent that of 'Abarim.

The limits of Amurru in 1100 were on the Mediterranean, as Tiglath Pileser I sailed in ships of Arvad upon "the great sea of Amurru." Asshur-nazir-pal (885) went to the great sea of Amurru, and received tribute all along the coast. Adad-nirari III names Amurru as between the Hittites and Sidon. Sargon (720) included the Hittites and Damascus in Amurru. Sennacherib (700) included Philistia and Phoenicia, Moab and Edom. Asshur-bani-pal (650) included Palestine in Amurru. The tendency was, therefore, to include only Northern Syria, and between 1100 and 650 to extend the name south until it included all Syria.

Now we can look at the position as it affects Egyptian history. From as early as the Pre-dynastic Age it is claimed that there has been a centre of Semitic influence and government in North Syria, that it had a full share in developing Babylonia, and that it lasted down to classical times, embracing what is known as the Aramaean kingdom. On the Egyptian side we find a large invasion from the East, founding the second prehistoric civilisation ; but this seems more likely to belong to the region east and west of Suez. A clearly Syro-Mesopotamian invasion was that which overthrew the Old Kingdom, as shown by the buttons with foreign devices ; with these must be noted the examples of symmetric scarabs, such as were later produced under Hyksos influence, but which are dated before the XIIth dynasty at Ehnasya (Pl. XIA) and Harageh. There is good ground for regarding this invasion as having come from North Syria or the Euphrates, and therefore as being Amorite. Then, after the Middle Kingdom, the same influence appears in the Hyksos invasion of Semites from Syria, who wielded a widespread power. Beside those recognised as Hyksos there are others who seem to have been their forerunners, Khenzer and Khandy, the latter of whom ruled over Syria and conquered Egypt, as shown on his triumphal cylinder (Univ. Coll.). Thus, there is good ground on the Egyptian side to look for a strong Semitic power in North Syria at the close of the Old Kingdom, and again at the close of the Middle Kingdom. This is in accord with Dr. Clay's position, and therefore on this side we welcome it as a gain to our historical view.

La Fin du Moyen Empire Égyptien, Étude sur les Monuments et l'Histoire de la période comprise entre la XIIe et la XVIIIe dynastie.—RAYMOND WEILL. 8vo, 971 pp., 2 vols. Picard, Paris, 1918.

This work has appeared in sections in the *Journal Asiatique*, 1910–1917, and the whole is here put together in a convenient form. As this is the only detailed attempt to contract the period dealt with, in the brief space of 210 years, demanded by Berlin, it should have the fullest attention. As a collection of the scattered material remaining of that period, it will in any case prove a work of permanent value, even apart from the author's conclusions. The length of it is rather deterrent, and it might have been less prolix with advantage ;

for instance, twelve lines of inconclusive argument deals with the identification of the cartouche of Neferhetep, which is all useless as the direct proof on a stele is stated in six lines more. A single line quoting the stele would have been all-sufficient. Also many examples of the simplest repetitions of a name are all set out in hieroglyphs at full length.

The serious question is how far we can follow, and rely on, the reasoning, and accept the conclusions. The main thesis is that a type of literary composition, deploring decay and devastation by foreigners, was started in early times and frequently re-used : the conclusion drawn from this is that such statements have no historic value. This is a position possible from a purely literary point of view, but the least knowledge of material history refutes it at once. The art and monuments of every land show a series of stages of growth and decay. In Egypt the periods of decay are obvious in two prehistoric ages, in the VIIth–XIth dynasties, in the XIIIth–XVIIth, the XIXth–XXIIIrd, and the Roman Age ; in all these we see great decadence, and in all these historic ages there is the absence of public monuments and the shortness of reigns, proving the disturbance, poverty, and trouble in the country. The evidence of foreign invasion is seen in the new types of production, the new connections with surrounding lands, the new names and characters of the people. From every material evidence we see that it is hopeless to claim that the re-use of classical expressions shows that the complaints about the times are unhistorical. How often have the declarations of Jewish prophets been re-used as applying to the fall of Rome, or by the Puritan party in England ? They are still felt to be the most vital expression of many of our troubles now. Shall we deny the historical truth of every account in which the phrases of Psalm or Prophet are used ? The material facts of repeated invasion of Egypt are externally attested—from the West the Fatimites, the Greeks, the Libyans, from the East the Tulunides, the Arabs, the Persians,—to say nothing of remoter times. To claim that a "theme of disorder" is only a rhetorical exercise, is to shut one's eyes to all the proved facts. It is impossible to accept this conception, which occupies a large part of the work, and underlies its whole fabric.

Another objection—perhaps more serious—is the way of treating basic documents. The account by Hatshepsut reads : "I have restored that which was in ruin, and completed that which was unfinished, since the stay of the Asiatics who were in the lands of the North and in Ha-naret with the Shemau among them, occupied in destruction ; they made a king for themselves in ignorance of Ra, and he did not act according to the orders of the god until the coming of my Majesty," according to Weill ; or the latter part according to Breasted "they ruled in ignorance of Re. He (the Hyksos ruler) did not do according to the divine command until my Majesty." Now this is not a claim to the conquest physically, but to the conversion religiously, of the Hyksos. It is the obedience to Ra that Hatshepsut obtained. There is nothing to contradict the previous expulsion from Egypt ; Hatshepsut only claims the restoration of monuments, and the obedience of the Hyksos to Ra, whether in Palestine or elsewhere. Capt. Weill goes on : "Hatshepsut has conquered the Asiatic destroyers installed in the Delta and in Ha-uaret . . . . . Therefore Hatshepsut lied. . . . She usurped without any right the merit of having expelled the Asiatics" (p. 38). This is a false rendering of the historical document.

A most strange treatment of a document, in a book professing to discuss history, is that accorded to the Turin Papyrus. Not content with ignoring its historic sequence, the whole of the lengths of reigns remaining in it are omitted. When publishing the text of it (pp. 590-3) not a single year is named. Yet there are twenty-four reigns still to be read in it after the XIIth dynasty, totalling 191 years, or an average of eight years. Can we take seriously any view of an almost contemporary document, when the most essential facts are omitted in discussing the very matter in question, namely, the years covered by the document ? To any reader who knew no better, it would appear that no years were stated. It seems impossible to accept any conclusions drawn from such treatment, nor can we take this elaborate work as more than the effort of an advocate who distorts and omits evidence.

If in 1910 it could be said (p. 25) that "social disorder has nothing to do with an entirely personal drama" of weariness of trouble and wish for death, that is not the sense of the world in 1919, when we know what social disorder means. We can see before us now how closely the miseries of social disorder touch the personal lives of those who suffer. The lamentations of the Egyptians might all be used by Serbs, Poles and Russians.

In discussing the record about the Hyksos kings, objection is taken (p. 182) that they are described as destroyers, and yet they set up monuments in Egypt. This ignores the 100 years of confusion of the conquest, before they were united under one rule ; this period is also overlooked when objection is made to recognising an interregnum in Africanus (p. 553).

In pursuance of abandoning awkward material, the dynastic divisions are entirely thrown aside (p. 183), "for us, who intend altogether to lose sight of the Manethonian dynasties in studying the monuments." Yet these dynastic divisions are pointedly shown by the monuments, not only in style and place, but by the founders of dynasties copying the titles of previous founders, and also by marked divisions in the Turin Papyrus.

A fundamental classification is made by what are termed the *Anra* scarabs (p. 191) ; a term used for all those with symmetric symbols and devices (P. 742). Because a scarab of Kha-nefer-ra Sebekhetep has such symbols (246), it is concluded that "the Sebekheteps have preceded Apepi, not far off ; but at a short distance" (p. 248), or, in the index, "the epoch of the group is that of Kha-nefer-ra Sebekhetep" (P. 932, and see p. 453). This position seems to be an entire misconception. First, the word (though usually badly copied) is not *Anra*, but *Da-ne-ra*, "gift of Ra" ("Heliodoros"), as commonly found on scarabs about the XIIth dynasty, and on examples figured here (P. 744) ; or in other cases perhaps *Ar-ne-ra*, "born of Ra," as on p. 250. Second, the symmetric style, as on the scarab of Sebekhetep adduced (p. 246), is found as early as Senusert I (p. 745), and continues on to Tahutmes IV (p. 739). That such scarabs are of the XIIth dynasty is shown by the peculiar light blue glaze of some, which is never dated later than the early part of that dynasty. How can any close indication of age be founded on a style which lasts from early in the Middle Kingdom to the middle of the New Kingdom ? Anyone who has collected scarabs on sites will know that symmetric scarabs are found almost wholly in the Eastern Delta : their style is that of a region, and not of a short period.

A further theory is that the symmetric scarabs of *Anra* type were made in Palestine (p. 732), because they are often found there. On the contrary the material, the glaze, the signs, are all Egyptian, and a far greater number are found in Egypt than in Palestine. That the Palestine scarabs are mainly of this type is to be expected, as it belongs to the Eastern Delta, nearest to Palestine ; but to suppose materials and workmen to be taken to Palestine, in order to export most of their products back into Egypt is fantastic.

The more important part of the work (pp. 276–514) is the discussion of the various families or groups, as shown by the parallel names of the same type. This is a useful principle ; yet as the author has to continue a single type of name, *Sekhem-ra*, over more than half the period between the XIIth and XVIIIth dynasties (p. 819) no close delimitation can be claimed. As a collection of material, with due connection of genealogic sources (as El-Kab tombs), this will be of permanent use to students, with the additions on pp. 226–251, 768–804. We may note in passing that the insertion of Ra with a personal name, as Ra-să-Hathor, is not merely a mistake of a scribe (p. 422, note 194), but occurs on contemporary objects of Ra-neb-taui, Ra-amenemhat, and Ra-sebekhetep. It seems to have been added as a token of descent from Ra. The general results of this discussion are put together in a *Livre des Rois* (pp. 818–880), which must be used subject to all reservations as to methods.

The crux of the whole work, to which all this material leads up, is the reduction of the documentary history of the Turin Papyrus and Manetho from a period of about 1,600 years to a period of 210 years, between the XIIth and XVIIIth dynasties. One or other view must be accepted, if the Sothic cycle and continuous kalendar are not rejected. The radical question is whether Egyptians placed contemporary dynasties in succession in a continuous list. The evidence that overlapping was avoided by Manetho is seen in the XIth dynasty, which lasted certainly over a century, but which has only forty-three years allowed, because the Xth dynasty was legitimate over the earlier part of the XIth. Again, Taharqa, who really reigned thirty-four years, is only allowed eighteen years by Manetho, because from that point the legitimate line was in Stefinates, great-grandfather of Psamthek I, and the XXVth dynasty could not be allowed to overlap the XXVIth. The examples that we can test therefore show that overlapping was not allowed in the history, and that a continuous single series of legitimate rulers was compiled. There is further evidence if we accept the Sebekemsafs, Nub-kheper-ra Antef, and others, as being of the XIIIth dynasty. They were important kings, and could not be placed as late as the decadence after No. 29 of the Turin Papyrus ; yet they are not in that list, nor is there any gap sufficient for them in the earlier part. They were deliberately omitted, and presumably as not being the legitimate line. If such kings were omitted, we cannot suppose far less important kings to have been inserted overlapping the reigns of others.

The Turin Papyrus is obviously in accord with Manetho, and they must therefore be taken as supplementing each other. In Manetho the XIIIth dynasty is of sixty kings, and in the Turin Papyrus after sixty kings is a break, beginning again with the formula " there reigned." Next, the XIVth dynasty is of seventy-six kings, and in the Turin Papyrus after seventy-three (or perhaps a few more) there begins the change to Semitic names, which correspond to the XVth dynasty of Hyksos in Manetho. The average of reigns of the XIIIth dynasty is seven and a half years in Manetho, and seven years in the ten reigns surviving in the Papyrus. In the XIVth dynasty Manetho's average is two and a half years, and the average of seven reigns left in the Papyrus is about three years. A closer correspondence of fragmentary material could not be expected.

The main attack on the continuity of the Turin Papyrus is made on the ground that a different type of name shows a change of dynasty. Apply this to well-known dynasties and see the result. In the XVIIIth dynasty there are two kings with Ra-neb-x, three with Ra-oa-kheper, six with Ra-x-kheperu ; in the XIXth three with Ra-men-x, three with Ra-user-x, Ra-ne-ba and Ra-ne-akhu. On the question of types of name we should have to split up each of these dynasties into three separate lines taken in irregular order. No canon of arrangement can be applied to obscure dynasties which will not give true results when applied to well-known periods.

Another line of attack is on the resemblances between the lengths of some dynasties. Elaborate theoretical stages of alteration of the text are presented to show how the existing figures arose from some very different form. The lengths of the dynasties in Africanus' version of Manetho, from the XIIIth to the XVIIth, are 453, 184, 284, 518 and 151. The only relation here is that the last is a third of the first. A change is made by adopting 259 from Josephus in place of 284 ; then 259 is half of 518. After this we find such theories as, although " we have suppressed " the XIIIth dynasty, yet take the sixty kings stated for that, add thirty-two kings of the XVIth dynasty, making ninety-two, double this (for no reason) and so get 184 *years* of the XIVth dynasty, which " is therefore artificial " (627). Now let us play with numbers likewise, about a period well known. The XXIInd and XXVIIth dynasties are each 120 years ; both foreign in origin ; evidently a duplication in history. The XXVth is sixty-one years, also foreign. Therefore there was but one foreign period of sixty years (XXVth) ; that doubled, for the reigns of the contemporary Egyptian rulers, made 120 years, and that is the origin of 120 years for the fictitious foreigners of the XXIInd and XXVIIth dynasties. This really fits much better than the numerical games played on the Hyksos Period ; and all being foreign dynasties the " Theme of disorder " would account for the whole, according to Capt. Weill's principles.

Such absurd treatment of historical records is what is set against the concordant statements of the Turin Papyrus, written only two or three centuries after the age in question, and the record of Manetho drawn from the material available while Egypt still had an unbroken continuity of literature. What is arbitrarily substituted for the ancient record ? The 1,600 years is cut down to :—

Contemporary Upper and Lower Egypt kings	20 years.
Thebans of Sekhem-ra group	90 ,,
Theban Sebekheteps and Hyksos ⎱	85 ,,
Later Sebekheteps and later Hyksos ⎰	
Theban and end of Hyksos	15 ,,
	210 years.

In these 210 years there must be compressed 133 kings of the Turin Papyrus, the great and lesser Hyksos and the XVIIth dynasty. Several of these kings we know to have had long reigns, enough of them to fill up the whole 210 years. Mermashau is placed as a Delta king, though his statues are of black granite from Upper Egypt. The reigns recorded for the Hyksos Khian and Apepi (who are agreed to have reigned over all Egypt, p. 207) alone occupy 111 years, and the whole of the great Hyksos kings total to 259 or 284 years. All this has to be suppressed, though it is certainly Manethonian history.

The wholesale disregard of the records, the suppression of the lengths of reigns stated (both in the Papyrus and Manetho), the fanciful theories of construction of the texts, the unhistoric treatment of the records of disorder and invasion, all prevent our regarding this work except as we regard the Egyptian history in Josephus, very valuable for reference, but without any reliance on the conclusions. This seems to be the best that can be done to destroy Egyptian history in favour of an arbitrary shortening that has no support in documents or in probabilities.

Le Musée du Louvre pendant la guerre, 1916–1918.—EDMOND POTTIER. 20 pp., 2 pls. 1919.

Those who have seen the back view of a mob of statues clustering in the bay of Demeter at the British Museum, and who have read of the strange holes in which our treasures have been secured from air attack, will like to hear how the French have fared. With them it was more a risk of plunder than of destruction. On the day of French mobilisation the director of museums met his colleagues and instructed them to put their treasures in safety for fear of Zeppelins. The rapid advance of German troops before the end of a month changed the orders to removal, packing and placing in southern cities. Toulouse was the centre, and a photograph shows the rows of cases and of railway wagons run into the church of the Jacobins for cover. Then, when immediate risks were less, the public demanded their museum ; and, as France could do its business without taking museums for offices as in London, several halls were re-opened after February, 1916. When the Gothas began to bomb Paris, all valuables were put under the solid vaulting of the ground floor. Next the Bertha bombardment began, and the pictures and marbles were sent off to Blois, and more sand-bagging was done at the Louvre. When the last struggle threatened to involve Paris, there was a scramble of museums and dealers to get packers, boxes, cotton and straw or hay to clear off everything, and near a hundred cases were got off in the last fortnight of June. After the armistice, in December and January, the cases were returned, and order was gradually restored.

Italy's Protection of Art Treasures and Monuments during the War.—SIR FILIPPO DE FILIPPI. 8 pp. (British Academy, 1918.)

We read here of the endeavours to preserve from modern barbarians the treasures which no invaders, however brutal, have yet wished to destroy. Two months before Italy's entry in the war, active measures were taken to protect monuments. The bronze horses of St. Mark's were taken down and placed in the Doge's Palace in a single day, sand-bagged and walled up. The great difficulty in Venice is the quaggy foundation, which prevents adding any great weight for fear of displacements. St. Mark's was covered with sand bags and sea-weed mattresses, which are light, elastic, and almost incombustible, also very effective in case of explosions. Canvas curtains are also a useful screen for glass or mosaics. All portable objects and the stained-glass windows were removed. At the Doge's Palace the portico arches were supported by masonry pillars, and the loggia with wooden props ; the sculptures were sand-bagged, and water pipes laid all over the buildings in case of fire. Venice was bombarded eleven times, specially on the churches. At Padua the Giotto frescoes were buried in sand bags ; the Gatta-melata statue, and the Colleone of Venice, were buried and boarded up, like Charles at Charing Cross. In all the other cities, Verona, Bergamo, Brescia, Milan, Parma, Bologna, the monuments, pictures, and treasures had to be protected.

Ravenna was an object of especial barbarism. There was no trace of military use there, hardly any population to be destroyed as civilians ; there was no purpose in attack, except the Germanic ideal of destroying all that gives national interest and historic sense to a people. To attack the churches of Ravenna is a depth of savagery which is only reached by the scientific development of psychological cruelty. The bomb which fell into S. Apollinare Nuovo, broke in the corner of the basilica, but happily did not destroy the mosaics. The whole tomb of Galla Placidia has been completely enclosed for protection, and San Vitale and the Baptistery strengthened throughout. At Ancona heavy shells were fired at the Duomo, high on the hill, and severely damaged it. The Arch of Trajan has been thoroughly built up with sand bags.

After their hideous depth of savagery, against all art and history, the Austrians are unabashed. A letter reached London lately from a Viennese stating that as he had excavated in Mesopotamia he would be glad to join in British work there. The reply was that the destruction of the library and apparatus of the University of Belgrade made it impossible for any Austrian to join in British work. That savage attempt to root out the intellectual life of a nation, was the clearest case of the degradation with which no civilised person could be associated.

F. P.

The New Catalogue of British Museum Greek Inscriptions relating to Egypt.

The editing of Section II of Part IV of *Greek Inscriptions in the British Museum* has been carried out by Mr. F. H. Marshall Hall, M.A., and the texts numbered from 1063 to 1093 are those acquired from Egypt and the Sudan, including one inscription obtained as late as 1914.

The volume is most beautifully printed and the facsimiles, or photographs (with the exception of that of the Rosetta Stone) finely executed ; it will be a great advantage to scholars to have this series of Egyptian records readily available, and to know where the originals may be inspected.

One of the most important texts in the collection is that from Syene, or Aswan, upon a column of red granite, which originally was erected at Elephantine. Much of the wording has been lost, but by the effort of several specialists a good deal has been restored, and it is found to comprise no less than ten documents concerning the later Ptolemies and their relations with the priests of the Chnoub Nebieb temple at Elephantine.

The records are either petitions from the temple servants to the king, or grants of privileges from the latter to the priests. The Syene quarrymen also put in their plaints ; probably, as worshippers of Chnoub, they also had their residences upon land leased from the temple, and thus sacred soil.

Although the documents concern kings as late as Ptolemy VIII and Ptolemy X, the latter in a letter dates it in the Macedonian month Dasios, equivalent to Egyptian Epiphi. Two generals commanding at Elephantine are mentioned, Hermokrates and Phommus. They are known from other papyri or inscriptions as being over the forces in the Thebaid.

Another historic monument is that found at Gizeh, which was erected by the citizens of Busiris in honour of Tiberius Claudius Balbillus, prefect of Egypt under Nero. The text from the dining hall of the Weavers' Guild at Theadelphia has been made of more interest by the evidence as to such associations recently supplied by the Oxyrhynchus Papyri.

A curious text is from the roadstead of Abukir, containing a dedication of a statue of the Phoenician deity Herakles Belos to Sarapis. The donor was not an Egyptian but a native of Askelon. One inscription is incised upon a gold plaque, and must have been deposited under the temple of Osiris at Canopus. It is a dedication of Ptolemy III Euergetes and Berenice his wife, daughter of Magas of Cyrène.

This Ptolemy was son of Ptolemy II, whose first wife was daughter of Lysimachus. Ptolemy II subsequently married his sister, Arsinoe, who adopted her stepson, afterwards Ptolemy III, as her son. This historical fact is now substantiated by this memorial, which calls Euergetes " son of Ptolemy and Arsinoe."

A similar votive plaque is in the Alexandria Museum. It preserves a dedication to Philopator and belonged to the Alexandria temple.

The next inscription chronologically is No. 1514. It is an offering to Ares, as a deity of hunting, by Ptolemy IV, dated about 206 B.C., and gives a text of six lines. It refers to elephant hunting, which sport the Macedonian monarchs much favoured, as it also supplied them with tame elephants for war equipment.

In this inscription Pisidian soldiers are mentioned, being another instance of the numerous countries from which the Ptolemies secured mercenaries. Mr. Hall provides what may be considered as the final edition of the Rosetta Stone, but does not refer to its partial duplicate of the Egyptian text, known as the Stele of Damanhour. It is a decree of the Council of the Memphis priests under Ptolemy V. All recent documents that throw light upon this superbly instructive text are utilised. Thus the hitherto mysterious mention of a thirty-year period is cleared up, by noting that that was the duration between the ancient royal *Sed*-festivals. The Egyptian version of the stone instead of " thirty years " reads " *Sed*-festival."

The allusion to the priestess of Berenice Euergetes, the child of Magas alluded to above, is illustrated by the Amherst papyri, whilst the financial matters in the Rosetta text are compared with the Tebtunis Ptolemaic revenue documents. Perhaps the review of the Rosetta Stone was written some time ago, because no reference is given to Otto, concerning priestly privileges, or to Lesquier for military matters. The worship of Arsinoe is illustrated by ostraca and a demotic document.

The last Ptolemaic record in a British Museum inscription concerns the eleventh of the Lagides. It comes from Paphos, in Cyprus, and quotes a letter of Alexander Grypus to Ptolemy Alexander, who was appointed governor of Cyprus by Cleopatra III. He is, however, styled Basileus in the text. Its date is 109 B.C., though he was not king in Egypt till 108 B.C. A single line upon a statuette base (*Memphis*, I, liii) entitles the Egyptian river god Νίλωι γονιμωτά(τω)ι. This expression is easily explained by the deity's statues depicting him surrounded by his numerous offspring.

A partly preserved slab from Antinoe, only obtained just before the war, gives the introduction to a panegyric upon a personage, said to have been a Platonic philosopher named Marcius Dionysodoros. He was also a councillor, and was one of the fortunate ones who for their erudition was maintained at, and by, the Museum.

Other epigraphical records and papyri refer to people so supported, including a text from Thebes and a Rylands papyrus.

There is one text from the Sudan which entitles the Nile " Oceanos," making the river a double of the Celestial Stream.

Several inscriptions, all short and fragmentary, are from Naucratis, including a poorly-composed poem upon a certain Herakleides who died just previous to the day upon which he was to have been married. (*Naukratis,* I, xxxi.)

These inscriptions, which would be a source of pride to any great museum, have been obtained by voluntary gift, purchase, or expensive explorations, and not as the loot of unjust wars of conquest. They form such a corpus of information regarding Egypt, that no history of that country in Gracco-Roman times will be complete without full consideration being given to them, and their editor is to be congratulated upon his work, which is a model for such a treatise.

JOSEPH OFFORD.

Cronologia Egiziana.—LUIGI PESERICO. 8vo, 71 pp. Vicenza, 1919.

This essay attempts to link various astronomical results with historical statements which would not usually be accepted. Results from Greek and Italian sources, especially the Parian chronicle, are here connected with Egyptian dates. The eclipse of 1411 B.C. is the date when the Pelasgi near Spina won a great victory over the natives. Eighty years after, in 1331 B.C., the Pelasgic *Sus* reigned, called Evander by the Romans and Perseus by the Greeks. Then we read of the invasion under Merneptah taking Tanis, a Pelasgic captain violating the queen of Merneptah, the plundering of the store cities of Pithom and Ramesses, a Pelasgic captain killing Seti Meneptah, only son and co-regent of Meneptah I. We may wonder where all this detail is to be found ; there is none of it in the Parian Chronicle. If it is in the author's translations of Etruscan documents, they need to be set out and established before they can be applied to history. In due course we reach the immigration of Abisha in the XIIth dynasty " whom some identify with the biblical Abram " ; a footnote adds that Ab-ram " father of elevation " is equivalent to Ab-shadu " father of height," which was Ab-sha. After going through Assyrian and Biblical chronology and the birth of Phaleg, there comes the " Rubble drift," which we usually call the " Noetic or universal deluge," beginning at some time in the four years 3048–3045 B.C. After this it need hardly be said that the writer has never heard of the Egyptian chronology, and depends upon Meyer for the possibility of a deluge at that date.

As a minor matter, the reign of Ramessu II is placed as beginning in 1325 B.C., which seems impossible. The date of 1300 B.C. agrees as well with the occurrence of a full moon on Mekhir 16. As the relation of lunations to Egyptian years of 365 days, and months of 30 days, cannot be easily worked except by compiling a table, and is wanted for any question of lunar dates, it is well to put it here on record. The years below are 365 days, months 30 days.

5 years 12 months = 2,185 days : 2185·22 = 74 lunations.
8 years 7 months = 3,130 days : 3130·23 = 106 lunations.
11 years 2 months = 4,075 days : 4075·19 ≐ 138 lunations.
19 years 10 months = 7,235 days : 7234·99 = 245 lunations.
25 years 0 months = 9,125 days : 9124·95 = 309 lunations.
111 years 2 months = 40,575 days : 40574·99 = 1,374 lunations.

Thus, every 25 years the lunations of a given month recur to the same day of the year, within ·05 day. At shorter intervals of 5, 8, 11 and 19 years a lunation occurs on the same day of some month. For reducing longer periods the cycle of 111 years 2 months may be used as correct to ·01 day, in the Egyptian kalendar.

PERIODICALS.

Académie des Inscriptions et Belles-Lettres.
Comptes Rendus, 1917.

MORET, A.—*Un Jugement de Dieu.* The stele published by M. Legrain in the *Annales du Service*, XVI, 161, is here retranslated. It has at the top a scene of priests bearing the barque of the divine Aahmes and Nefertari, and a priest Pasar standing before it adoring and praying " Oh judge who dispenses justice, let the owner of the house be justified, thanks to thee." Below is " Year 14 (or 18, or 26 or 34), 25th day under the Majesty of the king of South and North Usermaa-Ra, son of Ra, Ramessumeriamen, possessing life,—the day when came the priest Pasar with the priest Thay to enquire before the good god Nebpehtira. Came the priest saying ' As to this field it belongs to Thay, son of Sedemnef and to the children of Hayu.' The god remained unmoved. He returned to the god saying ' It belongs to the priest Pasar, son of Mesmen,' the god approved with his head very strongly, in presence of the priests of the good god Nebpehtira, the prophet Paaru, the front priest Yzanubu, the front priest Thanefer, the back priest Nekht, the back priest Tahutimes. Made by the priest, artist-scribe of the temple of Ramessumeriamen in the temple of Osiris, Nebmehyu."

This is a couple of centuries before the various other judgments known under the priest-kings. The case in question is connected with other documents from Saqqareh. Pasar is son of Mesmen, and under Aahmes I an ancestor of Mesmen named Nesha had received lands from the king. In the time of Horemheb quarrels had arisen among the descendants of Nesha, and some tried to partition the property, but in the direct line Huy, the father of Mesmen, had succeeded in keeping possession. Again under Ramessu II the collaterals attacked with false deeds, and got a decision against Mesmen, in favour of Khayuy. Here in this stele from Abydos is the sequel, that Pasar, son of Mesmen, got a divine decree in his favour, against the claims of Thay and the children of Huyu. The modification of *Kh* at Memphis to *H* in Upper Egypt is a known dialectic change. The name Thani is known in the Memphite family, corresponding to Thay in the Abydos text. Beside the conclusions of Prof. Moret, that divine decrees long preceded the priest-kings, and that such could supersede civil judgments, there is another extremely important conclusion. It has been usual to sneer at the decrees by the signal of the god as obviously only a trick of the priesthood. Here we have two priests appealing to the god-king. They must have believed that the decision was not manipulated, or neither priest would have agreed to be bound by it. In some way the decision did not depend on human interference, but was equivalent to drawing lots for a reply. The reason for an appeal to King Aahmes being recorded on a stele at Abydos is doubtless because his pyramid was there, and his worship would be carried on by the priesthood with a sacred bark and image to which the appeal could be made.

The Sculptured Stones found at Hal Tarxien, Malta, in their relation to Cretan and Egyptian Decoration.—EINAR LEXOW.   14 pp. Norwegian, 4 pp. summary in English.   (Bergen Museums, Aarbok, 1918-9.)

Dr. Lexow starts from the latest dating of Egyptian history, and accepts that there are no spirals before the XIIth dynasty, that is 2000–1800 B.C. according to him.   Hence he concludes that the spiral patterns originated long before in the Balkans, and not in Egypt.   This is very doubtful, according to the dating used by the Egyptians.   Next he proposes that the beautiful branching patterns found on the stones in Malta, were the earlier stage of the spirals also found there, and that such is the origin of spiral ornament.   Certainly it is very improbable that the formal spiral would give rise to the tree patterns, and therefore his main thesis seems likely.   There is no reason to bring in the dating to the question, as on any dating it seems that there was a large foreign admixture when the spiral appears in Egypt.

A Stamp Seal from Egypt.—WINIFRED CROMPTON.   6 pp., 1 plate.   (Journal of the Manchester Egyptian and Oriental Society, 1917–8.)

This seal of limestone has a rudely cut figure of a man and antelope.   Seals of similar design are quoted, and it seems likely that this is before the XIIth dynasty, and perhaps of the Old Kingdom.   The limestone stamps of the XIIth dynasty are less distinct in style and show a later stage of such work, which is clearly foreign.

Bulletin de la Société Archéologique d'Alexandrie.   No. 16.   The interest of the papers here is almost entirely classical, and so rather beyond our scope. The excavations of Col. Tubby and Lieut.-Col. James in the suburbs of Alexandria unfortunately miss the main question, as to how much is Ptolemaic and how much is Roman.   This might have been settled by the coins found, which are passed over as "unrecognisable," and "a few coins hopelessly oxidised." Anyone knowing coins could say within a century what their age was by the fabric alone.   The pottery, lamps, etc., would likewise have settled the date.   The only idea seems to have been searching for notable objects, and not settling historically the age of what was found.   Clear statement should be made as to whether the objects were contemporary with the graves, or only in the surface rubbish.

Dr. Granville gives an interesting biography of Henry Salt, the consul who figures largely in the early discoveries in Egypt.   A thoughtful looking man, with something that recalls Burns and Blake in his expression, he went to India and Egypt with Lord Valentia in 1802-6, as an artist and secretary.   In 1809 he was sent on a British mission to Abyssinia.   In 1815 he was appointed Consul-General in Egypt.   He there fell in with Burckhardt and Belzoni, and employed the latter for many years in excavations, from which come many of the older entries in the British Museum marked "Salt Collection."   He was in bad health, but could not leave Egypt owing to his duties.   He died in 1827 at the age of forty-seven, and is buried at Alexandria.   He was one of the valuable men who rose to the newer interests of his times, and was able thus to help in the early growth of research in Egypt.

1. ⎫ THE MALLON STATUE,
2. ⎬ FROM DEIR EL-BAHRI,
3. ⎭ EBONY.

4. ⎫ THE VIENNA HEAD.
5. ⎭
6. MENTUHETEP II, GEBELEYN.

ANCIENT EGYPT.

A MENTUHETEP STATUE.

THERE has lately been published by M. Paul Mallon, of Paris, a portfolio including some fine Egyptian figures. One of these is of much interest, and he has kindly allowed the head to be reproduced here. The figure is of ebony, twenty-seven inches high. The pose of the standing position is more thrown back than in the Old Kingdom, from the waist upward. The head has had inlaid eyes, now missing. The expression is marvellously vigorous and full of vitality, and it differs from other Egyptian figures not only thus, but also in the type. The very wide jaw, short chin, and high cheek-bone have hardly a parallel in other statues. It is clearly one of the great masterpieces, and of a rare style of work.

What period can be assigned for this? So far as external evidence goes, it is stated to have come from the XIth dynasty temple of Deir el-Bahri; and looking at the large slabs of sculpture which passed from the work there to the dealers, such a figure might more easily be taken surreptitiously. The nearest parallel for it is a head in Vienna, nine inches high, of green metamorphic stone. The views of this (borrowed from Bissing's *Denkmäler*) are here placed parallel to the Deir el-Bahri head. Allowing for the different school, working in different material, and the loss of the inlaid eyes, we see a close resemblance in the features. The wide short jaw, the proportion of the outline of the nose on the face, the high cheek-bone, the slope beneath the jaw, the squareness of the temple, all agree within near limits. The sternness of the work in polished stone naturally makes a different treatment and expression to the vivacity of the wood carving. The Vienna head is concluded to be of the Middle Kingdom by Bissing, who points out that the uraeus on it shows it to be after Mentuhetep II, who first wore it as in our Fig. 6.

Which of the Mentuheteps might the ebony figure represent? We will here follow the arrangement of Gauthier, as it seems to accord better with the artistic development than that of Naville, which puts Neb-taui-ra after Deir el-Bahri temple. The order of Gauthier for the Mentuheteps is as follows, stating the distinctive *ka*-name and Ra cartouche:—

I. Neter hezt.
II. Neb.taui   Ra.neb.taui.
III? Sonkh.ab.taui.
IV? Sma.taui   Ra.neb.hept.
V. Sonkh.taui.f   Ra.sonkh.ka.
VI.   Ra.mer.onkh.
            Ra.skho.ne.

Of these I is found at Deir el-Bahri, on sculptures from Gebeleyn, the head here No. 6. II is at Wady Hammamat. IV is the king of the Deir el-Bahri temple; according to Naville divided into two rulers writing the name by the oar and by the square, two homophones. V is the well-known Sonkhkara. VI is from a statue found at Karnak by Legrain. The last king here is not placed by Gauthier.

For the portraiture, though over ninety plates have been published from the temple, the royal portraits, unfortunately, have not been collected and reproduced efficiently on a full scale together. The complete heads on the British Museum sculptures do not all seem to have been published. The heads that are photographed in *The XIth Dynasty Temple of Deir el-Bahari* are in Vol. I, xii, xiii; Vol. II, v, vi; Vol. III, xii. None of them seem to have the prominent nose of the ebony figure, as these all agree pretty closely in having a slightly aquiline, massive nose, with little projection, a type seen now in some Sudanis. The Vienna head, when perfect, may have agreed with the Deir el-Bahri type. If so, the nose would not accord with that of the ebony figure. The Fig. 6 of Mentuhetep from Gebeleyn appears to be that in *XIth dyn. Temple*, I, xiiA. The general resemblance of this type to that of Ra.neb.hept shows that there was a family type; and it seems, then, most likely that the ebony figure, by its resemblance to the Vienna head, belonged to a successor of Ra.neb.hept, who dedicated his statue in the temple of his ancestor. When workmen are not well rewarded for the objects found, much is taken away without any record of its original place and connection. If we knew the position to which this figure belonged—the burial chamber—the royal shrine—the family shrines— or elsewhere—we might have fixed the historic value of one of the most striking portraits known from Egypt.

W. M. FLINDERS PETRIE.

ON THE USE OF BEESWAX AND RESIN AS VARNISHES IN THEBAN TOMBS.

IN some of the tombs in the Theban Necropolis it appears that wax was mixed with the colours used for the wall-paintings. The use of wax for this purpose has not been mentioned before, to the knowledge of the writer, but on turning over fragments of mud plaster from the walls of the tomb of Antef (No. 155) which had been buried in rubbish for some considerable time, he found that many of the colours were covered with a thin grey coating or skin. A brief examination on the spot proved this to be a wax, and a further investigation by Mr. Robert Mond in London gave the same result. A close examination of the walls of other tombs then revealed the fact that wax was fairly frequently used as a fixative or as a varnish in tombs ranging from the time of Amenophis I to that of Amenophis II. That the use of wax should be limited to this short period is interesting, but up to the present it has not been detected in tombs of either an earlier or a later date.

At the present day, the wax remains upon the tomb walls as a greyish and partially opaque skin which is readily detachable from the colour beneath, and thus gives impression at first sight that it was merely applied as a kind of varnish. Mr. Mond has however found in the sample submitted to him that the substance was as plentiful in the middle and bottom layers of the colours as on the surface, which suggests that the paint was mixed with the wax before being applied to the walls. The melting-point of the wax in the samples examined was 64° C., and as the melting-point of beeswax is 61° to 64° C., it seems probable that it was beeswax which was employed. Beeswax is. one of the materials imported into Egypt from the Sudan at the present day, and doubtless was in ancient days. The wax produced in Egypt is of a very poor quality and dark in colour. ' There is strong evidence that in some cases the wax was applied to the surface of the colours instead of being mixed intimately with them.

In several tombs, and notably on the walls of the inner passage of the tomb of Kenamūn (No. 93), the wax has been applied in this manner rather carelessly, and has encroached on, and slightly darkened, the white ground of the painted scenes. In the tomb of Antef (No. 155), the painter did not trouble to go round the small patches of the grey ground to avoid darkening them, but covered them also with wax.

There is no doubt that the application of wax was found greatly to improve the brilliance of the colours, especially the reds, blues, and greens. The re-melting of the wax on small painted fragments leads to the colours brightening up in an extraordinary way.

C 2

The question arises how this wax was applied, for even in a hot climate like that of Egypt it would never naturally be in a more melted condition than just pasty. It is, therefore, probable that it was mixed with some solvent, such as a volatile oil like turpentine ; the process of applying heated wax to the walls, as was done in the case of the Hawara portrait panels, would have been extremely tedious and uncertain. It would also take a considerable time to cover the walls of a tomb in this manner.

It is possible, of course, that an open brazier was held close to the portion of the wall to be treated, and a lump of wax then rubbed over the portion thus heated. A second application of the brazier locally to parts thus prepared would cause the wax to be well absorbed by the paint and plaster. If this method were the one adopted, it would perhaps account for wax being found right through a colour and not only on the surface, as well as overrunning the limits intended.

The following is a list of those tombs in which the waxing of colours has been observed :—

Tomb 179.	NEBAMŪN	..	..	..	HATSHEPSOWET.
,, 251.	AMENMŌSE	..	..	..	Early TUTHMOSIS III (?).
,, 155.	ANTEF	..	..	..	TUTHMOSIS III.
,, 39.	PUIMRĒ	..	..	..	TUTHMOSIS III.
,, 81.	ANENA	..	..	..	AMENOPHIS I–TUTHMOSIS III.
,, 82.	AMENEMHĒT	..	..	..	TUTHMOSIS III.
,, 86.	MENKHEPERRASONB		..	..	TUTHMOSIS III.
,, 93.	KENAMŪN	..	..	..	AMENOPHIS II.

The colours in the tomb of Puimrē are applied direct to the stone without an intervening coat of plaster.

In many tombs the wall paintings were covered with a varnish, which was made from some kind of resin, whose variety cannot, however, be ascertained as yet. In some of these tombs, the varnish is well preserved, though darkened in tone, but in others it has either scaled off through being applied too thickly, or it shows a badly cracked or fissured surface. Instances also occur where the varnish has become much blackened through age, more especially in those tombs which have been inhabited, a resin varnish apparently having a great affinity for smoke. Sometimes varnish was applied to the whole surface of a wall, but more usually only certain colours were treated with it, these being principally yellows and reds. It is difficult in some cases to distinguish between colours so treated, owing to the varnish darkening in tone (Tomb 150 and others).

There is strong reason to suspect that a varnish or similar medium was mixed with the pigments as well as applied to their surfaces, as some colours show a slight gloss combined with a peculiarly hard surface, the appearance of which is totally unlike that of a colour which has had a varnish applied only to its surface. It is to be regretted that up to the present only a few samples of varnished colours have been examined, owing to lack of material. It is highly undesirable to obtain samples direct from the tomb walls (which has been done in the past) and the only way is to obtain them from fallen fragments found in the course of excavating a tomb, which are either too poor to replace on its walls or whose proper position cannot be determined.

For those interested in this special question there is given below a list of some tombs whose paintings have either been varnished or possibly had a varnish mixed with their pigments :—

Tomb 40.	AMENHOTPE ..	..	Whole walls varnished.
„ 52.	NAKHT ..	..	Varnish applied only to limbs of some small female figures.
„ 64.	HEKERENHEH	..	Reds, blues, and greens, varnished.
„ 74.	THANUNY ..	..	Varnish applied to some of the greens.
„ 90.	NEBAMŪN ..	..	Yellows appear to have been treated.
„ 93.	KENAMŪN ..	..	Whole walls varnished and others waxed.
„ 130.	MAY	..	Reds and yellows varnished.
„ 139.	PERE ..	..	Reds varnished in places.
„ 161.	NAKHT ..	..	Many colours varnished.
„ 175.	(Name lost) ..	..	Reds and yellows varnished.

All the tombs mentioned above belong to the period of the late XVIIIth dynasty, the majority being of the time of Tuthmosis IV. Up to the present no examples have been found in the Necropolis of tombs of an earlier date that have been varnished wholly or partially, with the possible exception of yellows. A certain yellow used in the Theban Necropolis which was made from a compound of arsenic (orpiment) was generally applied over a white ground owing to its transparency. It thus acquires a glazed appearance which to the casual eye suggests a varnish.

There is not any known case of the employment of varnish for the purpose of protecting or enhancing colours in Ramesside tombs, with the one exception of Tomb 23, of Thoy or To. Probably varnish was soon found to be unsatisfactory as a medium for tomb decoration, though it was extensively used in the XIXth–XXth dynasties and later, for the decoration of coffins and funeral furniture.

The question now arises as to where the resin or resins were procured to manufacture such varnishes. Egypt does not produce any resin-bearing trees, with the exception of the acacia, and the nearest source of supply would be Syria and the North Coast of Africa, from which places sandarac and mastic are obtained.

Prof. Laurie has examined the question fairly closely in his *Materials of the Painters' Craft* (p. 31), where, in discussing a certain varnish found on a coffin of the XIXth dynasty, he concludes that the varnish used was a natural semi-liquid resin as obtained from the tree, like our Venice turpentine or Canada balsam, probably laid on after warming. He also states (p. 30) that a solid resin liquified by heat cannot be evenly spread on a surface, and it at once cracks on cooling. Now in Tombs 52 and 139, in which some female figures are thickly coated with a resinous varnish, it would appear that this was the method employed; for the varnish, besides being laid on coarsely, is now covered with numerous fissures and cracks (*see* NAKHT and PERE). In other tombs, also, the appearance of the varnish is very similar, which leads one to suppose that here again the resin was applied to the colours hot and not mixed with a solvent. On the other hand, there are tombs in which the varnish is fairly evenly spread and quite free from the blemishes mentioned above. One is, therefore, forced to the conclusion that in some tombs the resin was applied to the walls after being liquified by heat, and that in others a solvent was used with the resin to make a varnish either to coat or mix with the colours. What this solvent was it is impossible to say, as resin is only soluble in alcohol, turpentine or petroleum. If, as seems likely, turpentine was the solvent used, it could only have been procured from

C 3

Syria and the North of Europe, while petroleum, which is present in Egypt, could only have been obtained in an unrefined state.

Egypt's strong trade connection with Syria in the XVIIIth dynasty was probably responsible for the marked change observable in tomb decoration at that period[1] and for the introduction of the use of resin as a varnish. Syria at that time was exporting a quantity of material which may have been new to the Egyptians, and of which they did not properly understand the uses. The employment of varnish as a means of protecting colours, or perhaps for the purpose of brightening them, was a radical change which did not last very long, owing perhaps to the inborn conservatism of the Egyptian, or to the fact that it was found that a varnish did not in the end improve a colour but actually darkened it.

ERNEST MACKAY.

[The use of wax may be seen, mixed with dark green colour, as a filling of the hieroglyphs on the red granite coffin of Ramessu III in the Louvre ; also in incised figures on the wooden coffins (Univ. Coll.). This was probably the earlier stage of using coloured wax for portrait painting. The use of clear wax over colours was noted on the late sarcophagus of Ankhrui at Hawara ; this suggested securing the stucco by melted wax, and hence the excavators' system of using paraffin wax as a preservative. As to the use of turpentine as a solvent for wax or resin, the natural turpentine would be useless, being a thick syrupy resin. It is only the distilled oil of turpentine that would be of use. Pliny describes two rude methods of distillation. " From pitch an oil is extracted . . . it is made by boiling the pitch and spreading fleeces over the vessels to catch the steam, and then wringing them out." (XV, 7.) " In Europe tar is extracted from the torch tree by the agency of fire . . . The wood of the tree is chopped into small billets, and then put into a furnace, which is heated by fires lighted on every side. The first steam that exudes flows in the form of water into a reservoir made for its reception ; in Syria this substance is known as *cedrium,* and it possesses such remarkable strength, that in Egypt the bodies of the dead after being steeped in it, are preserved from all corruption." (XVI, 21.) From this it seems that in the later times, at least, an oil of turpentine was prepared in Syria for Egypt. The resin employed to coat paintings is described thus : " From the sarco colla (*Penaea Sarcocolla,* Linn.) a gum exudes that is remarkably useful to painters . . . similar to incense dust in appearance, and the white kind is preferred to the red." (XIII, 20.)—F.P.]

[1] Witness among other things—Floral friezes and ornamental ceilings and the use of the disc of the sun on top of the cheker ornament when that ornament was employed as a frieze.

THE KINGS OF ETHIOPIA.

THE journal *Sudan Notes and Queries*, issued quarterly since January, 1918, is mainly devoted to the customs and folk-lore of various tribes, a most needful help to administrators. The only articles touching Egypt are a series on the history of Ethiopia by Dr. Reisner, which is mostly familiar ground to our readers. The important new statement is the list of Ethiopian kings, as discovered and arranged from the excavations of the Harvard-Boston Expedition. Those with an asterisk are newly found.

	B.C.		B.C.
Taharqa	688–663	*Astabarqaman ...	466–463
Tanutamon ...	663–653	*Sa'asheriqa ...	463–443
Piankhy II ...	653–633	*Nasakhma ...	443–438
Atlanersa... ...	633–623	*Malewiyaman ...	438–408
Senkamanseken ...	623–603	*Talakhaman ...	408–403
*Anlaman ...	603–573	*Amanherinutarik	403–373
Aspalta	573–553	*Baskakeren ...	373–372
Amtalqa	553–538	* ?	372–368
*Malenaqan ...	538–528	* ?	368–348
*Nalma'aya ...	528–523	Harsiotef... ...	348–313
Netaklabataman	523–503	Piankalara(?) ...	313–298
*Karkaman ...	503–488	Nastasen	298–278

The order has been settled by the principle of sequence dating, the resemblances of one group of objects to another indicating their order of connection. The lengths of reigns seem to be approximations of ten or twenty years, or sometimes five or fifteen, arrived at apparently by the amount of work observed in each reign. The beginning and end of the list is fixed by contact with Egyptian sources. Any student of Ethiopic history will need this number (January, 1919), which can be obtained (3s.) at the Sudan Government Railways Office, 5, Northumberland Avenue, London, W.C. This journal may well be the basis of a national magazine of the Sudan.

NILE BOATS AND OTHER MATTERS.

(*Continued.*)

WE must now describe how this constructive difficulty, making a skin composed of many pieces into a continuous whole, one which could withstand longitudinal and transverse strains without yielding, was overcome.

Our wooden boats, whether " carvel " or " clinker " built, depend to a large extent upon the ribs which, however, would not maintain their verticality but for the skin of planks nailed to their outer sides : the ancient boat is a unit, a shell. The method made use of for holding the short planks one to the other becomes therefore a matter of the first importance. The keel plank (as I will call it) in the case of the Museum boats is made of but few pieces, so as to avoid the weakness of joints.

The wood of which these ancient boats are built is the same as that made use of to-day, very hard, but impossible to procure in straight lengths, hence the method of building up and fitting together of the parts as here described.

Iron was not made use of, perhaps not available in sufficient quantities.

We might have expected to find pins or pegs driven into holes prepared for them in the upper and lower planks, but if they are present in these specimens of ancient boat building they cannot be seen.[1] In the present case we find only dovetails with the occasional use of a species of tongue, which will presently be described (Fig. 5).

Countersunk recesses are prepared along the long sides of the planks and cut about half through their thickness (see A) ; into these the dovetails are forced, always on the inside of the hull. The butting joints of the keel planks are fastened together with large dovetails.

I venture to suppose that we should go wrong were we to assume that all boats of the period were built precisely as are the Museum specimens.

In the volumes before referred to on Beni Hasan, Part II, Plate XII, we see several boats differing in shape from those usually depicted. The hulls are deeper ; the greater draught must have enabled them to take considerable cargoes. In such boats the method of joining plank to plank with long pegs instead of with dovetails—which pegs and dovetails are now replaced by long iron nails, clinched, may have been employed. But, on the other hand, it must be kept in view that a clumsy draughtsman may be very responsible for a difference between one hull and another.

None of the ancient drawings are to scale.

In constructing a great barge such as that which is depicted at Deir el-Bahri and capable of carrying two obelisks, each of them some 32·0 m. in length, the construction of the hull must have been a matter of great care and no little science.

Denied the help of iron, and without the command of a variety of long straight timbers ; with the cross strains the structure must have been submitted

---

[1] In our own mediaeval carpentry we find magnificent roofs, held together entirely by oak pegs : for example at Westminster Hall.

to in getting the two immense monoliths on board ; in taking the chances of running on a sand or mudbank on the way down the river, and finally in unloading ; the hull must needs have been a really scientific combination of timbers. Whence came the large timbers ? Are we at all justified in supposing that there might have been more science displayed in building a barge in the XVIIIth dynasty than in the XIIth ?

We should bear in mind that long before the XIIth dynasty prodigious blocks of granite were brought down from the Aswân quarries for the Pyramids and for the temples at Saqqara.

As regards ship construction, it would probably be less difficult to support a great weight distributed over a large area, as in the case of obelisks, than it would be to support a similar weight concentrated, as in the case of a block, over a smaller area. It would seem impossible that dovetails alone could have held together the planks of the hull. The main strength of such a structure cannot have been merely in the skin, but must have been within, by making use of trusses and similar methods, clothed with the cleverly combined skin.

I may be pardoned if I make a short extract from a letter written me by the late Mr. Francis Elgar, Director of Naval Construction to the British Government. He says, " The two great obelisks of Karnak, 97 ft. 6 in. long, could be carried on a boat about 220 ft. long and 69 ft. beam, upon a draft of water of about 4 ft. 6 in. or not exceeding 5 ft." He was much interested in this question.

Some of the largest passenger steamers on the Nile approach this length but differ exceedingly in beam, they move on the river after its volume has considerably diminished ; but except at the very crown of high Nile, a barge of 69 ft. beam and 5 ft. draft would present great difficulties in navigation. As we have already said, merely to construct a vessel of such beam and yet of so shallow a draft under the limitations which pressed upon the ancient Egyptians must indeed have been a difficult matter. Whence came the necessary knowledge, at what remote period did the people begin to accumulate the experience which culminated in their power to deal with immense weights, lifting them, transporting them, unloading them, and this not only in the XIIth or XVIIIth dynasties, but in the IIIrd or IVth ?

It is not easy for those unaccustomed to deal with figured dimensions to realise merely by reading a statement of numbers of feet, how large a thing a barge would be, such as that mentioned by Dr. Elgar. Let me give an example. James Fergusson, in the monumental work, his *History of Architecture,* gives the following dimensions of Westminster Hall : 68 ft. wide and 239 ft. long. When we compare these with the dimensions required for the barge 69 ft. wide and 220 ft. long, we can realise what a serious business it must have been to build, to load, to tow, to navigate and finally to unload such a structure even under the best conditions.

To return to the boat in the Museum, which would be of very light draft and not intended to receive cargo. The dovetailing has been already described (Fig. 5). There is, however, another method by which the planks were held together, more akin to pegs and perhaps more effective (see Fig. 5).

Sometimes one, sometimes two tongues of wood are projected from the plank above and driven down into holes made to receive them in the plank below. In one case the tongue is 0.20 m. in length, 0.08 m. in thickness, and 0.15 m. in projection.

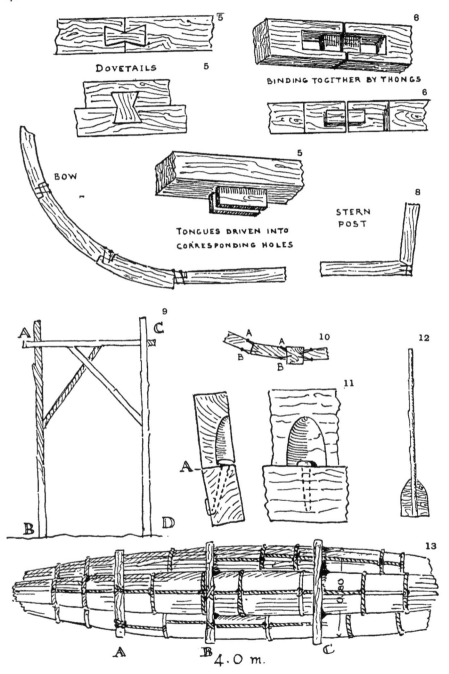

DOVETAILS   5

BINDING TOGETHER BY THONGS

BOW

TONGUES DRIVEN INTO
CORRESPONDING HOLES

STERN
POST

4.0 m.

The section of the boat (Fig. 1) shows that there is not, as we might have expected, a stout rim, or gunwale, forming a top rail to the hull (Fig. 6).

In this we see the ingenious method adopted by the boat-builders to tie together in their length the planks which form the gunwale—such as it is. No doubt a rope of fresh hide was bound tightly round the central tongue. The hide contracts in drying and in result an exceedingly close and strong junction is secured. The method is still made use of. The great yard of a dahabeah, usually made in three pieces and in length averaging more than 33.0 m., has the two largest pieces covered at their junction with a fresh hide, which, contracting as it dries and assisted by rope, withstands easily the great strain to which the yard is exposed under the tension of the sail. The yard of my own boat was fully 35.0 m. in length. This yard was on one occasion broken in half by the wind strain, but at the junction of the two heaviest pieces of the timber, one of which was broken, and which junction was fortified as usual by hide, no damage appeared.

It will be observed that the hull of the ancient boat is assisted to maintain its shape by eleven thwarts or cross-pieces, which are carried through the thickness of the skin of the hull and firmly fixed in position. They are visible from the outside. They support the deck planks.

A notable example of the way in which the thwarts were made use of in construction can be observed in the sculptures at the temple of Hatshepsut at Deir el-Bahari.[1]

On Pl. CLIII we see a considerable number of large rowing boats, which are being made use of to tow the barge which carries two obelisks. The ends of the thwarts are seen piercing the hull. On Pl. CLIV we see the great barge itself carrying the obelisks. The thwarts are in three ranges, one above the other, which is a proof that they formed most important members in the inner construction of this large hull.

In the case of the boats in the Cairo Museum, planks are laid, their ends resting on the thwarts and thus forming a movable deck.

This is a very usual method of forming a deck to-day.

At *AA* on the plan, Fig. 3, are indicated the places occupied by two posts to which the steering paddles were attached. Steering paddles—not rudders, as we understand them—are clearly shown on Pls. CLIII and CLIV *Deir el-Bahari* above referred to. The steering paddles were attached by ropes or thongs to the upper end of the vertical poles (see Pl. CLIV).

In the Museum boat there is no indication that they were provided with a mast. Had there been such we must find sockets on the centre plank at the bottom of the boat.

It is to be regretted that another illustration of boat building, in addition to that already referred to, is not known to us. Of boats already built and in use we have many examples. We must take refuge with Herodotus, who gives a short and not very illuminating description of how boats were built in the book *Euterpe*.

Of the passage in this book relating to boat building, various readings have been produced, none of them very helpful. Let us refer to that by Sir Gardner Wilkinson, *The Manners and Customs of the Ancient Egyptians*, new edition

---

[1] *The Temple of Deir el-Bahari*, by Ed. Naville. Part VI, Pls. CLIII and CLIV. Egypt Exploration Fund, 1908.

by Saml. Birch. Murray. Vol. II, p. 207. "The Egyptian boats of burthen are made of a thorn wood very similar to the lotus of Cyrene, from which a tear exudes called gum. Of this tree they cut planks measuring about two cubits, and having arranged them like bricks they build the boat in the following manner. They fasten the planks round firm long pegs and after this stretch over the surface a series of girths, but without any ribs, and the whole within is bound by bands of papyrus. A single rudder is then put through the keel, etc., etc." Wilkinson then gives a small woodcut (to which I refer the reader) which certainly does not at all agree with the Museum boat above described, nor with the way in which a **naggr** is built now. On p. 209 he gives a drawing of a boat the hull of which is constructed with thwarts as in the Museum specimens. None of the boats so beautifully sculptured in the reliefs at Deir el-Bahri, above referred to, suggest a method of construction such as that evolved from Herodotus by Wilkinson.

As I do not pretend to penetrate the mysteries of Greek texts, I have referred the question to my kind friend, Dr. Griffith, of Oxford.

He refers to a commentary on Herodotus by How and Wells, Oxford, 1912, Vol. I, p. 214. These commentators translate the passage in question as follows :

"The long bolts at frequent intervals were, so to speak, the string on which the short pieces were strung, they were driven in vertically to the layers." The words "string" and "strung" are not to be taken in the sense of tied together, but "attached," just as we find the word frequently used to-day. The bolts at frequent intervals were driven in vertically, as we see in the Museum boats.

If we may assume that the word "layers" should be taken to mean "horizontally laid planks," we find ourselves to be very near to some parts of the construction of the Museum boats, and also near to the method shown at Beni Hasan. Furthermore, we are very near to the method of construction as practised to-day, as we shall presently see.

Carey's translation is as vague as that of Wilkinson. How any boat can be "bound within by bands of papyrus," it is hard to say, but if the translator has put a wrong value on the Greek word and has translated as "bound" a word which should really be "caulked," he then describes that which is done to-day and must always have been done or the boat would not float.

The example of boat building before referred to from Beni Hasan (see Fig. 2) shows most clearly the planking formed of short pieces of wood and the vertical "butting" joints so distributed that, like bricks in a wall, no one joint comes immediately above the joint below. In this the description given by Herodotus is completely supported.

Seeing how fast many handicrafts making use of traditional methods are dying out in Egypt, it may be of interest to describe how I saw a naggr built in the year of grace 1911. The way differs not materially from the methods in use in the XIIth dynasty. I had the good fortune to see the business carried through under my eyes for the following reason. Sweet brotherly love does not always flourish between the inhabitants of neighbouring villages in Egypt. The two are very ready to fly at one another's throats. If harm cannot be done on a large scale it can be done on a small.

The noble and lofty principles inculcated by Mahomed are as thoroughly neglected as are the precepts of Christianity at home. There is the difference that the Egyptian is but emerging from the infamous misrule of the Turk ; he places but little confidence in the administration of the law ; he prefers to administer the law with his own hand. He begins with his tongue, his hands quickly follow, and violences are enacted. With us, happily, the law has a much greater power than in Egypt. We are forced to behave better.

In consequence of the above state of things and fearing that the wood, tools, etc., etc., might be stolen by way of revenge (no doubt the other side would call it justice), it was suggested that the naggr should be built on the river bank just below my house which, being at a considerable distance from the contending villages and having about it an aroma of the Government, there would be cast a halo of safety over both the materials and the operations.

I thus was introduced to some customs, more or less local, connected with carrying through the business which are not without their interest.

When it has been determined that a boat of this type shall be built, it is first necessary to select the builder, a craftsman who is classed amongst carpenters and confines himself chiefly to boat building. The carpenter, being instructed how many " dira " (yards) in length the boat is to be, agrees on a price. The " dira balady " or country dira is 58 centimetres in length = 23 inches.

The carpenter is paid at per " dira " of running length. Nothing is said about the beam of the boat or its draught. The carpenter carries in his head certain proportions of beam and draught in relation to length : a traditional system.

Judging by the clumsy tubs these boats always are, whether we meet with them at Omdurman, Dongola, Aswân or Assiût, we are justified in believing that the lines on which they are built are altogether traditional. A boat to take two masts is as clumsy in its proportions as a boat the building of which I am about to describe, taking one mast. The proportions differ materially from those of the boats in the Cairo Museum.

The naggr is built entirely for capacity. The draft and beam are, in proportion to the length, far greater than are those of the Museum boats. Of ancient boats there are countless models from tombs and as many drawings or sculptures upon the walls of tombs. In all cases there is shown a considerable part of the hull, both at the bow and the stern, out of the water. The difficulty of moving such a boat against a head wind must have been great (we have all doubtless experienced the difficulty in a gondola). The boats to convey merchandise, of which we see examples so carefully depicted in the Temple of Deir el-Bahri, are built on the same lines. The naggr of these days differs considerably.

In any case the existing form is evidently of very long standing. I would like to ask whether we are really justified in supposing that the models of boats in the Museums are at all correct. I do not believe that they are more than sketches. The same remark unquestionably may be made as regards the drawings or sculptures. They are symbols.

All students of Egyptology know the beautiful sculptured scenes on the walls of the Temple at Deir el-Bahri before referred to. The workmanship of the sculptor is so fine, so exact, and many details are set forth with such manifest accuracy that the impression at first received certainly is that here, at least, we stand before measured drawings: everything must be drawn to scale as in the drawings of an architect.

But the more the sculptures are studied, the more manifest it becomes that it is the method of delineation that produces the effect ; these beautiful works are, in fact, not to scale. Dr. Elgar told me he had come to the same conclusion as stated above and more especially is this the case with the delineation of the great barge bearing the obelisks, and he gave his reasons which were, to me, quite conclusive, but are too long to state here and too technical.

To return to building what I will call " our **naggr.**" There are sundry customs which cluster round the proceeding.

The carpenters go forth up and down the river to buy the wood.   This is, very usually, in the form of standing trees, which are carefully examined in regard to the possibility of cutting them into useful and handy pieces.

We must bear in mind that none of the wood is artificially bent ; all the curved pieces, such for example as the planks forming the bow, must needs be cut to shape by the skilful carpenter with an adze, and wonderful it is to observe the certainty with which he wields this instrument.   With the saw also certain slight curvature is obtained.   The wood, trees or planks, are purchased by the employer.   All surplus wood brought upon the ground belongs to the carpenter.

The carpenter is, further, entitled to be fed by the employer during the progress of the works, and that not with ordinary everyday durra bread and such like, but pigeons, chicken and other luxuries must be provided.

The neighbours of the employer are also placed under contribution ; they are supposed to consider that the building of a boat is a matter of interest and use common to all, so they frequently visit the work, consume a great amount of time in useless talk and bring as presents to the employer, but for the use of the carpenter, eatables of various sorts.

Custom further dictates that the carpenters (for in the case under consideration there were two) receive a complete outfit of clothes, such as people of their degree usually wear.   When the boat is ready to be launched, the carpenters receive a second suit.   Coffee is, of course, being freely administered to the carpenters and visitors during the whole time of construction.

The employer, in addition to the wood, has to find all necessary nails and bring them to the site.

The wood made use of is that of the *acacia Nilotica*, known on the Nile as " sunt," a slow-growing tree hard and close in grain.   The tree can grow to a considerable size, but it seldom gets a chance.   A stem of a metre in diameter is thought very large.   After purchase the whole tree stem, large branches and small, is brought to the river side after being in part. cut up to facilitate transport.   Having arrived, the pieces of wood are scientifically sorted, all the timber to be used for the naggr being laid on the slope of the river bank, just within.the water, so as to be kept always damp.

The carpenter brings his own saws, hammers, adzes and big augers, also a pair of gibbet-like affairs which are used with much craft to prop the timber for sawing.   A spot having been selected close to the river side (it must be understood that the work is usually undertaken during the going down of the Nile : if the Nile is rising the spot selected is high on the bank, so near as to facilitate the floating of the finished boat) a sufficient piece of land is made level, the naggr being built parallel with the stream.   Just north of it a little hut of durra straw is made to form a shelter from the prevailing north-west wind.   In this the interested parties live until the work is finished, thus keeping watch over the materials and the progress of affairs.

Let us say that the naggr, when finished, will be 24 ft. long over all.

A straight line is laid down on the levelled surface of the selected site, by the aid of a piece of string, its direction parallel with the river, and on either side of it, alternately, a small stump of a branch is fixed in the ground. In the meantime the keel, which is to rest on the before-named stumps, is being prepared.[1]

From small tree stems of a suitable size the longest available pieces are got : let us say three. These are, with the adze, worked smooth along the top. The two sides are dressed vertically but not very true : the under part is left rough and shapeless. The three pieces are halved together, drilled with the auger and mighty spiked nails procured from Cairo are driven in and clinched. The keel thus formed is placed on the stumps and is fixed to them by long nails.

It will be observed that in establishing a keel we have departed from the method of the Museum boats and it may be presumed, of the ancients, for neither in models nor wall drawings do we see anything that suggests a keel. As soon, however, as it was decided to make use of a hinged rudder and not of the steering paddle, a vertical stern post became a necessity. It must be presumed that with this change the keel also was introduced, as without that the stern post could hardly have been made firm at the bottom.

The carpenter now prepares the stern post. It consists of a straight piece worked square in section, by means of the adze, and halved at the bottom end to the keel. A spike nail or two is driven in, a fixing which seems very inadequate and indeed would be so were it not that by the method of building the hull every part of the structure assists in supporting every other part (Fig. 8).

The bow of the naggr is a more imposing affair than the stern. Having selected some knees from the wood lying on the bank, three curved pieces are cut and then shaped by the adze : they form when set together a somewhat imperfect quadrant. They are halved and nailed together in the way already described for the keel and the stern post, are quite neatly fitted, being finally dressed down with the adze after they are fixed in position (Fig. 7).

Where the curved pieces for the bow start upward from the keel, the bottom piece projects downward below the keel some four inches or more.

I could not ascertain that the carpenter knew why he made it thus. It seemed with him a matter entirely of tradition, but one can imagine that long since the advantage of such a projection was observed. When the keel strikes upon a sand or mud island, the projection would make a groove in the yielding surface, through which the keel would more easily follow.

Before the stern post or bow are permanently fixed, a piece of string is procured, also a piece of red ochre, which the sandstone hills in Upper Egypt provide so liberally. It is called " moghra." The ochre, in water, provides a red sediment : this is the pigment in which the string is soaked. The string is held along the middle of the upper surface of the keel and then plucked. The ochre is thus deposited in a straight line. In the same way straight lines were made, both vertical and horizontal, in remote times, as hundreds of tomb interiors still show.

By eye the stern post and rib for the bow are set up, a string is stretched from the top of the one to the top of the other, and by means of a plumb bob made of a heavy nail and a piece of string, the centre line or axis of the hull is established.

It is not a little fascinating to watch these effective but primitive methods being put into operation. Excepting in the presence of the iron nail, there is not one of these methods that by a study of the ancient drawings and buildings we cannot see to have been in use four or five thousand years ago.

---

[1] In Fig. 2, from Beni Hasan, we see the sticks set up so as to keep the hull in its place.

The Egyptian knew how to execute work, when he was called upon to do it, which in its perfection has never been exceeded, as, for example, the external masonry of the Great Pyramid.   Except in some of our finest metal work of to-day, screw gauges and things of that sort, we never approach it.   What absolute precision and mastery over the most stubborn materials, what fineness of modelling of the mouth and cheeks of a statue did he not attain !   We are still at a loss to know with what means he reached this perfection.

In other pieces of work where such accuracy was not required, he worked in a manner far more rough and undoubtedly the handiwork was, for the most part, guided by the eye alone.

The **naggr** we are now engaged upon comes under the last category. When one tests what the carpenter has done by a twentieth century standard and observes the tools and methods made use of, one is not a little astonished how so considerable a degree of correctness has been arrived at.   On the other hand, a **naggr** of but a few years old wears an aspect of hoar antiquity.

Worked, as all the surfaces have been, by the adze, the surfaces being without pitch, tar, paint or varnish, they acquire a silvery hue and distinctive texture that wood from the saw or plane never gets.   The rudder, although not belonging to the old order of things, is so rough in its make as to suggest a fragment of an old barn door, whilst the sails are usually the worse for wear.

The bow, stern post and keel connecting them standing complete, a little flag bearing the name of Allah is set up at the highest point of the bow and remains there during further building operations.

A reciter of the Koran, for a consideration, also attends occasionally : it is furthermore helpful to the success of the operations that pious and complimentary remarks should freely be made.

The large saw already mentioned as brought by the carpenter now comes into work.   A trunk of tree, after the adze has reduced it to a section more or less square, is marked with slightly curved lines, more or less parallel.   This is done by means of the string charged with " moghra " (red ochre) which is held by one of the carpenters in short lengths of perhaps 9 ins., and then plucked. The direction of the string is slightlv changed after each plucking until, at last, a long line somewhat curved is clearly marked.

We now come to the erection of the sawing frame.   Two fairly stout branches, selected from the stock of wood, have been set vertically, their ends buried deep in the alluvium of the river bank ; a cross piece joins them at the top, they are firmly roped together.   The piece of a tree to be sawn is tilted up against the cross piece.   The "gibbets" above referred to are placed under the other end of the piece to be operated on.   The diagram Fig. IX shows how the gibbets are used.

A, B and C, D are roped together tightly.   The trunk or log to be sawn extends from the cross piece first described and is rested on the cross piece of the gibbets A, C.   The whole affair, rickety as it appears, keeps steady.   One man stands on the trunk or log to be sawn, the other stands below.   A handy saw-pit is established but without the pit.   The contrivance can be set up almost anywhere.

The sawyer below observes the curvature of the red ochre lines which are above him ; directing the saw along these lines, three or four stout planks are produced to the shape intended.

In the case I am describing the planks were about 4 ins. = 10 cm. thick and as long as the trunk or log would permit.

Sundry planks, some 2 metres long, were obtained which were used for the bottom of the hull.

The planks are not nailed down on to the keel, but fitted against the sides which, as we have said above, were got to shape not by sawing but by the adze. The keel projects, when all is finished, but little below the skin of the hull.

It may be supposed that by the somewhat rough method of work above described, the sides of the keel are not very true. The difficulty is got over in the old Egyptian manner, as it was done by the masons. The piece of material to be set in place is fitted to the irregularities of the piece already established. None of the keel is cut away.

The way in which the adjustment of the planks to the keel is made is as follows. The sides of the keel are painted with a liquid mixture of Nile mud. Before this is quite dry, the plank to be adjusted is held in position against the mud paint. Where that paint comes off on the side of the plank, the discoloured surfaces are dressed away, very deftly, with the adze ; the process is repeated until the two fit very closely. The same process is repeated for all the joints throughout the hull.

The ready way in which the demands of the eye are responded to by the skilful hand is delightful to watch.

The plank, ready for fixing, being held in its allotted position, the carpenter arms himself with a small paint brush made from a piece of fibrous stick chewed at the end.[1] He dips this in the red ochre and marks the places for the nails (see Fig. X, A.)

A straight mark and a small circle indicate that the nails are to be driven in from above at A, or below at B, which when the hull is complete will be A the inside, B the outside (Fig. 10). The plank being set up edgeways on the ground, the holes for the nails are bored with a large auger. In this respect we have come away from the ancient dovetails but are not removed far from the pegs. The necessary curvature of the planks is gained entirely by the adze. This statement applies to those of less than two metres in length, which were in most cases sawn as before described.

The nails are of wrought iron, not very hard, tapering in form and with large mushroom heads : the nail must not be so stout that it cannot at the small end be bent over with some ease, as all nails are clinched.

In some cases a recess is prepared as at A, Fig. XI, giving greater facility to drive the nail diagonally into the next board B.

There are, near the top planks of the hull, pieces in the nature of thwarts set across from side to side and carrying a boarded deck. Quite half the area of the hull is thus covered in and the rigidity much strengthened thereby. Across the hull, just about the middle of its length, is fixed a stout beam, usually made from the stem of a tree, smoothed with the adze, but following all the inequalities of its shape. The thwarts above named are passed through the skin of the hull and are visible on the outside. The stout beam or tree stem is for making steady the short mast which has a socket in the keel and a strap or other form of stay to secure it to the beam.

The wooden structure of the naggr is now complete. The next duty is to enable it to float.

---

[1] See *Visits to Monasteries of the Levant,* by the Hon. Robert Curzon. Murray, 1850, p. 96.

We are accustomed to boats being caulked from the outside, but in the case of the naggr we find the same method employed as mentioned by Herodotus, the caulking is done from within ; but instead of " byblus " old clothes are preferred. There is a great merit in this system. To caulk a hull as we do it, the boat must be on land and attacked from the outside, but in the case of the naggr the traveller remedies the leak as he travels along, which indeed I have assisted in doing.

The proprietor sacrifices a strip of his " gallabea " or " camesa," or by preference, a piece of the traveller's clothes. This is vigorously pushed into the crevice, with the result that the boat becomes remarkably water-tight. This method of caulking adds to the ancient and ragged appearance of the hull. Little bits of rag are seen fluttering on the outside.

In these days the carpenter occasionally fortifies the hull by a few ribs, but these are in no way parts of a system attached to the keel, but are fixed to the interior of the skin, giving a little extra strength where the builder thinks it desirable.

The sail is always latine.

The naggr has now to be set afloat, but this is not a great piece of business —any inequalities in the surface of the sloping bank left by the retiring waters are smoothed down. The boat, its long axis parallel with the stream, is eased down first at the bow, then at the stern, and so it wriggles its way until at last it is afloat : imperfections in the caulking are made good ; the mast and cordage are set up, the sail is attached, and the new naggr at once takes its place amongst the antiquities of Egypt.

A study of what has been said shows that, as a matter of fact, the naggr of to-day must be a very direct descendant of the boats built some thousands of years ago, with the method of construction but little changed.

The saw plays a not very prominent part ; pegs and dovetails have given place to iron nails. The adze is now as it was long since, the most important cutting and shaping tool. Steering by a paddle has given place to steering by a rudder.

The progress of this type of boat, primitive as it is, depends still almost entirely on the sail, punting with a " midra " or long pole is still, as it always was, universal. The oar, when it is used, is no more than a bare pole, cut a little flat at one end.

The paddle, like the crocodile, has entirely disappeared between the sea and the Second Cataract. At Kareima, however, close to Gebel Barkal, just below the Fourth Cataract, I have had the pleasure of being propelled in the ancient manner as we see it in the models and on the wall sculptures. The side of the naggr in which I was travelling rose to exactly one metre above the water. Through a loop of rope, twisted round a thwart and projecting outside the naggr, was passed the shank of the paddle.

The loop acted as a rowlock. The paddle consisted of a fairly stout stick some two metres long, and at one end was fixed the blade (Fig. XII). The blade was tied to the shank. The paddle was used nearly vertical. Observing how the Kareima people used it, one understood the ancient models in the Museums with the extreme verticality of the paddles as there to be observed.

When in a swift stream additional strength was required, two or more men pulled at a rope attached to the paddle shank immediately above the blade, and thus, drawing the paddle towards them they very much augmented the force of the man who held the paddle.

I ask permission to insert the following from *Across Asia Minor on Foot* by W. J. Childs, Blackwood. I take the paragraph from the *Spectator* of March 3rd, 1917. It seems to me of peculiar interest as it shows that, if we go to the right place, we may see an ancient type of boat on the sea at the present day, square rigged :—

"A sight of this kind I watched one summer evening on the coast of the Black Sea, when a long boat, whose bow was shaped like a swan's breast, put off from the shore. Her stern projected above the hull and was curved into a form resembling roughly the head and neck of a bird preparing to strike. Upon the mast, hanging from a horizontal yard, was set a single broad square-sail, and under the arching foot could be seen the black heads of rowers, five or six men on either side, and a bare-legged steersman placed high above them in the stern." Mr. Childs sees in this, with great reason, the direct continuance of Greek tradition. May we not go further back and see the picture of this very ship in many an Egyptian tomb of far greater antiquity ?

There is yet one more machine for floating on the Nile which, exceedingly primitive as it is, is still in very general use. It is called "ramus." It is more than a raft which is merely a float; it is shaped to a certain extent and can be propelled, indeed it usually is so, by an imperfect paddle.

The ramus will take at least two people. It is made of boose—the straw of durra, which grows to a length of two, or two and a half, metres. The boose is tightly tied into long bundles, circular in section, diminishing towards one end, the bow of the machine. Three or more sticks, A, B, C, Fig. XIII, are tied across, so as to keep the structure steady. The largest of these sticks are 0.80 or 0.90 m. in length. I have measured the length of several of these ramus, all about 4 m. It is not curved upwards from the water at the bow end. The whole thing is made very rigid by being roped together, as shown in the sketch. A view of the fishermen working from these floats is given in the *Journal of Egyptian Archaeology*, IV, 255.

The passenger propels himself with a paddle made of a short piece of stick and a piece of flat board at one end. The thing is primitive but sufficient.

The ramus is much in use when cultivable islands appear above the retiring waters of the Nile.

Somers Clarke.

[The old-fashioned ship-building in England was not so very different to the Egyptian method. "Stocks.—A frame erected on the shore of a river or harbour whereon to build shipping. It generally consists of a number of wooden blocks, ranged parallel to each other . . . and with a gradual declivity towards the water " (*Encyclopaedia Britannica*, 1797). Had we the facility of a rising river to float off our shipping, no doubt the methods would have been still more alike.—F. P.]

REVIEWS.

—•—

Estudio de Arqueología Cartaginesa. La Necrópoli de Ibiza.—Antonio Vives
y Escudero. Madrid, 1917. 8vo, 189 pp., 175 figs., 106 pls. (Junta para
Ampliación de Estudios, Moreto 1, Madrid.) 20 pesetas.

This is a noble work of collecting materials for the "extension of study";
though based on the very varied contents of the Iviza Museum, all kinds of
collateral materials from Carthage, and some other sites, are brought in, and
briefly illustrated by sketches for comparison. The plates, 7½ by 4½ ins., are all
photographic, fine-grained half-tone or collotype, bright and clear. Unfortunately the industry of the author has had indefinite material to work upon.
The Iviza Museum appears to be a chance collection without any scientific data ;
not a single tomb-group, or association of objects is in evidence, not a single
dating is known beyond what may be guessed from appearance. It is of the
"curiosity" stage, like the Naples Museum, where no localities or groupings are
stated. What might be done in a single season's work by an archaeologist who
knew the dating in Greece and Egypt, would be worth all that is yet known and
collected. In the absence of any dating, it is only possible to note comparisons,
which we here do on the Egyptian side.

The earliest contact with dated material is in the curious pottery made
on a wheel, open below and finished off with head and arms above. This
style of figure is known from a tomb of the XIth dynasty (*Dendereh*, XXI) ; also
similar figures with hands to the breast from Cyprus (Cyprus Museum 5501–
5542, Sandwith Collection). Seeing how little is found in Iviza before the
Carthaginian period, it is very unlikely that such figures are of the XIth dynasty
age in Spain ; nor are they indigenous in Egypt. They seem to belong to some
centre—such as Cyprus—whence they were brought into Egypt in the XIth
dynasty, and into Iviza perhaps a couple of thousand years later.

Probably a similar connection accounts for the resemblance of the bird vase
(*Qurneh*, XII) of about the XVIIth dynasty, and the similar bird vase from
Gades (*Estudio*, XLVII, 4).

There is perhaps an echo of the early prehistoric Egyptian style in the bone
spoons with circular bowls, and the long hair pin (*Est.*, XXX, 7–9, 1); when
the close relation of the pottery of that age to the modern Algerian is considered,
there is no improbability in a style of ivory work lasting on in North Africa,
and passing thence to Spain, long after it ceased in Egypt.

Another similarity is in the multiple vases with Hathor head and cow's head,
found at Carthage (*Est.*, p. 130), and the group of vases with the cow's head and
disc, from the deposit of Tehutmes III (*Koptos*, XIV, 7). The Carthaginian
is also evidently related to the multiple vases on a ring as found in Egypt
(*Abydos III*, XVI, 4) about the XVIIIth dynasty, and known in Asia Minor
rather later. This type is foreign to Egypt, and may have been brought in there

at an earlier date than it was borrowed in Africa. All of these resemblances therefore indicate trade in common with centres of production, but not necessarily equal dates.

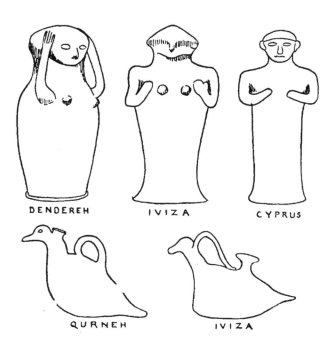

DENDEREH IVIZA CYPRUS

QURNEH IVIZA

The case is different when we reach the XXIIIrd dynasty, the early period of Carthage. Jars of this period are well known in Egypt (the parallels here are the nearest published, but others are closer), and are the same as found in Iviza and very common in Carthage (*Est.*, XLIII, 21–23, p. 118). The glass vases with variegated bands of colour found in Iviza (*Est.*, XXXII) are all of the later period of such glass, well known from the cemetery of Cumae, and generally assigned to the ninth century B.C. The glass beads, coarsely made of varied colour (*Est.*, XXXIV, 1–7) are common about the eighth century B.C. in Egypt. Cylindrical beads of coloured glass covered with knobs (*Est.*, XXXV) belong to the same factories and period. A cowry of glazed pottery from Carthage (*Est.*, Fig. 84) has the cartouche of Shabaka of the XXVth dynasty. Thus before the familiar Greek age of the XXVIth dynasty, there are plenty of connections with the remains known to be of the ninth to the seventh centuries B.C. ; but there is no direct connection before that, only joint borrowings from uncertain third centres of trade. The conclusion seems clearly to be that it was the Carthaginians who brought Egyptian things westward, and it was not until the Phoenicians had established the western connections that anything was regularly traded from end to end of the Mediterranean.

In the XXVIth dynasty the Egyptian products and influences were common. Glazed pilgrim bottles with new year wishes are found at Carthage (*Est.*, Fig. 78) ; circular mirrors (*Est.*, XI, 1, 5) ; triangular arrowheads (*Est.* XV, 4, 5) ; alabastra (*Est.*, Fig. 62) found at Carthage ; a finger-ring (*Est.*, Fig. 50) as found in Sardinia and Carthage ; a glazed ball with an uzat eye (*Est.*, Fig. 83) and scaraboids with a human head (Fig. 77), both from Carthage—all of these show the general spread of Egyptian things westward in the seventh century.

The usual little glazed amulets became familiar, and coarsely copied, in the West. That glazing was actually done at Iviza is probable from the occurrence of a lump of little balls of frit (*Est.*, XXXIV, 27), exactly such as were produced in Egypt, for the glaze factories to employ in making blue glaze. Perhaps, however, this may have been for making blue paste amulets ; anyhow it shows manufacture of amulets locally. A square amulet of bronze from Carthage (*Est.*, Fig. 58) shows a Phoenician adaptation of Isis and Horus, distinguished by the moon and sun respectively.

Coming later, the series of lamps runs through all stages—as at Naukratis—from the cocked-hat type of a flat pan folded over into a spout, through the central pivot-hole type, to the closed-in top, and then the addition of a side handle. There seem to be very few of the types with figures, only the two cupids and negro's head ; and there are none of the multitude of frog or palm types which abound in Egypt in the second to fifth centuries A.D. This seems to show that Iviza decayed after the first century, and ceased to import foreign goods, however common. There is no trace of the Byzantine types of lamps, so frequent at Carthage and in Sicily.

Of purely Roman age there is not much. A square metal mirror (*Est.*, XI, 4), some box handles (XVII, 3–6), a glazed dish with lions on the edge, from Carthage (Fig. 82), some bone hairpins (XXX, 10–14), little figures of cast glass (XXXIV, 20–23), and what may be a surveyor's mark, like those found in Egypt (Fig. 36), are all of them early Roman rather than late. Knowing how flourishing Carthage and Spain were in late Roman times, it is strange that more does not appear in this volume. One single earring from Cadiz, seems to be of Byzantine age (Fig. 17). The only conclusion is that purely Roman work had so completely driven out local or national style, that nothing remains but entirely Roman material, which the author has rightly discarded from a work dealing with Carthaginian archaeology.

Some good plates (XLI–XLIII) are given of the "indigenous pottery." This differs from what we know of the Italian, Greek or Egyptian. How far it may be in common with the Algerian or Spanish is not settled. Of the Carthaginian forms drawn there is but one which accords with the Iviza forms. The most peculiar products are the large masks of pottery, about 6 to 8 ins. high, mainly from Carthage, but also from Sardinia and Iviza. These have no descent from the Greek Silenus and other types ; they can scarcely be intended as merely comic absurdities, and rather suggest a use in regular plays or performances. If Carthaginian literature had survived we might have seen the clue to these.

The great characteristic of Spanish work in all ages has been a fulsome spread of ornament. The terracotta figures are examples of this, with headdress and tunic covered with rosettes and spirals (*Est.*, LXXXV, LXXXVII, 1 ; LXXXVIII, 3). This taste is what renders the mediaeval architecture of Spain so fatiguing in its details to those bred in plainer styles.

Some of the terms used here in classification are hardly exact. The scarabs named Mykenaean are by no means so early; those called Egyptian are all Phoenician imitations; the scarabs of so-called Assyrian style are rather the Persian edition; and those termed Carthaginian are mostly local variations of Greek design. The figure called neo-Punic (XCVII) seems rather to be pure Greek in a local school, probably Cyrenean.

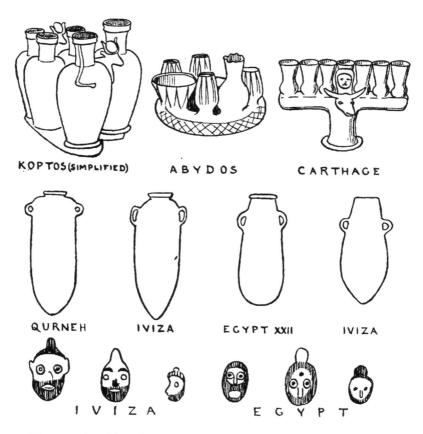

KOPTOS(SIMPLIFIED)   ABYDOS   CARTHAGE

QURNEH   IVIZA   EGYPT XXII   IVIZA

I V I Z A   E G Y P T

The general position then seems to be that there was little intercourse of the East with the Western Mediterranean till after the Trojan war; the traditional drift of peoples westward after that, in the reputed Trojan colonies, and the foundation of Cumae in 1050 B.C., began the movement which the Phoenicians carried on, and it was their trade that spread the taste for copies of Egyptian work. Scarcely anything of Egyptian make was traded West (the bust of Sekhmet, *Est.*, VIII, 2, is about the only piece), but there was a wide field for the Phoenician imitations, in scarabs and glazed ware, which flooded the trade, much as Naukratite imitations spread in the seventh and sixth centuries. Then after the Roman conquest there was a great collapse, and what little life remained in Carthaginian regions was completely dominated by Roman works.

The Tomb of Senebtisi at Lisht.—By A. C. MACE and H. E. WINLOCK. 4to, 132 pp., 35 pls., 85 figs.   New York, 1916.

At last we welcome the first volume of the results from the Expedition of the Metropolitan Museum of Art at New York, begun ten years before.   The scale and style of the present volume is delightful, but if one tomb claims such treatment, will the life of the explorers suffice to bring out the results of ten years ?   *Respice finem* is a motto which seems to be forgotten by most ex cavators.   They scarcely regard the fact that no one else is likely to find time to work up and publish their discoveries, if they do not find time to do so themselves.   Whatever a man does not issue of his own work will probably never be seen, and might as well have been left undone.   It will be useless to science, and lost to sight, like the plunderings by the European consuls a century ago.

This volume is a complete account of a burial of the XIIth dynasty, which had been attacked anciently, but was saved owing to the plunderers being interrupted before much mischief had been done.   The chapters deal with the general conditions, the clearing of the tomb, the coffins, the jewellery, the ceremonial stores, the pottery, and the dating.   The oblong pit, large enough to lower a coffin, and about 16 feet deep, and the narrow recess chamber, are all of the usual type, like dozens of such burials in any Middle Kingdom cemetery.   The great value of the account is in showing what a complete burial contained, and explaining the former contents of hundreds of similar tombs now empty.

Over the coffin, far from the loose rubbish that had fallen forward into the chamber, there was a pile of bricks and stones.   This seems to have been placed there by guardians of the tomb, to cover over the attempted attack on the coffins by the plunderers ; the same careful hands had filled up again the plunderer's hole down the shaft.   The coffin had been considerably decayed, but the original decoration was carefully preserved by treating it inch by inch with shellac or with paraffin wax.   On the outer coffin were inlaid eyes of alabaster and obsidian.   This coffin was of the usual rectangular form, with raised block ends and rounded top, such as began in the third dynasty.   Around the edges were gold strips, and down the axis of the lid an inscribed band, naming two women, Săt-Hapi and Senbtas ; there is no explanation of the occurrence of the first name, or whether these were two names for the same person, as was often the case for men.

The careful tracing of the arrangement of the bead girdle, the collar and other parts of the outfit, has added much to our stock of information.   It is an irony that the minute record of a much damaged burial should be worth more than the accounts of the perfect burials found by incompetent diggers.   The detailed discussion of the coffins and fittings, compared with those from other important tombs, makes this volume a text-book of the subject.

The inner coffin is claimed to be " the earliest definitely datable example yet known " of the anthropoid coffin.   Two questions are involved here.   First, the style of the decoration of bead collar and tresses of hair (frontispiece and Pl. XX)·seems to be far removed from a starting point.   The similar form of the spiral at the end of the tresses and the marking of the breasts, shows that copying had gone on long enough to lose the original idea : the formality and want of attachment of the rectangular beadwork below the collar, again, is evidence of repeated copying.   Second, how early is this coffin ?   Unhappily the evidence of date is not given : it is only stated (p. 114) to be " dated with great certainty to the early part of the XIIth dynasty," and to be connected with " the great wazir in whose tomb she was buried " (p. 49). Sometimes relatives are buried in a family tomb considerably older ; and here it is agreed (p. 32) that the technique and appearance of the coffin of King Hor is identical with this. Such resemblance takes us to the end of the XIIth dynasty, or more probably into the XIIIth.

This question of date is important as affecting a whole class of pottery. The application of white edging or stripes is well known, and is usually dated as after the XIIth dynasty ; occurring here, it is claimed as beginning early in the XIIth dynasty. The styles in this burial which do not agree with what is usually dated to the XIIth dynasty, are stated to be due to belonging to the ruling class, whose fashions were not yet generally copied. We need very certain proof before we can thus formulate a difference of fashion of several generations between the styles used in different classes of society. Such social viscosity has not yet been proved in other periods ; within a generation or two copying—however cheap or rough—takes a new style through all classes.

Let us hope that workers will devote their energies to publishing all their results, even if less luxuriously than in the present volume. No one ought to be allowed to turn up more material who is three years behind in publishing.

Études sur l'Origine et le Développement de la Vie Religieuse. I. Les Primitifs, l'Égypte, l'Inde, la Perse.—RICH. KREGLINGER. Bruxelles, Lamartin, 1919. 12mo, 370 pp. 6.50 frs.

This work is primarily written from the point of view of the study of recent peoples. It gives nearly half its exposition to these, then long sections on Egypt and India, and a shorter part on Persia ; " the other great religions, including Christianity, will be studied in subsequent volumes." If all the work is similarly carried out, it will be a most welcome text-book. The present volume is clearly arranged, well written, with logical development and sympathetic treatment. It aims at reaching the point of view of the primitive thinker, and realising the aspect of life as seen by those who are without our accumulated experience. It is well documented, giving a reference for almost every statement, and quoting important passages in full.

In the first part, on primitive ideas, realism is first considered, concluding that " savages do not think or perceive as we perceive and think ; with the more complex kind of life, experiences are multiplied and individualised, knowledge is widened, all the state of mind and mentality expands." To the savage mind impression constitutes reality, dreams are as real as waking impressions, drawings or statues are the equivalent of the bodies which they represent, the name is of the same effect as the person, and may give control of the person, the word of command creates the object or directs it. Magic rites are next described: of war, hunting, rain and sun. The basic idea of all these, is that man can control that which is beyond his reach by imitative actions. Under the head of Materialism are collected the instances of eating powerful men—enemies or friends —in order to acquire their abilities. The bones of oxen placed with the dead in Egypt are taken as being likewise to provide strength ; but as goats and other small animals are also buried, and offerings of bread and drink, it is more likely that the ox bones are also part of the food provided. The transference of sin or disease to an animal is also quoted from many lands. The possibility of telepathy and sympathetic influence is fully accepted, and examples are quoted of physical contact in teaching and conferring powers.

A full and important section is that on *mana,* or the pervading influence emanating from sacred objects and *tabu.* This influence can be transferred, and the rudest sense of it is as a fluid or wind which passes from the possessor to the recipient. The notion is found in Australia, Borneo, Annam, New Hebrides, Madagascar, South Africa, and North America ; it also lies at the root of Brahmanism. It should be added that this was familiar also in Egypt as the *sa,* or power, which was imparted by the god laying his hand on the back of the kneeling ruler. There was a class of *sa*-priests, who possessed this influence and imparted it. The essential value of it was protection by the gods, literally " backing," as *sa* was the " back " as well as the "influence." All kinds of objects may contain *mana*—stones, fire, wind, mountains, trees and weapons. The Dionysiac rites, and the eating of sacred animals, are parts of this system. The next section deals with the rites of contact with the earth, of fertility, and the marriage system.

Totemism is a valuable section, comparing and criticising the various definitions of the subject. The conclusion is " totemism is a belief that, in a society, certain persons or clans are connected, or identic, with species of animals or vegetables ; and it implies all the rites resulting from such a belief." It is remarked that nearly always a whole species, and not a single animal, is the totem. Here Egypt helps us by the names of early animal divinities being all in the plural, *khnumu* rams, *anpu* jackals, *bau* herons. The animal standards of tribes in Egypt, from prehistoric times, later fixed as the standards of the Nomes, seem to be on the same footing as the animal standards of the Hebrew tribes and of the various peoples in Italy and Greece. The eating ceremonially and rarely of the sacred animal is a rite of totemism, in order to maintain the bond of unity with it : to the examples quoted may be added that of the annual eating of the ram at Thebes, and the eating of the Apis bull at Memphis, of which only fragments of bone were left to be buried, in some cases. Some interesting points of primitive thought are quoted, showing the savage, like the child, disregarding his individuality and thinking and speaking of himself as a part of the species; this further may throw light on the aspect that animals bear to each other. " The social institutions of the present world find in these fundamental characters of ancestral mentality, their distant explanation, and often their sole justification."

The second part, on Egypt, deals with the soul, the king, and the gods. Here the author follows the view that the disseverment of the body was for fear of its return, and he calls it an act of impiety. This view, true in some countries, never was a motive in Egypt. The dead were often provided with weapons, unbroken and effective, proving that no dread of their action was felt. Moreover, after dissevering the body and cleaning the bones, they were carefully reconstituted in their original order. To prevent any action they would have been left in confusion. In the early texts it is stated that the body was cleaned in order to prevent decomposition, and to preserve it. The funeral prayers do not pray that the head may not be removed from the body, but that it may be returned to it, and the bones replaced ; this shows that the unfleshing of the body was not looked on as impious, but as part of a needful ritual of preservation. It is not the fear of division that prompts these prayers, but the fear of not being rightly re-united. The old idea is repeated that the contracted attitude of burial was embryonic ; there is no ground for this, as the attitude is that usual in sleep, and the dead were merely wrapped together as they lay in order to bury them. The dynastic people brought in full length burial, and that is the usual attitude of sleep among the Egyptian peasants in modern times.

A curious statement is given, without reference, that the Gizeh Sphinx was faced by another on the east bank of the Nile, forming a guardant pair to the entry of Upper Egypt. This needs to be verified, as it would clear up the meaning of the Sphinx, if correct.

The division of the hieroglyphs of animals, at the legs or neck, is supposed to be intended to prevent their injurious effect on the dead. This will not account for the removal of the feet of the harmless birds, which seems to show that mutilation was to hinder the animals from moving.

The earlier type of the ushabtis, as single figures of the deceased, is ignored, and only the later modification as servant figures is stated, though that did not begin till the XIXth dynasty. The idea of giving one for each day of the year was a late view in any case, and only rests on one or two having days named, which may be the day of death or of burial.

The *ka* being the family spirit, of which all descendants partake, is briefly stated ; but the African belief in the same family spirit should be quoted, as it is the strongest evidence of such a view.

In describing the gods, the local origin and worship of each is well enforced, and their local and tribal origin might be further illustrated by the compounding of gods together when different tribes were mixed. A worthy summary of the great advance of Akhenaten concludes this part of the work. The usual well-fixed lines of Egyptian belief are stated, and need not be repeated here, beyond the matters just named, which require further consideration.

. The third part, on the Religions of India, is a clear and well-arranged historical account of the changes that can be traced. Several long extracts give authoritative statements of belief. The gods of the Vedas and their origin are fully discussed. Next the system of Brahma, and the philosophical subtleties into which it developed. Lastly, the revolt of Buddhism, and the new morality and philosophy which it brought in.

The fourth part treats the kindred development of Zoroastrianism in Persia. The essential of this is the duality of the conflict of good and evil, which pervades the deities, the spirit world, and the actions of men. The date of Zoroaster is discussed, concluding that it cannot be later than about 1500 B.C., and that the movement originated in the Aryan homeland before the Hindu invasion of India. Though so closely akin to Hinduism, it reveals a violent antagonism in the opposite characters of the spirits. The Asuras are the good spirits in Persia, evil in India. The Devas are the evil spirits in Persia, the good in India. Indra is the great god of primitive Hindus, Andra is the worst of demons in Persia. Varuna the god of heaven in India is the demon of luxury in Persia. Vata, whose wind is the breath of life in India, is the demon of storm, snow, and destruction to Persia. " The religion of Zoroaster is one of the grandest doctrines which have ever been conceived, and which shines not only by the depth of the principles which the prophet discovered at the base of the world's evolution, but also by the admirable vigor of logic by which he subordinated all the details of his morals and eschatology to the first principles." After describing the struggles of good and evil for the possession of man, " We find thus in the religion of Zoroaster a grand conception which is not met with either in the Egyptian beliefs, nor in the profound speculations of the Hindus. The world has a history, it obeys the laws of evolution which from its present state lead it to an ideal stage toward which are tending all the forces that move it.   Neither in Egypt nor in India is the world conceived as progressing or developing ; each man only thinks of his own future—his own survival or annihilation—and the happiness which he seeks either in Paradise or Nirvana is only a distant future which he waits to realise. . . . For Zoroaster the world obeys a plan, it is in historic growth, a field of battle where a passionate struggle is waged between opposing forces, . . . the eternal and unquestionable opposition of good and evil, with one only hope—that of the victory of the good.   It is on this foundation, solid and simple, that his entire morality rests."

This little book, by its clear and sympathetic style, is worth more than most of the pretentious and prejudiced works which encumber the history of religions.

From the Garden of Eden to the Crossing of Jordan.—Sir WILLIAM WILLCOCKS 93 pp., 8vo, 4 maps.   1918.   5s.   Cairo.

When any work appears dealing with a large number of debatable matters, the first question is whether we must accept it as a final statement, or as material for consideration, or as suggestions to be criticised.   What value are we to assign to the statements of the author ?

We are met on the first page by a strong statement.   On Gen. ii, 6, " There went up a mist from the face of the earth," we are told " The word translated *mist* undoubtedly means free flowing irrigation," and " this Hebrew word occurred nowhere else in the Bible."   But it does occur also in Job xxxvi, 27, " For He maketh small the drops of water, they pour down rain according to the *vapours* [or ' free flow irrigation '] thereof which the clouds do drop and distil."   Now what has irrigation to do in a purely natural cycle here described ?   Also the word " *went up* a mist " is unquestionably *up*, and not *poured down* as a free flow irrigation.   Were all this merely a suggestion, it might pass as unfortunate ; but it " undoubtedly means " what we see to be impossible.   Close to this we are told, " Now no mist, not even a primæval one, will keep a garden alive." Yet in Palestine on the hills, crops of sesame are grown entirely by dew, without rain ; still more may this be the case in a low and damp situation.   On p. 4 we read that " the date palm has remained even to our day the tree of life " ; how then could the idea arise that the tree of life was not eaten ?

Another " undoubtedly."   " The letter E which precedes the names of the shrines (in Babylonia) is undoubtedly the same as the *yeh* which every Arab uses " as a vocative.   Now the E means the house or temple, the *yeh* is the common vocative Oh !   On p. 54 we read of " the salted lands near the lakes " of the Delta in Ramesside times.   But there were no lakes at that time, as the sea broke in at the time of Justinian ; till then there were marshes of the Nile stream, but no land under sea level.   Such statements as these must reduce us to considering each point on its own merits, without relying on the author's judgment.

The main matters of this discursive work will now be summarised.   The position assigned to the Garden of Eden is traced by identifying the four rivers which flowed from it.   The Pison is said to be the old Euphrates line from Ramadie to Kerbela : the Gihon, the Chebar or Pallacopas ; the Hiddekel, the Tigris ; and the present Euphrates passing Niffur.   The site of Eden, whence these streams divide, is claimed to be N.W. of Hit, the only position where a garden could be placed which could be irrigated by free flow irrigation all the year. But how much of this depends on the above views on the " mist " ?

The rise of the flood waters fifteen cubits is taken as showing an unusual Euphrates flood, which swept over the country, and stranded the Ark on a desert mound named Ararat. Why or where a rise of desert is so named we are not told. Much is said about the modern Arab *gebel*, meaning not a mountain but only desert land of any kind ; but this is beside the point, as it does not touch the meaning of the mountains named in the account of the Flood ; they are *har*, which always means a mountain, while there is an entirely different word *midbar* always used for a wilderness or desert.

Reaching the times of Israel in Egypt we are told of Joseph and Potiphar being at Zoan, but there seems no proof of this. The Auaris or Ha-uar camp of the Hyksos is identified with Hawara in the Fayum ; but probably this, and many other Hawaras, are named from the Howara tribe of Arabs. A strong point is urged that the control of the Delta and Nile irrigation depended on holding the entry to the Fayum, into which the Nile could be turned, and so cut off water from the country to the north of it. But the possibility of this view, setting aside the ancient acceptance of Ha-uar in the Delta, depends on the Egyptian account. In that campaign immediately after taking Ha-uar they besieged Sherohan, Sharuhen in the south of Palestine, and fought the Menti of Satet, or Bedawin south of Palestine. This implies that Ha-uar was near Palestine and not far away south of Cairo.

The plagues of Egypt are compared in detail with the seasonal changes of the country, as Osborn did sixty years ago. The course of the Exodus is then traced in a northerly route on the Palestine road, and Mount Sinai is supposed to be Kadesh Barnea. We read " Elim is undoubtedly Katia," but this phrase is not decisive. One of the main difficulties in the view of a northern Exodus is the mention of the Wilderness of Paran, which is obviously the same as the modern Feiran in Sinai, and cannot be the same word as Barnea, with which the author suggests its connection. This one site which can be identified by name seems to make it fruitless to identify unnamed sites on any other route. The objection that Sinai was " garrisoned by Egyptian soldiers . . more strictly garrisoned and more hostile to the wandering tribes of Asia than the Delta itself," is entirely untrue. There never was a garrison in Sinai, only armed expeditions occasionally visited the land for mining. Further, whatever Egyptians went there were only a small handful of labourers and a few soldiers, and they only occupied the actual mines, and never controlled the desert. The only valid reason for the northern route is the flight of quails, which are said never to pass far south of the Mediterranean. But that is not enough to gainsay the plain fact of the name of Paran.

Of course irrigation and water control often appears here in different connections ; but it is disappointing that a writer with so many ideas, and such experience of the East, should not have seriously taken stock of the facts ; thus he has missed making a valuable aid to understanding the many subjects involved.

PERIODICALS.

Journal of the Society of Oriental Research.

MERCER, Dr. S. A. B.—*Sumerian Morals.* (Vol. I, 2.) This is a long and careful study of the practical morals, as distinct from the theoretical ethics. First the family life is considered. Marriage was a civil contract and "there is no means of showing that it had any specific religious character." This accords with Egyptian usage, where the contract dealt with property as affected by a union, which apparently had no other legal status. The penalty for divorce was fixed, as in Egypt, at the marriage, and it could be performed at any time by the husband. Polygamy was possible but unusual. Polyandry was being extinguished at the time of Urukagina, before 3000 B.C. on the shortest reckoning. At that period women had an important position, the kings having the queens' names often with theirs in decrees. This looks as if an earlier matriarchal system was still respected.

In the matter of repudiation of a parent or a son, no notice is taken of the observation of Miss Simcox (*Primitive Civilisation*) that these included cases of adoption, and the separation of a child from his natural family by legal process. The system of adoption is described as regards the future position.

The business law was ample and detailed, and fully punished acts of carelessness which caused injury to others. Treaties between peoples were regarded as compacts made by the gods, under whom the rulers acted in war and peace. The ideal character attributed to the gods was high according to our ideas, much higher than that of the Greeks. So far as this reflects the ideals of the people, it puts the Sumerian above most races that we know. "Their gods were holy, righteous, just, truthful, pure, good, perfect, compassionate, merciful, mighty"; but they "were subject to the need of change and repentance, just as men are." In the summing up, "in spite of the presence of much materialism in their social life, and of much regard for ceremonial in their religious life, their moral ideals were singularly high."

A similarly exhaustive statement of all the passages of texts referring to *Early Babylonian Morals* (Vol. II, 2) seems to show very little difference from the earlier Sumerian ideas. The older population had set the standard adapted to the climate and the conditions of life in the country, and little difference could be expected, unless some great new ideals arose.

MERCER, Dr. S. A. B.—*Egyptian Morals.* (Vol. II, 1 ; Vol. III, 1.) In these articles the general character of the Egyptians is discussed, as shown by their ideals of life ; the difficulty as to the relation of the practical life to the ideal is hardly·touched. If the ideals of a people are pitched much above the average practice, there is too much hypocrisy ; but if there is no suggestion of hypocrisy, or a double standard, this points to a fair correspondance between the ideal and the practice. From this consideration it seems that we may fairly give the Egyptian credit for most of the virtues that he claims or commands. There is another line of evidence, not touched in these articles, the physiognomy of the nobles and kings, which—thanks to the great art of the early times—is known to us as familiarly as the portraits of modern statesmen. In these faces of the leaders of Egypt we see unmistakably all that is best and noblest in their ideals of action—the dignity, foresight, patience, and vigour, with usually kindliness, and sometimes humour. We feel it would be an inspiration to worthy life to be led by such men, we can credit them with all the virtues that they claim.

The different standards of action are dully realised by Dr. Mercer as limiting the quality of the individual. " He must be commended or condemned not on the basis of our code of morals, but on the basis of the morals of his own nation and times." Yet it is said of the standard itself that we must judge of it as better or worse than our own. Here there should be more reserve, due to the different conditions, climate and necessities of life in different lands. The relative proportion of qualities to each other largely depends on circumstances. Entirely different builds of character are now needed in New York or an English village, in Russia or in Spain, at the present time. What is a virtue in one country might be a vice of character in another. The morality of the ancient Egyptian is so closely fitted to the nature of the country, that it seems impossible to improve upon it for the present day ; all the faults of the people are so exactly reproved and countered in the admonitions, all the needs of character are so strongly stated in the claims to excellence, that any judgment of the moral standard by that of ourselves is inapplicable.

After classifying the various evidences of family qualities, social qualities, international and religious qualities, the general ideals are dealt with, the standards of good and evil, of free will and of right. The early Egyptian is concluded to have been " devoted to goodness, truth and justice. . . . . Considering the limitations of his time, he cannot be too highly praised."

The second article, on the morality of the Middle Kingdom, is on the same lines. The main development since the early times is in the individuality, the feeling of personal right. The decay of society at the close of the Old Kingdom, left a strong sense of the hollowness, insecurity and injustice of the course of life. The strong rulers who insisted on a high standard had disappeared, and those who sought justice stood alone. Falsehood, and the insecurity of life which it produces, were the great evil of the time. The evils of life had driven men to look for future compensation, and the ideas of different kinds of future existence grew and spread. The Kingdom of Osiris, with the personal judgment, began to take its place as a more reasonable prospect than the haunting of the graveyard. Dr. Mercer's articles give a summary which will be especially useful to those who make comparative studies with other lands. It might be an advantage to bring in the sidelights given by art and by ideals of the future life, to extend the view of character.

Report upon Archaeological Research in the College of Literature, Kyoto Imperial University. Vol. II. March, 1918. Though this does not concern Egypt, yet we must welcome the rise of archaeological work in Japan. There are 76 pages of Japanese text, 24 plates, and then mercifully a summary of 24 pages in English. The style of the excavations seems thorough. Plans and sections are given, the varieties of pottery and flint implements are photographed, and the skeletons are measured in detail and the skulls photographed. This is laying an excellent foundation for comparative studies, and we congratulate Prof. Hamada, who is the director of the work. He has also published—entirely in Japanese—a volume of his travels in Greece, with many photographs, 250 pages in all.

NOTES AND NEWS.

THE troubles which have befallen Egypt and the rest of the world have much reduced the number of excavations undertaken here, though the conditions of life in Egypt are better than elsewhere. Prices of labour and of food are high, but have not risen quite as much as in England. Gold and silver have vanished, and depreciated paper is the currency. All classes of natives seem to feel how misled they were in the outburst of a year ago, organised by Germany, and they do their best to regain their character for reason and politeness. The familiar station of Bedrasheyn is a heap of brickbats, and there are no tourists going to Saqqareh.

The American work continues with Dr. Reisner in Nubia, Mr. Winlock at Qurneh, and Mr. Fisher at Memphis. England is represented by Mr. Carter, working for Lord Carnarvon at the Tombs of the Kings, and by the British School at Lahun and Gurob. Dr. Grenfell has been out on a mission to acquire papyri for the British Museum.

The work of the British School has been carried on by Prof. and Mrs. Petrie, Captain Engelbach, Captain and Mrs. Brunton, Mr. Miller, Mr. Jefferies and Miss Hughes. The duty of fully working out and recording a site is incumbent on excavators ; and in clearing and planning the cemetery at Lahun, though the XIIth dynasty tombs were exhausted, there was found a cemetery of the Ist to IIIrd dynasties. A hundred graves of this period show the stages of development, from the prehistoric open pit grave, the pit divided for offerings, the shallow shaft and chambers, the stairway tomb with stone door slab, to the deep shaft tomb, which continued through all later times. Many stone vases and much pottery were found which will yield precise dating. One great tomb of the XIIth dynasty had been broken up ; but the fragments of inscription left were for Anpy, noble and chancellor, over all royal works throughout the whole land, and over the store of produce. Strange to say, he was a devotee of Sneferu, though living under Senusert II.

At Gurob the *sebakhin* have removed so much earth that graves are now found ranging from the XVIIIth dynasty back to the prehistoric, with many scarabs. A few large and important objects have rewarded the work at both sites.

Captain Engelbach is going to take up his duties as Inspector of Upper Egypt. Captain Mackay is in the army at Jerusalem, awaiting the development of the Service of Antiquities, which seems to hang fire, though destruction is rampant in the Hauran. The weather at Jerusalem has been as wild as else-where, with two feet of snow and great icicles.

1 : 1. GOLD URAEUS OF SENUSERT II. LAHUN.
1 : 4. MAGIC JAR OF ALABASTER. LAHUN.

ANCIENT EGYPT.

THE BRITISH SCHOOL OF ARCHAEOLOGY IN EGYPT, 1920.

AFTER five years of absence from Egypt, the conditions seemed to be suitable to resuming the work at Lahun last winter. No difficulties occurred, thanks to the goodwill of Lord Allenby, who has been kind enough to honour us by becoming the Patron of the School. The official world, both British and native, did all that could smooth our stay in the desert at Lahun. The party comprised Capt. Engelbach, R.E. (who was later joined by Mrs. Engelbach, and went on to Ghurob), Capt. and Mrs. Brunton, Mr. Eustace Miller, Miss Hughes, Mr. Jefferis, with Mrs. Petrie and myself. It seemed impossible to realise all that had passed since we left there, when we sat at mess in the same huts. We had nearly all of our older diggers, only two or three absent and doing other work.

The season opened with an interesting discovery before reaching the winter's work. At the north-east corner of Cairo, where the track strikes off for Gebel Ahmar, there are wide clearances of gravel, which has been used for road making. The flints are very large, mixed with blocks of fossil wood, much rolled, evidently washed down by floods from the Petrified Forest about twelve miles away eastwards. The high polish on these palaeoliths shows long washing with sand. A few very rudely flaked flints are among these, with large irregular slices knocked away to obtain an edge, without any definite form. These seem to be the earliest worked flints known in Egypt. When arrived at Lahun, we visited the gravels, full of boulders, which cap the hills between the Fayum and the Nile, all cut to pieces with sharp denudation valleys through 80 ft. of thickness ; but not a single worked flint could be found of that age of High Nile. The working seems to start when the Nile was about 100 feet over the present level.

On the edge of the desert at Lahun our best digger, Aly Suefy, had found a patch of ground about a couple of hundred feet across, thickly strewn with broken flints and many implements of Mousterian age. These were evidently in position as left on the surface, and had not been buried under deposits. The Nile, therefore, has not been above its present level since then, and the fluctuations have all been within the 50 ft. or more of the valley now filled up with deposits.

The entrance of the Nile waters into the Fayum was obviously a favourable place for fisheries, which would attract a population. We now find that from prehistoric times onward there have been settlements on both sides of the valley, at Lahun and at Ghurob. The early people seem to have been poor, but by the Ist dynasty a wealthy class had arisen here, and the graves have a full allowance of offerings, and vessels of alabaster. At the edge of the Lahun desert, close to the station of Bashkatib, we found a cemetery which had been partly attacked in modern times ; on the lower ground, covered by denudation wash, there were still a hundred graves which had only been attacked anciently. These burials comprise the whole series of forms, from the plain open grave of the prehistoric

E

to the deep shaft tomb which was usual in historic times.   The primitive grave was lined with brick, as a rectangular pit.   This pit was then sub-divided by brick walls, with the body at the northern end, head north, face east, in a contracted position.   The other compartments, from one to four in number, contained stacks of offering jars.   These jars were a continuance of the prehistoric ritual of placing jars of vegetable ash in the grave, many containing black ashes, but others having only black mud as a substitute.   The next stage was that of making a side recess to hold the body, instead of a roofed grave ; this form began in the late prehistoric age, and it was carried on here into the stage of providing a complete chamber opening from a shallow pit, which was the successor of the original open grave.   This form was placed where a thin structure of harder rock lay over a softer marl, thus a hard roof of a foot or two in thickness covered the chamber.   Not only was a place for the body provided, but also a second recess for the offerings.

When the burial took place in a chamber it was obviously useless to make an entrance pit equally deep all over.   A slope was therefore made down to the chamber, and this was formed into steps for easier access.   Thus a stairway tomb was developed, which expanded into a cruciform chamber, with side chamber for the burial and the offerings   From the stone vases and pottery, which are well dated to a single reign by the Royal Tombs of Abydos and allied groups, the age of these developments of the tomb can be fixed.   The open grave in this cemetery was made during the earlier half of the Ist dynasty.   The shallow chambered tombs are of the second half of that dynasty, and the stairway tombs are of the same age.

The stairway tomb was sometimes closed by a thin slab of stone over the doorway.   This was easily pulled forward by plunderers, so it was secured by being let into grooves in the rock at the sides of the pit.   This type, though beginning as early as the middle of the Ist dynasty, lasted on to the close of the IIIrd dynasty, as at Meydum, and was even copied in the archaistic tomb of the chief architect in the XIIth dynasty.   The deep shaft, with one or more chambers at the bottom, was the next type.   This type was also begun by the middle of the Ist dynasty, and probably continued here to early in the IIIrd dynasty, judging by the form of the offering bowls and the head-rests.   After that the cemetery declined, and nothing can be dated until the XIIth dynasty.   Thus, by the forms of pottery and stonework, which we know to have undergone rapid changes, we learn that the various developments of the grave were all started as early as the middle of the Ist dynasty, and continued side by side, until the greater security of the deep-shaft tomb caused it to supersede the other types ; it was favoured also by the increasing wealth of the country which enabled more costly tombs to be made.   This sudden appearance of several types of tomb rather suggests that the development had taken place elsewhere, and that the various stages belonged to different tribes, allied in the dynastic invasion.

The contents of these graves are of the usual forms of alabaster, basalt and pottery vessels.   The stone is mostly in the open graves, rarer in the shallow chambers and stairway tombs, and absent from the deep-shaft tombs.   This agrees with the scarcity of stonework in the tombs of the IInd and IIIrd dynasties elsewhere.   Some unusual objects were found : an alabaster vase surrounded with lotus petals of slate and alabaster, the forerunner of the glazed lotus vases of Hierakonpolis and later times ; three pottery vases of foreign origin, like those found in the tomb of King Den, and a small vase with black band, like that in

Tarkhan II, ix, 11. These confirm all this foreign pottery as being of the Ist ·· dynasty.

At Tarkhan it was found, on measuring the skeletons, that the group which · appeared to be that of the invaders showed a stature 8 per cent. shorter than that of the earlier people. Though not many skeletons could be obtained in suffi- ciently good condition at Lahun, the question was examined on six of the open- grave burials, against 18 in closed tombs. The result was that the closed burials were 7½ per cent. shorter in the leg, and 6 per cent. shorter in the arm. As these differences were three or four times the amount of the probable error of the contrasted quantities, there is good reason to accept them as veritable. This points to the open-grave burials being those of the prehistoric race, and the closed tombs those of the dynastic invaders, and thus corroborates the suggestion that the various types of burial were already in use before they were imported.

The large cemetery of the XIIth dynasty was the main object of work this year. Much remained to be done in exhausting chances of discovery, and in completely examining and planning the whole site. The interior of the pyramid of Senusert II was completely searched; in turning over the dust and chips lying near the sepulchral chamber, the gold uraeus was found, which must have been on the front of the crown. It is a massive casting, with inlay of carnelian and lazuli, a head of lazuli, and eyes of garnet in gold setting. Two stone lamps were also found in the pyramid, besides two or three already obtained from there.

The tomb of Princess Sat-Hathor-ant, where the jewellery was found in 1914, was further examined; behind the fine limestone lining a recess for offerings was found, containing common pottery and the great alabaster jar figured in the frontispiece. Perhaps this is the finest jar known. It bears a magical inscription stating that the princess would have everything that was produced on earth, and all she needed, in this jar. Such a form of magic provision is ⸗ not known before; it superseded all the offerings, the models, and the scenes of the tombs, by one comprehensive formula, which carried magic and the power of the word to its utmost extent.

Outside of the pyramid enclosure a great tomb was opened up, the tunnel of which ran toward the pyramid, ending in a chamber beneath the enclosing wall. This contained a splendid panelled sarcophagus of red granite, and a canopic box of granite. The sarcophagus, like that of Senusert, and of one of the princesses, was of exquisitely accurate work, with an average error of less than a hundredth of an inch. No name was found in this tomb. The position of the tomb shaft, 100 ft. outside the pyramid enclosure wall, suggested that other shafts might be hidden as far out as that. The whole ground on the north of the pyramid wall was therefore turned over down to the rock, moving a mass of chips which had been thrown into old quarries there, to a depth of sometimes 15 ft., but no other shaft was found. In the face of the enclosure round the pyramid there was an inserted stone, resting on another block inserted in the rock floor; but it proved all solid rock behind these. Opposite the queen's pyramid, a length of the brick wall was separated by vertical joints, as if it had been filled in later; this was removed, but solid rock was behind it. Then the whole length of the brick wall, as far as the great stairway, was cleared behind, to search the rock, which was all solid. Lastly, a shaft was sunk in the rock, 40 ft. deep, in the position most likely to intercept any gallery leading to tombs under the rock mastabas north of the pyramid; and cross-tunnels were cut from this to north and south in both of the strata where the Egyptians had elsewhere made galleries. All of these trials not reaching any passage, there only remains to be tried an extensive rock-drilling, to see if any chambers were actually cut under the small pyramid and mastabas.

While searching further in the platform built up of chips to the south-east of the pyramid, a stairway of brick was found, running diagonally to the pyramid corner. This was made before the great enclosing wall which cut across it, and it was the approach for the high officials during the course of building, to avoid the inconvenience of climbing over the waste-heaps.

On the top of the hill behind the pyramid, the foundations of a large building were found in 1914. At that time, and in 1920, many pieces of diorite statues and of a circular altar, limestone sculptures and architectural fragments, were found scattered about here. A most complete search failed to show any tomb shaft, and the fragments found were not like those of the mastabas. Considering that the *sed-heb* chapel of the apotheosis of Sonkhkara was on the top of the hill at Thebes, it seems probable that this was the *sed-heb* chapel of Senusert. At the corners of it were foundation deposits, with pottery, trays of reeds, and bull's head and haunch.

The town of the pyramid builders at Kahun was further searched, on the roads, and a few parts which had not been cleared in 1890. A large number of clay sealings were found, and a curious portico which seems to have been a place of domestic worship.

On a hill in view of the pyramid stood a great mastaba of brick, over a tomb with a steep entrance passage, and a great shaft for lowering the sarcophagus, like the VIth dynasty tombs of Dendereh. The tomb-chapel on the side of the hill, in front of the sepulchre, was like those of Beni Hasan. This curious combination was due to the taste of the chief architect of Egypt, Anpy, who was buried here ; he also cut off public access to the chapel by a deep pit, right across the court, and too wide to be jumped. Only some pieces of the inscriptions and of two statues remained, for the place had been ravaged for stone. Another curious preference is seen on his statue, where he is said to be devoted to Sneferu ; this devotion to the first pyramid builder may have been due to the architect's interest in building the Lahun pyramid.

In the XVIIIth dynasty there were some wealthy people, under the early kings. .Groups of scarabs were found dated to Aahmes, and four to Amen-hetep I ; with these are several scarabs which are clearly of the earlier time of the XIIth dynasty, probably obtained from the mastabas near by. The cemetery at Ghurob continued in use down to Ramessu II.

A puzzling monument is a granite sarcophagus of a prince " heir of the lord of the two lands, the king's son, Pa-ramessu." This was his style until the sarcophagus was nearly finished ; then on one panel of the body he is entitled " the king's son (Ramessu mery Maot) *neb uben maot kheru.*" Here a cartouche is assumed, and the addition *neb uben*, "lord of shining " ; while on all the other places where the name Pa-Ramessu occurs, there has been an erasure, and *neb uben* has been put over it. On the lid, the middle band has Pa-Ramessu, with the squatting man and whip determinative ; this is doubtless what has been erased on the body. The lid, having some spare space, was altered by putting on each side of the middle band "the king's son (Ramessu mery Amen) *neb uben* " with a cartouche. It seems then that an heir-apparent Pa-ramessu had come to the throne just before his sarcophagus was completed, and had the alterations made with cartouches. Yet he cannot have reigned long, or at the capital, because his burial was only in the outskirts of a small provincial town. Who this prince can have been it is difficult to decide. There were two statues of a Pa-ramessu, who filled the highest offices of state under Haremheb (ANCIENT EGYPT, 1916, 35–6), and who may justly be taken to be the same as Ramessu I. His father was named Sety. He cannot be the prince of Ghurob, as his tomb is known at Thebes, and he was not a king's son. Looking later, there is no prince Pa-ramessu, and if we accept the shorter from Ramessu (which occurs on the sarcophagus) there is no prince Ramessu except the second son of Ramessu II, who died between the twenty-sixth and thirtieth years of his father's reign, and who cannot therefore have succeeded to the throne. The later Ramessu princes reigned fully, as Ramessu III to XII, and therefore cannot be this obscure prince. Their tombs are known at Thebes, except that of Ramessu VIII. It is thus possible that this is the sarcophagus of Ramessu VIII, but unlikely, as his second cartouche does not appear. The so-called Ramessu IX, whose tomb is unknown, is really Saptah II, son of Sety II, and he would certainly have had Saptah in his cartouche. So far as we know at present, then, this sarcophagus belonged to some unknown prince who was the heir to the throne, and who hardly succeeded before he was over-thrown. Possibly he was an elder brother of Ramessu II. The sarcophagus is unique as having a sledge beneath it, carved all in one piece in the granite.

The season's work has thus given some entirely new results both of objects and of inscriptions, and the steady clearance of sites that are not reserved has now been carried as far south as the entrance to the Fayum.

W. M. FLINDERS PETRIE.

GRANITE SARCOPHAGUS AND CHAMBER, LAHUN.

E 3

THE ETHIOPIAN SOVEREIGNS AT MEROE.

DR. REISNER has restored for us the history of Ethiopia during the Napatite period. His archaeological work in the province of Dongola has been a remarkable achievement, and it has settled the chronology of the Sudan from the time when it began to be a world-power town to the epoch of Alexander, as well as the racial affinities of the dynasties who ruled at the time over Ethiopia. But the work done by Dr. Reisner at Napata and its neighbourhood, can be supplemented by the work done by Professor Garstang at Meroe.

Owing to the war only a bare outline of this has as yet been published. A considerable number of royal names, however, were discovered in the course of the excavations which carry back the history of Meroe to Dr. Reisner's IInd dynasty. Here is a list of them :—

(1) Atlenersa Ra-khu-ka, " king of Upper and Lower Egypt." On blue faïence found in the Great Palace. (Reisner : B.C. 650–40.)

(2) Senq-Amon-seken Ra-sekheper-en, " king of Upper and Lower Egypt." On blue faïence found in the Great Palace. Also on a blue object discovered at Memphis. (B.C. 640–20.)

(3) Aspalta Ra-mer-ka, " king of Upper and Lower Egypt." On stones of the Great Palace which he restored or enlarged, on a stela from the Sun-temple which he built, and on blue faïence. (B.C. 590–70.)

(4) The Horus Amtalqa Ra-uaz-ka, " king of Upper and Lower Egypt." On blue faïence and small pyramids of solid gold, probably tribute, found in the Great Palace. (B.C. 570–50.)

(5) Mal-neqen, " king of Upper and Lower Egypt." On stones from the Palace which he restored or enlarged, on small gold pyramids and on blue faïence. (B.C. 550–40.) He never has his Throne-name, but the personal name is sometimes written Mal-neq, and the determinative *nefer* is almost always attached to the first syllable, indicating that *malna* signified " good " in Meroitic.[1]

(6) Amon-kalbat, who seems to be Dr. Reisner's Netaklabat-aman, the leader of his IIIrd dynasty. (B.C. 535–15.) On blue faïence from the Palace.

(7) Amon-kalka, Dr. Reisner's Karkaman, the second king of his IIIrd dynasty. On blue faïence from the Palace. (B.C. 515–495.)

(8) Sa'heri ⌁. This must be Dr. Reisner's Saasheriya, the fourth king of his IIIrd dynasty. On blue faïence. (B.C. 475–55.)

(9) Amon-stykal. This must be Dr. Reisner's Astabarya-aman, the third king of his IIIrd dynasty, with the ox (*ka*) written instead of the sheep (*ba*). On blue faïence. (B.C. 495–75.)

[1] The Meroitic word must be *malna*, since in the inscriptions of Askhankherel in the North Pyramid 5, the name of " the Osiris Malna-[qen] " written *Malna*-NEFER.

Dr. Reisner's IVth dynasty is not represented at Meroe. But we have—

(10) Han . . . who may be a queen. On blue faïence.

(11) Amon-ardu[s]. On blue faïence from the Southern Palace.

(12) Amon-matleka[n]. On a stone from the south side of the City wall. To be distinguished from (4).

(13) Amon-ark Ra-khnum-ab, " king of Upper and Lower Egypt," whom I would identify with the classical Ergamenes, the builder, as I believe, of the great city wall. (B.C. 210–180.) Southern Pyramid 6.

(14) Amon-mer-Ast Ra-nefer-ankh-ab, " king of Upper and Lower Egypt." Southern Pyramid sand blue faïence from tomb 298.

(15) Ra-neb-kheper. On a scarab with deformed Egyptian hieroglyphs and AUG in Latin letters.

(16) Neb-hotep-... On yellow faïence from the South Palace.

(17) Neteg-Amon and Queen Amon-tari. On blocks from the temple of Amon and the sanctuary south of it. It is probable that Amon-tari also restored the Sun-temple. Neteg-Amon was buried in the Northern Pyramid 22.

(18) Agini-rherhe and Queen Amon-renas. On two stelæ from shrine south of Meroe, and on blocks from the Sun-temple. The stela records the Ethiopian invasion of Egypt. (B.C. 24–22.)

(19) Queen Amon-shabet. On an obelisk in the temple of Amon. She was buried in the Northern Pyramid 6, where Ferlini found jewellery (now at Berlin) of the late Ptolemaic or early Roman period.

(20) Toqrerhi-Amon. On blocks from the Lion Temple, and Northern Pyramid 27.

(21) Shen (?) On blocks from the Lion Temple.

(22) Ark-kharer. On a plaque obtained by the late Mr. Bishop from the temple of Amon. He appears as crown prince at Naga, and was a son of (17).

(23) Ya-baleq. On a fragment of stone (920).

To these may be added (24) Amon-khabil, " the Sun-god of Qash, ever-living, the Horus of the Reservoir," at Basa, the site of a reservoir and temple, a day's journey from Meroe on the road to the Red Sea.

Dr. Reisner has shown that the Napalite dynasties were of Libyan origin which explains the fact that in the sculptures of the Sun-god temple the Meroites are represented with the features of the blond race—Greek noses, high foreheads, and thin lips. The later sovereigns from Neteg-Amon onward are negro or negroid, and it is at this time that the queens take precedence of the kings. After the end of Dr. Reisner's IIIrd dynasty (B.C. 450, according to his chronology), Meroe either became independent of Napata or, more probably, was destroyed by foreign invaders.

Little chronological help can be obtained from the form or position of the existing pyramids. Each of the three groups contains pyramids of very different periods. In the Western group of those that remain, six are stepped ; the rest have straight and, in six instances out of nine, fluted sides. In two of the stepped ones the art belongs to a good period ; another with fluted sides was plastered all over, and surrounded by a walled court. The chapel of another fluted pyramid contained three seated figures instead of a false door. In two other instances a tablet was inserted in the centre of the false door, the tablet in one case (No. 15) being in Meroitic, and recording the name of Amon-tari. A Greek bronze lamp was found in one of these pyramids. In the Southern group all the existing pyramids are stepped, and the chapels have false doors, solar disks and boats.　One of them (No. 10), the joint tomb of " the Priest " (*kelni*) Kaltela Ra-ar-ta(?)a, " Lord of the Lake-land," and of Kalka, " the king " is of late date ;　another (No. 41) is the tomb of a "daughter of the king " ;　a third (No. 4) is the pyramid of Kenrethr, " the Sun-god of the South " ;　it is attached to another pyramid the chapel of which is destroyed, and is of considerably later date than the adjoining pyramid of Amon-mer-Ast.

In the Northern group the pyramid of queen Kentakit (Candace) Amon-ârti (No. 1) stands apart by itself.　That of Arkhenkherel Ankh-ka-ra (No. 5), who associates with himself an older king, " The Osiris Malna-NEFER," *i.e.*, Malneqen, is also intrusive, and has straight sides of peculiar form.　It may have been the first of the group to be erected.　The other pyramids with straight sides are No. 2, with four great bulls on each exterior side of the chapel, three images instead of a false door, and a representation of Hathor standing on the lotus ; No. 6, that of queen Amon-shabet (19), where Ferlini found his jewellery, the chapel of which has an arched vault ; No. 8 ; No. 11 which is very late and barbaric ; No. 12, with late reliefs and blank cartouches, a standing figure of the king taking the place of a false door ; No. 13, with late reliefs ; No. 14 ; No. 17 of king Amon-ton-m-Mari Neb-ma-ra (late) ; No. 18, with a court, of Amon-khetosen ; No. 19, of Triginal with full-faced king in place of a false door (very late) ; and No. 27, of...tera (?) Amon Kheper-ka-ra, with seated king instead of a false door (very late).　The sides of Nos. 16, 17, 18, and 19, though straight, are not fluted.　The stepped pyramids are :　No. 3 ; No. 4 (of Amon-...akha [Ra]-...n-ab) ; No. 7, of Alu(qa)-Amon Ankh-zeto-mer-Ast " lord of the two lands," who seems to have been a contemporary of Ptoleny IV ; No. 9, with a pylon ; No. 10, with pylons and winged bulls ; and No. 22, of Neteg-Amon, with the bier of Osiris in place of a false door.

That the Sun-temple—the first stage on the road from Meroe to the Red Sea—was built by Aspalta, we may conclude from the fragments of his stela that were discovered there.　It was subsequently restored, after partial destruction, by Agini-rherhe (18), perhaps with the spoils of his Egyptian campaign. But it is probable that the list of conquered or tributary provinces which adorns the eastern front of the temple was the work of Amon-tari, since when the cartouche accompanying it was first uncovered I was able to read the characters [A]m[on-t ?]r.　As the list was not quite correctly read from the photographs in Mr. Griffith's publication of it, and has since suffered severely from exposure, it is worth while to give it as it appeared immediately after excavation.

The first three cartouches are (or were) :—

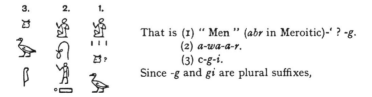

That is (1) " Men " (*abr* in Meroitic)-' ? -*g*.
(2) *a-wa-a-r*.
(3) *c-g-i*.
Since -*g* and *gi* are plural suffixes,

the three cartouches do not contain geographical names, but are merely an introductory formula :　" The men (*abrg*) of the countries " (*awar'*=*gi*) or something similar.

Then follow (or followed) the geographical names :—

(4) G-m-t-a ;   (5) T-'-s-n-a ;   (6) B-r-i-ḥa-a ;   (7) P-t-r (?) [or kh ?]-'-i ;
(8) A-n-rh[1]-' ;   (9) ...-rh-y-rh-y ;   (10) ...-wa-sh-' ;   (11) ...-...-n-q ;
(12) ...-t-r-a ; (13)...-rh- △ [perhaps a word signifying " cities "] ; (14) ...-g-to-' ;
(15)...-a (?) -q-' ;   (16)...-...- kh-' ;   (17)...-...-...-a.

One word more. Nastosen, who is placed by Dr. Reisner, B.C. 330–310, was a native of Bernat, usually identified with Meroe. But no trace of his name has been discovered there. Can he be the Amon-khatosen of the Northern Pyramid 18 ?   And is he further to be identified with " Aktisanes the Ethiopian," who, according to Diodorus, overcame Amasis and was counted among the Egyptian kings ?   We know that in the troubled earlier years of Ptolemy V, two Ethiopian kings, Harmakhis and Ankh-m-khu, ruled at Thebes, and the discordant medley of excerpts which take the place of Egyptian history in the pages of Diodorus would make anything possible.

A. H. SAYCE.

[1] The character which I transcribe *rh* is represented by *sd* in the transliteration of some of the names in which it occurs (*e.g., Merul* and *Mandulin, karhake* and *Candace*), though it remains *r* in the name of *Meroe* (*M-rh-e-u-i*) and interchanges with the ordinary *r* in two Meroitic inscriptions discovered by Prof. Garstang.   Hence we might have a name like *And* corresponding in Greek to *Anrh'*.

NOTES ON THE JEWELS FROM LAHUN.

THE jewellery found at Lahun by the British School of Archaeology—or rather all of it except those pieces retained by the Cairo Museum—recently arrived at the Metropolitan Museum of Art in New York, where it was placed on exhibition in December last. Without exception, those who have seen the treasure have been struck almost as much by the conscientious care and ingenuity shown by Prof. Petrie and Mr. Brunton in its reconstruction, as by the marvellous skill and taste of the ancient jewellers who made it. It was therefore with considerable diffidence that I suggested two changes in stringing. I would not care to dignify these suggestions with a published note, were it not that both Mr. Lythgoe and Mr. Mace, who mounted the jewellery for exhibition, have tested them out, verified them as correct and adopted them. This being the case it seems desirable that the reasons for the changes should be put on record in ANCIENT EGYPT, especially since the article which Mr. Lythgoe prepared to appear in the *Metropolitan Museum Bulletin*, December, 1919, at the time the jewellery was put on public view, did not seem to be the appropriate place to explain them in detail. These two changes, adopted in exhibiting the jewellery in New York, involve the stringing of the Senusert II pectoral and the cowries, and I have added a third, tentative, and as yet not finally adopted, change in the stringing of the lions' heads. This last is not susceptible of the demonstration which I believe can be presented for the first two changes.

To Mr. Mace I am indebted not only for many details on the particular jewels, but for numerous references and suggestions embodied in the following pages. I should state finally, that this note is written before the arrival in America of the definitive publication of the Lahun excavations by the British School, and that, therefore, reference can only be made to Prof. Petrie's preliminary descriptions[1] with the consequence that I may have missed a number of interesting points.

The point of departure for these suggestions was the string of gold cowrie-shells. Prof. Petrie has demonstrated that in the intervals between the eight large gold cowries, sixteen gold " double rhombic " beads should be strung, two in each interval. This arrangement is assured by the distance between the thread holes in the cowries and in the " rhomboid " beads—a distance which is practically identical in both cases. Now there can be little question that these cowries and " rhomboids " were intended to be strung tightly together, and if this is done they make a string 20¼ ins. in circumference, clasped. Because of the corrosion of the bronze cores of the cowries, threading them is now impossible and the only photographs of them which can be taken without the dangerous operation of re-drilling them, are somewhat deceptive. Each cowrie has two

Times, May 20, 1914; *The Illustrated London News,* June 20, 1914; ANCIENT EGYPT, 1914, p. 97; *Journal of Egyptian Archaeology,* 1914, p. 185; and *Catalogue of the Exhibition held at University College, London,* 1914.

thread holes through it, one slightly shorter than the other, but the difference in lengths between these two holes is so slight that it would take a string of cowries and " rhomboids " of 40 or more inches in length to make a complete, closed circle with all of the beads lying flat as in the photographs. In short, with this 20¼-in. string, when the clasp was closed, the beads would all be standing on edge, more or less vertically. If worn about the neck such a string of cowries would have the appearance of an upright collar, but a very ill-fitting one, for the circumference of a woman's neck is usually no more than from 12 to 14 ins., and this collar would therefore have hung almost upright an inch or so beyond, and under her chin. As all Egyptian necklaces were flat lying, except the tight

1. GIRDLE OF COWRIES, AS ARRANGED IN THE METROPOLITAN MUSEUM.

collars about the throat, it is evidently necessary to look for some other arrangement of this string.

After this conclusion it was inevitable that one should turn to those other " rhomboid " beads of carnelian and green amazon stone which had been strung with the " drop-pendants." Prof. Petrie had already considered this combination, but gave up the idea on two grounds.[1]

First. The size of these " rhombic " beads is such that, strung side by side, the space between the two threads would be greater than that between the two

[1] ANCIENT EGYPT, 1914, p. 98.

threads of the cowries and gold " rhomboids." This in many cases is true—in others it is not. In fact these hard stone " rhomboids " show a marked variation in size. While the gold beads were made mechanically either from dies or moulds, these stone beads were cut individually, and a larger error was tolerated in gauging them than was to be expected in metal work. Some of them are accurately made to take the strings of the cowries ; others will overlap slightly, but not objectionably, if strung on the same threads (*see* Fig. 1). Finally—and to me personally, this is conclusive—the variations among the " rhomboids " is not as great as that which exists between the big and little lions' heads from this find. Although of gold, variations in the distance between string holes of from 2 to 3 mm. actually exist among these heads, and yet there is no question but that they belong together.

Second. In Prof. Petrie's consideration the stone " rhomboids " are needed for the suspension of the " drop-beads," making a long, fringe-like necklace to be worn below and outside of all the other ornaments. This difficulty can be met satisfactorily I feel sure.

Two pectorals were found and one of them has been suspended on a string of amethyst ball-beads. Even if these latter are not employed as I suggest below, the second pendant is still to be provided for, however, and there can be little question that the " drop-beads," combined with the 20 gold and 12 green ball beads not otherwise strung, belong to it. Examples of such suspending strings of drop-beads are not at all uncommon on the monuments[1] (Figs. 2 and 3), and it is extremely interesting to find that at Dahshur, pectorals were associated with just such strings. De Morgan found in the First Treasure, with a pectoral of Senusert II, 30 gold ball beads and 37 drop beads of gold, carnelian, lapis lazuli and amazon stone,[2] and in the Second Treasure two pectorals, 43 drop beads and 98 ball beads, all of gold.[3] I suggested, therefore, that the drop and ball beads of the Lahun treasure made a characteristic pectoral suspender. Variations in the arrangement and number of spherical beads among the drops are found in all examples, and therefore the arrangement of this string was left to experiment. There were 73 drops strung together in the " fringe-necklace," and one other handed over separately to Mr. Mace by Mr. Brunton. Graded and arranged by colours it was evident that one more carnelian and one more lazuli drop were needed to make any consistent arrangement, and those two were restored. The small number of ball beads obviously was an enigma, but there is precedent for the omission of them between the drops, and they therefore were strung provisionally at the ends. The result (Fig. 5), is a double string of exactly the length to support the pectoral just over the lower chest where it

---

[1] A few examples at random are XIIth dynasty : Griffith, *Beni Hasan*, III, Pl. III, single string of alternating drop and ball beads, coloured blue, green, blue, yellow ; XVIIIth dynasty : Quibell, *Tomb of Yuaa and Thuiu*, Pl. XII, double string of drops alternating with balls in pairs ; L.D., III, 77A, triple string of drops alternating with balls in pairs ; Rosellini, *Mon.*, II, Pl. LXXX = Champollion, *Mon.*, IV, Pl. CCCXXXII, double string of drops alternating with balls, coloured green, blue ; Daressy, *Annales*, 1901, p. 5 ff. = Reisner, *Amulets*, 12196–12201, double and triple strings of dark and light blue, red and gold drop beads alternating with ball beads in threes ; XIXth dynasty : Caulfeild *Temple of Kings*, Pl. XVI, quadruple string of drops alternating with balls in threes ; XXth dynasty : Vernier, *Bijoux*, 52005, Pl. V.

[2] De Morgan, *Dahcḧour*, I, pp. 60, 63, Pls. XV, XVIII.

[3] *Ibid.*, pp. 64–5, Pls. XIX–XXII.

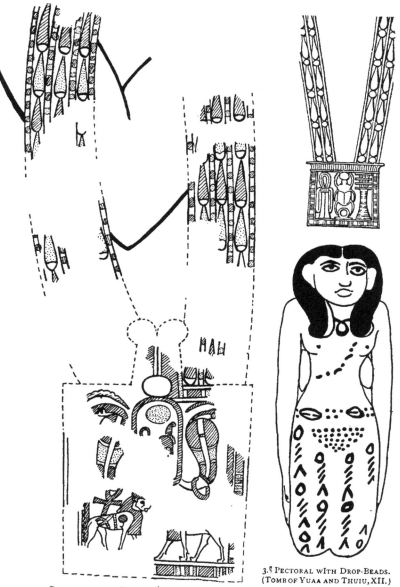

2. PECTORAL WITH GOLD-CAPPED DROP-BEADS.
(FRAGMENTS FROM TOMB 226. THEBES.)

3.ᵍ PECTORAL WITH DROP-BEADS.
(TOMB OF YUAA AND THUIU, XII.)

4. GLAZED FIGURE. LISHT.
(METROPOLITAN MUSEUM.)

should hang.[1] Furthermore, the materials of which it is made—gold, lapis-lazuli, carnelian and amazon stone—are exactly the same materials as those used in making the Senusert II pectoral.   This identity of colour scheme may be taken as evidence that the drop beads and this pectoral of Senusert II together make one jewel.   If no other use be admitted for the amethyst string, it may be assumed to have belonged with the Amenemhat III pectoral, now in Cairo.

Thus, with the drop beads provided for, we arrive at the point, where (1), the slight errors in size of the " rhomboids " can be explained by the conditions of their manufacture ;   where (2), the stone " rhomboid " beads are no longer necessary for the threading of the drop beads ;   and, where (3), they are in turn looking for a place.   It becomes a matter of necessity, therefore, to try them with the cowries, the previous stringing of which has resulted in an ill-fitting collar.

Sixty-one rhomboid beads, 31 of carnelian and 30 of green amazon stone, were strung with the drop beads and one more of amazon stone, presumably found later, was turned over to Mr. Mace by Mr. Brunton.   It does not seem totally beyond the bounds of possibility that, even with the most conscientious work in the tomb, two more should have escaped detection.   And still more likely, if these beads were worn by the Princess in life, that the strings might have broken at some time, the beads been scattered, and two of them completely lost before they were restrung again.   I see no strong objection to considering the set as having been originally 64 in all, made up equally of red and green.   Admitting this number, they divide readily into eight lots of eight each for the eight intervals between the eight cowries.   With the double gold beads they make a total of 96. For experimental stringing there was no further guide, and one is left to satisfy his own personal tastes.   An extremely attractive arrangement of gold and stone " rhomboids " between each pair of gold cowries is :   green, gold, red, red, gold, green.   Such is the arrangement shown in Fig. 1, and it may be said in passing that in its original colours it makes one of the most charming jewels ever found in Egypt.

The resulting string, when clasped, has a circumference of 33 or 33½ ins. If actually threaded, the beads, and particularly the cowries, would still stand more or less on edge when the clasp was closed, because experiment shows that there is not enough variation in the size of the rhomboids to make an inner row appreciably shorter than the outer.   The photograph of the beads lying flat is therefore still deceptive, and there can still be no question of the string being intended either for a collar or necklace.   In fact the one part of the human body where it would fit naturally and lie smoothly would be above the hips, for 33 or 33½ ins. is a normal measurement on a slender person around the top of the pelvis.

In other words, the cowries strung with the rhomboids seemed to make a girdle, and a very little research supplied the confirmation of this fact.   The Metropolitan Museum possesses a number of XIth and XIIth dynasty "dolls" of faience and limestone, most of them from the excavations in Lisht and Thebes, and I have found another of wood in the Boston Museum of Fine Arts, possibly of the same date—all wearing cowrie bead girdles.   The Boston " doll " (Fig. 6) is a remarkably striking example.   There can be no hesitation in recognising the cowries, because they are both modelled in relief and painted yellow to represented gold.   In scale they are correct.   In number they are identical

---

[1] Newberry, *Bersheh*, I, frontispiece.

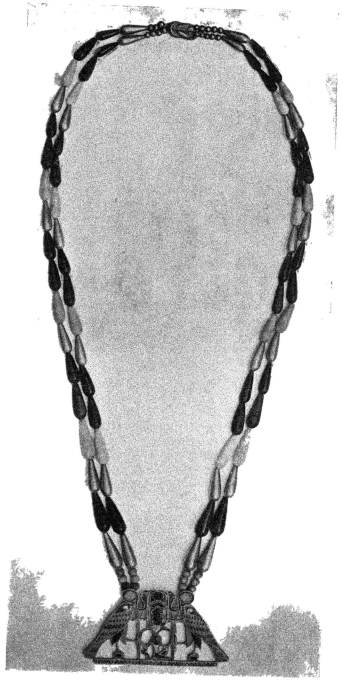

5. PECTORAL AND BEAD NECKLACE. AS STRUNG IN THE METROPOLITAN MUSEUM.

with the Lahun girdle, if in addition to the three shown in front and the three behind, two more were supposed to be hidden under the hands on the hips, which are unnaturally narrowed on the flattened " doll." Even the distance between cowries is as it should be if we are to suppose that the spaces now blank were once filled with dots of paint to represent smaller separating beads. If there never were such dots of paint, we must suppose that sometimes the cowries were worn with bare threads between, a method of stringing beads or shells which is not without parallel.[1] Most of the New York " dolls " represent the cowries in very rudimentary form, but all are perfectly recognizable in the light of the " doll " already figured. The clearest example in the Metropolitan Museum is shown in Fig. 4, like those in other museums. This " doll " is of faience, and like all of the others in this material, has accessories shown in black under the glaze. Here, not only are the cowries drawn to scale and properly spaced, but between them two strings of separating beads are plainly marked. To forestall a possible criticism, I should explain that the marks on the legs are pendants. Behind, one of them falls exactly between the two legs in a way that would be impossible if tatooing were intended, and as far as the belt itself is concerned, the Boston " doll " with its modelling in relief demonstrates the fact that the cowries are not tatooed.

The recognition of a girdle among the Lahun jewels leads to its recognition at Dahshur. In the First Treasure there were six large cowries, and apparently 98 " rhomboid " beads of gold (in pairs), carnelian, lapis lazuli and amazon stone.[2] The numbers are interesting in the light of those from Lahun. In the Second Treasure,[3] there is no mention of rhomboid beads with the cowries and, if none were actually found, we are forced to conclude that these cowries were worn, as the Boston " doll " (Fig. 6) may represent them, without connecting beads. In the Tomb of Khnumit there were found nearly 100 " rhomboid " beads, but no cowries,[4] which probably should be reconstructed as a bead girdle like that of Senebtisi. This last was made up of " rhomboids " only.[5] Buckles for two bead girdles were found in the Tomb of Ita,[6] and from the Tomb of Nubhotep comes an object which, while not the buckle of a girdle of the type here dealt with, was seemingly the fastening of a kind of cloth scarf, or sash, which crossed the shoulders and encircled the waist.[7]

A regular item of a Middle Kingdom court jewel-set thus was a girdle, and this girdle seems to have usually been made up of cowrie shells and rhomboid acacia beans,[8] either together or separately. Furthermore, even the less wealthy

---

[1] As for example the *šwt* beads described in Mace and Winlock, *Senebtisi*, p. 63, and the drop bead suspenders of the Rameses III pectoral in Cairo, Vernier, *Bijoux*, Pl. IV.

[2] De Morgan, *Dahchour*, I, p. 60, Pl. XVII.

[3] *Ibid.*, p. 65, Pl. XXIII.   [4] *Dahchour*, II, Pls. VII–VIII.

[5] Mace and Winlock, *Tomb of Senebtisi*, p. 68, Pls. XXII–XXIII. The other girdle was purely Osirian.

[6] *Dahchour*, II, pp. 52–3.

[7] *Dahchour*, I, Pl. XXXVIII, C. No description is given, but the illustration shows it to be identical, even to the colours, with the sash buckle of Neferure', in Rosellini, *Mon.*, I, Pl. XIX, 23.

[8] Mace and Winlock, *Senebtisi*, p. 68, note 1. Small silver and gold cowrie shells are sometimes found in the Middle Kingdom, but it would be difficult to say whether they are necklaces or girdles. *See* De Morgan, *Dahchour*, I, p. 66, Pl. XXIV ; Winlock, *Bulletin of the Metropolitan Museum*, 1914, p. 17, Fig. 8 ; Garstang, *Burial Customs*, p. 222, and Williams, *Jour. Egypt. Arch.*, 1918, p. 173, Pl. XXVIII.

women of the period wore girdles,[1] and the fashion passed over from the Middle Kingdom to the Empire. Thus Prof. Petrie has published the jewellery of a woman buried at Thebes during the Hyksos Period " around whose waist, outside the innermost cloth, was a girdle of electrum beads, 26 of semicircular

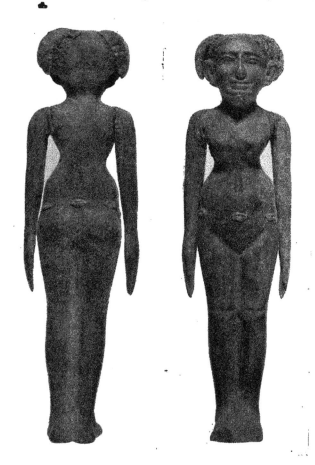

6. WOODEN FIGURE WITH COWRIE GIRDLE. BOSTON MUSEUM.

form, copied from a disc of leather folded over and stitched ; the spaces between these had two threads of six beads each, and in one case a space of seven beads. Three spaces had been gathered together by a tie of thread, so as to shorten the

[1] Mace has found two : one published in *Diospolis Parva*, p. 41, from Pit 90, which was a belt 10 ins. wide of faience and shell disk beads with a fringe of real shells ; the other at Naga ed-Dêr, which was a belt of twelve strings of disk beads of the same materials. Several others of the XIIth and XIIIth dynasties and of the XVIIth and early XVIIIth dynasties have recently been found at Thebes by Lansing. A preliminary report on his excavations is appearing shortly in the *Bulletin of the Metropolitan Museum.*

F

circuit of the girdle to fit the body.   The whole girdle was 31·6 ins. long, and was
shortened to 28·4 ins."[1]   A little later, about the middle of the XVIIIth dynasty,
a young woman found by Passalacqua in Thebes wore what must have been a
charming girdle of gold, lapis-lazuli and carnelian.   From his description, it
consisted of a series of " square-knots " similar to the little gold clasps found at
Lahun, spaced at intervals along a double string of smaller beads.[2]   Finally,
even in modern times Nubian girls are occasionally seen wearing belts of cowries
and beads very much like those worn by their ancient ancestresses.[3]

To consider now the way in which the girdle was worn.   Personally, I
have never seen a bas-relief or statue of a woman wearing a girdle over her
clothing.   Before the Empire the tight-fitting woman's shift descends from chest
to ankles in an unbroken line.   In the Empire a cloth sash is often bound over
it about the hips, but the many representations of bead girdles are always on
naked girls or occasionally worn by girls next their bodies, under transparent
garments.[4]   The " dolls," which, whatever their purpose in the graves, unquestionably represent dancing girls, are striking Middle Kingdom examples ;
dancing girls and maidservants are shown so attired in a woven bead belt at
innumerable banquets in the XVIIIth dynasty ;[5]   swimming girls on the toilet
spoons wear nothing more ;[6]   and it constitutes the sole article of apparel of the
ridiculous caricatures of negress slaves.[7]   It may be objected that all of these
little persons can hardly be compared with propriety to the Princesses of Dahshur
and Lahun, but at the time that the dancing girls and servants were wearing
such girdles two of the young princesses of the royal family, Neferubiti and
Neferure, daughters of Thotmose I and Thotmose III, respectively, appear clad
in jewellery identical with that from Lahun, including girdles very much like
this one of cowries—and nothing more.[8]   And then there is the very well-known
statuette in Turin (Fig. 7) of a charming little girl of good family who is clad
in the same way.   Like Neferubiti and Neferure she has not yet passed adoles-
cence.   On the walls of the belvedere of the harim at Medinet Habu, where no
one but the royal family could penetrate in ancient times,[9] we see full-grown
women of the court represented in sufficiently scanty clothing to tell whether
they wore girdles or not.   These decorations from the harim of Rameses III are

[1] Petrie, *Qurneh*, p. 9, Pl. XXIX.

[2] Passalacqua, *Catalogue raisonné*, p. 159.   The girdle was stolen from him, but he
describes it as having been of the same form as his necklace No. 599 which is Schäfer,
Goldschmiedearbeiten, p. 31, Pl. VIII, No. 35A.

[3] Roberts, *Egypt and Nubia* (1846), II, vignette.   Firth, who called my attention to
this picture, has seen such girdles being worn in Nubia in recent years.

[4] Rosellini, *Mon.*, II, Pl. XCVIII ;   Champollion, *Mon.*, II, Pl. CLXXV ;   Prisse,
Mon., Pl. XLIV, and *L'Art* (*Dessin*), Pl. VII ; Wilkinson, *Manners*, I, p. 501, Fig. 261.
What appears to be a girdle worn over or under the dress in L.D., III, 42, I take for the hem
of a short-sleeved shirt.

[5] Davies, *Tomb of Nakht*, frontispiece and plate XV are the latest published examples
of a very common scene.

[6] Prisse, *Mon.*, Pl. XLVIII, and *L'Art* (*Industrial*), Pls. XXI, XXIII.

[7] MacIver and Mace, *El Amrah and Abydos*, Pl. L.; Wainwright, *Jour. Egypt. Arch.*,
1915, p. 203, Pl. XXVI.

[8] The best copies are the earliest (Rosellini, *Mon.*, I, Pl. XIX, 23-24, and Champollion,
Mon., II, Pls. CXCIII-IV).   The later copies are all less detailed.

[9] Rosellini, *Mon.*, I, CXII-III ;   Champollion, *Mon.*, II, Pls. CXCIX–CC ;   L.D., III,
208 ;   Wilkinson, *Manners*, II, pp. 59-60 ;   Hölscher, *Hohes Tor von Medinet Habu*, Figs.
8, 40–42.

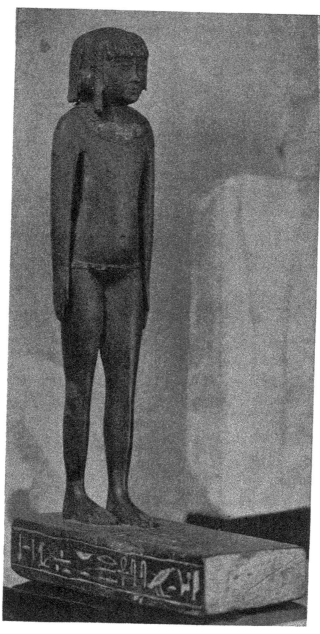

7. WOODEN FIGURE WITH GIRDLE. TURIN.

in fact unique, but if we are to take them literally we must conclude that in the seclusion of their private apartments the Egyptian ladies laid aside their hobble skirts and disported themselves at their ease, clad only in their jewellery, or at most in diaphanous garments, which were represented in paint only and have since been washed completely away. The fact that the ladies of this particular harim wear no girdles, need not be taken as proof that they, were not worn by higher-class women of the Empire.[1]

Having, as I believe, established the existence of girdles among the treasures of Lahun and Dahshur, I should like to conclude this paper with some consideration on the string of gold lions' heads. It is a subject of some difficulty, purposely avoided in the preceding pages. With the exception of the similar set from the Second Treasure of Dahshur, these heads are unique in Museums and, so far as I am aware, there is no representation of them on the monuments. In fact they appear to have been jewels whose vogue lasted so short a time that they never found their way into Egyptian pictorial art, and thus for any explanation of their wearing we are forced to rely wholly on practical consideration.

In the first place, their condition is such that Prof. Petrie was able to string them. This done, and the clasp closed, they have every appearance of making an upright collar, and such they have been unhesitatingly called. Only, when in New York the experiment was actually tried of putting them on a woman of normal size, one glance was enough to convince everyone present that they never could have been such a collar. Again it is a question of circumference. Clasped they should be worn on a throat measuring 16¾ ins. round, because, standing upright as they do, on an ordinary woman they sag down under the chin in a most unbecoming way. Now an upright collar, to be attractive, should be a fairly close-fitting one. If the wearer of this collar had a throat of such a size that the collar fitted closely, the uneven surface on the inner side would make it most uncomfortable, and to draw it in 1¾ to 2 ins., while clasping it, would be a painful operation if it was anywhere near the snug fit which one would expect. The tight, upright Egyptian collar of the monuments seems to have been designed like a bead bracelet and must have been clasped like a bracelet, with a buckle which does not have to be drawn in to be fastened.

Actual experiment, then, makes it seem improbable that the lions' heads should make a collar. Immediately one wonders how they could have been worn. The neck being practically eliminated—arms, wrists and ankles being out of the question—the head and waist remain the only parts of the body to consider. This is assuming with Prof. Petrie that the large and small heads belong together—an assumption which can be taken almost as an established fact.

The suggestion was made that they constituted a circlet. The answer to this appears to be that they present features both unnecessary for a circlet, and never found among Egyptian circlets. All known Egyptian circlets are, practically speaking, hoops, not jointed nor having a clasp, and being modelled or decorated on the outer surface only. The wearer's head is thus eliminated to all intents and purposes, and there remains only her waist to consider.

For the idea that the lions' heads constituted a girdle, naturally the inspiration was in all that has been written above. Again, size and workmanship class

---

[1] Were they customarily worn under the garments by grown women, they would unquestionably be shown sometimes at Tell el-Amarna, where the bodies are shown in full detail through the clothing.

them with the cowries. And finally, it is only around the waist or hips that it would be comfortable to wear anything that has to be shortened almost 2 ins. to be fastened. To be sure, it is impossible to advance arguments as convincing in this case as in the case of the cowries, but still it is an idea which has a great deal of probability. It remains necessary only to discover some method of stringing which would give a length approximating that of the cowrie girdle.

The experiment was tried, therefore, of lengthening the strings and spacing the beads equally on them, leaving bare thread between. Knots were made to hold the heads at equal intervals, and as authority for this arrangement the fact

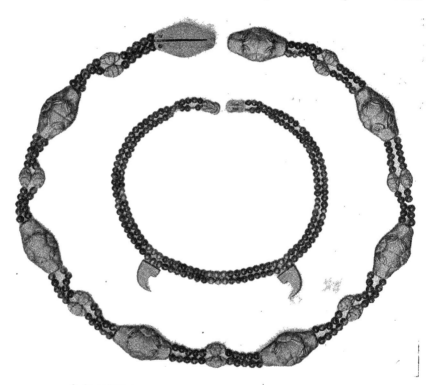

8. Claw Necklaces and suggested order of Lion-head Girdle.

was quoted that the cowries of the Boston " doll " and the Second Dahshur Treasure may have been so strung. To me, personally, however, the double line of bare threads did not seem in keeping with the fineness of the other jewels.

The suggestion was also made that small beads, such as are used in the bracelets and armlets, may have been employed. But of the little beads there are hardly enough for the requirements of these very bracelets and armlets even, and a double string, of the required length of twice 16 ins. more, could not possibly have escaped the painstaking and conscientious search of the finders of the tomb.

Hence, unless it is supposed that the lions' heads were not strung up when they were placed in the tomb, there is really only one set of beads which could have been used. The solution that I suggest, therefore, is that the lions' heads were threaded with the amethyst beads which formerly were strung with the Senusert II pectoral. This is a solution to be accepted with all reserve, and one which is for the present, at least, held in abeyance by Mr. Lythgoe and Mr. Mace. The latter, for instance, objects to this particular arrangement because of the size of the amethyst beads, in relation to the smaller lions' heads especially, and raises the point that up to the present no ball beads have been found strung in any way except as necklaces, in Egyptian tombs. Nevertheless, since there appear to be grounds for considering that the lions' heads cannot be a collar, and are probably parts of a girdle, there seems to be some point in setting forth in this place the result of the experiment of stringing them with the amethyst beads. At least by so doing I may be inspiring others to settle the matter one way or the other.

In the first place, when one puts the amethyst beads (on which was formerly strung the Senusert II pectoral) between the lions' heads, a girdle is made up 32½ ins. long, clasped. The length is near enough to that of the cowrie girdle to have been worn in the same way and the beads divide up excellently into sets, ten in each interval.[1] For this arrangement no mechanical objection can be raised. The diameters of the beads are such that they go perfectly on the threads passing through the lions' heads, and they stand, in thickness, midway between the big and little heads. Secondly, when laid beside the claw necklace there is a harmony of colour and workmanship which gives a wonderfully sumptuous effect (Fig. 8).[2] One gets the impression that the multicoloured cowrie girdle was to be worn with the pectoral and its polychrome string of beads, and that this gold lion-head and amethyst girdle was intended to be worn with the gold claw and amethyst necklace. As a matter of effect, aside from all other considerations, the stringing of the lions' heads and amethyst beads results in an incomparably magnificent jewel. Finally, the girdle so constructed conforms in type with the majority of those already quoted in having a series of large elements spaced along and joining two strings of smaller beads.

As has been said already the lions' heads from Lahun are paralleled nowhere except in the similar set from Dahshur. It is practically impossible, therefore, to demonstrate either the truth or falsity of this suggested stringing as a girdle. There is, however, one circumstance which is at least favourable to its correctness. The Second Dahshur Treasure, among which the other lions' heads were found, contained two gold claws and 252 amethyst ball beads.[3] Accepting 252 as a minimum (the actual number may have been considerably greater) it is quite possible to reconstruct the same combination of lions' head girdle and claw necklace in this case as well. Of course amethyst ball beads and claw necklaces are common enough without such girdles, and right in the First Treasure, 240 amethyst beads and two gold claws were found without any lions' heads.[4] And yet, while there is no positive evidence to be derived from the Second Treasure, at least it is suggestive to find that in the only two cases where lions' heads have been found the same combination is a possibility.

---

[1] This takes up 140 beads. One more was strung with the pectoral, but there is a place for that in the claw necklace, making a total of 152 amethyst beads in the latter.

[2] Showing the effect of a purely experimental stringing of the lions' heads. If they were thus strung as a girdle they were intended to lie flat on the hips. Hence in the photograph, where they lie flat on a table, the intermediate beads present an irregular appearance.

[3] *Dahchour*, I, p. 66, Pl. XXIX.

[4] *Ibid.*, p. 63, Pl. XVIII.

In conclusion, I should like to repeat that while I feel that it is possible to demonstrate rigidly the new stringing of the pectoral and the existence of the cowrie girdle, the proposed reconstruction of the lions' heads as a second girdle to go with the claw necklace, is purely tentative.

. H. E. WINLOCK.

[The evidence for the use of cowries in a girdle, seems good reason for accepting that arrangement in the Lahun series. The close similarity between the cowries and the lion heads, in size and fastening, leads also toward these having been in a girdle. The suspension of the pectoral by long drop beads is, however, a difficult matter. The dates of the examples quoted should be observed. From the IIIrd down to the XIIth dynasty, there seems to be no example of drop beads threaded in a long string. At Meydum there are long equiterminal beads and balls; in *Beni Hasan III*, iii, the same; in the funeral offerings (Lacau, *Sarcophages*, xlix-liii) the belt fringes are all of long and ball beads, the strings for collars are the same. In no case is there a drop bead in a long string. In the XVIIIth dynasty there was a great fall in taste, and a loss of the old ideals after Tehutmes III; then drop bead strings appear, with Tehutmes IV. The effect of the broad masses of drop beads close to the minute work of the pectoral is killing, and it is hard to believe that the refined taste of the XIIth dynasty would have made such a mistake.

As to the absence of clothing along with jewellery, note the account by Lady Mary Wortley Montague of the Turkish baths, where a large company of ladies will join in social functions, clad only in their jewellery. We must also remember that the Egyptian scenes were not of life on earth, but for life in a future state; even we should hesitate in a picture of heaven to introduce knee breeches, crinoline or hobble-skirts. At Deshasheh (Vth dynasty) the actual dresses buried for a woman were with tight long sleeves like a modern *ghalabiyeh*, and not at all like the low garment with shoulder straps figured in the tomb scenes of that age. The festive scenes of the XVIIIth dynasty tombs represented the joys of a future life, and need not be accepted completely as true in this world.— W. M. F. P.]

GENERAL MAUDE'S PROCLAMATION.

THE War has been responsible for many things—not all of them bad, and among the good ones may be counted the wholesale manner in which archaeology has been brought to the notice of the nation. Many thousands of men, who otherwise would never have thought of such a subject, have found themselves among ruins and other relics of past civilisations, when they were sent East with the various armies. A large proportion of these men have visited these remains, and have even been conducted round the museums of the larger towns, and some have been subjected to lectures in hospitals and elsewhere on the history, civilisation and art of the particular country in which they then happen to be. While no doubt the majority of such men could wish for more exciting fare, there is always a minority which is keenly interested and full of a thirst for information on little points which happen to have come before their notice; as for instance, where the horse came from, and when he first made his appearance in history; whether it was possible to cut hard stones with copper and emery, and so on; and it has even been the writer's pleasant lot at the Cairo Museum to be searched out by members of his previous week's audience, in order to certify themselves on various points, which had been so hotly debated during the interval as to have become somewhat confused.

This unexpected spread of interest in archaeology has its dangers, as the preservation of the past is essential to understanding it; and no one is competent to know what must be observed without a proper training. It was most satisfactory to see in the *Basrah Times* as early as August 6th, 1917, a fully conclusive proclamation signed by the late Sir Stanley Maude on May 22nd. It reads as follows :—

Whereas it is convenient to take over both for the preservation of ancient monuments, ancient objects of vertu, and relics movable and immovable of ancient times, hereinafter styled " antiquities," and also for the prohibition of traffic in forged articles falsely asserted to be antiquities; I, Lieutenant-General F. S. Maude, K.C.B., C.M.G., D.S.O., in virtue of the authority vested in me as General Officer Commanding His Britannic Majesty's Forces in Mesopotamia, do hereby proclaim as follows :—

(1) Throughout the occupied territories all antiquities, to wit, all ancient monuments, ancient objects of vertu, relics movable and immovable of ancient times, which formerly were the property of the Ottoman Government, or shall hereafter be discovered, are the property of the Administration of the Occupied Territories acting on behalf of the said Territories.

(2) The term " ancient " for the purposes of this proclamation shall be deemed to signify antecedent to the year 1500 A.D.

(3) Whosoever having discovered any antiquity fails to inform accordingly the nearest Assistant Political Officer in charge of a district within a period of 30 days shall be liable to a fine not exceeding 50 rupees.

(4) Whosoever having discovered any antiquity unlawfully appropriates the same to his own use shall be liable to a fine not exceeding ten times the value of the article discovered.

(5) Whosoever negligently or maliciously destroys, defaces, or in any way damages any ancient monument or any site which he has reason to believe to contain antiquities, shall be liable to a fine not exceeding 10,000 rupees.

(6) Whosoever traffics in or abets the traffic in antiquities, except under a licence duly issued by the Officer appointed hereto, shall be liable to a fine not exceeding 10,000 rupees.

(7) Whosoever, whether licensed or not licensed, sells or offers for sale as antiquities any article which he has not reason to believe antique, shall on conviction be liable to imprisonment for a period not exceeding six months or to a fine not exceeding 10,000 rupees, or both ; and his stock of antiquities or pseudo-antiquities shall be liable to be confiscated.

(8) Whosoever reports the discovery of an antiquity over which the Administration decides to exercise its right of property shall be duly compensated ; and when any such antiquity is relinquished by the Administration, the Administration shall deliver the said antiquity to the possession of the person appearing to have the most proper claim therein, together with a certificate enabling the said antiquity to be transferred in accordance with the terms of this Proclamation.

(9) The power vested in the Administration under this Proclamation together with power to perform all necessary acts subsidiary thereto are hereby delegated to the Chief Political Officer or such person or persons as he may appoint to act on his behalf.

Signed at Baghdad 22nd day of May, 1917.

F. S. MAUDE, *Lieut.-General,*
Commanding the Army of Occupation.

The law is admirable in conception and it is to be hoped that it may be effectively carried out.

Apart from the depredations of the mere plunderer, who goes to obtain saleable loot, Article 5 is framed to combat the ravages caused by the ignorance of two distinct classes of destroyers, at whose mercy antiquities only too often lie. These are, firstly, the ignorantly callous ; and secondly, the ignorantly keen.

The wrecking of the earliest sculptures of Egyptian history in Sinai was a sad case of the wanton destruction by modern " practical " men. They were too ignorant to know either the historic value or the market value of what they deliberately destroyed without any benefit to themselves. The late Inspector of Antiquities at Luqsor had great trouble with some " practical " engineers who had " no use " for what they knew nothing about. At Silsileh there is the great bed of sandstone which the ancients largely quarried, leaving numerous examples of their methods, and inscriptions of historical value, etc. Extensive as these records of the world's doings are, they by no means cover the whole available area for quarrying. Yet when these engineers needed sandstone for some work which they had in hand, they declined starting on a fresh piece of the cliff, but insisted on quarrying on the ancient sites, thus quite needlessly destroying for ever records of the world's progress which can never be replaced. Most fortunately the Department of Antiquities interfered in time to prevent any serious damage being done, and no doubt the necessary sandstone was obtained from the immediate neighbourhood.

Another kind of danger is also to be prevented by the clause about any who " negligently . . . destroys . . . or in anyway damages . . . any site." The amateur excavator usually damages or destroys more information than he preserves, and the hunting for something pretty or valuable is as destructive when done to amuse an amateur as when done for the profit of a dealer. A quantity of hunting is reported from various sites, even printed, with the melancholy result that the hunters could not in the least date what they were working at, or give any useful account of it ; while the date and proper record would have been an elementary matter to anyone educated in the subject. Even if everything is preserved and put in a local museum, the value of it is destroyed if there is no record of the relative positions and ages of the objects, no statement whether found in original position of deposit, or in ancient rubbish, or in modern tip-heaps.

Action such as this, while excellent in its intention, is deplorable in its results, for the novice full of his search all unwittingly does what is probably furthest removed from his mind or wishes, he destroys irretrievably more than he saves. It is not generally understood what a great range of facts have to be observed in excavating, how many subjects must be all promoted together, how varied must be the interests and view of the excavator, how ready he must be to succeed in preserving all he may find. Recently some great scholars—who were not trained as excavators—found some splendid bead-work of coloured figures, they could not preserve it, and it all fell to pieces. Anyone who knew his business would have easily preserved the whole of it complete ; but the great scholars had never even heard of using paraffin wax.

The encouragement of plundering by the purchase of antiquities from dealers is a difficult subject. The only proper rule is never to buy anything that is not of great importance to be preserved, where the information must not be lost. The ordinary objects, and specially any pieces of monuments recently broken, should be left on the dealers' hands. The encouragement of the chance finder to proclaim his accidental discoveries is most important ; it will put all honest possession on a legal basis, give the earliest notice to the Government, and provide an above-board supply of objects to the tourist and the foreign museums. The recommendations officially given for the new law in Palestine also recognises fully the rights of every chance finder, and encourages the open sale of all that can be honestly sold.

The activities of the forger are also heavily penalised. Large quantities of cylinder seals and cuneiform tablets have been produced in recent years, and a stiff hand must be put on such frauds. The manufacture of false antiquities has reached such proportions now in Egypt, that it may be considered one of the national industries, and indeed the Department of Technical Education includes a collection of modern " antiquities" among its exhibits of the crafts of the country. The result is that there are numbers of antiquity shops throughout Egypt in which a very large percentage of the objects exposed for sale are forgeries. Moreover, the trade in forgeries has not only reached extreme proportions in quantity, but also in quality, for the workmanship has improved so much in recent years that when a new line in statue heads or some other novelty comes on the market, it is quite likely to deceive the expert until he has examined it long and carefully. The writer well remembers accompanying one of the leading experts on Egyptian antiquities on a visit to a well-known up-country dealer. Before long two or three fine alabaster vases of large size caught his eye. They purported to be of late pre-dynastic, or of early dynastic, date, but after a long and detailed study of their form, material, and workmanship, accompanied by a critical cross-examination of the dealer, the prospective purchaser passed them over with the remark: " Twenty years ago I would have given you £25 for them, but to-day I dare not risk it."

The most obvious lesson of the whole wretched position of museums paying heavily to encourage the destruction of monuments for plundered spoils, with the loss of all archaeological history, is that properly recorded observation and excavation of certified and dated objects is the only right channel for either museums or the public to draw upon. The moral to those who stay at home, and to our local and national museums, is that every effort should be made to train excavators and to carry on the largest amount of proper excavation in order to save what little remains to us of the history and treasure of the past.

G. A. WAINWRIGHT.

REVIEWS.

———

Bulletin de l'Institut Française d'Archéologie Orientale. Cairo, 1918.

[We much regret that this will be the last contribution of our good friend, Mr. Joseph Offord, who died at the beginning of this year. He did much to spread the knowledge of the French works on Egypt ; both for his work and his genial personality he will be much missed and regretted.]

An important fascicule of the Bulletin is that of the first of Vol. XV, 1918. It contains some 140 pages, with about 25 hieroglyphic titles of Pharaohs and princes, to each page. It embodies the " Répertoire Pharaonique pour servir d'Index au Livre des Rois d'Égypte " of M. Henri Gauthier, that is to say, his great five-volume work in the series of the " Memoires de l'Institut Français d'archéologie Orientale du Caire." By issuing this Index in the comparatively inexpensive format of the Bulletin, with every royal name again reproduced in its hieroglyph form, the Institut has placed within the means of many students the opportunity of acquiring what is practically a catalogue of Egyptian royalties, from Menes to the Emperor Decius.

In Vol. XIII of the *Bulletin de l'Institut*, Mr. F. W. Read has a paper upon the precise sense of the word 𓏏𓏏 𓄿 𓃀 𓄋 𓏏, which Dr. A. H. Gardiner, in an article upon " The Egyptian Word for Dragoman," had rendered as " teacher of foreign languages." Mr. Read's view is that " scholar " would be a nearer translation of the title, and his main basis for this rendering is a passage in Chapter 125 of the *Book of the Dead*, wherein it is applied to Thoth the Scholar god *par excellence*.

Another essay of interest in the thirteenth volume is that by M. Henri Gauthier, " La Nécropole de Thebes et son Personnel." This refers to the inscriptions belonging to a considerable number of personages who were attached to certain priestly and lay offices for a site near Thebes known as 𓊹𓏏𓊖, " The place of Truth." Most of these people were buried in the hill of Deir el-Medineh, and a quantity of funerary objects and records of them have for many years been in the Turin Museum.

In the spring of 1917 the French Institut at Cairo carried out excavations at the hill site and found further tombs of members of the association or fraternity of the Place of Truth, enabling M. Gauthier to explain who and what they were more completely than Maspero was able to do, some years ago, when treating of them chiefly from the material at Turin.

Many of them were attached to the cult of the deified Amenhotep I, and it appears that his worship was certainly the origin of the confraternity of the Place of Truth.

Many of the office holders were also entitled *sotemu oshu* ⟨hieroglyph⟩
They wore special garments and headdresses as depicted upon the sepulchre
paintings and steles. Some were simply servants of Amon, the domestic for
hand washing, and the official for weighing silver and gold, and so on. One was
" serviteur de l'administration de la cuisson au bois (?) de la patisserie du palais,"
which reminds one of the chief baker in the story of Joseph.

M. Gauthier's researches show that the members of the Place of Truth were
permitted to serve living Pharaohs, in the administration and temples, or at least
that those determined as being *sotemu oshu* were so.

As far as we at present know, no female seems to have been a member.

M. Georges Daressy, in a long article, makes excellent archaeological use of an
Arabic work, which he entitles the " Livre des Perles Enfouies, et du Mystère
Precieux," an edition of which, based upon three manuscripts, was published by
Ahmed Bey Kamel some fourteen years ago.

Among the articles in Vol. XV of the *Bulletin* is one by Mademoiselle Chatelet,
a pupil of M. Loret, which is entitled " Le Rôle des Deux Barques Solaires."
The object of the thesis is to prove that the well-known Monzet and Mesketit
sun ships are not the vessels Ra occupies from sunrise to midday, and from noon
to sunset, but that one is used for a complete day, and the other for night.

The first evidence is from M. Jèquier's version of " Le Livre de ce qu'il a
dans l'Hadès," which states that at the twelfth night hour " the great god departs
from Hades that he may embark upon the Monzet."

From the inscriptions upon the tomb of Sety I, close to the representation
of the events of the first hour of the night is a line reading " This god in the
Mesketit barque which navigates in the *arerit* of this domain."

Another literary proof is obtained from the phrase in the *Book of the Dead*,
Chapter XV, Papyrus Ani, Pl. 20, reading " He sails in the Monzet, he ties up
(*amarre*) in the Mesketit."

A final proof is given from three of the pyramid texts given by M. Lacau
(*Rec.*, XXV, 153), which read " Thou passest the night in Mesketit, thou passest
the day in Monzet." Good cause for so rendering this sentence are quoted,
Mdlle. Chatelet summing up claims that the real myth was that the exchange
of vessels occurred at sunrise and sunset, but modestly adds that, perhaps accidentally at certain periods in variant theological schools, other views may have
been current.

Another interesting essay in this fifteenth volume is that by M. Gustave
Jéquier upon " Some Objects appertaining to the Funerary Ritual." The first
of these symbolic relics he treats of are the " Piquets d'amarrage " or the mooring
pegs for the dahabeahs of the dead. Illustrations of these are to be found upon
the Sarcophagus of Sâ-Uazet, published in *Riqqeh and Memphis VI*, Plate XXIII.
These special pegs thereon depicted, instead of having merely a knob, or spreading
a flattened top to support the driving blows of a mallet, terminate in a human
head and bust. It seems manifest without any literary proof that these sepulchral
mooring posts are deified in some sense. They are to be seen in the same form
emblazoned upon Theban tombs, but in two connections—the first as objects of
some funeral cult, secondly, as accessories at a ceremony relating to the due
presentation of the deceased to the gods of the dead. In the *Book of the Dead*,
in some illustrated papyri, one of these human-headed pickets is shown as securing
down the bird-catcher's net in the Elysian fields.

A more frequent picture of these objects is to be found in the representations of the Nile-boat voyage of the mummy (a favourite Theban theme at the XIXth dynasty era), to the shrine of Osiris at Abydos, of Anubis at Siout, and Amentit in Lower Egypt. In the rubrical texts for these scenes two pickets are mentioned, that of the prow and that of the poop. They are shown driven into the soil, and priests are rendering offerings unto them. Then another scene shows the boat being moored with ropes to the pegs, and libation offerings being made to them.   .

In these scenes, the pickets do not have human heads to them, but the rites with which they are worshipped are the same as those for a deity, and without doubt, M. Jéquier says, these objects are the Deésse-piquet of the Pyramid Texts, first recognised by M. Lefebure, the great Menat. They are also in some inscriptions identified with Isis or Nephthys.

Finally, these mooring pegs are mentioned, as might be anticipated, in descriptions of the voyages of the Solar barque.

M. Jéquier also writes upon the regal item of decorative costume called at various times Uatet, menkeret, and khebset, that is the animal's tail, worn by the Pharaoh upon ceremonial occasions, as shown in so many paintings and reliefs.

He proves by careful consideration that these tails are so accurately drawn that the usual idea that they are intended for lions' tails is erroneous, and that they are undoubtedly intended for those of a bull. This is confirmed by the frequent assimilation in Egyptian literature to a bull, and especially so by the figure of the king as a bull upon one of the prehistoric slate palettes from Hieraconpolis. The tail is always shown as being worn suspended from a waistbelt.

The syllable *set* of its name Khebset, M. Jéquier derives from a root *sed* or *set*, meaning tail. It forms the moiety of the word *heb-sed*, festival. The " Feast of the Tail " or Sed Festival, so often alluded to in Egyptian writings, and portrayed in reliefs, certainly seems to be a symbolical ceremony of the assumption of royalty or overlordship, and the putting on at that function of the belt and its appanage, being a similar performance to an act of enthronement.

M. Henri Gauthier has a lengthy article upon the title given to various personages of *Ami-Ra-Akhnute* and its diverse attributions. The question of interest he deems to have decided is not so much the official title of *Ami-Ra* as that of the complete significance of the term *Akhnute*, which many years ago Egyptologists decided was a definition for a particularly private chamber, or a select portion of some edifice, generally that of a royal palace.

M. Gauthier agrees with this rendering, but is also able, by carefully collected textual quotations, to prove that there were a number of other places, such as official bureaus, registrar offices, and safe deposit chambers, which were known to the Egyptians as *Akhnute*. In fact, he succeeds in citing from inscriptions the titles of some score of *Ami-Ra* officials belonging to as many different departments qualified as an *Akhnute* chamber, or department, in buildings of various characters.

The *Akhnute*, of which this personage was presiding officer, or custodian, appears to have been a " Selamlik," and so not a saloon of such a private nature, or of such forbidden access to the public, as the word usually signifies. For it is certain that as a rule admission to an *Akhnute* was only obtained for some special reason, or by privileged people. It should be mentioned it was sometimes used as a name for the royal nursery

When M. Loret wrote upon the subject he only enumerated some four or five different *Akhnutes,* but starting from the Hood-Wilbur papyrus, edited by Sir Gaston Maspero as the " Hierarchie," M. Gauthier gives some sixty instances of these officials, but without any distinctive statement as to the nature of their *Akhnutes.*

In his second chapter he gives those whose names are followed by determinative qualifications, such as *Ami Ra* of the " Preposé au Pays du Nord," and those of the " White House " and " Golden House."

One title new to us is that of the *Ami Ra Akhnoute* of the *Kherp hatu,* which M. Gauthier thinks applies to some further special palace apartments. Another chapter endeavours, by a comparison of numerous texts, to define what were the duties of the various grades of *Ami Ra* of *Akhnutes.*

The second fascicule of Vol. XVI, 1919, of the *Bulletin de l'Institut Française d'Archéologie Orientale* of Cairo is mainly occupied with the completion of Mr. K. A. C. Cresswell's article entitled " A brief Chronology of the Mohammadan Monuments of Egypt to A.D. 1517."

From the industrious pen of M. Henri Gauthier there is a description of a large number of inscribed Funerary Cones, found upon the eastern slope of the hill of Gournet el-Medineh at Thebes. The inscriptions upon them and upon those previously edited in various journals or museum catalogues now present some thirteen variant types of texts. Of these no less than six are derived from the numerous specimens now for the first time reproduced by M. Gauthier. He reproduces those of a *chef de bureau,* named Amonemapit (or Amonemat), who, like many other Egyptian people of importance, especially officials, enjoyed the honorific title of ⟨hieroglyphs⟩, and M. Gauthier thoroughly threshes out the probable meaning of it, rendering it *khrd kep,* "child of the nursery." That is to say, he had in youth been one of the playmates of the royal children, or perhaps it may mean that his mother having been wet nurse to a royal infant, he was also reared in the court nursery.

Two very valuable essays are provided by M. Jean Clédat, " Pour la Conquête de l'Égypte," and " Notes sur l'Isthme de Suez." The first is a full account of Egyptian methods of defence and offence upon the present Suez Canal route frontier, in ancient times, including the Ptolemaic and Roman periods. The geographical peculiarities of the district between the eastern Delta and Palestine are explained, quotations from papyri and inscriptions utilised, and notes upon various campaigns which opened or closed within this area are given, as well as quotations from the reports and diaries of travellers and officials, frontier officers and fugitives, such as Saneha.

M. Clédat is profoundly impressed by the splendid British engineering achievement by which fresh water is conveyed across the desert mounds and valleys, all the way from Kantara to El Arish. It carries the precious fluid for 150 kilometres, and is one of the most beneficent works of modern times. Yet British-like we have never even described its design and equipment, much less boasted of the matter, though the French journal *Illustration* has done so.

The notes upon the Isthmus of Suez are of much more importance than their title would suggest. The first is upon a Persian stele at Qabret. But few words remain of the inscription it once bore ; one of these is that for Satrap, and some others refer to the Tamahou country. The remains of a Byzantine fortress at the same locality are illustrated by a plan.

Two steles of Rameses II are described ; they mention the semi-Asiatic deities of Sutek, Anta, Baal and Sopdt, " master of the Orient land," who in a relief presents those countries to the Pharaoh.

Section 4 of this paper gives a ground plan and a detailed account of a Migdol watch tower fort, the innermost of three halls in which was employed as a temple in the time of Rameses II. Part was used as a storehouse, seven large vases being provided for holding grain.

Section 5 refers to the Israelite passage of the Red Sea, and because of M. Clédat's special knowledge of the districts concerned, is of very great value ; he gives an excellent map. He has been impressed by the very excellent work of the late M. Léon Cart, a Swiss archæologist and traveller, but M. Clédat addresses himself to ascertaining the true situation and the Egyptian title for every place-name in the Bible narrative. His work is additional to the previous attempts of this kind by Lieblein, Naville and Daressy, and previous to Dr. Alan Gardiner's treatise upon the City of Rameses, published this year in the *Journal of Egyptian Archaeology*. M. Clédat does not mention the topographical papyrus in the Cairo Museum summarised by Dr. Spiegelberg, but it is doubtless well known to him, nor the geographical details in the Arezzo manuscript of a Palestine pilgrimage, but he gives every important old Egyptian record its place.

The final paper is by Prof. Edouard Naville upon the " First Words of Chapter XVII of the Book of the Dead." After a long and convincing argument he decides for rendering them " I am Atum, I was alone (or the unique one) when I rose up from Nu. I am the past (yesterday) and I know what shall be the future (to-morrow)." The resemblance of the phrase to the " I am yesterday, to-day and to-morrow," and the priestess of Dodona's dictum, " Zeus was, Zeus is, and Zeus is to be," will naturally occur to many.

M. Naville takes the opportunity to enlarge upon the manner as well as matter of Egyptian monumental and manuscript writing. He concludes that wall inscriptions were executed vertically because engraved or painted from a ladder, and shows by the arrangements when copied upon papyrus, that the roll was placed upon the knees of the scribe, as is the case in Egypt to-day. He also gives valuable information as to the method and the results of the adoption of Demotic scripts. What he says about the appliance used for scribes or sculptors writing upon chamber or temple and palace walls is interesting, because if the Hittites used scaffolds going the whole length of the space to be covered, instead of ladders, it might account for their boustrophedon plan of writing. The scribe having got to the end of the wall, instead of walking back and recommencing at the other end, simply continued his text, working backward beneath (or above) the previous line.

The final essay is by the veteran M. Loret, " À propos d'un prétendu verbe irrégulier."

JOSEPH OFFORD.

NOTE.

WE regret to say that owing to the length of negotiations about the division of our discoveries at the Cairo Museum, it has been impossible to have an exhibition this year. The boxes have not yet arrived by the end of July, but we hope to include the objects from this year in next year's exhibition.

W. M. F P.

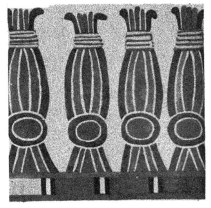

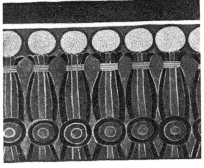

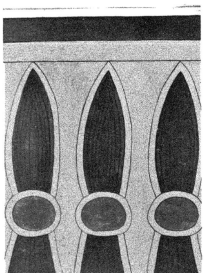

1. · XII, XVIII DYNASTIES, p. 111.
3. LATE XVIII, XIX DYNASTIES, p. 115.
5. XX DYNASTY, p. 118.

2. MID XVIII DYNASTY, p. 112.
4. TOMB 78. LATE XVIII, p. 117.
6. TOMB 71. MID XVIII, p. 120.

ANCIENT EGYPT.

THE GENESIS OF COPTIC TWISTS AND PLAITS.

A STUDY of the development of plaited ornament as a decorative motive is one full of interest, and one which, in the past, has occupied the attention of far too few. Work along these by-paths of research is often useful, and may always be considered as legitimately supplementing the pioneer work of the archæologist.

The wonderful spread—one might almost term it epidemic—of the use of plait motives throughout Europe in the early centuries has, of course, been noticed and commented upon. But Prof. Lethaby is, I think, the only one who has suggested[1] that it is to Egypt we must look for the rise and spread of this truly wonderful development.

This considered opinion of a man who has made a life-long study of the evolution of design needs no support from me. But, on the other hand, it certainly lends a greatly added interest to our study of Egypto-Roman art, insomuch as we now know that we are at work upon things more rare than usual, the early links of a chain of rich fancy, which has given us the beautiful interlacing of Celtic and Scandinavian art, the knots and borders of Longobardic sculpture, of the Roman pavements and Byzantine panels, no less than the clever grotesques of the MSS. of the Slavic races.

It is really a matter of regret that the Professor left his enquiry where he did, for clearly there must be an origin for the elements which are so frequent in the art of Coptic times.

The present paper, then, is an attempt to glean a sheaf of scattered vestiges from more ancient times, which, even though imperfectly, will nevertheless give indication of the probable sources from whence the Copts drew their early ideas of plaited ornament.

That the *invention* of the plait is not to be ascribed to the Copts themselves must be premised. Nevertheless we are here but a step removed from the centre whence the plait went forth to the enrichment of European art, and an enquiry into the origins of some of the forms as they are found frequently on Coptic cloths, will at the same time deal with the broader question of the cultural influences at work in Roman times in Egypt.

The simplest motive, and the one from which it would seem obvious that the plait must have originally developed, is the simple twist (Fig. 1). It is surprising, indeed, that so obvious and simple a decorative contrivance should

---

[1] Lethaby, W. R., " The origin of Knotted Ornamentation," *The Burlington Magazine*, X, 1907.

be so persistently absent from archaic art. Not, of course, that it is entirely absent ; but, considering the great frequency of, for example, the meander and fret in Greek, and even dynastic Egyptian art, it is notable that examples of the twist are curiously few and far between.

Nevertheless, there are well attested examples of the occurrence in pre-Coptic times of twists not only of single strands, as in Fig. 1, but also of double and triple strands that parallel the two twists of Coptic age shown in Figs. 2 and 3.

It is significant that, although not very frequently, it is found in Greek as well as Egyptian design, as witness Fig. 4, a twist of single strands from an early Attic vase in the Metropolitan Museum, New York (first half of the VIIth century, B.C.)[1] and Fig. 5, from a Corinthian vase in the Louvre (VIth century, B.C.) a twist of double strands. The single twist in Egypt may be exampled by Fig. 6, found rarely on scarabs of the Middle Kingdom, and Fig. 7 from a Kalum pot (XIIth–XIIIth dynasty). Fig. 8, a scarab of the Hyksos period may be looked upon as a link with the XIIth dynasty scarab, Fig. 9.

But it is to the Cylinder seals of ancient Babylonia that we must look for the earliest examples of the twist. In Syro-Cappadocian and Sumerian times it is of frequent occurrence. Yet here we are confronted, it would seem, with something more significant than a mere decoration. What exactly is the significance one cannot tell at present, but usually when it occurs on the cylinders it is not as a border. It is a complete figure, a twist of several nodes, the number varying from three to eight. Fig. 10, a twist of five nodes, is from a Sumerian cylinder[2] and is therefore at least as old as the VIth Egyptian dynasty ; fig. 12 is from the cylinder of the pre-Hyksos king Khandy, and 13 from a scarab of Apepy. Having found no twist of earlier age than these we are compelled to pause. As for its ultimate origin and symbolism it would seem probable that it may be closely associated with serpent worship (*see* Fig. 11) from a Sumerian vase.[3] Of the serpent I shall have something more to say. At present we may compare Figs. 10, 11 and 12 with Figs. 14 and 15 from Coptic cloths. I think the deduction is inevitable. As for the channel of influence, the occurrence of the complete twist in Greek art would suggest it. Fig. 16, from a plate in the Cabinet des Medailles, Bib. Nat., Paris,[4] is of VIIth century, B.C., and Fig. 17 from an amphora in the British Museum, dating from the VIth century, B.C.

Passing from the twist to the *plait* one must recognise that therein we have evidence of a distinct advance, not only in conception, but also in designing skill. This cultural step being obvious, it is all the more surprising to find that, if not actually on Sumerian, yet on Syro-Cappadocian cylinders, the genuine plait is already evolved (Figs. 18 and 19)[5]. Strangely enough, except for one example, the true plait seems to be quite missing from Egyptian decoration of pre-Roman days. As in the case of the twist, the vehicle of its introduction into Egypto-Roman art was doubtless the art of ancient Greece ; for it is not infrequent on Grecian mouldings, the *guilloches* (Figs. 20–22), and occasionally on pottery. Fig. 21 is from a fragment of a vase from Naucratis (VIIth century, B.C.)[6] and

[1] *Jour. Hell. Stud.*, XXXII, 1912, p. 370.
[2] Delaporte, L., *Cat. des Cylindres Orient,* 1910, Pl. XIII, Fig. 154.
[3] King, L. W., *Sumer and Akkad,* Fig. 29, p. 76.
[4] *Bull. Corr. Hell.,* 1895, p. 74, Fig. 2.
[5] Delaporte, L., *Cat. des Cylind. Orien.,* 1910, Pl. XXIX, Figs. 418 and 425.
[6] *Bull. de la Corresp. Hell.,* 1895, p. 81, Fig. 5.

Fig. 24 from a Proto-Corinthian vase of about the same century.[1] I give here a four-strand plait from a cylinder from Aîden which is perhaps a trifle older and probably Phœnician origin, Fig. 25 (*circa* 700 B.C.), and for comparison illustrate specimens of three- and four-strand plaits taken from Egypto-Roman and Coptic cloths in the Victoria and Albert Museum (Figs. 26–28).

Vladimir Bok in his monograph on Coptic Textiles[2] states that " The plait is met with on ancient Egyptian monuments beginning with the XIIth dynasty."

This statement would be more misleading than it is were it published in any less difficult language than Russian. As it is I am inclined to think that he must have had in mind the twist rather than the plait. And yet there is one un-doubtedly genuine example of ancient Egyptian plaitwork that can be seen any day at the British Museum. I refer to the plait design as it appears on the

[1] *Jour. Hell. Stud.*, XXXII, 1912, p. 341, Fig. 18.
[2] Бокъ, В. Г., *Коптскія узорчатыя ткани.* Москва, 1897.

fragment of the beard of the Sphinx. Fig. 29 gives the scheme of plaiting which is clearly visible on the specimen.

We will next consider an interesting group of figures which occur frequently on textiles of Egypto-Roman and Coptic date, and which, although they vary in many ways, are yet apparently all related. A typical example of the IIIrd–IVth century on a fabric from Akhmin is shown in Fig. 30. A portion of a similar design of IVth–Vth century is given in Fig. 31, while Fig. 32, although quite dissimilar, is most probably a derivative from the same parent source, its less pronounced cruciform shape being probably due to its earlier date (IInd–IIIrd century). The relation between these forms and the quite simple form, Figs. 33 and 34, will, I think, be apparent. But I imagine that in this simple form we have it in its pagan aspect. For it has persisted and is found in Celtic and Scandinavian ornament, where it was considered by Worsaae[1] to represent the earth with its four corners. Surrounding this Danish example is a serpent with its tail in its mouth, the great sea-serpent lying in the all-surrounding ocean. To revert to the Coptic examples, Figs. 30 and 31 have this form interplaited with the cross, no doubt used as a Christian symbol.

For the origin of this motive we must, I believe, again look to Sumer, although there are practically no directly connecting links, that I know of, if we except scarab designs of the type shown in Figs. 35 and 36 (after XIIth dynasty), and I think these are inconclusive. An interesting comparison may, however, be made with the Buddhist symbol shown in Figs. 37 and 38. This is one of the Eight Glorious Emblems or auspicious symbols frequently figured in Buddhist art and iconography.[2] It also occurs as the lucky diagram *Srîvatsa*, the symbol of the tenth Jina (Sitala) of the Jains, and in China as the Buddhist knot (Chang), or the sacred entrails (Fig. 39).

This Chinese sign was doubtless introduced by the Buddhist missionaries who reached China in the Ist century A.D. How the symbol arrived in Buddhist India one can only surmise ; but one cannot help remembering that Buddhism was still in its infancy when, in 329 B.C., Alexander made his momentous inroad, an event which impressed Indian art and decoration most strongly. Also we know that commerce was carried on between India and Babylonia from quite early times, and we find that in the IIIrd century B.C. the famous Buddhist Emperor Asoka claimed that missions sent by him to Greek kingdoms had resulted in conversions to Buddhism. These facts prove an amount of intercourse quite sufficient to account for the passage of this symbol. And although apparently not to be found in Greek ornament, yet if we look from these examples to that shown in Fig. 40, we cannot but notice their striking resemblance. Moreover, I think I may suggest (with probability on my side), that in this Sumerian figure we have the prototype of even the Coptic examples.

The figure is taken from one of the three most ancient specimens of Sumerian glyptic art yet known, one of the seals of the patési Lugalanda (about VIth–VIIth dynasties Egyptian). The somewhat laboured attempt at an interpretation of this sign by M. Allotte de la Fuije[3] may, I think, be put aside. It is far more likely to be the expression of a religious idea than a cryptic rendering of the artist's name. It may even contain the idea of Worsaae of the four corners of the

[1] " Danish Arts."

[2] Waddell, *Buddhism in Thibet*, p. 392.

[3] *Rev. d'Assyr.*, VI, No. 4. p. 117.

earth, but I believe that all these knot figures embody the idea of eternity, or perhaps, at least, longevity.

There is one more motive found on Coptic textiles of which I must speak. I have left it until the last because it is perhaps the most interesting of all. Figs. 41 and 42 show it as it appears on Egypto-Roman and Coptic textiles, and it will be recognised immediately as a familiar motive not only on these fabrics but also on Roman mosaics from the IInd century A.D. onwards. It is also of frequent occurrence later among Celtic and Scandinavian plaitwork as noticed by Dr. H. Colley March.[1] It is one of the seven World Ravishing Gems of Buddhism, and, in fact, is found so far afield as among the Mound builders of the American continent. It is sometimes called, in English, the duplex, in French *l'entrelac,* and Sarre enigmatically terms it the " Lieblingsmotive."

This motive, more elusive in archaic art than any, has yet I believe a history that may well be said to be more ancient than any other known symbol. For it is, I am convinced, derived directly from that ancient of days, the Swastika. That this is so can best be demonstrated by examples. Figs. 43 to 46 show the stages of development in as simple a form as can be. It could, of course, be proven at greater length, but the present is hardly the occasion. The Swastika is, of course, a universal symbol of fire and motion, *i.e.,* the sun ; and its derivative must be allowed to have, in some measure at least, a similar significance in pagan symbolism.

I have mentioned its occurrence on Roman mosaics, and this is most significant for our enquiry. For we are thus swept right past Coptic and Egypto-Roman art without touching it, so to speak, and we find it on a Ist century mosaic at Pompeii (Fig. 47)[2] in the Isis temple, which was rebuilt after the earthquake of A.D. 63.

There would seem to be an entire absence of this motive from both Greek and ancient Egyptian ornament, but I give an illustration of a gold ring from Selinous[3] (*circa* 1500–1000 B.C.), which is sufficiently like to afford comparison (Fig. 48). And from Egypt I give an impression of a Kahun sealing (XIIth dynasty).[4] The latter (Fig. 47) is certainly half way between the Swastika form and our figure.

But for the identical motive we must come to more recent times than this last. Again we go to ancient Babylon for our illustration, and we find here not indeed the simple duplex, but an artistic conception obviously based upon the same theme (Fig. 50). Incidentally it may be observed that this is, so far as my investigations have gone, the earliest example of knot work yet known. It might well be thought to be from some Celtic or Scandinavian cross so excellent is it. But it is taken from a Syro-Cappadocian seal (dated *circa* 1926–2225 B.C.), in the Bibliotheque Nationale.[5] The fact that this is a design more complex than the simple duplex argues that the latter must, at some period, have preceded it. But to find it in an earlier age we must look to pre-mykenian Crete.

Sir Arthur Evans[6] tells us that " of the origins of our complex European culture this much at least can be confidently stated. The earliest extraneous sources on which it drew lay respectively in two directions—in the valley of the

[1] *Trans. Dorset Field Club,* XXV.   [2] From Riegl, A., *Stilfragen,* 1893, p. 310.
[3] Fougères, G., *Sélinonte,* 1910, p. 42.
[4] Petrie, W. M. F., *Illahun,* 1889–90, Pl. X, No. 190.
[5] Babelon, E., *Guilde illus. du Cab. des Med.,* 1900, p. 32, and Delaporte, Pl. XXXVIII, Fig. 649.
[6] " New Archæolog. Lights on Orig. of Civilis. in Europe," *Smithsonian Report,* 1916.

Nile on one side, and in that of the Euphrates on the other." This being so we need not be surprised to find that here on the " doorstep of European civilisation " the duplex may be traced a step further back into the past. Fig. 51 represents the design of a steatite seal from Hagios Onuphrios,[1] and considered to date from the Early Minoan III period (IXth–Xth dynasties Egyptian). It will be seen that this design consists of the simple duplex with the addition of an interlaced square. If we now glance at the next figure we shall observe that the figures are identical, and yet this latter is from the IVth century Romano-British pavement at Wellow near Bath (Fig. 52). That the Cretan example is the prototype of the Roman there cannot be any doubt. A seal of ivory found at Hagia Triada, and dating from the second part of the Ist Minoan period, is illustrated by Mosso,[2] which appears also to be inscribed with this form.

Before concluding one more illustration must be referred to. It is shown in Fig. 53, and is taken from an asphalt relief discovered by de Morgan at Susa.[3] Dr. Capitan considers this to be an expression of the same idea, and it must be admitted that it is more than probable, for undoubtedly it is composed of two interplaited ovals. The fact of its being a representation of two serpents is, too, in my opinion, a point in favour of this. It is ascribed to the epoch of Naram Sin, equal to the IXth dynasty.

Looking back over the field of enquiry that has been covered it seems obvious that certain general conclusions may be deduced.

The Copts, and the Egypto-Romans before them, derived these decorative motives in their art, if not actually from Roman sources, at any rate from a common source with Rome. In this connection the significance of the evidence provided by the mosaics cannot be overestimated. For we know that the Romans obtained their art of mosaic from the Greeks about 80 years B.C. Moreover, we know that the source of inspiration was. *Alexandria*, which town passed under Roman rule at that time.

The decorative features we have been considering are in Egypt found with greatest frequency on the textile fabrics. But in Roman art they are most closely identified with the mosaic pavements. So much so that there is practically no doubt that the Romans derived them, with the art itself, from Alexandria.

We must therefore conclude that Egypt obtained her art inspirations from thence, also owing nothing to purely Roman but much to Romano-Alexandrian influence. What is more natural than that the city of Euclid should be the centre from whence these advanced designs should proceed, designs .which, based upon the symbols of archaic cults, were revivified and developed in the hands of skilled artists. Alexandria's position made it a focus of influences from East and West. Not only Greeks, Romans and Egyptians, but representatives of eastern lands congregated within its precincts. There is no doubt that many ancient cults were tolerated, and may have brought into its decorative art the symbolism of archaic faiths. Of these quite the most popular was the cult of the Serpent, the Agathodaemon and Uraeus, sacred to Serapis and Isis. Shrines existed there whereat the cult was practised, and the two serpents are frequent features on coins of the period.

---

[1] Evans, A. J., *Cretan Pictographs*, 1895, p. 107, Fig. 84.
[2] Mosso, A., *Palaces of Crete*, 1907, p. 249, Fig. 117A.
[3] de Morgan, *Recherches. Del. Perse*, XII, Fig. 394, and XIII, Pl. XXXVII.

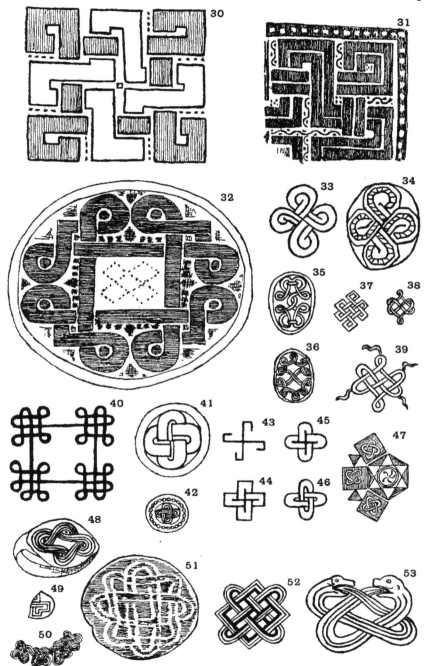

But we know that serpent worship was a prominent cult in the religious system of the Sumerians (refer back to Fig. 11), and with the ancient Persians we have seen that the two were linked into the prototype of the duplex. Space will not allow of exhaustive proof, but I am convinced that the motives we have been considering all originally embodied some phase of the cult of the serpent. The twist, the plait and the interplaited cross of ovals were all part of the ritual of the archaic counterpart of Isis and Osiris.

On Egypto-Roman and Coptic things they have, of course, lost their pagan significance, and are probably used merely as decorative motives—with one exception, the duplex. This, by virtue of its being cruciform and dual, was probably, as Dr. Colley March says, adopted as an emblem of the two-fold nature of Christ.

Whether this was so at so early a date is not certain. But it is certain that both in pagan and Christian art these non-terminate plait motives had the power of auspicious symbols, conveying the idea of good-luck. Particularly was this the case with the duplex; but we find, in these days, its popularity has waned—its parent, the Swastika, has outlived it.

Cyril G. E. Bunt.

[These conclusions on the Sumerian being the earliest forms of the twists and plaits accords with other facts of their distribution. The formula which seems to agree with all the cases is that the twist and plait is a Central Asian motive (*see* the wickerwork screens in Kirghiz tents); that from there it passed down the Euphrates, also into Syria, and first into Egypt under Hyksos influence. Plaits and twists were unknown in Italy until the Dacian captives were brought in and set to mosaic work; plaits were brought from the north into the basket-work capitals of Justinian, and the round plait in architecture only occurs in true Gothic work in Italy, the Lombard plait being angular, rushwork and not osiers. In Ireland the spiral is alone in the pagan age, and the plait only comes in after Norse influences of the Christian period.—W. M. F. P.]

THE SPHINXES OF TANIS.

IN the *Annales du Service*, 1917, M. Daressy opens the question of the peculiar type of art found in the sphinxes of Tanis, the fish-offerers and the Fayum statue. For figures of these see ANCIENT EGYPT, 1916, pp. 188–192, and plates. He points out that Zōn or Zoan is distinct from Hauar or Avaris in the Memphitic list, and that there is no reason to identify them ; and that the absence of any mention of Zon on the monuments of Tanis, and of any works of the great XVIIIth dynasty there, seems to show how unimportant the place was in early times. Suddenly in the XIXth dynasty it was started as a northern capital by Ramessu II, and filled with sculptures brought from other places. Of the early statues five have dedications belonging to *Onkhtaui* at Memphis, the later works of Ramessu II were made for the Heliopolitan gods, and a statue is dedicated to Upuat of Siut and Hathor of Dronkah near by. From El Kab has come a sphinx in white silicified limestone exactly like the Tanite sphinxes in work and dimensions. All these facts result in detaching this peculiar style of work from Tanis, and suggest that it is more probably southern.

HEAD OF TANIS SPHINX.   HEAD OF GALLA WOMAN.

The ground is thus cleared of an hypothesis that has confused the subject for fifty years past.   The southern source of such work at El Kab paves the way for our recognising in the " head of a Galla woman " (published in Maspero's " Struggle of the Nations," p. 233) the same type as in the sphinxes from Tanis. We require now an enquiry as to the sources and limits of this type in the south. Mr. Wainwright was struck by the similarity to the Tayesha, who were the body-guard of Osman Dagna, a Semitic African tribe.

If now we are to regard these sculptures as representing a Sudani people, it is clear that they belong to an invasion between the VIth and XIth dynasty, as there is no other period likely before the Hybros age when these figures were appropriated. The break-up of the Old Kingdom was due to Mesopotamians pressing in from the north—using button-badges, and to the Sudanis from the south, who took up Egyptian art for their own purposes. Similarly the break-up of the second prehistoric civilisation was both Elamite and Nubian ; the end of the Bubastite age was invasion from Ethiopia and Libya. To the weak, misfortunes seldom come single.

W. M. F. PETRIE.

ALEXANDRIAN WORLD MAPS.

As Alexandria was the centre of geographical learning where the world maps of Eratosthenes (*circa* 200 B.C.) and Ptolemy (*circa* 150 A.D.) were published, it may not be out of place to insert a short note on the possible survival of the former. The question of the authenticity of the actual maps accompanying the text of Ptolemy has recently been much discussed, but no one so far as I know has suggested the possibility that a copy of the earlier Hellenistic world scheme may still exist. There is in the Harleian collection in the British Museum a very remarkable map of the world drawn in the 9th or 10th centuries. It seems to be the work of an Anglo-Saxon scholar—that is, it must be his copy of an earlier map. The way the cities are represented within their walls has resemblances to the Madeba mosaic plan of Palestine, and the prominence of such places as Alexandria and Constantinople all show that there was a Byzantine or. Hellenistic original. Another point of interest is the fact that some of the places in North Africa, to which Prof. Petrie called attention as being mentioned in the old tradition of the peopling of Britain, are named on this map.

The map of the world given in Prof. Breasted's *Ancient Times* (1916) as the world according to Eratosthenes, seems to me to have more than an accidental resemblance to our Saxon map. In it we have an oblong world surrounded by ocean ; India is at one end, and the Mediterranean Sea enters at the other. It is still more remarkable in comparison with the Harleian map that the Caspian Sea is shown as connected with the ocean by an inlet from the north. Syria and Mesopotamia are near the centre of this world, which lies on the ocean as a rug rests on the floor. Furthermore, on the Saxon map there are a number of loosely-drawn lines, which are frequently roughly parallel, and at right angles to one another. The names of countries and cities seem to have been set down in relation to these lines, which indicate boundaries or position. Now Dr. Breasted writes of Eratosthenes : " His map of the known world, including Europe, Asia and Africa, not only showed the regions grouped about the Mediterranean with fair correctness, but he was the first geographer who was able to lay out on his map a cross-net of lines indicating latitude and longitude." It seems evident that the map in the Harleian collection must have had for its source a map with such lines upon it. It may be that the Saxon map follows some original constructed more or less in harmony with the theories .of Cosmas, the 6th century traveller, who published at Alexandria his Christian scheme of geography about 550 A.D. It is probable, however, that Cosmas reverted to the flat-land of Eratosthenes rather than inventing it afresh, and in any case the Saxon map is too detailed and, indeed, too correct to depend on anything but a classical source. There is a photographic reproduction of the Harleian map in Trail's *Social England* and a small text block in the *Encyclopaedia Britannica* (" Maps ").

W. R. LETHABY.

THE SUBTERRANEAN PASSAGES OF ALEPPO CITADEL.

ANCIENT Aleppo (the Egyptian Khalebu, the Greek Berœa) is supposed to have stood entirely on the partly natural, partly artificial mound now known as the Citadel, which measures 275 × 160 m. at the summit, and about 40 m. above the level of the town.   This seems probable since no pre-Arab remains are to be seen in the town, although Aleppo is known from Egyptian and Babylonian records to have been of extreme antiquity.

Under the Arab rule of Malik ez-Zahir, the mound was fortified, or more probably re-fortified ; a deep moat was dug round it and a strong defensive wall was built round the summit.   The wall of Ez-Zahir still stands, but the interior of the Citadel is in ruins, the only modern building of any size being a Turkish barrack.   The remainder is a mass of debris of Arab and Roman age which could easily be excavated now and would well repay a thorough examination.

ALEPPO CITADEL FROM THE S.S.W.

The Arab Commanding Officer told me that he had found the entrance to subterranean passages near the barracks, and invited me to explore it as he was not keen on doing it alone.   I accordingly called on him with Lieut. Lee-Brossé of the 1st Spahis.   He first led us to a chamber (A) close to his quarters, at the east end of which was a large rectangular well, the top being solid masonry and about 4.50 m. north and south, by 3.75 m. east and west.

The Arab Officer then showed us the entrance to a gallery built against the outside of the east wall of the chamber.   This gallery was almost stopped up with rubbish, and sloped downwards at an angle of about 20°.   It soon turned to the left at right angles, and began to follow round the outside of the well in a counter-clockwise direction with windows opening into the well at intervals in each circuit.   At first this gallery was in a very bad condition, but became better and freer of rubbish as we went down.   After two circuits we came to a small vertical shaft which we climbed down, after which the passage, now much larger, and with a well-cut staircase the whole of its breadth (about 3½ m.) continued to wind downwards.   At 16 m. depth the gallery was no longer built

in the rubbish, but cut in the soft limestone.   This gives an approximate idea
of the depth of artificial deposit on the Citadel.   Although the passage was now
in the rock, its tendency to crumble has necessitated arches and patches to hold
up and hold back the dangerous portions.   As we went still lower, the patches
were made in pottery bricks, 0.23 m. long by 0.03 m. deep, which seem to be
Roman.   The level of the commencement of the pottery revetting was 26 m.
below the ground level of the Citadel.   About this level a gallery, now obstructed,
appears to run southwards.   At 30 m. we again came to a gallery having a
masonry arch at the entrance, and then apparently running north in the rock.   It
is now totally stopped up with stones and rubbish.   At 37.80 m., a very small
passage opened out on the right of the main passage ; the roof had fallen in many
places and was very rotten.   I crawled in for about 25 m. almost due north and
found the end.   It apparently was a trial gallery left uncompleted.   A few metres
farther on the main gallery ends in a pile of rubbish, though it may continue
a little further.   Here we went down a small vertical shaft, which could be
covered by stone slabs which lay beside it.   At a depth of 3.50 m. we reached a
small horizontal passage (H) which went back under the main gallery for about
1.50 m.   Here a larger gallery ran left and right.   We first turned to the right,
and after about 3 m. we came to the well, being now almost at the bottom of it
(*i.e.*, within 7 ft.).   I was lowered down into it and could see straight up the shaft ;
this was 41.34 m. below the surface of the Citadel.   The curious part of the shaft
was that the four sides were corrugated, and gave the effect of looking up the
concertina extension of a kodak.   The bottom of the well was partly filled with
stones and filth dropped down from above, and beneath the shaft the depth of
the water varied from a couple of inches to a foot.   On the east, south and west
sides of the bottom of the well, large galleries about 2 m. high and 1·50 broad,
ran away for a unknown distance.   The entrances of these had masonry arches,
made without keystones, and the galleries themselves were well " rendered "
with cement.   I could not follow these more than about 10 m. as the water
became deeper owing to there being less rubbish the farther one goes from the
well-shaft.   The stench was bad, but with thigh boots one should be able to follow
these passages to their ends wherever they may be.   These are shown at (M, N, O),
in accompanying plan.   It seems as if these were gigantic water conduits for
the supply of the town.   With sufficient time I believe that the exits of these
conduits could be discovered even without following them internally, as they
must communicate with the river somewhere.   We only had three days at our
disposal so it was out of the question for us to search further, as we had other
work to do.   We then returned to the branch passage at (B) which, as has been
remarked, was about 2 m. above the water level of the well, and followed the
passage (BD).   The section of this gallery is shown at (Q), and the whole of it
is very finely " rendered," its primary object being obviously a water-channel.
After proceeding north for 58.50 m., it turns west for 31.40 m., and then south-
west and west-south-west as shown at (DE, EF and FG).   At (G) the passage
turns sharply to the right.   Here after 6.60 m. it is paved with large blocks.
Below these blocks there is a small channel, 0.35 by 0.35 m. protected by a strong
iron grating running forward.   The whole gallery is obstructed about 1.30 m.
further on, and no more progress was possible without excavation.   At this place
we found a limestone block 0.75 by 0.60 by 0.28 m., having a cufic inscription
on it in relief, the block being upside down and not belonging to the masonry.
Lieut. Brossé copied this as far as he could, and I can furnish a copy to anybody

who specializes in this class of inscriptions. At the point (J) there is a small
hole opening out of the gallery. I squeezed through this, and found myself at
the bottom of a circular shaft running vertically upwards (about 1 m. diameter,
and 5.10 m. high). I climbed up this and found the top covered by large slabs
of stone which I could not shift. I noticed the soil here was softer and more
crumbling and earthy, which showed that the top of the shaft was no great
distance below ground level. We then returned to the point (G) where a small
opening led into another shaft running vertically upwards. This shaft, 1.20 diameter, was 7 m. high. At the top of the shaft on the north there was a sort of
doorway of limestone about 0.80 m. wide, the jambs being smoothly dressed. We
could not see the height owing to its being partially filled up with stones and
rubbish. The right jamb of the door has a mason's mark, much resembling the

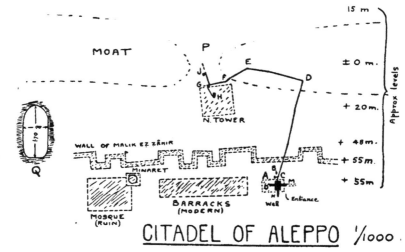

CITADEL OF ALEPPO 1/1000

Egyptian *'onkh*, 0.23 m. long. The chamber was almost entirely filled up, but
could easily be cleared. On the other side of the shaft running up at an angle of
about 50° and 150° east of north, was a large gallery roughly cut in the earthy
limestone and 10 m. long. At the top of this, turning to the left, we could just
squeeze into a small masonry antechamber (H). This was separated from an
apparently larger chamber by a heavy basalt door, leaning at about 60° outwards
from its frame which consisted of four blocks of basalt. The dimensions of the
door were 1.38 m. high ; 0.75 m. wide and 0.17 thick. On the west and on the
inner side there is a cruciform recess for a bolt. Above this lock recess is a hole
for the door pivot l The roof of the antechamber consists of a circular column
of basalt. The inner chamber was very much obstructed by rubbish, but by
crawling in I could see that the roof by the door consisted of basalt 0.42 m.
diameter, and a square sectioned block of the same material. The inner chamber
seems to lead into another smaller chamber roofed with slabs. This place was
too unsafe to examine thoroughly, without a certain amount of clearing and
shoring, which we had not time to do.

In the accompanying chart the dotted parts show the buildings, etc. above
ground ; they have been enlarged from a military map, and I do not vouch for

their accuracy. The underground passages were surveyed by us with a prismatic compass and are fairly accurate. It will be seen that the chamber at (H) comes nearly under the foundations of a small square Arab tower, now in ruins, on the slope of the Citadel. Point (H), however, must be at a much lower level, and be connected to the foundations of a more ancient building. (The Arab entrance to the north Tower was on its south side leading straight up into the Citadel. This was blocked up, and we could not find its other end in the Citadel.) At the point (J) the level of the moat is distinctly higher than elsewhere, and I do not think that the gallery at (J) is very deep below moat level. It is very probable that the passage runs out under the town.

I think the function of the gallery (B D E F G J) was to fill the moat. This would be done automatically when the water rose to sufficient height in the well. The subsidiary passages and shafts (J and H) were probably cut to connect buildings then standing with the Citadel, making the conduits serve a double purpose. That danger of invasion from these passages was apprehended is obvious, since in the spiral well passage small shafts, mentioned earlier, were constructed, so that the passage up into the Citadel could be easily blocked. As to the date, although the Arabs may have added and adapted certain parts of it, I cannot think that this was their original work. It certainly would repay a detailed examination, as all the rubbish could be basketed along into the well chamber and removed from there.

I can get no information as to whether this has been examined before; the local inhabitants are entirely ignorant of it, except that one old Arab told that the Citadel was connected underground with the Bāb Antakiyeh. It is possible that the Turks or Germans during the war may have examined these passages. I should be very glad to hear if anything is known further of this matter.

R. Engelbach,
Capt. R.E. (T.R.).

KHEKER FRIEZES.

[Number references are to the " Topographical Catalogue of Private Tombs of Thebes," by Gardiner and Weigall. A.E., *Ancient Egypt.* C.F.Y., Carnarvon, *Five Years' Explorations at Thebes.* D.P., Davies, *Ptah-hetep.* K. King's Tomb. L.D., Lepsius, *Denkmäler.* P.D.A., Petrie, *Decorative Art.* Q., Queen's Tomb.]

THE extreme upper portions of the walls of painted and sculptured tombs in the XIIth and XVIIIth dynasty, and also more rarely in later times, were usually finished off with a peculiar form of decoration, commonly known as the Kheker ornament.

The word Kheker occurs fairly often both in Old Kingdom and in later hieroglyphs in connection with the toilet, and also in the plural form as *Khekeru*, meaning *ornament*, which word has the figure of a Kheker as its determinative. It is this word for *ornament* that has given its name to this distinctive variety of Egyptian ornamentation.

The form of the Kheker most often thus employed in the Theban Necropolis is that shown in Fig. 1, where it seems to represent a series of reed or plant stems tied together at the tops and gathered in again close above the base, below which they spread out once more. Another suggestion for the meaning of this decoration is that it represents the fringe or tassel of a carpet or mat, the roundel above the base being a knot. The plant theory is probably the more satisfactory explanation of the form and was first suggested by Prof. Petrie, who wrote : " Suppose a screen of papyrus stems, the roofing stems tied on to the uprights and the loose wiry leaves at the head tied together to keep them from straggling over and looking untidy. Here we have all the details of the Kheker ornament simply resulting from structural necessity. The leaves are gathered together at the lower tying ; and there the end view of the concentric coats of the papyrus stems of the roof are seen as concentric circles, above which the leaves bulge out and are tied together at the top." (P.D.A., 101–2.)

This view of the origin of the Kheker ornament finds support in the fact that the Kheker frieze is practically always found at the top of a wall in a tomb. It occurs, moreover, in painted scenes as a free standing ornament to the tops of doorways and shrines when such are depicted on tomb walls (111 and Q. 36, 44, 52, 55). In three instances (Puimre, Amunezek, Menkheperasenb, and perhaps more), however, a row of Khekers serves as a kind of low square fence or enclosure in the scenes of funeral ceremonies in the inner chambers of Tombs 39, 84 and 112. It is also to be seen running down one side of the interior of a shrine in Tomb Q. 52, Thyti. In the tombs of the Old Kingdom no example is known of the use of a Kheker frieze to ornament the upper portion of the walls of a tomb, although it is employed to decorate the tops of shrines and doorways, etc., when such are depicted on the tomb walls. The Kheker is always of the pointed variety, very similar to that shown in Fig. 4, in shape but not in colour, but usually with two roundels at the bottom, placed one below the other, of which the lower one takes the place of the base of an ordinary Kheker (L.D. ii, 101). In the tomb of Ptah-hetep, however, a Kheker with the base as shown in Fig. 5 is used for the sign WSHT (D.P., I, xviii).

A peculiar headdress sometimes worn by dancers in scenes in the tombs of the Middle Kingdom is also suggestive of the Kheker ornament, especially its upper portion (C.F.Y. viii ; A.E. 1914, 126).

In the Middle Kingdom when the Khekers began to be employed as a frieze for tomb walls, the splay-topped form was that most commonly in use (Fig. 1). This variety is also the most common in tombs of the XVIIIth dynasty in the Theban Necropolis, though the pointed variety is still employed in minor positions. During Ramesside times, the pointed form reappears again as a frieze, but only in the Royal Tombs, the splay-topped form still remaining in use in the private tombs.

Splay-topped Khekers are always drawn at the top of a tomb wall in a row, with their bases touching, or almost touching, one another. The colouring until rather beyond the middle of the XVIIIth dynasty is constant, namely, blue outside, red inside and green between, the tie bands being similarly coloured with bands of blue and green above and below a middle band of red, five bands in all. The roundel at the base is also painted with an outer circular band of blue, an inner one of green and a red centre.

Towards the end of the XVIIIth dynasty and also in the Ramesside period, the roundels of the Kheker ornament were commonly painted of one colour only, red or yellow, though the remaining portion of the Kheker was coloured in the old way. We have, however, six exceptions in the Necropolis in Tombs 38, 76, 77, 91, 147 and K. 22. In the last of these tombs the Khekers forming the frieze at the northern end of the outer chamber are coloured blue, green and white. It is possible, however, that it was intended to eventually add red, and thus give the frieze the normal colouring. In the roundels of the Khekers in Tombs 76, 77, 91, 147 and K. 22 only two colours were intended and used, *i.e.*, red and blue,, the red being in the centre and predominating.

In some of the tombs of the end of the XVIIIth dynasty, and in most of those of Ramesside date, instead of being painted with the usual stripes of blue, green and red, the tie of the Kheker is painted entirely in yellow and the stripes or bands are indicated by lines of red or black (Fig. 2). The earliest date at which the yellow tie first appears in Khekers in the Theban Necropolis is the time of Thutmosis III (Tomb 112), but it appears more frequently in the time of Thutmosis IV, as may be seen in Tombs 58, 75, 76, 77, 89, 90, 91, 116, etc., though in some tombs of this date, and even later, the usual five coloured bands are still to be seen. In three tombs (76, 84, 112) Khekers with the usual blue, green and red ties are found on some of the walls, while on others the ties are coloured yellow. It is interesting to note that the lines drawn on the yellow ties to represent the former bands of colour are not always true as to number, showing that the old features were already being forgotten.

In most cases, as shown in uncompleted tombs, the Kheker pattern was set out with the aid of six horizontal lines, the top and bottom ones of which determined the height of the Kheker. The two lines below the top one marked out the proper width of the tie, and the remaining two fixed the position of the roundel at the base of the ornament. These lines were always set out with the aid of a cord soaked in red ruddle (21, 22, 43, 78, 82, 112, King Haremheb).

Owing to the irregularity of the ceiling, only five of these horizontal lines were drawn in some tombs, the usual top line being omitted, with the result that the height of the Kheker frieze varies considerably on the same wall. The usual

7, TOMB 88; 8, TOMB 255; 9, TOMB 51; 10, 11, TOMB 45.

reasons for this were either poor work or the excessive hardness of the rock which prevented a level ceiling being cut.

H

In Tomb 82 there are seven horizontal lines provided for the proportioning of the Kheker frieze, the extra one running through the middle of the roundel. There are also seven lines in Tomb 78, the seventh line marking the width of a disc over the Kheker.

It rarely happened that the artist kept strictly to these lines. The top of the Kheker frequently projects above the top line and the roundel is frequently below the space provided for it between the two guiding lines. It would appear, therefore, that these horizontal lines sometimes served as rough guides only and not as definite boundaries. Hence the great variation in the position of the roundel and tie that is often met with in the Khekers on the same wall.

The distance between the topmost and lowest horizontal lines is found to vary greatly. Taking a number of these distances and averaging them, it has been found that the three heights for the Kheker frieze that were most commonly in use were 180, 196, and 204 millimetres.

In careful work, three, and sometimes five vertical lines were also drawn on a tomb wall to ensure the proper width and proportion being given to each Kheker. In every case these lines were carefully drawn in red paint with a fine brush, which lead to their being easily obscured when the background was painted in. When three lines were used the middle one ran down the centre of the Kheker and the remaining two fixed its outer limits. In cases where five lines were employed, the additional two marked the inner edge of the blue stripe, which in most cases splays outwards at the extreme top of the Kheker. It is probable that these vertical lines were utilised in most of the tombs which show better workmanship, but, if so, they have in most cases been obscured by the background, which as a rule was painted in last, doubtless for this purpose. Tombs in which these lines can still be seen are Nos. 22, 87, 88, 112, 201 and 251.

Lines for the spacing of pointed Khekers (four in number) can be seen in Q. 38, and it may be noted here that as pointed Khekers have no ties, four lines are sufficient to set them out.

On one wall at least in the inner chamber of Tomb 42 (Amenmose), the Kheker frieze was drawn on similar squares to those used for the purpose of figure drawing. This was a very unusual proceeding in the Theban Necropolis, and there is apparently only the one example.

In rough work, the whole Kheker was merely outlined in red before the colours were applied, but in the more carefully finished tombs additional lines were added to mark the limits of the coloured bands (Tombs 42, 72, 77, 89, 201, etc.).

In most cases after the colours of the Khekers were painted in, a white line was placed over the edges of the stripes of colour to hide their junction and also to emphasise their colours. These white lines were very carefully put on in some tombs and in others very roughly, so that they vary much in thickness and regularity. The outside of the Kheker was rarely outlined in white, with the exception of the margin of the roundel.

In one tomb (42) the artist evidently ran short of red paint when drawing the outlines of his Khekers and employed blue instead for the purpose.

It seems that the Kheker ornament in a few of the better finished tombs was subject to definite proportions, as in the case of human figures. For instance, the top of the ornament from the tie upwards should be equal in height to that of the base as measured downwards from the bottom of the roundel; also the depth of the tie should be the same as that of the top and base. The diameter of the roundel was generally half as wide again as the height of the upper portion, base and tie of the Kheker when drawn perfectly round; in most tombs, however, it assumes a slightly elliptical form. The body of the Kheker appears not to have been subject to any definite proportions, hence the Kheker ornaments in various tombs on comparison show an apparent divergence in proportion, some appearing slightly attenuated and others the reverse in form.

The Kheker friezes in Tombs 45 and 260 present a peculiar feature which the writer has not been able to find in any other tomb, namely, three small black spots placed above the three middle bands of colours at the apex of the ornament and also a series of five similar spots down each vertical edge of the tie (*see* six on left of Fig. 1). It appears to have been a refinement in the decoration that was very rarely carried out, as, in the two tombs in which this addition appears, not all the Khekers were treated in this manner. As the two tombs in which these spotted Khekers appear are more than a mile apart and, curiously enough, similar tombs nearly always lie near together, it does not seem probable that they were the work of the same artist, neither do they agree in style.

A curious addition was made to the splay-topped Kheker at the close of the XVIIIth dynasty, namely, a round ball placed on the top of the ornament. (Fig. 3). The earliest date at which this is met with in this Necropolis is that of the tombs of Surere Ramōse and Ramōse,[1] and of one tomb in which the name is erased, the first two being of the time of Amenophis III, and the third and fourth of that of Amenophis IV. As this addition to the Kheker is not found in any tomb of earlier date than those mentioned above, it might well be possible that foreign influence had something to do with its appearance. There seems no doubt that this ball at the top of the Kheker represented the sun, or rather the disc of the sun, and on that account it was invariably painted red or yellow, and was always undecorated. This was probably due to the Aten influence shortly before; the new addition to the Kheker came into general use in Ramesside times, when the Kheker ornament, used in conjunction with other friezes, was a common feature in tombs, especially in those of the period of Rameses II.

It would appear that it became the custom in the period of Amenophis III–IV to colour the roundel of the Kheker either red or yellow and no longer to decorate it with the usual circular bands and centre of blue, green and red. The sculptured roundels of the Khekers in Tomb 48 (Surere) are unfortunately not painted, but, as they are not incised with the chisel in concentric rings, it would appear that they were intended to be painted one colour only. The roundels of the Khekers in Tomb 192 (Kharuef) were, however, both sculptured and ornamented with coloured concentric rings. This disc form of the roundel was also usual in Ramesside tombs, with the exceptions that in Tomb 216 the roundel is painted blue, and in Tombs 19, 35, 112, 134, 135, 220, 148 and 259 the old colouring is retained. A marked deterioration from the graceful shape of the early Kheker is noticeable in Ramesside times in the Theban Necropolis, not only in the smaller tombs, but even in the more important ones. For instance, probably owing to the non-use of the usual five or six horizontal lines which helped the

---

[1] There are two tombs with the name of Ramōse. One of these (No. 46) cannot be strictly dated, but has been assigned by Dr. Gardiner in consideration of style, etc., to the period of Amenophis III. In this tomb the ordinary Kheker with a yellow roundel and the Kheker with yellow roundel and yellow disc are both employed, the former in the outer chamber or corridor of the tomb and the latter in the inner chamber. (Nos. 48, 46, 55 and 188.)

artist to proportion his ornament, the Kheker tends to become more and more slender in appearance, especially at the top, where it is drawn in by the tie. Sometimes, also, the very order of the colours which was insisted on in the XVIIIth dynasty was altered by inserting an extra band of colour, as in Tombs 19, 31, 45, 106, 134, 135, 255, etc., or by the reversal of the greens and blues, the latter error being found in only one tomb (No. 30, Khensmōse).

There are two interesting examples in the Necropolis of Khekers outside the periods of the XVIIIth, XIXth and XXth dynasties. The first is found in Tomb 60 (Antefoker), which belongs to the XIIth dynasty. In every respect the Kheker ornament in this tomb corresponds with those of the later periods, with the one exception that the blue outer band, now almost faded away, is outside the tie and not within it. The second example is in Tomb 36 (Aba), which is of the XXVIth dynasty, where the Kheker conforms to the usual shape but the arrangement of the colours is different. Instead of the ornament being coloured blue, green and red, reading from the outside, the order of the colours is in this case, blue, red and blue, the roundel being correspondingly treated. In other parts of the same tomb the Khekers are painted entirely yellow.

It has already been mentioned that the Kheker ornament ran along the extreme top of a wall, but there are exceptions to be found in Tombs 35, 161 and 254. In the first tomb, the ornament is placed below a floral frieze and separated from it by a broad band of blue. The second tomb, on the western end, also has a floral frieze with a Kheker frieze beneath it, and the last tomb has a broad band of Chequer pattern above the Kheker frieze, consisting of seven rows of small coloured squares alternating with white squares, each row being of one colour only, blue, green and red. On the two side walls of the western end of this tomb there is also a band of yellow above the Kheker frieze.

A similar use of yellow may be seen above parts of the frieze in the inner chamber of Tomb 147 (no name), where owing to the irregularity of the roof, a wide gap occurs in places between the top of the frieze and the ceiling. Rather than leave this bare, the decorator of the tomb coloured it with yellow.

In the tomb of Queen Nefertari a border painted to resemble sand is placed above the Khekers on some of the walls.

In four tombs (40, 64, 76 and 253) there is a thin band of ornamentation just below the ceiling line, known as " Tail-edging." This form of decoration is very rarely placed above a Kheker ornament, though it is common as vertical bands for the corners of tombs.

When the Kheker frieze is painted on the walls supporting a barrel-shaped or arched roof, it is sometimes put wholly or partially above the spring of the vaulting, which makes it appear to be part of the ceiling decoration and not that of the wall. In such barrel-vaulted chambers, it should be noted that the frieze follows a straight line across the two end walls at the same height as on the side walls, no attempt being made to make it follow the curve of the ceiling, except in the shrine of 93. A semi-circular space is, therefore, left above the frieze on the end walls which is generally filled in either with two figures of the deceased for whom the tomb was made, adoring a figure of Anubis couchant on a pedestal or with various figures of gods and emblematic signs.

In a few cases (38, 40, 43, 75, 90, 253, 254 and 258), the Kheker ornament is only found on some of the walls of a tomb, the corresponding portion of the walls being decorated with floral friezes. Both the pointed and splay-topped forms of Kheker are to be found together in three tombs (Nos. 42, 106 and 253), the first case being especially interesting because the two kinds are actually to be seen on the same wall. In this connection, it should be noted that on one wall of Tomb 75 (Amenhotpe-si-se) a length of the Kheker frieze is found end to end with a strip of floral frieze.

Kheker friezes usually have a white or grey background, but there are exceptions, which may be seen in thirteen tombs (21, 26, 40, 46, 51, 55, 76, 89, 106, 130, 147, 253 and 259). In these tombs the colour of the background of the Kheker friezes is either red or yellow, in spite of the fact that the scenes below have the usual white or light-grey ground, except in the inner chambers or shrines of certain tombs, in which the background is yellow (21, 26, 40, 51, 55, 76, 89 and 253).

We even find in some tombs both coloured and white backgrounds for the Kheker ornament in the same chamber, though not on the same wall (76, 89 and 253).

The pointed form of the Kheker was the only form used in the Royal Tombs of Ramesside date, except in that of Sety I. It is also met with in nine of the tombs of the Nobles (39, 40, 42, 78, 85, 93, 106, 178 and 253), but, with the exception of four of these tombs (42, 78, 106 and 253), it occupies a very subordinate position. The pointed form first appears in this Necropolis as a frieze in tombs of about the time of Amenophis II (42, 85 and 93).

The colouring of these pointed Khekers varies considerably, and in no case does it resemble the colouring of the splay-topped, or ordinary type of Kheker, with the exception of Tomb 106 and the two Royal Tombs K. 22 and Q. 52. In five of the tombs of the Nobles (39, 40, 178 and 253) the pointed Khekers are only in two colours, either red (?) and blue, yellow (or red in 40) and blue, red and green or yellow and green, the arrangement being a broad mass of one of these colours in the middle of the Kheker, bordered on all the edges by a narrower band of a second colour. The roundels are treated in the same way, the centre of one colour being surrounded by a thin band of another colour. In two tombs (106 and 178) the roundels of this form of Kheker are painted wholly in yellow.

The pointed Khekers in Tomb 78 (Fig. 4) deserve special attention as nothing quite like them as regards the colouring is known elsewhere in the Necropolis. The middle portion of the upper part of the ornament is coloured in horizontal bands or rather blocks of blue, red and green separated by thin lines of yellow. The outer portions of the Kheker are painted yellow and the base is coloured in alternate bands of blue and yellow. The roundel, as will be noticed in the illustration, is a very elaborate one and consists of a blue centre surrounded by a ring of red with a ring of blue outside that again ; it is further decorated with white radii. The various bands of colours, with the exception of those belonging to the roundel, are edged with thin lines of dark red.

In the Royal Tombs the pointed Kheker is coloured in much the same way as those noted in the tombs of the Nobles, that is, in two colours, one of which was used as a border. These are, however, two variants which are not to be found used in a Kheker frieze in the tombs of the Nobles, the first being decorated with thin vertical stripes of blue, red, blue, green, blue and red, the last being in the centre. The roundel and base are similarly treated with these colours. Here we have an arrangement of colouring very similar to that of the ordinary splay-topped Kheker, except that there are eleven vertical bands of colours instead of the normal five.

H 3

The second variety is that shown in Fig. 5, a blue Kheker ornamented with fine lines (either dark blue or black) and edged with yellow. This can be seen in Tombs K. 11, Q. 43 and Q. 55, except that the colouring is in the first of these two tombs green and yellow, and in the second and third blue and red, green and blue predominating in the respective cases. In the tomb of Amenophis III, pointed Khekers are only present on the columns and are ornamented in exactly the same way as the ordinary Kheker, the roundel being painted red and edged with blue.

As a general rule, the colour of the roundels of the pointed Khekers agrees with that of the remaining portion of the ornament, but in seven of the Royal Tombs (Q. 42, 43, 51, 52, 55, Siptah, Rameses III) the roundels are coloured red, wholly so in three of these tombs (Q. 43, 51, K. 11), and edged with yellow in the remaining four, the body of the Khekers being painted either green or blue and edged with yellow or white. In the case of Tomb Q. 51, however, the Kheker is blue and edged with red.

It is curious that none of the roundels of the pointed Khekers in the Royal Tombs are wholly painted yellow, seeing that this colour was so popular for the purpose in the splay-topped Khekers. Yellow was also never used as the dominant colour in a pointed Kheker, but was solely employed as an edging.

In no case, either, was a ball or disc placed on the top of a pointed Kheker, as is so common with the splay-topped type.

In the Royal Tombs pointed Khekers are provided with either red or grey backgrounds, the former being the most popular colour. Yellow was never employed as a background for this form of Kheker, though it was so used with the splay-topped form.

In tombs in which the scenes are carved among the tombs of the Nobles, the Kheker ornament is usually either merely painted on the smooth rock face or the bare outlines, and sometimes the divisions of the colours, are incised. In some cases the frieze is carved in relief, as may be seen in Tombs 48, 57, 55, 106, etc. In many sculptured tombs, the Kheker frieze is merely painted on some walls and on other walls in the same tomb is both carved and then painted. The reason for this was probably the necessity of finishing a tomb as soon as possible, either because the owner found the cost of sculpturing the whole of the decoration of his tomb too much for his resources or because he died before his tomb was completed.

As most of the Royal Tombs are very heavily plastered, the Khekers are frequently found to be cut in this plaster as well as being merely painted. This is most common in the tombs of the Queens.

TOMBS IN WHICH KHEKERS ARE FOUND WITH A DISC AT THE APEX (AS FIG. 3).

TOMB.	COLOUR OF DISC.	COLOUR OF ROUNDEL.	DATE.
Seti I.	Yellow.	Yellow.	Seti I.
Haremhab.	Yellow.	Yellow.	Haremhab.
19.	Red.	Blue, green, blue and red.	Seti I.
23.	Yellow.	Red.	Meneptah.
26.	Yellow.	Yellow.	Rameses III.
30.	Red.	Red.	XIXth–XXth dynasty.
31.	Red.	Yellow.	Rameses II.

TOMB.	COLOUR OF DISC.	COLOUR OF ROUNDEL.	DATE.
35 (On cornice).	Red.	Blue, green and red.	Rameses II.
41.	?	Red.	Rameses to Seti.
46.	Yellow.	Yellow.	Amenophis III.
48.	Unpainted.	Unpainted.	Amenophis III.
49.	Blackened.	Blackened.	XIXth dynasty.
51.	Yellow.	Yellow.	Seti I.
55.	Yellow.	Yellow.	Amenophis III.
65.	Red.	Red.	Rameses X (?).
112.	Red.	Blue, green and red.	XIXth–XXth dynasty.
134.	Red.	Blue, green and red.	XIXth dynasty.
135.	Red.	Blue, green and red.	XIXth dynasty.
148 (Burnt).	Red (?).	Blue, green and red.	Rameses III–V.
157.	Blackened.	Blackened.	Rameses II.
158.	No colour.	No colour.	Meneptah.
159.	Yellow.	Red.	XIXth dynasty.
163.	Red.	Red.	XIXth dynasty.
178.	Red.	Yellow.	Rameses II.
188.	Uncertain.	Yellow.	Amenophis IV.
189 (Burnt).	Red (?).	Red (?).	Rameses II.
216.	Red (?).	Blue.	Rameses II.
220.	Red.	Blue, green and red.	XIXth–XXth dynasty.
255.	Red.	Yellow.	Haremhab.
259.	Yellow.	Blue, green and red.	Haremhab (?).

It will be seen from the foregoing list that out of a total of 25 tombs, after excluding the five, which are either blackened, uncoloured or doubtful, there are eight tombs with friezes of Khekers surmounted with a disc that still have their roundels painted in the old colours, namely, blue, green and red. In nine of the tombs the roundels agree in colour with that of their discs, and in five tombs the roundel is painted red if the disc is yellow or *vice versâ*. It may be gathered from this list, therefore, that the colouring of the new feature of the disc did not always influence the colour of the roundel.

In two of these tombs (Nos. 148 and 189) it is difficult to tell whether the colour employed for the discs was originally red or yellow, owing to the tombs having been badly burnt, thus causing a possible change of yellow to red.

At the close of the XVIIIth dynasty the Kheker ornament often appears in conjunction with other symbols. When it is used in this manner it is always the splay-topped form that is the one employed, there being but two examples (Q. 51 and new Ramesside tomb of Foucart, 1918) in Thebes where the pointed variety of Kheker is so used.

The commonest design in friezes where Khekers are used with other figures is a Hathor head alternating with figures of Anubis couchant on a pedestal, the figures and heads being separated from each other by two or more Khekers. Next in order of popularity is a row of figures of Anubis on a pedestal, the figures being divided by groups of Khekers.

Only one example has up to the present been found where Hathor heads appear alone with Khekers, and this occurs as a frieze on the southern wall of Tomb 45. The Kheker ornament is also used to form a frieze with the symbols

Dad and Thet in the inner chamber of Tomb 65. Sometimes a frieze, other than a floral one, was made up without employing the Kheker in any way, as can be seen in Tombs 14, 16, 45, etc. With the exception of one tomb (No. 71, Senmut), all such tombs are of Ramesside date, and for convenience sake the style of ornament and the order in which the ornaments appear are given in an appended list, which also deals with those friezes in which Khekers are combined with other figures.

KHEKER ORNAMENT IN CONJUNCTION WITH REPRESENTATIONS OF THE GOD ANUBIS COUCHANT ON A PEDESTAL.

Tomb 30. 1 Kheker, Anubis, 1 Kheker, vertical band of inscription, 1 Kheker, Anubis, etc.

,,   31. 2 Khekers, Anubis, 2 Khekers, Anubis, etc.

,,   35. (Inner chamber.) 3 Khekers, Anubis, 3 Khekers, Anubis, etc.

,,   189. Same as 35.

,,   Q. 51. 3 pointed Khekers, Anubis, 3 pointed Khekers, Anubis, etc.

KHEKER ORNAMENT IN CONJUNCTION WITH HATHOR HEADS AND ANUBIS COUCHANT ON A PEDESTAL, WITH OR WITHOUT VERTICAL BANDS OF INSCRIPTIONS (FIGS. 8, 9).

Tomb 41. (Shrine.) 1 Kheker, Hathor head, 1 Kheker, Anubis, 1 Kheker, Hathor head, etc.

,,   51. 1 Kheker, Anubis, 1 Kheker, Anubis, 1 Kheker, Hathor head, 1 Kheker, Anubis, etc.

,,   135. 3 Khekers, Hathor head, Anubis, 3 Khekers, Hathor head, Anubis, 3 Khekers, etc.

,,   148. 3 Khekers, band of inscription, Anubis, band of inscription, Hathor head, band of inscription, 3 Khekers, etc.

,,   157. 3 Khekers, band of inscription, Anubis, 3 Khekers, band of inscription, Hathor head, band of inscription, 3 Khekers, etc.

,,   158. 3 Khekers, band of inscription, Hathor head, band of inscription, 3 Khekers, band of inscription, Anubis, band of inscription, etc.

,,   159. Same as No. 158.

,,   178. 3 Khekers, Hathor head, 3 Khekers, Anubis, 3 Khekers, Hathor head, etc.

,,   255. Anubis, 2 bands of inscription, Hathor head, 2 bands of inscription, 2 Khekers, 2 bands of inscription, Anubis, etc.

KHEKER ORNAMENT USED IN CONJUNCTION WITH *Dads* AND *Thets.*

Tomb 65. (Inner chamber.) 5 Khekers, 2 Dads, 2 Thets, 2 Dads, 5 Khekers, 2 Dads, etc.

KHEKER ORNAMENT USED IN CONJUNCTION WITH HATHOR HEADS (FIG. 10).

Tomb 45. (South wall.)   3 Khekers, Hathor head, 3 Khekers, Hathor head, etc.

,,   58.   (Inner chamber.)   2 Khekers, band of inscription, Hathor head, band of inscription, 2 Khekers, etc.

,,   163.   2 Khekers, band of inscription, Hathor head, 2 Khekers, band of inscription, etc.

KHEKER ORNAMENT USED IN CONJUNCTION WITH FIGURES OF DECEASED ADORING ANUBIS.

Tomb 134.   (Inner chamber.)   Deceased, 2 bands of inscription, Anubis, 3 Khekers, band of inscription, deceased, etc.

FRIEZE MADE UP OF FIGURES OF THE DECEASED ADORING ANUBIS (FIG. 11).

Tomb 16.   (North wall only.)   3 bands of inscription, deceased adoring Anubis, 3 Nefer signs, Utchat eye, incense jar, Shen sign. (These symbols occupy the whole length of the wall and are therefore not repeated.)

,,   (? 7A).   Anubis, band of inscription, deceased and his wife, band of inscription, Anubis, etc.

,,   45.   (Eastern and western walls of southern end of tomb.)   Band of inscription, figure of deceased, band of inscription, Anubis, band of inscription, figure of deceased, etc.

FRIEZE MADE UP OF SMALL FIGURES OF DECEASED AND HIS WIFE ADORING ANUBIS AND A HATHOR HEAD.

Tomb 221.   Band of inscription, deceased and his wife before Anubis, band of inscription, deceased and his wife.

FRIEZE MADE UP OF *Dad* SIGNS ONLY.

Tomb 31.   (Two walls in outer chamber.)   2 Dads, 2 bands of inscription, 2 Dads, etc.

FRIEZE OF ANUBIS COUCHANT ON A PEDESTAL ALTERNATE WITH HATHOR HEADS.

Tomb 58.   (Inner chamber.)   Hathor head, Anubis, Hathor head, Anubis, etc.

,,   166.   (Jamb of entrance to shrine.)   Same as Tomb 58.

,,   149.   Hathor head, 2 bands of inscription, Anubis, 2 bands of inscription, Hathor head.

FRIEZE MADE UP OF ANUBIS COUCHANT ON A PEDESTAL WITH *Dad,* *Thet* AND OTHER SIGNS.

Tomb 14. Anubis, Thet, Dad, Thet, Anubis, Thet, Dad, etc.

FRIEZE OF HATHOR HEADS AND COLOURED CONES (FIG. 6).

Tomb 71. (Outer chamber.)

FRIEZE OF HATHOR HEADS WITH SUPPLEMENTARY *Nefer* SIGNS.

Tomb 6. (Second chamber.)

There are three tombs (Nos. 13, 166 and 184, outer chamber) in which the friezes are destroyed. The first one has only a vertical band of inscription and the front portion of an Anubis figure left of its frieze. The sole remains of the frieze in the second tomb is an Utchat eye on a Neb sign. In the third tomb it is just possible to see that Khekers in groups of three formed part of the frieze. The intervening signs or symbols between these Khekers are now entirely gone.

Numbers and names of tombs mentioned in this article :—

15. Shuroy.	65. Imisibe.	134. Thauenany.
19. Amenmōse.	71. Senmut.	135. Behnamūn.
21. User.	72. Rē.	147. Erased.
22. Wah.	75. Amunhetpesise.	161. Nakht.
31. Khons.	76. Thenuna.	166. Ramōse.
35. Bekenkhons.	77. Erased.	184. Nefermenu.
38. Zeserkarasonb.	78. Haremheb.	201. Rē.
39. Puimre.	82. Amenemhēt.	251. Amenmōse.
40. Amenhotpe or Huy.	84. Amunezeh.	254. Name lost.
42. Amenmōse.	87. Minnakht.	255. Name lost.
43. Neferronpet.	88. Pehsukher.	K. 11. Rameses III.
45. Dhōut, usurped by	89. Amenmōse.	K. 22. Amenhetep III.
Dhutemheb.	90. Nebamun.	Q. 1A. Setra.
48. Surere.	91. Erased.	Q. 42. Paraheremef.
55. Ramōse.	93. Kenamun.	Q. 43. Setymerkhepeshef.
57. Khaemhet.	106. Pesiūr.	Q. 51. Aset.
58. Unknown.	112. Menkheperrasonb.	Q. 52. Thyti.
64. Hekerenheh.	116. Erased.	Q. 55. Amenkhepeshef.

E. MACKAY.

REVIEWS.

Die Annalen und die zeitliche Festlegung des Alten Reiches der Ägyptischen Geschichte.—LUDWIG BORCHARDT. 1917. 64 pp., 6 plates. (Berlin, Behrend.)

In this study of the Palermo stone, and other pieces of the similar Annals, there is certainly one solution of the problem ; but we must ask, is this the only solution ? The main idea is that the five rows of year-spaces, each of different spacing, can only rarely coincide in the divisions, and therefore the terminals of these different series can be found by continuing them up to a coinciding position. This will be seen described in ANCIENT EGYPT, 1916, pp. 116–118 ; Dr. Borchardt protests that he was already on that track before—no doubt— and the English method of 1916 had been already worked here in 1902. The verdict in 1916 was that " the irregularities prevent accurate conclusions " at any great distance. This has been ignored by Dr. Borchardt, who states the breadths of spaces to five places of figures, while his actual measures were only to three figures (11 spaces in 78·25 mm., 9 in 83·6, 11 in 83·0, 11 in 70·1, 8 in 63·5 ; and, judging by the lower four registers, the first length was 77·25 and was misread). Much more serious is the variation in the regularity of the spaces, which vary as 65 : 70, 53 : 58, 45 : 50, 57 : 62. Hence there are several solutions fairly possible for coincidences of the lines of the registers; such as the numbers 24, 18, 22, 26, 21 ; or 81, 61, 75, 89, 71 ; or 146, 110, 135, 160, 128 (nearly Herr Borchardt's) ; or 162, 122, 150, 178, 142. There is yet more uncertainty due to all the measures being derived from photographs. Until there is an accurate direct measurement made of every line and thickness of each of the stones, it is wasted time to try for refinements. The best determination between the various possible number of spaces is the general character of the spaces on the back, belonging to the kings of the Vth dynasty. These agree to the length which is proposed, of 146, 112, 138, 163 and 131 spaces on the front ; so although there may be various solutions, there is a strong probability in favour of the one here set out.

A source of dating which is developed here is the high Nile being recorded in the latter part of the year, when divided between two reigns. As the times of high Nile are usually between 18 September and 7 October, and never more than three weeks beyond those limits, hence that part of the year must have coincided with a few months before the New Year. This gives the most effective result in the reign of Neter·ar·ka·ra, Vth dynasty, thus dated between 3120 and 3460 B.C., or perhaps a century further either way. Objection has been made that this writing of the high Nile in the second half of divided years was due to convenience ; but that could only be true of one case in the four which occur, the other three could equally well be written in either space. This date on the

Egyptian system—one Sothic period earlier—would be 4580–4920 B.C., or the extreme limits of 4480–5020 B.C., the first of which would just agree with Manetho's history. The result of the spacing of the Annals deduced above is also shown to be closely in accord with Manetho, and Dr. Borchardt concludes that "Manetho had really good sources, and his copyists have not altogether spoiled him." Yet however much he rehabilitates Manetho from the Ist to the XIIth dynasty, he will have none of him from the XIIIth to the XVIIIth, but keeps to the arbitrary setting of eight contemporary lines of kings in that period, to bring it down to two centuries.

One evidence against shortening the time stated for the IVth dynasty is the prodigious amount of building quoted. Even if those kings built twice as quickly as Sahura, they would need 50 years each to get through the tasks of Sneferu, Khufu or Khafra. The mention of 955 years in the Turin Papyrus is inconclusively discussed. The uncertainty of reading (755, 955, 1755 or 1955) and the very fragmentary state of the document prevent any result being more than a guess.

An interesting matter is the recurrence of a *zet heb*. It appears in the 70th, 190th and 350th year-space. The 70 and 190 being 120 years apart give rise to taking this as the festival of a shift of Sirius by one month; and the 350th would be 400 from a hypothetical start at 120 before the 70th, and thus a festival of the shift of 100 days. But there is no sufficient explanation of the term *zet* here; and as Uazet may be thus written, it would be more regular to take these as festivals of Uazet; the last example being also side by side with Nekhebt, the parallel goddess, would bear this out.

A matter which casts a serious shadow on this work is the "doctoring" of two ivory tablets on p. 53. A second version of one tablet has the gratuitous insertion of ⌒ put in for the sake of argument, of which there is no trace on the original. A second version of another tablet has a break smoothed out, and a perfectly clear incised line obliterated along with it, in order to make out a similar hypothetical group. Neither of these proposed readings has the least ground, and to propose fictitious readings only throws a shadow on all the rest of the material.

We may say then that there is a fair case for the rendering of the Annals here put forward; but it is much less exact and certain than it is stated, and the omission of some passages would have left the remainder in a stronger position. The dating concluded from all the sources discussed is: Ist dynasty, 4186 B.C. [or 5646]; IInd, 3938 [5398]; IIIrd, 3642 [5102]; IVth, 3430 [4890]; Vth, 3160 [4620]; VIth, 2920 [4380]; XIIth, 1995 [3455].

Imperial University of Moscow, Egyptian Collection I.—B. A. TURAEFF. Sq. 8vo, 84 pp., 12 plates, 10 Figs. text. Petrograd, 1917.

A melancholy interest attaches to the last works of civilisation that emerged from the welter of Russia. As the 48 heliogravures are the part easiest for reference, we note the inscribed and important pieces in order. I 3, a half-length of a king of XIIth dynasty, attributed to Amenemhat III, like the Karnak statue, a bad style from which the other statues redeem this king; also four anonymous heads. II, a gracious seated figure of a Vth dynasty priest of the Sun temple, Uzot·oher. A pair of seated figures, the woman Pernerek, larger than the man Sneferu·men, a child between them, IVth dynasty. III, a very early cross-legged figure, holding a papyrus across the knees, no name. A seated figure of

Sen·nefer, XIIIth dynasty (?). Seated figure holding a tablet with adoration to Amen, and prostration to Horakhti, by Tetares, early XVIIIth. Seated figure of Ren·onkh·em·o. IV, two boys wrestling, XIIth. Small figure of Amenhetep III from a group. Squatting figures of Asek, XXVIth (?). V, four wooden figures, not fine or inscribed. VI, cross-legged figure, papyrus on knees, XIIth. Statuette of a woman in very tight ribbed dress. Statuette of a XIIth dynasty woman inscribed on front. Statuette of Sebek·hetep, son of Mut. VII, pair of figures of Naiăy and Ast, daughter of Nefu ; fine work, mid XVIIIth ; amulet worn by man. Another fine pair of late XVIIIth of ...akhu, naming his sons Userhet, Tu·uaă, Aăy, and At·uah ("the hour multiplies"). VIII, three wooden statuettes of Pu, Rennăy by her daughter Ra·aă·kheper·ka·senb, and Amenhetep by the same. These last two are good examples of the transition from the early XVIIIth style. IX, Basalt torso of Hor·să·ast under Nekhtnebef, with figure of Maot worn as an amulet. X, head, probably of Ethiopian queen, Upper half of statue of XXVIth. Squatting statue of XIXth. Head of Nekht-horheb, nose unfortunately battered, a front view is to be desired. XI, Ptolemaic headless figure of Imhetep, son of Săm and Heronkh. Naophorus kneeling. ·Peda·mahes, wife Thent·ua, son Horusa. Squatting figure, headless, of Horkhab XII, anonymous heads, and Roman statuette holding robe, of good work for that age. There is a full index of names ; the text is entirely in Russian. The collection so far is what any dealer's shop might supply, without any selection for historic or artistic importance.

The Magic Papyrus Salt 825, of the British Museum.—B. A. TURAEFF. 8vo, 13 pp., 5 plates. Petrograd, 1917. A discussion and complete translation in Russian. We hope that Prof. Turaeff may survive the present disasters, and renew his contributions to this journal, which would be most welcome.

A Brief Chronology of the Muhammedan Monuments of Egypt to A.D. 1517. —CAPT. K. A. C. CRESWELL. 128 pp., 18 plates. (Bulletin de l'Institut Française d'Archéologie Orientale, T. xvi.)

For the work of the Arab period of Egypt this study will be an invaluable guide. The inscriptions and architecture are here viewed together, and the questions of the development of structural forms are placed on a firm foundation by the dated monuments. The buildings are noticed in historical order, with the dates A.H. and A.D. in the margin. The author states : "I have seen and examined every monument in this list (with four exceptions) in chronological order . . . in order to acquire a true historical perspective. . . . In this respect Cairo is unrivalled by any other city in Islam. What town, indeed, can show a series of monuments which, commencing in the IXth century, numbers over 220 before the year 1517 is passed ?" More than half of these monuments are actually dated by an inscription. Every date of alterations and rebuilding are here collected and discussed ; for instance, 11 dates for the Mosque of 'Amr, 8 dates for the Mosque of Ibn Tulun, 20 dates for El Azhar.

Though not in the usual scope of this journal, we may note points of general interest such as the use of pillars projecting as roundels on the face of walls is due to requiring bonding for a wall with a rubble core : the earliest armorial bearings on buildings are 1300 A.D., a time entirely under Central Asian domination, and the badges perhaps introduced from there ; and the earliest monumental date in figure is 1321, but on coin weights figured dates are found three centuries before. A matter of much interest, which the author does not touch on, is the close relation of style between Western Europe and Egypt ; the gateways of the XIth century at Cairo might belong to France or England in almost all points ; the pendentives of the XVth century show the love of short vertical lines of our perpendicular style ; the illuminated Qurans of the XIVth century in colour and flow of line might be French. Each century is more like its contemporaries in the West than like the next century.

Capt. Creswell has shown what a diligent student can do in leisure hours of two or three years ; what have hundreds of English officials done in ten times as long that they have been in Egypt ?

Levende og Døde i det gamle Aegypten.—By VALDEMAR SCHMIDT. 4to. 265 pp., with 1519 figures. 90 kr., or 120 frs. 1919 (Frimodt, Copenhagen).

At last the veteran curator of Ny Carlsberg has put forth his great collection of material relating to burial in Egypt from the prehistoric to the Roman period, extracted from all publications on the subject. While of immense value to students, it will also be very useful to experts as enabling styles and details to be readily compared. The figures are very clear and legible, and each has a full description and reference to its source—which may encourage the study of Danish. Such a collective work is the more needed as the literature increases, 400 serials and publications being listed here as references. The scope includes the tomb-plans, coffins of all kinds, mummies, funeral figures and statues, and the scenes and mythology figured on the coffins. It will save many a weary search for comparisons, and will prove to be one of the most useful works of recent times.

Ancient Survivals in Modern Africa.—By G. A. WAINWRIGHT. 8vo. 46 pp., 10 plates. 1919 (*Bull. Soc. Sultanieh de Géographie, Caire*).

These papers amplify the comparisons which were made in this Journal, 1914, pp. 115, 159. The resemblances between ancient and modern forms figured here are (1) Throwsticks, as in Monbuttoo. (2) Bows with reflex curve, as in Eritrea. (3) Falchion, as in Monbuttoo. (4) Leaf-shaped dagger of Greece, as in the Sudan. (5) Narrow leaf-shaped bronze spear-head, as in Eritrea. (6) Wide iron spear-head, as among the Baggara. (7) Barbed arrows of ancient Nubia, as on Upper White Nile. (8) Drums with cross bracing used anciently by Nubians, now in Eritrea. (9) Harp with wide bowl, and head on the top, as among the Niam-niam. (10) Lyre with diverging sides and bent top bar, as in Eritrea. (11) Head-rest, as in Eritrea, with pillar and saddle forms. (12) Revolving fan, as in Nubia. (13) Wide palm-leaf carrying basket, still identical in Egypt. (14) The coiled oval store-basket with lid, as in Nubia. (15) Sandals of palm-leaf, as in Somaliland. (16) Game trap of converging spikes, as on White Nile. (17) Double bag-bellows, as on White Nile. (18) Semicircular feather fans on long handles, as in North Cameroons. (19) Black-polished pottery, as in Central Africa. (20) Cups and bowls with a small spreading stem, as in Unyoro. Finally there are notes on the composite bows, and bows reversed when strung. Such papers as these build up the study of the descent of civilisations.

Une Station Aurignacienne à Nag-Hamadi.—By E. VIGNARD. 4to. 20 pp., 18 plates. 1920 (*Bull. Inst., Français d'Arch. Or. Caire*).

The station reported is on the west side of Diospolis Parva. It is claimed that the chelleo-mousterian work is only found on the plateau, and the aurignacian site is on the low desert. The aurignacian is stated to be also the age of many pieces from about Ramleh and Khan Yunis in Palestine. But we are told " the solutrean, the magdalenian, the campignyan were unknown in Egypt." Yet the very forms here published in pl. xiv 3, 4, have been found abundantly, see *Naqada* lxxi, 31, 35, 40, 43 ; and these ovoid forms were never found in the graves, but only in a site with ashes on the desert. The solutrean seems well known already in the great quantity of surface flints west of the Fayum ; the magdalenian flake is the type found in the prehistoric graves. Though we cannot thus accept all that is stated, we welcome these drawings of 116 flints from this site. In some final remarks on the steatopygous type, it is stated that Dr. Capitan has found it still in Tunisia.

Bulletin of the Metropolitan Museum of Art, June, 1920. (New York.)

This number is valuable as giving photographs of important specimens in the Museum. A diorite group of Sahura with a nome figure of Koptos ; a diorite portrait sphinx of Senusert III ; a basalt figure of Harbas holding an Osiris, XXVIth ; a sculptor's model of a ram's head ; and on the cover a charming Fayum portrait of a boy, with three lines of writing upon the dress, unfortunately not transcribed or noticed.

The Museum.—MARGARET TALBOT JACKSON. 8vo. 280 pp., 7 pls. Longmans, 1917.

Though this is rather a book for trustees and curators, much—or most—of it will appeal to any archaeologist. The questions of the site, buildings, fittings, and exhibiting are discussed, besides the matters about staff and students, which are so much more fully developed in America than in Europe. It is instructive to read of the new museum in Berlin, " So many mistakes have probably never been made elsewhere " ; it is on an island so cannot be enlarged, and with heavy express trains past it. It is on a quicksand, requiring 200 feet depth of concrete to fill it, the digging out of which almost upset the next museum. Some usual fallacies are not cleared away by the authoress. Lighting should always be direct from sky, and not diffuse from ground glass or ceilings. Floors should be of tile, and never of slippery waxed wood. Picture galleries need dark screens placed so that the pictures can reflect them, and so avoid bright reflections. Labels should not spoil the effect by harsh contrast, a brown label with darker ink is quite clear enough. A dust-trap, with free ventilation is needful for cases, as all airtight fastenings are fallacious. Though these points are omitted, yet all curators and museum frequenters should read this book for the systematic view of management.

Thirtieth Annual Archaeological Report, 1918. 8vo. 131 pp. (Toronto.)

This is naturally occupied with Canadian history, and pre-historic remains. A long paper by Dr. Harris deals with the ideas about a lost Atlantic continent. The undoubted civilisation of Peru and other countries is only evidence of a remote occupation of America. The real difficulty lies in the disproportion in age of any civilisation or tradition with the hundred- or thousand-fold age of any geological connection of land. The traditions are quoted from Central America and the Antilles, from Plutarch, Plato, Proclus, Diodorus ; but all of these cannot cover more than 3,000 or 4,000 years at the most. The age when the migration of animals indicates a land connection is the late Eocene or early

Oligocene (Gadow, *Wanderings of Animals*), and that is a matter of at least three or four million years, probably more. It seems hopeless to look at the traditional ideas as evidence of more than local disturbances of the coasts, unless geologists can allow of a change of an entirely different order to anything now granted.

Report upon Archaeological Research, Kyoto Imperial University.—By K. HAMADA. 8vo. 72 pp. (Japanese), iii + 8 pp. (English), 30 plates. 1919 (Kyoto University). As archaeologists we must welcome this gratifying extension of research by Prof. Hamada ; the prehistoric tombs were carefully excavated by him, the sculptures are reproduced in collotype with 5 plates in colour, and all the pottery is drawn accurately in section, giving a *corpus* of 173 types. The example given by European work has started our friends to equal it with their usual ability. Prof. Hamada has also published his travels in Italy and France, with a large number of photographs, as a popular volume, unfortunately for us entirely in his own language.

NOTES AND NEWS.

Mr. and Mrs. Brunton have already returned to Egypt to start on rock drilling in search of any chambers in the queen's pyramid and mastabas at Lahun. Mr. Miller and Mr. J. G. West will join the work, having obtained passages already. The rest of the party hope to obtain passages, namely Major Hynes, M. Henri Bach, Mr. Montgomerie-Neilson, and Prof. and Mrs. Petrie. It is hoped to continue the work southward from that of last season.

In Palestine the new School of Archaeology has begun work under Prof. Garstang at Ashkelon, where Minoan pottery has been found in the sea face of the mound of ruins. Unfortunately there is a great mass of mediaeval and Roman material to be removed before the more important strata are accessible.

The Egypt Exploration Society has left the great work at Abydos for the present, and Prof. Peet is to excavate at Tell el Amarna this winter.

Capt. Engelbach, R.E., has been appointed Chief Inspector for Upper Egypt, stationed at Luqsor.

Mr. Wainwright has been appointed Chief Inspector of Middle Egypt, stationed at Asyut.

It is to be regretted when societies criticise each others' affairs, as in a statement in a recent presidential address ; this compels us to consider the facts. It has been remarked that the Egypt Exploration Society "is practically alone in the study of Egyptian archaeology, with the exception of the Egyptian Research Account, and the Egyptian wing of the Liverpool University, both of which perform useful functions." Looking at the last fifteen years, since the Egyptian Research Account became the British School of Archaeology in Egypt, it has published, 1018 plates, nearly all discoveries of antiquities, while the Society which it is said "is practically alone in the study of Egyptian archaeology," has published 654 plates, mostly copies of known monuments and not discoveries.

ANCIENT EGYPT

1921. PART I.

CONTENTS.

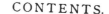
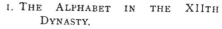

EDITOR, PROF. FLINDERS PETRIE, F.R.S., F.B.A.

YEARLY, 7s. POST FREE.

QUARTERLY PART, 2s.

MACMILLAN AND CO.,
LONDON AND NEW YORK;
AND
EGYPTIAN RESEARCH ACCOUNT,
BOSTON.

ANCIENT EGYPT. Net price of each number from booksellers is 2s.

Subscriptions for the four quarterly parts, prepaid, post free, 7s., are received by Hon. Sec. "Ancient Egypt" (H. Flinders Petrie), University College, Gower Street, London, W.C. 1.

Books for review, papers offered for insertion, or news, should be addressed :—
Editor of " Ancient Egypt,"
University College, Gower Street, London, W.C. 1.

Subscriptions, received in the United States by :—
Rev. Dr. Winslow, 525, Beacon Street, Boston.

NEGRO CAPTIVE FROM A THRONE.
BRONZE. XVIII DYNASTY. NEW YORK HISTORICAL SOCIETY.

ANCIENT EGYPT.

THE ALPHABET IN THE XIITH DYNASTY.

It is now eight years ago that the *Formation of the Alphabet* placed all the material of the primitive Mediterranean alphabet in order. Since then further evidence has not appeared until this year, except on the much later Semitic arrangement. Two seals of limestone that were obtained from the town mound of Illahun are

obviously of the Middle Kingdom, and one figured here bears a seated man holding a bird, with a rough fret-pattern over the head, and four signs (fig. 1) which are repeated here enlarged (Fig. 3). When clearing and re-arranging all the un-exhibited material at University College this summer, the box-full of pot marks collected at Kahun thirty years ago was sorted; among them some pieces of

A

a line of inscription were at last put together, and form a row of nine letters (the middle line of Fig. 4). The word of five letters (Fig. 2) was found and published in 1889 (*Kahun* xxvii, 85).

There are thus three inscriptions, each of which is dated by different means to the XIIth dynasty ; Fig. 1 by the style of the limestone seal ; Fig. 2 by being cut on a wooden tool which is only known in the XIIth dynasty, and found in a town of that age ; Fig. 4 by being from the same town, and on a jar certainly of that age. The signs are nearly all far older, being known in the pre-historic ages or 1st dynasty ; at those times they were probably owners' marks, and may have acquired sounds. But it is now evident that the use of these as letters for consecutive writing was fully established in the XIIth dynasty—that is, on the Egyptians' own dating, as long before the Phoenicians as we are after them.

It seems now fairly clear that there were three systems of writing in Egypt, and each of these is first known with a different race. The geometrical marks of the alphabetic system appear with the first prehistoric people, who seem to have been Libyans. They belonged to the west, and were the source of all the Mediterranean alphabets. Secondly, the later race of prehistoric times, seems to have come in from Syria, and brought in the word-signs, or ideographs, several of which used by them were common in later Egypt. Lastly, the dynastic race brought in letter-signs, by a group of which a word was spelled phonetically. The latter two systems mixed together became the later hieroglyphic system, while the oldest western alphabet continued in use among the foreigners settling in Egypt and perhaps among the lower classes. Long after all this, the Semite got hold of the alphabet and proceeded to spoil it. He degraded the vowels to be variable, owing to his phonetic inflections ; he used vague cursive forms in-stead of the clear uncial signs ; and he invented fancy names from the similarities of his shapes of the signs to irrelevant objects. This naming of the signs has nothing to do with their origin, but is like the Irish naming of all the letters from trees, in which there are enough resemblances to the Mediterranean names to show that both come from a common source.

How far is it possible to read these signs, may be asked? The group, Fig. 2, has been read by Dr. Eisler, and accepted by Prof. Sayce, as AHITUB ; this seems rather a jump at a well-known name, as the middle sign is not known else-where, either as a vowel or a consonant. The seal name, Fig. 3, seems to be in-tended to be read on the impress, or from the left on the seal, B, V, BH(?), G ; the third sign is not exactly known elsewhere, but is most like a sign of the pre-historic, and XIIth dynasty, which seems related to the South Spanish B, perhaps an aspirated form. The large inscription, Fig. 4, begins with a line of the usual formula " year 29, 1st month of Shemu"; then comes the line of alphabetic signs, the first of which is broken, TH(?) GOIF PŌRO ; below are Egyptian hieroglyphics again, *nes*(?), *per nesut* ; " belonging to the house of the king." Is this a bilingual version ? Can PŌRŌ be Pharaoh ? The O sign is found with this value in Karian and the Runes, and it does not appear in any other alphabet with a known value. As there can be no question of the O and I, the third and fourth letters, this serves to prove that the signs are alphabetic and not syllabic at this period.

Although the long priority of the alphabetic signs in Egypt leaves the tradi-tion of Phoenician origin out of the case, it is as well to point out how hopeless it would be to cling to it in any form. Even Diodoros did not believe in it, for he says : " There are some who attribute the invention of letters to the Syrians, from whom the Phoenicians learned them, and communicated them to the Grecians when they came with Cadmus into Europe ; whence the Grecians called them Phoenician letters. To these that hold this opinion, it is answered, that the Phoenicians were not the first that found out letters, but only changed the form and shape of them into other characters, which many afterward using, the name of Phoenician grew to be common " (v. iv). This account which Diodoros prefers is quite in accord with what can be traced. The Mediterranean alphabet was modified by the north Syrians (as shown by the vowel-endings of the names of letters), and the Phoenicians changed the forms from uncial to cursive. The order of the short Phoenician alphabet of 22 letters, in place of the full alphabet of 60 letters, was imposed on the world by their being used as numerals which became essential in trade.

When we see how widespread was the full alphabet, it is plain that the Phoenician had only a small part of the whole. There are 23 letters that were used in Egypt, Karia and Spain, all unknown in Phoenicia. There were 10 other letters which the South Arabian had in common with the Mediterranean and the Runes of Northern Europe, yet all unknown in Phoenicia. It seems obvious that there was a very widespread alphabet, from which at a much later time the Phoenician selection was formed.

The Greek maintained a part of this in the five letters which followed the close of the Phoenician series. The evidences for these, and many other details, can be seen in *The Formation of the Alphabet*, and briefly in an article in *Scientia*, December, 1918. The fresh material that we now have proves fully how the Mediterranean alphabet was in regular use for writing as early as the XIIth dynasty.

W. M. FLINDERS PETRIE.

THE LAHUN CASKETS.

THE accompanying plates show the Lahun jewellery caskets as recently reconstructed in the Metropolitan Museum, New York. A few notes as to the evidence
on which the restorations were based may be of interest.

It will be remembered from Prof. Petrie's account of the discovery (in *Ancient
Egypt*) that the wood had almost entirely disappeared. Nothing was left of the
caskets but a handful of ebony dust, a mass of broken ivory and the remains of
the gold decoration. The preliminary sorting of the material was carried out
at University College, and the general character of the boxes and outlines of
restoration was there determined. Arrived in New York, the first step was to
soak the ivory in water, to rid it of the salt which had already begun to work out
to the surface. This soaking greatly increased the work of mending, for the
pieces in some cases split into a number of thin slivers, and it was necessary to
siphon the water very carefully into the soaking dishes to prevent the smaller
fragments from floating out of position. It had the advantage, however, of
cleaning the surface, and making possible a much closer classification according
to colour and grain. It was estimated that upwards of two thousand separate
pieces of ivory and gold were involved in the restoration.

Large Casket (Fig. 2).

The wood had almost entirely disintegrated, but the powdery remains showed
that it had consisted of light streaky Sudanese ebony.[1] This particular variety
of ebony—known in the American trade as marble wood—has been used throughout in the restoration.

The size of the corner-posts was determined by the gold feet-coverings, which
had been preserved intact. The length and width between corner-posts were
settled exactly by the dimensions of the ivory slabs above the panels (*see* Fig. 2),
and the over-all measurements were confirmed by the cornice ivory, of which
hardly any had been lost. For the size of the panels themselves exact measurements were possible in some cases, and their number was determined by the 20
gold *dad* signs for the larger panels, and the 16 gold and carnelian squares for the
tops of the smaller ones. One of these carnelian squares was missing, but the
gold frame for it remained (filled in with coloured plaster in the restoration).
The blue glazed strips that had filled the smaller panels were still preserved,
but they had lost all their colour, so imitations in coloured plaster were inserted.
The width of the dividing strips of ebony between the panels worked itself out
automatically, by dividing into the number of spaces required the difference
between the slab lengths and the combined panel widths. For the height we
had as certain factors the ivory cornice, the gold torus-moulding, the width of the

---

[1] *See* Beauvisage, *Recueil de Traveaux*, 1897, p. 77. The word "ebony" itself is interesting, as being one of the few ancient Egyptian words that have come down into our own
language (𓉐𓆼𓂋𓈖𓏥).

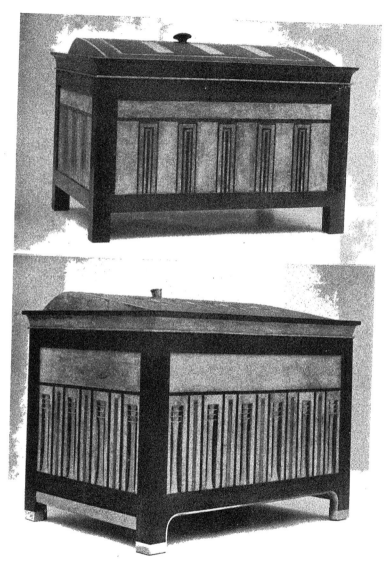

FIG. 1. LESSER CASKET, RESTORED. 1 : 4.
FIG. 2. GREATER CASKET, RESTORED. 1 : 4.

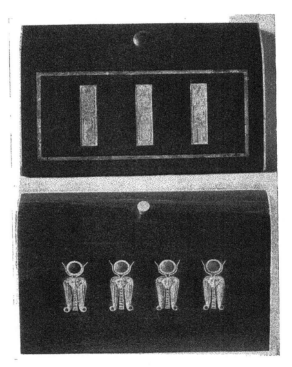

FIG. 3. LID OF LESSER CASKET, RESTORED. 1 : 4.
FIG. 4. LID OF GREATER CASKET, RESTORED. 1 : 4.

slab, the length of the panel, and the height of the gold foot. The ebony strip below the panels was shown to be necessary by the fact that the ends of the panel ivory and of the gold *dads* were left rough : the one above was needed, both for symmetry, and for providing a space for the side fastening-knob. The height of the legs was copied from a box of the same period in the Louvre. Fragments were left of the silver struts at the bottom of the box proper, and the exact shape was given by the rounded ends of the gold feet. The extra bars of ivory below the ends of the casket were a puzzle for a time, but their position also was shown by the Louvre box (No. 1392). It was evident also from marks on the ivory that the ends of the bars were meant to be covered. The narrow ivory strips at the top of the cornice could have gone nowhere else, for on fitting the pieces together a length was obtained which exceeded the measurement on any other part of the box.

The shape of the lid seems at first sight strangely unfamiliar, for on the monuments the tops of such shrine-shaped boxes always have the curve running lengthwise to the box. There was, however, in this case no question as to the direction of the curve, for the ivory that formed the ends of the lid came together almost perfectly. The Hathor heads (Fig. 4) were spaced out on the lid, and the shape of their wigs worked out from the tiny strips of gold. The discs are of carnelian, with encircling rings of gold and silver. The blue of the wig, six of the eyes, four of the carnelian wig-pendants, and the coloured part of the pectorals are restorations.

In addition to the ivory already mentioned there remained over—

(1) Two slabs about $28 \times 7 \cdot 3 \times \cdot 2 - \cdot 3$ cm.

(2) Two bars $25 \cdot 5 \times 1 \cdot 8 \times \cdot 4$ cm. Both ends of these bars had apparently been sunk into the wood for a distance of about 3 mm.

(3) A quantity of strip similar to that used at the top of the cornice. Of this strip there were at least 16 ends which showed marks of having been let into the wood.

These had no place in the exterior decoration, and must have belonged to the inside fittings. The casket may very likely have had a tray at the top for the mirror and razors, and a drawer to pull out below for the toilet vases.[1]

There were also preserved two copper fastening knobs—covered originally with gold or silver (?) and a copper bolt and staple.

Small Casket (Fig. 1).

Here there was much less evidence to go upon, and the restoration is in some points frankly conjectural. The bottoms of the ivory panels were irregular and obviously meant to be covered, and a well defined ridge on the face showed clearly the limits of the covering wood. Similar ridges at the bottom of the strip panels made evident the position relative to the wide panels which they occupied. It then became manifest that in order to complete the design the introduction of a third element, in addition to the ivory and ebony, was needed. This we supplied by making use of a red wood, very similar to rosewood, which is common on other known twelfth dynasty boxes. The covering of the bottom of the panels called for an ebony framework, similar to that on the large casket. The gold torus-moulding involved the addition of a cornice—of ebony this time, as there

---

[1] For an example of such drawers *see* Carnarvon and Carter, *Five Years.*

were no pieces of cornice ivory—and the ivory lid-ends determined the shape of the cover. The three ivory name-plates on the lid (Fig. 3) seemed lost in the expanse of dark wood, so the ivory and red rectangles were added, though their presence is purely a matter of opinion, as the ivory strip might equally well have belonged to the interior decoration.

In this casket also there was a good deal of ivory that seemed to have no place in the exterior decoration—

(1) A thin sheet 11·6 × ? × ·1 cm. The ends of this sheet were levelled off, whereas the sides were straight. This may have come from a tray.

(2) Two complete bars 14·5 × 1·1 × ·35 cm., and two incomplete shorter lengths. Of these bars one end only can have shown: the other was sawn irregularly, and must have been buried.

(3) More strips similar to that on the lid.

(4) Strip 12 + × ·4 − ·5 × ·35 cm. This must have been laid on edge, as the narrower face was the only regular one. One end of this strip was cut straight to show: the other was irregular.

(5) A few small triangular pieces, ·5 × ·3 cm.

(6) 3 complete oblongs 3 × 1·9 × ·3 cm.

(7) 1 complete oblong 7·2 × 1·1 × ·3 cm., and remains of at least two more. They were rough at one end, and were apparently meant to be buried 2·5 cm.

Many of the details of these restorations were worked out in consultation with Mr. Winlock, and to Miss Cartland I am indebted for much help in the actual work of reconstruction.

A. C. MACE.

THE BURIAL RITES OF WEST AFRICA
IN RELATION TO EGYPT.

NATIVE customs are very various in West Africa, as in other parts of the world, and there is no field in which the variations are greater than in burial rites ; this is owing partly to the fact that burial is largely a family matter in most tribes, and partly to the extraordinary facility with which burial customs seem to be borrowed by a people that will thereafter practise them unchanged for centuries. A comprehensive survey of West African burial customs would be an enormous undertaking, for which detailed information is for many areas almost wholly lacking ; even were this not so, the great number of tribes, and the diversities of custom within what is commonly termed a tribe, would make such an undertaking of necessity encyclopædic in bulk, for at a low estimate there are probably at least a thousand distinct negro tribes.

The term tribe is a vague one in Africa and does not really imply any political unity or even, in many cases, the possession of a common language ; for when we refer to the Ibo tribe, we are embracing under this head a congeries of peoples so diverse in language that two towns within a few miles of each other could hardly communicate with one another in pre-European days ; as the Ibo territory covers thousands of square miles and the people number some four millions, it is clear that the term tribe is, strictly speaking, a misnomer ; none the less, this is commonly the sense given to the term in Africa.

A cursory examination of the burial customs as recorded in the literature, old and new, of the coast, reveals the existence of elements in the burial customs which seem to be of very diverse origins. Some tribes practise rites indistinguishable from mummification as found in Egypt ; others formerly had similar customs but gave them up, sometimes under the stress of foreign invasions, soon after West Africa became known to Europe at the close of the Middle Ages. Side by side with these rites, but associated with them in a single complex we find undisguised cannibalism, which we can perhaps explain as an intrusion of older tribal customs on the sphere of the borrowed rite. A third set of practices, often associated with burial in an underground chamber, and therefore, *primâ facie* to be connected with the mummification portion of the complex, is the custom of orienting the corpse, usually facing east. Again, there is a large and important group of customs associated with the practice of removing the head of the corpse, either before burial or at a later period ; this may take the form of exhumation and storing the bones in a charnel house, of depositing the skull in a sacred grove, where ancestral cults have their home, or of handing the skull to a king or chief as the emblem of sovereignty and also the visible embodiment of the spirit of his predecessor.

In certain parts of West Africa we find associated with this custom a well defined practice of head hunting, that is to say, of taking the heads of enemies for the sake of the magical powers associated with them ; how far these two customs are to be regarded as independent, how far as associated, either both imported or lineally related, it is not easy to say.

This is by no means a complete catalogue of all the burial rites of importance ; we have, for example, a widespread custom of human sacrifice ; in Nigeria, west of the Niger, what is commonly termed a totem is sacrified at the burial ceremonies, or at least killed and eaten ritually ; and there is in most tribes a custom of second burial, that is to say, the actual interment is followed at an interval of months or years by a second rite, in which there is a second interment of some object representing the dead man.   It is a matter of great interest to determine the relation of this element to the features previously mentioned ; for it may be interpreted as a burial of the remains which were originally exhumed in order to take the skull or bones for ritual purposes ; but it may likewise be regarded as a ceremony intended to send the dead man to his own place ; it is, however, possible that these two interpretations are in reality one—simply two sides of the same rite ; but on this point further evidence is needed.

We come to a wholly different cycle of customs in the cult societies, most frequent perhaps in Nigeria, where they form the germ of such powerful secret societies as Oro in the Yoruba country, and from small beginnings have spread beyond their own immediate area, growing in power until they have like the Ogboni, actually become the supreme government of the realm.

In some tribes these customs take the form of dressing up the dead man, in others we get a stage further and find that for the corpse is substituted one of his relatives ;, on another line of development a masked figure takes the place of the corpse.   All these customs appear to be connected in some way with the practice of dismissing the dead man to his own place, or of calling him to his house to take his place among the worshipped ancestors.   They are therefore bound up with one aspect of the rite of human sacrifice ; for over a wide area in West Africa is found a custom of selecting a favourite slave or other person, with whose well being was bound up the life of the person concerned—in other words as a double or human representative of the genius, which was on the Gold Coast known as *kla* or *aklama*.   In view of the widespread Egyptian influence traceable in reincarnation beliefs no less than in burial rites, this word seems to be referable to the Egyptian *ka* ; there is a common suffix *li*, of uncertain meaning, which often assimilates its vowel to that of the root ; the root vowel is not infrequently dropped, and it is therefore clear that *kla* is a regularly formed derivative of *ka*.

In connection with the reincarnation belief may be mentioned the Kisi custom of putting upon the grave steatite or other statuettes, regarded as the representatives of the dead man.

I have mentioned above the use of an underground chamber ; we may perhaps regard as a variant of this the provision of a side chamber to the grave. often shut off, before the earth is put back, by branches or logs ; the usual native explanation is that it is intended to keep the earth from coming in contact with the body, but this may be of the nature of an aetiological myth.   In a variant of this custom we find what I propose to term a hood grave, in which a lateral cavity is provided for the head.   Also connected with the underground chamber complex is perhaps the tumulus, commonly of earth, raised above the grave, or sometimes above the body deposited on the surface and covered with the roof of a hut.   In certain areas we find monoliths and stone circles associated with burial ; but there is no evidence, except in the Northern Provinces of Nigeria, that these burials were the work of an indigenous race.

In a certain number of cases canoe burial is found ; in others the corpse is placed in a pot, or covered with a pot.

In a few cases, notably that of the *griot* or musician among the Mandingo, the corpse is placed in a hollow tree, the explanation being that if it were placed in contact with the earth, a drought would be the result. It is possible that the *griot* is an immigrant, and that in this rite we have a reminiscence of his native mode of burial. In certain other cases, for example, those of women who die in pregnancy, those who die of " bad diseases," or those who die in debt and have no relatives who will undertake the responsibility of disposing of the corpse and shouldering the burden of debt, the dead body is exposed.

A few tribes west of the Niger put cowries or gold in the mouth of the corpse, and explain the custom as intended to supply the deceased with ferry money with which to pay his passage across the river of death. In one case gold plates are or were put over the eyes, mouth and nose of the corpse ; but this is clearly associated with a different cycle.

As regards the position of the grave and similar questions, there is a good deal of variation. Some tribes bury a man in his own house and abandon it, others bury him in the house and continue to use it ; many bury in the fields or bush, some by the way side, some, especially in the case of chiefs, in the bed of a running stream. There may be a vault for all the members of a family, or an area set apart for their graves, or certain localities may be reserved for those of a certain rank or age.

More or less independently of all these elements varies the actual position of the corpse, which may be extended on its back, upright, squatting, lying on its side in a contracted position or otherwise. It frequently happens that the precise orientation of a body is not ascertainable for lack of data as to the position ; a further difficulty arises from the fact that we cannot compare, in respect of orientation, the customs of a tribe that lays the corpse on its back with those of a tribe that lays it on its side, at any rate without direct evidence as to what view the native takes of the matter. If a man is buried with his head to the west, it may or may not be true that he is supposed to be facing the east. For if at one time the corpse was laid on its side, for which was substituted at a later period extended burial on the back, it is clear that the orientation would be changed unless the orientation of the grave underwent a simultaneous alteration.

It is impossible to discuss here in their relation to Egyptian practices even a small proportion of the customs here passed in review. It will be enough to deal with three or four items, mummification, decapitation, orientation and the like.

Regarding mummification customs it is perhaps hardly necessary to argue at length the Egyptian origin as an alternative to convergence ; no theory of convergence will account for agreement in non-essential details, though it is of course possible that one or two such cases are pure coincidences. A few cases, however, of mummification may be cited. In Sierra Leone, then known as Bulombel, early in the fifteenth century when an important man died his body was opened at the side and the entrails taken out and washed ; the cavity was filled with sweet-smelling herbs like mint and the body rubbed with palm oil ; meal and salt were added to the herbs introduced into the body cavity.

This custom is now no longer practised, so far as I know ; it seems to have disappeared after the Manes invasion of the sixteenth century, which imposed on most or all indigenous tribes paramount chiefs of alien birth, whose burial rite was that still in use at the present day.

This present system is the burial of the body in the bed of a running stream, and we may suspect that it was also accompanied with decapitation ; for in the present day the Temne chiefs, or some of them, preserve the head of their immediate predecessors as a magical instrument.

On the Ivory Coast the Baule take out the entrails of a dead man, wash the cavity with alcohol, and introduce a mixture of alcohol and salt to replace the entrails ; the orifices of the body are plugged and gold plates put over the eyes, nose, etc.

The Asanti kings, the Ata of Ida and other potentates, were or are mummified and their bodies preserved for years ; it is of interest to note that in the case of the latter, who is of the Igara tribe, the bodies of four Ata remain unburied ; for it is the custom, it appears, for the dignity to pass in rotation to four families, and the Ata of each family must have in his keeping the body of his immediate predecessor of the same family.

Among the Jukun, whose king is or was slain by his successor, the entrails are removed, and the corpse is smeared with butter and salt ; then it is dried over a slow fire for two or three months ; finally the death is announced to the people, and the slayer of the dead man takes his place, stepping over the corpse in the course of the accession rites.

In the Kukuruku country the king of Ijeba is inhumed for a fortnight after being rubbed with alcohol ; this temporary measure may or may not be related to the custom of mummification. The simpler and more widespread practice of drying the body over a slow fire, recorded among the Gambia tribes, in several parts of Nigeria and probably elsewhere, is also of uncertain origin.

I have alluded above to the hybridisation of customs ; this is very marked in the case of some of the rites in the mummification complex. On the Gambia the corpse is dried over a slow fire, then buried in a side-chamber grave, the aperture of which is closed by the door of the dead man's house ; a few days later it is exhumed, boiled with rice and eaten by the relatives. There can be very little doubt that in this case there are traces of customs belonging to several distinct systems ; this is equally clear in the case of the Baya of Central Africa, who bury the corpse in a stream after disembowelling it.

In the present day we often find that smoke-drying the corpse is resorted to, if the burial is delayed for any reason, such as lack of funds for the necessary feasts ; in other cases the body is quietly buried and the rites postponed till funds accumulate. This may be one of the origins of the custom of second burial mentioned above.

It is of course possible that some of these rites are indigenous, but it seems hardly possible to maintain that the procedure of mummification—disembowelling by a lateral opening, treatment with alcohol, sweet-smelling herbs, salt, honey, etc.—has been evolved independently. At the same time there is scope for enquiry into Egyptian origins ; for there is the possibility that both sets of customs go back to a common source. If the Egyptian origin of the complex discussed above seems manifest, the case is very different when we come to the decapitation rite ; there appears to be evidence that the same practice prevailed in Egypt at an early period ; but there is comparatively little evidence that it was also common in historic times. In any case there is little reason to associate it with the mummification complex. We cannot therefore argue that the ascription of an Egyptian origin to mummification, as practised in West Africa, necessarily entrains the attribution of a like origin to other customs, not in themselves typically Egyptian, nor associated with those Egyptian customs and beliefs for the transmission of which we have good *primâ facie* evidence, merely on the ground that at some period a custom of decapitation, which outwardly resembled that of West Africa, was known in Egypt.

Two grounds have been assigned for the Egyptian custom of decapitation : it was intended firstly to facilitate the entry of the deceased into the other world ; secondly, to prevent his return to this world. So far as can be seen, neither of these motives is operative in West Africa. The corpse which is beheaded is that of the witch, and the motive is to prevent its return to the scene of its malefices ; but in the case of the ordinary man, an invitation is given him to enter his house and join the body of ancestors to whom prayers and sacrifices are addressed. The admission of the negro to the other world is facilitated by the due perform- ance of burial rites, including sacrifices, not by mutilations of the corpse. Where the latter take place, they are associated with the preservation of the skull in connection with the cult of ancestors.

On the whole it seems probable that the Egyptian explanations of the custom are secondary. If the rite was practised at an earlier period, the reason for it must have been forgotten, or lapsed with the introduction of a new cycle of ideas. It is virtually impossible to derive from Egypt the skull customs of the West African area, even if we only include in our survey the rites that have to do with the heads of relatives. It becomes still more impossible to associate the customs with those of Egypt when we take account also of the ceremonies con- nected with the skulls of enemies ; for there is, so far as I know, no evidence that head hunting was ever an Egyptian practice.

As regards orientation, it is well to remember that the orientation of the grave is necessarily different from the orientation (*i.e.*, the facing) of the body, unless the latter is on its back ; in the latter case the term orientation is used in a vague and somewhat anomalous way, for the direction in which the corpse would be facing if it were stood upright. It is noteworthy that some authors confuse this point ; one author for example records that the Mascagnes of Senegal grill the body with rice, remove the skin and bury it in a pot, which is put in a side-chamber grave ; but when he adds that the grave runs east and west and that burial takes place with the face to the east, it is not quite clear what he means.

Generally speaking, when the corpse lies on its side, it faces east ; this is the case with the Mosi, the Mandingo, the Wolof, the Serer and the Bambara in the west, and with the Dakakari, the Hona, the Kerikeri, the Nupe and other tribes of Nigeria ; as exceptions, the Kilba and Marghi bury their dead facing west.

Where we have to infer from the wording of the report that the corpse is on its back, there is more variation ; the Gbandi bury with head to the west, so do the Mumbake of Nigeria. The Dukawa and Mumuye of Nigeria bury the body with head to the east, the Kamberi with head to the south. While the Miriam turn men's heads to the north, women's to the south, the Kaje turn men to the west, women to the east, and the Kisi on the borders of Sierra Leone reverse the positions.

If it is true that the orientation of a corpse is in the direction from which the tribe originally came (or possibly in the direction from which the custom practised by the tribe originally came), it is of much importance that, in the comparatively small collection of scattered notices, complete agreement is found among the western tribes, and that the tribes of Nigeria should for the most part follow the same custom.   As to the signification of the direction in which the head is laid, it is possible to speculate at length without arriving at results of much value.   First and foremost we need to know the native view on the matter.   If the statement as to the direction of the dead was made *sua sponte* by an informant, it is one thing ; it is quite another if the answer was elicited by a leading question.

I do not propose to discuss here the relation of the rites briefly described in this paper to those of Egypt ; but it seems desirable to note the close agreement of many of them with the customs of Indonesia, which has, on grounds of material culture, been regarded as connected with the West African area.   First of all, the skull cult and associated head hunting finds its explanation far more naturally in this culture than in Egypt or North Africa, though it must not be forgotten that head hunting is also a Balkan amusement.

The preservation of the body pending the performance of the final cere-monies is likewise Indonesian ; and it is the practice to close the apertures of the body as a protection against evil influences of a magical nature ; we have seen that this is also done in West Africa, though the grounds for the custom are not stated.   The treatment of the body by fire is practised in Timor as a means of hastening the process of decomposition, *i.e.*, in order to separate the flesh from the bones, without which the final rites cannot be performed, which send the soul to its own place.

Cannibalism, associated with rites of another order on the Gambia, is a method of disposing of the flesh in Indonesia, and likewise a ritual repast.   The reason for not consigning the body to the earth before decomposition is ended, is that the earth is holy and may not be polluted ; this recalls the side-chamber grave and the precautions taken to prevent earth from touching the body.   This ritual is commonly interpreted in West Africa as being in the interest of the corpse, but this may well be an afterthought.

In Indonesia the chief's successor is not appointed till decomposition is finally ended.   In Sierra Leone the new chief is secluded for a period and the death of the old chief not mentioned, though it is probably no secret ; an analogous case has been mentioned above.   These customs find their natural explanation in the Indonesian rite and its explanation.   An interregnum for the death of the king is also common to parts of Indonesia and West Africa.   Finally, ossuaries, which are known to the Wolofs in the far west, and also to some of the Ibo east of the Lower Niger, are an Indonesian custom.

It may appear a bold hypothesis to derive important elements of West Africa belief from an area comparatively remote like Indonesia.   I put forward the hypothesis tentatively in the first instance, conscious as I am of my ignorance of matters Egyptian ; but if Egyptologists find it impossible to explain the rites common to Africa and Indonesia by reference to well-established Egyptian customs, practised at a date that makes transmission to other parts of Africa probable, I submit that the Indonesian hypothesis may be accepted as a working explanation of the data.

I need hardly recall the fact that musical instruments, weapons, architec-tural features, and other elements of West Africa culture have also been traced to Indonesia.   For these the question arises whether they were transmitted direct, or *via* the south coast of Asia. We have also to solve the problem of whether they were carried by people of whose culture they formed an integral part, or whether they were transmitted much as manufactured goods in our own day pass from hand to hand. Architectural resemblances are perhaps less easily explained in this way than similarities in readily transportable material like weapons ; but it seems still more difficult to account for the transmission of burial customs independently of the movement of peoples, in large or small numbers. The field of burial rites therefore seems to be on the whole a favourable one for arriving at a definite decision, and I put forward these facts and suggestions in the hope that Egyptologists may furnish valuable material for the final solution of the problem.

NORTHCOTE W. THOMAS.

A NEGRO CAPTIVE.

(*See Frontispiece.*)

PIECES of royal furniture are so rare, outside of the Cairo Museum, that we should notice a figure in the collection of the New York Historical Society. This figure of a kneeling negro, with his hands bound behind him, evidently has been for some object like a royal footstool. The king Amenhetep II as a boy is shown resting his feet on a group of captives, five beardless negroes and Hittites, and four bearded Syrians, making up the traditional nine subdued peoples, often shown as nine bows beneath the king's feet. The negroes of this footstool, figured in the tomb of Ra (Lep. D*enk.* III, 62), have the elbows tied behind them, and are kneeling as here. The casting of a bar between the feet was doubtless to provide for attaching them to the furniture round which it was to be ranged with other captive figures.

The casting, from its complexity, must have been modelled in wax, and cast *cire perdue.* It is said to be " exceedingly heavy " which seems to show it to be a solid casting without a core. The specific gravity would settle that. The head has been burnished, the front partly so, but the back between the arms is left with the original skin of the casting. From the absence of polish on the knees it does not seem ever to have been actually mounted and used, as any wear of handling and cleaning would have smoothed the prominent part. Probably this has been found as left behind in a workshop. The illustration here is of the actual size, for which I have to thank Mrs. Ransom Williams, who has lately been describing the collection of the Historical Society.

W. M. FLINDERS PETRIE.

ON QUEEN TETISHERI, GRANDMOTHER OF AHMOSE I.

In a well known inscription from Abydos, King Ahmose I recounts how he erected a pyramid-chapel in the Sacred Land to "the mother of his mother and the mother of his father, the Great Royal Wife and Royal Mother Tetisheri, triumphant," whose tomb was in the Theban Necropolis, and whose cenotaph was already built in the Thinite nome.[1] The King first expressed a desire to accomplish this act of piety while talking with his wife Ahmose-Nefretiri "seeking the welfare of the departed." There is, it is true, no definite statement as to how long the grandmother of King Ahmose had been dead, but one gets the impression that she had died several years before, and that the cenotaph already erected in Abydos was either beginning to fall in ruins or that it belonged to an earlier reign and was therefore not as sumptuous as Ahmose thought fitting for his ancestress. In other words, it would seem fair to say that she was not only genealogically two generations earlier than Ahmose, but that historically she belonged wholly to that earlier age.

I must confess that some time ago in beginning a study of the XVIIth dynasty I started on this supposition, but I eventually concluded that such an interpretation of this text was impossible. About twenty years ago Erman discovered (*A.Z.* 1900, p. 150) that an XVIIIth dynasty *Book of the Dead* from Abusir, and now in Cairo, had been written upon a piece of papyrus which had already, at the beginning of the dynasty, been used for some farm accounts. At the end of these he could make out :

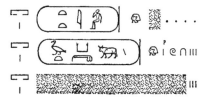

Erman judged that reference was here made to actual estates of Sitkamose and Tetisheri rather than to their chapels or tombs, and nothing to the contrary appears ever to have been advanced. Taking this as the case, then Tetisheri and Sitkamose were endowed with estates presumably near Abusir, for it would not be very likely that a scrap of paper of this sort would travel a great distance from its point of origin.

The interesting point is that the only villages to-day called "Abusir"—I base this statement on the Baedeker maps—are in the Fa'yum and north towards Memphis, and that of these the "Abusir" of the Cairo Museum records is doubtless the well known one in the Memphite Necropolis. As late as the reign of Kamose

---

[1] Gardiner in *Abydos* III, pp. 43 ff ; Breasted, *Ancient Records*, II, pars. 33 ff ; Sethe, *Urkunden des 18ten Dynasties*, p. 26, translations, p. 14.

this region was well within the domain of the Hyksos whose southern frontier was Cusae-Meir (*J. E. A.*, 1916, p. 108–10). Since Tetisheri was a Theban princess she could scarcely have held title to land in the North until after the expulsion of the Hyksos. I was therefore forced to the conclusion that Tetisheri survived the expulsion of the Hyksos, or in other words, that she lived into the reign of Ahmose. The only alternative solution of the difficulty would have been to suppose that the campaign of Kamose was pushed to the point of taking or beleaguering Memphis and thus freeing Abusir and its neighbourhood, but of this there is no other evidence. Having come to the conclusion that Tetisheri survived until the reign of Ahmose, it was very gratifying to me to have it confirmed by an unpublished fragment of a stele in University College, London, pointed out to me by Prof. Petrie, who bought it in Egypt some years ago, and through whose courtesy I am able to bring it out at this time.

The stele has a semi-circular top with the usual winged disk in the lunette. Its width is thirty-eight centimeters. The lower part is entirely broken away. The very brief inscription announced that "[*In the . . . Year*], *IVth Month of Summer*, 17*th Day, of His Majesty The King of Upper and Lower Egypt Nebpehtetre', Son of Re' Ahmose, given life,* [*he built*] *anew this wall as his monument to his father Montu Lord of Thebes, the Bull in the midst of Hermonthis.*" On the left can be seen the tops of the plumes of "*Montu, Lord of Thebes.*" On the right is the peak of the White Crown worn by "*The Good God, Lord of the Two Lands* [*Nebpehtetre'*] *Son of Re'* [*Ahmose*] "

Behind Ahmose there stood a Queen whose figure was, properly, shorter than that of the King, and whose name is given as "*The Royal Mother Tetisheri*" in which the first ⌒ and the ◊ are unquestionable, as Prof. Petrie demonstrated to me, and the lacunae impossible to fill satisfactorily except with another ⌒ and 𝄞.

Here Tetisheri is surviving the coronation of Ahmose and participating in the restoration of the Temple of Montu in Thebes. The Abusir farm accounts show that she lived to see the Hyksos expelled, and on that occasion received from her royal grandson an estate in the reconquered North. Her death, of course, took place before the reign was out, and even before Ahmose contemplated building an extension monument in Abydos ; because a first cenotaph was put up there in her honour at the time of her burial at Thebes. It was only toward the end of the reign, while the King was erecting his false pyramid and tomb in the Sacred Land, that he erected the second cenotaph found by the Egypt Exploration Fund in 1903.

There is one more point to be remarked. In what we must presume was an important official function, the Petrie Stele shows the Dowager Queen Tetisheri accompanying the reigning king to the exclusion of all others. In the same way on a temple built for Ahmose shortly after his conquest of Nubia, the viceroy has caused the King to be shown with the Dowager Queen Ahhotep alone (*Buhen*, p. 87, xxxv), and one is naturally led to remember that in Karnak Ahmose set up a proclamation, in the course of which he decreed that Ahhotep be shown practically the same deference as was shown himself.[1] In short, the terms of the document (an endowment of the Amon Temple of Karnak), sound very much like the declaration of a regency during the king's absence from Thebes, or a republication of the proclamation of regency on the occasion of the endowment of the temple. Late in the reign this prominent place in affairs was taken by Ahmose-Nefretiri, the wife of King Ahmose. It is she who shared with the King the honour of building Tetisheri's second cenotaph, and she who appears with the King on a dated monument of the twenty-second year,[2] and following her husband's death she occupies the place of honour throughout the reign of her son Amen-hotep I, and even appears on the coronation stele of Thotomose I.[3] Taking the clue given by Ahhotep, we may conclude that these queen-mothers appear on the monuments because they are·the regents or potential regents at the time. This would be Tetisheri's position in the " Year   . . ." of the Petrie stele, a year to which we must unquestionably give a low number.

Tetisheri must be looked upon therefore, as in every way a predecessor of that remarkable line of XVIIIth dynasty queens whose rights and prerogatives were so high that they were virtual rulers of the country. Presumably it was in them that the family strain was purest and through them that the inheritance passed. Most of them survived their husbands, and in widowhood held enhanced influence. For about a century the royal family was to all intents and purposes a virtual matriarchate. The active, warlike functions and the ritualistic offices were the men's, and officially they took precedence, but a large share in actual government evidently lay in the hands of this line of women.

Tetisheri is not only the earliest of this line whose name has survived—she must have actually headed it, for she was by birth a commoner whose parents were known by the simple styles of the Honourable Tenna and the Lady Neferu (*Ann. Serv.*, 1908, 137). Lowly as her origin may have been, however, she was the ancestress of a line of women famous in Egyptian history : Ahhotep, Ahmose-Nefretiri, Ahhotep II, Ahmose and finally Hātshepsut with whose ambitions the female line of the royal family reached its climax and suffered its eclipse.

H. E. WINLOCK.

---

[1] Legrain, *Ann. Serv.* IV, pp. 27–29 ; Sethe, *op. cit.*, p. 21 ; translations, p. 11.
[2] Breasted, *A. R.*, II, pars. 26 ff ; Sethe, *op. cit.*, p. 24 ; translations, p. 13.
[3] Sethe, *op. cit.*, p. 80 ; translations, p. 41.

REVIEWS

Leçons sur l'Art Égyptien.—By JEAN CAPART. 1920. 8vo. 541 pp. 20s (Vaillant-Carmanne, Liége).

This is the text for the 200 plates which appeared in 1911 as *L'Art Égyptien:* when conditions improve in the world a special series of illustrations are promised, and this is called a provisional edition. After an historical introduction, the early civilisation is described, the oldest monuments, the sources, materials, and forms of architecture, the conventions and ideas of the Egyptians. The temples, tombs and statuary of the Old Kingdom are described. The architecture and art of the Middle Kingdom come next, and then a fuller treatment, on the same lines, of the material of the New Kingdom and the later period. New ground is broken by the enquiry as to the connecton of the scattered statuary without a history, which was dispersed by Mariette and others without record. The work is full of remarks or critical detail, which cannot be summarised, but need full consideration ; such reading will well repay attention, however much others may feel a different appreciation of the questions. Unfortunately there is no index, and only a scanty table of contents.

Le " Pseudo-Gilgamesh " figure sur le couteau Égyptien de Gebel el 'Arak du Louvre.—By J. CAPART. And *Note de M. G. Bénédite.* 8vo. 15 pp. (Comptes Rendus Acad. Ins. 1919). The hunting scene on the seal of Den, and the sign *qes* of Cusae, are here produced as Egyptian parallels to the hero and lions on the handle. Further, the personal names Qesmer and Qes-em-hot are quoted as evidence that Qes was a deity. The phrase " Cusae leads " is, however, like that of " Memphis for ever," yet we do not say that Men-nefer was a god. This endeavour to regard the hero and lions as Egyptian in origin entirely ignores the striking dress which is northern and not Egyptian, and the cold-climate fur of the lions. These alone would prove a northern origin, regardless of the form of the' group.

M. E. Pottier remarked that the aspect of the group was Asiatic, above all in the hair, dress and long beard of the figures. To this Dr. Capart replies inconclusively.

M. Bénédite replies that the *qes* figure is the old group of restraining the long-necked panther, as on the palette of Narmer, and is not a lion-hero : also that the royal figure in a quilted robe (*Abydos* II, xiii) is more Asiatic than Egyptian in style. He asks how can we escape from the fact that the more Egyptian art is seen in its primitive aspect, the more evident is its relation to Mesopotamian art ? In this, however, only the art leading to the dynastic age is considered ; the art of the true prehistoric is outside of this comparison.

Bericht über die grabungen . . . auf den Friedhöfen von El-Kubanieh-Süd. Winter 1910–1911.—By HERMANN JUNKER. 4to. 1919. 227 pp., 56 pls. (Akad. Wissenschaften in Wien).

The site of this work was nine miles north of Aswan on the west bank of the Nile ; the periods of the cemeteries described are prehistoric, XIIth dynasty, and

Byzantine. Of the prehistoric age 24 plates are occupied with views of 96 burials 8 plates are of pottery of dynasties 0–1, all common ; 7 plates are of slate palettes, ivory pins, comb, and falcons, finger rings, beads and shells, flint flakes, and a rectangular copper axe, two bracelets, tweezers, fish-hook and needle, all of copper. Of the XIIth dynasty are 8 plates of burials, 3 of beads, a few scarabs and cylinders and bone armlets, harpoon, wand, and *user.* Five plates are of Christian burials. It is sad that such excellent and careful work was not rewarded by a single object of importance, the lavish publication only concerning material quite familiar and usual. The best object is a white-lined bowl (in the text) with a spotted disc in the midst, from which radiate 23 palm branches. A few pot marks are mostly of animals, and a few signs. The catalogue of graves is not in any order, so reference is difficult, and the pottery is insufficiently typed.

The graves of the XIIth dynasty were shallow rectangular pits in the rock, or lined with bricks. A cylinder of Amen-em-hat III, another of the XVIIIth dynasty, and 5 usual scarabs of XIII–XVth dynasty were found. There were fragments of many cartonnage masks, pottery, and four small alabasters, all as usual. The date, by the cylinder and one cartonnage, probably extends to the XVIIIth dynasty. When there are so many important sites still needing record, it seems that the care and publication spent here should be given where it is needed, rather than to a poor cemetery of this kind.

Prehistoric Cultures and Races of India.—By PANCHANAN MITRA. 8vo. 88 pp. (Calcutta University Journal, Dept. of Letters, 1920).

This paper by the professor of prehistoric archæology needs notice, as it concludes that "the pre-dynastic Egyptians and the chalcolithic Indians very probably belonged to a common 'Erythraean' race ; the home of that ancient race was most likely Punt in Ta Netar, which though finally located in Africa, had also a counter-part on the Indian shore of the Arabian sea ; and Ta Neter, the land of gods, was probably an early colony from pre-'Aryan' southern India and Punt from the Pounnata of Ptolemy in Southern India."

The existence of a long age of copper is recognised in India, but as it is all pre-historic it attracts less attention than the iron age. Iron is named in the earliest writings, but as the Vedas are not earlier than 1200–800 B.C. this does not precede iron in the west. It is claimed here that the iron age in South India was active in 1600–1500 B.C., and spread thence to Mesopotamia, but no evidence of so early an age is given. The iron-using people were agricultural, had weaving, gold and bronze (? copper) ornaments, and kept buffaloes, sheep and goats. Iron was wrought as swords, daggers, spears, javelins, lances, hatchets and spades. Rude stone monuments were erected. Two modes of burial were followed ; mostly urn-burial under megaliths, or in long cists, less usually by cremation.

The similarity of the pottery to that of Egypt and East Mediterranean, and a like series of owners marks, is the main ground for a connection. This connection would be with the prehistoric Egypt, and not the dynastic, whereas the theory given is that the Sumerian (or dynastic Egyptian) was linked with the Dravidian. The resemblance of Punt to Pounnata in India is not much to rely on ; and that of Ta Neter to Teu Nodr " country of the gods " will not work, as it is not *nodr* but *teu* that means god. Before granting an Egyptian-Indian connection we must see clearly which of the races on each side is specified, and how far India, undated before 1200 B.C., can be linked with stages in Egypt thousands of years earlier.

PERIODICALS.

———

Aegyptus; revista Italiana di Egittologia e di Papirologia.—
1920. 30 lire ann. (R. Accademi Scientifico-letteraria in
Milano via Borgonuovo 25.)

We must welcome fresh activity in our science on the Italian side, in this
journal, which is to be issued quarterly, to comprise 400 pages annually, though
the first two numbers indicate more than 500 pages for the output. The classical
age and the papyri are naturally the main interest to Italy. Prof. Calderini is
the chief editor.

LUMBROSO, GIACOMO.—Comments on Arrian's account of the founding of
Alexandria (III 1, 4) and on the Heroeion to Hephaistion at Alexandria, and in
Pharos (VII 23, 6).

FARINA, GIULIO.—*I popoli del mare.*—This is a review of the various lists of
foreign peoples. The analysis of the 87 articles belonging to the Keftiu, of which
60 are Syrian, is set aside because we do not know all the products of countries
in 1500 B.C., and artists may have made mistakes. It is just this looseness of
treatment which Wainwright exposed, by showing that the artists were consistent,
and that confusion arose by the mistakes of commentators. The conclusions
reached are that the Luku were of Lykaonia, the Shardena of Pisidia, the Pulosathu,
Zakkaru and Daanona of Lykia, and thence the two former settled on the coast of
Palestine.

ARANGIO-RUIZ, VINCENZO.—*Applicazione del diritto Giustinianeo in Egitto.*—
A discussion of the law as shown by the Byzantine papyri, published by Jean
Maspero.

CALDERINI, ARISTIDE.—*Ricerche sul regime della acque nell'Egitto greco-*
romano.—This recites the various attention to canals and water-works in Egyptian
history, beginning with the director of the inundation under Azab ; there is,
however, an earlier one under Den, and the mace-head of the Scorpion king,
pourtrayed making canals before the Ist dynasty. The reference to canals in
the Greek papyri are all collected and discussed, with a list of names of 50 canals,
and restored plans of properties along the canals.

NORSA, MEDEA.—*Un nuovo prossimo volume di paperi della Società Italiana.*—
This volume will contain 140 more Zeno papyri, and 80 of Roman and Byzantine
age.

DE FRANCISCI, PIETRO.—*Il papiro Jandanae 62.*—A Byzantine business letter
discussed with the Justinian law.

BRECCIA, E., gives a summary of the Staff of the Cairo Museum, an abstract
of Dr. Reisner's recent work, a report of museum work and accessions, and results
at Alexandria. Reviews follow, mainly on papyri. Lastly the outline of a system
of bibliography, and 361 entries classified, of recent publications.

PART 2. LUMBROSO, GIACOMO.—On the letter of Aristaeus, referring to
animals unclean among the Jews. This seems now to be accepted as genuine.

MAROI, FULVIO.—*Un documentob ilingue di* datio tutelae *dell' egitto greco-romano.*—This Greek and Latin document published by Grenfell has a formula of initials, which is here amplified thus :—d (escriptum) e (t) r(ecognitum) e (x e (xemplari) b (ibliothecae) t (abul.) s (uper) s(scripto).

NORSA, MEDEA.—*Scolii a testi non noti.*—A fragment of a text naming Neoptolemos and Achilles, with scholia.

SEGRE, ANGELO.—*Misure tolemaiche e pretolemaiche.*—A summary of what is well known on the cubit and systems of long measure. Also a statement of *Kite* (*qedet*) weight, with a few dozen weighings of examples—not a tenth of what are known ; also an outline of the capacity measures. So far this is familiar ground, but the latter part dealing with the Ptolemaic system used in papyri will be useful for that period.

CALDERINI, ARISTIDE.—(Continuation of paper on water works). A list of the embankments, and the system of maintenance, gathered from papyri.

HUNT, A. S.—*P. Mahaffy.*—A careful appreciation of the great Provost of Trinity College, Dublin.

Short papers and reviews, with a continuation of the bibliography.

New York Historical Society, Quarterly Bulletin.

In the days of Mehemet Aly, an important figure in Cairo was the American Dr. Abbott, who used his opportunities to collect many fine antiquities. This collection is now with the New York Historical Society, and Mrs. Ransom Williams has been publishing illustrations of the important objects.

January, 1918. The Ushabtis include some of the finest class, such as an inlaid coloured glass figure of a lady Săt-ta of late XVIIIth dynasty. Another fine one of limestone is in a model sarcophagus, name Auy. There are examples of queens Mehti-en-usekht and Karama Mut-em-hat; and, illustrated, Amen-em-apt, chief artist of the temple of Amen, and a treasurer Psamthek. A mummy case with ushabtis and a roll has been given in ANCIENT EGYPT, 1920, p. 18. We hope a full catalogue of the whole series will be published.

April, 1918. The head of Semenkhu-ptah, appeared in the number just quoted. A large piece of a temple scene of Sankhkara, with the upper part of figures of the king and Uazet, is of the same style as the sculptures of Menthu-hetep and Senusert I, of artistic, but not historic interest. It is clearly the same as Brugsch gives (*Thes.* 1455) as his copy is incomplete, which shows that he did not see it, owing to its being sent to America before he went to Egypt, and he only obtained a copy.

July, 1918. Bronze statuettes. A fine kneeling figure of one of the " Spirits of Pe " is 6·7 ins. high, cast *cire perdue*. A solid bronze Hathor standing, with cow's head, disc and horns, was dedicated by Ast-resh, son (?) of Penptah, about the XXVth dynasty. Figures of Bastet are cat-headed and human-headed ; a cat and kittens, and a standing Harpocrates, with a shrine before him closed by a hinged lid, are all without names. A lion-throne of Harpocrates was dedicated by Pen-khepra, son of Peda-amen. The kneeling negro bronze appears in this number of ANCIENT EGYPT. A standing bronze of a man in a kilt, head shaven, may probably be of a priest ; the arms are cast separately and dowelled on, which seems to show a rather early date.

October, 1918. Wooden statuettes of gods. The illustrations are of a jackal-headed figure 13·6 ins. high, with cavity for papyrus in the back ; an

Osiris figure 20·7 high with cavity from the base upward ; seated figures of Bastet and Osiris with cavity in throne ; an Osiris-khent-amenti figure of late date, with cavity for a dummy serpent mummy ; a large Bastet squatting on a lotus, a case for a mummy cat still in position. Of solid wooden figures there were three of Osiris and two of Isis and Horus, painted or gilded.

April, 1919. A *cire perdue* bronze of seated Horus of Roman age, was thrown aside as a defective casting, with the core in it and the mould round it. After removing more of the mould and cleaning it, the defect in the flow of metal round the back of the head is well shown as an instructive technical example.

July, 1919. There are about 320 figures of gods in the collection, of which there are illustrated a seated Harpocrates, a triple aegis of Osiris, Isis and Horus, a seated Maot in bronze ; and in blue glass a double-fronted Bes(rough) and a pantheistic Sokar-ram-hawk.

The descriptions given of these objects will spread the interest in them, and make Egyptian matters more intelligible to the public. Let us hope the whole collection will be published for the benefit of science, and not for the amusement of book collectors with the abnormal extravagance which lately besets American issues.

Bulletin of the Cleveland Museum of Art, Oct.–Nov., 1918.

The well-known High Priest of Memphis under Shashanq I, Shedes-nefer-tum dedicated a stele which is figured and described by Mrs. Williams. The central figure is Harpekroti, seated on the lotus, perhaps the earliest example of this subject. Adorations to the Memphite gods are made by Hora, *x* descended of Psheri-mut, Senkhrenf and Yufonkh.

Bulletin of the Metropolitan Museum of Art. New York.

December, 1918. An exhibition of daily life of Egyptians, by objects and drawings, shows the right museum development, and the attention to the history of civilisation, which no country but America has properly followed. The work of this museum has opened three dwelling sites lately, a town of the XX—XXIIth dynasties at Lisht, the palace-city of Amen-hetep III at Thebes, and the town of Hibis in Khargeh Oasis. We hope that all these results will be fully and quickly published.

February, 1919. A pair of seated figures from about the end of the XVIIIth dynasty was found in a tomb at Asyut. The persons are Auy and his sister Rennut. His parents were Amen-hetep and Rennut, and those of his wife Aäy and Yaă. Their figures are in relief on the back of the group, receiving offerings from a younger Auy, and a sister Hathor. It is a charming piece of best work of the age. The tomb chapel and another statue are in the local museum at Asyut.

August, 1919. A fine bowl of millefiori glass recently acquired, leads to a discussion of the nature of " murrhine " vases, and the conclusion that they were of this glass. They were said to come from Alexandria, and this points to glass work, and is considered to outweigh the statement of Pliny that murrhine vases were dug from the earth. What if *morria*, the Greek form of the name, *myrrhites* the Roman, is really from *myria*, a myriad, and the name *millefiori* carries on the same idea ?

Museum of Fine Arts Bulletin.   Boston, October, 1918.

These 15 pages give a very brief account of Dr. Reisner's discovery of the burials of the Ethiopian kings in their pyramids.   All the tombs had been robbed of their gold, but many pieces were accidentally left behind, and all the ushabtis. These bear out the view that the Ethiopians had a finer standard of work than the Egyptians of the VIIth century, which is suggested before by the sudden rise of style under the Ethiopian rule in Egypt, both in ushabtis and scarabs.

The tomb chambers were all inundated, but by diligent baling the water was reduced, and the hundreds of ushabtis recovered.   The group of pyramids is at Nuri opposite to the capital at Napata.   The tombs found include that of Tabarqa, with over a thousand ushabtis; Tanut-Ȧmen; Senkamanseken, with blue ushabtis and the chamber walls covered with the negative confession; Amtalga ; Hariotep; Astabargandu, Nȧstasan ;   Amlaman ;   and others as yet unknown.   Tombs of fifty-three queens and princesses were also found.   The lid of the granite coffin of Aspalta is copied from the wooden coffins of that age, with upright corner posts, and a small jackal and hawk standing up on it.   Foundation deposits were found at the corners of the pyramids, as in the XIIth dynasty.   When may we hope to see a full publication for reference of all Dr. Reisner's undertakings ? The little sketches are welcome enough, but that is not what is due for scientific work.

Crocodiles in Palestine.—By Prof. G. BUCHANAN GRAY.   8vo. 10 pp. (Quarterly Statement, Palestine Exp. Fund, 1920, p. 167).

The ancient, mediæval, and modern statements about crocodiles inhabiting the river Zerka are here discussed ; though the reported views of the animals were extremely brief and dubious, yet the general belief, and the production of the remains by one of the natives, seem to warrant accepting this as a habitat.

L'exode et le passage de la Mer Rouge.—By G. DARESSY.   8vo.   23 pp. Map.   1919 (*Bull. Soc. Sultanieh de Géographie, Caire*).

This is mostly dealing with Sir W. Willcocks' views as to a northern route of the Exodus.   On geographical grounds, these views are firmly contradicted, and the traditional understanding of the route is upheld.   The papyrus list of twenty places in the eastern region is detailed in support of this.

Annales du Service des Antiquités de l'Égypte.   XVII, 1917.

DARESSY, G.—*Fragments de deux cercueils de Saqqarah.*   Parts of two coffins of Ptolemaic age were brought by Mariette from Saqqareh, and have not yet been published.   That of Apollonias has parts of chapters 127, 133 of the Book of the Dead, also various figures of gods with brief legends.   The coffin of Khayf has many figures of genii with their names, scenes of the sun during the twelve hours of day alternate with the transformations of the dead in the twelve hours of night, altogether 178 subjects beside texts.

DARESSY, G.—*Statues de Mendès.*   The first is Peda...amen, son of Pama, born of Ymhetep, the second a son of the great judge Rere, the third is Tefnekht, born of Nes-nebhat.   A few geographical details here should be utilised in dealing with this nome.

DARESSY, G.—*Le lieu d'origine de l'arbre āsh.* The article debates the meaning of *Remenen*, usually identified with Lebanon. Such permutations of *l* and of *b* are stated to be unknown. As a final *n* is used for *l*, it is proposed to read the name as Ermil ; and this would be Hermil, the actual place of the forest on Lebanon.

DARESSY, G.—*Les titres du Grand Prêtre Piankh.* This priest-king seems to have had only secular titles in his youth, fanbearer, scribe, vizier, general, royal son of Kush, keeper of the southern lands, keeper of the granaries, commander-in-chief, as recorded in a letter on an ostrakon from the Tombs of the Kings.

DARESSY, G.—*Deux canopes provenant de la Moyenne-Égypte.* These were bought at Mellawi, probably from Meir, and are Persian or early Ptolemaic in date. They belonged to Pa-du-hor-mehen, son of Set-ar-bu, and give religious titles. A head of another jar was for Pedu-horen.

DARESSY, G.—*Deux grandes Statues de Ramsés II d'Héracléopolis.* South of the well-known temple is a plain, on the east of which is the mound Kom al Aqareb; in this the two statues have been found, with a granite building probably part of a temple gateway. On one block is the name of Queen Sebekneferu, on another Senusert III is named. The statues appear to have been of the XIIth dynasty, appropriated by Ramessu II, and one of them, later, by Merneptah.

DARESSY, G.—*Poids Égyptiens.* Three rough stone weights, inscribed in ink, from the Tombs of the Kings, show units of 130·2, 145·9, 139·7 grains. The first is on the daric standard, though marked *deben* like various other standards, merely meaning a unit. The other two are of the usual qedet standard. A bronze couchant bull from the Fayum marked 5, is on a standard of 137·3 grains, perhaps a very light qedet.

DARESSY, G.—*Le Roi Tèôs à Athribis.* A re-publication of Sharpe's *Egyptian Inscriptions*, pl. 43, from a copy by Harris.

DARESSY, G.—*Stèle du roi Pefnifdubast.* A limestone stele from Ehnasya is dated in the tenth year of the same king who dedicated the gold statuette (*Ehnasya*, front). It records a donation of land by Aruath, born of the royal daughter and wife Takhredt-ne-ast. The solar cartouche being Nefer-ka-ra, it is suggested that he was a vassal of Shabaka. If so, he would be the grandson of Pef-du-bast, of the time of Piankhy.

DARESSY, G.—*Le Dieu de Toukh el Malaq.* A black granite statue of a bull-headed god, with a disc and uraeus between the horns, has a prayer to Shu in the temple of Hat-amen. Tukh el Malaq is 12 kilometres from Benha, and the place Hat-amen may be Kom Atrun, 3½ kilometres west of Tukh.

DARESSY, G.—*Une Stèle de Xois.* A stele probably of Augustus dedicated by Imhetep-să-ptah.

LEGRAIN, G.—*Rapport sur les Nouveaux Travaux exécutés à Louqsor.* Oct. 1916–Mars 1917. After an account of the Thebaid under the Romans, and the martyrs of Thebes, there follows a statement of the course of work in clearing the Roman Forum of Thebes. Pedestals were found with dedications to Julian by the Governor Aurelius Ginns, A.D. 360. A triumphal arch, and a gate of the Forum, led up to the four pedestals, and the cross-road through them led into the Ramesside court at Louqsor.

DARESSY, G.—*Legende d'Ar-herus-nefer à Philae.* M. Barsanti copied this inscription in 1896. It is an adoration of the god, dated under Tiberius, and should be considered, in disentangling the later mythology.

DARESSY, G.—*La Statue No.* 35562 *du Musée du Caire.* This is the lower part of a small seated figure, with four signs like those of early date from Sinai. It was found west of Aswan, with objects of the XVIIIth dynasty, beneath a rock inscribed at that period.

DARESSY, G.—*Débris de Stèle d'Hor-em-heb.* This represents an offering to Osiris, and gives the complete titles of Horemheb.

LUCAS, A. *Efflorescent Salt of Unusual Composition.* Silky efflorescence on terracottas from the Fayum proves to be butyrate of lime. The source of the fat is unknown.

DARESSY, G.—*Inscriptions Tentyrites.* 1. Stele of Pa-haf, the first prophet of Hathor, governor, son of Nes-Min, and Ta-khred-tehuti. Nes-Min had the same office, and a notable point in the reading is that the *nesut* plant is used for writing *nes.* 2. Stele of a prophet of various gods, Her-taui, son of Pa-khred, son of Pen-khred, son of Nes-Min, the latter written as before. He went to Osiris at 70+x years, probably 90+x. 3. Stele, name lost, naming fifty religious posts held by one man, a pluralist of pluralists. 4. Feet of a black granite statue, name lost, with many religious titles. 5. Stele of about the time of Sety I, of Pa-nezem (?), engraver of Panopolis, in honour of Hathor.

DARESSY, G.—*Sarcophage Ptolémaïque d'Assiout.* Hard limestone coffin of Dut-nefer, born of Sät-bastet. A hymn of Ra entering the underworld, apparently unknown except on a wooden coffin from Qau, the variants of which are given here.

DARESSY, G.—*Rituel des Offrandes à Amenhetep I.* The upper half of a roll of papyrus, with ritual of Rameses II offering to Amenhetep I. This is mainly of interest in connection with other details of offering services ; comparison is made with those of Unas, Sety I, and Paduamenapt. Of general interest are points in the Osiris legend, as that Isis was delivered by a negro wise-woman of a feeble infant ; and in the Greek legend a negress-queen, Aso, helps Typhon to attack Horus.

DARESSY, G.—*La " Demeure Royale " en Basse-Égypte.* A lintel from El Damayin, 3 miles S.W. of Faqus, names a royal house ; it is supposed to have been brought from elsewhere, and the final conclusion is that Faqus may be the place of the palace of Sety II. The geographical discussion of this region will be useful in future research.

DARESSY, G.—*Inscriptions du Mastaba de Pepi-nofer à Edfou.* An Old Kingdom mastaba, the inscriptions of which are now in Cairo, is here published. Pepy-nefer, with a good name Mery-Ra-nefer, was a young man under Teta, passes over Aty in silence, and then became superintendent of the South, to the general benefit of the people, and especially in managing the supply of cattle from the nomad shepherds. Two limestone statues—one perfect—were also found.

ELIAS, GIRGIS.—*Inspection de l'Oasis de Dakhleh.* This records four town sites and three temples, only one of which is inscribed, with names of Nero, Vespasian, and Titus.

MUNIER, HENRI.—*Fragments des Actes du martyre da l'Apa Chnoubé.* Though in Sahidic, this martyrology refers to Bubastis, and names the canal passing through the city. There is no indication of date, but from the character of the persecution it was probably under Decius or Diocletian.

MUNIER, HENRI.—*Une Lampe Chrétienne de Karnak.* This lamp of fine red pottery is inscribed for Abba Loukios and Abba Arsenios, Martyrs. These names are known and celebrated on 16th Khoiak as Syrians who suffered at

Ekhmim. Loukios is a corruption of Eulogios. Other lamps are quoted, as one of "Alexander Archbishop," who was patriarch of Alexandria 312–328 ; one naming "Ioudas and Iakobos Apostles," from Thebes ; and one from Kom Ombo, naming "The Saint Michael."

MUNIER, HENRI.—*Note sur le Village de Hagé.* Zawyet-el-Meyitin is proposed as the site of Hagé, on the strength of that being the birthplace of the father of a man whose tomb is found at Zowyeh.

DARESSY, G.—*L'Art Tanite.* Maspero recognised five centres of sculpture, Thebes, Hermopolis, Memphis, Tanis and Sais. The importance of Tanis is attacked here. It is shown that five of the statues of Tanis all refer to Memphis, proving that Ramessu II plundered Memphis to adorn his city of Tanis. Another statue names Hathor of Maz, or Dronkeh, showing that statues were brought from as far as Siut. Many monuments came from Heliopolis. Even the well-known sphinxes were imported, as part of an exactly similar sphinx of the same size was found under the floor of a temple at El Kab. M. Daressy concludes that these sphinxes came from Upper Egypt; that some at Memphis were inscribed by Apepi, and later they were taken to Tanis by Ramessu II. The bearers of offerings of this same type are placed by M. Daressy in the XVIIIth dynasty, and refer all the peculiarities of hair and beard to their representing the king as the Nile Hapi. He confesses, however, that the type of face is that of the sphinxes, and does not try to reconcile this with the type of the kings of the New Kingdom. The later artist's trial-pieces and small work at Tanis is the same as such elsewhere. The conclusion is that there was no special school at Tanis. We have dealt with this question with illustration in the last number.

CHABAN, MOHAMMED.—*Le puits du général Ankh-uah-ab-rè-si-nit à Saqqarah.* The pit was beneath one of the pillars of the church of Jeremiah. When excavated four chambers were found at 60 feet deep opening from a hall; in this hall another pit descended 15 feet further to three more chambers, all anciently pillaged. The glazed ushabtis number 384, and give the usual chapter with name and title of general; 367 other ushabtis are for his mother Astkheb, born of Thet-Hor. The general's father was Psamthek, and his grandfather a general Nes-aoh. A few small vases and scraps were also found. Near the mouth of the pit were blocks of the XIXth dynasty, with inscriptions of Ptahemheb, Amenemhab and Ra-mes.

DARESSY, G.—*L'origine du Sceptre uas.* A stick of this form was observed to be used in hooking in bunches of dates for cutting, also used in carrying a bundle by a negro. If M. Daressy would visit Sinai he would find such a form of stick carried by all the Bedawin. The extent of the use of it should be studied.

DARESSY, G.—*Bas-reliefs d'Athribis.* Four pieces of a remarkable scene of Ramessu II, supposed to be part of the Osiris mysteries. There are figures of Hapi, standing and kneeling on running water, offering to the Bennu in a tree; Anubis preparing four canopic jars with human heads; filling a pot by a syphon from a jar (see the drawing of syphons on the Satiric Papyrus of Turin, *Auswahl,* xxiii). In a list of offerings the round-headed sistrum is distinguished from the naos-headed Hathor wand.

DARESSY, G.—*Stèle de Karnak avec textes magiques.* A text on pieces of a stele from the great pit at Karnak, differing from any on the steles of Horus: too much broken to be translated.

DARESSY, G.—*Les formes du Soleil aux différentes heures de la journée.* Six lists of the emblems and divinities associated with the different hours are here compared.

EDGAR, C. C.—*On the dating of early Ptolemaic papyri.* This deals with the complication of the Egyptian and Macedonian kalendars, and the starting point of the regnal years, from the Zeno papyri at Cairo ; but the whole of the group scattered in various collections needs to be used. . One disturbing result is that the provincial " was often five or ten days wrong when dating by the two calendars."

DARESSY, G.—*Deux naos de Qouss.* A naos in red granite of a prince, judge, and vizier Shema is of the Old Kingdom. The second naos is of Philadelphus, already published in *Description de l'Égypte*, Champollion and Lepsius.

DARESSY, G.—*Chapelle de Mentuhetep III à Dendérah.* A small chapel of Mentuhetep Neb-hap-ra was found standing in the rubbish mounds. It had suffered from salt and corrosion, and was further damaged after discovery. The king grasps a papyrus stem twined round with convolvulus, apparently representing Lower and Upper Egypt. There are added inscriptions of Merneptah.

DARESSY, G.—*Monuments d'Edfou datant du Moyen Empire.* 1. A stele of a *kher heb* of Hor-behudet, royal son, Ab, son of Iuf, born of Ab ; his wife Hor-mes, born of the royal sister Iuf and the prince of Edfu Apu. 2. Altar of offerings for the same Ab, son of Iuf, and his wife Hor-mes. 3. Stele of a *kher heb* Hora, son of Hor-any, son of Neferhetep, born of Senh ; his wife Hor-săt, daughter of the prince Abaoi, born of the princess Ast ; his son Sebekhetep. Figures bear other names, of Iuf-senb, Neb-ant, Nubududu. 4. Altar of offerings for An(y, born of) Nubdudut ; his wife Senb ; Antef-hetep ? ; and Anher. 5. Stele of Iuf. 6 and 7. Statuettes of yellow limestone of Ayni.

DARESSY, G.—*Alexandre Barsanti.* This Italian had been the handyman of the Cairo museum since 1885. Originally sculptor-modeller, he repaired and mounted objects, managed the removals of the museum, transported the heavy monuments from various parts of the country, repaired buildings, cleared buildings and carried on excavations. He organised a working staff competent for all these enterprises, and he wrote numerous accounts of work and discoveries in the *Annales du Service.* In every part of the country the people were familiar with the work of " Skander," as he was called. At fifty-nine years, such incessant and heavy work ended in a brief heart attack. The Service will hardly find another such active and efficient worker ; but we may hope that different men will be employed in these tasks of museum repairer, architect and excavator, which each require very different training and abilities.

RONZEVALLE, SEB.—*Sur le nom Égyptién du Liban.* This defends the old rendering of Remenen as Lebanon, and disputes the equivalence with Hermil proposed by M. Daressy.

RONZEVALLE, SEB.—*Notes sur les Statues No. 31919 et 35562.* A figure of red granite from Aswan with Aramaic inscription of Bel-sar-usur. On the front is a sign supposed to be the lance of Marduk. Probably of the VIth century B.C. A figure of sandstone described by M. Daressy as having a proto Semitic inscription like those of Sinai, is read as Gaash (*see* Jos. xxiv 30 ; Jud. ii 9). " There is no ground for dreaming of Asiatic writing, as M. Daressy has suggested, seduced by the theory of M. Alan Gardiner, on the monuments yet undeciphered of Sarbut el Khadim. The essay at decipherment, attempted by MM. Gardiner, Cowley and

Sayce, of the texts, which are so important for the history of the Semitic alphabet, does not appear admissible."

BOVIER-LAPIERRE, PAUL.—*Note sur le traitement métallurgique du fer aux environs d'Assouan.* De Morgan had observed limonite iron ore near the monastery of St. Simeon, but had not seen any workings. Now, up a side valley, small remains of iron smelting have been found, but fuel would always be a difficulty, and probably most of the ore was sent away.

DARESSY, G.—*Le Convent de Nahieh.* This name of the Arab treasure hunter is now identified with Ed Deir, near Abu Rowash. The ruins there cover about 50 acres ; the deir had columns of granite, marble work and mosaics.

DARESSY, G.—*La porte de Beltim.* Parts of a doorway from Kom el Ashaàr at Beltim on the extreme north of the Delta, bear a dedication to Uazet of Pu and Depu (Buto and Phragonis) ; figures of Isis and Nebhat adoring the *Zad* ; names of places seem to refer to the coffin of Osiris having landed at that site from Byblos.

TOME XVIII, 1918.

STRAZZULLI, A. ; BOVIER-LAPIERRE, P. ; RONZEVALLE, SEB.—*Rapport sur les fouilles à Eléphantine.* Previous hunters had only turned over the Persian layer in search of papyri. Now the stuff has been completely sifted over with good result, the lower layers also cleared, and all the houses planned. " The history of the fortress of Yeb would have been perhaps possible, if entirely dis-interested excavations had methodically occupied the whole site, and ended in establishing strata of uniform periods. None of the expeditions which have worked at the Kom have had such an aim." This is the criticism of the irregular and unscientific work that has gone on. Search was made for the site of the Jewish temple, unsuccessfully. On the plan (1 : 500) is noted the position of each object discovered in place ; these comprise a wooden statue of the Old Kingdom, on the rock, a prehistoric bird palette, a polished prehistoric bowl, and some tombs and other objects of later periods.

BARSANTI, ALEX.—*Rapport sur les travaux exécutés à Saqqarah,* 1912. Repairs of the Serapeum and tombs.

BARSANTI, ALEX.—*Rapports sur les travaux exécutés au Ramesseum.* Res-toration of a column, and repairs at Tombs of the Kings.

BARSANTI, ALEX.—*Rapport sur les monuments de la Nubie.* Details of small repairs needed ; the most serious causes of damage are the collisions by boats over-throwing walls and columns when submerged, and the gradual decay of the sur-faces by repeated wetting and drying, which will finally efface the sculptures—as might have been expected, in spite of all interested assurances by the Engineers.

DARESSY, G.—*Position de la Ville de Takinach.* This city of the inscription of Piankhi is identified with an irrigation basin, Diqnash, in the region of Feshn where it was expected.

DARESSY, G.—*Samtaui-Tafnekht.* The socket of a statue of this prince has been found at Ehnasya, naming him son of a royal son ; the leg of a statue was found with it. There is also a statue of him from Sais. He is named as the admiral of the fleet of Psemthek I. Two other men of this name may be descendants of the prince.

DARESSY, G.—*La localité Khent-nefer.* A lintel with this name was found at Qantir, near Faqus ; but other references place it near Gizeh, and probably the lintel has been moved in later times. It is proposed that it is the Ta-khencfretis of the Memphite nome mentioned in a Greek letter, and perhaps represented by Shenbari, a village east of Ausim.

DARESSY, G.—*La chapelle de Psimaut et Hakoris à Karnak.* The clearing of this chapel has shown the order of the dynasty to be as stated by Manetho. The inscriptions uncovered are not of importance.

DARESSY, G.—*Monuments d'Edfou datant du Moyen Empire.* 8. Stele of Iuf surnamed Ab, son of Iuf and born of Iuf. The title *kher heb* is reduced simply to the *heb* basket. 9. Stela of Ab born of Ta-akhred, naming also Adu born of Ta-urt, and his son Iuf; also Ab and his son Adu. 10. Statuette, seated on the ground with one knee up, of Adu, made by his son Iuf. 11. Part of stele of Nubu-ne-ab, daughter of the prince Hor-em-khau born of Urt; his son Sen-rau. 12. Stele of Iuf, son of Dudunub, made by his brother Horemhat.

DARESSY, G.—*Deux statues de Balansourah.* Seated figure of a prince of Nefrus, Any, made by his brother Mahu. Seated figure of Mutnefer, wife of the preceding. Nefrus was therefore at Balansureh, where one of the four sacred rams of Egypt was worshipped as Khnumu. Near to it there is also a place El Birbeh, where the temple of Nefrus probably stood.

EDGAR, C. C.—*A further note on early Ptolemaic chronology.* Continuance of the discussion with fresh material. " I think it will be found impossible to avoid the conclusion that at least two and more probably three different systems of reckoning the year were in common and rather indiscriminate use at this period."

MUNIER, HENRI.—*Un Éloge Copte de l'empereur Constantin.* " This text is a sequence of that at Strasburg, both being in the Sahidic dialect. For one finds, amid a sea of invocations and praises, the apparition of a cross to Constantine, the explanation of it by a Saint Eusignius, and allusions to the Council of Nicaea."

MUNIER, HENRI.—*Vestiges chrétiens à Tinnis.* This site was large, with many churches and mosques, baths and ovens ; Arab writers describe it with admiration. The bishop attended the councils of Epheseus and Chalcedon, A.D. 431 and 451. By 535 the sea had covered part of the land, forming the lake of Tinnis, and the extent of it increased every year. Then came the flooding of Lake Menzaleh in A.D. 554 by subsidence of the Delta. Yet the town survived till it was taken at the Arab conquest, 641. By 1193 the inhabitants were ordered to remove to Damietta. The flooding of the catacombs at Alexandria is 9 feet, and they were probably well above water-level when cut (*see Comp. Rend. Acad. Sci.,* 16 June, 1917). This gives the best information we possess on the gradual subsidence, which seems to have been continuous from 500 to 1200, though the greatest visible effect was on the breaking of the sea walls, and flooding of large areas, in 554. A few columns of granite and grey marble have been removed in 1912, and one has a figure of St. Procopios, the martyr of Caesarea in Palestine.

DARESSY, G. —*Une statue du taureau Mnévis.* A figure published by Griffith is here discussed, with reference to the chancellor Bay named on it.

DARESSY, G.—*La gazelle d'Anoukit.* On an ostrakon a gazelle is adored, with inscription of adoration of Anuket, and *nesut da hetep* to Anuket, by the royal scribe of the *ast maot,* Ahayt. This explains the quantity of mummies of gazelles in the hills near Komir, between Edfu and Esneh.

QUIBELL, J. A.—*A visit to Siwa.* This was by steamer to Mersa Matruh, and then south by military motor. An interesting account is given of the conditions of life and the physical details of the Oasis of Amon, which was conquered by the Egyptians a hundred years ago. There are some small temples of the IVth century B.C., quarries, and much-plundered tombs. The ground is too salt and damp for antiquities to be well preserved, unless gold. Worked flints are found only near the lagoons. Regarding the retrocession of the fauna, the ostrich was extinguished only two generations ago. A Siwan vocabulary and sentences are added.

DARESSY, G.—*Statue de Zedher the Saviour.* This is a black granite squatting figure, fitting in a base with an altar before it ; the whole is 37 inches high. It is covered with minute inscriptions of magical texts. The translations and description of these fill 46 pages of the Journal. This will be a principal source of texts of the steles of Horus on the crocodiles. They refer particularly to protection from scorpions and serpents. The man's father Zedher had two wives, one Ta-khredet-ahet mother of Zedher-pa-shed of the statue ; the other wife Tayhes, daughter of Pedu-ne-hor and Ta-nefert-hert, whose children by Zedher were Pa-ru-ahet, Zedher-pa-asheru, Ta-khredet-ahet, Khut, and Ta-khredet-ne-ta-asut. This is given with vast prolixity of repeating parents' names and titles every time. Evidently the object was to " make talk " on the figure. Why the name is translated " the Saviour " is not clear ; *shed* might as well be " the saved," or " the suckling," or " the reader." The latter is suggested by a reference to his doing good to men by means of the writings of this *shed* who is in Ro-sat-zatu ; also he claims that " no fault has been found before the master of the gods (Khenti-khati) in all the things that I have done according to the books." These passages seem to show his ability in reading the sacred books, and hence his title of " the reader," *pa shed.* Another person named is Uah-ab-ra son of Dun-s-pa-nefer, born of Kho-s-bast. Ro-sat-zatu, named above, was near Athribis, where this figure was found. The texts are, of course, essential in any study of magic formulæ, but are not of other interest.

EDGAR, C. C.—*Selected papyri from the archives of Zenon.* A great find of papyri of Zenon, who had been a private secretary of the State Land Agent, was found in 1914-15 at Philadelphia in the Fayum. Like most large finds it was split up, and the papyri are scattered in Cairo, Italy and various other countries, much to the hindrance of a consecutive study of them. As they date from the time of Ptolemy Philadelphos, they are the earliest large group yet found. The more valuable part of the correspondence refers to Palestine and Syria, during four years. Zenon was a Carian Greek, and some of the letters refer to affairs at Kalynda. Among other business we find that he was away east of Jordan, where he bought a young slave girl for 50 drachmae, and several other papyri mention shipping slaves from Syria to Egypt. Another matter was trying to get money from a Jew named Ieddon, which only resulted in insults and blows. There is a description of difficulties officially in getting in old gold for coinage. Gold plate was offered to be coined, but there was no regulation of its value.

DARESSY, G.—*Inscriptions Tentyrites.* 6. Stele of Padu-hor-sam-taui who in his 80th year went to Osiris. He was wise in the sacred writings, and those which covered the wall of Heliopolis, and the wisdom of Safkhet are named. 7. Part of a stele naming Antefa, a governor of the South, in the XIIth dynasty. 8. Black granite statue of Menkh-ne-ra, son of Pa-ashem, who was general of the southern nomes, and a great pluralist in religious offices. At some time the base has been changed, as it has a demotic inscription naming the "great statue of Kirgis the strategos " (*see* ANCIENT EGYPT, 1917, p. 132). 9. A group of two nude figures side by side has the limbs hidden by the coils of two serpents ; one is a child, Horus-Apollo, the other a woman representing the moon.

GAUTHIER, H.—*Les stèles de l'an III de Taharqa.* Of the stele at Cairo a duplicate has been seen by Mr. Offord in London.

DARESSY, G.—*Une Mesure Égyptienne de* 20 *hin.* This has been put together from fragments found in the pit of Karnak. It has the name of Tehutmes III, but no mark of quantity. From the form it appears to be a standard measure of 40 hins, not 20 as described. It is estimated to have contained 1,231 cubic inches, giving a hin of 30·8 inches. Other marked examples vary from 25·0 to 33·0 for the hin. These are only secondary markings on vases made for other purposes. The best mean value is 29·2 cubic inches.

CHAABAN, MOHAMMED and DARESSY, G.—*Rapport sur la découverte de la tombe d'un Mnévis de Ramsès II.* An interesting discovery of an unopened burial, largely decomposed, however, by water. To the north of Heliopolis the stone roof of the tomb chamber was found 20 inches under the surface. Two walls could be traced on the surface ; these probably belong to the court or chapel for the worship of the bull, as the steles which were placed in the chapel were found sunk outside the walls of the tomb, facing inward, so the chapel inside must have been larger than the tomb outside, or 25 feet wide. The tomb is 23 × 16 feet outside, the chamber 207 × 121 inches, or 10 × 6 cubits. The walls are roughly built, and have been repaired in parts, as the door jamb. The doorway is still blocked as originally. The stones used by Ramessu II had come from a building of Tut-onkh-amen, re-used by Horemheb. Strangely, the figures of Amen and Khousu had been erased ; if the name of Tut-onkh-amen is not placed over that of an earlier king, this would show a triple conversion of that king. There were two sets of canopic jars, the order of which is usual, but turned with north in the place of east (*Riqqeh*, 31). The sculptured scenes on the burial chamber walls are of Ramessu II offering to various gods, and the spirits of Buto and Nekhen. Two limestone ushabtis were found 8·6 inches high, parts of bronze fittings of the funeral couch, which is figured in a shrine on the walls, and various small amulets and pottery.

DARESSY, G.—*La tombe du Mnévis de Ramsès VII.* This tomb is nearly identical with that under Ramsès II (*Rec.*, xxv 29). The scenes are here re-described with the assistance of the previous tomb.

DARESSY, G.—*Un décret d'Amon en faveur d'Osiris.* This is a papyrus of the Persian age. It is analogous to the decrees of Amen in favour of Nesi-khonsu and Panezem. The assumptions of the high priests could not go beyond this : " Speech of Amen Ra...' I divinise the august soul of Osiris Un-nefer, I give well-being to his body in Kher-neter, I preserve his body, I divinise his mummy.' " This ! to Osiris, god of the dead. M. Daressy politely supposes that this only referred to a dead man and his family under the names of Osiris and his family. There is, however, no hint of any human being concerned in this.

EDGAR, C. C.—*Selected papyri from the archives of Zenon.* The system of dating the Macedonian year is still obscure. The letters here published do not seem to be of intrinsic interest, but will be valuable for combining with the rest of the group in restoring a full view of official life day by day. The details are technical matters of the duties and relations of officials.

GAUTHIER, HENRI.—*Les " Fils royaux de Ramsès."* This is a study of the various descendants of the Ramessides. The persons and sources discussed are as in Petrie, *History* iii, 242, except the last.

(1) Nemarth, son of the daughter of the great chief of the mountains, Pa-nreshens. Further, he is said to be a royal son of Sheshenq Meramen, presumably Sheshenq I. This name has been left unexplained, but a possibility should be here noted : *nr* is the Egyptian mode of writing *l*, so the name is " The Leshenes," which is fairly equivalent to Lissaenos, " the man of Lissos," that is, probably, Lissos in Crete. As to being a royal son of Sheshenq, it seems incredible that if Sheshenq had married his mother the royal descent should not appear on his statue at Miramar, nor on his bracelets in the British Museum, but only on his statue in Cairo. This seems to show that he was a royal son by adoption or officially, like the " royal son of Kush " and others. If we accept this, we get a light on the frequent title in the XXIInd dynasty, " Great prince of the mountains " ; it referred to any foreigner from a hill country, and perhaps was predominantly Cretan.

(2) Zed-hor-auf-onkh, son of the royal daughter Zed-anub-es-onkh, whose plaque was made by Sheshenq I.

(3) Zed-ptah-auf-onkh, known by mummy, coffins, boxes, ushabti and papyrus, from his burial at Deir el Bahri, in the 10th or 11th year of Sheshenq I.

(4) Uasarken (?), high priest of Amen, in the 28th year of Sheshenq III, on a stele in Berlin.

(5) Auuapuat, with a foreign sign after the name, on a fragment of alabaster vase in Cairo museum.

(6) Pa-shed-bastet, chief of the Mahasu, on a stele from Abydos, at University College, London, dated in the 36th year of Uasarken I. M. Gauthier concludes he is not the same as Pa-shed-bastet, son of Sheshenq III.

(7) Ast-(em)-kheb on a stele under Uasarken I, Paris, apparently a woman.
The position is accepted that these were descendants of the Ramesside family.

GAUTHIER, HENRI.—*Trois vizirs du Moyen Empire.* Res-senbu and his brother Ymeru were both viziers, and sons of the vizier Onkhu. Onkhu married Merryt, daughter of Hentpu. Ymeru had a sister Senbhenas, who married Upuat-hetep, son of Khnumu-hetep and Tahent. Upuat-hetep's children were Khnumu-hetep, Neshmet-hetept, Khensu and Amen-hetep. The question is whether Onkhu, vizier under Sebek-hetep III, is the same as Onkhu, vizier under Khenzer; either they were different, or Khenzer was not placed in the Turin papyrus. Another vizier, Hennu, has been omitted in A. Weil's *Veziere*, as well as Res-senbu.

DARESSY, G.—*Rapport sur le déblaiement des tombes 6 et 9 de Biban el Molouk.* An unpublished report of 1888, naming some small objects found, and the ostraka, since published in the Cairo catalogue.

DARESSY, G.—*Antiquités trouvées à Fostat.* In clearances at Old Cairo there have been found (1) part of the base of a diorite statue of Khafra, doubtless from the pyramid temples ; (2) part of a black granite obelisk of Ramessu II ;

(3) a Ptolemaic basalt torso of Senti, son of Pen-sebek ; (4) part of a Coptic epitaph.

DARESSY, G.—*L'emplacement de la ville de Benna.* This town, which is given in a Coptic list of bishoprics, as part-successor of Leontopolis, is to be sought near Tell Moqdam. It is named by Maqrizi as Benu, and though destroyed before 1375, the name remains in Binnai, an irrigation basin.

DARESSY, G.—*Une statue de Deir el Chelouit.* Near this little temple, south of Medinet Habu, a black and red granite statue was found of the XIXth dynasty, of Seta, a prince, royal sealer, and treasurer.

MUNIER, HENRI.—*Deux recettes médicales Coptes.* Written on the back of an Arabic paper letter. The purpose is not stated, so they seem to be a physician's prescriptions.

NOTES AND NEWS.

The work of the British School in Egypt began this season early in November when Mr. and Mrs. Brunton went to Lahun to search beneath the Queen's pyramid and royal mastabas, to which no entrance had yet been found. Tunnels have now been run diagonally beneath the pyramid and in other directions, so far without result. Mr. West joined in this work.

The main party, consisting of Major Hynes, Mr. Miller, Mr. Neilson and Mons. Bach with the Director and Mrs. Petrie, assembled at Ghurob at the beginning of December. During a fortnight the work there showed how little now remains to be done at that site. A black steatite cylinder of Pypy of the 1st dynasty, some bowls of the IIIrd dynasty, a few burials of the XIXth with usual alabaster and pottery, and some granaries with protective amulets, were all that was found. Half a dozen graves at Zeribah, four miles south, proved to be of XXIInd dynasty, all plundered.

The camp was then formed at the great cemetery of Herakleopolis. This has been largely cleared by various authorised and unauthorised diggers, but no plan or details are published. A systematic working of it has now been started, and remains of the Ist, IIIrd, IXth, and XIXth dynasties are already in hand. The great tombs have several chambers on different levels, and seem to have been for families. One has yielded parts of sarcophagi, steles, figures, canopics and ushabtis of the two viziers, Parahetep and Rahetep his son, under Ramessu II ; another of the same age is of the keeper of the cavalry Pahonneter ; a man of the same office and name, buried at Hibeh under Ramessu III, was probably his grandson. Sarcophagi of red granite are very massive and coarse ; one of black granite—of which parts remain—was thin and finely carved. This excavation continues the regular clearance of the western side of the Nile, southward from Dahshur ; in such systematic work the fat and the lean must be accepted as they come, but the historic importance of the city here promises to repay work on its cemetery.

Of other excavations there is little news yet to hand, but the excavations for New York continue under Mr. Winlock at Thebes, and also at Lisht under Mr. Mace.

ERRATUM. In ANCIENT EGYPT, 1920, p. 105, 9 lines from botttom, *for* HBYROS, *read* HYKSOS.

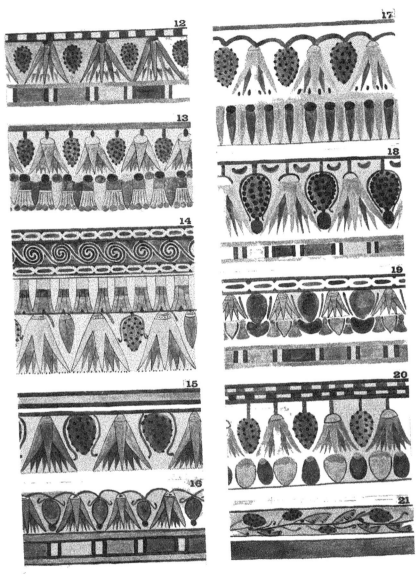

BORDERS OF THEBAN TOMB-PAINTINGS.
LOTUS FLOWERS AND BUNCHES OF GRAPES.

COLORS IN ORDER OF TINT ; YELLOW, GREEN, BLUE, RED, BLACK.

1420—1330 B.C.

TEHUTMES IV TO HEREMHEB.

ANCIENT EGYPT.

THE BRITISH SCHOOL OF ARCHAEOLOGY IN EGYPT.

THE work of the British School has been moving southward, in the course of a systematic clearing of the western bank of the Nile valley. At Lahun the search beneath the small pyramid of the queen of Senusert II occupied Mr. Brunton most of the season. Tunnels were cut at two levels, in the most likely strata, running diagonally and to the faces, but no chambers or passages were found. It seems, therefore, as if the burials were all on the south side, and the small pyramid and mastabas on the north were cenotaphs. A few remaining tombs were also cleared at Lahun.

While this was going on, the rest of the party were finally searching the cemetery of Ghurob, where a few more graves were found, including some of the earlier dynasties, one having a primitive black cylinder of a man named Pypy. The other graves were of the XIXth dynasty. Several granaries were found, some of which had blue glazed amulets put in them for protection. One rare find was a perfect wooden sickle. This site, worked at by various diggers for over thirty years, seems to be practically exhausted.

The main camp then moved south to the cemetery of Herakleopolis, now Ehnasya, which had been wrecked anciently, and worked by Dr. Naville and several later searchers, but without giving plans or record. There was, however, much to be done by careful and complete clearance, which well rewarded us, and after this it may be regarded as exhausted. The site has a remarkable history. In the geologic past the Nile had found an exit to the Fayum about ten miles south of the Lahun entrance. The strata collapsed into the worn channel, and lie tilted up at 45 degrees. This break in the ring of the Fayum basin gave later an easy access from the west into the Nile valley. Through this gap various waves of Libyans have come, the best known of which are the Libyan chiefs of Herakleopolis in the XXIInd dynasty. Doubtless that city was founded at first by such an invasion, which accounts for its unusual position, far from the Nile. In recent times it is likewise the seat of a large and unruly Libyan invasion, from Tunis and the Oases. Looking at the flatness of the desert opposite to Herakleopolis, it seems likely that the two miles of mud now between the Bahr Yusuf and the desert have only recently been flooded, and probably the canal ran along the old desert edge, and the city was founded on the opposite bank. This would have been in prehistoric times, as it is a city of the earliest class, having the worship of the Corn Osiris (*Historical Studies*, II, pl. ix). The first cemetery is therefore probably below the present cultivation.

Upon the desert the oldest graves are of the Ist dynasty. Of the IInd dynasty there are many, including large tombs with stairways, sometimes turning at right angles. A few of these were found intact, with characteristic stone vases. The objects found will be described in the next part of this journal, as, owing to robbery of some boxes on the Egyptian railway last year, it is undesirable to publish objects until in England.

The great period of the cemetery began in the VIth dynasty, with the tombs of some nobles, and continues till a maximum was reached about the IXth dynasty, of which age there were hundreds of graves. They contained principally pottery, and in many instances the bodies had been spitefully burnt in the graves or entirely removed. This points to an extreme hatred of these people by later residents, and indicates that they were foreigners. No trace was found of the burials of the great men of the IXth dynasty which centred on Herakleopolis. It is certain that no large group of their tombs can have escaped us there, and it seems as if they lay in some other district. Strange to say, the flourishing age of the XIIth dynasty, so abundantly active at Lahun, has not left a single grave that can be dated by any remains. The site seems to have been deserted at that age.

The XVIIIth dynasty began again here about the time of Tehutmes I or II, and from that age on to Ramessu II there were frequent and rich burials. Of these some were left of fine quality. One of the earlier tomb chapels was complete, with a large painted stele of the finest work, representing four generations of the family ; before it was an altar inscribed, and in front of that a kneeling figure with a tablet of adoration. The whole group is now in the Cairo museum. The greatest tomb was that of the two viziers of Ramessu II, Parahetep and Rahetep. It had originally a large chapel on the 'surface, of which pieces were found widely scattered and reused. The various statues and steles of the family had been defaced, broken up, and partly thrown down into the tomb. The extensive family of these nobles (see *Student's History*, III, 90) has had a few more names added to it from these monuments.

Though the XXIInd dynasty generals were so largely of Herakleopolite titles, not a single fine burial of that age was found. This suggests that their connection was purely titular, like our Prince of Wales, and not of local authority. Only a few of the usual coffins were found, with illiterate inscriptions belonging to the period. The late tombs of Roman age were very poor, and some dozens that were worked yielded nothing. The surprise of this site is the prominence of the IInd dynasty, and the deficiency of the XXIInd.

The number of well-dated skeletons gave opportunity to compare them with those of sites on either side, at Medum, Tarkhan and Deshasheh. The main results are that the IInd dynasty heads were longer and narrower than in the VIth. Those of the VIth dynasty were larger in all ways than skulls of other ages and places, perhaps owing to their being those of nobles. In the IXth dynasty the heads diminished, but yet were larger than others of that age. The limb bones are larger in the IXth dynasty than in any other time or place ; the leg 3 mm. longer than at Deshasheh, 7 mm. longer than at Tarkhan ; the arm over 4 mm. longer than at other sites. The people of the IXth dynasty were therefore distinctly larger than the Egyptians elsewhere, in head and in limbs.

The party of workers this year consisted of Major Hynes, Mr. Neilson, M. Bach, Mr. Miller, with the Director and Mrs. Petrie. Later Mr. West came over from Mr. Brunton's work, which he had assisted, and joined us for a short time. Subsequently Mr. Brunton took over the excavation at Herakleopolis, and Mrs. Brunton has taken a large part in the drawing of objects. The exhibition will, it is hoped, be held during the four weeks of July, 4th to 30th, at University College, London.

W. M. Flinders Petrie.

ORIGINS OF SOME SIGNS.

THE variants in the form of the ḤN sign show that the root-meaning of the word is " Young, youth." The sign represents the young leaves or flower-buds of a plant ; though the species of plant varies, the essential point is never forgotten. The earliest example (Fig. 1) is from the tomb of Rahotep at Medum, and represents the sprout of a marsh plant ; similar plants occur in the tomb of Nefermaat (Fig. 2) the slight variations being due to the drawing by different artists. The open flower, of which the hieroglyph represents the bud, is seen on the head of the boatman (Fig. 3), also from the tomb of Nefermaat. This example shows that the plant was a flowering rush, perhaps *Juncus acutus*. Figs. 1, 2 and 3 are taken from Prof. Petrie's original facsimile drawings, and are reproduced half-size. Figs. 4 and 5 appear to me to be the same plant drawn with a good deal of artistic licence ; the tombs at Meir show that the artist's sense of the dramatic often overpowered his sense of truth, both in the scenes and in the hieroglyphs, and these two examples seem to be a case in point. Fig. 6 is another flowering rush, *Juncus effusus*, coming into blossom ; it appears to be a form of the sign used in the XIIth dynasty, for it occurs both at Beni Hasan and at Meir ; I am not aware of its use at any other period. Figs. 7 and 8 represent the young sprouts of a succulent plant such as grows after rain in the desert at Saqqara, near the tombs in which it is represented ; it is probably a *Zygophyllum*. Figs. 9–13 are clearly representations of one species of plant, but without sufficient definition for accurate identification. Fig. 9 may be one of the *compositae*, but it also suggests *Cakile maritima*. This is the form which was in common use as a hieroglyph, and became gradually conventionalised ; Fig. 12 shows the usual hieroglyph of the XVIIIth dynasty, and 13 a slightly varied form of the XIXth dynasty.

Neith has two emblems ; one is certainly two arrows across a shield, and many suggestions have been made as to the meaning of the other. The most usual explanation is that it represents a shuttle, thus connecting the goddess with weaving. But the shape of the emblem shows that it cannot be a shuttle. A shuttle must of necessity taper at each end in order to pass freely between the warp threads, whereas the emblem shows two projections curving outwards at each end. Such an object, if thrown like a shuttle between threads, would inevitably catch in the threads and entangle and break them. Again, there is no proof that the shuttle was invented so early in the history of Egypt. The use of the shuttle presupposes some mechanical method of alternating all the warp threads at once ; the earliest process of weaving was by laboriously passing a ball of thread in and out of the warp threads by hand. This method was continued even after the invention of the shuttle, as the width of the cloth shows ; the cast of a hand-thrown shuttle is at most 4 ft., while the cloth in the tomb of the Two Brothers in the Middle Kingdom was 9 ft. wide ; this must have been made by the slow and laborious method of passing the thread in and out by hand, but the skill shown proves that the weaver was well accustomed to the process. The emblem in question then is not a shuttle ; the hieroglyphs of the Old Kingdom, which give the sign in detail, show that it represents two objects, curved sharply at each end and lashed back to back in a kind of case. The only object which at all resembles these things in shape is a bow of the type of Fig. 15, which

C 2

is itself a stylised form of the bow carried by the men in the Hunters' palette, and is carved on the scorpion vase of Hierakonpolis (Fig. 16). The curious folding of the bow-string in the Hierakonpolis example seems to indicate that the material was a strip of thick leather, which became " goffered " by pulling. Prof. Petrie, however, suggests that the bow-string has had beads threaded on it to be used as a primitive musical instrument, a kind of early sistrum for rhythmic rattling. Both emblems of the goddess are therefore weapons of war ; the one is the crossed arrows and shield, the other the two bows.

The 𓊋-sign occurs as early as the Ist dynasty, where it appears on a stela from the Royal Tombs (Fig. 17). It appears to represent a bead tassel, with a single tie. This is in accordance with later forms of the sign, and also with representations of the actual object. The sign as a phonogram reads *āpr* 𓂝𓊪𓂋 , and means, " To equip, to provide." The actual object was an ornament or tassel of beads which was attached to the two ends of the bead-collar and hung down the back of the wearer ; as an ornament it is called *mānkht* 𓆤 𓊽 𓈖𓐍𓏏 .

In the IIIrd dynasty the form shows two ties (Fig. 18), but is without the characteristic pendant beads ; this example is from the monolithic granite false-door in the tomb of the Sheikh el Beled at Saqqara. In the Old Kingdom the actual object is often represented, and always among the jewellery with the neck-laces (Figs. 19, 20) ; on Middle Kingdom coffins (Figs. 21–24), it occurs beside the necklaces in the representations of the property of the deceased, each necklace having an *āper* matching it in colour and material; if the necklace has hawk-head or plain semi-circular terminals, the *āper* has the same (Figs. 23, 24), this may account for the third hawk-head found in the tomb of King Hor at Dahshur (de Morgan *Dahshur*, p. 100) ; two of the hawk-heads were obviously the terminals of the necklace, and de Morgan supposed the third to be the top of the flagellum, though he acknowledges that the supposition is doubtful. In the same tomb there was a model of a collar with plain terminals, and a model *āper* in gilded wood, also with a plain terminal (p. 100). In the tomb of Nub-hetep there was again a third hawk-head terminal, which must have belonged to the hawk-head necklace of the princess (p. 114). On statues of the Middle Kingdom the *āper* is represented with plain terminals (Figs. 25–31) ; the greater number of examples on both coffins and statues are finished with a row of pear-shaped pendant beads, but Figs. 30, 31 have hanging lotus-blossoms instead. Fig. 32 is from the remarkable cartonnage found at Beni Hasan, probably of the early XVIIIth dynasty. Later in the dynasty the hieroglyphic sign (Fig. 33), shows a reversion to the form with a single tie, in use in the Middle Kingdom (compare Fig. 21). Fig. 34 from the " tombeau des graveurs " at Thebes, shows lotus-blossom terminals with a lotus-blossom *āper* to match. The long narrow type of the actual object, as represented in the Old Kingdom, is found again in the example from Abydos (Fig. 35), where King Sety is offering it to Ptah. Fig. 36 is one of the amulets in the list at Dendereh. On comparing it with Fig. 22, it is seen that the type has persisted from the XIIth dynasty to the Ptolemaic era. Figs. 37–40 are from bronze figures of gods in the collection at University College ; only one, Fig. 37, has the characteristic form of the *āper*, the others possibly represent some other kind of ornament.

The actual method of attaching the *āper* to the collar is not easy to understand. In Figs. 22 and 36 the strings are arranged in loops through which perhaps

the strings of the necklace were passed, but the method of making the loops is not shown. Fig. 27 shows in detail what is presumably a reef-knot with the ends of two strings hanging down; this can only represent an instance of the *áper* with a loop at the top, either made of its own string, or being actually part of the terminal. The strings of both the necklace and the *áper* are made of the threads on which the beads are strung; the terminal is pierced with several holes along the base which unite in one hole at the top. The threads on issuing from the top of the terminal are twisted together; in the case of the *áper*, they form sometimes one string, sometimes two. The method of attachment in Fig. 28 is

C 3

inexplicable, the loop at the top serving no purpose whatever. Figs. 41–43 show the *āper* in use ; Thothmes III as Osiris wears an *āper* with a long tie ; a short-stringed *āper*, as long as the collar is wide, is worn by the Horus-hawk at Abydos (Fig. 41).

The *āper* is generally found among the ornaments of men, very rarely among those of the women. This is probably on account of its position on the person ; the woman's hair or long wig would cover it, while on a man it would be easily visible. In early times it seems to have been worn only by nobles of high rank ; in and after the New Kingdom it appears to have been confined to a few gods and to the King as god.

Its amuletic quality is indicated by its dedication to Hathor, who is called at Dendereh ▽ Lady of the Āper (Brugsch, Wtb. 182). As an amulet it was for protecting the wearer from the assaults of spirit-foes, and was part of the great spiritual armoury by which evil demons were repelled and routed. With a powerful amulet placed between the shoulder-blades—one of the most unprotected parts of the body—the wearer would be fully " equipped " against unseen and ghostly enemies. For this reason it survived as a small amulet, generally carved in hard stone, down to the Ptolemaic period.

The actual object made in beads has never been found, but at the Ramesseum a model *āper* was found (Fig. 44). It is made of leather embossed to represent beadwork, and was attached to a leather *menat* and leather braces. Though this dates only to the XXIInd dynasty, the use of the *āper* and braces together goes back to the Old Kingdom. Fig. 45 shows a procession of bearers of offerings, each carrying a jar and a personal ornament ; the first holds a necklace, the second an *āper*, and the third has the wide beadwork braces on his arm with the strings hanging down. Fig. 20, from the same tomb, shows a man in full dress wearing a necklace and braces, and standing beside tables loaded with beadwork ; on the lower table are laid a collar, an *āper*, and two braces.

M. A. MURRAY.

THEBAN BORDERS OF LOTUS AND GRAPES.

(See Frontispiece.)

A VERY popular border was a design of lotus flowers and bunches of grapes, which is to be seen in twelve tombs (Nos. 8, 38, 49, 64, 74, 75, 90, 147, 151, 175, 181 and 249 ; for names see *Ancient Egypt*, 1920, p. 122). The simplest form is found in tomb 175 (Fig. 12), where open lotus flowers alternate with bunches of grapes, the latter appearing to be suspended in mid-air. On the western walls of tombs 38, 175 and 249 there are very similar borders, but it is probable that they are unfinished, and that it was intended to complete the stems, as there is a blank space left above the flowers and fruit. On the whole this design, as illustrated in Fig. 12, is very stiff and uninteresting.

It was somewhat improved, however, in tombs 8, 74, 75, 151 and 249 (Figs. 14, 15) by the addition of tendrils to the bunches of grapes. A further addition, and what appears to be an attempt to improve on Nature, is a series of looped stems joining the lotus flowers and clusters of grapes together, as may be seen in tombs 49, 90, 151 and 181 (Figs. 16, 17).

The borders of this type in tombs 151, 181 and 249 differ from the others in having a red spot just below the tip of each grape cluster. As the bunches of grapes in tomb 181 do not show the spots which usually serve to represent the separate grapes, it has been suggested that it was really intended to represent cornflowers, but the presence of the tendrils hanging down on either side of the bunches makes any question as to whether or not grapes are here represented quite superfluous. The red spot below each grape cluster in tomb 249 has a black base, and is probably an attempt to represent a poppy petal (Fig. 18).

It will be noticed that in tombs 8 and 90 (Figs. 13, 14, 17) there is a border of another design either above or below the floral border, a circumstance which will be more fully dealt with later in this section.

The floral border in tomb 8 (Fig. 14) has the additional feature of lotus buds alternating with the lotus flowers and grape clusters, and is the only example at present known in the necropolis, of lotus buds occurring in conjunction with both lotus flowers and grapes. The end of a stem showing on the right of the calyx of each flower is also only to be seen in this tomb. The whorl pattern between two rows of tail-edging ornament above this border is curious, but there is some doubt as to whether it belongs to the ornamentation of the border proper or to that of the barrel-vaulted roof.

In tomb 64 (Fig. 19) there is a border made up of a row of crescent-shaped ornaments, which may represent lotus leaves, alternating with mandrake fruit and cornflowers (?) below a row of lotus flowers and grape clusters. The cornflower is probably the species *Centaurea depressa*, Bieb., now only found in Asia Minor, the Caucasus, and neighbouring countries. This species has been found in ancient wreaths and garlands of the XVIIIth and XXth dynasties and again in the Fayum in the Graeco-Roman period. See article by Percy E. Newberry in *Proc. Bibl. Arch.*, May, 1900.

The same crescent-shaped ornament, but without the mandrake fruit, is to be found in tombs 147, 151 and 249 (Fig. 18). The crescents form the upper part of the frieze in the inner chamber of tomb 249 and the outer chamber of tomb 147, while in the shrine of tomb 249 they occur both above and below the

C 4

other components of the border. In tomb 151 (one wall) they form the lower portion of the border.

There is an auxiliary band of alternate mandrake fruit and rounded red objects, which may perhaps be identified as poppy flowers or petals, to be seen in the frieze in the inner chamber of tomb 151, and the whole frieze is further widened by two rows of chequers in red and black from which the lotus flowers and grapes depend (Fig. 20).

The design on part of the north-eastern and north-western walls of tomb 151 differs somewhat from that on the remaining walls. The grape clusters have no tendrils, and are connected by looped red stems with the lotus flowers on either side of them, instead of hanging down from straight stems as shown in the previons illustration (Fig. 20). A narrow band of yellow on which is placed a row of crescent-shaped objects, again suggesting lotus leaves, also replaces the mandrake fruit and poppy petals, and is repeated above the frieze between it and the chequer bands.

Tomb 147 has an effective border in its inner chamber which is, however, too much blackened to be copied. It is composed of the usual alternate lotus flowers and grape clusters suspended by short red stems from a single line of black chequers on a yellow ground, and between the flowers and bunches of grapes there is a series of red objects which are practically the same in form as those in tomb 151. Below the main design is a row of yellow mandrake fruit on a blue ground, and above the single band of chequers a green-margined border.

A very free treatment of grape clusters and vine-leaves as a running pattern is to be seen in tombs 149 and 259 (Fig. 21) ; in the former tomb, on the northern wall of the outer chamber above the Hathor and Anubis frieze. In tomb 259 it is found above a Kheker frieze on the north-eastern wall at the northern end of the tomb. This design, therefore, can hardly be accepted as being a border in the strict sense, for it was merely used to fill up a vacant space between the border proper and the ceiling of the tomb. In both tombs the design is painted on a yellow ground and forms a very distinctive ornamentation, all the more to be valued on account of its extreme rarity in the necropolis. There is also a very similar border, but coarsely executed, on the eastern wall of the inner chamber of an unnumbered tomb a little to the west of tomb 154, which belonged to the XIXth or XXth dynasty. The illustration is taken from the design in tomb 259 (Fig. 21), which is practically identical with that found in tomb 149, except that the latter is more roughly painted and has rather more angular stems. Both tombs are of late date, the former belonging to the period of Haremheb and the latter to the XIXth or XXth dynasty. E. MACKAY.

[If we look at the historical order of these borders, the earliest is Fig. 15 of Zenuni, under Tehutmes IV, a simple and complete design. Similar, though obviously unfinished, is Fig. 12, of Tehutmes IV (?). Next come the group with a flower and seed border, Figs. 18, 19, 20 ; of these 19 is attributed to Tehutmes IV, but as Heqerheh was tutor to Amenhetep III, it is likely that his tomb was not decorated till Amenhetep III. Figs. 18 and 20 are dated to Tehutmes IV (?) ; but the flower and seed borders are scarcely as early as that, and seem to belong to the naturalistic schools of Amenhetep III. The borders with rows of bouquets (Figs. 13, 14) are obviously later ; of these 14 and 17 are of Amenhetep III, and 18 probably the same date. The loops connecting the lotus flowers in Fig. 17 are developed further in Fig. 16, which is dated to late XVIIIth dynasty, and is obviously degraded in its Pompeian style.   Lastly, the old design vanishes under the influence of Akhenaten's realism, and Fig. 21 shows a degraded running border, probably of the time of Heremheb, which continued in other examples into the XIXth or XXth dynasties.   Thus there is a consistent development in these borders, which ran through all their changes in about a century.—F.P.]

FRIEZES OF LOTUS FLOWERS AND BUNCHES OF GRAPES.

1. WITHOUT TENDRILS OR STEMS; PLATE 12

Tomb 38. Northern wall of western end of outer chamber. Tuthmosis IV.
  " 175. Northern, southern and eastern walls. " "(?).
  " 249. Western wall of outer chamber. " " ".

2. WITH STRAIGHT STEMS ONLY; PLATE 13

Tomb 90. Western end of southern wall. Amenophis III.

3. WITH TENDRILS; PLATE 14 15

Tomb   8. Side walls of vaulted chamber. Amenophis III(?).
  " 74. Southern end wall of outer chamber. Tuthmosis IV.
  " 75. Right hand jamb of entrance to inner chamber. " "
  " 151. South-eastern wall of north-eastern end of inner chamber. " "(?).

4. WITH LOOPED STEMS CONNECTING FLOWERS AND GRAPES; PLATE 16 17

Tomb 49. Inner chamber. Early XIXth. dynasty(?).
  " 90. Eastern end wall and western end of Southern wall. Amenophis III.
  " 151. North-western wall of inner chamber. Tuthmosis IV(?).
  " 175. Western wall. " " "
  " 181. All walls of outer chamber. Late XVIIIth. dynasty.

5. WITH LOTUS LEAVES(?); PLATE 18

Tomb 147. Above false door at southern end of outer chamber. Tuthmosis IV(?).
  " 151. North-western wall of inner chamber. " " "
  " 249. Inner chamber and shrine. " " "

6. WITH LOTUS LEAVES(?), MANDRAKE FRUIT AND CORNFLOWERS(?); PLATE 19

Tomb 64. Northern end of outer chamber. Tuthmosis IV.

7. WITH POPPY PETALS AND MANDRAKE FRUIT; PLATE 20

Tomb 147. Inner chamber. Tuthmosis IV(?).
  " 151. South-eastern wall of inner chamber. " " "

8. WITH POPPY PETALS(?) AT BASE OF THE FRUIT; PLATE 16 18

Tomb 181. Outer chamber. Late XVIIIth. dynasty.
  " 151. North-eastern end of north-western wall of inner chamber. Tuthmosis IV(?).
  " 249. Inner chamber and shrine. " " "

9. WITH AUXILIARY PETAL BAND; PLATE 14 17

Tomb   8. Side walls of vaulted chamber. Amenophis III(?).
  " 90. Ends of southern wall of outer chamber. " " "

10. RUNNING DECORATION OF GRAPE CLUSTERS AND VINE LEAVES; PLATE 21

Tomb 149. Northern end wall of outer chamber. XIXth.-XXth. dynasties.
  " 259. North-eastern wall of chamber. Haremhab(?).
  " (?). (a little west of Tomb 154). Eastern wall of inner chamber. XIXth.-XXth. dynasties.

A HEAD OF A BARBARIAN FROM EGYPT.

THE marble head represented in the accompanying plate was brought from Alexandria by Mr. Alfred E. Rand, now a student in the Architectural Department at University College, who was serving in Egypt during the war. The following facts as to its discovery are kindly supplied by him ; we also have to thank him for his permission to publish the head here. " The head was found in sandy soil, about 10 feet deep, whilst a trench was being excavated in connection with an ammunition dump at Mex—a short distance from Alexandria. As far as I could ascertain no further portions were discovered."

There appears then to be no external evidence as to the nature of the monument or other work of sculpture from which the head has come ; but there are some indications in the head itself. It is about half life-size. A thick iron cramp is fixed by lead into a hole in the top of the crown, and must have served to attach the figure to a background or to a projecting cornice. The left side of the head is only roughly blocked out. It is therefore clear that the head must have been part of a figure in high relief. Its portrait character is obvious, and it most probably comes from a tombstone ; many tombs of Hellenistic or Roman date have been found in this region.

The head itself is in several ways remarkable, chiefly for its heavy square shape and the peculiar treatment of the moustache. This is, so far as my own observation and memory goes, unique in an ancient work of sculpture. I shall be very grateful if any reader can point out a similar instance. It is true that Gauls and other " barbarians " often wear a moustache only, the rest of the face being shaved. But these moustaches are of a quite different character. They are usually long and drooping, as in the famous " Dying Gaul " and the Ludovisi group. Here the moustache is short and bushy, and apparently brushed up at the ends in a way familiar to us in modern Germans and in some Indian races. It therefore affords us no definite clue as to the racial character of the subject. The shape of the head itself, however, appears distinctive, and indicates the assignment of the man to the so-called " Armenoid " race,[1] which spread from western Asia into eastern Europe in the early centuries of the Christian era, and which is now most familiar to us in the Prussian type. The resemblance which strikes one at first between this head and that of a Prussian soldier is therefore not fortuitous. There were probably many barbarians from northern and central Europe in the Roman garrison of Egypt during the second and third centuries of our era, the period to which this head apparently belongs. And it therefore need not surprise us to find such a racial type and such a fashion in wearing the moustache on a monument erected to one of these barbarian mercenaries. There is nothing Egyptian about the style of the head, which is an ordinary product of later Graeco-Roman art.

ERNEST A. GARDNER.

[1] I am indebted for confirmation of this identification to the high authority of Prof. Elliot Smith

[The peoples engaged by the Romans as auxiliaries in Egypt comprised the Franci and sub-tribes Sugambri and Chamavi, which are perhaps too western for the above type; but it might represent one of the Germani, Alamanni, Vandali, Rhoeti, Quadi, or Sarmatae. None of these were stationed in Alexandria, but a veteran might well have retired there from the upper country.]

MARBLE HEAD OF A NORTHERN TYPE, PROBABLY A GERMANIC SOLDIER.
ALEXANDRIA.   ROMAN PERIOD.

THE TRANSMISSION OF HISTORY.

SURPRISE has been expressed that the various Greek versions of Egyptian history should show divergences in the lengths of the reigns and the totals of dynasties, and that these again differ so much from the amounts of the Turin papyrus, and the details that can be collected from dated monuments. We must remember that all these Greek versions are manuscripts, subject to all the corruption found in other manuscripts of such ages : there is no reason that in such manuscripts early Egyptian history should be better preserved than that of any other period. To see what the actual state of manuscripts is for a well-known period we may look at the various versions of Ptolemaic history. These are published in the *Monumenta Germaniae Historica, Chron. Minores*, where the later annalists are given in full, leading on to European history : the volumes and pages are, Column A, Laterculus, III, 448 ; B, Beda Chronicon, III, 275— ; C, Isidorus Chronicon, II, 451— ; D, Prosper Tiro, I, 398—; E, *Computatis* cccclii, I, 52 ; F, *Lib. Gen.* I, G, *Lib. Gen.* II, of Chronographer of cccl, I, 137.

			A.	B.	C.	D.	E.	F.	G.
		reign							
Soter,	began 325 B.C.	40	20	40	40	40	42	42	22
Philadelphus,	285	38	38	38	38	38	...	38	30
Euergetes I,	246	26	25	26	26	26	26	30	27
								F.25	
Philopator,	221	17	17	17	17	17	18	17	
Epiphanes,	204	23	24	23	24	24	20	23	20
Philometor,	181	36	35	35	35	35	11		17
Euergetes II }	145	28	29	29	29	29	27		25
Physcon }							F. 1	F.11	F.25
Soter II } { 117–108		10	36	F.17	17	17	E.27	E.26	E.26
Lathyrus } { 88–81		7							A.15
									S. 30
Alexander I,	108–88	20		10	10		19	20	28
				P. 8	8	8	S.19		
Alexander II,	19 days						19 d.	18 y.	24
									P.20
Dionysos }									
Auletes }	81–51	30	29	30	30		29	29	17
Cleopatra,	50–30	20	22	22	2			25	
Total ...	295			295			244	346	335
added up ...			(275)	(295)	(276)		(239)	(304)	(327)

These various writers are placed here in the general order of accuracy. The known reigns are stated with the names in the first column. Variations in the names are marked in the other columns : in A, Alexander is omitted, and 36 years all given to Lathyrus ; in B, Lagus is Largus, after Euergetes II, Fiscou 17 (really Lathyrus), then Ptolemy 8, which is the latter half of Lathyrus. C and D follow the same order. In E, confusion begins with Fiscou I and Euerceta 27 ; after this, Alexander 19, Soter 19. F gives a fictitious brother of Euergetes I 25 years ; and 11 years to Fiscon, omitting two previous reigns. G is the worst with " Iunior " 26, Fusci 25, Euergentis 26, Alexi 15, secundus Sotheris 30, Alexi 28, Alexandri 24, Ptolemy 20, Dionisi 17, a jumble which we need not speculate upon.

The main result is that by A.D. 350 there was complete confusion in some authors about the reigns of some of the greatest line of rulers living only four centuries before. Further, none of the totals stated agree with the sum of the reigns, except in Bede. Of all these writers there is not one which is as exact as Bede : beyond assigning the 10 + 7 years of Lathyrus to a duplication called Fiscou, and repeating the 7 years as 8 of a Ptolemy, cut away from Alexander's 20, and making up the total correct by giving the 2 years over to Cleopatra, there is no other error ; in the complication of the later reigns, with continual changes, it is pardonable to have strayed thus far. The surprising thing is that Bede, writing in the remotest corner of the former Empire, long after the other writers, and after the great breaks of the invasions, succeeded in getting a more correct version than any other chronicler.

This is Egyptian history, and the conclusion for us is that we must not be surprised at finding equal confusion and errors in the transcriptions from the earlier history of Manetho. Such errors do not reflect on the accuracy of the original writer, nor do they entirely vitiate the general scale of history. The average errors of all these writers for the total length of the dynasty is 35 years, or less than one-eighth of the whole period.

W. M. FLINDERS PETRIE.

A CARTOUCHE OF AUGUSTUS.

M. Daressy published in 1908 a stela containing a cartouche which has been the subject of some controversy.[1] The inscription commemorates one of the sacred bulls of Hermonthis, and is drawn up in the style of the much better known Apis-stelae. It begins with the date of the bull's birth : Year 33 under the majesty of the king of south and north, lord of the two lands, ⬚. We are then told that the animal was enthroned in year 39, and that he died in year 57, having lived 24 years. The stela, as M. Daressy remarked, cannot be older than the Ptolemies ; and there is no Ptolemy or Roman Emperor who reigned 57 years. There is, however, a method of computation (the era of the κράτησις), the starting point of which is the taking of Alexandria on 1st August, 30 B.C., commonly named the Actian era. The years of this era were later reckoned from 29th August (the Egyptian New Year's day) in order that they might coincide with the regnal years.[2] The year 57 according to this computation would fall in the year 13 of Tiberius. M. Daressy calls attention to the unusual arrangement by which the words " year 33 " are made to stand by themselves (on a level with the bull's seat in the tableau), above the first full line. As he well remarks, to the mind of an Egyptian a date was inseparable from the indication of a king's name, and the scribe took this means of combining the two ideas.

We may now consider the cartouche, which is as follows :—

Like the whole inscription, it is wretchedly engraved, and at a first glance is quite unintelligible. Daressy proposes to read the middle signs as 𓏞𓇳𓎟𓎟 , *Autokrator*, supplying the first △ and correcting ⎯⎯ into ⬭. In the characters at the end of the cartouche, together with the first two (misplaced) signs, he sees 𓏞𓇳𓎟 △ , *Augustus*, with the correction of ııı into ⎯⎯ .

Prof. Spiegelberg sought to explain the puzzle in a wholly different way.[3] He admitted that Daressy was correct as to the era, but contended that in that case the year should not be followed by a king's name, and he pointed out that no such cartouche as Autokrator Augustus was known. His view was that the scribe had endeavoured to express in hieroglyphs the Greek formula : ἔτους *x* τῆς Καίσαρος κρατήσεως θεοῦ υἱοῦ. The signs △ are doubtfully equated with τῆς, though the doubt seems rather out of place in view of the daring correspondence which follows. The two bungled strokes, it is suggested, express Καίσαρος. The whole of the remaining signs are for κρατήσεως, 𓏞𓇳 (*ι*) being the helping vowel before the double consonant *kr*, and 𓎟 or 𓊖 = εως, perhaps

---

[1] *Rec. de trav.*, XXX, p. 10.

[2] Gauthier, *Le Livre des Rois*, V, p. 16, note 1.

[3] *Ä.Z.*, XLV, p. 91.

with correction into ⊕. The last two words of the formula are to be found in the title 🝔, " Son of the Sun-god," preceding the second cartouche. Prof. Spiegelberg concludes by saying that the practice of the Egyptians in expressing dates will explain why the era was treated as a king's name.

The cartouches have been again published by M. Gauthier in the final volume of his splendid collection of royal names, where he has for the first time ventured to transcribe the second cartouche.[1] This is even more badly engraved than the rest of the stela, and is rendered specially illegible by the crowding of the characters at the end of the line. As, however, it begins with a clear ⌒ and contains a fairly recognizable 𓊪, there need be little difficulty in accepting M. Gauthier's view that Καίσαρος is intended. He regards Spiegelberg's explanation as more satisfactory than Daressy's, but places Καίσαρος as the last word in the Greek formula, in agreement with his reading of the second cartouche.

It seems to me, on the contrary, that the objections to Spiegelberg's view are, in their cumulative effect, overwhelming.

(1) The titles before the first cartouche are completely ignored, while " son of the sun " before the second is regarded as translating two Greek words.

(2) 𓇋𓏤 is explained as the helping vowel (*i*) before *kr* ; but it is surely very unlikely that the easy combination *kr* should require a helping vowel when the *Ps* of " Psammetichus " and the *Pt* of " Ptolemy " did not.

(3) If we are to see Καίσαρος in the second cartouche, it cannot very well be also found as part of the first ; and in that case we leave two characters unexplained, besides departing from the usual order of the words in Greek.

(4) Instances have been found by Gauthier and Spiegelberg where the era of the κράτησις is actually expressed in Egyptian (not Greek), while the second cartouche of the Emperor (Καίσαρος) alone appears without any of the usual titles.[2] These facts are clearly against the suggestion that the Greek formula would be put into a cartouche. It may of course be argued that they also show that some words were required to indicate the era ; but Daressy's explanation that this was done by placing the number of the year in a separate line seems a highly probable one. It may also be remarked that dating by an era is not altogether unknown in Egyptian inscriptions. Not to speak of the famous " Stela of 400 Years " (the meaning of which is still doubtful), there is the mention of year 59 of Horemheb, which is generally agreed to have been counted from the death of Amenhotep III.[3]

Whatever may be thought of the different opinions so far discussed, it will presumably be admitted that the two strange signs following ⌒ have not been satisfactorily dealt with. Daressy gives no account of them at all ; and it is difficult to attach much value to Spiegelberg's suggestion that they stand for Καίσαρος, since they do not in the least resemble any known method of writing that word. If we admit Gauthier's much more reasonable view, that Καίσαρος is to be found (as might be expected) in the second cartouche, the two signs in question are again unaccounted for. Here, then, lies the crux of the problem. The suggestion I have to offer is that these two vertical strokes are simply a very bad attempt (in keeping with the character of the inscription as a whole) to write

---

[1] Gauthier, *Le Livre des Rois*, V, p. 14.

[2] Gauthier, *loc. cit.*, V, pp. 10, 18.

[3] Inscription of Mes, line S. 8, published by Loret, *Ä.Z.*, XXXIX, p. 1 = Gardiner, " Inscription of Mes," in Sethe, *Untersuchungen*, IV.

the common phrase [symbol], "deceased." There are many instances of these words (which would be readily supplied by the reader) being reduced almost to mere lines, even in better executed work than our stela.[1] It is even possible that the bend in the first of the two strokes may stand for the angle in the lower part of [symbol], but naturally we cannot lay much stress on this in such bad work.

If the above argument is valid, Daressy's original interpretation s the only possible one. We should, then, correct the cartouche into

[cartouche] [symbol]; and the complete date of the bull's birth will read : " In the year 33 (of the κράτησις) and under the majesty of the king of south and north, lord of the two lands, Autokrator Augustus deceased, son of the sun, lord of diadems, Caesar."

F. W. READ.

The head on the cover of this journal is from one of the bearers of offerings, found by Mr. Winlock in the great group of models of the XIth dynasty at Thebes, see " Notes and News," p. 64 here. Illustration and discussion of this group will appear in a subsequent number.

[1] Several examples will be found in Ahmed Bey Kamal, *Stèles ptolémaiques et romaines* (*Catalogue général du Caire*). The worst written are Nos. 22197 (line 1), and 22212 (line 10), both of which must be very close in point of date to the Hermonthis stela.

REVIEWS.

Balabish.—By G. A. WAINWRIGHT. 1920. 4to. 78 pp., 25 pls. 42s. (Egypt Exploration Society.)

This is a detailed account of a small site, on the east of the Nile, about equidistant from Abydos and Farshut. Not much was found that is new to us; but the careful working allows scope to Mr. Wainwright for two comprehensive discussions, of the Pan-grave people and the foreign pottery of the XVIIIth dynasty, which give value to the book.

The graves equivalent to those called " Pan-graves " at Diospolis were here deeper and of three forms, cylindrical and oval with contracted burials, and long with full-length burials. Yet no exclusive difference could be traced between the objects buried, which would show different dates or races. The burials of this kind are found from Rifeh near Assiut, up to El Khizam, south of Thebes. An earlier invasion of probably the same people, with much the same pottery, extended north to Herakleopolis in the IXth dynasty, as found this year. The contracted bodies at Balabish were lying on the right side, with head to north and facing west. The generality of the material is already well known, old vases of the middle kingdom re-used, leather work, shells and shell bracelets, ostrich-shell beads, and the peculiar pottery as at Diospolis. Two new classes were, however, found ; the archers' wrist-guards of leather with incised patterns, and the curved horn implements, which appear to be strigils. Two copper axes that were in the graves are the thin fighting axe and the stout, long-backed, carpentry axe. Some things were probably continued in use like the kohl pots, from the middle kingdom, such as the fly amulets, the much worn carnelian beads, the amazonite beads, and perhaps the blue glazed crystal and black manganese-glaze beads, all of which are familiar in the earlier period. There appear to be three classes of peoples whom it is difficult to identify :—(1) The " Pan-grave " people ; (2) the C-group people of Nubia ; (3) the Kerma people having their fine pottery with trumpet mouths. There are difficulties in connecting any of these ; and as the XVIIth dynasty and early XVIIIth fought against Nubia, it is also barred from being identified with (2) or (3). Whether there are connections or identities of any of these contemporary peoples is not yet clear.

The cemetery of the XVIIIth dynasty did not produce anything unusual, except an alabaster figure-vase, of a girl playing on a lute. One of the penannular white stone rings was found in position on the ear of a mummy ; this proves that such rings were used on the ear, although other examples have so narrow a slit that only hair could possibly be passed into them. If such rings were tied on to a hole in the ear the slit would have been inconvenient. It is certain, therefore, that the penannular rings were for both ears and hair.

The presence of types of foreign pottery gives rise to a useful summary and discussion of the extent of each variety and its limits of date. The *bilbils*, little

D

straight-necked flasks, with conical foot and lip, were found in south-west Palestine and Cyprus, as well as widely in Egypt under Tehutmes III ; they do not belong to north Syria, Asia Minor, or the Aegean.   The remark that this type has not been found to contain ointment is superseded by an example at Herakleopolis.

The long tubular bottle, otherwise called spindle-shaped, is found in Cyprus, Crete (Gournia), and Gezer; the clay is not Egyptian, but its source is unknown. An example of double the usual size was found at Herakleopolis.

The pilgrim-bottle type is found in south Palestine, rarely in the north, and is only in Cyprus at a later date.   It cannot be dated in Egypt before the swamp of Syrian influence under Tehutmes III.   The occurrence of a similar form in the stone vases of the second prehistoric age, which is Asiatic in its source, suggests to the author that the origin is probably eastern.   As the form is probably copied from leather, it might be that it was seldom made in more permanent material until it was adopted by a stone- or pottery-using people.   Thus it might be native to Nabathaea and south Palestine without leaving a trace.   The sites in south Palestine, which were certainly ancient cities by their names, have not a scrap of pottery upon them ;   only leather and wood were in use.

The false-necked vase, or *bügelkanne*, is known in the Aegean and Cyprus, and was probably brought thence into Egypt.   It was copied there in blue glaze (Univ. Coll.).   The globular forms with broad bands are the earlier, about Tehutmes III and Amenhetep III (Naqadeh and Ghurob), and the flatter forms and narrower bands are of the close of the XVIIIth dynasty (*Illahun*, xvii, 28 ; xx, 7, 9).   The ring base to vases is not Egyptian, but is found in Syria and Troy ;   also the hollow conical foot.   The present position is tantalising ;   we have several distinctive forms foreign to Egypt, and do not know the source of any of them, owing to our lack of enterprise in Asia.   There is nothing more promising in archaeology at present than a search over the early pottery of sites in Syria and Asia Minor, to find the extent, and trace the source, of the various styles of pottery.   This will give the key to the relations of countries more readily than any other work.

The Oxyrhynchus Papyri, Part XIV.—By B. P. GRENFELL and A. S. HUNT. 1920.   244 pp., 3 pls.   (London : Egypt Exploration Society.)

This volume contains about a hundred papers on business and letters, and about fifty abstracts, another large slice of the enormous mass of material now in hand.   Who will extract all the results that can give a social and economic view of the country ?   Some interesting details appear at first sight.   The very long date-formulae, naming all the Ptolemaic priesthoods, were cut short by saying, in such a year of the king " and the rest of the formula as written at Alexandria." The last day of the year and the new-year-day were both kept as holidays (p. 172). In mentioning children it was usual to say " the unbewitched," probably as a prophylactic against the evil eye.   A son urges his father to avoid danger, and to have an identity mark, to verify his body if he were killed.   A long list of all the operations of a vineyard is given in a contract (p. 18).   Christian phrases appear in saying that there was no witness to a loan, but God and the sister and wife of a man, and a letter is written jointly by Didyme and her " sisters in the Lord."   The monstrous depreciation of the copper substitutes for silver coin appears again in a contract to pay a donkeyman 2,000 drachmae a day, showing a depreciation of at least 1,000 to 1, only rivalled now in Russia.

The Hittites.—By A. E. COWLEY. 1920. 94 pp., 35 figs. 6s. (Schweich Lectures, 1918, British Academy.)

This is the most valuable summary and study of the Hittite question, describing the localities, the history, the questions of race, of language, and of decipherment. The interest in this people started with the allusions in the Old Testament. This was greatly increased by the identification of them with the Kheta of inscriptions and sculptures in Egypt. The discovery of the Hittite capital at Boghazkeui, and the archives, with the cuneiform duplicate of the treaty with Egypt, the many letters in Hittite language, and to crown all, the discovery of the names of Indo-aryan gods there, has made this a subject of the highest importance. The Czech scholar Hrozný has urged the Aryan relationship of the Hittite language, mainly from grammatical forms which can be detected in the cuneiform versions, though the roots of the language are still unknown. To this Dr. Cowley barely assents, though it has been largely accepted by others.

The whole question of the hieroglyphic inscriptions is entirely separate. Here Dr. Cowley starts from the Tarkondemos boss, as everyone else has done, assuming that the Hittite signs there are equivalent to those in cuneiform. Unfortunately the linguistic scholars have not had any technical knowledge of workmanship. The centre part of the silver boss was never wrought in metal; the cutting is that in stone; it is a silver cast from a stone seal. Then when this silver was cast, a broad flange or border was cast around it, and on that was punched the cuneiform inscription, so strongly as to come through on the back. There is thus no proved connection of the two inscriptions, but rather a reason for a difference in age and sense between them. It is like the case of a Roman intaglio being put in a mediaeval setting, inscribed for a seal. The whole of the structures of interpretation which have started from the six signs on the central seal must remain in suspense until some firm basis can be proved. The guess at some of the often-repeated city names gives more hope; but the best chance is in the immense mound of Carchemish, which seems as if it must contain some cuneiform bilingual, or perhaps even a Hittite hieroglyph version of the Egyptian treaty. At the end of the volume is a list of over a hundred signs. The work is essential for anyone dealing with Oriental history.

Ancient Egyptian Fishing.—By ORIC BATES. 1917. 73 pp., 26 pls. (*Harvard African Studies*, Vol. I. Cambridge, Mass.)

This important collection of materials is the last work of one who promised to be a leader in the organising of knowledge. His comprehensive study of the Eastern Libyans (*Ancient Egypt,* 1914, p. 181) will scarcely be superseded in its fullness of detail and reference; and the present work systematises all that can be gleaned from the monuments, and from actual specimens, published in dozens of works. Had his life been spared, doubtless he would have become more accustomed to deal with facts, rather than rely on the opinions of those with whom he was familiar.

For the prehistoric age, it is suggested that the animal form of palettes—especially of fish—was intended to convey a magic value to the paint ground on the palette, as Pliny says that those who hunt crocodiles anoint themselves with its fat. Thus malachite ground on a fish palette might convey power over fish to the wearer; and in support of this it may be noted that all the animals represented are used for food—Barbary sheep, hartebeest, stag, elephant, hippopotamus, hare, turtle, birds, fish; the only exceptions are two falcons and a crocodile in later time. The great royal palettes were for the war-paint of the king, to enable him to overcome his enemies, as figured on the palettes. The importance of fisheries, and the veneration of some species, are fully described.

The means of fishing by papyrus rafts and papyrus boats is minutely detailed. The *sa* amulet sign is linked with the loops of papyrus stems, which are often shown beside fishers or worn by them over the shoulder. This agrees with its meaning of " protection," and the examples of it in use seem to leave no doubt as to its origin. The harpoon is next discussed at great length ; the rise of the copper harpoon is placed too late, as it is certainly of the first prehistoric age by the graves where it has been found. The bident is described, and all the variety of fish hooks. Fish traps, hand nets, casting nets and the seine, are next considered in all the detail of working. The lead net-sinkers are dated too late, as they abound in towns of the XVIIIth dynasty. The curing of fish, the sale of fish, and the social position of the fishermen, complete this study, which will long be the work of reference for the whole subject.

Worship of the Dead as practised by some African Tribes.—By J. ROSCOE. 1917. 15 pp. (*Harvard African Studies*, Vol. I.)

This is an illuminating comment on Egyptian usages, from the customs of Uganda at present ; the more so, as the writer recounts from an English rectory what he observed without any reference to Egypt. The great concern for a sick man, and the gifts and sacrifices at burial, are held to be due to a wish to stand well with the ghost. The cemetery is the property of the clan, and only those of the same totem may be buried in it. In no case may two bodies—even of mother and infant—be placed in one grave, as in the second prehistoric age. At the head of the grave a small shrine is erected in which offerings are placed, like the soul-houses of the Xth dynasty. On the death of a king the war drum is beaten, and there is a state of anarchy, since peace, law and order cease with the king's life. Pillage and war follows until another king rules. The queen must be a princess, if possible a sister of the king and daughter of the previous king, as in Egypt. The body of a king is disembowelled, all the juices are pressed out into sponges of fibre till the body is dry and hard ; the entire mummifying takes six months. The body is placed in a shrine, and widows, chiefs, and personal servants stand around it and are clubbed to death. In the second courtyard outside, four or five hundred victims are executed. This is like the burial of Hepzefa, and the rows of burials of servants around the tombs of the Ist dynasty kings. An extraordinary feature is that the shrine of a king's mummy is guarded by a group of his widows, who are replaced when they die, by others of the same clan, so that the worship is kept up for even hundreds of years. A widow may, however, retire and marry, if she can get a substitute. This seems to explain the frequent cases anciently of a wife being a *nesut khaker*, or adorner of the king. These were girls who had been brought into the harem, and after the king's death had adorned the body, but married after a time. At the back of the shrine lives the medium, a man who had been familiar with the king, and who is subject to the king's spirit, passes into trances, can ask questions of the king, and receive the answers. This may be parallel to the *neter-hon* of the king. Ghosts are expected to be re-born. Each child when a year old is tested to find which family ghost animates it. Then the shrine of that ancestor is left to decay, as his spirit is reincarnated. Among the Basoga, north of Lake Victoria, the new chief opens the grave of his predecessor after a year, takes the skull out, cleanses it, wraps it tightly in skins, and places it in a temple with a medium to speak for the ghost. In common burials the objects buried are broken " to free the spiritual essence that it may escape to their late owner," like the broken offerings in Egypt.

The Paleoliths of the Eastern Desert.—By F. H. STERNS. 1917. 35 pp., 18 pls. (*Harvard African Studies*, Vol. I.)

The 120 worked flints here figured came from the desert between Qeneh and the Red Sea. They are of the forms already familiar in the flints from the plateau of the Nile valley. It is to be noted that there are scratches on these flints like those which have been attributed to glacial action, or to ploughing, in England ; as neither method can have acted in Egypt, so neither need be true in England.

Notes on Egyptian Saints.—By R. H. BLANCHARD. 1917. 11 pp. (*Harvard African Studies*, Vol. I.) This paper describes some of the principal festivals, pointing out the primitive nature of them, and that most are connected with fertility charms.

A new Solution of the Pentateuchal Problem.—By M. G. KYLE. 1918. 39 +18 pp. (*Bibliotheca Sacra*, January–April, 1918.)

The new idea presented here is that there are three different types of law, always distinguished by different names. (1) The Judgements are decisions of judges, often old traditional law, expressed in a proverbial style, as a mnemonic aid, and concerning law between man and man. (2) The Statutes, which are decrees or regulations, of legal offences which are not criminal, but only *mala prohibita* ; also laws of offerings. (3) The Commandments, which are fundamental laws and moral principles. A different style of writing naturally goes with each type of law, a brief proverbial style, or description, or hortatory, and this style belongs also to the narrative portions connected with each type of law. These styles are then found to correspond with the three main divisions already proposed, the JE documents, the Priestly and the Deuteronomic. The argument then is that this division of character accounts for the distinctions already proposed, and is consistent with the single date for the Pentateuch. The name Elohim belongs to the legal phraseology, while the name Yahveh is religious. Here is at least a fresh criterion brought into critical questions, and all such are welcome.

Die Griechisch–Ägyptische Sammlung Ernst von Sieglin. III teil, Die Gefässe in Stein und Ton, Knochenschnitzereien. By RUDOLF PAGENSTECHER. 1913. Folio. xi + 253 pp., 60 pls,, 188 figs. (Leipzig.)

This volume deals with material from Egypt in various German museums. Sumptuous as this is (weighing 16 lbs.) it is disappointing to find so few unusual or important objects in such a work. First there are nine plates of purely Egyptian stone vases of all periods. A few good prehistoric are all catalogued as Old Kingdom. A canopic jar (p. 2) has Bissing's description of it quoted as a translation ; it is really of a palace official, Huy. The only notable vases are two of alabaster with names of Pepy I and II. Only seventeen pages refer to the Egyptian remains, and 225 are given to Hellenistic and Roman pottery. Scarcely any dating is assigned to this material, which varies over six centuries. The only self-dated vase of importance is a blue glazed flask with applied relief figures having the name of Ptolemy Philopator (225–205 B.C.), which gives a fixed stage of such work. The variety of design in the IIIrd century vases from Hadra is the most artistic product, as given in pp. 34–52, pls. xv–xviii. There was a school with good sense of form, and passably good decoration, without the vulgarity of the late Italian work : it is the most creditable result of Alexandria. The difficulty of trade during the war has prevented this work reaching us till this year.

Nekropolis, Untersuchungen über Gestalt und Entwicklung der Alexandrin-ischen Grabanlagen und ihrer Malereien.—By RUDOLF PAGENSTECHER. 1919. 4to. 216 pp., 127 figs. (Leipzig.)

This elaborate work is the historical comparison and summing-up of the results of the Ernst von Sieglin expedition at Alexandria. It is a kind of study that is much wanted in all subjects, bringing together material from the collateral examples, and drawing conclusions about sources and dating. The wielding of classical material seems complete, but in some earlier matters wider search would have been useful. More use might also have been made of some of the pottery models of buildings, such as are in University College.

The first chapter deals with the type of monument on the surface. This is of three classes, Hellenic, Asiatic and Egyptian. The Attic stele is the source of the Hellenic class. The earliest cemetery contains coins of the Satrapy and Ptolemy Soter, and cannot be placed later than 250 B.C. There seems, indeed, no reason why it should not be before 300 B.C., as there must have been a cemetery within a generation of the founding of the city. The stele, though starting with Attic tradition, was in very different conditions from the original. It was no longer a free-standing monument, but was only the decoration of a larger structure, of an altar-shape. This may be due to the influence of the Egyptian tomb, in which the false-door was only a part. Another large difference from the Attic steles was that the painted relief sculpture was simplified as a mere painting on a flat panel. In the earliest cemetery—of Chatbey—there are twenty-one painted steles and only eight sculptured. The steles of the earlier date have whole length figures ; later there are some half-length figures in a naos border, and in the western cemetery are busts of stucco. In the tumuli over the tombs there are small vases and statuettes in the earth ; these are supposed to have been deposited on the tumulus, and to have been covered over by disturbance of the soil. More accurate observation is evidently needed, to see if the positions agree to this, or if the objects were placed in the earth at first, which seems the more likely course. The larger monuments have statues around them. There are commonly altars by the tombs, of a large size and square in the chambered tombs, or of a small size and round, by the tumuli. These suggest the continuance of offerings of incense or of food for the dead, as in ancient times in Egypt. The placing of the stele varied considerably : it was at first on a high base, then upon steps, or on an altar over the grave, or on a long rectangular base, or a square base, or placed upon a short column. The type ascribed to Asia Minor is the cubic die placed upon steps. This began about 250 B.C., as dated by two black-figured vases in such a grave. The stepped form of monument is stated to be devoted to gods and heroes. The great cenotaph of Hephaistion at Babylon was in five stages, probably borrowed from the *ziggurat* of the country (DIOD. XVII, xii). Next reference is made to the pyra of Pertinax and Severus; but such funeral pyres in stages are figured on coins from Antoninus to Saloninus.

Another omission is the heroic character of the Mausoleum, as the stepped pyramid had the chariot of Mausolos at the summit. If there is any precedent from early times in these Roman forms it is hardly in the solitary step pyramid of Saqqarah, but rather in the *ziggurat* copied by Alexander for Hephaistioṅ.

The Egyptian form of monument is expressly stated to be the horned altar, that is to say, with triangular elevations at the corners. It is called " a real Alexandrian type," and said to be " the first form by which the impress of Egypt became perceptible." This view is astonishing, as the form is unknown in Egyptian work. The example of brickwork towers, quoted from the Praeneste mosaic, has nothing to do with this form, as the top edge is curved in a circular sweep, due to the usual curved courses of Egyptian brickwork ; the horned altar has sharp triangular corners. A parallel to the grave-altar, with doors partly open on the upright face, is in a Pompeian fresco where a tower some 18 feet high has an open doorway, and triangular corners at the top. Such altars of pottery on a small scale are common in Roman tombs (see *Hawara*, XV, 8; *Roman Portraits*, XV, 6, 7), and they have burnt marks on the top, showing that they have been used as fire altars. It seems clear that in Roman times towers were sometimes built over graves, with a way to ascend to the top, for burning offerings; and small models were placed in graves. This form of monument was copied in relief at the tombs of Medain Saleh in Arabia (26½ degrees N.) of the first century A.D., so it was known to Semitic people. It is not Babylonian, as the altar on the cylinders is a column with a pile of flat loaves on the top (HAYES WARD, *Cylinders*, 824, 826, 827), or a bowl (876). It appears, however, as a Persian altar (*Cylinders*, 1144). Long before that, it is figured in the seventh century B.C. as the altar of a high place, on an Assyrian relief (*Botta*, 114, copied in WARD, *Cylinders*, 1258). Possibly it is the form intended by the rough figure of a fire-altar on cylinder 1260. The horned altar, being expressly a fire-altar, can hardly be separated from the rock-cut fire-altars of Nakshe Rustem (DIEULAFOY, *Art Antique de Perse*, III, v), which have corners raised and three pinnacles along the sides. These are dated before Cyrus, as the earliest monuments of Persia, akin to Assyrian work (p. 8). All of these have their parallel in the horns of the altar of burnt offering and of incense ; while the table of shewbread had no horns, being probably like the Babylonian altars with a pile of round loaves. The horned fire-altar was then certainly known to Sargon in the eighth century B.C., and probably used by Israelites centuries before that ; it was adopted as the Persian fire-altar in the sixth century ; next, enlarged as a tower over a tomb, with an entrance to lead to the top, it was copied in central Arabia and in Pompei, and used in miniature over the graves in Alexandria, while in the form of pottery models it was, down to the third century A.D. a common offering in Egyptian graves. In the later Ptolemaic tombs at Alexandria a portrait was painted on the side of the fire-altar.

A truly Egyptian loan was the pyramid over a tomb. This appears in late Ptolemaic time, of the steep form then fashionable, as seen at Meroe, the cemetery of Hawara (about 68 degrees, *Ro. Port.* 19), the pyramid of Caius Cestius (67 degrees), and Pompeian frescoes. The pyramid form had attracted Alexander, who intended to build a pyramid equal to the greatest, as the monument of his father Philip (DIOD. XVIII, i). Altars in the form of a truncated pyramid were found at Alexandria, but only 9 inches high. An error should be noted on p. 29, as the pyramids represented at Qurneh are not on columns, but on tomb chambers.

The Egyptian naos or shrine, often with a cornice of uraei, was a favourite memorial, with a figure or bust of the deceased person occupying the shrine. Such were made in the second century B.C. to the first century A.D., and spread from Egypt to Sardinia.

The painted steles are classified according to the figures. There is a resemblance to Pompeian frescoes in some of the attitudes, probably both drawn from some celebrated pictures that were familiar. The work is but poor and careless, always upon local limestone, and without any background or accessories. A most interesting census of the origins of the Alexandrian population is given by the ethnic names. Thirty-nine are recorded, and of these fourteen are Europeans (six being Thessalians), four islanders, only three Africans, and eight Greek Asiatics, with ten Galati and Kelt. This prevalence of Keltic mercenaries is mentioned when Philadelphos had 4,000 (PAUS. I, 13), and later in 213 B.C., 4,000 Thracians and Gauls were enlisted from settlers, and 2,000 more imported. That a quarter of the burials are Keltic shows how largely northern the Alexandrian was.

The covers of the loculi are often painted, with various forms of double doors ; some with lattice in upper part, mostly with ring handles or heads. Sometimes one door is drawn as partly open. The Egyptian ideas remain in an instance of a full-length figure standing in a doorway, with groups of gods and the deceased down the sides.

The plans of the tombs are classed as (1) the Oikos type, from Europe, with a burial chamber and antechamber ; (2) the Peristyle type, from the Egyptian house and temple ; and (3) the Loculus type of Roman origin. The Oikos type is compared with the Greek house, an example from Priene having a close agreement with a tomb at Chatbey in the position of the chambers. The decoration is elaborated at Ras et Tin, with the walls painted in squares of marbling, and Egyptian niches and cornices. The use of horizontal divisions on columns is noted as Egyptian (bands at Beni Hasan). The Peristyle type has a peristyle court, open to the sky between the pillars. This is compared with the Egyptian buildings for the living ; but no tomb in Egypt has an open peristyle court, and closed peristyle halls are very unusual there. It seems doubtful if an Egyptian house or temple plan would be intentionally adopted as a new type of tomb by the Greeks. This type appears in Cyprus, but whether before or after the Alexandrine tombs is not settled. In any case the open peristyle court is at least as familiar in Greek and Italian houses as in Egyptian, and the Greek source is much more likely to have been copied by Alexandrians. Various other tombs are described, the greatest of which is the catacomb at Meqs ; the great hall there is 52 feet square, with side chambers having three tiers of loculi, while the axis continues to a hall 23 feet across, with a cupola and side chamber, with places for nine sarcophagi. Certain criteria are stated, as that there is neither peristyle nor cupola in any tombs fixed to Roman age ; also that loculi began to be made in Hellenistic times. The Meqs catacomb is placed to the first century B.C. In the Roman tombs the loculi are arranged in rows along corridors. A summary gives the dates of tombs as Chatbey 320–250 B.C., Anfushy 270–200, Station cemetery fourth to third century, Hadra 280–150, Antoniadis and Meqs first century.

The last chapter deals with Alexandrian painting. Chatbey, the earliest cemetery, has no colour left. The vertical division of wall surfaces into painted panels, by half-columns, began as early as the third century. Later the system was by horizontal division into zones. Marbling became usual, and there was a great use of blue colouring, especially for ceilings. At Suk el Wardian there is pure Greek work of the late fourth century style. At Anfushy (Ras et Tin) the surfaces are painted in squares of marbling copied from inlays. The ceilings are plain at Chatbey; at Sidi Gabr long coffering appears; at Suk el Wardian square coffering; and at Anfushy decoration in the coffering.

The whole subject is of value as showing the gradual swamping of purely Greek work by native style, in some respects, though hardly as much as the author suggests. The changes to the Roman Pompeian style moved as in Italy, showing the unity of feeling round the Mediterranean. The endeavours of the author to reach definite dates and criteria are most welcome.

Catalogue of Textiles from Burying-Grounds in Egypt. Vol. I.—By A. F. KENDRICK. 1920. 142 pp., 33 pls. 5s., posted 5s. 6d. (Victoria and Albert Museum, S.W. 7.)

This catalogue is valuable for the historical and technical introduction which occupies half of it, and discusses the dates and origin of the decorated garments of Roman age in Egypt. After an outline of the history of the period in question, the various sites where textiles have been found are described. The nature of the burials, the various preparations of the body with cartonnage, painted cloth, or portrait, and the dates of some garments, are fully stated. The technical weaving is noticed and the use of silk. The tunics, which are the main subject for decoration, and the large hangings or cloths, are discussed, with other material for comparison. The subjects of the woven tapestries are then catalogued in detail, under Gods, Portraits, Horsemen, Huntsmen, Warriors, Dancers, Vintage, Playing Boys, Animals, Plants and Ornaments.

The broad conclusions are that these patterned textiles were not peculiar to Egypt, but belong equally to the whole Roman Empire. A further evidence may be given for this from the gold-in-glass figures of the third and fourth century, which are apparently Italian and not Egyptian. The circular tapestry patches on the knees are shown on these figures. The date of this work is assigned to the latter part of the third century and onward. The main difference between this dating and that of Gayet is in the circular purple patches worked over in fine thread in interlacing square patterns. Here they are placed, like the figure work, to the third to fifth century, while Gayet put them into the Arab period. This work by its complete discussion of the materials will be a standard textbook for long to come. We hope the succeeding volumes will be as thoroughly treated.

The Life of Hatshepsut.—By TERENCE GRAY. 8vo, 260 pp., 13 pls. 14s. 1920 (Heffer, Cambridge).

This work is described as ' A Pageant of Court Life," and " A Chapter of Egyptian History in Dramatic Form." It is a serious attempt at historic reconstruction, using the actual documents that can be connected with the subject of the Great Queen. Let it be said at once that this is entirely clear of the ill-informed absurdities which have been produced when trying to exploit Egypt for the stage. The scheme is well arranged, and the various scenes reasonably fulfil the actual conditions. In this form the striking historic position will doubtless interest many who might not read the scattered records at first hand. With the dramatic quality of this work this journal is not concerned; but we may note the difficulty of treating the long-winded pomposity of official formulae in harmony with a conversation. Some familiarity with the talk of modern Egyptians might have given more likely phrases than " Thou hast no further theory," or " the magnificence of this great civilisation," which we cannot imagine put back into vernacular intimacy of talk. This alternates with too sharp a contrast of very intimate talk of royal persons. It does not accord with the XVIIIth dynasty for courtiers to " smell the earth," only foreigners did so then, and courtiers bowed. We may regret to see the Greek form of termination Tahutmosis put in the mouth of an Egyptian, and Amen called Yamoun, a form impossible at that time, and perhaps at any other. There is much thought and perception in the stages of antagonism of Tahutmes III, and it is hard to say if such episodes could be better treated.

Bantu Methods of Divination.—By REV. NOEL ROBERTS. 12 pp., 3 pls., 1917. (South African Journal of Science, April, 1917.)

Everything that can be gleaned from African beliefs and customs that have any parallel in Egypt is a priceless key to understanding the mute evidences that we find, especially those of prehistoric age. This description of the apparatus and methods of divination may interpret some of the slate and bone objects, such as are figured in *Prehistoric Egypt*, xliv–xlvi. Mr. Roberts begins with an outline of magic and its purpose. " Among all primitive people who practise magic, however, we find the belief that a *rapport* exists between the *name* of a thing and the thing itself—in fact, a man and his name are often regarded as identical." This is well known in Egypt, where an object, such as even a walking stick, had its name, and nothing really existed unless named.

" Almost every Bantu tribe is distinguished by the name of an animal or other natural object, and that animal or object is regarded as *taboo* to all members of the tribe which bears its name. This identity of man and totem is expressed not only by vocal imitation of the animal, but also by gestures of a more or less conventional type, which are supposed to represent the characteristic movements of that animal. These gestures are woven into the ceremonial dances, so that the tribal origin of a man may be ascertained by noting his actions during the dance." In Egypt the animals representing the different tribes are well known ; on the slate palettes the standards are shown of the falcon, jackal, lion and scorpion, while later on, the nome signs include the falcon, hare, gazelle, jackal, ibis and bull. Can we trace any of the gestures or other imitations of animals in representations ? Certainly the women taking out offerings to the tomb at early dawn imitate the howl of a jackal, as heard in 1892 at El Amarna.

The casting of lots for divination is fully described. The knuckle-bones or astragali are mainly used for this, and they are called by Boers " toy oxen," *dol-ossen*, hence the English term dolosses for such casting pieces. " As a rule the set contains the astragali of the totem animals of the neighbouring tribes. In the case of larger animals some other bone or part of the body is used to replace the knuckle-bone. Thus in the case of the lion one of the phalanges is usually chosen, and parts of the carapace of different species of tortoise are commonly seen. . . . From what we know of magic and totemism, it is clear that each bone or object in the set represents the animal of which it once formed part, and hence the *tribe of which that animal is totem.*" One end of the knuckle-bone is recognised as the " head," the convex side as the " back," the concave side as the " belly." When the bones are thrown, they may fall with the " head " facing either towards or away from the operator, and with one or other of these faces uppermost . . . . the various positions assumed by the bones may be generally classified as follows :—

(1) *Anterior position.*—Head away from the operator = " lost," " strayed," etc., generally *negative* character.

(2) *Posterior position.*—Head facing toward the operator = " will be found," etc., generally *affirmative* character.

(3) *Dorsal aspect.*—Back uppermost indicates " health," etc. ; *and*, by a grouping of ideas, " success," " prosperity," etc.

(4) *Ventral aspect.*—Belly uppermost, representing " death," " failure," etc.

(5) *Right pectoral aspect.*—Right side uppermost.

(6) *Left pectoral aspect.*—Left side uppermost.

Either pectoral aspect may represent " sleep," " sickness," " uncertainty," and hence " try again."

Now here are three aspects, back, belly or side up ; or, with a pair, six aspects. The use of astragali for playing games is certain in Egypt, as a pair have been found in the drawer of a gaming board. The three or six types of throw here were all simply indicated by the players calling out that they have three or six in the throw, and by the game boards being three squares in width across, so that a throw of three gives an advance of one row. It is remarkable how games have been derived from divination. Here the throw of astragali, and hence of dice derived from them, is for divination ; the throw of four arrows, the early Chinese divination, is the source of the four suits of cards ; the diviners' bowl with divisions all round it, to which a floating object may point, seems to be the parent of the roulette table.

How remote a connection of ideas may seem to us, appears in the throwing of a plate of the carapace of the tortoise ; if this falls back up, it is in the walking position, and as the proverb is " the tortoise only walks when it rains," the position indicates rain.

Various tablets are also used for divination. Unfortunately Mr. Roberts has been misled by Churchward's " Signs and Symbols." The tablets quoted from Egypt are clearly the labels of offerings, all from one tomb, and that of a queen of the 1st dynasty, found by De Morgan, and not from " Naqada and Ballas." The set of tablets used in several different districts in Africa are of a tongue shape, with a guilloche twist on one, a zigzag border, rows of zigzags across, and rows of triangular hollows. These four types are associated, by the Malaboch, and slightly varied by degradation among the Mountha and Matala. We need to recognise any parallels to this system that may turn up in Egypt. The guilloche twist may be the degradation of the two serpents—caduceus fashion—on the prehistoric handles. (*Prehis. Eg.* xlviii, 4, and Berlin.)

The paper concludes with figures of two diviners' bowls, with signs around the edge representing different tribes. The bowls were filled with water, and seeds or buttons thrown in to float ; the position which they took in relation to the signs on the edge served to give the answer.

Prehistoric Arts and Crafts of India.—By PANCHANAN MITRA. 8vo. 66 pp. 10 pls. 1920. (University of Calcutta, Anthropological papers No. 1.)

The comparative studies of the author have already been noticed here (p. 18), and the present work is a more systematic account of prehistoric India. It is fortunate that zealous research is being given to these remains, though much more is needed for so vast a region. The earlier chapters discuss the glacial period on the north, and the contemporary river terraces, the palaeoliths, and the rock paintings of hunters. In this connection there are on pl. VI two pieces of decorated pottery obviously of Islamic age. Regarding the earliest date of pottery it must be considered that the favoured civilisations of the warm river valleys of Mesopotamia and Egypt were probably far in advance of savage Europe in starting various arts. For the resemblances stated between Egyptian and Indian pottery, we need to see a series of forms of each set side by side in plates, before we can weigh the evidence. The occurrence of the " chess-board patterns " in India, like those of Elam and Anau, is fair ground for a general Asiatic connection ; such pattern is always foreign to Egypt.

On coming to the age of metals, there are many questions on which more precise details are needed. No dates, even approximate, are given for the earliest examples in India. It is useless to say that iron is known in " primitive India," when the earliest assignable date is not before the early European iron of 1200 B.C. In India as in Africa we must have definite evidence of a date before that, if the European origin of iron is to be set aside ; it is useless to speak of a " primitive " age, in regions developing later than the Mediterranean. It is claimed that wootz steel is electrum, " where we get the very same name." What name ? Greek *electron*, shining like the sun, or Egyptian *uasm* ? We read " we think steel, especially wootz, was imported from India in (to) Egypt as objects of high value in those early times about three to four thousand years before Christ." How is such date reached for Indian wootz, or where is it found in Egypt ? A reasonable passage is quoted from Dr. Coomarswamy that " the most ancient part of Indian art belongs to the common endowment of early Asiatic culture," and he speaks of a " Mykenaean facies " and designs " of a remarkably Mediterranean aspect." This is reasonable enough for about 1000 B.C., but it will not take back India to any comparison with early Egypt, still less to originating anything of Egyptian culture. The author has a wide field of the greatest interest, on which we all want to have exact information, and any proofs of connection, or still better of priority, will be heartily welcomed.

PERIODICALS.

Journal of the Society of Oriental Research, Chicago.

In October, 1919, Prof. Mercer discusses the question *Was Ikhnaton a Monotheist ?* The definition of monotheism is drawn very rigidly: " there is but one God, whose being and existence pervades all space and time " ; this involves attributes which have nothing to do with the denial of any other gods. Taking such a rigid view, and looking for any survival of notice of the other gods, it is not surprising that Akhenaten is reduced to the position of " a clever and self-centered individual henotheist." This seems rather too theological a view of a change, which was hedged about with continual difficulty, and which had to be carried out practically and not merely discussed in the study. If some minor inconsistencies remained, if there were political views on the suppression of the priesthood of Amen, yet these cannot hide from us the intense fervour of the adoration of the Aten, and the repudiation of tolerating any other god. The figure of Maot used for *truth* cannot be adduced as a divinity, as Maot was never worshipped ; not a stele nor a temple belongs to her, she was only an impersonation like a figure of Justice at present. Dr. Mercer not only denies the king the name of monotheist, but also " especially ethical monotheist." Now the insistence on all occasions of his personal motto " living in truth," utterly unknown before or since, may give him the right to be valued as an ethical reformer. We cannot expect any one of his age to have the keen sense of congruity which has been developed in us by centuries of dogmatic discussion of rival creeds and heresies.

The " Eye of Horus " in the Pyramid Texts is studied by Prof. Mercer in March, 1920. He concludes that the sun and moon were originally regarded as the eyes of Nut, the sky goddess. Later they were named the eyes of Ra, and as the sun was Ra, so the eye of Ra was Ra himself. Then the consuming eye of Ra became transferred to Hathor, Tefnut, Sati, Bast, Sekhmet, and the Uraeus. Osiris was popular at the early date and usurped the place of Ra. Here we must require strong evidence for such a sequence, as the worship of the Osiride group appears to precede the Ra worship ; no proof of the precedence of Ra is given. The loss of the eye of Horus, in combat with Set, made the Horus-eye one of the most sacred symbols of sacrifice. It became the synonym for every kind of offering. As the eye-sun became identical with the Horus-sun, so the eye was Horus ; and as the king was Horus, the eye was the king. In short, the vagueness of Egyptian thought and lack of consistency, led to the eye being taken as " anything that was construed sacrificially " ; it was conceived, born every day, lived and addressed the king, avenged the king, and sat before the king as his god. These views were probably never all held as one, but they show the meanings that different worshippers might attach to the sacred eyes so abundantly found in house and in tomb, and the scenes of the king offering the eye.

Journal of the Manchester Egyptian and Oriental Society. IX. 1921. 18 + 56 pp. 5s. (Longmans.)

The Egyptian article in this is *The Problem of Akhenaton*, by T. ERIC PEET. In this Dr. Mercer's denial of Akhenaten's monotheism is discussed, and the general influence of that king. The principal matters are that Aten worship was already started under Amenhetep III, both at Thebes and as a transformed Ra worship at Heliopolis. It is therefore the exclusiveness of Aten worship that was due to Akhenaten. The attempts to show that other gods were recognised by the king are all reduced to mere conventions of speech (as Aten being the Nile, the king being the " strong bull "), which have no religious authority. The artistic reform is rather hesitatingly attributed to the striving after truth, professed by the king. It is surely late in the day to debate the unity of the religious, ethical and artistic revolution carried out by the king who " lived in truth." It is curious to note how nothing has modified the summary of dates and changes stated in *Tell el Amarna* (Petrie), twenty-seven years ago. Nothing has been found—not even from the mummy of the king—to alter or amplify that outline.

Bulletin of the Metropolitan Museum of Art. Part II. October, 1919. New York.

This supplement is a monograph on the statues of Sekhmet from the temple of Mut at Karnak. These figures were so abundant that they are found in many museums, and rather lose their attraction by familiarity. The whole history of them here put together is, however, an interesting outline of the general exploitation of antiquities in the past. Anyone who remembers the temple of Mut some years ago, will know the zigzag line of black granite figures, half buried in the salt soil, and tipped about at various angles in various stages of decay. Mariete estimated that there had been 572 of them originally. They were set up by Amenhetep III, as well as many others in his own temple at Qurneh. Later on, many of these statues were appropriated by the pirate kings, Ramessu II, Panezem II, and Sheshenq I. The modern stripping of the place began in 1760, when one was sold for an exorbitant sum to a Venetian. The French expedition found, and removed to Alexandria, many of the figures. The next stage in the clearance of Egypt was when Salt arrived in 1816 as British Consul-General. He had known Belzoni, who was then in Egypt as an engineer. Burckhardt proposed to Salt to employ Belzoni to bring down the bust of Ramessu II from the Ramesseum, later presented by Salt and Burckhardt to the British Museum. Drovetti, the French Consul-General, was also employing agents to collect at Thebes, so Belzoni set earnestly to work, uncovered a whole row of Sekhmet figures, and began active transportation of them. Next year, in 1817, Belzoni continued work with a young Greek from the Consulate, Yanni Athanasi. The excavations went on with various changes till 1819, when Belzoni retired from the work. Salt went on employing Athanasi, mainly at the temple of Amenhetep III, on the western bank. Many more Sekhmet figures were found there, also the two colossal heads of the king in quartzite, now in the British Museum. Salt died in 1827, and without his protection Athanasi found his work impeded. Much of Salt's gatherings were sold to the French Government in 1827. It appears that the sale in 1833 in London was also of Salt's things, mixed up with Athanasi's management. At this sale, seven of the complete Sekhmet figures were too heavy to go into Sotheby's rooms, and were placed in the recesses of Waterloo Bridge. A relic of this sale is the head of Sekhmet which stood for years over one of the entrances of Sotheby's sale rooms. Of the seven figures, one was sold for twenty guineas (not the cost of transport), the rest were bought in. All seven were, however, re-united as a group in the great collection of all kinds in the hands of that eccentric *virtuoso* Dr. Lee of Hartwell. They appear in his catalogue, published in 1858. By 1865 they were in the collection of Mr. Tyssen-Amherst at Didlington, later Lord Amherst. From thence in 1914 they were acquired for New York.

The great mass of Salt's gatherings were gradually unloaded. In 1823 he sold much to the British Museum. In 1826 a far larger amount to France. In 1833 came the first sale at Sotheby's, followed by another in 1835, and a final sale in 1837 was perhaps entirely of Athanasi's separate work. It is easy now to revile Lord Elgin, Salt and others who brought away so much from ancient lands. They were great benefactors; they saved much from destruction, and they secured it for study and the education of western people, which would never have advanced without some striking appeal to popular imagination. They did vastly less harm than Layard and other explorers in Assyria, who destroyed most important documents and remains from sheer ignorance. Little could be lost by moving away statues from the temples; and until whole buildings were pulled to pieces by French speculators, there was nothing to detract from the benefit of such salvage work.

It may well be asked how it came about that such an immense number of statues of Sekhmet should be made by Amenhetep III. They were not placed in a temple of that goddess, but in temples of Mut and of the king. They were sheerly stacked together, touching side by side and even placed row before row. They were not, therefore, required for the place where they stood, but were merely stored. There is no evidence in other remains of any special devotion of Amenhetep III to Sekhmet; her name only occurs on one of fifty great scarabs, and on a hundred smaller she is never named. It would really seem as if an unlimited order had been sent to the quarries of black granite, to make Sekhmet statues, and it was never revoked, but was left to go on in forgetfulness, the official staff hoping that such a permanent job would not come to an end They may have turned out about thirty a year, and despatched them to Thebes, where they were stacked till further orders. Afterwards it was no one's business to move them, and even the appetite of Ramessu for piracy was quenched by 700 or 800 black Sekhmets.

NOTES AND NEWS.

The excavations of the British School on the desert of Herakleopolis were continued till April. The division of the heavy sculpture and most of the objects was carried out in March by the Keeper of the Museum and the Inspector of Middle Egypt, after which the Director and Mrs. Petrie left, and Mr. and Mrs. Brunton closed their work at Mayana and took charge of the main camp. The continuance of the work brought to light more of the groups of servant figures and boats. Major Hynes then left, and three weeks later Mr. Neilson and M. Bach concluded their work. Mr. Brunton remained to see to the final arrangements of transport. The old system of a weekly steamer is practically cut off ; the Italian line involves much difficulty, and the only certain and easy line, by Marseille, goes but once in three weeks.

At El Amarna the Egypt Exploration Society has been represented by Prof. Peet and Mr. Hayter. We hope to give an account of the results later on.

The work at Thebes, for New York, has been brilliantly conducted by Mr. Winlock. Last year, in a tomb which had been recently cleared, and left as finished, he detected a lower chamber, and found the most amazing series of models. The great group, about four feet long, shows the dais under a colonnade, where the owner sits with his scribes, while his cattle are counted before him. Another model of a tank, surrounded by sycamore trees and a portico, is of exquisite work. Some of these will be illustrated in one of our future numbers. This year Mr. Winlock came to the conclusion, in studying Dr. Naville's and Mr. Hall's publication of the XIth dynasty temple, that there must be another tomb there. On looking for it, the place was obvious, and in that was another great sarcophagus with scenes carved on it, like that of Kauit, now at Cairo, and a wooden statue and mummy of the Princess Aashait. Also in the northern shrine Mr. Winlock found a secondary burial with five silver and gold necklaces.

Prof. Schiaparelli has been working at Gebeleyn, and brought much away. Unhappily nothing is published of the Italian work in the past, but it is to be hoped that the Department of Antiquities will ensure a complete record being produced, according to the regulations.

The earliest example of graphite known is a large lump found at Ghurob, probably of the XVIIIth dynasty. Mr. C. A. Mitchell, who has been studying the history of graphite, has kindly supplied the following analysis of this specimen. Graphitic carbon and moisture, 37·4 per cent. ; mineral matter, 60·6 ; of the latter 47·6 per cent. is of silicates insoluble in acid. This is similar to some of the Swedish graphite. The source of this specimen is unknown ; it is now at University College.

The free public lecture (without ticket) on the results of the year, English and American, will be given, with illustration, on Wednesday, 25th May, at 2.30, at University College, Gower Street, W.C.

The annual exhibition will be at University College, during the four weeks of July, 4th to 30th, 10 to 5.

YOUTHFUL FIGURE OF MERY·RA·HA·SHETEF.
VI DYNASTY.   EBONY.   SEDMENT.

ANCIENT EGYPT.

DISCOVERIES AT HERAKLEOPOLIS.

THE British School in the past winter has made a complete clearance over the cemetery of the city of Henen-nesut, now Henasieh or Ehnasya ; owing to the Greeks identifying the local god Hershefi with Herakles, the city was known in classical times as Herakleopolis. The cause of its position and importance at different periods has been noticed in the preliminary account in this journal, p. 33. Here we are describing the objects discovered.

The earliest part of the cemetery on the desert is of the Ist and IInd dynasties. The tombs are cut in the marly rock, with descending stairways. The most complete tomb contained all the offering vases at the end of the chamber, stacked together, the burial being in a recess at the side. These offerings comprised five bowls of alabaster, one of porphyry, three cylinder jars, two large spheroid vases made in halves, a table, and a large disc table, all of alabaster ; also two bowls and two ewers of copper, in all seventeen vessels. Happily, the copper was in perfect condition, scarcely tarnished. This is the largest and most perfect group known of the IInd dynasty. Another group contained seven alabaster vessels, and a copper basin and ewer, placed on a wooden tray, in front of the recess where the body rested. Another group was of six large alabaster vessels, and various others were also found. More than a dozen skulls of this age were also obtained in good condition.

In the VIth dynasty there were several important burials, one of which happily remained intact. A rock chamber containing two coffins of women had been plundered, but a shaft in the corner of the forecourt had escaped destruction. At about 12 ft. down there were found, buried in the sand filling, three ebony statues of a man, 2 to 2½ ft. high, another of a woman, and three groups of servants. These figures were all carefully ranked in order against the back face of the shaft, standing upright. Continuing the clearance downward, the chamber was found, more than 40 ft. deep, too damp for the preservation of the coffin, but containing an alabaster head-rest of fine work, with an inscription, thrice repeated, of the titles and name of Mery-Ra-ha-shetef, thus dating this burial to the middle of the VIth dynasty. The work of the statues varies ; evidently they were not made by the same hand, and they represent different ages ; the best is equal to the finest Egyptian work in anatomical observation, the poorest is far better than what the Cairo Museum already has of this age. The third and largest of the figures has been kept at Cairo. The meaning of having three figures is shown

E

by the difference in age and dignity. The youngest is a fresh, active youth ; the next is the estate-owner with his long staff ; the largest is the chief of the clan with the *kherp* sceptre in his hand. These explain the figure of King Pepy accompanied by a youth, found at Hierakonpolis. Such reduplication was to give the soul the choice of the freshness of youth, the activity of manhood, or the dignity of rule.

In the above group, the servant figures were carefully made, with smooth stucco surfaces, equal in appearance to the limestone figures of the IVth and Vth dynasties. This was also the case with the servant of a man Nena, whose wooden statue was set up in a recess of his tomb chamber. Such figures led on to the less finished figures of the IXth and Xth dynasties. These models of servants and of boats are sharply limited in age ; they are rare before the VIth dynasty, and are never found in the XIIth dynasty or later. Conversely the ball beads, so characteristic of the XIIth dynasty, were never found in this cemetery with the servant figures. The two characteristics are entirely exclusive one of the other, and mark different periods. The IXth and Xth dynasties were important at Henen-nesut, as this city was their original seat. The foreign character of the people is seen by the cartonnage busts having whiskers, beard and moustache painted ; and the utter destruction of the bodies from many graves of this age shows how bitterly they were hated. This accords with the violent character assigned to Khety, the founder of the IXth dynasty. The principal objects of this age are the groups of models of servants and boats. These show the bearers of offerings, granaries, various preparation of food, setting of a table, and the carrying-chair borne by porters. The graves also contained head-rests, sandals, bows and arrows, sets of delicate models of tools, and, rarely, pottery offering tables. None of the more developed pottery soul-houses were used here, like those in the contemporary graves at Rifeh, 140 miles further south. In graves dating from the VIIth to the Xth dynasty several scarabs were found, of different types, each of which will take with it classes of scarabs hitherto undated. There are the spirals of C and S forms interlinked, the wide spirals of broad shallow work, the double *net* with crowns or vultures, the lion, the *hes* vase in fine outline on dark green jasper, and others. The only objection raised to dating scarabs before the XIIth dynasty has been the absence of them in recorded graves. Now that difficulty is removed, and the evidence otherwise of early dating stands unquestioned. Such discovery of early scarabs does not stand alone. Several were found at the temple of Ehnasya, dating before the XIIth dynasty (*Ehnasya*, ixA), at Kafr Ammar (*Heliopolis*, xxvi), and others at Harageh, not yet published.

The pottery of the early cemeteries passes by gradual stages from the late versions of Old Kingdom forms used in the VIth dynasty to some which border on the forms of the early XIth dynasty. The most marked forms are the cups with straight sides and a foot, the long pots with a funnel neck, the pointed pots of whitish-drab pottery, and the various pentagonal forms of bowls and cups. The cups have been dated before at Rifeh, but the other forms are new to us. Now that we have the whole series of the IXth and Xth dynasties fixed, it will serve to identify tombs of this age found elsewhere. The total absence of any burials of the Middle Kingdom, XIth to XVIth dynasties is remarkable, between two ages of which there are abundant remains.

The revival of Henen-nesut in later times is first shown by a coffin rudely hollowed out of a block of wood ; the lid, which is similarly cut, made up a

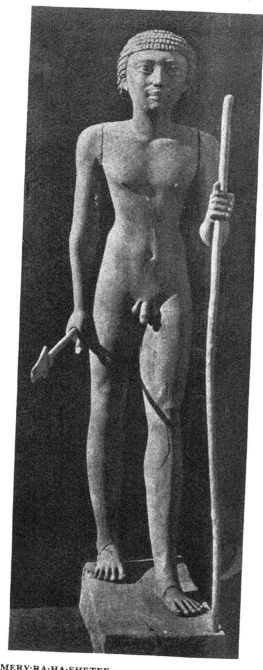

MERY·RA·HA·SHETEF AS HEAD OF HIS CLAN.
VI DYNASTY.   EBONY.   SEDMENT.

cylinder with the body. It was rudely inscribed in bands, naming the four genii, and a little picture of the deceased Tazerti, seated, was drawn on one shoulder. This was probably of the XVIIth dynasty, and is now in the Cairo Museum. Inside the coffin was a basket containing a kohl-pot and a scarab, laid near the head.

COFFIN OF PASAR, FOLLOWER OF AMENHETEP II.
BLACK GRANITE.   SEDMENT.

A remarkable tomb chapel of the XVIIIth dynasty contained a large stele, 3½ ft. high, standing in position in a niche with the altar before it, and a kneeling figure with a tablet in front. The stele is finely carved, with four generations of figures, and the colours are fresh and bright. The head of the family, Sennefer, bears a plaited lock of a royal son, and was high priest of both Heliopolis

E 2

and Memphis; probably he was a son of Amenhetep I, and three generations later would lead to the reign of Tehutmes III, to which the style of this points. Sen-nefer's daughter was Sherat-ra, who married Neb-nekhtu, son of the prophet of Hershef, Amen-mes and Auta; the father of Amen-mes was Aohmes; the stele was erected by Amenhetep, son of Neb-nekhtu. The name of Neb-nekhtu, at the end of the inscription on the base, has, curiously, only the determinative of a frog. The altar before the stele was for Amen-mes, the grandfather; the kneeling figure holds a tablet of adoration to Ra by Min-mes, who does not occur in the family list; perhaps he was a son of Amenhetep, who put his figure later into the tomb. For the size and brilliant work of the stele, and the completeness of the whole group, this discovery seems unparalleled. Strange to say, no tomb-shaft or burial could be found in connection with this chapel. Another burial in open ground in the same hill was in a coffin with ridge roof, unpainted, now in Cairo Museum. Five Nubian baskets in the coffin are in perfect condition; they contained six alabaster vases and kohl-pots, several Cypriote *bilbils*, a very rare oval red vase imitated from leather-work, a casket with panels inlaid with squares of ebony and ivory, and another casket with two sliding lids and a sloping lid bingeing for the various compartments. These are in perfect condition, and are dated to Tehutmes III by the presence both of kohl-pots (which ended in that reign) and kohl-tubes, which first appear then.

A toilet-spoon, with the figure of a girl carrying a vase, is one of the most beautiful of such figures for the breadth and natural character of the work. Another figure of a swimming girl carrying a dish with a lid is of good work. Two hemi-cylindrical toilet boxes have the usual hunting scenes on them; one with lid was also found at Ghurob, containing a ring of Ramessu II. A pen-case bears the name of a scribe, Men-kheper. A gaming board was found, of the 60-hole game in a human outline, such as is known from Kahun (*Kahun*, xvi), Thebes, Gezer and Susa (VINCENT, *Canaan*, III, 2, 3). The present example stands on three legs, and has on the under side a door with bolt, closing a recess to hold the game pieces.

Portions of a magnificent papyrus of the Book of the Dead were found, partly unrolled, and thrown in the dust at the door of a rock chamber. This dust had preserved the papyrus far better than if left in a chamber. The paintings in it are of the finest quality, better than those of the Ani papyrus, which it resembles in the writing. It is hoped that most of the 40 ft. of it which is preserved can be restored to order. One XVIIIth-dynasty burial had 15 scarabs and plaques upon it, mostly of the finest green glaze of Amenhetep III. Another burial had almost as many scarabs and a turquoise-blue bowl.

Some large steles were found with successive scenes of offering, more or less broken up. The earliest is of the fan-bearer on the king's boat, Neb-em-Khemt, about the time of Amenhetep III. Another is of the divine father of Hershef, Amenemhot, probably of the same age. Parts of a very large stele belonged· to a general of cavalry named Pa-hen-neter under Ramessu II. He had appropriated an earlier figure-coffin belonging to Pasar, finely executed in black granite, and placed his titles and name over the erasures.

The largest work of the XIXth dynasty was the tomb-chapel of the viziers Ra-hetep and Pa-ra-hetep. Portions of columns were carried away to be built into other tombs, and a large lintel with figures of the vizier adoring the cartouches of Ramessu II, was coated with plaster and re-used. Since removing the plaster, the stone is in perfect condition. On the destruction of the chapel, the monuments in it were broken up and thrown into the tomb. The red granite altar of Rahetep was found perfect. The family stele of basalt, finely engraved, was mostly complete, and is now at Cairo. A great shrine with the figure of the vizier was much broken, but groups of the family are on the sides. Various other parts of monuments were with these, and ushabtis of different kinds. Great quantities of ushabtis of the XIXth dynasty were found in other tombs, along with much funeral furniture of canopic jars, head-rests, amulets and other objects. One tomb, of a general named Sety, had been cut in soft rock requiring support, and half a dozen stout limestone pillars were placed in it, with his titles of royal scribe, over the body-guard of the king, and general. These bore dedications to Ptah (7), Osiris (6), Anubis (4), Hathor (2) and Isis (1). Some of the titles of the gods seem new, such as Ptah *yu beb neheh*, " going around eternally," or *mes ubău.*

The pieces of Aegean and other foreign pottery are mostly of new types, and the comparison with the Greek examples will be of much interest.

The exhibition of this collection, and that of last year from Lahun, will be held at University College, July 4th to 30th (hours 10 to 5); with two evenings (7 to 9) on the 15th and 25th.

W. M. FLINDERS PETRIE.

SURVIVALS OF ANCIENT EGYPTIAN IN MODERN DIALECT.

A COMPARISON between the spoken Arabic of Egypt and that of Syria, and other Arabic-speaking countries, shows that the difference between them does not exist only in the mode of pronunciation and accentuation of the words, but that it is more profound and goes as far as the actual use and choice of the words, the phonetic values of the different letters, and the grammatical expressions and the turn of the phrases. That the colloquial idiom of Syria is much purer Arabic, and much nearer to the classical language, is undisputed, and it would be interesting to know the causes of this difference, remembering that the influence of the original classical Arabic has been similar in all countries.

A Syrian in speaking Arabic drawls the end of the words, accentuating the last syllable. He often replaces the final nasal *n* by an *m*. The final *t* which is always dropped in the idiom of Egypt, or softened into an aspirated *h*, or replaced by a short *ă*, is often pronounced fully by the Syrian. The final *ă* (= fatha) is often changed into an accentuated *é* before the final *t*. Thus the word ketābă in Egypt is pronounced ketābét in Syria. The letter *g* is always softened in Syria, whereas in Egypt it is only so (and in quite a different manner) in Upper Egypt or among Arabs, but it is hard in Cairo and almost the whole of Lower Egypt. The phrase " Ya Girgis ta'āla hena " of Egypt is uttered " Ya Jirjis ta'āl hôn " in Syria.

But it is the colloquial speech of Egypt that concerns us in this article.

There is a distinct difference between the idiom of Upper and that of Lower Egypt. Again, there is a distinction between the Arabic of Alexandria and that of Damietta, and between that of the Dakahlia and that of the Sharkia Provinces. In Cairo the dialect stands unique, and its pronunciation has been officially adopted throughout Egypt by the Government in the matter of names of villages and towns.

From Cairo the dialect gradually changes as one goes south. First in Beni-Suef, where the idiom is most marked in Bush, Ehnasiah, etc. ; second, in Minia, particularly round about Mellawy and Ashmunên. Between this last and that of Asiut the difference though characteristic lies in the intonation only. The Girgah one is most marked in the whole province, and is particularly so in Akhmim. Then comes that of Luxor and Keneh as far as Esneh. Lastly, the Asuan dialect merges into Berberin. The Fayum dialect has lost most of its characteristics lately, but in the outskirts of the province it resembles that of Beni-Suef.

We will now consider those dialects in detail. The Alexandrian dialect is distinguished by the constant and almost invariable use of the first personal pronoun plural for the singular, where a person speaking, calls himself *ueḥna* (not *'iḥna* as in Cairo) instead of *'Ana*. It must be remembered the population of Alexandria has been always of the most cosmopolitan and heterogeneous type possible. At the present day the Italians and Greeks are predominant, and the colloquial dialect has been enriched by many Greek and Italian words.

The dialect of Damietta, and that of the neighbouring towns down to Mansurah, has the peculiarity of placing a final accent on the words almost amounting to an intonation, which it is very difficult to represent in writing. It is also distinguished by the distinct pronunciation of the letter T. It often replaces with them the harder letter D. It is often followed by a slight aspiration (*siffle*), which makes it more like the English ' ch" in" child'" than the ordinary simple T.

The Sharkia dialect much resembles the rest of those of Lower Egypt, with the exception that in some parts of the province (in the outskirts of Zagazig) the uneducated fellahîn pronounce the hard letter *q* ق, as it ought to be. Again, the letters ك, *k* and *g*, hard, are often softened into ش, *sh*.

The dialect of Cairo is, so to speak, the most refined of the colloquial languages of Egypt. It has peculiar characteristics which distinguish it from the rest of the idioms of Egypt, and is undoubtedly influenced in acquiring its present form by more factors than one. Its most salient characteristics are first, the total dropping of the letter *q* ق wherever it exists and its replacement by the hiatus (hamza). The word قال *qâl*ᵃ is uttered *'Âl,* *qird*, قرد, is pronounced *'Ird*. Second, the letter *g* is never softened into *j* but is always hard. There is no special accentuation or intonation of the word. In the choice of words there is, one might say, a special vocabulary for Cairo. Gutturals are as far as possible eliminated and there are hundreds of words which, if not purely European in their Italian form, are yet not known in Upper Egypt.

Then, as to the most important group, that of Upper Egypt, we can distinguish the following divisions :—

(*a*) The Beni-Suef group.
(*b*) The Minia group, including that of Asiut and Ashmunên.
(*c*) The Girga group.
(*d*) The Luxor to Asuan group.

The most important characteristic of the first group is the dropping of the terminal letter of the words, the drawling of the final vowel, and the vocalisation of the letter *q*, ق, wherever it exists, its right guttural pronunciation, and the hardening of the letter *g*, ج. These characteristics are found *in toto* round about Ehnasiah, in Bush, and in Beni-Suef. The best illustration of these peculiarities can be shown in writing, thus—

$$\text{qad}\ ^{d.}\ \acute{e}\breve{s}\qquad قد أيش$$

whereas in Cairo the same phrase would be pronounced 'Ad êh—or to take a longer phrase يا واد يا احمد هات القله و حطها جنب would be pronounced in Beni-Suef thus—Ya wād yaḥm [ad] hāt el qullah w' ḥuṭṭaha gam [bi] whereas in Cairo it would be uttered like this—Ya wād yaḥmād hāt el wllah w'ḥuṭṭaha gamby.

Thus the letter ق is entirely dropped in Cairo and replaced by the ٢ hiatus or Alef hamzatum. It is replaced by the hard *g*, ج, in Upper Egypt, whereas

E 4

it retains its real value in the Beni-Suef dialect. The letter *g* is hardened in Cairo as *g* in English " good." In Beni-Suef it is also pronounced hard, but not invariably so. In Upper Egypt from Minia upwards it is always softened, but in quite a peculiar manner which makes it different to the sound of the English *j*, and yet it stands between the hard *g* and the soft *j*. One has to hear it uttered before one can have an idea of its value.

In the Minia and Asiut group the letter *q*, ق, is hardened to *g* wherever it exists, whereas the letter *g*, ج, is softened to *j* or something like it ; but it is the letter D that takes the value of the English *j* when it is in the middle of the word. Thus q^{a}lb, قلب is pronounced g^{a}lb ; q^{u}tt قط is pronounced g^{u}tt, but ادلع 'Idd^{a}ll^{a}c is pronounced 'Ijj^{a}ll^{a}c ; the name Kostandy is uttered Gostanjy ; the word Brostandy for Protestant is pronounced Brostanjy.

The Girgah group has the peculiarity of replacing the *d* by *g* and the letter *g* by *d*. Thus the word gabál, mountain, is pronounced dabal, and the word g^{u}wwa, جوا, inside, is vocalised d^{u}wwa. The name Girgis is uttered Dirdis, but the word 'Idd^{a}ll^{a}c, ادلع is always pronounced 'Ijj^{a}ll^{a}c, اجلع. The *g* being always softened in the manner described above.

Foreign words introduced into the spoken idiom of Upper Egypt receive different treatment in the different districts of Egypt. Metathesis is very common in Upper Egypt. 'Isbitalia for hospital is pronounced 'Istibalia. This sometimes happens in purely Arabic words ; d^{a}r^{a}g^{a}h is uttered garadah. The letter *d* sometimes replaces the letter *p* ; lampa is said lamda. The letters *u*, و, and *b*, stand for the *v*. Babur or wabur stand for " vapeur." *M* might take the place of *p* ; mantalón for pantalón. For a Cairene or a Lower Egyptian it is sometimes possible to pronounce the European letter *p*, but never so for an Upper Egyptian.

As regards the use of the vowels we find in certain cases that the round *o* is always preferred in the idiom of Upper Egypt and Lower Egypt, whereas in Middle Egypt the open *a* is always used instead. To take a very common word used as an exclamation, " 'Iabôy." It is pronounced thus in Upper Egypt. In Lower Egypt it is Iabôuy, whereas in the Fayum and Beni-Suef it is always Iabāy. There are many other examples, but time and space do not allow me to multiply them.

Now, having considered the particular characteristics of the different dialects in the whole of Egypt, it becomes interesting to speculate about the causes and factors of these differences. The facilities of communication of the present time, and the thorough intermixing of all the population of Egypt, ought to help these differences to disappear entirely, whereas to all practical appearance they seem to be fixed and enduring. On examination of the vocabulary used in the vulgar Arabic of Egypt one is struck by the great number of words which can be easily traced to an Ancient Egyptian or Coptic origin. These words are much commoner in the dialects of Upper Egypt than in those of Cairo and Lower Egypt. At the end of this article I have collected a few words which are commonly used. Again, the expression and the turn of the phrases used in Upper Egypt can sometimes be literally translated into Coptic without its being necessary to make in Coptic any grammatical changes in the relative position of the different members of the phrase. For instance, the curious correspondence of the pronunciation of the different phonemes in the modern vulgar Arabic of the Sa'id with their old values in Coptic, such as the pronunciation of the letter ج, exactly like the Coptic ϫ, different to its pronunciation in all .other Arabic-speaking countries. The value of a hard *g* given to the Arabic letter ج was the same phenomenon that happened when the ancient Egyptian language was written in Greek letters to form the Coptic language; the same play on, and the interchange of, the vowels is seen in the different modern dialects of the vulgar Arabic as in the different dialects of Coptic, such as the prolongation of certain vowels in Upper Egypt when they are shortened in Cairo, or the dropping of certain terminal letters in both dialects, betraying the custom of doubling the vowels in Sahidic Coptic when they were only single in Bohairic ⲟⲩⲁⲃ Boh., and ⲟⲩⲁⲁⲃ Sahidic, or ⲕⲁϩⲓ Boh., and ⲕⲁϩ, Sa. All this, in fact, induces me to believe in the influence of Coptic on the spoken Arabic rather than *vice versâ* as most authors hold to be the case. Those authors believe that it was through the influence of Arabic, that the difference between ⲛ and ⲃ was lost in Coptic, and that the vowels ⲁ and ⲉ came to have the same value, whereas we know from demotic, and even from the Graeco-Roman hieroglyphic that these changes had already been effected in the language.

A glance through some of the Christian Arabic MSS. shows them to be teeming with mistakes in their Arabic grammar and syntax. A careful analysis of these mistakes shows that most of them are really due to literal translation from Coptic by a scribe who was not a master of Arabic.

Masculine words are treated as feminine if they happen to be of a feminine gender in Coptic, *e.g.*, the word الارض is feminine in Arabic but masculine in Coptic, and so it is thus treated. There are two words for evening in Coptic, ⲧⲣⲟⲩϩⲓ and ⲛⲓⲉϫⲱⲣϩ, both translated by one feminine word in Arabic الليلة; but we often find the Arabic word treated as masculine probably when the original Coptic word used was the masculine one ⲛⲓⲉϫⲱⲣϩ. These examples can be multiplied, and a reference to their existence is enough to serve our purpose.

We can again remark quickly the differences between the different Coptic dialects from the point of view of similar differences in the modern vulgar dialects. The letter ⲕ was commonly changed to ⲅ in Sahidic. In the ancient language the letters ⊂⊃, ⌐ and ◠, ⊏⊐ and their syllabics often interchanged as they do now in the Minia group and the Dakahlia dialect (see above).

Metathesis occurred more commonly in Sahidic Coptic than in Bohairic. The drawling of the vowels and their lengthened vocalisation is explained by their doubling in Sahidic when compared with Bohairic, and the dropping of the terminal vowel is similarly located. Lastly the preference for the open vowel *a* to the closed one *o* is again shown in the dialects of Middle Egypt, where we had ⲉⲃⲁⲗ, F., ⲉⲃⲟⲗ, S., and all these phenomena exist in our own days in the modern vulgar dialects of Egypt.

The fact mentioned above of the occasional pronunciation of the hard ⲕ and the hard ϫ in Lower Egypt as *sh*, ش, is proved to have existed when the Arabs transliterated the names of the towns in these localities in Arabic letters. Notice ϫⲁⲃⲁϭⲉⲛ written now شباص and ϫⲉⲃϫⲏⲣ شبشير, ϫⲉⲃⲣⲏ شبرا, and others.

Some Egyptian Words remaining in Modern Use.

ٮٮٮ, ᴀᴧ, " small stones." At the present day there is a game played with ·small pebbles by boys in the streets called the game of the Āl, لعبة آل.

 oⲧⲱ = واوا a word commonly used to babies with the meaning of painful or burning.

ʙoᴧ, " out, outside," may be the origin of the colloquial بَرّا in the saying اطلع برّا " go out."

ᴛнᴛᴀᴀʙ طياب, in the language of the crews of Nile boats, meaning a good breeze.

кᴀı " bone," кⲱc " to bury," the word كاس is often used in the sense of death and burial.

معديه at the present day is the name given to a ferry boat.

رومس is the name given to a plank of wood used as a small boat.

مشنه is the basket (couffe) in which dates are carried.

ɴᴀпʙı is used in speaking of cultivation. " We cultivated our field *nabary*," meaning any of the grains, wheat, barley or other.

ᴀхп, " hour," وجبد a certain length of time, an hour.

ⲩᴀoⲧⲱⲩ " eat," always used to babies.

ɸopı بورى fish.

The names of some of the fish рнı, راڭ, ʃɛᴧqᴀı, ʃɛᴧʙᴀı شلبه, أنومة.

ᴛⲱʙɛ " brick," طوبه. This word, meaning brick, has passed even into Spanish.

хᴧoᴧ " vase," قلة. The ordinary drinking pot.

ʃⲱʒп, " to burn," *cf.* cᴀʒϯ both used as شوب and صهد meaning " hot " day.

ʒⲱʙ, " work." This occurs in small songs and in appeals, etc., amongst the fellahin or the boatmen on the Nile. هوب هوب تتلن لهشوب or هوب ياشغل لهنوب; the first is sung when the work becomes killing on a hot day, and the second is a song of the wheat harvest.

ⲭⲟϥ, ⲭⲁϥⲭⲉϥ, " cold," جغيف, or the noun جِفّة, meaning rigour, chill.

🐟🏺🐊 ⲟⲩⲭⲁⲓ, " to be safe " or " well," is used when crying for help, جاي ; one can hear the word almost any day in the streets.

ⲍⲁⲗⲱⲩ, " cheese," حالوم is the Upper Egyptian name for cheese.

ⲗⲉⲃⲩ, " straw," لبش, in talking of sugar cane ; it is always counted by the *libshah.*

ⲁⲓⲃⲁⲛ, " cord," amongst the rigging of a boat on the Nile, لبان.

⳨, ⲩⲟⲩⲛⲉ, " barn, storehouse," شونه, a large storehouse for cotton, wheat, etc.

ⲙⲁⲣⲏⲥ, " south," ماريس, " southern," when talking of the wind for boats, or anything that comes from the south.

ⲙⲏⲧⲉⲙⲥ, مدمّس, anything cooked in the oven by a continuous fire. There is the مدمس فول, beans, a very common dish.

ⲡⲉⲥⲟⲩⲣⲱ, بصارة, another kind of cooked beans, something like a purée.

🐟 ١١, الفايتان, two poles in the forepart of a boat.

ⲙⲉⲍⲓⲱⲥ, " full of quickness," مهياص, a very common word, " busybody," one who talks and moves a great deal without doing anything.

ⲩⲫⲏⲣ, B., ⲩⲡⲏⲣ, S. اشبار, a common expression in the language of women when trying to excite pity, اشبار علي, meaning " I am to be pitied," or " Dear me," or " I have become miserable." The Coptic word means " wonder."

🦅, ⲡ, ⲉⲣⲡⲉ, S., ⲉⲣⲫⲉⲓ, B., ⲡ, " temple," برب, a common word in Upper Egypt for any old temple or chapel.

ⲧⲉⲣⲉⲗⲉⲁⲓ ترالّي, in the expression عقله ترالّي, meaning " he is become dotty," a " simpleton."

ⲧⲉⲁⲧϩⲁⲓ, " to dribble, to drop," in the expression انامتلتل, meaning " my nose is running."

ⲩⲛⲟⲩϥ, " basket," شنفه, measure for hay or straw ; شنيف تبن, net for straw.

ϥⲱⲥⲓ, " hatchet," فاس, the usual pick for field work.

ϥⲟⲩⲧⲉ, فوطه, a towel.

ⲧⲍⲉⲁⲓⲥ, ⲧⲉⲛⲍⲉⲁⲓⲥ, اتهيلصا, a cry of boatmen on the Nile when their boat sticks in the mud ; the meaning is literally " we have stuck in the mud." So also when they call each other to work, ⲍⲉⲁⲉ ⲍⲱⲃ هيلبوب, " come to work."

〰️, " to open " ; شنيشه, *shenisha,* a hole in the wall.

The above list gives a few examples of the hundreds of words which are in common use in the dialects of Egypt, and which have remained in the common language and could not be replaced by Arabic words. They do not exist, nor are they understood, in other Arabic-speaking countries, such as Syria or Algeria. They do not occur in the Arabic dictionary of the classical language.

Geo. P. G. Subhy.

ORACULAR RESPONSES.

In Part I (1920) of Ancient Egypt, p. 31, there is an article on Monsieur A. Moret's "Un jugement de Dieu," in which the following comment is made: "In some way the decision did not depend upon human interference, but was equivalent to drawing lots for a reply."

In connection with this vexed question of the means by which the gods of ancient Egypt communicated their wishes to men, the last article published by the late Mons. Charles Legrain is of considerable interest.

It was published early in 1917 in the *Bulletin de l'Institut Francais d'Archéologie Orientale* under the title "Un miracle d'Ahmes à Abydos sous le règne de Ramses II." It consists of a detailed examination, in that gifted writer's best style, of the relief and inscription of stela No. 43649 of the Cairo Museum *journal d'entrée*, and is published with a plate. Shortly, the relief represents the bark of the god-king Ahmes, borne on the shoulders of eight priests, four to each pole, before which "the priest of Osiris Psar" raises his hands in reverence. "Paari, true of voice," standing in the midst leads the company with his hand extended to the nearer pole of the ark. The sacred image is hidden from view by the usual embroidered curtains which are held together in front by a small kneeling figure of a king.

The text, which is given in full with Mons. Legrain's rendering of it, lacunae in brackets, shows that the scene represents the arrival of the sacred object, the oracle of Nebpehtra, upon a plot of land, to decide a case of disputed possession. The translation given runs as follows: "The year 14 second month of Shat day 25 in the reign of the King of Upper and Lower Egypt (Ramses II) day of the arrival of the priest Psar with the priest Jai to bring (the oracle of) Nebpehtra. The priest Psar arrived on the field which belonged to (my) son. He heard the (acclamations?) of the children of the people. The god was to establish (the right?). The god arrived, saying, 'it belongs to Psar the son of Mes,' and the god *weighed down* very heavily in the presence of the priest (of the king?) Pehtinebra, the prophet Paari, the front priest Inoujabou, the (rear?) priest Janofre, the rear priest Nakht, the rear priest Thotimes. Made by the priest, scribe, sculptor of the temple of Ramses II in the domain of Osiris Nebmehit."

The critical words in the translation are those in italics, as they are Legrain's rendering of the word Hen ⟨glyph⟩ which is usually translated "to bow the head." The word is sometimes followed by the determinative of a head, as shown above, but not always; in fact the arm determinative alone is much more common, which led M. Brugsch to suggest that the will of the god was expressed by a gesture of the arm. M. Legrain suggested very plausibly that the head determinative where it occurs in the significance under discussion, has been mechanically inserted by the scribe from association with the homophonons word meaning "skull."

M. Legrain pointed out that the image is hidden by the veiling curtains, held together by the little figure. How then, even supposing the Egyptians were able to make mechanical figures of this nature (of which no example has ever been found) could the spectators see if the head nodded ? Another very strong point he makes is that unless his explanation is correct, namely that the bark *weighed down* or became heavier on one side than the other, there is no reason apparent for the mention of the names of five of the bearers.

But M. Legrain's suggestion is put out of the reach of refutation, practically, by the singularly apt example he furnishes of an almost identical " marvel " similarly attested in writing from modern Egypt, having occurred in fact barely two months before. The phenomenon (if one may call it so) is fairly well known to residents in Egypt, and in the case in point is connected with the burial of the Sheikh el Said Yussef, descendant from the holy Sheikh Abu Agag, whose ancient white mosque stands on an eminence of unexcavated earth in the midst of Luxor temple. The Arabic statement, dated November 6th, 1916, describes how, when the body borne on the shoulders of three men was passing a certain spot by the Nile, the men suddenly felt the bier[1] weighing heavier upon them, and they could not walk on. They put it down and after reciting a prayer, continued under normal conditions. This happened twice again during the progress to the burial. The names of the three bearers are given as witnesses.

About ten or twelve years ago I saw an excited hurrying crowd passing along one of the main streets leading to the southern part of the native quarter of Cairo, and was told in reply to my question that " the corpse was running." Similarly, I have seen a bier with a crowd collected round it in the middle of a field of clover, into which it had insisted upon going. If possible the body in these rare circumstances is buried on the spot in which it seems so emphatically to indicate its wish to be interred. But in this case the crowd of relatives, among whom no doubt was the owner of the field by that time, seemed to be waiting for the all too conscious corpse to change its mind, and relax its determination to be buried in a spot so eminently and obviously undesirable for the purpose.

It may be emphasised, a point which M. Legrain apparently did not seize upon, that the determinative of the word Hen is an arm; perhaps the arm of the bearer or the priest so often represented placing his hand beneath the pole as he walks.[2] We may suppose that at least four signals could be registered, namely, from the front, rear, left and right. In this case the weight is attested by the four rear men.

To refer such " facts " as those related above to the similar phenomena called psychical or spiritualistic, would make this note needlessly long; M. Legrain does no more than allude to it. But it may be remarked that automatisms could be quoted, which, in so far as they constitute messages or statements and are veridical, can to a large extent be referred (their conformity with fact that is) to telepathy. Bribery and corruption were doubtless as common in ancient Egypt as they are to-day, but it is, apparently, perfectly possible, if one may believe the reports of accredited scientific researchers, that the feeling

---

[1] The modern Egyptian bier is in the form of an oblong box, in which the swathed body is placed. The bier is carried on two poles attached to it.

[2] The feeling of additional weight would cause the bearers to " give," and the priest, Paari, in this case (see above), would thus attest it. The bearers would behave as though the weight had suddenly and normally increased.

of weighing down should be subconscious and take effect as though it were due to material causes, and that it should coincide with, or respond to, a telepathic stimulus, unconsciously given, from some person present. We may, however, be sure that the priest Psar was exerting considerable psychic pressure, in the form of hope or prayer, on behalf of his family during the ordeal !

ERNEST S. THOMAS.

[There was the same belief in Sparta, as to divine intimation by weight. At the scourging of youths by the altar of Artemis " the priestess stands by during the operation, holding the wooden statue, which is generally light by its smallness, but if the scourgers spare any young man at all in his flogging, either on account of his beauty or rank, then this wooden statue in the priestess' hand becomes heavy, and no longer easy to hold, and she makes complaint of the scourgers and says it is so heavy owing to them." Pausanias III, XVI.—F. P.]

NAWRUZ, OR THE COPTIC NEW YEAR.

THE Nawruz, or the Coptic New Year as it is called in English, is the day of the High Nile, and fell this year on September 11th.

The word Nawruz is from the Persian *Naw* " new," and *Ruz* " day," an appropriate term for the beginning of a new year. It is not clear why a Persian phrase should be used to signify a purely Egyptian festival, nor is the exact date known of its introduction into general use in Egypt. Maqrizi, writing towards the end of the fourteenth century, employs the word as the usual term for expressing this special festival. Previous to Maqrizi, the only Persian influence in Egypt was during the two Persian invasions, one in the sixth century, the other in the seventh. As these were of short duration, and as the invaders were held in great detestation, it is not likely that a word from their language would be adopted throughout the country for a national custom. It would seem then that the word must have become acclimatised during the Persian dominion which began with Cambyses, when the Persians actually ruled Egypt. It is possible that the ancient name for the festival was sufficiently like in sound to its Persian supplanter to make it possible for the Persian word to supersede the original Egyptian. Such a word has, however, not yet been recognised in hieroglyphic or Coptic.

The festival of Nawruz is traditionally very ancient. Maqrizi says that Ashmoun ben Qobtim ben Masr ben Beïsar ben Ham ben Noah instituted it in Egypt. As the first three names are those of towns—Ashmouneyn, Quft and Cairo—it appears that the festival was universal in Egypt ; and that it was known from an early period is indicated by the genealogy which takes the first institution as far back as five generations after the Flood. It would seem probable then that the festival went back traditionally to prehistoric times.

Maqrizi mentions three consecutive festivals of the Nile : " C'est habituelle-- ment en Mesori qu'on ouvre le Khalig ; l'eau y pénètre et monte jusqu'à une écluse, où elle s'arrête jusqu'à ce qu'on ait arrosé les terres situées au-dessous du niveau de l'eau arrêtée dans ce canal ; puis l'écluse est ouverte le jour de Nourouz et l'eau s'étend jusqu'à une autre écluse où elle est encore arrêtée pour permettre d'arroser les terrains situés en contre-bas de son niveau. Cette seconde écluse est ouverte à son tour le jour de la fête de Salib, dix-sept jours après le Nourouz ; l'eau gagne une troisième barrière où elle est encore arrêtée pour permettre d'irriguer les terres situées au-dessous de son niveau ; enfin, cette dernière barrière étant ouverte, l'eau va plus loin arroser d'autres terres et finalement se jette dans la mer."[1] Maqrizi does not give the interval of time between the first and second festival, but the date of the third discloses an interesting fact. Nawruz falls always on the first of the month of Thoth, and in ancient times. the seventeenth of that month was the festival of Uag, one of the chief of the Nile festivals, christianised later under the name of the *Id es Salib*, the Feast of

---

[1] Maqrizi, Pt. I, ch. 16, p. 159, Bouriant's translation.

the Cross. It is generally supposed that it was on this festival that the sacrifice of a girl was celebrated, but Maqrizi[1] gives the twelfth of the month Paoni (June 11) as the date of the sacrifice. Paoni is the month when the Nile is at its lowest, an appropriate time for a sacrifice to cause the water to rise.

The modern celebration of the festival of the Nawruz in Cairo is too well known to need description ; the cutting of the Khalig, the processions, banquets and fireworks have been described by all travellers. Klunzinger,[2] who was in Egypt from 1863 to 1875, gives an interesting account of the Nawruz celebrations, which he says took place in " every little town " in Upper Egypt. He describes the mock kings who ruled their respective towns for three days, and on the third day were condemned to death by fire ; the royal insignia were burnt, but the wearers escaped unhurt. This custom does not appear to survive now, at least not among the Copts of the west side of the river. It is possible that it may yet be found on the east side ; for, as the Nawruz occurs always in the hot month of September, few Europeans remain in Upper Egypt or visit the villages at that time of year, therefore there is no one to record the customs, and this most important survival of the ceremonial death of the king has as yet been described, very inadequately, by only one observer.

There is, however, another method of celebrating the Nawruz, which takes place at the little Coptic town of Neqadeh, on the west side of the Nile, in the mudiriyeh of Keneh. Of this custom there is no record in the accounts of travellers, for I am told that Neqadeh is the only place which retains this ancient and traditional method of keeping the festival. By the kindness of Negib Effendi Baddar, omdeh of Neqadeh, I had the privilege of witnessing the celebration at that town.

In the early morning, from about half-past two until dawn, the inhabitants of the town, men, women and children, Copts and Moslems, went down to one of the four places on the river bank where the women come to fill their pitchers and the farm animals are watered. The people came in family groups, parents and children together. The women waded into the river and stood knee-deep in the water ; they then lifted water in their hands and drank nine times, with a pause between every three mouthfuls ; or they dipped themselves nine times under the water with a pause between every three dips ; or they washed the face nine times with a pause between every three washings. The men sat on the bank and performed their ablutions or drank the water in the same way ; a few big boys and young men flung themselves into the stream and swam about. The children were dipped nine times or had nine handfuls of water poured over their heads by their mothers. Friends greeted one another with the words " Abu Nawruz hallal " or " Nawruz Allah." The whole ceremony is essentially religious, the women especially pray the whole time, either to obtain children or for special blessings on their children, in the belief that prayers made on this occasion, and when the worshipper is actually standing in or drinking the Nile water, are particularly efficacious.[3] The reverence and simplicity, the heartfelt faith of the people, made this ceremony one of the most beautiful and touching that I have ever seen.

---

[1] *Ibid.*, Pt. I, ch. 17, p. 164.
[2] C. B. Klunzinger, *Upper Egypt*, p. 184. Glasgow, 1878.
[3] I saw one woman remain stooping over the water for a considerable time, evidently praying. When she had finished, she beat the water nine times with the corner of her garment, and then came out. I do not know the significance of her action.

The extreme antiquity of this water festival is manifest from the allusions to it in Pharaonic times. These allusions have not been understood, but the ceremony which takes place at Neqadeh at High Nile makes it possible to identify two ancient festivals which have not been recognised hitherto.

The graffito of Amen-em-hêt in the tomb of Antef-oker in the XIIth dynasty records his desire to " sniff the breeze out of the Netherworld and to drink water upon the swirl of the New Water."[1] The expression, " the New Water," clearly refers to the inundation, and the drinking of the inundation water must be an allusion to a ceremony such as I have described above.

In the *Book of the Dead* and in funerary inscriptions the gods are frequently petitioned that the votary may " breathe (or smell) the sweet breezes of the north wind from the Netherworld (*khert-neter*) and drink water from the eddy of the stream."[2] *Khert-neter*, or the Netherworld, which the sun entered and passed through during the hours of the night, was anciently supposed to lie to the north of Egypt, either in the Mediterranean or still further north among the islands of the Aegean. Hence the idea that the north wind came out of the Netherworld.

In most of such ancient prayers the breathing or smelling of the north wind is usually coupled with the drinking from the eddy, and the modern custom shows that two festivals still commemorate these practices; they are both called " Coptic " festivals, and are observed by Copts and Mahomedans alike. The first is known in English as the Coptic Easter Monday, the second as the Coptic New Year; while in Arabic the first in March is named *Nawruz es sultani*, the royal New Year, the second, in September, *Nawruz Allah*, the New Year of God.

The Nawruz es sultani, the Coptic Easter Monday, has yet another name, *Shem-en-Nessim*, and is celebrated on the 12th of Barmahat (March 22nd), at the beginning of the period when the north wind begins to blow steadily. The name Shem-en-Nessim, literally " Smelling the Breeze," refers clearly to the custom mentioned in the ancient funerary prayers; thus showing that both the Nawruz festivals are of early origin, and are survivals of two popular festivals dating back at least to the Middle Kingdom.

Then, as now, they belonged to the populace and not to the priests; they were celebrated in the open and not in temples; they were in honour of un-changing natural phenomena and not of the gods; they were for the living and not for the dead. For these reasons they have remained almost unaltered for more than forty centuries, surviving changes of religion, government and, to a great extent, of race.

M. A. MURRAY.

[In the *Zar*, or women's hypnotic dance for curative purposes, the special words connected with the ceremony are also of Persian origin, perhaps from its possible introduction from the East by itinerant fortune-tellers in ancient times.—H.F.P.]

[1] DaVies, *Tomb of Antefoker*, p. 28.
[2] *Book of the Dead*, chapters XXXVIIIA, LVI, LXVIII, CXXXVIA, CLXIV, CLXV; *Recueil des Travaux*, I 202, II 122, IX 99, etc.

PERIODICALS.

Annales du Service des Antiquités de l'Égypte.
Tome XX, 1920.

BARAIZE, E.—*Rapport sur la mise en place d'un moulage du zodiaque de Dendérah.*—The French Government having supplied a cast of the zodiac, which was removed from the temple of Denderah in 1822 by M. Saulnier, this was placed in the position of the original, which is now in the Cabinet des Médailles of the Bibliothèque nationale at Paris. M. Baraize has restored the appearance of the chamber as nearly as possible to what it was a century ago.

DARESSY, G.—*Bas-relief d'un écuyer de Ramsès III.* This is on a lintel in the Cairo Museum from the tomb of Pa-neter-nahem at El Helleh opposite Esneh. The deceased is shown standing, holding the strap of a horse ; he is entitled " chief of the stable of the king," and *nesut up er semt neb,* " royal messenger unto all lands." Quotations are given of the *up* to specified countries.

DARESSY, G.—*Les Statues ramessides à grosse perruque.* These statues are described in three groups : (1) those with two ensigns, one in each hand, (2) those with one ensign, (3) those holding other attributes. It had been suggested that these figures were of the XIIth dynasty, and appropriated by the Ramessides. M. Daressy concludes that none of these were of the Middle Kingdom, and though some might be as early as Amenhetep III, yet there is no re-appropriation, and all was probably made between Ramessu II and VI.

DARESSY, G.—*Le scarabée du cœur de la grande prêtresse Ast-m-kheb.* Engravings of this are published as a tail-piece to the preface of Zoëga's work on obelisks in 1797. It is stated to have been in the Borgia collection ; but it is not in the Vatican catalogue, though it may be in the Naples museum, to which some of the Borgia objects passed. It is described as of green porphyry. There is no peculiarity in the inscription, but it is strange that the mummy had been robbed of the scarab before being placed in the pit at Deir el Bahri, and the scarab had not been renamed for another burial, as was so often the case.

EDGAR, C. C.—*Selected papyri from the archives of Zenon.* These are dated from year 36 to the end of the reign of Philadelphos. After business notes about pigs and wheat, vines and goats, there are letters about the billeting of troops in Karia, and exemptions are claimed by Government officials in Egypt for their friends, by direct request to the *Boule* and *Demos* of the city.

LEFEBURE, G.—*Le Tombeau de Petosiris.* This long article of 81 pages should have more than two illustrations of sculpture if it is to be a substitute for a volume memoir on this interesting structure. There is some hope held out of a great publication, but on a scale for which time and money is wanting. The tomb is in the cemetery of Hermopolis, opposite El Bersheh, and is assigned to the middle of the fourth century B.C., the end of the XXXth dynasty. An outer court, or pronaos, has the palm leaf columns still standing complete, and the curtain walls between them. Behind that is the naos, a hall with four pillars around the tomb shaft. In front of the building is an altar, free-standing, with triangular corners or horns, of Asiatic origin (see last number, p. 55). The examples of the sculptures show that the old scenes were repeated, but the cloth-ing was copied from the life of the time, the man wearing a loose tunic to the knees. The inscriptions refer to eight High Priests of Hermopolis in five genera-tions, Zed.tehuti.auf.onkh, Seshu, Pef.nef.neit, Zed.tehuti.auf.onkh, Petosiris, Zedher, Tehuti-rekh, and Petu-kem.

The façade has scenes of offerings, with the king officiating, above a dado with Nile figures offering. Petosiris appears playing draughts. In the pronaos all the scenes belong to Petosiris. Workshops are figured, with coppersmiths, gilders, gold weighing, perfumers, carpentry and basketwork. Some new forms of tools should be carefully copied. Scenes of agriculture and wine-making follow, and the great group of Petosiris and his wife receiving offerings from their children, with sacrifices of cattle.

The chapel or naos was for Seshu the father, and Zad-tehuti-auf-onkh, the elder brother, of Petosiris. There are two registers of scenes, beginning with the father and brother before Osiris. There is a great funeral procession, after which the brother adores groups of divinities of nine different places. After this are nine cynocephali, who acclaim Ra in Duat; the twelve hours are represented as women standing, alternately in red and in blue dress; twelve uraei follow as the divinities who lighten the darkness in Duat. The next scene is of two bulls of Amen and Osiris, each with a mummy, following which is the judgment scene. There is an address of Petosiris to his brother about the beauty of the tomb, and then a row of 25 servants with offerings, and 28 more, alternately men and women, the latter sometimes carrying infants.

The pit of the tomb is 26 feet deep, and leads to many chambers below, filled with broken fragments of rock and sarcophagi. Among these was found the magnificent lid of one of the three body-coffins of Petosiris, bearing long columns of inscription, entirely wrought in coloured glass hieroglyphs, inlaid in the ebony. It is the most brilliant example of glass work, like a fragment— hitherto unique—in the museum of Turin. The subject is the 41st chapter of *The Book of the Dead.* Let us hope that this remarkable tomb will soon be copied in full-size facsimile (by dry squeeze), and ·published; it must not be allowed to perish like the late tomb at Gizeh, cleared in 1907, and soon after broken up by dealers.

DARESSY, G.—*Deux stèles de Bubastis.* One is of a Thanure or Thal; the other of Ptah.kho, born of Nespamok and Bast.renen, with brothers Ta pesh.her, Onkh set.her, Nuty . . . her, Ta khred.bast, and Ta da nut.

DARESSY, G.—*Un groupe de Saft el Henneh.* This group of the close of the XVIIIth dynasty was accidentally found. The inscription is supposed to be an appropriation of the Bubastite age; it records the general, chief of archers, chief of the serfs of Ra, prophet of Sepdu, Sa.uas; his wife Onkhs.mut, son Her, and daughter Thent.amen.

DARESSY, G.—*Un " fils royal en Nubie."* This is a stele from Abydos, of the XIXth dynasty. It was made by the " overseer of the southern lands, royal son in Nubia, overseer of the works of the temple of Amen, chief of the Maza land, Any." At Abu Simbel Any is called " royal son of Kush, of the people of Henennesut." The temple of Wady Sebu'a was named " the Temple of Amen." A long discussion on Maza Land is of value for Nubian geography.

DARESSY, G.—*La princesse Amen.mérit.* A figure from Karnak, of a tutor with a princess, Amen.meryt, evidently belongs to about the time of Tehutmes III ; and as he is represented with his daughter Amen.meryt at Deir el Bahri, this serves to date the figure.

TODA, E.—*La découverte et l'inventaire du tombeau de Sen.nezem.* This account, published in Spanish in 1887, is here translated by M. Daressy. Signor Toda was one of a party taken by M. Maspero on his voyage of inspection in 1886. The tomb was found by a native, and at once searched by Maspero. After 35 years the French Institute is stated to be intending to publish the scenes and inscriptions. The tomb contained 9 bodies in coffins, and 11 others laid on the sand. The latter all broke up in moving, and only the heads were preserved. The bodies in coffins and all the contents of the tomb were carried to Maspero's boat. Ushabtis of 13 different persons were in the tomb. More than 40 boxes of painted wood were found, and a set of instruments, measure, squares and plummet (*Tools and Weapons*, XLVII). This magnificent set of tomb furniture has been scattered in the Cairo Museum, and many pieces were sold to the collections of America and Europe. Altogether 26 names are recorded from this tomb :—Sen.nezem, Ya.nefer.tha, Kho.bekhent, Sătha, Bun.khetef, Pa.kharu, Ra.hetep or Pa.ra.hetep, Khensu, Tămokt, Ra.mes, On.hetep, Ra.nekhu, Aru.nefer, Tă.aosh.sent, Tăyna, Hetepu, Rusu, Rămo, Thără, Tăan, Rămo, Tă.osh . . ., Tutua, Mesu, Tăau, Hent.urt.

DARESSY, G.—*Un groupe de statues de Tell el Yahoudieh.* Two figures of a man and woman standing, roughly cut, of the Ramesside age. He was royal fan-bearer, over the lands of the south, Piaăy ; his wife was Tăuser. He holds a staff bearing a ram's head.

DARESSY, G.—*L'animal Séthien à tête d'âne.* The writer had previously proposed that the Set animal was an arbitrary combination. Set appears with an ass's head in the XIIth dynasty and Roman times. Now a coffin of Nesi. amen, one of the priests of Amen, shows the sun-bark drawn by three jackals and three animals with ass's heads.

DARESSY, G.—*Fragments Memphites.* These have been found in the temple area between the village and the colossus. They are :—(1) a black granite figure of Ramessu II in many pieces ; (2) block of limestone with his cartouche ; (3) another block with part of a Ptah figure ; (4) part of an alabaster base of a column, with the name of Ramessu.user.pehti (*Student's History*, III, 37, after No. 23) ; (5) two blocks from a chapel of Sekhmet built by Sheshenq II, with a figure of his son, the High priest Takerat ; (6) a block naming a priestess of Mut and Neferatmu, Bast.au.seonkh ; (7) a sandstone door-jamb of Amasis.

DARESSY, G.—*L'évêché de Saïs et Naucratis.* In the Coptic lists the bishopric of Sais is stated to be Sa and Satf. Sa is Sais, and now it is proposed that Satf in Coptic would be an easy corruption of Gaif, the modern name of Naukratis. .

DARESSY, G.—*Un Sarcophage de Médamoud.* This belonged to Her.pa.ast, otherwise Borsha, son of Hetabu and Tharden or Tarudet. [The name Bor is the usual Baal, and Sha is a divine name ; thus Baalisha, " my lord is Sha," is parallel to Elisha, " my god is Sha."]

EDGAR, C. C.—*Selected papyri from the archives of Zenon.* Among these we get a light on the currency difficulties. Zenon owed 400 drachmae, payable in copper ; but he gave 400 in gold as security. After that the receivers refused to exchange it. 400 of gold was equal to 416 in silver, and that was equal to 460 in copper. Another papyrus on exchange raises further difficulties, yet unsolved. Elsewhere there was the risk of the Government being paid both by the debtor and his surety, and " you know well that it is not easy to recover money from the Treasury." Other affairs about goats and pigs and bees wait to be dealt with as a whole view of rustic life.

LEFEBVRE, G.—*Textes du tombeau de Petosiris.* The piece of coffin in Turin, inlaid with coloured glass, is here compared in its text with that of Petosiris. It belonged to a son of Seshu and Nefer.renpit, and was probably taken from the tomb of Petosiris. The texts published here refer to the funeral ceremonies.

LEFEBVRE, G.—*Le dieu* "Ηρων *d'Égypte.* The god Hero on horseback is shown on two steles of late Ptolemaic age published here. The lintel of a temple of Hero has been found at Theadelphia ; two frescoes from the Fayum and a lead amulet from Alexandria also refer to Hero. The connection of the god's epithet Subattos with Sopd, and of his position with Atmu, are discussed.

LEFEBVRE, G.—*Inscription grecque du Deir-el-Abyad.* This is on the inner face of a lintel : " To the eternal memory of the very illustrious count Caesarios, son of Candidianos, the founder."

PERDRIZET, P.—*Asiles gréco-égyptiens, asiles Romains.* An asylum decree of Ptolemy XI is here discussed, and its relation to Christian rights of asylum. The Ptolemaic right of asylum extended to 50 cubits around. The churches of Gaul had the asylum 60 paces round large churches, 30 paces around the small.

Revue Égyptologique, Nouvelle Série, Tome I, 1919.

We have to welcome after many years' silence a revival of this journal, in new hands and with a different manner. It is in two yearly parts, called Fascicule 1 and 2 and Fascicule 3 and 4, although each part has no division in it. The part dated January, 1920, appears in 1921. The scope of the articles is mainly philological and Graeco-Roman.

MORET, A.—*Monuments égyptiens de la collection du comte de Saint-Ferriol.* These were mostly given to the museum of Grenoble in 1916. (1) Stele of two women, Uotn and Nebent, with brief list of offerings, fully discussed here. An interesting addition to the few works of the IIIrd dynasty. (2) A seated figure of Amenhetep, who was director of the prophets of Tehutmes I, and servant of the statue of Men.kheper.ra and of the statue of Men.kheper.ka.ra, the two forms of Tehutmes III. It is remarkable that both forms are stated together, as if simultaneous. The parents of Amenhetep were Nezem.ast.Her and Tua.Her. The figure was placed in the temple of Amen to receive the benefit of daily offerings to the god. (3) Stele of the vizier User and wife Thuau adored by their son Sămenkht, and the vizier Oamtu and wife Taoamtu adored by their son Merymăot. The main interest is that User was one of the priestly porters who bore the image of the god and heard the oracles, showing that this method of consulting the gods was already in use in the XVIIIth dynasty. (4) Stele of Hemert, prince, eyes and ears of the king, and architect, adoring a sphinx on a pedestal, approached by steps. The Uzat, and orb with one wing, above. (5) Stele of Kuban of Ramessu II, the well-known account of making a cistern on the road to the gold-mine of Akita, fully published and translated.

SOTTAS, H.—" *Mnw* " = *Socle.* This note discusses the rendering of *mnw* as depth, and proposes that it is the name of the object, a socket or pedestal for a figure. This agrees with *menu* as apparently " bases " in the Book of the Dead, c. 172.

LEFEBVRE, G., et MORET, A.—*Un nouvel acte de fondation à Tehneh.* The tomb of Nek-onkh, son of Heta and Debet, contains a deed of endowment for offerings. All his children are made a company of *ka* servants, with food-rents from which to provide for the table of offerings at the festivals, " under the hand " of the eldest son, Em-ră-f-onkh, who was constituted *kherp* or chief. Thus, at the beginning of the Vth dynasty, in all that concerned family matters there was a head of the family with the title of *kherp*. This gives the meaning probably to the bearing of the *kherp* sceptre in the hand.

BLACAS, LOUIS DE.—*Une statue d'Osiris de la XXIII⁵ dynastie.* This grey granite standing figure, 38 in. high, was found at Memphis, and is in the collection of Count de Blacas. The interest of it lies in giving four generations of a family, with 28 names. It is probably of the XXVth or early XXVIth dynasty, as shown by the names of Amenardus and Shapenapt.

VITELLI, G.—*Trimetri Tragici.* A papyrus with 18 mutilated lines, of the IIud or IIIrd century A.D., appears to belong to an unknown tragedy earlier than Euripides.

JOUGUET, P.—*Les Βουλαί égyptiennes à la fin du III⁵ siècle après J. C.* A senate, or *curia*, was set up in each nome under Severus. The reasons for this, and the system, are here studied in full detail, mainly from a report of proceedings at Oxyrhynkhos.

ROUSSEL, P.—*Les Sanctuaires égyptiens de Délos et d'Érétrie.* The remains of these shrines refer principally to the worship of Sarapis.

COLLART, P.—*L'Invocation d'Isis d'après un papyrus d'Oxyrhynchos.* This refers to the list already analysed in ANCIENT EGYPT, 1916, pp. 40–3.

A section of *Notices et Bulletins* contains an appraisement of the work of Revillout, English papyrology during the war, and the same for Italy. Finally come reviews of books.

The second part, called Fascicules 3–4, is of similar quality.

SOTTAS, H.—*Remarques sur le "Poème satirique."* This is a fresh study of this obscure and much-debated demotic fragment. The translation given is expressly free of all attempt at restoration. As to the sense, it reads like the most inconsequent passages of Petronius.

LANGLOIS, P.—*Essai pour remonter à l'original égyptien du terme sémitique désignant l'Egypte.* The source of the Arabic *Maçr,* cuneiform *Muṣur,* and Hebrew *Mitzri* (adj.) is here sought. The Persian is *Mudrâya,* and this is compared with the *d* inserted to strengthen *zayn* in Ezra = Esdras, and 'Azrb 1 = Hasdrubal. It is thus suggested that the *sad* here has replaced a dental ; and this dental is deduced from the *tera* sign after the well-known Ta-mera as the name of Egypt, pointing to a value approaching *metra.* This dental influence is thus proposed as the source of the *tzaddi* in the Semitic forms. Many cognate questions are discussed in illustration.

MORET, A.—*Monuments égyptiens de la collection du comte de Saint-Ferriol.* Continued with 6, figure seated cross-legged, with libation altar in front, in sandstone, of Nefer-renpet, mayor of the palace. 7, limestone stele of the chief goldsmith Amenemhot, XVIIIth dynasty, with his sister Then-asheru and six children. 8, limestone stele of Nem-ptahmo, son of Hat and Nub-nefert, sons Renty, User, Pupuy and Nub-nefer. 9, limestone stele of Yrrā and his sister Yrrāres. 10, limestone stele of Peda-ast, son of Arhapy and Tenat. 11, pieces of sandstone reliefs of Tehutmes III. 12, 13, fragments of statues. 14, fragment of limestone figure of a noble, Arneptah. 15, five pieces of the granite sarcophagus of the celebrated Amenhetep, son of Hapu ; another piece is in University College, London. 16, anthropoid coffin of Psemthek, son of Sebă-rekhtu. 17, anthropoid coffin of Nehems-menth, son of That-unth and Tadathnebha. 18, lid of wooden coffin of Ta-nekht-ne-tahat. 19–22, ushabtis, names Psemthek (of 16) and Psemthek-neb-pehti, born of Khnem-nefer, daughter of Psemthek. 23, imitation vases of the chief goldsmith Nefer-heb-ef. 24, ushabti box of Ta-pa-kheut and Rames. 25, bronze of Roman Anubis. An excursus of M. Perdrizet deals with the jackal or dog origin of Anubis, the funerary and the heavenly Anubis, the Hermanubis and the Roman forms. 26, a Karian stele, described by M. Autran.

CAVAIGNAC, E.—*La Milice égyptienne au VIe siècle et l'Empire achéménide.* This starts from the passage in Herodotos (II, 164–8) recounting the Kalasires and Hermotybies, garrisons of the Delta and Thebaid. The passage is concluded to have been drawn from some Ionian writer of the time of Amasis, and the number of Kalasires is more exactly given in Her. II, 30, as 240,000 men, with 160,000 Hermotybies, or 400,000 military fiefs, of about 6 acres each, or 4,000 square miles. This was not, however, all in the Delta, as the writer assumes, since there were troops in the Thebaíd. The 400,000 men with families and serfs are taken as 1½ to 2 millions of population. The area of Egypt being (in 1880) 11,342 square miles, with the Delta lakes and marshes (since formed) it would be about 13,000 square miles. Thus the military fiefs were nearly a third of the land, in agreement with the statement that the land was held equally in thirds by the military, the priests, and the civilians. This implies a total population of about five or six millions. With this compare seven millions under the Ptolemies, three in the decadence, five about 1880, and eleven millions under British rule now. All the earlier estimates depend on the number of servile population attached to the military, which is very uncertain. The writer proceeds, on still vaguer ground, to take the tribute of Egypt to the Persians as not including any tax on the priests, and so to estimate the tax as 700 talents on two-thirds or one-third of the population, hence the tax as a didrachm per person. This, by the bye, was just the Roman poll tax in Palestine (Matt. xvii, 27). From this basis the whole population of the Persian empire is estimated by the tribute as 25 to 30 millions. Against this should, however, be set the fact that Egypt was one of the richest lands, and most regions could not yield a half or a quarter of the rate of tax in Egypt. All this estimate must be taken with much reserve.

BELL, H. I.—*Some private letters of the Roman period.* This gives text and translation of four letters selected as examples of more intimate and personal expression.

CLOCHÉ, P.—*La Grèce et l'Égypte de 405/4 à 342/1 J. C.* This is a long and critical article dealing with all the sources of history from the XXVIIIth–XXXth dynasties. The summary of the discussion concludes that in 405 Amyrtaios became independent, but sent troops to aid Artaxerxes II, and a prince Psammetichos acted also in Persian interest. In 399 Naifaaurud I succeeded, who leaned on Sparta as against Persia (396). Hakar succeeded in 393 and warred with Persia 389–387, a situation which ended in 381/0, a little before the death of Hakar. Psimut and Naifaaurud II reigned in 380–379. Nekht-neb-ef had begun some usurpation in 381, and reigned from 379 to 361. The aggression of Pharnabazos and Iphikrates was in 374 or 373. Zeher reigned 361–359, and began plotting with the Asiatic satraps, seeking help in Sparta and Athens, and received Agesilaos and Chabrias about the end of 360. War broke out in Syria, 359, and was checked by the rebellion of Nekht-her-heb. Zeher fled to the Great King. Chabrias returned to Greece and acted for Athens in the war on Thrace, 358. Nekht-hor-heb conquered a usurper in 358 by help of Agesilaus, who left at the beginning of winter, 358/7, and died. In 351 a Persian expedition was checked, and this led to a revolt in Phoenicia and Cyprus, which was crushed in 350. Ochos began long preparations to attack Egypt, and in 344/3 got the neutrality of Athens and Sparta, and the military help of Thebes and Argos. The war began in 342, and in that, or the beginning of 341, ended by the Persian reconquest of Egypt. All of these dates accord with those given in the *Student's History*, except the rise of the XXXth dynasty being a year earlier. The inversion of Nekht-nebef and Nekht-her-heb rests on the evidence of their building at El Khargeh:

An eulogy on Prof. Mahaffy, and reviews, complete the number.

Vol. II. GAUTHIER, H.—*Le dieu nubien Doudoun.*

This is an important study of a god who often appears on the borders of Egyptian mythology, and deserves full consideration. The foreign gods are noticed, as the cow-goddess Hathor of Punt, or Somali Land; Bes from east

Africa ; Neith of Libya ; and in the XVIIIth and XIXth dynasties the Semitic Baal, Astarte, Reshef and Qadshu. From Nubia come the goddesses Anuqet and Satet, as well as Dudun. Thirteen various spellings of the name are quoted, in which are three entirely different signs for the first syllable, and as many for the second. These emphatically show that the name was entirely foreign, and had no root in Egyptian. There is no sign for the first vowel, which has been supplied by transliterators in every form ; so, with our usual convention, it is better to spell the name Dedun. In the pyramid texts of the VIth dynasty the king is promised the perfume of Dedun of the south, coming from the land of the bow, or Nubia. The bird determinative after the name seems like the *ur*, great, and so equal to the later epithet the *neter oa*, great god ; but it is suggested that this is really the sign of being a bird-god, like the falcon-Horus, and—as only a coincidence—there is quoted a bird named in Upper Egypt as *zuzun* or *susun*. It is remarkable that three other southern gods, Khas, Aãhes and Sopdu are associated with Dedun in providing the ladder by which the king is to ascend into heaven. This looks as if this idea of the ladder was Ethiopian ; may it not be derived from the ladder by which the huts of Punt were entered (Naville, *Deir el Bahari*, LXIX, LXX, LXXI) ? This would relieve the Egyptian belief from its absurdity ; the ladder was simply the means of entering a dwelling, and to enter heaven the normal means of access were naturally quoted. In another passage, Pepy is identified with Rahes or Abes, god of the south land (Sudan), Dedun god of the bow land (Nubia) and Sopdu.

In the Middle Kingdom Senusert III built a small temple to Dedun in the fort of Semnah, along with Khnumu of the cataract. This obscure king Ugaf of the XIIIth dynasty (?) likewise was " beloved by Dedun.". In the XVIIIth dynasty Tehutmes III carried on the worship of Dedun in Nubia, and the god promises him the control of the Anti and Mentiu, nomads of the eastern and western desert, as a reward for building his temple. The offerings of corn and cattle originally established by Senusert III, were renewed by Tehutmes III. The feasts there were on the new year (1 Thoth), the second season of the year (1 Tybi), the slaughter of the Antiu of the bow-land, Nubia (21 Pharmuthi), and the third season of the year (1 Pakhons), the feast of queen Merseger called " feast of chaining the desert folk," and the feast of Senusert III. Dedun is first represented in Egypt at Deir el Bahri, but only as belonging to southern scenes. Sety I incorporated this god in a group of purely Egyptian deities at Karnak, between Ptah and Horus ; as Dedun is the only foreign god there, this selection is the more marked. Although Ramessu II built so many temples in Nubia, yet Dedun is never represented in them ; nor did the earlier Ethiopian conquerors ever name him. Tirhaqa revived his worship at Napata and Karnak, where Dedun typifies the south. Later the kings of Ethiopia, Atlanarsa and Aspalta, continued the adoration of Dedun, who is called the god of Kush.

In the Graeco-Roman age Dedun is figured at Philae, by Nekht-nebef, and by Ptolemy VII and his successors. There seems to have been a triad at Philae of Ari-hems-nefer, Tehuti and Dedun. As the name was evidently foreign, it seems useless to try to deduce for it an Egyptian meaning ; nor is a mixed origin, *Tod*, young (Nubian), and *hun*, youth (Egyptian), less unsatisfactory. M. Gauthier firmly rejects the assimilation of Dedun to Ptah-Tanen, which he declares cannot be identified with Dedun ; yet there is the form ⚊ 丁丁 〰〰 which duplicates the dental. Tanen is said to bring the inundation from Elephantine, and he was a creator-god, like Dedun, being linked with Khnumu. There is thus enough resemblance still to leave an open question whether Tatnen was not a form of Dedun.

Another question is raised about Tithōnos. The legend is that he was a Trojan prince, beloved by Eos (dawn) and carried by her to Ethiopia, where they had two children, Emathion and Memnon. Tithonos in the time of Aristophanes is used for a very old man ; and Hesychios (IVth century) states Tithōnokomon to be " a black race over all the body, but with white hair." Thus Tithōn is strongly connected with Ethiopia ; yet that is but vague in position, and might mean only the south of Phoenicia. There are thus several questions remaining about this god Dedun, which still seem open to further evidence.

GARDINER, A. H.—*On certain participial formations in Egyptian.* This discusses the two renderings of the same phrase *hessu-neb-f*, as an imperfect passive participle "one (being) praised of his lord," or as the relative form " one whom his lord praises." These being the same, the result is "that we are clearly wrong in classifying the Egyptian verb-form under two separate heads." In short, the grammar has been over-elaborated by the moderns. After many points which are raised, it is concluded " that the transformation of the passive participle into the relative form takes place by gradual stages." Next is discussed the passive of ⏤ 𓏭 𓄿 𓂝 ; and the conclusion is that ⏤ 𓂝 𓄿 must have meant something like " the fact of his not having done," and ⏤ 𓂝 𓇋𓇋 𓂝 " the fact of there not having been done."

MONTET, P.—*Sur quelques passages des Mémoires de Sinouhit.* This discussion of some passages leads to amending " an offspring of the Setiu " to " a thrower of the boomerang of the Setiu." The sign *khet* is stated not to be a branch, but " the iron of a harpoon " ; on the contrary, it has clearly the branching of twigs, and is used for wood and not for metal. Other remarks on the products of Syria are inconclusive.

COLLINET, P.—*Le P. Berol. gr. inv. no. 2745 et la procédure par rescrit au Vᵉ siècle.* The evidence of date points to 468–477 A.D., and the papyrus completes our knowledge of the procedure by imperial rescrit to a judge.

CLOCHÉ, P.—*La Grèce et l'Égypte de 405/4 à 342/1 avant J. C.* The previous part of this memoir (see above) was devoted to the chronology ; in this continuation the political detail of the Greek connections are set out. A long enquiry is on the Persian seizure of the Mendesian mouth, the desire of Iphikrates to push on to Memphis while it was undefended, the timidity of Pharnabazos, waiting for reinforcements, and the failure by delaying till the rise of the Nile. In all this M. Cloché does not point the close parallel to the invasion by Louis IX : he landed at Damietta, only 20 miles difference ; his one chance was to push on to Cairo before the Nile rose, but he waited months to collect troops, while the Saracens rapidly recovered, and planned resistance. Pharnabazos, more fortunate than Louis, had an open retreat, and could regain Syria without a total wreck, by keeping command of the sea. The war of Zeber is detailed, his betrayal, and flight to the Persians whom he had been attacking. The final assault by the Persians under Ochos is studied at great length, and the fall of the Egyptian kingdom. Nowhere is the Greek policy seen to be more futile

.and useless than in the alternate support of Egypt and of Persia. Egypt was
no menace to any Greek interest, and if the Greek assistance had been given
·continuously to Egypt, the Persians would have been defeated and reduced long ·
before Alexander.

LESQUIER, J.—*Les nouvelles études sur le Calendrier ptolémaïque.* This is a
·study of the relation of the Egyptian and Greek calendars in the latter part of the
reign of Philadelphos, as shown by the Zeno papyri. The relations are greatly
·complicated by the uncertainty of intercalation, and the use of a fiscal and a
regnal year-system. Much remains still doubtful, as the uncertainties and
unknown factors exceed the scope of the material. A biennial intercalary lunar
month was used, so that the year alternated between 354 and 384 days, averaging
·therefore 369. How the 4 days' surplus was eliminated is not stated. It would
have needed suppressing the intercalary month every 9 years. But there is no
trace of this rectification in the table of connections, and without this the lunar
months would slip through all the series in 94 years.

Zeitschrift für Aegyptische Sprache, LIII, 1916.

SPIEGELBERG, W.—*Briefe der 21, Dynastie aus El-Hibe.* Dr. Spiegelberg
·publishes some papyri which were bought together at Luxor more than twenty
years ago. The papyri are fragmentary and there was no provenance, but from
internal evidence he finds that they come from El Hibeh, about 13 km. north
of Tehneh. The papyri consist chiefly of letters, which, by the names, must
be dated to the XXIst dynasty. The principal correspondent is a divine father
and Temple-scribe, Hor-pen-êsë of the Camp. Two letters are from him. The
first letter refers to soldiers, the second to horses ; both begin with flowery
salutations and prayers for the welfare of the recipient. In one of the letters
.addressed to Hor-pen-êsë, mention is made of ·Masaherte, the well-known
High-priest ; he was suffering from illness and sought help at the hands of the
·god of El Hibeh. Another fragment alludes to Isi-em-kheb and Pasebkhanu.
Unfortunately the papyri are too fragmentary to translate completely, but
sufficient remains to show that the letters were chiefly official correspondence·
·Spiegelberg publishes the fragments in the hope that some, at least, of the
missing portions may yet be found in other collections.

SPIEGELBERG, W.—*Der demotische Papyrus Heidelberg 736.* The writing
·of this papyrus is of the Ptolemaic period, about the second century B.C. On
the *recto* are the remains of a story concerning a magician named Ḥen-naw,
·son of Hor, and two birds of heaven. Fortunately an almost complete version
of the story is preserved, written on potsherd. In this story the magician's
name is Ḥi-Ḥor, and he possessed two birds. On one occasion, when the birds
were absent, he was seized and imprisoned at Elephantine. The birds found
him and induced him to write out his history on two rolls of papyrus, which
they then carried to Pharaoh in his palace. The end of the story is lost, but
·undoubtedly he was released and lived happy ever after. The *verso* contains
.a hymn to Isis, apparently to be sung at a religious procession.

SETHE, K.—*Die historische Bedeutung des 2 Philä-Dekrets aus der Zeit des
Ptolemaios Epiphanes.* Revillout was the first to call attention to two kings

who reigned in the South for twenty years, and he placed the end of this short dynasty in the nineteenth regnal year of Ptolemy Epiphanes. Sethe recounts all the proofs for this discovery of Revillout's, and adds some further details which throw light on this obscure period. The two kings were called respectively Harmachis and Anchmachis, and Sethe shows that the general who overthrew the latter was called Amuos, and that the final battle took place near Thebes, and he also proves that these two kings were of Nubian origin.

SETHE, K.—*Zwei bisher übersehene Nachrichten über Kunstwerke aus Kupfer aus den ältesten Zeiten der ägyptischen Geschichte.* (1) Sethe makes the very interesting suggestion that the entry on the Palermo Stone, which he, in common with all other scholars, has read " Birth of Kha-Sekhemui," should have an entirely different meaning. The two signs which occur in the inscription under the word *mes* have hitherto been neglected. The first is the sign for metal, which must be read with the word *mes*. The second is divided from the first by a wide space, and is the hieroglyph ⌓, which in its root meaning reads " High." Sethe brings together instances to show that ⌓ followed by a king's name refers to a building or some work of art, in this case a standing statue, as the phrase is determined by the picture of the statue. Reading the word *mes* as " fashioning " and not as " birth," the result is " A metal-fashioned [statue called] High is Kha-Sekhemui." Sethe cites the great copper statue of Pepy I as proof that the Egyptians were masters of the art of metal working by the VIth dynasty.

(2) In the reign of Nefer-ar-ka-Ra, of the Vth dynasty, the Palermo Stone records that various objects were made in electrum, and also an obelisk of eight cubits in copper and a solar Morning-boat and Evening-boat in the same metal and of the same size.

SETHE, K.—*Ein ägyptisches Denkmal des Alten Reichs von der Insel Kythera mit dem Namen des Sonnenheiligtums des Königs Userkef.* A little bowl in " white marble " was found in excavations in the island of Cerigo and was published in the *Journal of Hellenic Studies,* XVII, 349. The signs inscribed on it have been supposed to be Mycenæan or Cretan " alphabetic characters." Sethe, however, identifies them at once as the name of Userkaf's sun-sanctuary ☉⊗⚒, which was built, according to the Palermo Stone, in the fifth or sixth year of that king. Sethe now reads the name of the sanctuary as *neḫen Ra,* " the court of offerings of Ra," the sign ⊗ being the same as ⊂⊃.

STEINDORFF, G.—*Die blaue Königskrone.* In the Old and Middle Kingdoms the white and red crowns, the double crown, and the striped head-dress with lappets, are all worn by the kings, but it is not until the New Kingdom that the *khepersh*—the so-called war-helmet—appears. The first to wear it, as far as we know at present, was Kames, but it became the usual head-dress of the Pharaoh, either in war or peace. The form is well known ; it is represented as covered with rings or discs, and is uniformly coloured blue. Steindorff holds to the opinion that it is, as has always been supposed, a head-dress of leather with metal rings. Borchardt, however, holds that it is a special method of hair-dressing, and that the rings are a stylised representation of curls, and quotes a relief in the Temple of Abydos showing Sety I wearing what might be a wig—

it is very similar to the style of chignon that Queen Nefert-ythi wore—covered with rings like the *khepersh*. Borchardt also points out that the hair of kings and gods is often painted dark blue, the same colour as the *khepersh*. Steindorff brings forward a good deal of evidence from literary sources, showing that the *khepersh* was considered, by the Egyptians themselves, to be a crown and not a form of hairdressing, as it is usually mentioned with the crowns of Upper and Lower Egypt, with the double crown, and with the *atef*-crown. Steindorff also points out that at Dendereh a procession of gods and goddesses carry crowns as offerings, and the *khepersh* is the fifth, coming after the white and red crowns and before the *atef*. The origin of the word *khepersh* is discussed, Semitic scholars such as Max Müller and Zimmern inclining to the belief that it is a foreign word introduced from Syria or Assyria. Steindorff thinks that their derivations are possible but not probable, and points out that the word is always spelt out in the orthography of Egyptian words and not in the special forms reserved for foreign words. If, therefore, the word was not foreign, the crown itself was not foreign either. It is not found before the New Kingdom, but, as Steindorff says, our knowledge of the representations of Pharaohs of the early periods is confined to statues, and even in the New Kingdom the royal statue very seldom wears the blue crown ; it is represented almost entirely in reliefs and paintings, where the king is shown offering in the Temple, taking part in great ceremonies, or in company with his wife and children. It hardly seems likely that a foreign head-dress, newly introduced into the country, should be so completely adopted ; it is more probable that it was an ancient head-dress, the use of which more or less superseded the other crowns for ordinary wear in the New Kingdom. Another possibility is that it is the leather case for the red crown, the outline of which would fit it.

RUSCH, A.—*Der Tote im Grabe.* There are, in the Pyramid Texts, four groups of texts which contain a reference to an ancient funerary ritual.˙ In these the dead man is called upon to raise himself from his left side and to lie upon his right, in order to receive certain offerings ; he is called " my father," and the reciter speaks of himself as " thy son, thy heir." As the records of excavators show, the usual position of the body is facing west with the head to the south ; the cemetery being in the western desert, the offerer would come from the east ; the dead man is therefore exhorted to turn over in order to receive the offering of food and drink. Rusch suggests that the harvest text, which sometimes accompanies the exhortation, is a later addition to the more primitive form, though it also contains a reference to the son. Another son-text is obviously Osirian ; this Rusch considers to be later. He states the chronological position thus :—

1. The son as the ritual priest for the father (the son speaks in the first person).

2. The living king brings harvest offerings at certain festivals to his dead father (the son is spoken of in the third person).

3. Horus as the *nd-ti* of his father (the son again spoken of in the third person).

KEES, H.—*Ein Onkel Amenophis' IV Hoherpriester von Heliopolis ?* Borchardt has suggested that Āanen, the brother of Queen Tyi, who was second prophet of Amon at Thebes, was also High-priest of Heliopolis, on account of his title

"Greatest of seers." Kees calls attention to the fact that even as early as the beginning of the XVIIIth dynasty the title was no longer confined to Heliopolis, but is found in Thebes. The Ra-cult with its priestly title was established chiefly at Hermonthis but also at Thebes, where several High-priests of Amon bore the title of "Greatest of seers."

EMBER, A.—*Kindred Semito-Egyptian Words.* (New Series.) This paper is a continuation of a series, of which the last is in Vol. LI. It is a list of words with kindred words in Arabic and Hebrew. It is an important contribution to the study of the ancient Egyptian language, and contains many interesting points, amongst others the suggestion that the word *ka,* "food," and *ka,* "protective genius, double," are intimately connected with the Semitic word meaning "to sustain, provide," and with the modern Arabic "to guard, protect."

SPIEGELBERG, W.—*Varia.* 1. The title *ddtw n šnb* probably refers to the playing of a musical instrument in the temple ; from the determinative of metal, which accompanies the word *šnb,* it is possibly a trumpet.

2. Horapollo, as an interpreter of hieroglyphs, is regaining his lost credit. He clearly knew the late forms of the writing, and many of his statements are therefore very illuminating for students of the late period. A title of Hathor in late times is *Mistress of sixteen.* Horapollo says that the word for *joy* was written with the numeral sixteen ; therefore the title reads *Mistress of joy.*

3. In discussing a new legend of the birth of Horus, Spiegelberg disregards the facts of anthropology. This makes some of his remarks rather out of date, though the greater part of the article is interesting.

4. The derivation of the Coptic ⲟⲟⲧ, "to be angry," is from the Egyptian ![glyph] which by analogy with other Coptic derivatives must have been a triliteral verb ![glyph], the two alephs coalescing. But the spelling of ![glyph] and similar words show the triliteral root.

5. Maspero first pointed out that the inner rooms of houses, temples, and even of tombs, were decorated to represent the world, with the sky above, and the earth underfoot. Visitors to the temples wrote in their graffiti that they found the temple "like a heaven within, in which Ra rose." The two pylons of Edfu are called Isis and Nephthys, "who raise the God of Edfu (*i.e.,* the Sun-god) when he shines in the horizon." In a temple orientated east and west, the sun could be seen rising between the pylons, which would be considered as the entry of the god into his heaven in the temple.

6. Brugsch has given the meaning of ![glyph] as the reliquary which held a relic of Osiris. Spiegelberg agrees that it is a receptacle of some kind, but proves from literary sources that it contained a document bearing the titles of the god as ruler of Egypt. In the case of Horus it is the "last will and testament" of his father Geb by which Horus obtained the kingship of Egypt. The kings carried the same object as being themselves divine, and also as successors of Horus. Spiegelberg suggests that the shape of the object is due to the material of which it was made, probably soft leather, which was squeezed in the middle by the pressure of the hand. The word *mïks* ends in *s* as do so many other words which refer to the royal insignia.

7. By analogy with the Coptic derivatives of Egyptian words, the Egyptian 🦅 "mother," probably contained another consonant such as 🦅 which was not written. It is suggested that the name Mουθ, of the vulture-goddess of Thebes, has nothing to do with the word for "mother," but perhaps meant simply "vulture." The reading of the word ⊗, "town," was also probably *niwt*, *i.e.*, with a weak consonant.

8. Spiegelberg corrects von Lange's translation of the inscription of Antef, now in the British Museum. Von Lange translates " [I gave to him] a measure of land of watered ground to reap every year." Spiegelberg reads this as " I gave to him the produce of one arura after the annual inundation."

9. In the early periods each year was called after some event ; this custom continued till late times, the most interesting example being " the year of the hyaenas, when there was famine."

10. The translation of a papyrus, now in the Berlin Museum, shows that it is a letter from a landowner to a tenant. The tenant had been evicted, but at the intercession of the landowner's wife he is permitted to retain the land. The letter is not merely to announce the fact, but is to serve as legal proof to the authorities that the lease is still in force.

11. The ancient Egyptian specialists in medicine were the eye-doctors, who are known from the Old Kingdom onwards, and the curers of intestinal troubles.

12. Griffith has already published a record of Admiral Semtutef-nachte, and Spiegelberg here publishes an inscription copied from a statue which he saw at a dealer's in Cairo. It is interesting to find a reference to the rather rare god Her-shefi, as the admiral also held the office of the overseer of the prophets of that deity.

13. A formula of good wishes is found in the expression, " May he have the duration of Ra." It is the stereotyped phrase after a king's name, " Gifted with life like Ra for ever," and it is also the usual greeting in demotic letters.

14. There is a *ushabti*-figure in the Berlin Museum with an unusual inscription. Instead of the words " to fill the channels with water," *i.e.*, by the hard manual work of the *shaduf*, the text gives a variant ⟨hieroglyphs⟩ Roeder translates this as " to sail round the fields," but, as Spiegelberg points out, this does not carry out the idea of agricultural labour. He therefore suggests that, as *ḳd* can mean a " wheel," the reference here is to the method of raising water by a wheel, such as is in use in Egypt at the present day.

15. The rib of the palm leaf was used as the sighting rod of astronomers, and was called ⟨hieroglyphs⟩, which means palm-stick, in Coptic **ʙᴀ** : **ʙᴀı**.

16. On a statuette of the Theban priest *Ke-te-Mut*, he is called " Great chief of the *Māhasaun*." Spiegelberg identifies these people with the Libyan Massylioi.

17. The Egyptian name for the so-called " Maxims of the Wise " is practically the same in the early examples as in New Egyptian, and can be translated " Educational precepts."

18. The phrase *nfr-ḥr*, applied to Ptah and other gods, is usually translated " beautiful of face," but would be more correctly translated as " gracious of face."

SPIEGELBERG, W.—*Demotische Miszellen.*   1. The Egyptian word *nm̔w* apparently continues into Coptic as ⲡⲩⲍⲉ with the meaning "free."

2. The demotic script of the Rosetta Stone seems to have been done by two hands, the first as far as the end of the protocol, the rest by the second. The use of the word "teaching" in the sentence "the rest of the people, who were in another teaching during the disturbance which reigned in Egypt," reminds one of the same use of the word under Akhenaten. "Those who are in another teaching" were always the enemies of the king.

3. Spiegelberg proposes to recognise in No. 1,326 of Mariette's *Catalogue des Monuments d'Abydos* an inscription relating to the embalming and burial of a dead falcon.

4. Two demotic ostraka in the British Museum are receipts for the cemetery dues paid to a certain Panas and paid by him to the Overseer of the Nekropolis.

5. Spiegelberg proposes to read an enigmatical group in the London Magical Papyrus as 𓏲, the Coptic form being given in the papyrus as ⲱⲉ. The whole sentence would then run, "A snake of the brood of Atum, which lies as uraeus-snake on my head."

6. Examples are given of Greek words spelt out in demotic, or literally translated. *Sẖ n giḏ,* "handwriting," might also be translated directly into English.

7. The word *ḥsy,* determined with the Sun-god, means "drowned," the determinative not being read. In demotic the usual *maā-ḫrw* formula after the name is also determined with the Sun-god. The dead were identified not only with Osiris but with Ra, whom they accompanied in his journey. The hypocephalus, so common in late times, is also connected with Ra worship. Schäfer has suggested that the hypocephalus originated as the object which is represented in Middle Kingdom coffins, and is there called *ḥnmt wrt;* it may be a kind of cushion.

8. Demotic, as also Ptolemaic hieroglyphic texts, introduce a new absolute pronoun to denote the object, except in the third person singular and plural, where the old pronoun is retained. The new pronominal form is found in the Persian period, and even as early as the inscription of Piankhy and the story of Wenamon. In Piankhy the form is simply ⳤ before the suffix, but the usual writing is 𓂝𓏲 before the suffix. It is possible that this is the origin of the Coptic imperatives which take a ⲧ between the verb and the object; and possibly also the ⲧ of the objective pronoun of the first person singular, which follows infinitives ending in ⲧ or ⲁ, may result from the use of the demotic pronoun with imperatives.

9. Greek titles are sometimes literally translated into demotic, sometimes merely transcribed. In one case the demotic scribe paraphrased the Greek syn-genês as "Brother (sen) of the genos."

(*To be continued.*)

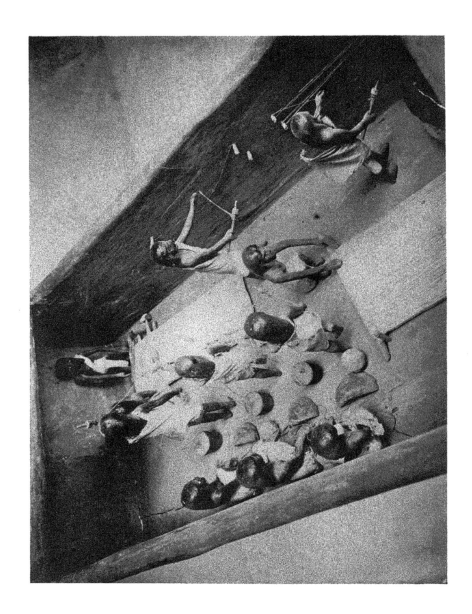

ANCIENT EGYPT.

MODELS OF EGYPTIAN LOOMS.

PHOTOGRAPHS are now available of the model illustrating Egyptian textile methods discovered in an XIth dynasty tomb recently by Messrs Winlock and Burton. The model is a remarkable one and well worth a full description, but in writing this it must be remembered I am only dealing with photographs and not with the actual model, and that disarrangement of the yarn, etc., even slight, must be allowed for. For comparing the model with what we have already learnt, or are not clear about, from illustrations on the tomb walls already made public, I have chosen the illustration of the wall drawing in the tomb of Tehuti-hetep, XIIth dynasty, issued in Prof. Percy Newberry's *El Bersheh*, I, pl. 26, and reproduced as Fig. 11 in my *Ancient Egyptian and Greek Looms* ; see here Fig. 1.

—Tomb of Tehuti-hetep. Date about 1939.—1849 B.C. From Professor Percy Newberry's *El Bersheh* I. Pl. 26.

FIG. 1.

In Winlock and Burton's model (frontispiece and Fig. 2) there are three squatting women manipulating some raw material, probably flax, and having at their service a couple of balls of the raw material, while in front of each woman there is a small platform in shape like a truncated slice of a sphere. The three squatting women appear to be preparing the material for its being drawn upon by the three women standing in front of them. In the top left-hand corner of the Tehuti-hetep illustration can be seen two women with similar appliances, and apparently engaged in similar work, but the platform's position is reversed.

G

The function of the little platform is not very obvious ; it may be like that of the επινετρον or ονος used by Greek women, but these women must have done their manipulation *on top* of their instrument, while according to the Egyptian model the Egyptian women drew the material *from under* their instrument—unless the articles on the model have got misplaced in transit, which I rather doubt. It is possible the little platforms may have been used to hold down the material as it was drawn upon.

Between the two sets of women there are three pots which are possibly tension pots, from which the standing women are drawing the so-prepared material, and twisting it on to a sort of distaff held in the left hand. From this the sliver (so far prepared material) is lightly spun by means of the spindle in the right hand and the thigh, the action being indicated by the raised right leg. The furthermost standing woman appears to be working with three slivers or rovings, the middle one with two, and the last or nearest woman with one only. They are, in fact, doubling (twisting, folding) ; in so doing are thinning out the yarn until the correct fineness is attained, and the rovings spun into finished yarn.

On the opposite wall are two women engaged in warping, that is, arranging the yarn for beaming, which is putting the so-arranged warp on to the loom. The more centrally-placed woman appears to be warping with " sisters " (yarn placed more or less side by side in contrast to doubling where two or more yarns are twisted into one). In some specimens of mummy cloths from Theban tombs, given to Bankfield Museum by Sir E. Wallis Budge, we have warp which is doubled as well as warp which is " sisters." The nearer warper is apparently working with an ordinary doubled yarn.

On the floor are two models of horizontal looms, with the two beams held in position by the usual pegs, and provided with single heddles, shed-sticks and the now well-known curve-ended beater-in. Other details are not sufficiently clear to warrant description. Prof. Garstang's discovery of a smaller model with the loom merely indicated by lines on the floor was the first to prove that the XIIth dynasty drawings of looms before the Hyksos invasion were horizontal and not vertical looms, and the present model confirms this in a striking manner. Messrs. Winlock and Burton are to be heartily congratulated on their discovery in their work for New York, which from the textile point of view is extremely interesting and important.

H. Ling Roth.

During my stay in the Sudan (winter of 1920–21) I made some study of the very primitive methods of spinning and weaving in use there, and I gladly attempt here to answer the question put to me by Prof. Petrie on my return home— whether I had seen anything similar to the processes shown in the wonderful newly-discovered weaving model, which I had marvelled at when passing through Cairo.

I have seen groups of women working with just such a loom, one of their number weaving ; another with her hand on the heddle rod ; the third—how admirably faithful the artist of the model was !—controlling that tiresome back beam that will ride up as the web grows. I have seen women spinning with the spindle rolled on the thigh and dropped whorl uppermost ; I have seen women warping in similar fashion to the two at the wall, winding the warp on the pegs one thread at a time from the spindle. While I have watched such groups of women, with their hair braided after the fashion of Ancient Egypt, their surroundings and belongings—mud-walled huts and courts, bedsteads, mats, and baskets—equally archaic in character, I have been seized with the emotion of Elroy Flecker's vision of the " Old Ship," and I have felt as if I saw a scene—

> " of some yet older day
> And, wonder, breath indrawn,
> Thought I—who knows—who knows, but in that same—— "

—yes, it must have been in that same way that the women of Ancient Egypt wove the linen that won them fame. How simple their tools and methods were, and yet how beautiful and good the result. When you look at the little figures in the model (Fig. 2), preparing and spinning their flax, you see *why* it was so good. In hand-spinning the heckled flax was put directly on the distaff, and the spinner took which fibres she liked to spin up. She could choose, the machine can't, and experts still allow that her gentleness and intelligence could produce a better

FIG. 2. SIDE VIEW OF FRONTISPIECE.

thread than the violence of the spreader, the rover, and the hot water trough of the spinning machine. But where are the fine spinners of Egypt now ? I cannot help thinking that a sympathetic observer among the women of the Fayum (where flax is still grown) might find much of the ancient craft still living, and give better parallels to the processes of the model than I can ; striking as those I have seen in the Sudan are, they cannot be taken as exact, for they are all concerned with wool and cotton, while those of the model are to do with flax. In the absence of such observations I have been encouraged by Mr. Ling Roth to place this note on some of the processes I have seen, with his description of the model itself.

Warp Laying.—In the Sudan the fine hand-spun cotton warps for the pit treadle loom are laid on pegs knocked into the wall of the courtyard or house.

The woman warping walks up and down, spindle in one hand, laying one thread from it with the other, exactly after the fashion shown in the model. One of the Bersheh figures appears also to be doing the same thing, marked X in Fig. 1.

Fig. 3 shows a usual arrangement of the pegs, the number of which, with their zig-zags, vary with its length. The warps on the wall in the model have but three pegs, so I take it that they represent the exact length of the looms. The crossing is not seen, but in the absence of a special peg (peg B in the diagram) to hold the crossing it would not be very noticeable in any case. It is an easy matter to lift so simple a warp off the pegs and slip it on the loom beams.

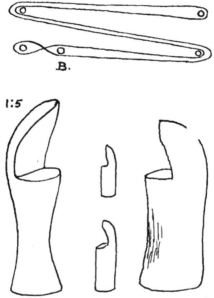

FIG. 3. SUDANI COTTON WARP.
FIG. 4. WOODEN WEAVING IMPLEMENTS.

The Loom.—The looms in the model are very like the horizontal two-beam looms used in the Sudan for the weaving of woollen goods such as tent cloths, blankets, fringed bags, and patterned camel girths ; also by Bedouin in Egypt for very similar purposes. I recognize the four pegs planted in the hard beaten floor of court or house, the two beams laid behind them, the rod heddle, and the shed rod between it and the back beam, the long rod with its double function of shed opener and batten. Sudani women, working with clinging woollen threads, use also a sharp-pointed stick or gazelle horn to beat up with, but this would not be so necessary with flax threads. One very essential part of the Sudani loom is missing, the heddle rod supports, which are various in kind, stones, baked clay pillars, Y-shaped sticks, etc. Is it possible that the curious wooden implements lying on either side of the loom were used for this purpose ? This seemed to me at first a probable suggestion, based on the absence of any support under the heddle and the presence of four wooden objects of sufficient solidity to serve the purpose, but the shape of the implements does not make it at all convincing. They are much more like tools used in the hand to adjust something. But what is there to adjust in a loom of this class ? The warp beam in the model is quite clearly fixed ; was the cloth beam possibly a revolving one as some experts think is the case in the loom of the Tomb of Khnem-hotep ? I could see nothing in the model to indicate this. As usual, the new discovery has raised a new problem. I have asked Prof. Petrie to republish a drawing of originals of similar implements from the Univ. Coll. collection in the hope of finding a solution (Fig. 4).

This simple type of loom has one great virtue, the warp is well stretched, but it needs a strong one, and no doubt this is the reason why so much of the ancient linen has the warp threads doubled ; Sudani woollen warps are also made of doubled yarn. Another virtue is its mobility. You can pick up the whole concern, roll up the web on the beams, walk away with it and peg it down somewhere else if required. Again, and this is a point which is not without interest in considering the evolution of the Egyptian loom : you can, if you wish, weave vertically instead of horizontally on it ; you have only, as the Navaho Indians do with their similar loom, to tie one of the beams to a support above instead of the floor to gain whatever it is that can be gained by the change of position. Further, the very crudity of the loom gives the weaver freedom ; all textures, all patterns, are his (or hers) to create, given time and the necessary skill. To watch a primitive woman weaving on such a loom—say a Navaho woman turning out her patterned belt 10 inches per hour--or (as I have done) a Sudani woman figuring out a black-and-white camel girth, or more startling still, a Cairene weaver of intricate braids, virtuoso in colour combinations, supplementing his already elaborate set of heddles by a reversion to primitive practice, his fingers flying among the threads as a pianist's among the keys, gives the clue to the fine work of ancient Egypt ; the secret is not altogether lost, but is still revealed to the children of the world, and beauty is still won by patience and simplicity.

G. M. CROWFOOT.

[The figure on the cover is from Beni Hasan ; it shows how the spinner worked with four threads and two spindles, standing on a height to allow of a long spin before winding up, and rolling the spindle on the thigh. The two pots in front belong to another spinner ; the front threads are drawn from a yellow mass (Rosellini).]

THE DATE OF THE MIDDLE EMPIRE.

AN ounce of archæological evidence is worth more than a ton of subjective speculation, and that evidence is now forthcoming for settling the date of the Middle
Egyptian Empire, or at least its relation to Babylonian history.   I have recently
been examining the two alabaster vases inscribed with names of kings of the
Babylonian dynasty of Akkad, which are now in the Louvre.   They are the only
genuine ones as yet brought from Babylonia, with the exception of one of older
date from Lagas, lately acquired by the Ashmolean.   But there is more than one
forgery existent, though none of the forgeries I have seen is sufficiently good to
deceive the expert.

The Louvre vases are of Egyptian alabaster.   No. 2 bears the name of
Naram-Sin, No. 1 that of Rimus, the son and successor of Sargon, the founder
of the dynasty of Akkad.   Both vases are of Middle Empire (X–XIVth dynasties)
form ; I found many examples of No. 2 in the Xth dynasty graves which I
excavated at El-Kab.   We now know from the annalistic tablets of Nippur, as
completed by the recent discoveries of M. Legrain (*The (Pennsylvania) Museum
Journal*, December, 1920), that the date of Sargon of Akkad was about 2800 B.C.,
with a few years' difference more or less.   Before that date, therefore, the Xth
Egyptian dynasty will have already been upon the throne.

The cuneiform texts discovered by the German excavators at Assur have
shown that relations already existed between Babylonia and Egypt.   Among
them is the copy of a sort of geographical survey of his empire by Sargon of
Akkad, giving the distance in double miles of one part of his dominions from
another (*Keilschrifttexte aus Assur verschiedenen Inhalts*, 92).   In this, after stating
that Anzan (southern Elam) was 90 *beri*, or double miles, in extent, he goes on
to say : " To the Tin-land (and) Kaptara (*i.e.*, Krete) the countries beyond the
Upper [Sea] (the Mediterranean), Dilmun (Tylos) (and) Magan (Northern Arabia
from the Persian Gulf to the Sinaitic Peninsula) the countries beyond the Lower
Sea (the Persian Gulf), even from the lands of the rising sun to the lands of the
setting sun, the hand of Sargon the king in 3 campaigns has prevailed."   I learn
from Dr. Forrer that a still more important text, not yet published, is a stele of
another Sargon, the *patesi* of Assur 2180 B.C., who claims to have conquered Egypt,
then under a foreign Sudani dynasty, as well as Kaptara or Krete, where his
commissioners received tribute from the Tin-land (KU-KI) " beyond the sea."   The
Sudani occupation of Egypt explains the name of the XIVth dynasty king Nehesi,
as well as the black-topped Sudani pottery which I found at Ed-Dér, opposite
Esna, between XII–XIVth and XVII–XVIIIth dynasty graves.

But as far back as the Old Empire—not to speak of the prehistoric period
with its seal-cylinders—there must have been indirect intercourse between Egypt
and Babylonia.   On the one hand, Babylonian civilisation was introduced into

Asia Minor at an early date, and in the age of the IIIrd dynasty of Ur (2400 B.C.) eastern Asia Minor was in possession of the Assyro-Babylonians, who worked the mines of the Taurus and whose merchants and postmen traversed the roads that had been made through the country. On the other hand, Prof. Petrie has found Old Empire gold which, according to Prof. Gladstone's analysis, would have come from Asia Minor. The intercourse must have continued with little break; Prof. Maspero told me that the XIIth dynasty coffins found at El-Bersha were made of juniper-wood, which must have come from Krete and Asia Minor.

A. H. SAYCE.

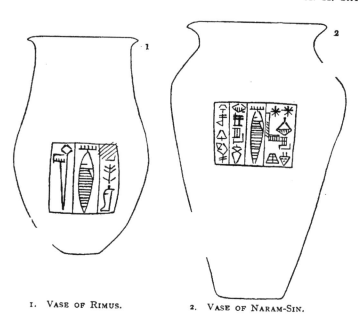

1. VASE OF RIMUS.   2. VASE OF NARAM-SIN.

[The form of the vase of Naram-Sin is known from other instances as belonging to the Xth dynasty; the comparisons which have been made with a vase of the VIth dynasty from Mahasnah and one of the Ist dynasty are incorrect. A vase might have been made in Egypt long before its export to Babylonia, and when we are certain of the date of Naram-Sin there will be a lower limit for the Xth dynasty. A similar case in the opposite direction is the lazuli cylinder, lately sold in Cairo, with cuneiform inscription, which may have been of any age before it was exported to Egypt as lazuli, and engraved for Amenemhat I.—F.P.]

THE TREE OF THE HERAKLEOPOLITE NOME.

⌊Dr. Bruijning, the Director of the Station for Seed Testing in Holland, visited London this summer. Unhappily he was seized with illness, and died on his return to his home at Wageningen. Sad to say, this is the last paper of his, and the present form of the translation has not received his final revision.]

1. The Pomegranate. 2. The Oleander. 3. Climate. 4. The *nårt* nome. 5. The Pomegranate. 6. Form of the nome-sign. 7. The *aåm* palm.

1. Professor Newberry in the *Zeitschrift* (L, 1912, p. 78) has put forward the view that the tree worshipped in the Herakleopolite nome was the pomegranate (*Punica granatum*), which he reads in the nome-sign ⚬ as ⚬ (B.D.G., 313), or ⚬ (B. *Thes.* VI, 1251). He does not admit of Loret's opinion that it is an oleander. He writes: " In figures 1–6 I give the various forms of this nowe-sign, as they appear on the monuments.[1] The first example, from a IVth dynasty stele of ⚬, explains the ill-defined appendage of the later forms ; it is *clearly a tree with projecting branch on one side terminating in a flower or fruit*. This projecting branch was already becoming misunderstood in the Vth dynasty, and taking the form of an arm holding a ⚬. Later, in the XVIIIth dynasty, the arm has become separated from the tree sign, and in the hand is a ⚬ ring. Among the cult signs occurring on the prehistoric Decorated pottery we find a tree-branch terminating in a flower or fruit (Fig. 7), evidently the early way of representing the Herakleopolite tree. The shape of the fruit or flower, and the form of the tree of the IVth dynasty example, certainly shows that we cannot identify it with the oleander, but it very closely resembles the pomegranate, as will be seen on comparing it with a drawing of a pomegranate tree in one of the Tell el Amarna tombs (Davies, El Amarna, I, Pl. 32). I think, therefore, that we may safely identify the sacred tree of Herakleopolis with the pomegranate (*Punica granatum*, L.), which may well have been indigenous in Lower and Middle Egypt."

Objections may be raised to both Newberry's and Loret's opinions, which I now proceed to consider.

2. Loret's view rests on the occurrence of the oleander in Egypt, at any rate in the later periods, and on the name ⚬, Coptic ⲛⲉⲣ being Nerium (Oleander, L.), while the tree *når* was the nome sign of Herakleopolis.

That the Nerium Oleander occurs at present in Egypt is unquestioned ; it is cultivated throughout the country, and its range extends from Mesopotamia to

---

[1] Footnote by Newberry. " In an example from Tehneh figured in *Annales du Service*, III, 76, the flower or fruit issues from the top of the tree." We shall refer to this afterwards.

Spain. It is, however, an open question whether this plant, now typically south Mediterranean, was known in the Old Kingdom, or even at an earlier date. Probably this must be answered in the negative. Nerium is one of the oldest sympetals, fossil traces of which go back as far as the Eocene. The northern limit was then in the north of England and in Bohemia, whereas it is now south of the Alps. It is not a rash view to say that the tree came to Egypt by way of Syria, under human influence. In regard to Egypt, it is an intruder unknown among the original flora of the Nile Valley. Indeed, there is no indication that Nerium was known in the early dynasties. Representations of it do not appear, nor are there any remains of it from the Old or Middle Kingdoms, nor is it among the interesting finds of Flinders Petrie, described by Newberry (*Kahun,* ch. vii, and *Hawara,* ch. vii)

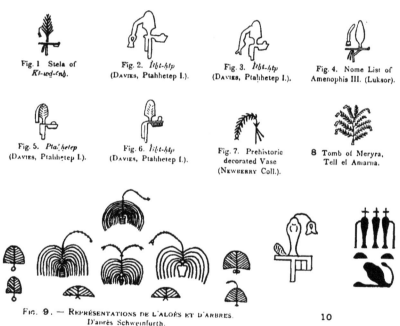

Fig. 1 Stela of *Kt-wd-ᶜnḫ.*

Fig. 2. *Itḥt-ḥtp* (Davies, Ptahhetep I.).

Fig. 3. *Itḥt-ḥtp* (Davies, Ptahhetep I.).

Fig. 4. Nome List of Amenophis III. (Luksor).

Fig. 5. *Ptaḥhetep* (Davies, Ptahhetep I.).

Fig. 6. *Itḥt-ḥtp* (Davies, Ptahhetep I.).

Fig. 7. Prehistoric decorated Vase (Newberry Coll.).

8 Tomb of Meryra, Tell el Amarna.

FIG. 9. — REPRÉSENTATIONS DE L'ALOÈS ET D'ARBRES. D'après Schweinfurth.

10

3. Here another consideration must come in which bears on the question of the pomegranate and the sacred tree. It is generally assumed that the climate of Egypt has not materially changed in the last 4,000 years, nor the vegetation. Blanckenhorn, to whom we owe the best geological study of Egypt,[1] is of the same opinion, but admits the possibility of the climate having been somewhat moister in the pyramid times, in accordance with the opinion of O. Fraas. Such estimates are but vague. The IIIrd dynasty is 800 years earlier still,[2] so it is quite possible that at the time when the nome-signs were adopted the climate

---

[1] M. Blanckenhorn, *Neues zur Geologie und Palaeontologie Aegyptens,* IV, *Das Pliocaen und Quartaerzeitalter in Aegypten,* Zeits. Deut. Geol. Gesellschaft, 53, 1901, p. 457.

[2] [2,800 years earlier according to the Egyptians.]

was different, somewhat moister, and perhaps warmer.   A difference of climate would involve a different vegetation.   As far back as 1874 Schweinfurth expressed the view (*Im Herzen von Africa*, I, pp. 74–5 ; also *Le piante utili dell' Eritrea, Boll. Soc. Afric. d'Italia*, Napoli, X, Nos. 11, 12) that the climate of Egypt is slowly changing from a tropical to a Mediterranean type.   Many plants which grew spontaneously in ancient Egypt are now found blooming on the White Nile.   Such are the papyrus and the *Acacia Nilotica*, now only found as cultivated plants in Egypt, where formerly they were as common as they now are on the White Nile.

It would be going too far at present to enter on the historical and geographical distribution of plants which is here involved ; but it must be deemed improbable that a nome-sign should be connected with a plant for which climatic conditions were not favourable in ancient Egypt.   This alone would indicate that the nome-sign was not likely to be the oleander, nor—as we shall see below—the pomegranate.   A view of the more ancient forms of the Herakleopolite sign excludes the possibility of its being an oleander.

Let us now distinguish the two questions, first, whether the oleander was (as Loret says) the 𓏤𓏏𓆱, ΝΕΡ or ΝΗΡ, Dioscorides' νήριον, and secondly, whether the nome was called *nâr*.   Loret's theoretical view has not been opposed, so far as I know.   If it be granted, then, as we have to assume that the tree in the nome does not represent the oleander, but that on the contrary 𓏤𓏏𓆱 may be identified with Nerium, consequently *nâr* cannot represent either the name of the tree or that of the nome.

4. How, then, is the nome to be read, if this be the case.   In his study of the nomes Steindorff[1] speaks of the *nârt* nome, divided into the former and hinder *nârt* nomes, XX and XXI.   But probably *nârt* rests on a misunderstanding. Brugsch in earlier works considered 𓏤𓏏𓊖 as another name for 𓏤 𓏤𓊖 Herakleopolis, as in his essay "𓊪𓊪𓊪𓊖 oder Mendes " (*Zeits.* 1871, 81–85) and in his " Religion " of 1891 (pp. 193–4).   But it seems rather that it was not the name of the city, but of a sanctuary in the neighbourhood.   Wreszinsky, in his work on the London medical papyrus, No. 10059 (1912, 12, 9, p. 195), translates as " ich will dich noch *n'rt* bringen," taking it to be the name of a locality.   In the hymn to Osiris, Budge translates, " Thou art the soul of Ra, his own body, and hast thy place of rest in Henensu.   Thou art the beneficent one, and art praised in Närt " (*Pap. Ani*, I, 1913, p. 59 ; see also his *Gods of the Egyptians*, II, p. 148).   Indeed, Budge has expressed himself quite clearly in the matter (*Dictionary*, 1920, p. 1,004) and designated Nâr as " a district of Henensu (Herakleopolis)."   He still has doubts about it, as he reads 𓏤𓏏, 𓏤𓏏𓆱, " sycomore tree (Laurier Rose, *Rec.*, 15, 102), Copt. ΝΗΡ, νήριον," and " a sycomore tree in the Tuat sacred to Osiris " (*Dict.*, p. 347).   The reading " sycomore tree " and " Laurier Rose " are certainly erroneous.   Others also have their doubts, as, for instance, G. Röder (in his *Urkunden Relig. alt. Eg.*, 1915), where he reads " Baum oder Stadt " (p. 22), but also " Er liegt in Süd-westen von Naret " (p. 132).   We cannot go further into the literature, but it is

[1] *Die aeg. Gaue* (Abh. phil.-hist. Königl. Sächs. Ges. Wissen., XXVII, No. XXV, 1909, p. 878).

evident now that the tree sign of may actually represent two quite different species, so that Loret's version of the determinative of *nårt* may stand, while it is decidedly wrong in regard to the nome-sign, the sacred tree of the XXth nome, with which we are now concerned.

5. This tree was not the oleander ; was it then, according to Mr. Newberry's view, a pomegranate ? I will try to answer this question. Schweinfurth's original opinion was that the pomegranate had been grown in Egypt from the earliest times. It was supposed—with many other plants—to have passed in a primitive age from South Arabia to the Semites on the north, perhaps with the sycomore and persea (Schweinfurth, *Verh. Berl. anthrop. ges.*, 1891, 649–669). The cultivated species would have to be derived from the *Punica protopunica*, Balf., only known in Socotra (J. B. Balfour, *Botany of Socotra*, pp. 93–96). Schweinfurth supposes that this wild species " eigentlich nur durch die Blätter verschieden ist." Also Buschau (*Vorgeschichtliche Botanik*, 1895, p. 159) is of opinion that the original home of Punica is in Arabia Felix, rather than in North-western India, Persia or Baluchistan. These views would be in accord with Mr. Newberry's, but they are no longer tenable.

As early as the Pliocene of southern France (Meximieux) a fossil species is found which is scarcely distinguishable from *P. granatum*, the *P. Planchoni*, Sap., and it is obvious that the latter—like Nerium—has moved southward. Also the pomegranate may have come to Egypt through the Semites, and many circumstances seem to bear this out. Decandolle sought its origin in Persia, Afghanistan or Baluchistan, where presumably the plant had been grown for 4,000 years ; but this is no proof of origin, as it would only go back to the XIth dynasty. However, it may be accepted that the pomegranate is found growing wild in clefts of the calcareous mountains of Avroman in Shahu (Persian Kurdistan), and likewise in Baluchistan, Afghanistan and North-western India (V. Hehn, *Kulturpflanzen* . . ., 8th ed., 1911, p. 246). Thence the tree has moved southward through Syria to Egypt, and has been cultivated there at a rather late period. The earliest occurrences are of the XIIth dynasty, from Dra-abul-negga.[1] Loret quotes as the oldest text naming the pomegranate, that of Anna of the XVIIIth dynasty (*Flore phar.*, 1892, p. 76), but as that is funerary, he rightly supposes " que le grenadier n'était pas un arbre tout à fait nouveau pour les Egyptiens." The view that it was a Hyksos importation is barred by the examples in the XIIth dynasty. By so late a date as this Mr. Newberry's theory is condemned, as also by the representation of apparently leafy branches depicted on the prehistoric vases, ending in something like a flower or fruit, and looked upon as Punica. The comparison does not hold good, as it is not made with a complete figure, but only with a partial drawing on the pottery. On looking closer at the drawings, especially those of *Naqada*, 1896, XXXIV and LXVII, it is apparent that the leafy twigs evidently represent the racemose inflorescence of the leafless and rootless plants also occurring in these drawings, and identified by Schweinfurth, with great probability, as the Aloe. To show this we may refer (Fig. 9) to a collection of such figures given by Capart (*Débuts de l'Art*, Fig. 81). These show the probability of Newberry's branches being the inflorescence of the Aloe, certainly neither flower nor fruit-bearing branch of the pomegranate.

---

[1] Schweinfurth, *Dernières découvertes*, in *Bull. Inst. Eg.*, 1887, No. 6, pp. 256–8.

For the sake of completeness we should mention some brief philological observations. In the later Iranian languages the pomegranate is called *når* (Pers.), *ćnar* (Kurd.), *nurn* (Arm.) (see Hehn, *Kulturpflanzen*, p. 247), which names might be connected with ϭρϻⲁⲛ or ϩⲉρϻⲁⲛ (Copt.), and finally with *når*. Compare the opinion of Burchardt (*Altkanaan. Fremdworte*, II, 1910, p. 5, No. 71), who renders *anhmn* as " a fruit tree and its fruit," quoting from *Urk.* 4, 73 ; Ebers, 19, 19–20 ; Harris, 56A, 5, etc. In view of the comparisons by H. Zimmern (*Akkad. Fremdworte*, 1915, p. 545) of *armannu* (akkadian) as a fruit tree, *rimmon* (heb.), *rummånå* (aram.), *rummān* (arab.), *remmān* (ethiop.), Burchardt denies the connection with the iranian group of Moldenke,[1] and supports Loret's identification of the *Punica* with $\cap$ and $\cap$! This connection might agree with Newberry's view more or less, but hardly enough to allow us to read the nome-sign as *når*. I must not, however, lose myself in conjectures about such questions, which are not in my own line of work. The older renderings of *når*, such as " persea " (Birch) or " acacia " (Brugsch), need not be discussed. See Levi, *Vocab.*, III, p. 90.

From the above I should be inclined to infer that the Herakleopolite nome tree is neither a *Nerium Oleander* nor a *Punica granatum ;* that its name should not be read *når*, and that the nome therefore cannot be denoted as the *når* nome. A further inference is that the nome tree in question need not be found in Egypt at present ; on the contrary, the ancient nome-signs go back to the very first periods of Egyptian culture, so that, on the strength of the above observations on climate, it is quite justifiable to seek the nome tree more to the south, on the Blue or White Nile, to which region it may have retreated, like the papyrus and hippopotamus.

6. The various forms of the nome-sign seem to be characterised by a conspicuous inflorescence. In the drawing of Fraser from Tehneh (*Ann. Serv.*, III, 1902, p. 76), also cited by Newberry, this inflorescence, though conventionalised, is very obvious (Fig. 10). The examples before quoted (Figs. 1 to 5) are in accordance with this. The small differences between the examples are only what are commonly found in such figures, and need not detain us. We can accept that the tree had a large and conspicuous drooping inflorescence. The tree was, further, worshipped as a sacred one. Of such trees it was presumed (to quote Erman, *Religion*, 1909, p. 28), " die Stätte einer himlichen Göttin seien, die den armen Toten Essen und wasser reichen und die man Nut oder Hathor en rennen pflegt."

7. This conception must lead us to the practical conclusion that they were trees-" die wohl am Wüstenrande standen " (Er., *Relig.*), and of some use, as they produced food and drink. If we combine this view with the typical form of the tree, there is hardly any conclusion but that it represents a Raphia or wine palm : not a leafy tree but a palm, the *adm* palm, Raphia (*Monbuttorum Drude*). This should be noted because Sethe names the *adm* tree as a leafy tree (*Urk.*, 18th *Dyn.*, I, 1914, p. 38). In the text of Anna published by him (*Urk.*, 18th *Dyn.*, I, 1906, p. 73), he mentions, however, that the name of the tree is nearly obliterated, only the tip of the first sign remaining. He relies, therefore, on other texts, of which that of Brugsch (*Rec. Mon.*, I, 36, 1) is the most familiar :

$\cap$ ⲓⲓⲓ. In the same text three other trees are determined with the sign

---

[1] C. T. Moldenke, *Ueber die in Altaeg. Texte erwähnten Bäume* . . . Inaug. diss. Leipzig, 1886, p. xii.

✻, namely ⟨ ✻ *bnrt*, date palm ; ⌐⌐ ✻ *mămă*, dum palm ; and ⌐⌐ 𓏲 *mămă-n-khănnt*, *Medemia* (*Hyphaene*) *Argun*. We should consider, therefore, why the tree named by Anna has not been recognised as a palm. Brugsch (*Dict.*, pp. 66–67, Rev. Arch., 1865, 206) thought that *aăm* was a date palm. He was, however, wrong, as Dümichen and Moldenke perceived (*Altaeg. Texten erwähnten Bäum*, 1886, pp. 60–65), who stated ⟨ 🦉 ◊, ⟨ 𓏏 ◊, etc., to be a palm, and discussed whether it were the date palm. In accounts and lists, and in the Ebers papyrus, *bnrt* and *aăm* do not interchange. I presume that the Anna text

FIG. 11. RAPHIA MONBUTTORUM DRUDE. VICTORIA NYANZA.

is an erroneous transcript from hieratic, as is often found in sculpture. Moldenke, however, goes too far when he ascribes all the six variants of ◊ 🦉 to being errors for 𓏪. In hieratic *aăm* is rightly determined by a palm tree ; for instance, ⟨ 🦉 🦉 ✻ (Blackman, *Mid. Kingdom Religious Texts*, *Zeits.* 47, 1910, p. 125). The passage in the Ebers papyrus is well known (47, 11) ; see also Möller, *Hier. Palaeographie*, 1, 1909, No. 265. Probably in the papyri the palm determinative has been confused with the leaf-tree, so that it is not conclusive, and the less so if transcribed into hieroglyphics. So the determinative in the text of Anna is of little significance.

F. F. BRUIJNING.

(To be concluded with the discussion of the botany.)

THE CEREMONY OF ANBA TARABO.

THE ceremony is performed over a person bitten by a dog, in order that there may be no ill effects from the bite. As the proportion of fatal cases of dog-bite is only 15 per cent., even when the dog is mad, and as the greater number of bites are received from dogs which are not mad, the ceremony is naturally considered highly efficacious among a people who know nothing of percentages. There is, however, a curious nervous condition which bitten patients sometimes develop. To anyone who has been actually bitten by a dog, whether mad or supposedly so, such a condition is easily understandable. The horror and terror produced by the expectation of possibly dying the most agonising of all deaths is enough to upset the most balanced nervous system, and the mental agony is reflected, of course, in the physical condition. The symptoms of this pseudo-hydrophobia are not unlike the actual disease. Osler describes them thus : " A nervous person bitten by a dog, either rabid or supposed to be rabid, has within a few months, or even later, symptoms somewhat resembling the true disease. He is irritable and depressed. He constantly declares his condition to be serious, and that he will inevitably become mad. He may have paroxysms in which he says he is unable to drink, grasps at his throat, and becomes emotional. The temperature is not elevated and the disease does not progress. It lasts much longer than true rabies, and is amenable to treatment. It is not improbable that the majority of cases of alleged recovery in this disease have been of this hysterical form." (Osler, *Principles and Practice of Medicine*, p. 371, ed. 1912.)

It is this condition for which the ceremony of Anba Tarabo is a certain preventive, especially to the patient who has faith in it.

The words of the ritual are already known to students of Coptic, and also probably to many people who have studied modern Egypt. Two versions have been already published, one by Emile Galtier, *Bulletin de l'Institut français d'Archéologie orientale*, iv. (1905), pp. 112–127 ; the other by W. E. Crum, *Coptic Manuscripts in the Rylands Library*, pp. 236–7.

As far as I know, nothing has yet been published by anyone who has actually seen the ceremony performed, and the " manual acts," which form so dramatic a part of the rite, have obtained little or no attention.

It is, however, these " manual acts " which impress the imagination of the patient, and so effect the cure of the nervous condition The onset of the real disease is usually within six to eight weeks, but the nervous condition may super-vene at any time, even months afterwards. The ceremony of Anba Tarabo to be effective must be performed within forty days of the bite.

At least four Christians must take part, even if the patient is a Moslem. In the service I am about to describe, which was performed over myself, the Christians were the patient, the *omdeh* of the village (a Copt), and two Coptic priests.

The patient was asked her Christian name and that of her mother, and was referred to in all the prayers as " Margaret, daughter of Margaret." She sat on the ground, the *omdeh* at her right hand ; in front of them was a wooden stool on which rested a basket tray, thus forming a kind of low table. On the tray were dates, cakes of unleavened barley-bread, and a coffee-cup with some oil. The dates and cakes were counted, seven of each were placed on one side of the tray for use, the others piled together on the other side out of the way. Any uneven number would have done, but seven is considered the most efficacious. Two *qullehs* filled with water were placed on the ground, one on each side of the stool. The two priests stood on the other side of the table, facing the patient. When all was ready, they recited the service together, but the pace at which they went made it difficult to follow the mixture of Arabic and Coptic. The younger priest, standing opposite the patient, signed to her to hold out her hands, palms uppermost, which he then tapped five times gently with his ebony staff. He inserted the point of the same staff into the mouth of the *qulleh* on his right, moving it clockwise round the rim ; after which, both priests placed their fingers in the same way in the mouth of the *qulleh*, thus blessing the water. The exact place in the service at which these " manual acts " took place could not be accurately ascertained, but the dramatic part of the rite occurred after the recitation of prayers was ended. Seven boys, all with one exception under puberty, were called up to represent the dogs of Anba Tarabo. They joined hands by interlocking the fingers, the palms being held upright, and formed a circle round the patient, the *omdeh* and the table, the priests standing outside the circle. They were told to go round clockwise, repeating words which sounded like " Bash, bash, stanna," and which were said to be Coptic. After doing this about seven times, at a given signal they reversed the motion and went round widdershins. At another signal they stopped, and all with shrieks of laughter fell on the patient from behind, pretending to bite her on the arms and shoulders, and growling like dogs. The younger priest then sprinkled the *omdeh* and the patient with water from the *qulleh* that had been blessed, the patient being sprinkled three times ; he anointed the *omdeh* with the oil out of the little cup, on the forehead, throat, and the inner part of both wrists. The patient was anointed on the forehead and wrists only, not on the throat. Meanwhile the elder priest was nipping a little bit out of each of the seven barley loaves and the seven dates, which pieces he gave to an attendant with instructions to tie them in a piece of cloth and bury them in the desert. The ceremony concluded with the patient and the *omdeh* each eating one date and a piece of one of the barley loaves, and drinking some water out of the blessed *qulleh*.

It is believed that if any animal finds and eats the bits of date and barley-bread which were removed by the priest and buried in the desert, that animal, especially if it be of the dog species, will take the disease and become rabid ; if a person eats them, he will bark and bite like a dog. But whether the pieces are eaten or decay naturally, the disease is now completely removed from the patient. The rest of the dates and barley loaves were anointed with oil and distributed to the assembled company to bring a blessing upon them. There is a very strong belief that if anyone is bitten and the ceremony is not performed over him within forty days, he will go mad and will bark and bite like a dog. As these are not the symptoms of rabies, it is evident that this statement must refer to a form of the nervous condition mentioned above, and the length of time—about six weeks

—also suggests that it is the pseudo-hydrophobia, and not the real disease which is cured by this ceremony.

In the book of the service of Anba Tarabo, published by Galtier, the " manual acts " differ from those I have described. Probably there are local variants in different parts of the country. Galtier's version gives the following directions : " On a Saturday take seven unleavened round loaves, seven cheeses, a little good oil and a little wine, light a lamp, and take seven innocent children who are fasting. Make a little bag and hang it round the neck of the patient, and let the priest speak and make the children go round seven times to the left and seven times to the right, and let him say, ' Welcome to all of you, children, who ask healing from God and the holy abba Tarabo ; may God grant healing to you.' Afterwards, first of all, the thanksgiving is said, incense is burned, and the Epistle of St. Paul and the Gospel are read in Coptic and Arabic. Then the children shall go round the patient, and each time that they go round, make the sign of the cross with oil upon the face of the patient, saying (so that it shall not be heard), ' Eloï, eloï, eloï, elema sabachthani,' until the seven turns are finished. Then give to each of the boys a loaf and a cheese, and he shall bite off a mouthful with his teeth, and shall make a noise like a mad dog. Then read Psalm xc : ' Whoso dwelleth under the protection of the Most High.' Then read the life of the holy abba Tarabo completely, afterwards make the boys go round and make the sign of the cross three times over the water and say the following, followed by the sign of the cross : ' Understand and thou shalt do well, and it is God who is the help.' [Then follows the religious service. At the end] : Add, ' O Lord, hear my prayer and my petition. It is I, abba Tarabo, who implores thee this day and this hour. Show thyself pitiful towards thy servant, N. son of N. (fem.), help him and save him from the bite of a mad dog, let not his body be either sick or wounded, let not evil seize him, let him have nothing to fear either from him [the dog] or his evil, let him [the dog] not be able to do harm under thy protection either in body or soul, let not his [the patient's] body be enfeebled, let not his members suffer, but let him be strong, thanks to thy holy power, for Thou art He from whom comes all healing and to whom praises are due for ever. Amen.' "

It is noteworthy that in this as in my version, the filiation is to the mother, and not to the father.

Crum gives only a summary of the ritual, which is as follows : " A widow's only son being bitten, is sent by his mother to Abba T., bearing a present of seven unsalted loaves, seven fresh, unsalted cheeses, seven bunches of grapes, and a little olive oil and wine, all wrapped in a white cloth. On learning his need, Abba T. summons seven pure boys, and bidding them follow him and respond to each word he shall say, he sets the widow's son with his gifts before him, placing in front of him the oil and wine and a jar of fresh water. Then he turns seven times round the bitten boy, followed by the seven children, to whom he says : ' Welcome, children ; peace unto you,' while they reply, ' And unto thee peace, O master.' He : ' What seek ye ? ' They : ' Healing we seek for this unhappy one, that the mad dog hath bitten.' He : ' Depart in peace. The Lord shall cure and heal him, for His trusty promise unto me, His servant, that do confess His name.' Here follows a long prayer by Abba T., including Ps. xc. The ceremony concludes with further ritual. The first of the seven boys approaches the priest, the whole congregation meanwhile joining hands, and says, ' Peace unto thee, O teacher of teachers.' The priest replies, questioning him as before; but here healing is sought for all such as may have been bitten. Then, as each time they repeat their circuits round the supplicant, seven to right and seven to left, they say, ⲛⲓⲥⲟⲉⲛⲉ ⲛⲓⲥⲟⲛⲉ. Then the priest takes the first boy's hand, and all bark like dogs and bite at the unleavened bread until it 'is consumed, the victim standing in their midst the while and saying, 'By the prayers of the saintly Abba T., may the Lord accept your prayers and grant me healing speedily,' after which the priest dismisses them with his blessing.'' A footnote gives a quotation from the copy of the service in the Aberdeen University Library, which dates back to 1795 : '' And he (*sc.* the victim) shall eat the piece of unleavened cake that has been placed in the oil and taken from the boys' mouths, and shall be anointed with the oil, and shall drink of the water and wash therewith ; so shall he be made whole by the blessing of the saintly Abba T. Therefore the priest shall say the blessing, &c.''

Though the date of the earliest published manuscript of this service is only of the eighteenth century, the whole tenor of the ritual suggests a pre-Christian origin. The most obvious comparison is with the Metternich Stele, which is one of the best-known magical texts for the cure of poisonous wounds. It appears to be the standard text of a temple, possibly Heliopolis, and seems to contain several '' services.'' Most of these are to cure the sting of a scorpion, but the ⲓ animal is also mentioned. From the determinative this is presumably a mammal of some kind, and the word may be a late spelling of , '' Wolf.'' An animal, known as a wolf, is still found in Egypt. Bites from a rabid wolf are peculiarly virulent ; the number of cases of hydrophobia in persons bitten by mad wolves is 40 per cent. as compared with the 15 per cent. of cases amongst those bitten by dogs. The danger of wolf bites may have been known, and the wolf would therefore be taken as the typical animal whose bite was to be cured.

There are several points of contact between the Metternich Stele and the service of Anba Tarabo besides this suggestion as to the wolf. In the versions published by Galtier and Crum the actions of the saint are not differentiated from those of the priest who performs the ritual, and the widow's son of the story coalesces with the patient over whom the ceremony is performed. In the same way, in the inscription, the speaker of the words of healing is sometimes Thoth, who invokes Ra, sometimes Ra himself, sometimes someone else, apparently a priest, who invokes both Ra and Thoth, just as the Christian priest invokes both God and Tarabo. The inscription gives Horus, son of Isis, as the patient, and the real patient is so completely identified with him that it is a little difficult to be always certain which is being referred to. I would suggest that the reason why Anba Tarabo's patient is called a widow's son is that Horus was essentially the son of Isis, and that when in course of time the divinity of Isis was forgotten, she would be thought of as a woman whose husband was dead and who had only the one child.

In the version which I have given above, the boys repeated the words '' Bash, bash, stanna '' when circling round the patient. In Crum's version the word is written ⲛⲓⲥⲟⲉⲛⲉ ⲛⲓⲥⲟⲛⲉ. It seems probable that this is a corruption of some Egyptian word and not of Greek origin as Crum thinks. I would suggest that it is a mispronunciation of the words ,' ' Fear not, fear not,'' which form part of the ritual given on the Metternich Stele.

The saint of the Christian ritual, Anba Tarabo, is entirely unknown to bagio‑ logists except in this one connection. It has been suggested that he is the same as a certain St. Therapòn, with no further reason for the identification than the similarity in the sound of the name. It is possible that Tarabo might be a personification of healing ($\theta\epsilon\rho\alpha\pi\epsilon\acute{\upsilon}\omega$) ; but if so, one would expect to find him as the healer of other diseases, not of dog-bite only ; this, however, is not the case. As he is not found elsewhere in Christian Egypt, or in Christendom in general, it is advisable to search for him in pre-Christian times, especially as the ritual seems to be derived from a pre-Christian and purely Egyptian source.

In the Magical Papyrus of London and Leyden, which, though belonging to the third century A.D., is undoubtedly copied from some much older source, there are two remedies for dog-bite. The first throws no light on the matter, but the second is called " The exorcism of Amen and Triphis." Triphis is a rare goddess, but her name is enshrined in the name of the southern Athribis. Gauthier (*Bull. de l'Inst. fran. d'Arch. orient.*, 1903, III, 165) has collected all that is known about her, and his researches appear to me to show that though she is hardly mentioned in inscriptions, her cult was a popular one. The mere fact that an important town in the south was called Athribis, " House of Triphis," would be sufficient to prove this. Gauthier shows that the personal name ⲧⲁⲧⲉⲧⲣⲓⲫⲓⲥ is formed, as so many personal names were formed, with the elements ⟨hieroglyphs⟩, followed by the name of a deity, the meaning being " the gift of " that deity. Gauthier identifies Triphis with a goddess ⟨hieroglyphs⟩, who seems to have been a local form of Isis at Akhmim ; but this identification does not account for the origin of the name of the town, nor is it borne out by the demotic equivalent. In demotic the name is *t·rpy·t*, which, when transcribed into hieroglyphs, as at Athribis, is ⟨hieroglyphs⟩, " the heiress." There is also a goddess ⟨hieroglyphs⟩, who is always characterised as ⟨hieroglyph⟩, " the great." It is well known that the queens of Egypt were often represented as goddesses, and it is presumed that they were considered divine, though there is no literary evidence of the fact till the deification of the Ptolemaic queens. But Nefertari is represented as being worshipped at Thebes, and her cult seems to have continued long after her death. The title of " the great heiress " is fairly common for queens between the XIIth and the XVIIIth dynasties, and it is possible that the immediate heiress to the throne may have been credited with divine powers, among which would be the power of healing some specific disease, as was the case among our own monarchs. If then " the great heiress " was the healer of dog-bite, and the title ⟨hieroglyphs⟩ is the origin of the name Triphis, we have the continuation of the cult of the queen as late as the Magical Papyrus of London and Leyden, which is within the Christian era. And as in the words ⟨hieroglyphs⟩ there are all the elements of the name of that otherwise unexplained saint Tarabo, I would suggest that we have, in this service for the cure of dog-bite, the survival of an ancient liturgy which reaches back perhaps to the XVIIIth dynasty, or perhaps even to a still earlier period, and that the name of the saint carries on the cult of an ancient Egyptian divinity.

M. A. MURRAY.

REVIEWS.

Nile and Jordan.—By Rev. G. A. Frank Knight. 1921. 8vo, 572 pp. 36s. (Clarke.)

The purpose of this work is to show the connections between Egypt and Canaan during the whole of the Biblical ages. An index of 1,800 references to all parts of the Bible will show how closely every connection has been noted, and will long serve as a text book for exegetical use. The industry of the author has resulted in references to some 1,700 different publications, showing an immense amount of reading and compilation. It may seem a hard saying, but it is in this studious collection of opinion that the danger lies. The authors rather than the facts are piled in the balance ; for instance, for the number of campaigns of Sennacherib fifteen authors are stated in favour of one, and twelve in favour of two campaigns. " The problem is thus fairly evenly balanced." It is not the problem but the piles of authors that are here balanced. What are the facts on which they build ? Are their differences due to facts or to arguments ? How many of them have followed one after another like sheep ? All through the work perfectly baseless or erroneous assertions of one writer are given equal credit with the most careful and accurate work of another. This is the natural defect of a literary treatment, not in touch with the basic facts. It does not matter what opinions are, compared with what the facts are. The original works are less referred to than the various Journals, which often give incomplete statements.

The need of reference to the facts is seen where a carving is said to be from the cataracts, though it was from the Royal Tombs (p. 41) ; or where certain authors are said to deny that Amenemhat III was buried in the Hawara pyramid, while it is certain that his canopic jars and fragments of a coffin were found alongside of the sarcophagus there (p. 89). On p. 175 we read, " the silver mines of Egypt were said to produce annually 3,200 myriads of minae " ; but what is really stated by Diodorus is that in the ruins of one temple (not annually) there were found 3,200 talents, of 60 minae (not a myriad). No silver is known to be produced in Egypt. Tanis is said to have been built " in the dreariest and most desolate part of the Delta, on the extreme northern edge of a vast morass." It was built in the most beautiful and flourishing region, which only sank under sea level in the time of Justinian (p. 238). Gold vases are said to have been found in the tomb of Rameses III (p. 259) ; but this refers to figures of vases painted on the wall, which might be of copper or pottery. These are examples of the misunderstandings due to second-hand sources, which recur far too often through the work.

A summary is given of the complex German theories about the Thothmides ; but a hint is needed that the whole pile of theory depends on the assumption that no ruler ever restored the name of a predecessor, though we know that such restoration was done, as by Sety I. The few stray examples of iron in Egypt are quoted as proving that it " was one of the very first countries in the world to mine and to use this metal " : whereas probably all the early examples are meteoric, and Egypt was far behind other countries in the adoption of iron Much more might be noted, but we will turn to the general view.

Palaeolithic and Neolithic men are first dealt with. Then the early dynasties, where the bungle over Mena being " a composite figure " is unfortunately given currency, as well as the errors about Khent or Seshti for the name of Zer, and Besh being supposed to be a king. The pyramid period is fully described, with parallels between Ptah-hetep's and Solomon's proverbs, and also between the pyramid text of Pepy II and the Chaldean creation, which are notable. In the full description of the XIIth dynasty the Lay of the Harper is set parallel with Ecclesiastes. The Hyksos age is granted the extent and importance assigned to it by the Egyptians. In the XVIIIth dynasty the questions of the Exodus are introduced, the author taking a very decided position that it was about 1445 B.C., in the reign of Amenhetep II. This is based on the 480 years stated between the Exodus and Solomon's temple ; and the chance of this being due to misunderstandings must be weighed against the absence of any reference in Judges to the conquests of Sety I, Rameses II and III, and the uniform length of the four priestly genealogies which indicate a date of about 1220 B.C. for the Exodus.

The Egyptian influence on the Hebrews is discussed, and the Hymn of Akhenaten to the Aten is set parallel with the 104th Psalm. The later history is fully dealt with, and does not give scope for so many different views. A chapter is devoted to the Egyptian origin of the Book of Job. Some of the main reasons are, the parallel between Job's confession and the Negative confession, and the description of the ostrich, hippopotamus, and crocodile, which are all African. The conclusion is that it was written by Jews in Egypt about the Persian dynasties. The Ptolemies are very fully described, and the century of Roman rule until the fall of Jerusalem.

As a summary of the literature of such a vast extent the work is remarkable, and could hardly be surpassed ; we may hope that it may be improved in future by a critical valuation of the facts and arguments, without depending merely on authors, and by avoiding many of the confusions and errors of previous writers.

L'Humanité Préhistorique.—By J. DE MORGAN. 1921. 8vo, 330 pp., 190 figs. (*La Renaissance du Livre,* 78 Boul. St. Michel, Paris.) 15 frs.

Here is a noble start on returning to pre-war prices of knowledge. Such a volume of original writing, with such full illustration, would be brought out here at three times the 7s. at which it is priced. Over half of the volume is assigned to the various stages of flint and metal working. A preliminary chapter deals with geologic conditions, the ice age, and the scale of time. Each successive period is then described, with full illustration of types. After this there is a section of 30 pp. on dwellings, clothing, agriculture, and animals. A long section of 120 pp. deals with paintings and carvings, pottery, design, burials, beliefs, monuments, emblems, writing, trade, and relations of races. Thus the whole field is fairly noticed ; as a general presentation it is an excellent outline, and the details which invite notice below do not impair its value for general instruction. The author's view on various debated questions is what will be most of interest and value.

Perhaps the most important question at present is how far similarity of form of flint work was contemporary. In noting the contemporaneousness of

Achulean and Mousterian forms, it is said : " Ces similitudes dans la formes des instruments portent à penser que ces industries se sont, aux mêmes époques, étendues sur la majeure partie de l'Europe occidentale et centrale " (p. 54). This sides with the single-period view. On the other hand there is a strong protest against the types of one style being supposed to be synchronous (p. 32) ; the resemblances in different countries are referred to similar thoughts and material, while absolutely independent (p. 105) ; synchronism cannot be admitted for the same industry in all regions (p. 297) ; and we must strike out of the archaeologic vocabulary the words *age, epoch, period* (p. 305). The difference of these positions needs consideration. What seems to be the needful view is that, while the conditions and the results of necessity may be of widely separate age in different lands, yet the artistic features of form and treatment are not re-invented, and show a connection not far removed in time wherever they are found. The artistic appearance of American stone work differs from anything in the Old World, while the exact similarity of characters all round the Mediterranean seems to demand a real connection of culture in each stage ; and though the more remote countries might lag behind, they would not exactly repeat artistic detail independently. In accord with this is the remark that there is no Chellean period in the Far East (p. 309) ; if invention had repeated the same course it would be a needful prelude. There is required here some outline of recent views as to styles belonging to different races, who swept into Europe and other fields of action.

In other respects also the results of the last ten or twenty years are not taken into account ; the pre-Crag flints, the Gebel el Araq knife, the complete series of flint types in Egypt, including Aurignacian, Solutrean, and Magdalenian (which are expressly denied), the results from Anau, the evidence in the Vedas of migration from Central Siberia, the alphabetic signs all being early known as pot-marks, the definiteness of geologic age from radium, the use of sequence dating—in ignoring all of these the book might as well have been written twenty years ago. Some detail about the mammalia, shells, and plants, typical of each human stage should also have been given.

The age of metals might well be treated more definitely, in its general outline (p. 112), and in the detail of the known sources of tin in Saxony and Hungary (omitted p.124), in bronze not being regularly used till long after the IIIrd dynasty (pp. 135, 309), in the confusion of sometimes recognising the copper age, and otherwise ignoring it (159, 189), in iron being only sporadic in Egypt until Greek times, and bronze ploughshares preceding iron. There is confusion about the Sinai sources ; really no copper ore or smelting is known in Maghara or Serabit, but an immense quantity of copper came from the Wady Nasb, as the slag mounds show : this is contrary to pp. 123, 291.

In the dating of Egyptian material there is the same attribution of historic objects to prehistoric times, which disfigured earlier work of this author. On p. 101, Fig. 19 is of the XIIth dynasty ; on p. 110, Figs. 2, 3, 6, 7, 9, 27, 30 and 31 are of the XIIth or XVIIIth dynasties ; on p. 180 the sickles found were not prehistoric but of XIIth and XVIIIth dynasties, and the teeth never extended to near the point ; on p. 186 no cotton was known in the IIIrd dynasty, nor till Arab times ; on p. 192 it should be said that scarabs were often mounted in rings, and the single earring in the top of the ear is a modern Nubian fashion. The mistake about the early kings' tombs being incinerated burials is perpetuated, though the burning was only the act of destroyers. The sources of ornament on prehistoric pottery are mis-stated (p. 189). In all these points some familiarity with the historic archaeology is needed. A printer's error in inverting two blocks, pp. 280, 296, should be remedied.

Some notable remarks are made about the spiral patterns being of Magdalenian age (p. 314), and hence theories of later migration are beside the mark ; also the distribution of dolmens, and their cultural ages, bar the diffusion of them either way (p. 252), and show that the megalithic idea naturally started at various centres (p. 254). This book is an essential and stimulating outline for general reading, though verification at the sources is desirable before accepting all the details.

Motya.—By JOSEPH I. S. WHITAKER. 1921. 8vo, 357 pp., 118 figs. 30s. (*Bell.*)

The elusive Phoenician has left very little that can be accepted as distinctive of his abilities or his taste. Nearly all his cities have passed into other hands and been covered with the work of later times. The author has succeeded in acquiring a unique site, which should give a clearer view than any other place, of the work of the Phoenicians. This is their principal city of Sicily, Motya, 5 miles north of Marsala, destroyed in 397 B.C., and desolated so that there is no trace of the later Greeks or the Roman rule.

The Phoenician—a true sea-trader—always established himself in island cities near a mainland, and preferred an island small enough to be entirely walled, and leave no footing outside of it for attack. Tyre, Aradus, Motya, are the proto-types of Singapore and Hongkong. This book is an introduction to the Phoeni-eian question, dealing with a summary of the Phoenician colonies, the early Sicani and Siculi, the Phoenicians in Sicily, the Greeks, and the fall of Motya. A second part describes the remains of the fortifications, and the contents of the museum on the little island, which is only about 3 furlongs across. There is very little that is dissimilar to the Greek work of the same age ; the flat-bottomed cylindrical bottles with a handle are about all that is not met with elsewhere. The traces of Egyptian influence are the scarabs set in rings, which seem to be the usual Naukratite or Rhodian, and the amulets of the sacred eye, Apis, Ptah, Bes and Uraeus, all probably foreign copies. It is much to be hoped that when Mr. Whitaker carries out his intended clearance of the site we may have a detailed plan of the city, and register sheets of all the objects found, for it is not only the best site to get Phoenician work, but will be of much value for dating Greek work before the limit in 397 B.C.

PERIODICALS.

Zeitschrift für Aegyptische Sprache, Vol. LIII, 1916.

(Continued from p. 96.)

SPIEGELBERG, W.—*Koptische Miszellen.* 1. The transcription of Pharao for the Coptic ⲛⲉⲣⲟ and the Egyptian ⌐⌐ can be traced in full, the aspirated P showing that the Hebrew and the Greek forms were taken from the dialect of Lower Egypt.

2. The verb ⲛⲟⲧⲧϥ, translated as "to laugh," by Peyron, means simply "to loose." The full expression is "to loose the mouth with laughter," but occasionally the contraction is used.

3. The word ⲉⲧⲛⲓⲍ, "ashes," which occurs only in Clement of Alexandria, derives from the Egyptian [hieroglyphs], "dust of fire." This derivation may also explain the very puzzling word ⲕⲉⲛⲉⲫⲓⲧⲉⲛ "ash-bread," *i.e.*, "bread of the ashes."

4. The suffixed pronoun -ⲥⲟⲧ or -ⲥⲉ of the Sahidic dialect is usually supposed to be the remains of the Egyptian [hieroglyphs] Spiegelberg suggests that the s is euphonic between two vowels, or between a vowel and a half-consonant.

5. Spiegelberg suggests the derivation of ⲝⲁⲛⲉ, "water-flood," from [hieroglyphs] though he acknowledges the difficulty of proof.

6. When the holy Shenoute fulminated against Aristophanes, he accuses him of having filled books ⲛⲁⲧⲛⲩⲩⲏⲧ with silly words. Spiegelberg proposes to derive the description of the book from two Egyptian words meaning "true, or good skin," *i.e.*, parchment. The costliness of the material as compared with the worthlessness of the words written on it certainly gives point to Shenoute's remarks.

7. This is merely a note to show that the two causative verbs ⲧⲥⲟ and ⲧⲩⲩⲟ can take a direct object without the connecting ⲛ.

8. Spiegelberg here traces the variations in vocalisation of IIIae inf. verbs. He gives nothing really new, but merely supports Sethe's investigations.

9. The Coptic word for "sandal" was either masculine or feminine, but the masculine, in the dual form, survived. In the construct form the meaning changed and can mean "bosom," hence ⲛⲉⲧⲍⲓⲧⲟⲧⲱ = "the nearest," is literally "He who is in the bosom of."

WIESMANN, H.— [hieroglyphs] =: ⲟⲧⲓ-ⲍⲣⲁ =. A large number of quotations are given with the result that the derivation of this expression is evidently from [hieroglyph] "the face," and not from |, "the voice." The meaning is "to be busy with, to be engaged in," with the underlying idea of "unruliness," hence "dissipation, laughter, entertaining."

VON BISSING, FR. W.—*Die " Gottesstrasse."* In the dream-stela of Thothmes IV mention is made of the Road of the Gods. Brugsch, in a passage to which little attention has ever been paid, notes that the Road of the Gods occurs also in the inscription of Piankhy, where it is called the Road of Sep, and led apparently from Heliopolis to the town which was the origin of the modern Cairo. The god Sep is known in the Book of the Dead, and the name is also preserved as an epithet of Osiris, and is closely connected with Heliopolis. The road appears to have been on the east side of the river.

Miszellen.

1. STEINDORFF, G.—In the Metternich Museum at Königswarth are two wooden coffins of the New Kingdom. One, of the XVIIIth dynasty, is mummy-form, and is painted black and yellow; it belonged to a certain ⟨hieroglyphs⟩, The other is of the XIXth or XXth dynasty, is coloured a golden yellow, and is covered with religious pictures and short texts. It still contains the mummy, who was an *uab*-priest of Amen called ⟨hieroglyphs⟩ " He of the watch house." It looks as though the coffin came from the great mummy-pit of the Theban priests at Thebes.

2. WIESMANN, H.—A further example of nouns formed with the qualitative and peϥ- (see LII, p. 130), is peϥcɴт, "astrologer."

3. WIESMANN, H.—The phrase ɴe⋀т ⋀ɴⲕⲁⲍ is translated by Horner, " ends of the earth." But as ɴe⋀т is without the definite article, the genitive ɴтe- should be used. It is perhaps a kind of proper name which carries its own definition. The etymology is not known.

3. WIESMANN, H.—An unusual use of the word ⲙⲙⲟɴ shows that it introduces the apodosis in a conditional sentence.

4. BISSING, FR. W. VON.—This is a suggestion that the artists who decorated tombs in the Old Kingdom had a " book of patterns " out of which they chose the designs, including the animals led as offerings by the servants, and that the name of the animal was sometimes wrongly copied.

5. BURCHARDT, M.—Two interesting parallels with Egyptian legends are given here. One is from the collection of *märchen* of Sidhi Khūr : a woman bathed in a stream, which carried away two locks of her hair and left them on the bank where they were found by a maid of the king's. The king finally carried off the lady. The second story is from the collection of Ardshi Bordshi Khan : An army of ghosts demanded human victims. The rescuer set a pot of brandy before each ghost, who became drunk and all were then killed by the king's son.

Zeitschrift für Aegyptische Sprache, Vol. LIV, 1918,

SETHE, K.—*Zur Komposition des Totenbuchspruches für das Herbeibringen der Fähre (Kap. 99, Einleitung).* The chapter of " The Bringing of the Ferry-boat " is found in the Middle Kingdom ; and Sethe has traced, from the examples remaining, many of the changes which crept in and altered the conception. The main idea of the chapter is that the dead man (addressed as " O magician "), calls to the celestial ferryman to bring his boat. The ferryman makes various objections, as that the boat is all to pieces (𓂝 ⸺ 𓂋 𓏴 ⟍), but is finally overruled. The original ferryman was *Ma-ḥa-f*, " He who looks behind him," but later he becomes merely the person who answers the dead man. The ferryman, in what is evidently the later version, is called the Āķen ; and the dead man tells *Ma-ḥa-f* to " Awake me the Āķen." When the Āķen is finally roused, he answers, " What is it ? I am still asleep." On which the magician replies, " Bring me that [*i.e.*, the boat], if you will be provided with life. Behold, I come." The *Āķen* then tests the knowledge of the would-be passenger : " Which are the two cities, O magician ? " " They are the Horizon and the *shesemt*, I think." " Dost thou know those two cities, O magician ? " " I know them." " Which are those two cities, O magician ? " " They are the D*uat* and the reed-field." The Āķen, as a last resource, objects to ferrying over a man who cannot count his fingers ; the magician refutes this by triumphantly repeating a finger-counting rhyme. The order of development is shown thus :⸺(1) A short summons to an unnamed ferryman to bring the boat. (2) A similar but longer summons to the celestial ferryman, " He who looks behind him," originally the ferryman who brought the boat and who made the objections as to the boat's condition, but who is now only required to awake the Āķen. (3) A similar conversation between the dead man (known as the magician) and a being whom he meets on his arrival in heaven. This personage is called " He who looks behind him," although he is not the ferryman and is only the awaker of the Āķen. (4) A summons to the celestial ferryman, the Āķen ; this contains certain elements like those in No. 2, as well as the polite refusal to bring the boat, and the epithet " magician " applied to the dead man. It is needless to say that in a paper written by a master of the language, such as Professor Sethe, every statement and suggestion is of importance, both as to words and grammatical construction. [Trouble with the ferryman was evidently as familiar anciently as it is in modern Egypt.]

SETHE, K.—*Ein altagyptischer Fingerzählreim.* In the foregoing article mention was made of a person who, if he could not count his fingers, would be refused transport into the presence of Osiris. When the magician says that he can count, the celestial ferryman retorts, " Let me hear you count both your fingers and toes." Whereupon the magician recites a finger-counting rhyme of the type of " This is the one that broke the barn," or " This little pig went to market." The Egyptian rhyme is full of puns on the numbers : " Thou hast taken the one ; thou hast taken the one as the second ; thou hast extinguished it for him ; thou hast wiped it away for him ; give to me then ; what is smelt in my face ; loose not thyself from him ; spare it not ; thou has illumined the eye ; give me the eye." The lines go in pairs, each pair ending with the same word, with the exception of lines 5 and 6, which make a rhyme in our sense of the word, *i.e.*, two words of which the termination has the same sound. This is evidently done purposely to mark the change from one hand to the other. Sethe suggests that the whole rhyme refers to the Eye of Horus ; that " the one " of the first line is the Eye, and that the feminine pronoun, which I have translated as " it," also refers to the Eye. As parallel examples of some of the phrases can be found in the Pyramid Texts, Sethe dates the composition back to the Old Kingdom. It is a well-ascertained fact that children's rhymes often originated in ancient religious ritual ;. and it is extraordinarily interesting to find an original for one of these rhymes. This is actually the oldest known example of finger-counting verses.

SETHE, K.—*Das Pronomen* I. *sing.* " *n-nk* " *und die Eingangsworte zum* 17. *Kapitel des Totenbuches.* The seventeenth chapter of the " Book of the Dead " contains the well-known phrase 〔hieroglyphs〕 " I am yesterday and I know the morrow." In the religious texts of the Middle Kingdom the sentence begins 〔hieroglyphs〕, which has usually been taken as a variant of 〔hieroglyph〕. The introductory words of the chapter are 〔hieroglyphs〕 〔hieroglyphs〕, which is often translated " Let the word come to pass. I am Atum." Sethe points out by various examples that 〔hieroglyph〕 is not the same as 〔hieroglyph〕, but means " Belonging to me." At the same time he shows that 〔hieroglyph〕 is not the name of the god, but has in this connection its original meaning of " complete, all." The sentences then would read " To me belongs yesterday and I know the morrow," and " Let the word come to pass, [for] to me belongs all." The New Kingdom texts have completely lost this sense, which is preserved in the Middle Kingdom. Sethe takes the form of 〔hieroglyph〕 to be a compound of *n-i inwk*, the *n* of the dative followed by the pronoun of the first person singular (omitted in writing, as is so often the case) and emphasised by the absolute pronoun. This use of an emphatic pronoun is common in Coptic ; the parallel phrase would be ⲚⲀⲒ ⲀⲚⲞⲔ, and it is also found in Arabic, لِي أنا, The position of a prepositional phrase at the beginning of a nominal sentence is rare ; this reversal of the usual order of words is also clearly for emphasis. The use of the form 〔hieroglyph〕 appears to have been confined to the Middle Kingdom.

SETHE, K.—*Die angeblichen Schmiede des Horus von Edfu.* Brugsch first identified the 〔hieroglyphs〕 of Horus of Edfu with the Coptic ⲂⲀⳠⲚⲎⲦ, and explained the word as " smiths " or " metal-workers." Maspero suggested— and his suggestion has been universally accepted—that, in the campaign of Horus of Edfu and his " smiths " against Set, we have the far-off echo of the invasion of a flint-using people by a metal-working race. Sethe now proposes to jettison this theory, which practically rests only upon Brugsch's identification. The word 〔hieroglyphs〕 is used from the Old Kingdom down to Ptolemaic times for a sculptor in stone or wood ; it probably read Ḳstr, and has nothing in common with the name of the companions of Horus except the bone-sign. The usual way of writing the name is without the 〔hieroglyph〕, *i.e.*, *msnw*, therefore the identification with 〔hieroglyphs〕 and with ⲂⲀⳠⲚⲎⲦ falls to the ground. In the earliest example, which is of the Middle Kingdom, the word is written *msnw*, and a parallel text gives the sign 〔hieroglyph〕 as the determinative. Brugsch and Maspero both saw in the place-name 〔hieroglyphs〕 a workshop or forge erected in the temple of Edfu for the

" smiths " of Horus, and read it as *MSNT*-city. But the sign can also read *bb*, which is an implement used in hippopotamus-hunting. The word *msn* can be determined with the sign of wood as well as the bone-sign. From the literary evidence the word seems to mean a harpooner, or the whole tackle of a harpoon. If this is so, the sign is easily explained by the fact that in predynastic times bone-harpoons were commonly used. Sethe suggests that the word *msn* is a form of the name of the two-barbed harpoon ⎥ *sn* with prefixed *m*. [Sethe does not explain the sign ⟊. I would suggest that it is the case in which the sharpened harpoon-points were carried. I do not think a reel was ever represented among any fishing-tackle, otherwise the presence of the cord wound round the object and tied in a knot would suggest the reel. The harpoon had long been made of copper before the text in question, and therefore cannot be called a " bone-sign." This leaves Maspero's position unaltered.]

SETHE, K.—*Zum Inzest des Snefru.* Sottas has called in question Sethe's translation of the well-known genealogy of Nefermaat, which shows the closely consanguineous marriages so common in early times. Sethe brings forward further proof that Nefermaat was the son of Snefru ; Nefermaat was " king's son," a title borne only by an actual child of a king, the son of a king's son being merely a " royal acquaintance." He also points out that, though the word " son " is sometimes rather loosely used, the meaning in a genealogy is always strictly limited to the actual son.

VAN DER LEEUW, G.—*External Soul, Schutzgeist und der ägyptische Ka.* The *Ka* has been a subject of much controversy, and Herr van der Leeuw brings forward evidence to show that it is (1) the life principle, (2) the double, (3) the guardian spirit. As the life-principle, the soul-power, it is not unlike the Melanesian *mana*. To be parted from one's *ka* is nothing else than to die. But the *ka* continues to exist after death ; and the evidence seems to show that it is born with the man and governs his mortal life, but its real life begins after death. But a soul which can be severed from its body is a kind of external soul ; and if the dead wished to share in a higher life, they were said to go to their *kas*. The *ka* as the double is well known in representations of the king. As the guardian spirit the *ka* is that form of the life-principle which is external to the body and for security's sake is hidden away in a secret place. As long as it remains hidden the person to whom it belongs is immune from death ; but if the hiding-place is found the person has no means of defence. This duality is shown in Egyptian examples : " Thou (the God Geb) art the *Ka* of all gods . . . thou art God, for thou hast power over all gods." Geb has here secured the safety of his soul by uniting it with the gods. If the *ka* of the gods dies, Geb dies ; but conversely, if he dies, the gods die. Therefore he protects them and they protect him. [The last word is far from being said on this complex subject. Further light might be thrown upon it by a study of the *qarina* of modern Egypt, the " double " of the opposite sex which comes into the world with each child. The African belief in the " ancestral spirit," which is partly incarnated in each successive generation, serves to explain completely the *ka* as external and also in-dwelling (see *Anc. Eg.*, 1914, 24, 162).]

SPIEGELBERG, W.—*Ein Heiligtum des Gottes Chnum von Elephantine in der thebanischen Totenstadt.* As a great number of granite-workers from Aswan must have gone to Thebes in the course of business, it is natural to suppose that there must have been a sanctuary of their local god, Khnum of Elephantine, in the Theban necropolis where they worked. There is proof of this in several monuments from Thebes, either dedicated to Khnum in words or with representations of that god being worshipped. Spiegelberg publishes a small wooden stela, painted with a representation, in the upper register, of the god Khnum seated; a worshipper kneels in the lower register; and the dedication is to Khnum by 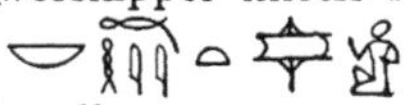. "Master of the North Wind," *i.e.*, a man who knows wind-spells.

SPIEGELBERG, W.—*Die Darstellung des Alters in der aelteren aegyptischen Kunst von dem Mittleren Reich.* In comparing the two portraits of Ra-hesy on the well-known panels, it will be seen that one represents a much older man than the other; the sharpened features, the wrinkle from the nose to the side of the mouth, the hollow under the cheek-bone, all show the advance of age. In the case of stout elderly men the wrinkle is but lightly indicated, the face being almost dropsical in its fatness. Figures in the round also represent old age. The best known of these is the ivory king from Abydos, which represents the bent attitude, the hanging mouth and the withered skin of old age; the large, warm, quilted cloak is another sign. In the slate statue of King Khasekhem from Hierakonpolis (Quibell. *Hierak.* XLI) the characteristic nose-to-mouth wrinkle, though not very deep, is still clearly marked. One of the best examples of the representation of a man at two stages of his life can be found in the two statues of Rahetep, high-priest of Memphis. One of these shows this "prince of the church" in the flower of young manhood, the other shows the same man when past his prime. The celebrated scribe of the Louvre is another case in point; the flabby body and the sharpened features represent a man verging on old age. Spiegelberg, like Capart, inclines to the belief that these representations of old age were not intended as portraits. He maintains that the great sculptors of the Old Kingdom did not make portraits but types, these types representing men at two different stages of life.

SPIEGELBERG, W.—*Eine Bronzestatuette des Amon.* This bronze statuette represents the god Amon in human form with a ram's head. The figure is nude. Nude figures are not uncommon in the reliefs of the Old Kingdom, but nude figures in the round are rare at any period. The statuette is of bronze, originally overlaid with gold-leaf, and inlaid with gold wire; the eyes had also been inlaid. The ram's horn remains on one side of the head, and proves that the animal is the *Ovis Ammon.* It has always been remarked how wonderfully the Egyptians managed the anatomy of human figures with animal heads; in this statuette it is the anatomy of the face which is remarkable. The upper part of the face—forehead, eyes, ears and cheek-bones—are human, it is only the muzzle which is animal; and under the creature's chin is the beard which is appropriate to the gods. Spiegelberg puts the date of the statuette at the XIXth dynasty.

SPIEGELBERG, W.—*Der Maler Heje.* Schäfer has suggested that drawings on potsherds and limestone-flakes are not always free sketches, but are often memory-copies of some original, and Frau Luise Klebs remarks that the artist only noted down what interested him artistically. Spiegelberg here publishes a sketch which was found in the neighbourhood of its original, at Deir el Medinet. In this cemetery is the tomb of Huy (Heje), a great artist who lived under Rameses III ; and on the wall of the tomb is a portrait of the artist, probably by himself. The sketch on limestone, found in a tomb close by, reproduces the figure with sufficient fidelity to make it possible to recognise it even if the inscription had not been copied also. It is evident that it was the representation of the artist's streaming hair and of his upturned foot, as well as the flowing lines of the whole figure, which attracted the copyist.

BONNET, H.—*Die Königshaube.* The *nms* headdress of the King is made of cloth, which is taken straight across the forehead and behind the ears, and covers the whole of the head ; at the back it ends in a roll of the material, the so-called pigtail, in front a long lappet falls over each shoulder ; on each side it is pushed out into a rounded form by the mass of hair below. The cloth is pleated in folds of varying dimensions. A similar headdress is the ⌐⊚⌐, which differs from the *nms* in being perfectly smooth and having no lappets, the pigtail is flatter and broader. The *ḫꜣt* was worn by women, and according to Borchardt was worn by all Egyptian ladies under the wig. [In this they would resemble their modern descendants who, when in native dress, wear a handkerchief tied over the head in a peculiar way under the veil.] The *ḫꜣt* is represented in the lists of property on Middle Kingdom coffins. On statues and reliefs the *nms* is known as early as the IVth dynasty, but the *ḫꜣt* is not found till the New Kingdom. Still, the method of arranging the headdress shows that the one is the simpler, and therefore probably the earlier, form of the other. In the *ḫꜣt* the cloth is not folded in any way, but in the *nms* the folds are a characteristic feature ; in the *nms* also the cloth is held in place round the forehead by what appears to be a metal band.

SPIEGELBERG, W.—*Eine Totenliturgie der Ptolemäerzeit.* The papyrus 25 of the Egyptian collection at Vienna has been published by von Bergmann as a list of gods. But it also contains a very interesting funerary liturgy written in demotic for a lady named 𓅂𓂝𓏤𓊨𓏤 Artemisia. It ends with the instruction to carry the bier with the body to four places, probably shrines ; at the first, the head shall be to the north, the feet to the south ; at the second, the head shall be to the west, the feet to the east ; at the third, the head shall be to the east, the feet to the west ; at the fourth, the head shall again be to the north, the feet to the south. Various offerings and ceremonies probably took place at each shrine. Then follow these words : " Afterwards comes Horus. He smites the wicked one, while the children of Horus are in the hall. . . . There appears this god Osiris, appearing in the Nun." Spiegelberg takes this as a direction to perform the mystery-play as part of the funeral ceremony.

SPIEGELBERG, W.—*Der demotische Papyrus der Stadtbibliothek Frankfurt a. M.* This is a marriage-contract in which a concubine is raised to the position of a wife. The eldest son, who at the time of the marriage, was already in existence, is mentioned by name ; this being the only instance known of such mention by name. The child is, by authority of the parents, to inherit equally with any future children. Dr. Joseph Partsch adds a short legal commentary on this contract, in which he points out that it is of the usual late type. It is worth considering whether a son born after marriage ranked as the eldest son, or whether that position belonged to a child born before marriage.

SETHE, K.—*Zum partizipialen Ursprung der Suffix konjugation.* Sethe derives all the forms of the suffix-conjugation—*sdmf, sdmn-f, sdmin-f, sdmḫr-f*—from participles. The literal translation of *sdm-f* would be "he is hearing"; in *sdmn-f* the *n* is the preposition, "is heard by him." The *in* of *sdmin-f* is also a preposition, and is commonly used in that way with other forms of the verb. So also *ḫr* is a preposition. This explains why in the relative form with *n—sdmwn-f*—the *pronomen relativum* is not expressed, although the object of the verb, ⟦hieroglyphs⟧ "The voice which I heard," literally "The voice which was heard by me."

SPIEGELBERG, W.—*Der aegyptische Possessivartikel.* The Egyptian ⟦hieroglyphs⟧, ⟦hieroglyphs⟧, and ⟦hieroglyph⟧ are the origin of the Coptic ⲡⲁ, ⲧⲁ and ⲛⲁ, "He of, she of, they of." In the Middle Kingdom they were used with the genitive ⟦hieroglyph⟧, and from the New Kingdom onwards the masculine is usually written ⟦hieroglyph⟧, but at the same time in other examples the genitive *n* is dropped out; so that "He of Abydos" can be written ⟦hieroglyphs⟧ or ⟦hieroglyphs⟧. These forms are used, in combination with gods' names, as personal names; and in late times can express filiation, instead of the older ⟦hieroglyph⟧, thus ⟦hieroglyphs⟧ for ⟦hieroglyphs⟧ "Horus, son of Isis." In the feminine the pronoun is written ⟦hieroglyph⟧, ⟦hieroglyph⟧, or ⟦hieroglyph⟧; the last when combined with the genitive becomes ⟦hieroglyph⟧. But in this connection it is necessary to note that in many personal names, the ⟦hieroglyph⟧ is a combination of the demonstrative pronoun with a relative particle following, "The one who."

SPIEGELBERG, W.—*Demotische Kleinigkeiten.* 1. This is a contract for mummification and burial. Thotortaios has handed over to Phagonis all the materials for embalming the body of his son. Phagonis undertakes the commission, and engages that the form of mummification already agreed upon shall be carried out by the choachytes of Thotortaios. There is to be a forfeit of money for non-fulfilment of the contract.

2. An acknowledgment of a debt of two silver *deben* and half a *kite;* the debtor engages to repay in seven months. If he should delay to do this one month beyond the appointed time, he must pay one and a half times the outstanding amount as a fine. He pledges his house as security for the debt.

3. Four demotic examples from Hermonthis of receipts for the payment of a tax are given. The tax is known as λογεία Ἴσιδος, and was for the benefit of the priests of the bull Buchis and the goddess Isis of Philae, who had a sanctuary at Hermonthis. All four receipts are to the same man, Pi-buchis.

4. This interesting fragment records the dedication of a gift in the temple of Isis of Philae. The gift was apparently in fulfilment of a vow, and Spiegelberg suggests that the pilgrimage to Philae was an atonement for some sin.

5. The fragment here published belongs to the demotic inscription of Parthenios, published in Vol. LI, p. 81.   The date of the inscription was in the last line of this fragment, but unfortunately the actual numbers are broken away.

6. The name which in Greek is written Θουτορχῆς is derived from the Egyptian 𓏞𓎛𓂋𓏏𓅱 "Thoth   him."   Griffith has tentatively suggested that the Greek name Θοτρωῖσις is derived from the above, but Spiegelberg thinks that its real origin is 𓏞𓎛𓂋𓇋𓇋𓁹 "Thoth watches," a form of name which is not uncommon.

7. A mummy-label in the British Museum has a demotic and Greek inscription.   The Greek gives the date in the co-regency of *Publius* Licinius Valerianus and *Publius* Licinius [Valerianus] Gallienus when a third *Publius* Licinius Cornelius (Saloninus) Valerianus (Gallienus) was Caesar.   The abbreviation, which refers to the three rulers of the same name, occurs only on this label, and may be a popular designation.   The date is May 3, A.D. 256.

8. This is a note on the demotic writing of the name of the goddess *R'-t-t3wy*, "Rā-t of the two Lands," Ra-t being the feminine form of Ra.   Rā-t t3wy was the local goddess of Hermonthis.

SPIEGELBERG, W.—Τηιουχῶνσις.   At the end of the New Kingdom there are found personal names which mean "Portion, or half," of a god, *e.g.*, 𓂝𓃠𓂋𓏏 *dni* 𓈖 𓏏𓏏𓏤 *ti-t* "The part of Bast," or 𓂋𓇋𓐎𓏏𓏏 "Part of Khonsu."   The interchange of ꝫ and ⳁ shows that the *n* had already been lost in pronunciation.   The *t* of the definite article would coalesce with the first letter of the noun, and the name *T3-dni-t n Ḥnsw* would become in Greek Τηιουχωνσις.

SETHE, K.—*Die Bedeutung der Konsonanten verdopplung im Sahidischen und die Andeutung des ě durch den übergesetzen Strich.*   Sethe is against Erman's explanation of the doubling of consonants in Sahidic, and points out that it occurs only after the short *e* which is indicated by a stroke over the letter.   The doubling occurs with the letters ⲃ, ⲗ, ⲙ, ⲛ, and ⲣ.   According to Sethe this is not phonetic, but is an entirely graphic convention, which came into use before the introduction of the stroke.   Thus a word written ⲍⲩⲩⲟ must be pronounced *hěmě*; without the reduplication it might have represented the sounds *hmě*, or even *ěhmě*.

SPIEGELBERG, W.—*Koptische Kleinigkeiten.*   1. The Coptic ⲍⲏ "Quarry" is derived from the Egyptian word 𓃭𓏏 which has the same meaning.   In the Coptic version of Judges vi. 2, when the Israelites sought refuge from the Midianites, they dwelt in dens, and caves, ⲛⲛⲍⲏ ⲛ̄ϣⲁⲧⲱⲛⲅ " The quarries of the quarry-men."

2. The word ⲛⲥⲁϫⲧ following a proper name has hitherto been considered as an epithet meaning "the abstemious."   Spiegelberg now points out that the man's trade is often mentioned after his name, as "Father Jacob the builder," or "Phibammon the carpenter."   ⲛⲥⲁϫⲧ then probably means "the weaver" from ⲥⲱϫⲉ "to weave."

3. The Coptic ⲟⲃϣⲓ has hitherto had no known derivation. Spiegelberg has already shown that ⲧⲃⲁⲓⲧⲱⲧ is the Coptic form of 𓏤 ⳤ ⲧⲃⲁⲓ or ⲟⲃⲁⲓ would then be a Nisbe-form meaning "to be upon."

4. In the Coptic inscriptions from the convent of Jeremias at Sakkara, published by Sir H. Thompson, a man is given the epithet of ϥⲁⲧⳉ, which is left untranslated. Spiegelberg thinks this is a variant of ⲛϩⲁⲩⳉⲉ, "the carpenter," and quotes a similar form, ϩⲁⲧⲛⲟⲧⲃ for ϩⲁⲩⲛⲟⲧⲃ "Goldsmith," in support of his suggestion.

5. The Coptic ϫⲱⲣⲙ, "to wink," is derived from an Egyptian original,

⳥ 𓀢 𓁹. This appears as early as the coffin-texts published by Lacau (where, however, it is copied as 𓁹 𓀢 (?) 𓁹, the ⌒ being doubtful), and also in the tomb of *Tẓi* at Thebes.

SETHE, K.—*Miszellen.* Sethe does not agree with von Bissing as to his suggestion that the word 𓃀 is a mistake for 𓈖 and has been wrongly used by the Egyptian artist. On the contrary, 𓃀 is rightly used for a female goat, the name of the male being 𓃀𓃝. The word 𓈖 means the wild cow; the wild ox is *smȝ*, and is the animal whose feet, made in ivory, support the furniture of early times, and who was hunted by Amenhetep III. Its name, *smȝ*, seems to be connected with the word *smȝ* "to slay." It is not the hartebeest or bubale with lyre-shaped horns, which is called 𓌞𓈖𓏏𓃝𓅆 in Egyptian. A characteristic peculiarity of the *smȝ* is that in standing its tail is held between the legs, but in sitting or lying down the tail is held stiffly out.

SETHE, K.—The two Nile-gods, who bear respectively the symbolical plants of Upper and Lower Egypt on their heads, are represented as uniting the Two Lands. They are themselves the personification of the two parts of Egypt, as Gauthier and Jequier have already pointed out. On the statue of Amenemhat III published by Maspero, they are actually called Upper Egypt and Lower Egypt.

MÖLLER, G.—A lazuli figure of Taurt, bought at the Kennard sale, shows the goddess in her usual form as a hippopotamus standing on her hind-legs. It was not intended to be worn as an amulet, but under the feet is a short peg to fix it into a base. Through this peg a cylindrical hole has been bored up through the legs into the abdomen of the figure. The hole is filled with a doubled-up tube of thin gold which contained a few shreds of linen. This was an offering from an expectant mother for a safe delivery. Another figure of Taurt in wood had had the abdomen hollowed out and finished with another piece of wood, which was glued on after the insertion of a piece of a garment. A faïence figure shows the goddess in the act of suckling, the right paw holding the left breast. In place of the nipple is a hole communicating with a hollow inside the figure. If milk were put in this hollow it would trickle out of the hole. The idea seems to be that the dedicator of the figure would thus ensure adequate nourishment for her offspring.

ANCIENT
EGYPT

1922. PART I.

CONTENTS.

EDITOR. PROF. FLINDERS PETRIE, F.R.S., F.B.A.

YEARLY, 7s. POST FREE. QUARTERLY PART, 2s.

MACMILLAN AND CO.,
LONDON AND NEW YORK;
AND
EGYPTIAN RESEARCH ACCOUNT,
CHICAGO.

ANCIENT EGYPT. Net price of each number from booksellers is 2s.

Subscriptions for the four quarterly parts, prepaid, post free, 7s., are received by Hon. Sec. "Ancient Egypt" (H. Flinders Petrie), University College, Gower Street, London, W.C. 1.

Books for review, papers offered for insertion, or news, should be addressed :—
Editor of "Ancient Egypt,"
University College, Gower Street, London, W.C. 1.

Subscriptions received in the United States by :—
Miss Helen Gardner, Art Institute, Michigan Boulevard,
Adams Street, Chicago, Ill.

END OF SARCOPHAGUS OF PA-RAMESSU.

AT THE LEFT HAND SEE THE CARTOUCHE AND *NEB UBEN* NOT ON ERASURE.   TO THE RIGHT ARE
THE EARLIER CARVINGS OF PA-RAMESSU WITHOUT CARTOUCHE AND *NEB UBEN* OVER ERASURE.

HEAD OF WORSHIPPER. PTOLEMAIC STELE, ABYDOS.

ANCIENT EGYPT.

THE TREE OF THE HERAKLEOPOLITE NOME.
(Concluded.)

Let us now consider the subject from a botanical point of view. The species Raphia[1] is characterised by large penniform pinnate leaves, surpassing the trunk in size. The trunk is so short in proportion that Wurming writes of " the almost stem-less Raphia-palms " (*Lehrbuch d. ökologischen Pflanzengeog.*, 1918, p. 616).

In this it differs from the tall-stemmed slender species, mainly of date palms. In accordance with the Raphia is the determinative showing a short stem and a strongly developed crown of leaves. Agreeing with this is Dümichen's view quoted by Moldenke (*Alt. texte erw. Bäume*, p. 63) that " dieser Baumname, wenn auch nicht die Dattel palme, so doch möglicherweise eine andere Palmenart bezeichnen könne, vielleicht die Zwergpalme. Mit Bezugnahme auf die dem Worte *äm* auch zustehende Bedeutung ' das Kind,' ' die Kleine ' (Brugsch, *Wörterb. Supp.*, *äm*, p. 64), determiniert durch das Bild des Kindes) wurde des der Zwergpalme gegebene Name ' Die Kleine ' eine durchweg entreffende Benennung gewesen sein."

Such a surmise is rather dangerous, as it leads one on to another possibility. May this be connected with the name of Herakleopolis ⸢hieroglyphs⸣, *hnn-neswt*, " the palm-grove of the king " ? Note also that the Coptic ⲣⲛⲉⲥ, ⲣⲛⲏⲥ ⲥⲣⲛⲏⲥ and ⲣⲛⲁⲧ is " rami palma⸱ vel vitis in quibus sunt dactyli adulti, et uvae " (Peyron, *Lex.*, p. 355), and the form ⸢hieroglyphs⸣. Even now at Khartum the Raphia Monbuttorum is called *nakhl el Faraun*, or " the royal palm " (Schweinforth, *Herzen von Afrika*, 1918, 104). This palm was found by Schweinforth on the Jur River, a branch of the Bahr-el-Ghazal, 8° N. 28° E., where it seems to have its northern boundary. But, comparing the recession of other plants, this probably extended further northward, though it is now entirely extinct in Egypt. It might have been artificially retrieved as far north as Middle Egypt, after it had receded to the south. The Raphia palms, which flourish in moist soil, are more likely to have survived on the swamps of Middle Egypt and the Fayoum, than in the drier conditions of Upper Egypt.

[1] A. Engler, *Pflanzenwelt Afrikas*, 2, 1908, p. 227 ; Engler and Prantl, *Natürl. Pflanzen-familien*, 2, 1889, 3, Palmae von O. Drude ; Martin's *Hist. nat. Palmarum*, 3, 9, Raphia, p. 216, 1836–50.

Besides the short stem the Raphia is especially characterised by the enormous drooping inflorescence. The length of this is about one metre, and is the more conspicuous by the stem being less than a metre and a half high. Compare Fig. 11 with Fig. 1, where the spadix has already passed into a drooping inflorescence. This change is more marked in the Tehneh example (Fig. 10). Before going further we should consider why the Raphia is not figured with an obviously large spadix. There might well be representations of the wine-palm without inflorescence, merely as a short-stemmed palm, such as that on a seal of Sakham-ab-Perabsen (*Royal Tombs*, II, xxii, 189) Fig. 16, and the palm in the name of the princess Bener-ab (*R.T.*, II, iii, 1) which might equally read Ama-ab, Fig. 12.

Raphia is monœcious, the spadix having both male and female flowers, in separate bracts of the same branch, see Raphia Ruffia in Fig. 14. In this 1 is a blossoming branch, female flowers below and male above ; 2, two female flowers half covered by the theca-form bracts ; 3, male flowers with bract and first leaf ; 4, seed, back ; 5, seed, section ; 6, branch with ripe fruit, and flowers below. (Engler and Prantl, *Pflanzenfamilien :* 6 also in Maout et Decaisne.)

It should be noted that the sheath-like bracts in which the flowers lie, are like the perianths often figured in the New Kingdom (Günther Roeder, *Blumen der Isis*, Zeits. 48, 1910, pp. 115–123). They appear as determinatives of *más* ⌐⌐ ⏀ ⚏ (Levi, *Vocab.* 2, p. 272, " mazzo di fiori, collane di fiori, che entrano l'uno nell' altro ") 🦅 ⏀ ⚏ (Budge, *Dict.*, p. 287) and ⌐⌐ ⚘ *más* " bouquet, bunch of flowers."

There may be some connection between the form of the seed of Raphia, and the " fruit d'un palmiste indéterminé " carved in green stone, found in the Aha tomb (De Morgan, *Tombeau de Négadeh*, Fig. 714). On the offering table of Sărenput, son of ati-hetep, there is an indistinct figure which might be connected with Raphia (De Morgan, *Cat. Mon. Haute Eg.* 1, 1894, p. 155).

12. PALM OF BENER-AB.
13. SPADIX OF RAPHIA VINIFERA.

It may be compared with the fruit-bearing spadix of *Raphia vinifera* in Fig. 13.

Thus we see various grounds for the supposition that the tree of the Herakleopolite nome was wine-palm or *Raphia*. The correctness of the reading *amă* in place of *năr* is in accord with de Rougé reading *am-khent*, and Brugsch *am-khnti* and *am-phwu* (*Aegyptologie*, 447). The wine-palm also satisfies the condition that it must have been known in Egypt in the earliest period. The

Pyramid Texts, which descend from remote ages, and which have but few tree-determinatives, yet name the *ámā* palm among the palm-wines. There was already some confusion in determinatives, see Teta 334, or Pepy 826 and Meryra 249 and 704 (Sethe, *Pyramidentexte*, 1908, 380). In Pepy, 826, the determinative is the same as the sycomore 🔲 ⚘. In Meryra 113, " the wine-palm follows " ▭◫▱━▱▱━▱▱, this figure is a short-stemmed tree with thick foliage. This palm-wine, well known in later lists, occurs also in the pyramid texts, as in Teta 120 a ◫▱▱▱▱▱ (Sethe, P.T. 55).

The nature of palm-wine should be noticed, as some confusion has arisen between the true palm-wine and that fermented from dates. The true palm-wine is obtained from the sap of various species, drawn by incisions in the spadix, or the head, or by cutting off the spadix. The sap, collected in a very primitive manner, is fermented to produce wine. In Mesopotamia this sap-wine was

14. FLOWERS AND FRUIT OF RAPHIA RUFFIA.

collected from the date-palm, but in ancient Africa this was probably not the case. It seems probable that the date palm became more valued for fruit, the sap-wine was only drawn from other species; and this may have tended to exterminate these in the northern habitat.

The use of dates for wine, was like that of other fruits; the ripe fruit was mashed with water, pressed or boiled, and then fermented. To avoid confusion it is best to call this date-wine, as in Egyptian ◫▱▱▱▱ (Ebers Pap, x, 2; Pliny xiv, 9; Wiedemann, *Herodots zw. Buch*, 355). The true palm-wine *arp-amā* constantly recurs in lists of offerings, along with *arp mı̄*, *arp ábsh*, *arp amt*, *arp śnw* and *arp hámw*. The reading " wine of Buto " for palm-wine originates from Brugsch; but as Bollacher remarks (Pliny xiii, 9) this seems groundless. It is, however, evident that when Raphia was extinct in Egypt (save in a few oases) the name of palm-wine might be extended to other products of palms.

As the palm-wine was the refreshing drink from the sacred tree of Herakleopolis, so the palm-cabbage was also valued in Egypt as a food. This terminal bud and leafage, otherwise called the ' heart" or '"brains " of the tree, was taken from many different species, and probably also from the wine-palm. It has a sweetish taste, was much appreciated anciently, and is still sold as a dainty in Cairo. Regarding the name of the palm-cabbage Moldenke (*Altaeg. Texte*, 55) supposes that the name was 〔hieroglyphs〕 " Blättenwerk der Dattel-palme," or elsewhere (p. 64) " Blätter[1] oder Blatt spitzen." Joachim (Pap. Ebers. Berl. 1890) rendered 〔hieroglyphs〕 as " Zweige vom *äm*-Baume." But it is possible that we should read this as the leaflets of the large penniform compound leaves of the wine-palm, or 〔hieroglyphs〕 as the same leaflets of the date-palm, rather than the palm-cabbage.

For 〔hieroglyphs〕 Moldenke renders " Flower of the *amă* palm " ; but this seems unlikely, and it might rather mean the living part of the tree, the so-called palm-cabbage.

〔hieroglyph〕 may also be written 〔hieroglyphs〕, determined by an ear, or shell-shaped organ, which is found in various plants as well as in the palms. In the Hearst papyrus (Reisner, 1905, xiv, 14, to xv, 1) 〔hieroglyphs〕 is rendered by Wreszinsky " sycomore seeds, napeca seeds, *amă* tree seeds, acacia seeds." (*Lond. Med. Pap. und Pap. Hearst*, 1912, p. 125). Reisner read 〔hieroglyph〕 as " leaf " of a plant "written either with or without the determinative 〔hieroglyph〕 applying to the expressions as a whole " (*Hearst pap.* vocab. pp. 14 and 17). Perhaps both renderings may be partly right. 〔hieroglyph〕 should probably not be read here as *ad* but as *onkh*, according to the Berlin medical papyrus, where 〔hieroglyph〕 is given in full (Wreszinsky *Med. Pap. Berl.* V, 4, 5 ; and p. 10). On the other hand if we accept Reisner's view and suppose that this represents a leafy organ, resembling an animal's ear, and hence resembling the sheath of a palm enclosing the spadix, it would be inapplicable to the syco-more or acacia. Hence, I conclude that it simply means " buds," shaped like an ear, out of which the life of the plant emerges. This would apply equally to the terminal bud of the palm or buds of an acacia. The 〔hieroglyphs〕 would then be the palm-cabbage of the date palm.

Another difficult term to define is the 〔hieroglyphs〕, or 〔hieroglyphs〕, an organ thus found in such different trees as the palm and the vine, the sycomore and the napeca (Wreszinsky, *Lond. Med. Pap.* 10059, in Pap. Hearst I, 14). Various renderings of *ashed* have been proposed, apricots (Murray), *Cordia Myxa* (Dümichen, Loret, Moldenke), *Balanites* (Maspero), grapes (Reisner); and later it seems to be a general term for a fruit or group of fruit. [It might well mean simply " gathering " or " fruit " in all cases.—ED.] Thus, I propose to read *ashdt nt ams*, clusters of fruit of the wine-palm.

---

[1] As also Wreszinsky in the case of willow leaves (*Grosse med. pap.* 3038, 1909, 7, 12).

Another general term is $\bigcirc$ o or $\bigcirc$ 🗊 🐍 o, *kh sá*, as $\bigcirc$ o ◊ 🐍 ◊, *khsá-n-amá*. Joachim and Wreszinsky both render it "fruit of the *ám* tree." It has probably a wider meaning as core, or kernel of a large size. The terms of botanic morphology in Egypt will need much research before they are fully understood.

To return to the palm-cabbage, Woenig calls it a " very excellent vegetable," obtained by the Egyptians from the so-called " brain of the palm, that is from the young, tender and juicy shoots of the leaves " (*Pflanzen in alten Aeg.* 1886, pp. 221 and 312). Though usually precise, this writer here states no more than did the ancients. It should be noted that it is not found in the lists of offerings, but no more are many other vegetables. Maspero remarked in 1897 that no vegetables are specified except onions, but they are only included in some general rubric at the end. On the other hand there are many figures in sculpture which seem to be palm-cabbage.

These have been taken for artichokes by C. Pickering (*Races of Man*, p. 371); but F. Unger[1] doubts this " Wenn von allen diesen Darstellungen etwas für Palmenkohl in Anspruch genommen werden könnte, so wären es nur Fig. 27 und 28, die allerdings von den übrigen bedeutend abweichen. Aehnlich erscheinen in den ägyptischen Alterthümern die Darstellungen der Blüthensträusse, von welchen ist die Artischoke nur durch den meist gekrümmten Stiel und durch den Mangel der Ringelung, was bei den Straüssen den Bindfaden andeuten soll, zu unterscheiden weiss." As far back as 1834 Rosellini (*Mon. civ.* p. 388) had recognised the palm-cabbage at Beni Hasan (see Leps., *Denk.* II, 129). Unger takes this figure to be *Raphanus sativus* (*major*), horse-radish, " Die nach oben erweiterte Wurzel trägt Narben von entfernten Blättern, von denen die innersten und jüngsten noch in einem Buschel vorhanden sind. *Allerdings spricht das mehr für Beta als für Raphanus, allein für Palmenkohl am wenigsten.*" The latter words, which I italicise, are a notable opinion from so serious and accurate a botanist as Unger. I never met with a Raphanus or a Beta bearing leaves up, or nearly up, to the top of the root. Schweinfurth doubted the appearance of Raphanus in ancient Egypt.[2] The reference to an inscription on the pyramids by Herodotus must be taken with all reserve as to what he was told by others, however accurate his own observations may be. Loret takes the figures named above to be *Lactuca sativa*,[3] and Schweinforth and Buschan[4] agree with this. These figures are but exceptional; and in my opinion those published by V. Bissing (*Gem-ni-kai*, xxvi) and Reno Muschler[5] are by no means Lactuca.

In other cases there may, perhaps, be figures of unnoticed species ; but the older interpretations—such as pine-cones—must be set aside. We return now to the question about artichokes. Woenig is surprised at De Candolle doubting about Egyptians having *Cynara scolymus*, or its prototype *C. Cardunculus ;* but he after all doubts whether *C. Scolymus* was known in Egypt. It is almost certain that the south European *C. Cardunculus* is the prototype of *Scolymus*.

---

[1] In *Botanische Streifzüge auf dem Gebiete der Cultur-geschichte*, Sitz. Kais. Ak. math.-natur., Classe I, die Pflanzen des alt. Aeg. 38, pp. 69–140.

[2] In *Ver. Berl. Anthrop. Ges.* 1891, 665.

[3] *Flora Phar.* 1892, 68, No. 113.

[4] *Vorgeschichtliche Botanik* 1895, 144.

[5] *Elaüterungen an den Pflanz.* 41.

Originally the hard and unpalatable flowers of *Cardunculus* were used as food. The artichoke proper was described by Theophrastus, who reminds us of the resemblance between the thalamus and the palm-cabbage. This, however, is much later than the Egyptian figures. The spread of the artichoke was very slow ; in 1466 from Naples to Florence, and not till 1548 to England (H. Phillips, *Hist. Cultiv. Veg.* I, 23) ; but there is no reason to expect it in early Egypt. We may, indeed, meet in reliefs with plants which we cannot determine, because of imperfect execution, especially in provincial art ; moreover, the figures are often damaged. Again, repeated copying, regardless of the original subject, may cause wide divergence. We must therefore be cautious, and restrict ourselves to comparisons of repeated forms which are not very divergent. Any wide deviation must be specially considered. As Schweinforth remarks, " Il faut une profonde

15. RAMES SEATED HOLDING A BOUQUET OF LEAVES.

connaissance du style égyptien, de la symbolique figurée et des plantes du paÿs pour être à même de bien interpréter la signification de ces images. De plus, c'est une tâche qui doit être supportée autant par le savoir que par la critique. Il s'y agit parfois de reconnaître, parfois de deviner. La détermination d'une plante comme espèce est souvent déjà difficile quand on a sous les yeux une gravure de nos jours, elle l'est bien plus lorsqu'il s'agit de dessins aussi grossiers que ceux de la sculpture " (G.S. *Flora phar.* Bull. Inst. Eg. 1882, No. 3, p. 9).

We should therefore restrict our field to the regularly recurring forms, which have only slight divergences from a normal type. Any considerable or strange deviations must be carefully considered. When we look thus critically at the artichoke resemblance, we see that it is impossible, and only two sources seem likely, an artificial bouquet of leaves, or else the palm-cabbage. As against the bouquet, we see that such are either straight or curved. For instance,

Khay seated before Rames (Fig. 15) holds in his left hand a bouquet of leaves. [This is generally accepted as a palm spathe.—F.P.] Something similar but very primitive is seen from Hierakonpolis (Quibell, *H.* xlvi, 1), where the leaves are reduced to ✎ few lines. In the mastaba of Gemnikai (Bissing, *Mast. Gem.* 2, pl. 1) one of the offering bearers is preceded and followed by a man carrying a palm-cabbage in the left hand (Fig. 17). Bunches of flowers or leaves tied together are sometimes placed in the graves, as that of Nekht-ef-Mut at the Ramesseum (Quibell, *R.* xvii, 10). Leaf-bouquets are sometimes figured in the New Kingdom, as in Lepsius, *Denk.* III, 236A; VI. 123A, 78, which latter Unger describes as a bouquet wrapped in a leaf. There are many representations of the palm-cabbage, and probably in the Old Kingdom they already knew of various species, and perhaps indicated them in figures.

16. PALM ON SEALING, IIND DYNASTY.
17. PALM-CABBAGE CARRIED.

As early examples of the palm-cabbage see the fine steles in Leyden of Khu and Antefaqer (Boeser, *Beschrijving . . Eg. Versam,* pls. xxix, xxx; ii). Also those of Upuatu-a (pl. iv) and Upuatu-nekht (pl. xxviii). Earlier instances are at the tomb of Ti (Steindorff, *Grab des Ti,* 37), and that of User-neter (Murray, *Saqq. Mast.* xxiii), while it appears later at Deir el Bahri (Naville, *D. B.* I, xv).

Far the greater number of so-called " artichokes," on the funeral offerings, undoubtedly represent palm-cabbage. At least one relief may be quoted, from the tomb of Akhet-hetep (Davies, *Ptah-hetep and Akhet-hetep,* xvii), where the man is seated with food before him, eating the palm-cabbage (Fig. 18), in a way which clearly proves that it is not an artichoke. We may note, by the way, that the palm-cabbage was never used to make palm wine, as Scheil has supposed. (*Tombeaux Thébains,* V, p. 562.)

I have tried to point out the probability that the tree of the Herakleopolite nome is a wine-palm, *Raphia Monbuttorum,* which has since then retreated southward. It has doubtless kept its place longest where the conditions were more favourable, and a warm air and soil gave a damp atmosphere. Among such sites are particularly the Oases. In support of these views there is a state~ ment by Sethe (*A.Z.* lvi, 44–54) that the " field of *aăm* trees " is not a special oasis but a general term for the Oases (p. 52), as sources of palm wine, defined thus in the Edfu text, "he brings to thee fields of *aăm* palms, making intoxication with its wine." (De Rouge, *Ins. Edfu,* II, 99, 14.)

A 4

I cannot leave the subject without disclaiming any special study of the archaeology, as my work has been widely apart from Egyptology. Having been for more than twenty-five years in practical botany, especially agricultural, an investigation of the ancient botanic material of Egypt brought me into contact with Dr. Boeser, who has revealed to me the civilisation of the Pharaohs. The interest once aroused was unquenchable, for the Nile has an irresistible attraction ; and my own subject gave material enough to stimulate research. I soon realised that the application of physical science to Egyptology demands a knowledge of both sides, especially in the language and literature. On the other hand, I would emphasize that the philologist requires sufficient scientific acquirements

18. MAN EATING PALM-CABBAGE.

to follow the physical side of his subject. This, however, does not diminish our gratitude for what has been done by great scholars in Egyptology. The domain of this science has gradually become so wide that it is nearly impossible to deal with all aspects of it, as is likewise the case in other sciences. We cannot work now without specialising, in order to obtain a critical interpretation of the material, and to render the structure of the subject not only wider but more substantial. It is desirable then that not only philologists but medical men, agriculturists, botanists, and other technical students who feel the charm of our historic knowledge of ancient civilisation, should acquire the necessary view of this subject, which will prove not only instructive but fascinating in its scope.

F. F. BRUIJNING.

THE SARCOPHAGUS OF PA-RAMESSU FROM GUROB.

Was He the Heir of Seti I ?

The red-granite sarcophagus found by the British School of Archaeology in Egypt in the season 1919–20 has a somewhat curious history. Photographs of the sarcophagus and cover, now in the Cairo Museum, together with the plan of the tomb and full description, are being published in the forthcoming volume of the School, entitled *Gurob 1919–1920*; a summary description will therefore suffice here to introduce the question of the identity of the prince.

About twenty-eight years ago eight men worked out a large shaft at Guroh and discovered, on reaching the burial chamber, that it was flooded, the mummiform lid of a very large red-granite sarcophagus only being visible above the surface. A Greek antiquity dealer was summoned to see this cover, and he offered £50 if it could be broken into sufficiently small fragments to make it transportable. The finders broke off the head and part of one arm, and, from what I can hear, got it to the surface. The secret of this find had,. however, leaked out by this time, and the party of eight had become forty, all eager for a share in the loot. A fight ensued, and finally the affair was given away to the then Inspector of Antiquities of the district, who arrived on the scene, seized the lid, and in due course sent it to the Cairo Museum, where it was registered as No. 30707 " 4ᵉᵐᵉ fils du roi Rameses II." There it has remained ever since, until recently fixed up against a wall.

The knowledge of the position of the pit seems to have been completely lost, and we had to take the largest and most prominent pit and chance our luck. The first pit proved to be the one, and we found the plan closely resembled the royal burials in the Tombs of the Kings at Thebes. After bucketing out the water in the chamber and clearing out the rubbish from the tomb we were surprised to find the sarcophagus was represented as being on a sledge, coffin and sledge being in one piece. The inscriptions on the sarcophagus present no special peculiarities, except in the spelling of the name of the owner, who is called Pa-Ramessu and Ramessu, and whose titles are " Royal Son," " Vizier," " Hereditary Prince of the Lord of the Two Lands " and " Commander of the Bowmen."

The name of the prince is written in various ways, an analysis of the name showing the following peculiarities, (and variants) always and only for the titles " Vizier," " Hereditary Prince of the Lord of the Two Lands " and " Commander of the Bowmen "; (never with " Royal Son ")

with " Royal Son " but with no other titles.

and with " Royal Son " or without title.

As we have already remarked, in whatever form the name occurs, the epithet has been added.

Apart from the title " Royal Son," the other titles occur each singly and in combination, the title of " Commander of the Bowmen " where in combination never being in the first place. Otherwise, we have been able to recognise no system in the arrangement of the titles.

The title " Royal Son " never occurs with any other title, except the added " *Neb Weben.*"

We believe that this prince cannot be the 4th or any son of Ramessu II for the following reasons :—

While admitting that *Sa nisut* ⟮ Ramessu - mer - Amen ⟯ *can* mean " Royal Son *of* Ramessu," in this case it cannot be so, as no name follows the cartouche although this phrase occurs seven times, so that it cannot be a chance mistake. We should, therefore, read it Royal Son ⟮ Ramessu - mer - Amen ⟯, and recognise in it a prince, entitled to use the cartouche, which happens to be identical with the personal-name cartouche of Ramessu II. Further, each cartouche, and in consequence each name on the sarcophagus, has been altered to render it different from that of Ramessu II by the addition of the phrase *Neb Weben.* Who then would object to a cartouche exactly similar to his own ǀbut Ramessu II ? " If Ramessu objected to anyone having his cartouche, (or in any case,) he would not have permitted one of his sons to take it.

Since Pa-Ramessu was not the son of Ramessu II, his actual identity must be determined. We cannot put him after Ramessu II as : (*a*) We have practically no graves after that date at Gurob ; (*b*) No one after Ramessu II would care if his cartouche resembled that of Ramessu II or not ; (*c*) The style of work on the coffin and the objects are all characteristic of the late XVIIIth—early XIXth dynasties, and (*d*) There is no position into which we can fit Pa-Ramessu after Ramessu II.

It seems that the fact of the name being written in a cartouche should give the key to this puzzle. In the full publication of this tomb, we shall give a list of all the princes of the XVIIIth to XXth dynasties with their most important titles. Under the heading of " cartouche " will be found the number of times the name of the prince is written in a cartouche as a fraction of the total number of times the name occurs. These are all taken from Gauthier's *Livre des Rois*, II and III. The kings entitled " Prince of Egypt " from the Kheta Treaty will be omitted.

From this table it will be seen that from Thutmose III until the end of the XXth dynasty, every prince whose name is known written in a cartouche became king ; in other words, was the heir. The only exception being that of Ramessu-kha'-em-Wast, son of Ramessu III. Even this can be easily explained by the fact that his name is a combination of the family name Ramessu and should be grouped among such names as Men-kheper-Ra-senb, etc. The rule then seems absolute that the name in the cartouche indicates the *heir.* It may be noted that in the 37 times the name of Kha'-em-Wast, an admittedly favourite son of Ramessu II, occurs, in no case is the name found written in a cartouche, although he has all the most important titles.

As to the title " Hereditary Prince of the Lord of the Two Lands," although we have not been able to find another example, those borne by Horemheb before his coronation (*Livre des Rois*, Gauthier, II, p. 384), Merenptah and Sety II are of practically the same meaning.

We have, therefore, a prince, heir to the throne, before the time of Ramessu II, with a cartouche exactly resembling his, changed probably by him, by the addition of an epithet. We suggest that we have here a son of Seti I and an elder brother of Ramessu II or at any rate the heir of Seti I, who died before Ramessu II's succession. Whether this is the prince (or one of them) whose figure was introduced into the Karnak reliefs of the wars of Seti I, and whose figure was changed to that of Ramessu II, is not certain. As regards titles, it is *possible*. That the prince in question is Amen-nefer-neb-f, as held by some, is at least a doubtful supposition, the only foundation being the possible presence of a *neb* after the name, and the fact that he has the title " First Royal Son of his Majesty." This title goes for very little, as it occurs with *two* of the sons of Ramessu III and even in the titles of the non-royal Amen-nakht, son of Amen-kem-s (*Livre des Rois*, III, p. 397), each of whom has the title " Chief Royal Son " ; neither is it of first importance, as Amen-her-unem-f, son of Ramessu II, only uses it once in the three times his name occurs.

The titles of the unknown heir (?), according to Gauthier, are :—

(1) Hereditary Prince and Mayor (*Erpaʿ-hatiʿ*)
(2) Chief Royal Son of his body.
(3) Fanbearer at the Right of the King.
(4) Royal Follower into Retennu.
(5) Royal Scribe.

In examining the titles of those princes whose tombs are known, one is struck with the fact that the military titles shown in great detail on the temple lists are nearly absent from the tombs (*cf. Livre des Rois* III, pp. 176, 177). Of the titles of the unknown prince set out above, Numbers 3, 4, and probably 5 were of a purely military nature and might well have been omitted in the tomb or on the sarcophagus. As to the title " Of his body," one has only to look through the titles of the princes to see how unimportant it was considered except among the lesser known sons. For example, Merenptah, in styling himself
omits altogether the phrase " Of his body " after the words " Royal Son," although he is known to have this title.

From this we see that, as regards titles, Pa-Ramessu *could* be the unknown prince. We do not insist on this, but he seems to have been undoubtedly the heir to the throne.

Legrain, in the *Annales du Service*, Vol. XIV, pp. 17–26, discusses two statues (now at the Cairo Museum), found by Pylon X at Karnak in 1913, of a person called Pa-Ramessu, son of Seti. He suggests that this man became Ramessu I, and I believe that this is now generally accepted. Assuming Legrain's hypothesis and ours to be correct, we have the following sequence :—

Sethi

Pa-Ramessu who became Ramessu I, Men-Pehti-Rēʿ.

Seti I

Pa Ramessu also called Ramessu and [Ramessu - mer - Amen].

The Gurob Pa-Ramessu and King Seti I, each being named after his grand-father, a common Egyptian custom. The Gurob Pa-Ramessu may have retained the alternative spelling, and his titles of " Vizier " and " Chief Bowman " on his coffin, in honour of his grandfather ; the slight change of the Prince (*erpa'*) of the whole land into the Prince (*erpa'ti*) of the Sovereign being due to the royal birth of the grandson.

A list of the titles of the Karnak Pa Ramessu, with those of the Unknown Prince of the Karnak reliefs and the Gurob Pa-Ramessu, is not without interest.

Karnak Pa Ramessu.	Unknown Prince.	Gurob Pa-Ramessu.
1. *Erpa'* of the Whole Land.	*Erpa'-hati*.	Erpa'ti of the Sovereign.
2. Vizier.		Vizier [1]
3.	Royal Son.	Royal Son.
4.	Chief Royal Son.	—
5. —	Chief of his body.	
6. —	Royal Son of Kush.	
7. Royal Fanbearer.	Royal Fanbearer	
8. Commander of Bowmen	—	Commander of Bowmen.
9. Royal Scribe	Royal Scribe	—
10. —	Royal Follower into Retennu.	
11. Royal Groom		
12. Royal Charioteer		
13. Chief of the City		
14. Ambassador		
15. Judge		
16. Chief Canal Engineer		
17. Chief of Fortifications		
18. Chief Priest of all the Gods		
19. President of Council		
20. Royal Acquaintance (?), etc.		

It shows the great resemblance between the elder Pa Ramessu's titles and those of the Karnak Prince and the Gurob Pa-Ramessu.

Numbers 3, 4, 5 and 6 are almost exclusive to Royal Princes, but Pa Ramessu has both the titles Royal Fanbearer, Royal Scribe, and Royal Groom, so often held by the Princes. As to Number 10, Pa Ramessu could not have held it, as it only dates to Seti I's wars. The remainder of the Karnak Pa Ramessu's titles are those of a great soldier and statesman, but are not usual in the titles of Royal Princes. It is curious that the Karnak Prince omits the title of Chief Bowman and Vizier. Limit of space on the wall may well account for this as he is sure to have had many more titles. Another and more probable reason is that, assuming he and the Gurob Pa-Ramessu are one and the same, he would not insert non-royal titles on a temple wall although he may have had reasons for doing it on the sarcophagus.

As to the significance of the epithet *Neb Weben*, we have to take refuge in conjecture. Assuming the genealogy stated above to be correct, it seems possible that the Gurob Pa-Ramessu, on being declared heir, had taken for his personal cartouche the name that Ramessu II wanted after his death. Deciding to take his elder brother's name, his instinct, from what we know of him, would be

---

[1] This is the only case I can find where a Royal Son has the title of " Vizier."

to cut out the cartouches of the heir. Here we may see the restraining influence of the friends of the late prince whom Ramessu II, so early in his reign, would not risk offending. The conversion of the cartouche into a laudatory phrase by the addition of a word like *nakht* or *senb* would have been almost as bad, and the party of the prince would have been even more incensed at his cartouche being used to praise the younger heir, who probably hated him. It seems, then, within the bounds of possibility, that the epithet *Neb Weben* was added with an ambiguous intent, perhaps conferred posthumously, ostensibly as a title of honour and meaning "Lord of Brilliance," Ramessu II trusting to posterity to read it as Ramessu (II) *is* the Lord of Brilliance. This may be far-fetched, but we can suggest no other to meet the facts. If we are right, it is a subtle move well in keeping morally with what we know of the character of Ramessu II.

We are unable to comment on the reason why Pa-Ramessu was buried here at Gurob, as we have not sufficient data as to the burials of the XVIIIth—XIXth dynasty princes, to say if it is unusual. Gurob is possibly near his personal estates.

R. ENGELBACH.

[The history of the sarcophagus appears to be that it was engraved for the king's son Pa-ramessu *maokheru*, without cartouche. The lid was finished and all of the body but one panel. Then, either on his becoming co-regent, or his accession, in the remaining panel the name was put in a cartouche with *neb uben*, not over an erasure. On the other parts the *maokheru* was erased, and *neb uben* substituted. On the lid there was space enough to add, down each side of the middle band, a fresh column with the name in a cartouche and *neb uben*. On Ramessu II succeeding he adopted his brother's cartouche, which enabled him to appropriate any monuments already erected ; he denied to him burial with the kings, and erased all trace of him.—F.P.J.

KNOTS.

THE Egyptians of the early dynasties seem to have been averse to making representations of knots. In the Old Kingdom knots are hardly ever seen, and it is only in the Middle Kingdom that the reef-knot first appears.

Various devices were used for fastening ropes on boats, such as lashing with the loose end tucked in. Strings for garments and personal ornaments must have been tied in some way, but the knot is either not shown or is conventionalised out of recognition. As the Egyptian artists, in both the Old and Middle Kingdoms, were accurate in their detail, we can only suppose that these subterfuges were intentional, and were due not to incapacity on the part of the artist to represent so small an object but to some religious or superstitious feeling in representing a knot which could never be untied.

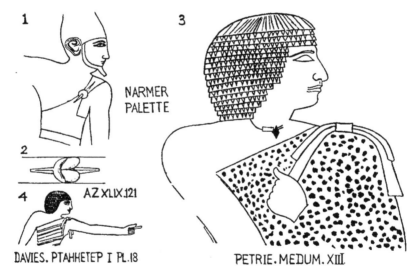

1

3 NARMER PALETTE

2

4 AZ XLIX.121

DAVIES. PTAHHETEP I PL.18

PETRIE. MEDUM. XIII.

The earliest examples of the fastening of garments are on the slate palette of Narmer. No. 1 shows the fastening of the curiously shaped garment worn by the king. A piece of the garment is brought over the left shoulder and meets on the left breast another piece which comes from below the right arm. It is uncertain whether the fastening is a conventionalised knot, or whether it represents, as Montet suggests (*A.Z.* xlix, pp. 120–121), a kind of leather fastener (No. 2), which developed into a metal ornament in the Middle Kingdom. As the Narmer example is the earliest known, and as the shape of it does not correspond with Montet's suggestion of the method by which the fastener was held in place, it seems likely that Narmer's garment is knotted, and that the conventionalised knot of the early periods was imitated in the late Old Kingdom in leather or other material.

When a garment was fastened on the shoulder, it appears to have been tied there with four strings, as in No. 3, the huntsman in the tomb of Ptahhetep. Another form of shoulder-fastening was used only by priests of high rank, for it is the method of tying on the panther-skin. This is seen in No. 4, Rahotep seated at a table of offerings and dressed in a spotted robe to imitate a panther skin. The detail of the tie is perhaps more clearly shown in another figure of Rahotep, No. 5, where he holds one end of the tie in his left hand. This attitude is seen again in the figure of Urarna I (No. 6), who holds the long end in his hand ; he also wears a panther skin. In the case of Gemnikai (No. 7), the details of the fastening are not given. Two similar figures (Nos. 8 and 9) clothed in panther skins and with the tie on the shoulder are of Ukh-hotep, and show that this portion of the priest's ritual dress continued into the Middle Kingdom. The fastener is used as a hieroglyph from the 1st dynasty onwards (Nos. 10 and 11), and reads $k3p$, or kp. On examination, it is clearly seen, both in the hieroglyph and in the object itself in use, that it is not a tied knot though it is intended to represent some method of fastening strings securely. No. 5 shows two loops and two ends, which suggests the ordinary bow, the others, however, have four ends and no loops. But whether loops or ends, they appear to pass through a leather or metal tube. Such a tube would be quite unpractical and could not hold the weight of the panther skin dragging on the strings. We are then forced to conjecture either that this is the conventional representation of an ordinary bow-knot, or that it is an ornament made up and sewn in position, like our shoulder-knots.

Another form of the shoulder-knot is worn by the panther-clad official in attendance on Narmer (No. 12). This is the nearest approach to the true representation of a knot which occurs before the Middle Kingdom, although the cleft in the middle of the cross-over (No. 13) shows that the artist did not desire to represent the knot with accuracy and truth. A similar shoulder-knot is worn by User-neter (No. 14) when clothed in a panther skin. Here the hemispherical objects are perhaps used to prevent the strings from slipping through the tube through which the ends are passed.

Turning from this clearly artificial fastening, we come to another part of the costume in which a knot is essential, *i.e.*, the girdle ; yet here again the artist carefully abstains from any truthful representation. On the slate palette of Narmer the king is in the act of smiting the , who wears a girdle only. This girdle (No. 15) consists of a belt round the waist, the ends of which fall in long loops in front ; the little projecting knob above the girdle seems to indicate that the girdle itself and the loops were tied together in one knot, though judging by the drawing one might almost suppose that the bunch of loops were separate from the belt and were pulled through the band which held them in place. The angle at which the belt is worn precludes such an interpretation of the drawing ; the bunch of loops, if separate, could not have retained their position unless they actually formed part of the girdle.

Another type of girdle is worn by Narmer's personal attendant (No. 16). In this, the method of fastening is studiously concealed. Yet another type of girdle is found on the ivory figure from Hierakonpolis (No. 17), where a single loose end is brought over the waist-band and falls down the front of the loin-cloth ; its connection with the loin-cloth or with the belt is impossible to determine ; the method of fastening is obscure.

5 · PETRIE.MEDUM.XV.

6 · DAVIES. SHEIKH·SAID.VI.

7 · BISSING. KAGEMNI.II PL.2

8 · 9 · BLACKMAN.MEIR.II PL.16

10 · PETRIE.ROYAL TOMBS.II PL.22

11 · PETRIE. MEDUM.XV

12 · 13 · NARMER PALETTE

14 · MURRAY SAQQARA MASTABAS I.PL.23

15 · NARMER PALETTE

16 · NARMER PALETTE

17 · QUIBELL HIERAKONPOLIS.VII

18 · QUIBELL.RAM: XXXII

19 · QUIBELL RAMESSEUM. XXXIII

20 · 21 · MURRAY. SAQQ: MAST: I PL. 11 · PL.12

22 · BISSING KAGEMNI.I.PL25

23 · QUIBELL RAMESSEUM.XXXII

24 · MURRAY SAQQ: MAST: I PL.22

25 · DE MORGAN DAHCHOUR I PL.16

26 · NEWBERRY EL BERSHEH.I PL.15

In the carefully detailed representations in the tombs of Rahotep and Ptah-hotep, the same avoidance of knots can be observed (Nos. 18, 19 and 20) ; the girdle is clearly tied, but the method of tying is left to the imagination.

So also in the case of ropes by which animals were secured. In No. 21 the rope is simply curved round the creature's front leg, and in that position could not have held the animal for a moment. In No. 22 a bow-knot is indicated, though it and the leading-rope have no apparent connection with the rope-collar encircling the animal's neck. Again, in the rope attached to a hoop in the ground, used for securing a calf (No. 23), the knot is only vaguely indicated. The elaborate rope appendage worn by the sacrificial ox (No. 24) may have been spliced to the leading-rope as there is no visible join. But though splicing may account for some of the joins this method could not have been used in No. 21, where a knot of some kind was essential.

The first attempt to represent a knot truthfully occurs in the XIIth dynasty jewellery, both at Dahshur and Lahun (No. 25). Here the reef-knot is clearly, though not accurately, indicated ; and the mere fact that it occurs as a jewel shows that the ordinary fastening of strings of beads was by a knot. At the same time, representations of knots in ordinary life are as studiously avoided in the Middle Kingdom as in the earlier periods. At El Bersheh the ropes, by which the colossus is dragged, are merely bunched together without any connection (No. 26) ; this must be intentional, as the most careful attention paid to detail in the rest of the scene shows that the artist could have represented the knots had he wished. Tehuti-hotep's daughter (No. 27) wears an elaborate head-dress consisting of a wide fillet with pink lotus-blossoms ; at the first glance the fillet appears to be tied in a bow with wide loops, but a closer examina-tion shows that the ends of the fillet pass apparently through a metal clasp in which lotuses are fastened. As such metal fasteners have never been found in any of the numerous Middle Kingdom burials, it can only be supposed that this is merely the conventional representation of a knot.

At Meir, Senbi wears a girdle (No. 28) twisted several times round the waist and fastened by what purports to be a knot though in reality it is nothing of the kind. The cross-belts which pass over the shoulders are fastened at the back with the ends hanging down, but the knot itself is discreetly hidden. The Ukh sign (No. 29) also shows a knot which is no knot, the loop being coloured blue while the ends are white with a little red ; this suggests that the loop and ends have no connection with one another. In a bird-catching scene at Meir, the two ropes which close the net are fastened to the pulling rope (No. 30), the knot is given with great detail, but it is not a real representation of a knot. On the same wall is a scene of boat-building, and here the knots are almost accurate (No. 31), showing that the artist could indeed draw a knot if he so desired.

In the temple of Mentuhetep, at Deir-el-Bahri, the ropes at the side of the boat (Nos. 32 and 33) are so arranged that the method of fastening cannot be seen. It is evident that they are not knotted, therefore they must have been either spliced or lashed.

In the hieroglyphs, the same aversion to knots is equally evident. The sign *ts*, which means a knot, is never represented as a true knot. In the VIth dynasty (Nos. 34 and 35) there is no attempt to show the structure of a knot. Even in the XVIIIth dynasty (No. 36) there is only the indication of the form ; sufficient, however, to give the general effect of the method of joining two bandages used frequently in the Middle Kingdom (No. 37). Other hieroglyphs show that

B

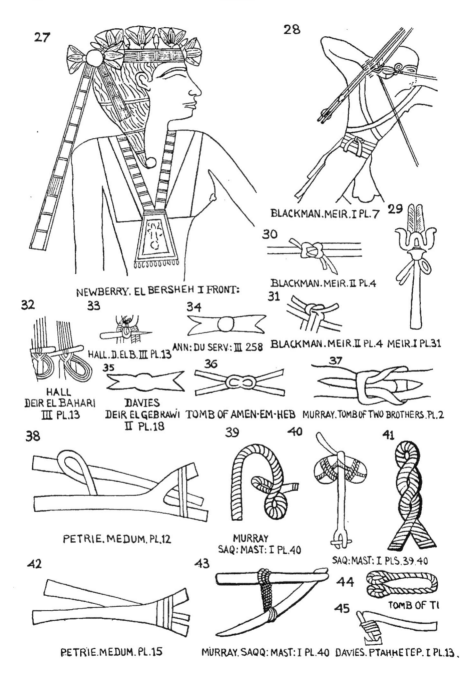

27

28

BLACKMAN.MEIR.I PL.7   29

30

NEWBERRY. EL BERSHEH I FRONT:

BLACKMAN.MEIR.II PL.4

31

32   33   34

HALL.D.EL.B.III PL.13   ANN:DU SERV: III 258   BLACKMAN.MEIR.II PL.4   MEIR.I PL.31

35   36   37

HALL
DEIR EL BAHARI   DAVIES
III PL.13   DEIR EL GEBRAWI   TOMB OF AMEN·EM·HEB   MURRAY.TOMB OF TWO BROTHERS.PL.2
                II PL.18

38   39   40   41

PETRIE.MEDUM.PL.12   MURRAY
                SAQ:MAST:I PL.40

                SAQ:MAST:I PLS.39.40

42   43   44

45

TOMB OF TI

PETRIE.MEDUM.PL.15   MURRAY.SAQQ:MAST:I PL.40   DAVIES.PTAHHETEP.I PL.13.

ropes were not knotted, but were lashed round an object and the loose end tucked in. The *šn'*-signs (Nos. 38 and 42), in the tomb of Rahotep, show this lashing in common use. The *wȝ*-sign (No. 40) is one of the most interesting of the cord-hieroglyphs, as it represents the loops used in forming a clove-hitch ; here the cord is only in position, the knot itself is not completely made. In the *ḥmtỉ*-sign (No. 40) the ropes appear to be fastened by lashing, as no sign of a knot is visible. In the *ḫ* (No. 41) the ends are obviously tied to prevent their spreading, but the method of fastening the ties is not given. In the fine example of the *mr*-sign (No. 43) the rope is looped three times round the blade and round the handle, the loose end is then twisted round and round the three strands and probably pushed under one of the loops where it was held firm. In the rope handle (No. 44) the loops appear to be made by lashing ; and in the *stp*-sign (No. 45) the blade of the adze is securely lashed to the handle without the sign of a knot.

From the evidence before us, it seems, therefore, that in the early dynasties knots were never represented. In the Middle Kingdom, though the same prejudice still existed, there was a movement towards an accurate presentation of the knot, showing that there was a change and that the old ideas were beginning to pass away.

M. A. MURRAY.

PERIODICALS.

Zeitschrift für Aegyptische Sprache, Vol. LIII, 1916 (continued from 1921, p. 128)

SPIEGELBERG, W.—In the " Two Brothers," whose temple was near the Serapeum at Oxyrhynchus, Grenfell and Hunt see the Dioscuri. But Spiegelberg thinks they really belong to the Egyptian pantheon, for personal names are combined with two, three and even four " brothers." The divine name Psosnaus is in Coptic ⲡⲥⲟⲛⲥⲛⲁⲧ " two brothers," and Chemsneus is " three brothers."

SCHÄFER, H.—Commenting on Spiegelberg's proposed discovery of the mention of a water-wheel on a ushabti-figure, Schäfer quotes Marti's translation of Deut. xi. 10, " The land, whither thou goest in to possess it, is not as the land of Egypt, from whence ye came out, where thou sowedst thy seed, and wateredst it, like a garden of herbs, with thy foot [-driven water-wheel]." The explanatory addition in brackets should rather be " watering machine," as there is nothing to show that it was a wheel. It is, however, important to find that a water-machine worked by the foot was known as early as the seventh century B.C. So little is known to us of the ordinary life of the Egyptians in the first millennium before Christ that we are largely dependent for our knowledge on foreign sources.

Zeitschrift, Vol. LV, 1918.

SCHÄFER, H.—*Altes und Neues zur Kunst und Religion von Tell el Amarna.* Prof. Schäfer's paper on the Art and Religion of Tell el Amarna fills nearly half of this number, and is a criticism of Borchardt, with whom he disagrees on most points. Schäfer is frankly conservative in his estimate of Akhenaten, regarding him as a great reformer both in religion and art, whereas Borchardt's opinion is adverse to the heretic king.

Schäfer divides the royal portraits of the Tell el Amarna period into three classes : (1) Portraits with the name of Akhenaten but drawn in the conventional Egyptian style. These are usually said to have been made before the king instituted his reforms, but Schäfer now concedes that Borchardt has now proved that they are portraits of Amenhetep III and not of his son. It is inexplicable how this can be asserted in view of the youthful Akhenaten of conventional Egyptian style, with cartouches, adoring the radiant sun (Prisse, *Mon.* X, 1). (2) The hideous portraits, often bordering on caricature, of the king and queen, emphasizing their physical defects. Here Prof. Schäfer stops to point out the two characteristic features of Akhenaten's face—the hanging chin, and the nose-line continuous with the forehead. These two features are found in the real portraits of the king, but Schäfer is obliged to confess that there are so many variants of the royal face that it would be impossible to recognise them unless they were named. Akhenaten and his queen are represented with long thin necks, but Akhenaten's is always distinguishable by the slight arching of the nape. The mummy of Akhenaten shows that he had a tendency to hydrocephaly with the back of the skull enlarged, a condition which appears in his daughters.

Borchardt contends that Queen Nefert-ythi's head was not of this shape, and that all figures of queens with "bladder-heads" represent someone else; but Schäfer refuses to admit this. It is interesting to find two learned professors disputing over a matter which a woman would settle at once, after seeing the photograph of the exquisite figure in the Berlin Museum, shown on Pl. VI, 2. The shape of the head is clearly a method of arranging the hair, which is either rolled on itself, as is done by Tamil women in Madras, or is taken back smoothly over a cushion, as was worn by many people a few years ago. The smoothness, which is an essential in this style of hair-dressing, could not be expressed by an Egyptian artist except by colour. The princesses are represented with the same kind of hair-dressing, for even little girls wore wigs like their mothers throughout the historic period of Egypt. (3) The third group of portraits shows the same features as the second, but less markedly pronounced, and are distinguished also by the earlier age of the royal couple. The beautiful statue, numbered Berlin 20496, is said by Borchardt to be of Tutankh-Amen. This is strenuously disputed by Schäfer, who points out that in the five known portraits of Tut-ankh-Amen the line under the chin is straight, whereas Akhenaten always has a hanging chin, a feature clearly shown in this statue. The retreating forehead, the slightly arched nape, and the backward curve of the skull are also very evident, and prove the accuracy of Schäfer's ascription. In the Berlin relief No. 15000, which Borchardt attempts to prove is of Akhenaten's daughter and her husband, the hanging chin of the king stamps it at once as the portrait of Akhenaten himself.

The representations of domestic life among the royal family are not peculiar to this period. There is a fragment of ivory now in the Ashmolean Museum at Oxford, which shows a king of the Ist dynasty with his queen on his knee. Erman has also remarked that the kings of the New Kingdom took pains to show that they were human, and were often represented in the ordinary dress of the period.

As regards the religion of Tell el Amarna, it is generally acknowledged that the Aten-cult was practised at Heliopolis and was known in other parts of Egypt. Maspero considers it a local cult raised to the supreme place. It is very certain that Amenhetep III called his boats, his palace and his army after the Aten, and his own name was "Nebmatre, the glittering Aten." The inscribed block at Berlin was found at Karnak, and shows the Aten as a hawk-headed man. This is dated by Borchardt to Amenhetep III, and shows that there was a place for the worship of the Aten before the time of Akhenaten. But though the Aten was worshipped earlier, the representation of the sun with rays ending in hands begins in the reign of Akhenaten, and is peculiar to that period only (see Prisse, *Mon.* X, 1, quoted before). Schäfer does not agree with Borchardt that the block came from Hermonthis, but thinks that, as it was found with other blocks built into the pylon of Horemheb, the Aten-temple must have been at or near Karnak. Borchardt also maintains that even before Amenhetep III there was a city called "Horizon of the Aten" at Tell el Amarna, with a large part of the temple and palace. Schäfer strenuously denies this, quoting Akhenaten's own words when he says that he found the place belonging to no deity or ruler, "The king raised his hand to heaven and to his Creator, and swore that in no other place would he establish the city." Borchardt's chief argument, however, is a fragment published by Wilkinson, showing Akhenaten offering to the Aten, with the inscription, "The living Aten, in the temple of Men-khepru-Ra in the Aten temple in Akhet-Aten." Schäfer's refutation is that the temple of Thothmes IV is another name for one of the chantry chapels, called "Shadow of Ra," which

Akhenaten built and dedicated in the names of his relatives. Borchardt brings forward another argument in the fact that in the tomb of Huya (Davies III, Pls. X, XXV) statues of Amenhetep III are represented, and suggests that Akhenaten tried to efface the memory as well as the name of his father. Schäfer points out that Akhenaten destroyed only the personal name of his father, in which the hated word Amen occurred, and that the statues of the father were set up in the temple by the filial piety of the son.

Borchardt will not even allow that Akhenaten appears in "the glory of a reformer." Schäfer thinks that, from the evidence of the Tell el Amarna tombs, the king was the moving spirit and himself preached the new doctrine. He ascribes the failure of the reform to an under-estimation of the power of traditional religion, and also to the fact that it was too philosophical for the mass of the people. At any rate it is the figure of Akhenaten which stands out as the chief Aten-worshipper, without whom the Aten would have been to us but one out of a hundred other obscure gods.

Though Borchardt lays stress on the fact that Egypt's foreign power fell, and the country itself was reduced to chaos, neither he nor Schäfer appear to have considered the possibility that the whole movement may have been political as well as religious. Throughout Egyptian history, whenever a glimpse can be obtained of the underlying forces at work, there is manifest a struggle for supreme power between Church and State. It is seen in the Old Kingdom, when Khufu and Khafra bridled the power of the priesthood, and were branded as tyrants by the priestly recorders. In the XVIIIth dynasty the magnificent donations of the victorious kings to the temples, especially that of Amen, gave enormous power into the hands of the hierarchy, who were never slow to combine the spiritual and temporal kingdom. Akhenaten was not a Khufu to defy the priesthood, but he made a gallant stand; and by removing the capital from Thebes to Tell el Amarna he struck a blow at the prosperity of the great priesthood from which it would never have recovered had he lived longer or had his successors stood firm.

Prof. Schäfer has unfortunately seen fit to end his very interesting paper by some sarcastic remarks, made without verifying the facts. Arrows of sarcasm shot from the bow of inaccuracy are apt to injure the archer more than the quarry.

SCHÄFER, H.—*Die angeblichen Kanopenbildnisse König Amenophis des IV.* Prof. Schäfer here discusses the portraiture of the four human heads of the canopic jars found in the tomb ascribed to Queen Tyi. They were first said to be portraits of the queen herself, but Maspero brought forward arguments to show that they were the portraits of Akhenaten. Schäfer agrees that they are not Tyi, but also refuses to admit that they are Akhenaten. In his previous paper he has proved that the one constant feature, from the best to the worst portraits of Akhenaten, is the hanging chin, whereas each of these heads show a straight line under the chin. The retreating forehead is common both to Akhenaten and his wife, who bears a strong resemblance to the king; but their respective portraits can usually be distinguished by the difference in the shape of the chin. Schäfer compares the profile of the canopic heads with the profile of the Berlin figure of Nefert-ythi, and concludes that they represent the same person, namely Akhenaten's queen. As the so-called "Tomb of Tyi" was evidently used as a hiding place for royal mummies, Schäfer thinks that some of the costly tomb furniture was also secreted there.

BURCHARDT, M., und ROEDER, G.—*Ein altertümeln der Grabstein der Spätzeit aus Mittel-ägypten.* This stone bears an interesting inscription for a man named Ānti-ḥetep. He held various offices, many of whose titles are rare, such as ▽ 🐦 �, "Lord of Gladness," which occurs always with the place-name ⌷. The style of the stela, and the careful work, is so fine as to approximate to Middle Kingdom sculpture, and Middle Kingdom influence seems to be apparent even in the inscription. The name of the man, for whom the stela was inscribed, is 🐦, which has often been read *ḥrti*, but Sethe now reads it as *'nti*, a form which would be hellenised as Antaios.

SETHE, K.—*Zu den mit 🐦 wr "der Grosse" beginnen den alten Titeln.* There are a whole series of titles beginning with 🐦, always showing very high rank. These have always been read as (*e.g.*) "The Great One, the Leader of the Craftsmen," "The Great One, the Seer," and so on. Sethe now proposes to read the word *wr* in this connection as the superlative, "The Greatest of the Leaders of Craftsmen," "The Greatest of the Seers." This reading is particularly happy in the title of the High-priest of Hermopolis, "The Greatest of the Five of the House of Thoth," and of the High-priestesses of male gods, "The Greatest of the concubines."

MÖLLER, G.—*Ein koptischer Ehevertrag.* Coptic marriage-contracts are rare, only four having been published. The one, which Möller now publishes, is in Sahidic, and is dated, by the mention of John Patriarch of Alexandria and Michael Patriarch of Antioch, to about A.D. 1208. This example gives the bridal dowry as one hundred gold solidi, of which twenty were paid down, but no time limit is set as to the payment of the remainder. In the contract published by Sir H. Thompson (*P.S.B.A.* XXXIV, p. 173) the bridal dowry was also one hundred gold solidi, of which twenty were paid at the time of the marriage, the remainder to be paid in five years. For a much humbler marriage see *Gizeh and Rifeh*, p. 42.

WIESMANN, H.—*Koptisches.* Herr Wiesmann has published some highly technical notes which are interesting to students of Coptic, especially of Boheiric. He has collected special uses of negatives and peculiar meanings of words.

MÖLLER, G.—*Mḫbr* = Μεγαβάροι. In a demotic marriage-contract of the time of Ptolemy Philopator, one of the contracting parties is "Pabus, the *mḫbr*, who was born in Egypt." Spiegelberg has already suggested that the word is an ethnic name from Nubia, and Möller now connects it with the Megabaroi, who are mentioned, under various spellings, by several Greek and Latin authors. These Megabaroi are said to have lived in Nubia, and were neighbours of the Blemmyes. Möller identifies them also with the modern Mekaberab who live on the east bank of the Nile, north of Meroë.

SCHÄFER, H.—*Nubisches Aegyptisch.* In his study of the inscription of Nastesen—an Egyptian text from Nubia—Dr. Schäfer explained the numerous extraordinary faults of spelling and syntax which it contained, by reference to the same kind of mistakes made by Nubians of the present day when writing Arabic. In support of this theory he publishes an Arabic letter from his own Nubian servant, showing exactly the same kind of grammatical and orthographical faults as in the inscription of Nastesen.

Spiegelberg, W.—*Ein Brief des Schreibers Amasis.* Ten years ago Maspero published two fragments of a papyrus, which attracted little notice, though belonging to the beginning of the XVIIIth dynasty, at which period documents are rare. The papyrus is a letter from a man named Aāhmes, a scribe in the service of a certain *Pnūti*, who is already well known as having lived in the reigns of Amenhotep I, Thothmes I, Thothmes II, Hatshepsut and Thothmes III. The writer complains that a slave girl has been taken from him, and given to someone else, and her mother has written to ask why her daughter has been removed against the girl's own wish.

Erman, A.—*Ein orthographisches Kriterium.* Any help towards the exact dating of an inscription is always welcome. For practical purposes, one of the best means of dating is in the spelling and writing of common words. Prof. Erman illustrates this with the root ⌷⌷⌷ ∿∿, which as preposition and adjective took, in the Middle Kingdom, the determinative ⌷. The determinative properly belongs to the word only when it means Face. As often happened, the determinative became confounded with, and was used instead of, the correct phonogram. This occurred occasionally in the Middle Kingdom ; the use revived in the latter part of the XVIIIth dynasty, and was common in the XIXth and XXth. Therefore any inscription, in which the spelling ⌷ occurs, would belong to the XIXth or XXth dynasty, or at earliest to the XVIIIth. Curiously enough, hieratic papyri do not show this spelling till after the New Kingdom.

Spiegelberg, W., und Sethe, K.—*Das Grundwort zum Lautzeichen* ⌷ *d.* This is a double paper. Spiegelberg begins by pointing out that the alphabetic sign is derived from the word ⌷ ⌷, ⌷, which—as the single line shows—is a picture of the creature and not a phonetic. Sethe and Gardiner have identified ⌷ with ⌷, but Spiegelberg points out that in the Pyramid Texts the two snakes are sharply distinguished : ."This is the viper (⌷) which came forth from Ra, this is the uraeus (⌷) which came forth from Set." He suggests that the Coptic ⲁϫⲱ, ⲉϫⲟⲧ *Viper* is derived from this word, which in its original form must have been *ꜣdit*, only the strong consonant ⌷ surviving as an alphabetic sign. The second part of the paper is by Sethe, who while agreeing that the origin of ⲁϫⲱ is ⌷, will not admit that his derivation of ⌷ from ⌷ is wrong. He brings forward several proofs, of which the most convincing is the writing of the royal title ⌷ on the "Menes-Täfelchen" of Naqadeh. He therefore considers ⌷ as an early form of writing the venomous snake which is usually written ⌷. The difference would be between the uraeus in peace, as the goddess Uazet, and the uraeus reared up to strike in judgment, as the king.

Lidzbarski, M.—The demotic word *mtkte* "army" seems to have been introduced into the language from the Assyrian at the time· of the Assyrian conquest.

SCHÄFER, H.—According to Horapollo, the number sixteen, whether spelt out or written in numerals, means Joy or Pleasure. Hathor is called ⟨hieroglyphs⟩. Schäfer suggests that the Egyptian word must be sought in some word beginning with ᴜɪɪᴛ- or ᴜᴇᴛ-. As an addition to a previous paper (*A.Z.* XLII, p. 72) he mentions that at Denderah the number nine is written ⟨hieroglyph⟩.

SPIEGELBERG, W.—The phrase ⟨hieroglyphs⟩ " to enter a house " is probably an idiomatic term for marriage, and comes down from the XIXth dynasty, or even earlier.

MÖLLER, G.—The word ⟨hieroglyphs⟩ was recognised by Goodwin as meaning " wife." Möller suggests that it means "the covered-up one," and cites a Nubian marriage custom in support. The bride comes alone to the bridegroom closely wrapped up in cloth, and resists all attempts to remove the covering till she receives the bride price.

Comptes Rendus, Acad. Inscr. et Belles-Lettres.
15 Oct., 1920.

LACAU, P.—*Les Travaux du Service des antiquités de l'Egypte en* 1919–1920. —At Denderah work interrupted in 1914 has been resumed. A *mammisi* has been unearthed, older than the well-known one of Augustus. It was built by Nekht-hor-heb, and under the myth of Horus commemorated the divine birth of the king as a son of Amen and Hathor. By the side of this is a Christian basilica, built from the spoils of the *mammisi* of Augustus. The sacred lake has been found ; it is 31 by 25 metres, with a gate at each corner opening on a stairway. The walls are 3 metres thick. The Ptolemaic water level was 2 metres lower than at present. The sacred lake was the parallel to the tank of water which was essential to any private house. A well adjoins it, for drawing water to serve the temple. The store-chambers have been found in the south-western corner of the great enclosure.

The tomb of Petosiris is next described, which has been noticed here in the abstract of the *Annales du Service.*

At Hermopolis the cemetery of the ibis has been opened, and 200 metres' length of gallery has been explored, containing thousands of burials. Most of these are placed in jars, but others are in loculi, or in small sarcophagi of stone.

Comptes Rendus, 17 Dec., 1920.

G. JEQUIER.—*L'Enneade Osirienne d'Abydos et les enseignes sacrées.*—After describing the well-known enneads of Heliopolis and Hermopolis, the ennead of Abydos is described from the great stele of Tehutmes I. At the head was of course Osiris, then Khnum of Antinoe, and of the Cataract ; Thoth Chief of the gods, and of Hermopolis ; Horus of Letopolis, and avenger of his father ; Upuatu of the South, and of the North. The worship and sacred objects of these gods were established by Tehutmes I, and three centuries later in the temple of Sety I there is figured the sacred head of Osiris, and before it the eight ensigns of these gods. Such ensigns are only found in scenes which are, or may be, religious, and they seem therefore not to be military or tribal. [Yet we must remember that the tribe was denoted by its god in the earliest times.]

Museum of Fine Arts Bulletin, Boston, April–June, 1921.—This contains a report of 18 pages, more than two years after date, of the discovery of the pyramids of the XXVth dynasty. Such an interval ought to have sufficed for the complete publication, instead of adding to the ever-increasing pile of future obligations for volumes. Behind the village of El Kur'uw, about as far north of Barkal as Nuri is south of it, lies the pyramid field. There were but weathered heaps of débris, yet these covered the tombs of Kashta, Pionkhy, Shabaka, Shabatoka and Tanutamen. Beside these are other tombs, on what appears to be the more obvious part of the site, and therefore earlier. Dr. Reisner estimates these as extending back to 900 B.C. These earliest tombs contained many finely chipped arrow-heads of flint and chalcedony. Such suggest that the rise of this family was from the Libyan desert. These had been very rich in gold, judging by the quantity which the plunderers had dropped as negligible. Fragments of fine Egyptian work showed an active trade in objects of luxury. Tombs of the queens have also been found, and the tombs of the horses of the kings, four of Pionkhy's, eight each of Shabaka and Shabatoka, and four of Tanutamen. They were of a short and rather small breed, and were buried upright in the graves. Though no trace of a chariot was found, it seems that the numbers four and eight suggest pairs or fours to draw chariots. Beside the views of the site and tombs, with ritual chapters inscribed on them, there are figures of a blue bowl with reliefs of bulls ; gold, garnet and carnelian necklaces ; silver amulet figures and vessels, a " canopic " figure of crystal and gold, faïence plaques and necklaces, alabaster vessels of the early stages of the alabastron type ; blue glazed relief and openwork figures ; ivory carvings ; alabaster canopic heads ; a gold band collar of a queen ; bronze bed legs resting on a goose, of Shabatoka ; the heart scarabs of Shabaka and Tanutamen ; a silver mirror hawk with four statuettes of gods around it ; and a bronze gazelle. Beside the historic interests, there is the artistic outlook of the Ethiopian adaptation of Egyptian work and motives. As a matter of taste, the changes are all to the bad, yet the African taste for fat women did not spoil many of the designs, and there is a good deal left to admire.

REVIEWS.

The Kalahari or Thirstland Redemption.—By E. H. L. SCHWARZ. 8vo,
163 pp., 14 pls. (No date or price.) Blackwell, Oxford.

Though the purpose of this book is a matter of economics and engineering,
it has so important a bearing on the history of the Nile valley and historic changes
of climate, that it should be understood by our readers. The abundant data and
facts related here, as well as the author's public standing, show that the conclusions deserve the most serious consideration. The broad position is that the
table land, about half a mile high, of South Africa is so nearly flat, that small
impulses of storms, surface denudation, and other transient changes, suffice to
spill a river discharge one way or the other in a few years. Also that the short
coastal rivers are eating back and tapping the head waters of the internal drainage,
so as to remove the rainfall rapidly instead of letting it feed flood-lakes. The
actual total of rain is of much less import than the spread of it over a longer
season, and thus keeping a moist atmosphere during the period of growth.
The system which such a form of land needs is that of large drainage lakes which
can evaporate, and so produce fresh precipitation and moist atmosphere, instead
of deep gorge-rivers, which are useless. The author's remedy of dams does not
concern us here, but rather his reading of the history of North Africa, in view of
what is rapidly going on in the South.

The Nile history is started with the discharge of Lakes Tanganyika and
Kivu into the Nile, extending its course about 700 miles. Such discharge has
recently been cut off by volcanoes arising, and thus forcing the lake to rise and
spill over into the Congo. How recent the change may be is suggested by a
native belief remaining that Tanganyika did discharge northward. The change
may well be within Egyptian history. Another volcanic change was when the
old direct channel of the Nile, from near Khartum to Ambukol, was blocked at
the south end, and the Nile had to make a long detour through Berber. Lower
down, the early Nile is stated to have run through the oases of Khargeh, Dakhel
and Farafra. The Atbara was an independent river running down to Abu
Hamed, and on through a great desert valley to Korti or Aswan. The Atbara
then worked back a side stream (? Abu Hamed to Ambukol), and so tapped the
Nile, and drew it off from the present oasis line to the present Egyptian course,
which was the old Lower Atbara.

The author considers that the earliest Congo discharged northward through
the Saharan region, and the evaporation of lakes along its course would maintain
fertility there. It was the tapping of the Congo westward which ruined the
Sahara. All of these changes have to be kept before us when considering the
changes visible in the excavation of the Nile valley, and the conditions of man in
the palaeolithic ages.

The Earliest Internationalism.—By J. H. BREASTED. 8vo, 23 pp. (Lecture
at the California Celebrations, 1918.)

After referring to the shipping of pyramid times, Sanehat, and the Ship-
wrecked Sailor, Dr. Breasted remarks on the commanding position taken by
Egypt in the XVIIIth dynasty, holding the land link of Asia and Africa, crossed

by the water link of the Mediterranean and the Red Sea. The flow of foreign products, trees and herbs, animals and foreign men into the Egyptian capitals must have been a strange surprise. The reforms of Akhenaten and his religious change are looked on as part of a movement of internationalism. The letters of his age show how treaty rights extended to private property of foreigners. The importance of Asia Minor and the Hittite land in controlling the flow of Asia southward down Syria, is strongly insisted on. The resemblance of the ancient strategic position with that of our own day is well described. A remarkable letter has come to light from the widow of one of Akhenaten's successors, offering to take a Hittite husband, and so unite the Asiatic power with Egypt.

It was the Assyrian menace which led later to the treaty between the Hittites and Egypt. Dr. Breasted has made a very careful study of the great marriage stele at Abu Simbel, which recorded the festivities of the Egypto-Hittite alliance. With Egypt clearly decadent, the Hittite later looked to Babylonia, and stirred up there an attack on Assyria. This only led to the capture of Babylon, and the power of the Assyrian to entirely overthrow the Hittite power and civilisation.

A History of Sinai.—By LINA ECKENSTEIN. 8vo. 202 pp. 22 figs. (S.P.C.K.) 1921. 8s. 6d.

It is remarkable that no general history of Sinai has hitherto appeared. The interest of so many races and religions has not produced any summary of the many different periods which are there commemorated. This volume is all the more welcome as dealing with all the ages of the peninsula. The first third is occupied with Egyptians and Israelites, the next with Nabatheans and Christians, the last third with the history under Islam. After describing the nature of the country, the moon cult is discussed, the temple of Serabit and its surroundings are described, and then the history of the Egyptian occupations and their remains. The chapter on the early people and place names deals with the Anu, the Mentu, and the Retennu. The last, so well known in Egyptian inscriptions, remained down to the Raithenoi of Ptolemy, and the Retheny, who were the attendants on the mosques at Gebel Katrin as late as 1816. Various other tribes are mentioned in the Pentateuch and later writers. Two chapters deal with the Israelite questions, the author taking the new view that Serabit was the mountain of the Law. The historical position of Moses is here followed, and placed in a setting of locality and circumstance which renders it the more physically probable. How far this will fall in with the whole account needs full consideration.

The interesting commercial rise of the Nabatheans is summarised, and then the Hermit period, and life and writings are described. The history of the Convent follows, and the earlier settlement of Pharan. The strange episode of the introduction of the worship of St. Katherine the Alexandrian saint is described. Why she should have been so fervently accepted in Sinai is strange. Is it possible that her name fitted near enough to Hathor for it to carry on an older worship then near its end ? There is plenty of varied interest in this book, and it will make a long-familiar name far more real to many readers.

Fishing from the Earliest Times.—By WILLIAM RADCLIFFE. 478 pp. 28s. (John Murray.) 1921.

" And first for the Antiquity of Angling, I shall not say much," wrote Isaak Walton. Mr. Radcliffe, on the other hand, has written many delightful pages, which are certain of appeal to lovers of folk-lore, archaeology and fishing. A dexterous blend of learning and anecdote fulfils a promise of grace of treatment, which is implied by quotation in the dedicatory lines of Andrew Lang's appeal to Persephone to " grant that in the shades below my ghost may land the ghosts of fish." The book is generously illustrated, and the numerous notes and references to the latest authorities are an additional delight. Selection is difficult from such a mass of interesting matter. With chapters on Egyptian, Assyrian and Jewish fishing ahead, one may be tempted to hurry through the section on Greek and Roman times, though one would not willingly miss the account of the discovery by two unlettered French fishermen of the modern method of breeding fish, nor the recapitulation of the old theories on the vexed question of the propagation of eels, which was not solved until 1920. Excellent historical summaries usher in the Assyrian and Jewish sections, and the discussion of the reason why these nations apparently knew not the rod in spite of intercourse with Egypt. The fish which leaped out of the river and would have swallowed Tobias (R.V.) introduces an interesting account of misconceptions of the *jus primæ noctis* and its connection with " Tobias' days." Possibly the Chinese chapter contains some of the best anecdotes, for example, that of Chang-Chih-ho, that " glittering example of humorous romantic detachment and carelessness of public opinion, who spent his time in angling, but used no baits, as his object was not to catch fish."

L. B. ELLIS.

NOTES AND NEWS.

WORK AT ABYDOS.

ABYDOS is an oppressive site, as the enormous extent of hundreds of acres of cemetery far exceeds what any living person could hope to work out. Moreover, at present it has been so far exhausted that there is scarcely any obvious lead of importance, and most of the area that is not piled with past clearances, is deeply cumbered with late tombs, which have been nearly all plundered, and which in no case add materially to history or to collections. All that successive excavators can do is to select some definite and limited aim which can be attained, and complete that.

Some twenty years ago the Royal Tombs of the Ist dynasty were entirely cleared and examined, and later work done there did not add anything further to the results which I had found. In the course of later work, about ten years ago, yet another party cleared a part of the northern cemetery, near the old fortress of the IInd dynasty, known as the Shunet Ez Zebib. Most of the tombs and graves were of the XIIth dynasty, but amid these were some lines of graves which were recognised as being of the Ist dynasty. Nothing was done to complete the plans of these ; and, though carefully recorded, the account ends, " Whether these are isolated or connected phenomena, and what their significance is, are questions which cannot be answered." However this may be, the close resemblance of these lines of graves to those around the royal tombs, a mile or two distant, made it desirable to examine them completely ; and as ten years had passed, and nothing more was done, it seemed worth while to step in and clear up these remains.

The British School accordingly began work on this part of the cemetery in December. In two or three days another line of Ist dynasty graves was found, but the site is slow to work in, as it is encumbered with ten feet of later structures of tombs built over it, large buildings have been placed cutting through the lines of graves, and the ground is riddled with long graves of the XIIth dynasty, which scarcely ever contain anything. Little by little we have won out a long front line of over thirty graves, and a side line at right angles almost as long is now appearing. The central burial pit had been cleared out, and deepened with five large trench tombs in the XIIth dynasty, for a noble Uahem-Shenu and his family, one of whom had four of the Ist dynasty stone vases laid over her body. Similarly, we have found two sides of the second great tomb circuit, long lines of graves, all anciently plundered, but containing enough of pottery and fragments to date them. The central tomb of this has not yet been attempted, as it is deeply covered with heaps from other excavators ; but so soon as the circuit of graves is clear, we shall know where to sink for the centre. The pottery of the first tomb was evidently within a reign of the time of king Zer, and this was confirmed by twice finding his name and also that of a queen Mer-nesut. The Ist dynasty is so completely known in the royal tombs of Umm el Qa'ab that there cannot be other tombs of kings of that age ; so it seems likely that the queens were buried here, and the fortress near by was built two or three centuries later.

Such is the definite piece of work that the British School intends to settle, without any ambition to undertake the whole site. Of course, various later things are thrust upon us in the clearance of superimposed burials, but nothing of importance or value. One piece of a stele of Greek period is curious for the naturalistic figure of the worshipper, which is here reproduced. When the site of the Ist dynasty is cleared up, it is hoped to move down to Middle Egypt, and resume the regular clearance of the western side from last year's work at Sedment. The camp will be at Oxyrhynkhos, which has hitherto only been worked for Roman papyri, but a nome capital should have temples and cemeteries of many ages to be sought for. The subject of the distribution of prehistoric flints is being thoroughly worked over, at Abydos, by Miss Caton-Thompson, of the staff of the School.

Though the excavation of the British School is expressly limited to the north part of Abydos, we have naturally visited the massive structure behind the temple of Sety, which was opened up in 1914, and which remains in the condition in which it was then left. As I had the advantage of discussing it with Mr. Wainwright (now Inspector of Antiquities for Middle Egypt), who managed the excavation, it may be as well to sum up what seems to be ascertainable about this unique building. It was entirely subterranean, as the stratified layers of marl thrown over remaining parts of it show that it was completely covered. The roofing of the middle hall was of a type unknown elsewhere ; on each side cantilever blocks projected, sloping below, in order to carry great roof beams, which stretched across. There is no proof that any water was originally in it ; for the general water-level of the country has risen so much that it would have been sixteen feet lower in the XIIth dynasty, to which date this building probably belongs. The walls of quartzite sandstone were partly dressed smooth, having an excess of two or three inches when built in, to be later reduced by dressing. The end of the hall was finished smooth and was afterwards utilised by Merneptah. The sides were partly smoothed at the top, and the surplus left below. The doorways of the cells around were never completed, and were therefore never closed. The sandstone floor blocks beneath the walls have never been smoothed at the edges to receive a close-fitting flooring across the halls ; this does not preclude a floor having been put in, as the Egyptian was careless about the fitting of floors.

Though many uncertainties still remain, we may outline what seems likely to have been the history of the site. The grey granite used for the enormous pillars, architraves and roofing, was a stone which was rarely—if ever—used before the XIIth dynasty. The same is true of the quartzite sandstone, which was used for the walls, and for the floors which carried great weight ; as it was lavishly used in the tomb of Senusert III here, it also points to the XIIth dynasty date. Certainly there is nothing like all this material to show in either the Old Kingdom or in the New Kingdom, and as it was all familiar in the Middle Kingdom it is to that period we must ascribe this building. The purpose of the four or five courses of hard stone foundation under the walls and pillars was to obtain a firm base to carry the enormous weight of the structure. The bay of hills at Abydos is filled with a deep mass of water-laid sand, with occasional patches of gravel. Such was too frail a bed for great weights, and foundations were laid in—probably down to the rock bed—for the superstructure. In the spaces between the walls no such strength was needed for carrying a floor, and probably this was filled up to floor level with blocks of limestone, which were all used abundantly as filling, between the outside of the walls and the sand ground. The floor being thus completed, Merneptah would have been able to utilise the building ; while such limestone floor would be the first thing to be removed when the building became a quarry. Since then the rise of water level has filled up the spaces between the wall-foundations.

When Sety planned his temple here, he seems to have been aware of the subterranean building as he followed the same axis. But there was not enough length for the whole of his temple and its courts between the cultivation and the subterranean, so the back part of his plan was cut off and placed at the side of it, as described in " The Temple of the Kings." After that, Merceptah added a long approach sideways behind the subterranean, and sculptured the end wall of the great hall. This approach was cleared and published as " *The Osireion.*" The use of this building continued till Ptolemaic times, as is shown by the inscribed block found as a foundation deposit, under the gateway of the enclosure wall. In Coptic times it became a quarry, the limestone floor was all removed, the granite beams of the roofs were broken up, and parts of the architraves and pillars were split to pieces, to cut out millstones.

At Thebes, Mr. Winlock's party are continuing the study of the temples and tombs of the XIth dynasty ; Mr. and Mrs. N. de G. Davies are copying and recording the painted tombs ; and Messrs. Fisher and Mackay have begun work on the top of the hill of Drah abul Nega. Regarding the uncertainties of the political situation here we must trust to the judgment of the British authorities as to the desirability of continuing our operations, for we can but rely on their opinion and wishes.

W. M. FLINDERS PETRIE.

32.

ENGRAVED GLASS JAR, 1 : 2.
OXYRHYNKHOS. VIth CENT., A.D.

ANCIENT EGYPT.

THE BRITISH SCHOOL IN EGYPT.

SHORTLY before the War there was published an account of a row of graves of the Ist dynasty, which had been discovered near the fort of the IInd dynasty at Abydos. They were said to be inexplicable, and no attempt was made to search out their extent. As that region had been abandoned for eight years, there was no reason for other excavators not examining it. The British School therefore applied for this place, and has now worked over about 500 graves of the earlier half of the Ist dynasty. As such graves of royal dependents have not been known except around the Royal Tombs, this was probably the last great group of that age in Egypt.

At first we only anticipated finding a square of graves, around a larger burial, like the graves around the Royal Tombs a mile to the south of this. The work, however, continued to expand more and more until we had cleared a square of 350 × 400 feet, formed of 269 graves, an area large enough to hold all the royal tombs known before ; a second square, 250 × 380 feet, of 154 graves ; and a third square, less complete, 260 feet wide, with 76 graves. The graves around the royal tombs had diminished in number as the dynasty progressed, Zer having 326, and the succeeding reigns 174, 61, 131, 63, 69 and 26. The numbers of the new squares were therefore like those of Zer and Zet, but the size of the squares was much larger as the graves were in single or double line, and not in blocks. The pottery found in these graves showed that they belonged to the reign of Zet, or very near that ; and the royal names found on objects here were of Zer, Zet and Merneit. While, on one hand, the number of graves was far greater than was expected here, on the other hand there was no central burial. In one square there was a large pit, with burials of the XIIth dynasty in the floor of it ; but this was nearer to one end and much nearer to the east side. However, in one of the XIIth dynasty tombs were three stone vases of the Ist dynasty which might have come from a disturbed burial. In the largest square the whole area was searched, but no considerable pit could be found within it. The third square was deeply piled with sand heaps, but the centre of it and a long stretch near that were bared without finding any early burial. The search over all these squares was difficult as the ground had often been re-used, especially about the XIIth and XXXth dynasties, so that there was hardly room for another tomb. In the later time many large vaulted burial chambers had been inserted which destroyed all that went before them. The repeated building of surface chapels had retained much blown sand, and more had been thrown up

C

by digging, so that the Ist dynasty grave pits were buried under 3 to 6 feet of loose sand and later deposit. A large part of our time was swallowed in clearing these later burials, which at least produced three large steles of the XIIth dynasty ; but our attention was kept on the early graves to ensure that the really important subject was thoroughly worked out.

Most of these graves were empty or had only fragments of pottery. About a sixth of them still contained skulls and bones and some complete pots. Only a few were undisturbed, and had copper or flint tools. No gold or silver were found ; yet from such a large number of graves the total produce is considerable. Eighty skulls were obtained and measured, and have been soaked in paraffin wax to preserve them for transport. About half that number of skeletons were found and the long bones all measured. While the whole of the facial bones are the same size as those of the Ist–IInd dynasty at Sedment, the median overall size of the skull was about 4 mm. less in each direction, and less also than at Tarkhan. This may be due to the greater warmth of Upper Egypt. From the burials around the Royal Tombs having been made rapidly in large numbers, it was concluded that the courtiers were despatched at the death of the king, like the Nubian custom exemplified at the burial of Hepzefa (ANCIENT EGYPT, 1916, pp. 74, 86). Among the burials found this year were several which seemed to have been made while conscious, and one shows clearly the struggle to get the head clear, the skull being twisted round over the back, which lay upward. These instances suggest that the men and women were stunned and then placed in the shallow graves, in the usual contracted position, and earthed over, so that they were smothered. This would be a painless death, and therefore the most likely for the unoffending courtiers. Even later in Rome, if a master were murdered, all the slaves in the house were killed.

The most remarkable object was a large ivory comb with the name of king Zet, over which was the bark of the solar falcon flying upon wings. Another unique piece was a large ivory wand for a dancer, ending in a ram's head. These were, of course, kept in Cairo. Ivory gaming pieces were found, eight or ten lions, some in fine condition, and sets of pieces for the prehistoric game. One draughtsman had the name of a queen on it, Mert-nesut. More than a dozen large flint knives were found, half of them thick for scraping, half thin and wide for cutting ; also many copper adzes, long knives notched on one side, axes, small curved knives pierced to hang at the girdle, and innumerable copper needles and ivory arrow heads. Some ivory labels of Zer and Zet were found ; four wooden cylinder seals, which will serve to date such things ; and half-a-dozen limestone steles, with the names of officials in relief, one being of Hetep-neb, the carver, denoted by a flint knife. The graves contained several alabaster cylinder jars and bowls of the usual form. Two remarkable pots came from some foreign source ; they are of very hard thin pottery that rings when struck, one, a two-handled jar like the foreign ones in *Royal Tombs* II, liv., but taller, much wider and dark brown, the other a cylinder jar or stand, fluted round the outside, only part of the top remaining.

The XIIth dynasty there are three large steles, found in wide pits with graves in their floor, half-a-dozen small steles, and an altar with 43 names of one family. In the groups of small objects there is a necklace of carnelian claws and ball beads, and a brilliantly glazed kohl pot with manganese veining. A tomb for cats had in the recess many little offering pots, presumably for milk.

Of the later times are found the ebony inlays of a shrine of a high priest of Osiris named Unnefer (see *Abydos* II, p. 45). A piece of a small stele has the wish expressed, not for the material offerings, but that the gods would grant " a sweet heart every day to Aanya." There were several later steles, none of them important.

IVORY LION.   EBONY CYLINDER SEALS.

In a distant valley of the high desert we found a Coptic hermitage, complete down to the stove and cooking pots. In a natural cave the entrance was walled across, and a chamber arranged, open along the top, with a sleeping bench and a cooking bench ; an inner chamber opened on one side of it to a larder. At the back was a wall across the cave and a door leading to a chapel, with a window, and an altar recess in the eastern wall. On the front wall and inside the chapel were many Coptic inscriptions, elaborate crosses and decorations. All of these were copied in facsimile, full size, and also photographed. The whole place— in living room, larder and chapel—abounded with pegs of wood, bone and flint stuck into the wall—forty we counted. The hermit seems to have been very tidy and to have had a place for everything. The precision, tidyness, brilliant whitewash and decorations are far from the common idea of unkempt misery. Altogether this cave gives a more personal view of a hermit's life than any of the literature.

The desert, both at Abydos and Helwan, was very carefully searched for flints by Miss Caton-Thompson ; in this way the hermitage was found. The flints were all levelled, classified and tabulated, to study the distribution. We may hope that this is the beginning of a scientific study of this subject, which has hitherto been the prey of the looter and the casual collector.

After this work we moved down to Oxyrhynkhos to examine that region Nothing dynastic had been found there, and the reason for this silence of a nome capital was unknown. We verified that there is nothing before Roman age above water-level both west and south of the present town of Behnesa, which is bounded on the east by the Bahr Yusuf. In a search over twenty miles of desert to north and south only Roman remains were observed. The ground is so flat that half a mile back to the west the Roman foundations are now at water-level. It seems that the older city must have been very little above water-level, and the whole of it, with its cemeteries, has been submerged by the dozen feet of rise since the New Kingdom. The early cemetery may be beneath the wide extent of the mounds of Roman age ; no tombs earlier than Roman were found on the desert, except one or two of about the XXXth dynasty at the south end.

Some columns which stood up in the ruins were traced out by deep digging. At last we reached to No. 28 in the line, which probably joined up to another line at right angles, at a distance equal to 54 columns further. The column shafts were 18½ feet high, 12½ feet centre to centre in the line, and 18 feet apart between the two lines. The whole colonnade was apparently 850 feet long or more, and 22 feet high over the capitals. The question arises whether the colonnades here and also at Antinoe, Alexandria and Palmyra carried a timber and matting roofing, like that over the bazaars in a modern town. This would give a purpose to these costly constructions, providing a shady way for public loitering. The long colonnade here ran toward the theatre, though not quite directly.

Another column suggests a third colonnade, but this region is so deep in Coptic and Arab rubbish that it would be very costly to clear. The work will be done before very long by the natives digging for nitrous earth. Even in a month or two I saw a huge crater cleared out close to the town, exposing an early Arab mosque, which would soon be destroyed. The rate at which the *sebakh* digging goes on is astonishing. A light railway has been carried from the bridge of the Bahriyeh oasis line (now abandoned) round the whole back of the mounds, and a long train of over a hundred tons of earth runs every morning in the season. Other light railways run down to the canal, and within a lifetime there will probably be nothing left but sifted potsherds over the site of some two square miles. Of course papyri are being turned out, and I secured hundreds of fragments, beside doing some digging for them. These have not yet been examined, but none were dated be earlier than Augustus. There are some Hebrew fragments of the third century, which seem to be the oldest Hebrew manuscripts known. Dr. Hirschfeld is preparing to edit them in our publication, and they appear to be liturgical poetry.

A large area of sand and chips which I had looked at twenty-five years ago, before I handed the site to Dr. Grenfell, proved to be the theatre. The ruins are buried under 10 to 15 feet of sand, and to clear the whole would be very costly. We have done what seemed reasonable, to find the general dimensions and the detail of the stage. The diameter was about 401 feet, length of stage 200 feet 5 inches, width of orchestra 100 feet. The relation of these dimensions is notable, though we do not know of any ancient measure commensurable. At each end

EBONY INLAYS OF UN-NEFER.

of the stage was a spiral stair, exactly on the mediaeval pattern, with centre newel cut in one block with two steps, and the under side a smooth spiral twist. These stairs did not give access to the stage, but the one best preserved led to a gallery opening as a window 6 feet above the stage, and the stairs continued upward. Along the back of the stage were pilasters, and opposite the alternate ones were polished granite columns, 2 feet in diameter and about 13 feet high. Between the columns were draped statues of heroic size, probably of the Muses. The stage was flanked at the ends with a wall bearing attached columns and pilasters. The benches, with a footrest to each, were in bands of five with pass-ways between. From the slope of these it appears that the outer wall must have been about 100 feet high. Around the top it had a very bold and deeply cut band of flowers and foliage. The capitals and friezes of the stage were of good work for this period, about the IInd century A.D. Examples of these will be exhibited. At the end of the stage there was an outside portico 52 feet wide, which did not open into the building. The whole of the seating must have held 10,000 people or more, a larger accommodation than that of the theatre of Herodes at Athens. This gives a great idea of the importance of this remote provincial town at that time. It is hard to see what supported so large a town or such immense cost of building, on the desert side, without any great trade.

The cemetery is immense, reaching at least a couple of miles each way and all of Roman age. There are four different types of tombs, apparently between the IVth and VIth centuries A.D. Probably the earliest is that with a sub-terranean chamber, reached by a stairway, and ground level chambers, with some painted decoration. This lower chamber is a continuation of the tombs commonly called *birbiyeh*, made in the XXVth dynasty and onward. There are sometimes stairs going to an upper storey, now destroyed. This type lasted on to the late Vth or VIth century, and also contained small graves in the ground floor chambers.

Next there are ground floor chambers with shallow graves. These are usually along a wall and covered by a bench of brickwork, with a raised end like a couch. Sometimes there is a stairway to upper chambers. In various tombs we have recovered a good deal of decorative sculpture.

The apsidal type is remarkable. There is a semi-circular apse about 7 feet wide, sometimes with niches in the sides, stuccoed and marbled. On either side of it is a small chamber with a door. Across the apse in one case was a low screen of slabs of stone on edge with an opening at one end. A few feet in front of the apse was a wooden screen across the chapel, sometimes with stone pillars in the line. The hall before the screen sometimes has a stairway to an upper chamber. Burials are in the hall. In this arrangement there seems the intention of having a chapel; the screens seem to show that there was some altar. There is not any mark or break on the back of the apse, nor any altar structure. As the Coptic Church uses a wooden table altar and places it with a clear passage behind it, such a table in the tombs would leave no trace. The frequency of tomb chapels seem to explain the Coptic statement that there were 316 churches in Oxyrhynkhos. Such a number could not be in the town, but if every tomb chapel was counted it might well be reached.

A very different type of tomb was also found. Burials were made in the open desert in shallow graves. Around these, chambers were built with the brickwork rough inside and still rougher out. These walls were banked up with gravel as they were built, as upper walls often run far off the lower part, and could not be built without support. At about 10 feet high a flooring was laid, and the walls above that were plastered. A doorway at this level gave access. These upper rooms were for funeral offerings, and fragments of a statue of the deceased were found. The chambers were roofed, and a stairway led to the top. The whole was piled over with gravel, so as to appear as a tumulus with a door half way up. The gravel cover still remains, and unshifted, as we can see by the fragments of many glass cups that had been thrown away on the top, after making libations. They prove that the top surface has only been weathered down by wind and rain, but retains its materials in place. In other instances, the glass cups were found on the top of great ash heaps of a funeral pyre. The largest was

80 feet in diameter and 15 feet high, and we collected 15 pounds' weight of glass fragments on the top, the remains of much over a hundred vases. This custom was probably Egyptian, as I found on the top of a VIth dynasty mastaba at Dendereh the original offering pots lying in place, exposed for about 6,000 years. In one of these Roman tombs a very large engraved glass bottle was found, now in Cairo.

An unexpected result was found on visiting some rock tombs back in the eastern desert opposite Oxyrhynkhos. A chamber of the VIth dynasty, with traces of fresco, had been used about the Vth century B.C. by Jews, who had left several long Aramaic inscriptions on the walls. Though much scraped and damaged it might be possible to recover much, or most, of them if some one thoroughly familiar with Aramaic were to live there for a few weeks. We much hope that some scholar will rescue these documents.

Varied as the season's results have been, they advance our knowledge and help to fill up the picture of ancient civilisations. The exhibition will be held at University College, Gower Street, during the four weeks of July (3rd to 29th), hours 10 to 5 ; and open on the evenings of the 5th, 15th and 25th, 7 to 9. Admission free, without ticket.

W. M. FLINDERS PETRIE.

THE SET REBELLION OF THE IInd DYNASTY.

So far as is at present known from contemporary monuments, the following kings reigned in Egypt between the end of the Ist dynasty and the accession of Neterkhet Zoser, the first king of the IIIrd :—

1. The Horus-king Hetepsekhemui, the [hieroglyphs] Hetep.

2. The Horus-king Nebra.

3. The Horus-king Neterimu, the [hieroglyphs] Neterimu.

4. The Horus-king Sekhemab[1] Perenmaat.

5. The Set-king Perabsen, the [hieroglyphs] Perabsen.

6. The Horus-king Khasekhem, who was afterwards[2] called the Horus-Set-king Khasekhemui, the [hieroglyphs] Hetep-Wnef (or Nebui-Hetep-Wnef).

An inscription on the shoulder of the Archaic Statue No. 1 of the Cairo Museum (Borchardt, *Statuen von Königen und Privatleuten*, No. 1) is our authority for the sequence of the first three kings. That they and Sekhemab preceded Perabsen[3] is certain, for objects inscribed with their names have been found in the Set-king's tomb at Abydos (*R.T.* ii, pl. viii, 8–13, and pl. xxi, 164–172). That Zoser was later than Perabsen is proved by a sealing of the latter being found in Zoser's tomb at Bêt Khallâf (Garstang, *Mahasna and Bêt Khallâf*, pl. x, 8), and that Khasekhemui must have preceded Zoser is evident from the fact that his queen Nemathap, " Truth belongs to Apis," is called " Mother of the King's Children " on a sealing found in Khasekhemui's tomb (*R.T.* ii, pl. xxiv, 210), and " Mother of the [hieroglyph]-king " on a sealing discovered in Zoser's tomb (*Mahasna*, pl. x, 7). Sealings of Khasekhemui and Neterkhet (Zoser) have been found together in the old Shunet el Zebib at Abydos (Newberry, *Annals of Archæology and Anthropology*, ii, p. 136, pls. xxii–xxiii). A granite door-jamb of Khasekhemui and sealings of Neterkhet were discovered at Hierakonpolis (Quibell, *Hierakonopolis*, pls. ii and lxx), and an architectural fragment of granite inscribed with the name of Khasekhemui has been recorded from El Kab (*Annales du Service*, VI, p. 239).

The first two kings are believed to have been buried at Sakkara, where sealings bearing their names have been found (Maspero, *Annales du Service*, III, p. 182 seq.). Neterimu's tomb was perhaps at Gizeh, where many of his sealings have been brought to light (Petrie, *Gizeh and Rifeh*, pl. v, E). Of Sekhemab there are numerous sealings from the tomb of Perabsen (*R.T.*, II, pl. xxi, 164–172), but his burial place has not been located. Perabsen and Khasekhemui were both interred at Abydos (*R.T.*, II, pp. 11, 12). Zoser's tomb was at Bêt Khallâf.

It will be noticed that the first four kings of our list are all Horus-Kings, but the fifth assumes an altogether new title, and one that is never found with any other king of Egypt. Instead of placing the Horus Falcon upon his palace-sign, he puts the animal [4] of Set, thereby declaring that he was an adherent of the god Set, not of Horus, the tutelary deity [5] of the legitimate kings of the Ist and IInd dynasties. Perabsen, however, bore the titles 〰〰 〰〰 showing that he held sway, or at all events claimed to hold sway, over all Egypt. The placing of the Set-animal upon the palace-sign indicates that this king was not only an adherent of Set, but that he was in origin a Set Chieftain, that he came from the Set, not the Horus, country. Now the god Set is from the Pyramid Age onwards often called 〰〰 " Lord of *Ta-shema* " (*e.g.*, *Pyr.* 204), and *Ta-shema* certainly meant in the Pyramid Age the whole of Upper Egypt from Lisht to Aswân.[6] In the Archaic Period, however, the region under the influence of Set did not, I believe, extend south of Gebeleyn, for from that place up to Gebel Silsileh was the region of Horus.[7]

The chief seat of Set's cult was Nubt (Ballas), and it was from that city that he derived his common appellation, *Nubti*, " He of Nubt." This must have been an important city in early times, for near it was the burial place of one of the earliest Ist dynasty queens, and sealings of the IInd dynasty have been brought to light from amongst its ruins (Petrie, *Naqada and Ballas*, p. 65, and pl. lxxx, 28–35). The southern boundary of the original Horus kingdom, as I have said, was Gebel Silsileh, beyond which extended Bow-land. The northern boundary was somewhere between Esneh and Gebeleyn.[7] The early capital of the Horus kingdom was Hierakonpolis. The country from Gebeleyn to Rifeh was mainly under the influence of Set, and to the north was the kingdom of the Reed 〰〰 with capital *Het-nyswt*. The Set country from Gebeleyn to Rifeh was, I believe, divided up into administrative nomes by King Zoser. The great importance of Set in the Ist dynasty is clearly shown by the title of the queens : 〰〰 " She who sees Horus and Set " (*R.T.*, II, pl. xxvii, 129), and this title proves that there was then no enmity between the two gods of Upper Egypt at that date.

Now at Hierakonpolis, the old capital of the Horus kingdom, have been found a series of monuments of the Horus-King Khasekhem, who was in all probability a contemporary of Perabsen. These monuments consist of two seated statuettes, one in limestone, the other in slate (*Hierakonpolis*, I, pls. xxxix–xli) ; also a granite jar, an alabaster jar, and a piece of an alabaster bowl (*ibid.*, pls. xxxvi–xxxviii) ; and, lastly, a fragment of a stone stele (*ibid.*, II, pl. lviii). All these monuments bear the name of Khasekhem, and, with the exception of the last-mentioned, bear inscriptions recording victories over rebels of the north. On the vases the vulture-goddess Nekhebyt of El Kab reunites for Khasekhem the symbolical plants of Upper and Lower Egypt with the legend " Year of Victory over the rebels of the north." The two seated statuettes show the king wearing the white crown, and on the bases are figured heaps of dead, with inscriptions giving the numbers of northern rebels slain. On one statuette the number is 47,209, on the other 48,205.

These monuments, as Meyer (*Histoire de l'Antiquité*, Paris, 1914, p. 155) has recognised, show that the unity of the empire had been broken up for a time, and that Khasekhem reconquered the kingdom of the north.[8] It was then that he united the two opposing peoples, the Companions of Set and the Followers of Horus, placed over his palace-sign the Set-animal by the side [9] of his tutelary deity the Horus-falcon, and assumed the name Khasekhemui. To make this reunification of the country secure, he took, just as Menes had taken in earlier days,[10] and perhaps under somewhat similar conditions, a northern princess to be his queen. This princess was Nemathap, who has long been known from inscriptions in the tomb of Methen (Breasted, *Ancient Records*, I, p. 78), and is now generally recognized as the ancestress[11] of the IIIrd dynasty line of kings.

The preceding notes give all that is known, from contemporary sources, about the rebellion of northerners at the time of Khasekhem. But there is a much later inscription which, I believe, preserves a record of this war : this is the Ptolemaic inscription in the Horus Temple at Edfu, which is usually known as the Myth of Horus of Edfu. I do not mean to suggest that this later document is historically accurate in every detail, but I do contend that it contains, like most myths, much historical truth, and that it refers to the Set rebellion of Perabsen of the IInd dynasty. My reasons for this view are the following :—

First, immediately preceding the text is a figure of King Zoser's vizier Imhotep[12] (Naville, *Mythe d'Horus*, pl. xi), facing to the right, and reading from a scroll as though he were actually reading a record of the war written in the lines of inscription in front of him. Behind the vizier stands the figure of a king with blank cartouches above him ; we cannot, therefore, determine who this king is, but, as he stands with Imhotep, he may perhaps be Zoser himself. In front of Imhotep stands a priest (*mnḥw*), who is cutting up a hippopotamus. The hippopotamus is a well-known Setian animal,[13] and here probably symbolises the country of Set, which Imhotep directed to be cut up, and the parts distributed among the gods.

Secondly, when the rebellion broke out, we are told that the Horus-king was with his army in Bow-land (Nubia) suppressing a rebellion there (Naville, *l.c.*, pl. xii, 1, 2). This statement may be compared with the record on a fragment of a stele of King Khasekhem (*Hierakonpolis*, II, pl. lviii), recording that king's conquest of Bow-land.

Thirdly, the outbreak of the rebellion is dated (Naville, *l.c.*, pl. xii, 1, 2) in the 363rd year of Horakhuti, "Horus of the Horizon." This is obviously an era dating,[14] *i.e.*, it gives the number of years from the establishment of the monarchy by the Horus-King Menes to the time of the outbreak of the Set rebellion recorded in the text. If we had accurate chronological data for the Archaic Period, it would be a simple matter to check this era date, but the Turin Papyrus is too mutilated to be of any real service, and the text of Manetho is hopelessly corrupt. Our best source would be the Early Annals of the Kings of Egypt, but of these only the Palermo, Cairo, and University College fragments remain. It is very unfortunate that there is no adequate publication of the Cairo fragments in Gauthier's plates[15] : all accurate measurements have been omitted, so that it is useless to try to work out with precision[16] the number of year-names in the various registers. But several tentative attempts to compute the original size of the Annals Stone have been made, and in my judgment Edward Meyer's restoration (Meyer, *Aegyptische Chronologie*, p. 197) is much the most satisfactory.

The first two registers of year-names give the Annals of the kings of the Ist dynasty.[17] The third register of the Palermo fragment gives part of the Annals of King Neterimu of the IInd dynasty, and the fourth register preserves the year-names of the latter part of the reign of King Khasekhemui.[18] This last king reigned at least seventeen years. Now, according to Meyer's computations (made from a study of the Palermo fragment alone), the first two registers contained 210 year-names, and the third 135, making for the first three registers 345 year-names. The Palermo fragment is placed by Meyer a little to the right of the centre of the entire block, so that the year-names of Khasekhemui begin about thirty year-names from the right-hand side of the entire block. Adding these thirty years to the 345 of the first three registers, we obtain a total of 375 years from the accession of Menes to the beginning of the reign of Khasekhemui. We have thus on Meyer's conjectural restoration a difference of twelve years between it and the era date at Edfu. Meyer's restoration, it must be remembered, does not claim to be absolutely precise, but, even if it were, the twelve years might easily be accounted for by the ancient chroniclers only taking account of the reign of Khasekhemui from the time he reunited the whole country, and not from the time when he, as Khasekhem, was fighting the Set usurper Perabsen. But however this may be, I think that we have in an era date of 363 years an important new fact that must be taken into account by any future student who endeavours to reconstruct the chronology of the first two dynasties.

There still remains one more fact in favour of dating the Horus-Set war to the end of the IInd dynasty. The difficult title ⟨sign⟩ first appears with King Zoser (*A.Z.*, 1900, p. 20). Sethe (*Mahasna and Bêt Khallâf*, p. 19) discussing a sealing of Neterkhet (Zoser), in which the sign ⟨sign⟩ takes the place of the ⟨sign⟩ name of later kings, says : " here Neterkhet being placed over the ⟨sign⟩ may possibly mean Neterkhet who has conquered the · god ⟨sign⟩ (Set of Ombos). This would agree with the Rosetta translation ἀντιπάλων ὑπέρτερος (" victorious over his enemies ") for the royal title ⟨sign⟩ .

THE EDFU ACCOUNT OF THE HORUS-SET WAR.

Shorn of its fantastic etymologies and some unimportant details, the Ptolemaic account of the Horus-Set war runs as follows :—

In the year ·363 of Horakhuti, the Horus-King returning from a military expedition into Nubia finds that a rebellion has broken out in Egypt (Naville, *Mythe d'Horus*, pl. xii, 2). He lands in the *Uthes-Hor* nome, where, before Edfu, he attacks the rebels, who are routed and flee northwards (pls. xii, 3– xiii, 8). The Horus-King pursues them to Zedmet, south-east of Thebes, and defeats them a second time (pl. xiv, 3). The rebels then retire to the north-east of the crocodile nome (pl. xiv, 5), and here another battle takes place, many of the enemy being slaughtered. Still flying north, the rebels are defeated in the Hermopolite[2] nome, and a battle is fought at Hebnu (pl. xiv, 8–13), where again many of the enemy are slain. Up to this point in the record the enemy are described as hippopotami and crocodiles (both Setian animals), but now they are called *smayw nt Set*, " Companions of Set " (pl. xv, 1), and the Horus-King engages in battle and defeats them, first on the water of the Oxyrhynchite nome (pl. xv, 1–3), where they are led by the Set-King himself (pl. xv, 5), then at *Per-rerhehw* (pl. xvi, 2), and at Ast-abt on the southern side of Herakleopolis (pl. xvii, 1–2). The enemy is then driven northwards to Heliopolis (pl. xviii, 1), and finally defeated at Zaru on the eastern frontier of the Delta (pl. xviii, 1–3). The Horus-King then returns south, goes into Nubia, and overthrows the last remnants of rebels at Shasheryt (pl. xviii, 6). He then celebrates a great festival at Edfu (pl. viii), and later divides up the country that had been under the influence of Set, and distributes it amongst his own followers (pl. xi).

NOTES.

1. There is no evidence whatever that Sekhemab was the Horus-name of Perabsen, as stated by Sethe (*Beiträge zur ältesten geschichte Aegyptens*, p. 36) and Gardiner (*Abydos*, III, p. 39). A fine sealing of this king is published in *Abydos*, III, pl. ix, 3.

2. This was originally suggested by Naville (*Rec. de Travaux*, XXIV, p. 118), and, in spite of Sethe's criticisms (*Beiträge*, etc., pp. 34–35), I think it most probable.

3. A fragment of a bowl with Horus-name Nebra almost erased, and re-inscribed with the name Neterimu, was found in the tomb of Perabsen (*R.T.*, II, viii, 12). A stone bowl found in the Mykerinos temple at Gizeh, bears the names of Hetepsekhemui and Nebra (Borchardt, *Klio*, ix, p. 488).

4. In *Klio*, xii, p. 397 ff., I identified this animal with the wart-hog, but since that paper was written I have accumulated much evidence to show that the Set-animal was in fact a pig, probably an extinct species, from which the domesticated animal was originally derived. On sealings of Perabsen *R.T.*, II, xxii, 178) and Khasekhemui (*R.T.*, II, xxiii, 199) the deity is represented in human form with Set head, and is named Sha. At Dêr Rîfeh (Griffith, *Siut*, pl. 18) Shau is described as "Lord of Shashotep," a city name which means 'Pacifying (the god) Sha," and this city was the capital of the 𓈙𓈙-nome. (*Cp.* the name of the Nubian city Sha-s-heryt, "Terrifying Sha," where the last remnant of the Set rebels were defeated (*see* p. 43). Now *Shau* is a well-known Egyptian name for swine, and in the *Book of the Dead*, ch. 112, it is said that Set transforms himself into a black *sha*. The greyhound-like appearance of the Set-animal might be thought to militate against any identification with a species of pig, but several correspondents have pointed out to me that when the domesticated variety runs wild it reverts to a thin long-legged greyhound-like creature, and one variety in Ireland is actually known as the "Irish greyhound pig" (*see* G. Rolleston, *Scientific Papers*, II, p. 541). The erect tail is a very characteristic feature of many species of *Sus* when they are at all angered. Often on Egyptian mounts the Set-animal is represented with a feathered arrow tail (l), and Mr. Winlock has drawn my attention to the following passage in Darwin's *Variation of Animals and Plants*, Ed. 1905, p. 95 : " The wild boar of India is said to have bristles at the end of its tail arranged like the plumes of an arrow." *Cp.* Note 13 below.

5. On the Horus title of the kings of Egypt see Newberry, *P.S.B.A.*, December, 1904, p. 295 ff.

6. For conclusive evidence on this point see Moret, *Une liste des nomes de la Haute Égypte*, in *Comptes-rendus*, Acad. des Inscr., 1914, p. 565 ff.

7. The nome of *Uthes-Hor*, "the raising of Horus," with Edfu as its capital, extended some little distance to the north of Edfu. Then came the 𓈙 nome. The early capital of this nome must have been 𓈙 *Nekhen*, Hierakonpolis, for the city name is written with the sign of the

nome cult-object. Later the capital was transferred to Nekheb, El Kab, on the opposite bank of the river. That this nome extended northwards as far as Gebeleyn is indicated by the titles of Paheri, who was Mayor of Nekheb and of Ani (Esneh), and as scribe of the accounts of corn " filled the heart of the king from Per-Hathor to El Kab " (Griffith, *Paheri*, pls. iii and ix, I, 9). Per-Hathor = Φαθυρίς at Gebeleyn (Griffith, Ryland, *Demotic Papyri*, III, p. 422).

8. Trouble in the north was already brewing under Neterimu, who in his thirteenth year records the " hacking up " of two northern cities (Palermo Stone, Obv. register 3, entry No. 8).

9. It should be noted that in the titles of Khasekhemui the Set-animal and the Horus-falcon, as well as the Vulture and Uraeus in the *Nebty*-title face one another.

10. Newberry, *P.S.B.A.*, 1906, Feb., pp. 69–70.

11. A title which occurs on her cylinder seals, " If she says anything, it is done for her," is found also with Queen Mertityôtes, the ancestress of the IVth dynasty (E. de Rougé, *Inscr. hiérogl.*, I, 62) ; with Queen Aahmes, ancestress of the XVIIIth (Naville, *Deir el Bahari*, pl. xlix), and with Satra, Queen of Ramses I (Maspero, *Etudes de Myth.*, IV, 329), ancestress of the XIXth dynasty.

12. See Sethe, *Imhotep der Asklepios der Aegypter.* Leipzig, 1902.

13. Apet (= Taûrt) was the hippopotamus goddess of Thebes, and in Ptolemaic times there was a small temple erected to her in that city. On her name *see* my note in *P.S.B.A.*, 1913, p. 117. Set himself is sometimes represented as a hippopotamus (Lanzone, *Diz. mit.*, pl. ccclxxx : Eusebius, *praeparat. evang.*, III, ch. 12). The female hippopotamus was also named *rert*, and this name in the light of note 4 above is interesting, for swine were called *rer*, Copt. ⲣⲓⲣ.

14. The only other Ancient Egyptian era dating is the 400th year of Set on the Tanis stele of the reign of Ramses II, in the Cairo Museum (*Rev. Arch.*, XI (1865), pl. iv).

15. Published in *Le Musée Égyptien*, III (1915), pl. xxv.

16. Borchardt's attempt (*Die Annalen und die zeitliche Festlegung des Alten Reiches der Aegyptischen Geschichte*, Berlin, 1917) has been ably criticised by Peet in the *Journal of Egyptian Archæology*, VI (1920), p. 149 ff.

17. The Cairo fragment (*Le Musée Égyptien*, III (1915), pl. xxv, gives in register I, King Zer Athi, and in register 2 I thought I could read the name Az-ab Mer-pa-ba, when Sir Gaston showed the fragment to me in 1914. The second register of the Palermo fragment, as Wainwright and I proved in 1914 (ANCIENT EGYPT, 1914, p. 148 ff.), gives the annals of Wdymw (Den).

18. Following Schäfer (*Ein Bruchstück*, etc., p. 27), I at first believed (Newberry-Garstang, *Short History*, 1904, p. 27) that the entry No. 4 of the fourth register referred to the birth of King Khasekhemui, but Sethe has since shown (*Journal of Egyptian Archæology*, I (1914), p. 235) that it really records the making of a copper statue (*msw·t·bya*) of Khasekhemui. The first six year-names of this register therefore refer to the reign of Khasekhemui, and not to his predecessor.

19. Seymour du Ricci (*La Table de Palerme* in *Comptes-rendus : Acad. des Inscr.*, 1917, p. 107 ff.) computes 275 year-names for the first three registers, and

thirty more in register 4 to the accession of Khasekhemui, making 305 years from Menes.

20. In Naville's edition of the inscriptions, the important text that runs along the base of the wall upon which the myth is recorded has been omitted. It is printed by E. de Rougé (*Edfou*, pl. lxxxv), and gives a summary of the long text above it. After the record of the defeat of the rebels north-east of the crocodile nome, the longer text says that they fled to the *pehu uaz-ur* (pl. xiv, 7–8, *cf.* xv, 1) ; this is not the sea, but the *name* of the lowlands of the crocodile nome (*see* de Rougé, *Edfou*, pl. xix). The summary gives the names of the places where the battles were fought in the following order : Edfu, Zedmyt to the south of Thebes, ⌒ 𓏏𓇌𓌂 ⊗ on the east of the Crocodile nome, then Wnt (Hermopolis), Hebnu (Minieh) 𓊖 ⊗, Ast-aby, Herakleopolis magna, the western and eastern *Mesens*, and, finally, Shasheryt in Ta-Wawat.

PERCY E. NEWBERRY.

EGYPTIAN WORDS REMAINING IN MODERN USE.

(*Continued from* p. 75, Part III, 1921.)

ⲀⲦⲬⲀⲀ, B., ⳓⲀⲦⲬⲀⲀ, S., حَوْجَل " anchor."

ⲀⲀⲀⲕ, B., ⳓⲀⲀⲀⲕ, S., " ring." Late Ptolemaic. ⸗⸗ *v.* Griffith, *Catalogue of Demotic MSS.* Rylands, Vol. III, Glossary, p. 370, late Egyptian ⌷ ☐ ⲙⲁⲕ ا ; حَلَق . Classical Arabic, قُرْط adj., مُقرْطَق .

Ⲁⲩⲉϣ, B., Ⲁⲩϣⲉ, " whip " ⳓⳓ / أَمْشَا .

ⲀⲩⲉⲛⲦ, B., ⲀⲩⲉⲛⲦⲉ, S., The West; the land of the dead, ⳓⳓ , ⳓⳓ أَمَنْدى in the expression داهية توديك الامندى = " an Evil that sends you to Hades." This expression is becoming rare, and is used only in certain circles.

Ⲁϣ, أَش " what ? " ⳓⳓ and Ⲁⲓⲣ, B., Ⲁⲣ, S. Very common in the Fayum and Beniseuf.

ⳠⲀⲀⳓⲰⲀⲅⲉⲙ, B., بَلْغِم " to bluff in words," " to prevaricate," " to speak in jargon " ; name of the Blemmyes, who spoke a language not understood by the Egyptians.

ⲂⲀⲣϣⲟⲧⲣ, B., مِنْشَار ,وارشور " saw " (the instrument).

ⲂⲀϣ, B., Ⲃⲉϣ, S., and doubled form ⲂⲉϣⲂⲱϣ, ⳓⳓ ; ⳓⳓ انا اتبشبشت مية , بَشْبَش ,بَاشْ " to be wet, wetted " in the saying, " I was wetted with water."

Ⲃⲱϣ, B. and S., " to be void " ; " to be empty " ; used metaphorically in the sense of loss ; طلعنا بوش " We turned out empty handed," etc.

Ⲃⲉⲣ, B. and S., ⳓⳓ, " fall down " ; وِرّ in saying نزل يورّ " fell down," " dropped down."

Ⲃⲣⲏⳓ, " lightning," بَرْق . These two words are probably of an early Semitic root. All words marked with an * are probably of similar origin.

*ⲈⲓⲟⲦⲀ, " stag," أَيِل ⳓⳓ.

*ⲈⲀⳓⲱⲂ, ⳓⳓ , لِيديب مرمراحم " to burn."

ⲈⲦⲛⲓ, B., " mill," طاحونه in the song: يا طاحون الرحاية أوني أوني. .

Ⲉⲱ, Ⲁⲱ, حمار " donkey " ⳓⳓ ; عَا in Upper Egypt—calling for the animal يَوَّى .

ⲈⲛⲕⲟⲦ, B., " to sleep," in the expression ⲦⲈⲛⲕⲟⲦⲕ = أَنُكْتَك " I make you fall down " ; or انتكت نام " lie down and sleep."

*ѲѦѦⲓⲤ, تلّيس "sack."

*Ѳѧⲗ, تل "hill, mound."

ѲѦϥ, B., ⲧѦϥ, S., ⲧѦϥⲧѦϥ, ⲧѦϥⲧⲉϥ, B., Ѳⲟϥⲧⲉϥ, S., "spit" تَفَّ, تَفْتَفَ

ѲѦⲃ, Ѳⲱⲃ, B., ⲧⲱⲣ, S., ثَمِلَ, "drunk," شرب طانح, very common expression meaning "drank until he became drunk."

ⲩѦⲟⲧⲟⲩ, B., حَمْ, "eat," imperative, in giving food to babies.

Also, ⲩ̄ⲙⲓⲩⲟⲟⲧ, اِمبُو, for offering water to babies.

ⲚⲟⲧⲚⲟⲧ, نونو, "baby, anything small and young."

Ⲛⲟⲝⲣⲏ, B., "big sun," "strong sunshine," نَفَر. "Do not walk in the strong sunshine," ماتمشيدش في النفر. It is interesting to notice the ⲝ becoming a غ in Arabic. The Coptic word is Ⲛⲟⲝ, "big," ⲣⲏ, "sun."

ⲟⲧⲱⲓⲚⲓ, B., عوانيه, "a big date palm."

Ⲛⲓⲃ̣ⲟ, B., ⲚⲉⲭѦ, S., ⲚⲉⲭѦ, B., سبخة, "the handle or the edge of a plough."

Ⲛⲓⲃ̣, افريت, late Egyptian : غ., "afrit," is used to frighten someone.

ⲓⲓⲓⲚⲉⲓ, S., Ⲛⲓⲫⲉⲓ, برغوت, "flea," often called in Arabic بيبه, particularly when talking to babies. The fact that most addresses to babies remain in Coptic until to-day is most significant, and means that the Coptic language has lingered long in use in private homes.

*Ϥѧⲩⲩ, ⲚѦⲃ̣, ⲚѦⲩⲩ, فَشّ, "trap," root (?)

Ⲛⲱⲣⲩⲩ, Ⲛⲱⲣⲃ̣, Ϥⲟⲣⲩⲩ, B. and S., "to stretch out"; برش a kind of small mat used in many ways.

*Ⲛⲓⲟⲧ, S., Ϥⲱⲧ, B., نَطَّ, "jump," "run," ⲗ.

*ⲣⲱⲧ, روض, "garden," "park." Common in the names of towns, ديروط, ⲧⲉⲣⲱⲧ, etc.

ⲉ̄ⲚѦⲧ, ⲤⲚѦⲧⲉ, سباطه "a bunch of dates."

*Ⲥⲱⲃ̣ⲉⲩ, ⲤѦⲃ̣ⲉⲩ, سخّم, "to defile, to dirty."

ⲤѦⲣⲧ, ⲤѦⲣⲧⲉ, صيد, "heat," الصيد طالع حامى.

* (Ebers, XLVII, pp. 12, 13), صداع, "migraine."

Ⲥⲱ, B., ⲤѦⲟⲧ, S., سدّه, "to drink," شرب،ا; in Asiut, in calling for water they say (سيّا).

Ѳⲱⲩⲩ, ⲧⲱⲩ, حد, طاش, "boundary."

ⲧⲱⲣⲓ, طورِيه "hoe."

ϥⲱⲥⲓ = فاس "pick-axe."

ⲧⲕⲧⲕ, الطبيخ تكتك, نَكَتَك حَمضَ "gone bad"; for food, نَكَتَك.

ѲѦⲣⲩⲉ, ⲧѦⲣⲩⲉ, "to invite," دعوق، طهمه, "invitation."

ϯⲁⲩϩⲓⲡⲓ, دميرة, " inundation,"

ϯⲟⲩⲓ, طَمْى " the Nile mud."

ⲩⲑⲁⲩ, ⲩⲑⲟⲩⲥ, اُشْدُوم, " dam,"; different from στώμα.

ⲩⲁⲣⲕⲉ, شراقى, " low Nile "; deficiency (of water).

ⲩⲉⲣⲟⲕϩ, " wood for burning," شرَاق .

ⲩϩⲓⲓ ⲗⲉⲗⲟⲩ, " small boy," شملول, " dandy," " young man."

ⲩⲉⲛ, شَن, , " blow the nose."

ϧⲁⲓⲡⲓ, ϩⲱⲓⲡⲓ, خرَاء, fæces, in the expression يهر, " having diarrhœa."

, ⲭⲁⲓⲉ, شايه, " the shirt of a baby."

ⲭⲓⲡ, صيْر, " small fish "; also in the sense of acid they say, حادق صير, " very acid."

ϩⲁⲗⲟⲧⲉ, هلوس, " spider's web."

ϩⲁⲭⲱⲥ, هجّاس, " chatterbox."

ϩⲏⲧⲕ̄, حرّاك, " by your side."

(*To be continued.*)

GEO. P. G. SUBḤY.

D

REVIEWS.

The Palace of Minos at Knossos. By SIR ARTHUR EVANS. Vol. I. Sq. 8vo, 721 pp., 8 pls. coloured, 11 pls., 542 figs. and map. 1921. (Macmillan.) 126s.

The harvest is now put into our hands of all the work begun more than twenty years ago in Crete, and the first volume we hope will be soon succeeded by the two other volumes which are promised. This is far more than an account of Knossos, as the results and objects found by other excavators elsewhere are incorporated, to complete the material of each period, thus rendering the work an entire view of Cretan civilisation. Here will be stated an outline of the work and its relations with Egypt especially.

It is truly said that this was a pioneer work. There was very little known of mere loose objects, and there was no pre-Hellenic building which could serve as a pattern for the excavation. The whole of the sequence of civilisation had to be worked out from the material as it came to light. After a preliminary sketch of the general connections of Cretan civilisation with other lands, there is a first chapter on the neolithic period. The series of superposed palace ruins are really a terrible encumbrance of a great neolithic site of the first importance. Even on the shortest dating of the palace period, the neolithic would in proportion extend to 8000 B.C. This great mass of 23 to 26 feet depth of ruins contains the early history of civilisation, perhaps more completely than elsewhere. Though the later remains above it must be preserved, yet it might be possible to tunnel it at different levels, and recover the stratified series of deposits. So far only a few pits have been sunk. From these the lowest stratum yielded polished stone implements, and pottery with a good burnished face. In the middle strata is found the beginning of the incised decoration, some with white filling ; figures of animals appear, and human figures with stump limbs and heads, mostly squatting women. On some of these is the zigzag line pattern so usual on the prehistoric statuettes of the first period in Egypt. The figures are thus placed in relation to those from the Aegean region. The later period at Knossos is marked by the pear-shaped and orange-shaped stone maces, like those of the second age in Egypt Thus we may take as contemporary :—

Knossos.	Egypt.
Early neolithic.	. . .
Middle neolithic.	First prehistoric age.
Late neolithic.	Second prehistoric age.

The ages in which metal was used are divided into Early, Middle and Late Minoan, roughly corresponding to Old, Middle and New Kingdoms in Egypt, and each age is divided into three parts, numbered I, II, III, according to the well-known system of the author.

The Early Minoan I is marked by polished black ware, as found in the Ist dynasty at Abydos, bowls on stands as in the IInd dynasty, a chalice apparently copied from a lotus cup (19 D.), globular jugs with long spouts, and heavy stone bowls imported from Egypt, beside imitations of such.

In the second age (E.M. II) the main material is from the cemetery of Mochlos. It is remarkable for the beauty and variety of the stones, which are, however, all soft, limestones and steatite, and not hard silica minerals as in Egypt. The pottery is of cloudy colouring of black, orange and red, varied by oxidation in burning, like prehistoric Egyptian ware. Conical cups with short spouts resemble the Old Kingdom forms, and cups on stems are like the cups of the IXth dynasty. Imitation rivets, copying metal ware, were similar to Egyptian of VIth dynasty. The double spouts of the IInd and IIIrd dynasty were copied, as also the bowls with deeply curved lip, "carinated," which are of the IIIrd–Vth dynasties. A marble vase is taken from the form in the VIth dynasty.

The third period (E.M. III) was one of deterioration. A great domed chamber, cut in the rock, is the prototype of the "Treasury" tombs. Painted pottery now became much commoner than stone vases, and spiral ornament begins to appear. This was probably preceded by the earliest spiral in Egypt, of Zed-ka-ra in the Vth dynasty. But it is not regularly adopted till the Xth or XIth dynasty. We may agree with Sir Arthur in supposing that it came from the north by way of the Cyclades. Along with the spiral comes in the squared form, the "fret" or "meander" pattern. The Cretan adaptation of button-badge patterns from Egypt shows that they must belong to the VIIIth dynasty ; the pattern is degraded, and the original did not start till late in the VIth.

The period of Middle Minoan I is especially the Age of palaces (M.M. I). Upon the blocks of stone are many signs, referring to the quarry or the destination ; we shall notice these below. Of this age is the substructure of a great square tower, built in a cellular form with deep blind chambers, which were filled up to make a high platform. It is 46 × 51 feet, which is much less than the platforms of forts at Daphnae (140 feet) or Naukratis (190 feet), but it belongs to the same system, which was expanded later. The drains of the palace are of the earliest laying out. The pipes were 30 inches long, and 5 inches tapering to 3-inch bore. On the narrow end was a stop-flange outside, and in the wide end an internal collar, so as to give a wide bearing on the flange. Some had two pairs of handles outside, in order to move such heavy things safely. Pottery modelling of figures was common. A new type is of jars with two handles, either joining the neck vertically, or rising from the shoulder at both ends. Painted imitations of stonework are common, and foliage decoration begins to be freely used. Scarabs are first imitated in this age, and are of the style of the XIIth dynasty.

The next stage (M.M. II) is marked by the laying out of the palace plan on a large scale. The great drains were built of stone, 30 × 15 inches, catching the rain from the open courts and light wells, into which the roofs discharged, and also draining the latrines. The pottery was highly developed. There are enormous oil jars with knobbed pattern and taller than a man, and there is also an egg-shell ware, with striking decoration and brilliant colouring. This pottery was also adapted to imitate metal vases, in form and polish. The patterns are the most perfect and brilliant of any period. From the fragments found at Kahun, and the vase from Abydos, this style is dated to the end of the XIIth dynasty. Towards the close of this period the leaf patterns become mechanical repetitions of a formal kind. Seals with hieroglyphs of Cretan origin were much used. A good dating point is gained by a diorite seated figure of Egyptian work

found with pottery of this age at Knossos, and belonging to the late XIIth or
XIIIth dynasty. It represents Ab-nub, born of Uazet-user. The serpent of
Uazet is placed on a stand to show that it represents a god, like a falcon on a
stand for Horus.

The relations of trade between Egypt and Crete lead to attributing the
great harbour works at Alexandria to Cretan enterprise. These works were
found by M. Jondet, Chief Engineer of Ports, and mapped by him. He published
them in 1916 at the *Institut Égyptien.* They comprise an inner and outer
breakwater in front of Ras et Tin, and running west, and a back breakwater
behind, enclosing a harbour now over 20 feet deep. Before the sinking of the
coast this would not be over 10 feet, but the ancient shipping was of very light
draught, as it needed to draw in close to shore. Before the Pharos island was
joined to the mainland by Alexander it would be a convenient point for traders,
like Hongkong, clear of the Egyptian shore. The basin of the harbour was about
150 acres in area ; the front of it was outside the present harbour, and the back
of it along the present breakwater and beyond the bend of it, on to the islands
and shoals.

A notable view of the life of this age comes from the pictures of houses,
modelled in glazed pottery and inlaid in some general scene, which included
trees, water, animals, warriors and negroid figures. The houses were of three
or even four floors, the windows sometimes divided into panes. Most were built
of stone courses, others of wood, with round poles for flooring and partitions.

The latter stage (M.M. III) of this great period was marked by a catastrophe,
which was " so general that the palace sites both at Knossos and Phaestos may,
partially at least, have remained for an appreciable time uninhabited and have
existed as mere heaps of ruins." Though in writing, seals and architecture,
changes appear, yet these are more as developments than as new motives. It
seems that the break was caused by a people of lower ability, who did not bring
in new ideas. There was widespread conflagration and plundering of the palace.
The renewed life here, of M.M. III, is dated by the alabaster lid with the name of
Khyan, belonging to the XVth dynasty. There was a distinctly later taste in
the pottery, applied modelling stuck on, and sprays, which remind us of the style
of 1870. A greater degree of luxury appears in the inlaid crystal, ivory and gold,
gaming board, the abundance of coloured glaze ware for inlay, as the goats,
cows or fish (long before Akhenaten), and the free and delicate drawing of the
frescoes. A weird variety of monsters were devised on the seals, and a new
decoration of great lily plants rises life-size up the sides of the tall jars. The
religion is shown in the figures of the snake-holding goddess, the marble cross
and the emblem of the double axe mounted on a stand. The writing changes
to a more cursive form of the earlier hieroglyphs, due to a free and common use
of reed pans. Beyond this the volume does not go, the late Minoan stages and
other subjects are for future issue.

Some general matter remains to be noted. The strong artistic instinct of
the Cretans led them to decorate pottery and walls with a great variety of plants
and figures. To these no magic purpose would be assigned. Why then attribute
a magic intent to the less perfect decoration by other peoples. Let us credit
lower races with having æsthetic desires, such as can undoubtedly be observed
at present. The examples of multiple beads from Egypt, Crete and Britain are
well illustrated, but it might be added that the exact fabric of the Wiltshire beads
is only paralleled in the multiple beads of 1210 B.C. in Egypt.

The signs used by masons on blocks of stone are nearly all well known about the Mediterranean, where they probably had regular sound values. Out of 15 single signs, 13 are known in Spain, 11 in Egypt, 4 in Karia, 3 in Lydia and 2 in Lachish. In the fuller list of all the advanced linear signs in Crete about 36 are geometric. Of these 27 are known elsewhere, 25 in Egypt, 16 in Spain, 12 in Karia, 8 in Lydia, 6 in Lybia, and 5 in Lachish. Thus the connection with the opposite ends of the Mediterranean is closer than with the neighbouring Asia Minor coast. With regard to chronology it is to be regretted that the knowledge of the Egyptian dating seems to have been forgotten, and the consistent system which they have left us is regarded as a mere supposition of the present time. The Berlin dating here followed is a total impossibility; the XIIIth dynasty alone, of well recorded kings, would overlap the XVIIIth on that supposition. Not a single advocate of the reduced dates has ever attempted to show how the known reigns can be compressed into the time.

It will be most desirable to trace out the system of design of the buildings, what parts were laid out to measure and what were of mere resultant lengths. So far as a few measures are given, the standard seems to have been the Persian *arish*, divided into three feet of 12·83 inches. This was in use in Asia Minor. The weights also must be published, especially an accurate weighing of the great octopus standard.

A great problem is that of the future of Knossos. It is largely built of gypsum, which is very soluble and was protected anciently by roofing or lime plaster. Without any plaster it will now all perish in a few generations. The ancient construction has been largely repaired by modern work, needful to put the place into accessible state. This will, in a century or two, be blended and confused with the original work. To keep the site really safe it needs much more reconstruction and roofing. Left as it is it will largely perish, without the proteeting coat of earth that has saved it for 3,000 years.

Les Indo-Européens. By ALBERT CARNOY. 1921. 256 pp., 16mo, 7 frs. (Vromant, Bruxelles.)

This work deals with the linguistic point of view, set out by Max Müller sixty years ago. The author disclaims at once the idea of an Indo-European race being defined by the language, yet little or nothing is said as to the various racial sources of the peoples who adopted the language. There is a chapter on the centre of dispersion, but beyond stating that it included Central Asia, Russia and Germany, nothing more is attempted. Tilak's work, which would place the Aryans at least as far north as Tobolsk, is not mentioned. The increase of cold in Scandinavia at the beginning of the bronze age is noted, but the connection of that with the submergence of the same period should be mentioned. In general the physical side of the subject is hardly developed, but the linguistic evidence is fully described with examples dealing with each branch and most dialects of Indo-European speech. The evidence from community of words is classed under all the various heads of zoology, dwellings, utensils, food, clothing, arms, &c., and the beliefs and mythology are fully described. This is a useful outline of the subjects with which it deals.

The Septuagint and Jewish Worship. By H. St. J. THACKERAY, D.D. 8vo,
143 pp., 1922. (*Schweich Lectures, Milford.*)

This course of British Academy lectures is mainly occupied with the
influence of liturgical use on the minor books of the Old Testament, the incorporation of rubrics, and transformation of such into parts of the text. The
results of the author's study on the Gracco-Egyptian version, known as the LXX,
concern us here. He remarks on its value as being made from MSS. older than
the formation of the orthodox recension of the Masoretic text, and far before
any remaining MSS. of that. It is very difficult to counterpoise the value of two
opposite kinds of material. In the received Hebrew text, late construction, but
excessive care ; in the Septuagint, earlier construction, more varied material,
but lack of precision and careless transmission. The Pentateuch was first
translated, by a small group, in the third century B.C. The language is the
popular Greek, and not literary, hence it was for general use and convenience,
and not done for library purposes. The familiarity with Egypt shows that it
was prepared there. Next the Prophets were done by another group in the
second and first centuries. To them were gradually added the Psalms and lesser
books, translated by individuals, and more as free paraphrases than as formal
renderings. The whole was then subject to various editing, and versions
made in the Asiatic schools of the second century A.D. ; in fact, the translation
of some parts seems, from peculiar words, to have been made in Asia Minor.
Of the earliest MSS. the Vatican is the best, the Alexandrian (Brit. Mus.) being of
mixed origin.

*Synoptic Series of Objects in the United States National Museum Illustrating
the History of Inventions.* By WALTER HOUGH. 8vo, 47 pp., 56 pls. (*Proc.
U.S. Nat. Mus.*)

Though this collection scarcely touches on Egypt, it is of great interest for
comparison, as showing independent lines of invention in America, covering the
variety illustrated in the University College Catalogue of Tools and Weapons of
the Old World, and continuing the evolution down to the present day.

Catalogue of Textiles from Egypt. Vol. II. By A. F. KENDRICK. 8vo,
108 pp., 32 pls. 5s. (*Victoria and Albert Museum.*)

This is the continuation of the catalogue noticed in ANCIENT EGYPT, 1921,
p. 57. It deals with " The period of transition and of Christian emblems." The
transition is that from Graeco-Roman to Coptic art, during the fifth and sixth
centuries. The old skill was waning, the old notions were being discarded, the
sense of ordered disposition was giving way to the attraction of bright colours.
The catalogue begins with many examples of woven crosses. On comparison
with the accurately dated examples of forms of the cross, the dates in the
catalogue average 150 years too early (*see* ANCIENT EGYPT, 1916, p. 103). This
suggests that all these textiles have been dated a century or two too early ; it
does not appear that there are any absolutely dated examples as a basis.
A generally later dating would accord more nearly with Gayet's statements.
It is well that the materials should be so clearly illustrated and described,
and this will long serve as a book of reference on the patterns and methods
of work.

Capitals and Bases : a theory of their evolution. By F. WELMAN. 6 pp. (Journal of Royal Institute of British Architects, 22 October, 1921.)

This theory mainly refers to Greek forms of capitals, but also includes some of the Egyptian. As it is a new possibility it needs consideration. The idea is that a wooden architecture is made more durable by damp-proof layers of bitumen, and that the architectural details of design have originated from such bitumen layers retained in place by cloth wrappings and cords. Thus the features of the Doric capital and Attic base are well accounted for, and, less distinctively, the Ionic and Corinthian capitals. The evolution of forms is a difficult subject owing to our ignorance of the series, of which we only know the final product, and here and there a few of the earlier stages. This is as true in architecture as in zoology.

The basic question is where the forms were developed, and whether bitumen was known there. So far as we know there is no trace of bitumen used in any Mediterranean country for building purposes. Can the forms have arisen farther east. In Assyria there is something like the volute (Botta, Pl. CXIV), and in Persia is the prototype of the Ionic echinus. The latter, however, is obviously a leaf pattern in the long drooping form at Persepolis (dieulafoy II, xxi), otherwise there does not seem to be any oriental source for the forms attributed to the use of bitumen.

In the dry climates of Egypt and Greece there would not be the same inducement to use damp-courses that we have in the north. Yet the forms suggest a soft material held in place. May it be that the purpose was to keep a bedding material in place to equalise pressure, and that clay was so used. The suggestions of origin of the features of Egyptian architecture is not in harmony with materials used in ancient or modern times, reeds, maize stalk, mud, cord, lotus, papyrus stem and palm leaves. Nor will the suggested origin of the spiral accord with the earlier examples as surface decoration on small objects. The fret is the spiral squared up in weaving patterns, as seen on the earliest example, on the borders of dresses of pre-Persian statues.

Die Cheopspyramide. By K. KLEPPISCH. 8vo. 74 pp. 1921. (Oldenbourg, München.) 15 marks.

This work by a Polish engineer deals mainly with the external form of the pyramid, and the various mathematical properties that co-exist in that form. Here we meet the old difficulty, how many such properties are accidental ? or did the constructors select the form from a wide knowledge of such properties showing them that this form combined many different ideas ?

The proportion of the radius to circumference, or approximately 7 : 44, for the height and circuit of the pyramid is accepted ; but the author takes up the old and erroneous measures of the base in order to make out that the slope $+ \frac{1}{2}$ base $= 1,000$ English feet. Really the actual measures give 11,871 to 11,888 inches for this amount. Wiping out this, there remains principally the mean proportional relation of $\frac{1}{2}$ base : height :: height : slope ; which results in many relationships, such as area of face = area of height squared ; or base area : face area :: face area : whole area base and faces. Another proposal is that, taking the height as 280 cubits and $\frac{1}{2}$ face as 220, the slope is 356·090, or slope $+ \frac{1}{2}$ base $= 576·090$, almost a regular number, 24^3. It seems very unlikely that such relations determined the Egyptian to select the radius and circle proportions. That the Meydum pyramid is 7 and 44 × 25 cubits, and Khufu's pyramid is 7 and 44 × 40 cubits gives the strongest reason for accepting that on the originating purpose ; all else is therefore only coincidence.

The Origin of Letters and Numerals. By PHINEAS MORDELL. 8vo. 71 pp. 1922. (Philadelphia, 4137 Leidy Ave.) 2 dollars.

This essay deals with the Sefer Yetzirah, a mystical tract on the nature of letters. The author distinguishes an early edition, which is pre-Talmudic, of about 600 words, and later editions with targums, of two or three times the length, which may be of the fifth to ninth century A.D. Apart from the Jewish interest in the mystical allusions, this tract is of general interest regarding the Semitic alphabet. According to the original edition, the alphabet consisted of ten double letters which had modified values ; *aleph* (e and o), *beth* (b, v), *gimel* (g, j), *daleth* (d, dh), *vau* (u, w), *kaph* (k, kh), *pe* (p, f), *resh* (r, gh), *shin* (sh, zh), *tau* (t, th) ; the other twelve letters had single uniform values. Thus a total of thirty-two letters is reached. The Sefer states that the tetragrammaton Yhvh consisted of vowels, so that all the letters rendered as vowels in western alphabets were also recognised as vowels in Hebrew. It was not till mediaeval times that the consonantal view came in. The modern values according to Mordell's comparisons are :—

	aleph	yod	vau	'ain
Sephardic (Spanish)	a	e, i	o, u	
Ashkenaz (German)	e, o	i	u	a

The Svastika and the Omkāra. By HARIT KRISHNA DEB. (*Journ. Asiatic Soc., Bengal*, N.S., XVII, 1921, No. 3.) " The syllable *om* . . . is part and parcel of the Vedic religion." As it is pronounced with a long *ō*, the author suggests that the sign for *o* (a " pothook " with square ends) was duplicated, one across another, and so originated the *svastika*. At first sight this may seem merely a guess, but it is fortified by other evidence. The *svastika* goes back to Panini, in the VIIth century B.C., when it was a cattle mark ; another reference is well before 528 B.C., and it is on a gold leaf in a vase found with relics of Buddha. On Indian coins of Eran the *svastika* has the letter *m* added to each terminal, thus making *om*, and a variant of this is on coins of Ujain. Two of the Asoka edicts have corner marks of the *svastika* and letter *m*. Albiruni (1030 A.D.) states that an ∽ sign is read as *om*. Thus the connection of the *o* sign, *om*, and *svastika* is strongly indicated. The meaning of the *svastika* is " that which signifies well-being " or " brings blessing," like the *onkh uza senb* in Egypt. The earliest example known is on the spindle whorls from Troy, in the third city, about 1800 B.C. It is frequent on Greek vases about 600 B.C. Among some rather uncertain conjectures in the latter part of the paper there is a striking comparison of the names of Gilukhipa, sister of the king of Mitani, with Guruksepa, who was the third successor of Brhadbala, who fell in the Bhārata war about 1450 B.C., another Indo-Aryan link with Naharain.

PERIODICALS.

———

Comptes Rendus, 1921. March—June.

CAPART, J.—*Un mythe Égyptien dans le Roman de Renart.* In the XVIIth chapter of the Book of the Dead is the description of the combat of Horus and Set. For this combat the regulations described are like those of the judicial combat in the Romance of Petubast. The eye of Horus was injured, and was restored by Thoth, and then became *uza*, whole or healthy. The details of the combat between Horus and his uncle Set are the same as those in the fight of Renard and his uncle Isengrin. The animal gods of Egypt easily gave rise in their mythology to folk tales about animals.

Lettre de M. Montet à M. Clermont-Ganneau. This outlines the history of Byblos, *Keben.* As the port for obtaining timber for shipbuilding, it was essential to trade, and the pinewood from there was used for furniture. Various fragments of Egyptian monuments have been found there, the names are of Tahutmes III and Ramessu II. An earlier block, with scenes of a kneeling king offering to Hathor, is dated to the XIIth dynasty by the spelling of *Keben.*

A mosaic floor of a synagogue of the IIIrd century has been found about four miles from Jericho. The chariot of the sun is surrounded by the signs of the zodiac, and figures of plants and animals. The Jewish character is assumed from the Ark of the Law, the Holy Lampstand, and Daniel between the lions. The presence of figures would rather point to the building being a church, the subjects named being often found in Christian art.

July–October.

Rapport de M. Lacau . . . sur les travaux exécutés pendant l'hiver 1920–21. The Nubian temples are withstanding inundation, but the gate of Hadrian at Philae will need reconstruction, and the small temple of Tafah will need to be completely rebuilt on higher ground. At Denderah the whole surroundings of the great temple are being cleared. The lake and wells, and the mammisi are all cleared. The fore part of the latter was removed anciently to build a church, but the plan remains traced on the foundations. The protection of the roofs against rain percolating was most carefully provided for in the construction.

At Karnak, one of the most important excavations in the world, work has been resumed. M. Pillet has taken up the work left at M. Legrain's death, and the intention is to publish all architectural parts that can be considered as finished. A large clearance must be trenched deeply to see if any monuments lie under it before using it as a space for arranging and reconstructing the blocks of the Amenhetep temple and other buildings. The stairway of the great pylon has been opened up, and a row of relieving chambers found in the upper part.

At Saqqarah nothing had been done for seven years, and now Mr. Firth has renewed the work. It is first intended to clear the funeral chapels of the pyramids of the VIth dynasty, and then to clear around the mastabas to examine exteriors. The mastaba of Kagemna has a figure and texts upon it. On the south face small tombs were inserted in the Middle Kingdom, with statues of the deceased squatting at the base of the stele. The pit led to a chamber covered with figures of offerings ; the funeral furniture included alabaster canopies of fine work, and many rock-crystal model vases left solid. The clasp of a gold necklace shows that jewellery had been buried here.

At Aswan the great unfinished obelisk has been cleared to 118 feet length, without reaching the end. At Thebes the sarcophagus placed by Hatshepsut in her cliff tomb in the Queen's Valley has been removed to the Museum, and stands by the side of her sarcophagus from the King's Valley. At Tuneh the sculptures of the tomb of Petosiris have been copied for publication.

At Athribis (Benha) a tomb has been found of a priest of the sacred falcon, of Greek period. An enormous limestone sarcophagus was built round with great blocks, on the ground surface. There was neither chamber nor pit, as the water level did not allow of sinking.

At Tell el-Yahudieh more Jewish-Greek steles have been found, many dated in the reign of Augustus.

November–December.

November 9. M. Montet found many alabaster vases at Byblos, one with the name of Unas (p. 332).

December 23. M. Montet found inscriptions of Menkaura, a colossal figure of Egyptian style, and fragments of two other statues (p. 363).

January–February.

M. Montet found a large group of things near a temenos wall : lions couchant and standing, cynocephali, scarabs, kneeling figures, flies, model table of bronze, bracelets and rings of bronze, gilt-bronze statuettes and a coin (illegible) ; a cup full of beads of rock-crystal and carnelian. In another place was a large quantity of alabaster vases and pottery. On one vase is the name of Unas, beloved of Ra, " over the lake of the Great House," supposed to be a royal lake, but *per oā* at that time might refer to a temple. On a piece of a vase is the *sed heb* of Pepy, and on a cynocephalus vase is the name of Pcpy II. A vase of Menkaura goes back to the IVth dynasty ; and still earlier is a cylinder, two inches long, with three gods upon it, naming " the lady of Byblos," the hieroglyphs of which are irregularly placed, as in the IInd and IIIrd dynasties. There is a circular wall a metre thick, round a paved area ; also a temple with four colossi before it, standing and seated ; they are broken away above, but a head was found. There are no inscriptions, and it is supposed to be Phoenician. This is the last report issued, when the work was stopped in January by the rains.

Palestine Exploration Fund, Quarterly Statement, April, 1922. A cubical bronze weight from Petra, described by Mr. E. J. Pilcher, bears on it *Khamsheth* or " five," showing it to be a weight of 5 qedet, on the Egyptian standard of 140 grains. The form of writing is the Edomite Semitic alphabet, and it points to trade from Egypt through Nabathaea as early as the sixth century B.C. There is also in this April number a summary of all the archæological work in Palestine by Prof. Garstang.

Metropolitan Museum of Art, Bulletin, Part II, 1921.—This is entirely devoted to a fairly full account of the excavations of season 1920–21. At Lisht —described by Mr. Mace—there was a pre-dynastic village with fragments of pottery and stone vases. A later village built against the side of the pyramid yielded stone figures, tweezers, rasps, harpoons, combs, like those from Kahun. Among these were incised black vases of Hyksos age, and one of the same family of buff pottery with birds and dolphins in dark red, outlined by white incisions. This is a new style of this Syrian pottery. There were also engraved ivory wands, and a weight of Senusert with the number 23¼ on it, evidently a converted weight, but the amount is not stated. As regards the pyramid of Amenemhat I there is great confusion, as blocks are found (1) with Old Kingdom reliefs, (2) from earlier work of Amenemhat I, (3) of the final temple, and (4) temple reliefs copied from older monuments. Under a corner of the pyramid was found a foundation deposit, exactly like that under a temple (*Abydos* II, p. 20). The tombs of four princesses proved to have been entirely plundered.

The copying work of Mr. Davis at Thebes has been devoted to the tomb of Neferhetep, which contains some well-known scenes (Wilkinson, Pl. LXVII).

The Theban excavations are described by Mr. Winlock. After finding the tomb with the magnificent set of models, the rest of that valley was thoroughly explored, but nothing further appeared. To the south was the platform for a royal temple, and the causeway leading to it, which ran across the site of the future Ramesseum. Only one small tomb—perhaps never finished—was found here, and the great tomb temple was never built, probably because the court moved away to a new centre. Some much later tombs were found, one being of the charioteer Atefamen, with three fully decorated coffins in a painted sarcophagus.

An entirely different enterprise was in the XIth dynasty temple of Deir el-Bahri. The work of the Exploration Fund had bared the foundations of six shrines of princesses, and tombs beneath four of them. But, strange to say, no search had been made for the burials beneath the other two shrines. On looking at the paving it was obvious where the pits were, by the sinking over them. On opening that of Oashyt her coffin was found complete, with the mummy and wooden statue, in a limestone sarcophagus. Outside, this was decorated with scenes like that of Kauit, now in Cairo ; but inside, instead of being plain, it was also sculptured and painted with scenes. The wooden coffin is highly painted with rows of funereal offerings, and figures of the constellations, the thigh, Orion, and Isis. This is certainly the most splendid burial of the Middle Kingdom, in its furniture. The jewellery had, alas! all been robbed anciently. The sixth shrine, that of Mayt, proved to be of an infant. Some strings of beads were found in her wrappings with a cartonnage over the head, in a plain whitewashed box, in her coffin. Among the beads are some of blue glass, extremely rare in the Middle Kingdom. We may add that this year Mr. Winlock has found the foundation deposits of the temple. It is to be hoped that he will soon publish all of these finest products of the temple, the sarcophagi, the deposits, the wooden statue of the king (ANCIENT EGYPT, 1920, p. 33), and as many as possible of the fine blocks of sculpture which crowded the dealers' shops during the previous excavation. This is necessary to supplement the publication by the Fund.

A search in the convents of the Wady Natrun has been made by Mr. Evelyn White, and plans and photographs secured. A quantity of leaves of early works were rescued, which belong to books previously obtained by Tattam and Tischendorff. Altogether this bulletin is the record of a fine harvest of new results, and we earnestly hope it will soon be followed by complete publication.

Annals of Archaeology. Liverpool, 1921.

GRIFFITH, F. LL.—*Oxford Excavations in Nubia.* This work was at Faras, a third of the way from Abu Simbel to the Second Cataract. The earliest object here was a drift type palaeolith of quartz, the only one known so far south. A village and cemetery of the end of the pre-dynastic age contained pottery which was entirely of the age before Mena. It is unfortunate that the absolutely dated series of pottery of the Royal Tombs is disregarded in calling this " protodynastic." A thin layer of ash and charcoal marked the settlement, which was probably of wicker booths. The pottery of distinctive forms is between 75 and 78 S.D. With this was also the soft black-bodied Nubian pottery with parallel incised lines, of the class which was brought down into Egypt after the VIth dynasty and after the XIIIth. The palettes were thin oval slabs of quartz. Copper adzes (mis-called chisels) and axes were found ; also a cylinder seal of ivory of local design unlike the Egyptian, and beads of crystal, carnelian, garnet and serpentine, and ostrich eggs. So far as the skeletons could be discriminated, the men had axes and chisels buried with them ; the beads, armlets and copper piercers were with women ; the palettes were with both. These settlements of the late prehistoric age died out very soon in Nubia ; various causes are suggested, but the most obvious would be that these were groups of the prehistoric folk driven out by the dynastic invaders, taking their goods with them, but unable to continue their old handiwork, and gradually becoming lost in the native population. This would account for the absence of anything belonging to the dynastic culture.

After this comes the Nubian civilisation contemporary with the Middle Kingdom, stated to range from the end of the VIth to the XVIIIth dynasty, the so-called C group. The graves were surrounded by a ring-wall of stones, filled up with sand and topped by slabs. The pottery was placed outside of the graves as offerings, as in Egypt (*Tarkhan* II, xiv–xvi). The contracted bodies are all on the right side, head between north and south-east, whereas the prehistoric bodies were—like the Egyptian—on the left side, head south. There was one instance of a dismembered body, with bones broken. There were armlets of shell, ivory, marble and alabaster ; finger rings of ivory, horn and shell ; amulets of a turquoise hawk, carnelian foot, silver *onkh*, and a rather geometric figure on a hemi-cylinder, of the usual post-sixth style. The beads were of gold, quartz, carnelian, diorite, steatite, shell and blue glaze. Patterned beadwork in squares was also found (the drawing has the heraldic shading reversed). A curious kind of pot is conical, about five inches long and one inch wide at the mouth ; the inside is smooth as if it were a mould ; these are like pots of double the size found elsewhere. Some such—but not all—have a hole in the bottom, and have been thought to be tuyers ; they are too long for crucibles apparently, and have no trace of slag in them. Another suggestion is that they were moulds but there are no moulded objects of this shape and size.

Considerable remains of the New Kingdom were discovered. A temple to Hathor seems to have been built by Hatshepsut. Another temple was built by Tahutmes III, of which various blocks and fragments remain. A third temple was built by Tutonkhamen, which still shows half the columns of the forecourt, and nearly all of the hypostyle hall. .Huy, the governor, built it at the request of his sister, who was head of the harem of the king. There is the greater part of a granite stele with figures of Tutonkhamen and a god. Lastly, there is a grotto of Ramessu II and the governor Setan, which may be a tomb, made for Merapu son of Pa-mer-ah. A new variation in transliteration appears in using *j* for *z ;* as many people follow the German use of it for *y*, it is confusing, and *j* is better omitted altogether, as it is so ambiguous. This report is very welcome, though eight years old, and the twenty-five plates record the main things sufficiently.

Annals of Archaeology, Liverpool, 1922.

MACE, A. B.—*The Influence of Egypt on Hebrew Literature.* The lack of interest in Egyptian literature is mainly due to the imperfection of translation, and loss of the spirit and rhythm of it. This is illustrated by a supposed future version of a sonnet of Shakespeare. The comparisons of Egyptian and Hebrew writings are set out in parallel columns—the Proverbs of Ptah-hetep with Abikar, the Hymn to Aten with Psalms, Ptah-hetep with Proverbs, Ani with Proverbs, Khakheper-res-senb and the Song of the Harper with Ecclesiastes. Some of these comparisons were made in *Nile and Jordan.*

Other important articles on megaliths by Mr. Thurlow Leeds, and on Asia Minor, Syria and the Aegean by Mr. Woolley, do not touch on Egypt.

Journal of the Society of Oriental Research, Chicago, 1921.

MERCER, S.—*Egyptian Morals of the Empire.* This article is in continuation of two previous articles upon the earlier periods, which were noticed in ANCIENT EGYPT, 1920, p. 62. Regarding marriage, examples of two wives are quoted, but at Hagarseh six wives are represented ; the chief wife had no children, and this may have led to the large number otherwise (*Athribis*, vii). The sister-marriage, which was usual in royalty, is said to be of uncertain frequency in the lower classes ; it is often found in family records, though it was not usual. The habit of speaking of a wife or lover as a sister at least shows that it was an ideal, like first-cousin marriage in Egypt at present. The close family affection is noted, like that of the modern Oriental, and the emphasis on children being the gift of the gods, theophoric names being commoner than in early times. The ideal character was of a high standard, much above the actual standard of any modern country ; but there was, of course, a continual slipping away from it, especially in lax reigns, only to be compensated by an uncomfortable tuning up under an able ruler, such as Heremheb. (There is a strange allusion by the author to *coin* of that time, whereas there was no coinage till many centuries later.) Slavery was not unmitigated, and though slaves were sold and hired out, yet they could rise to wealth and power, as in modern times. The ideal of life was *maot*, truth or straightness, most prominently stated by Akhenaten " living in

truth." Lying and deceit were reprehended, and there was a strong belief in
honesty ; whether this was more effective than at present may be doubted. The
modern Egyptian is remarkably honest to his equals, but has no feeling for his
inferiors. We can, however, readily believe in the virtues of the Egyptian, as
they are seen in many races at present—such as the North-American Indian—
who have not much intellectual growth. One judgment of the author seems far
too strong when he writes of "their excessive cruelty." The Egyptian was a
very kind man, to whom the infliction of punishment was distressing, and there
was a great delicacy of feeling about referring to any unpleasant subject (*Ptah-
hetep*, 26 ; *Any*, 63 ; *Ptah-hetep*, 29). The only signs of cruelty are in the treatment of captives ; but then war is war, and there were no tortures beyond the
needful binding of the arms to prevent resistance. The figure of a king clubbing
a group of captives is only an emblem of victory continued from primitive times.

MAYNARD, J. A.—*Were the Phoenicians a Semitic People ?* This is a review
of M. Autran's book, the conclusions of which and their discussion we may briefly
note. The idea is that Egypt and Mesopotamia were not favourable to external
energy, and are not likely to have greatly influenced the world ; the greatness
of their works and their brilliant qualities seem, however, to show that for the
native the climate was not enervating. The Phoenicians are compared to the
Northmen for their activity, and are regarded as having gone south to Palestine.
In the Phoenician area of colonisation there are no Semitic names in Sicily,
and very few in the Aegean. The archaic words in Greek are neither Semitic
nor Egyptian, but probably come from the older Mycenaean. The Greek gods
are of Asianic origin, and a few Phoenician words in Greek authors are not Semitic.
But how about Carthage, the great Phoenician colony, with entirely Semitic
speech ? The primitive name of Karia was Phoinike, but this proves nothing
as it may lead either way. According to M. Autran it was the Karians who were
the fount of civilisation, and settled in Syria. The place names of Syria are
claimed as of Aegean origin. Maynard's conclusion is that there was a large
Aegean element in the Phoenicians, which might be only due to a small ruling
caste like the Franks ruling the Gallo-Romans. Altogether there is a whole
wilderness of theories : Puni from Punt, or from Karia ; the leaders in civilisation, yet without a single distinctive art and merely copying their neighbours ;
autochthonous Semites, or intrusive Philistines from Crete ; everywhere, and
yet leaving remains nowhere ; with a capital, Motya, without anything eastern
and merely inferior Greek work ; with an age-long reputation and nothing to
show for it. Let us hope that serious excavation in Phoenicia, with careful
archaeological discrimination, will clear up some of this confusion.

NOTES AND NEWS.

Capt. Engelbach has been clearing the great obelisk in the Aswan quarry, and finds that it is 133 feet long, which is more than any obelisk that has survived. It was abandoned because of fissures, and there are various plans for dressing it outlined upon it. The official report will give many interesting details.

The French excavations at Edfu have produced a jar full of Coptic documents of the VIIIth century.

Mr. Winlock, for New York, has found at Thebes a batch of letters of the XIth dynasty, as well as the foundation deposits of the XIth dynasty temple at Deir el Bahri.

Mr. Fisher and Mr. Mackay have found a group of demotic contracts at Drah abul Negga. Altogether, with the large quantity of Greek papyri and the earliest Hebrew obtained by the British schools, this may well be called the year of papyri.

At Amarna a palace on the south of the plain at Hawata has been further traced out by the Egypt Exploration Society. There was a stone hall, gardens, with cowsheds and dog kennels ; a lake with buildings about it, strewn with flower beds and tanks. Another clearing was done on the workmen's village, which had long, straight streets like Kahun ; many small things were found, and it was occupied until Tutonkhamen. At Hagg Qandil remains of a temple were found under the village, and this region continued to be occupied down to the XXVIth dynasty. A glass factory was found in the town, and the house of the vizier Nekht proved to be well inscribed, and to show some fresh kinds of decoration.

The remains from Byblos (Jebail) are now in the Louvre. Prof. Sayce states that the vases of the IVth—VIth dynasties were under the floor of the later temple. With them was a small seated figure of early Sumerian work, like a figure on a Tello relief, belonging to the time of Urnina, which is about 3600 B.C. As this is according to the Egyptians about the Xth or XIth dynasty, it might agree with the burial of Old Kingdom objects. The earliest object is a cylinder seal, with Thinite hieroglyphs belonging to a king Khoam, apparently a Babylonian or Amorite, naming Ra and Hathor as lord and lady of Gebal.

The Louvre has also recently obtained, from Cappadocia, at Topola, near Nevshehr (the ancient Soanda), the largest Hittite inscription yet discovered, about 16 feet by 10 feet.

Prof. Newberry's very interesting paper in this number adds a fresh datum to the early history, which will doubtless receive full discussion. The presence of the sealings equally of Sekhem-ab and of Per-ab-sen in the tomb at Abydos, and the absence there of any of Per-ne-maot, has caused the first two names to be looked on as belonging to one king, of whom the name as ruling the Horus people was Per-ne-maot. If Khosekhem is the same person as Khosekhemui, it is strange that there were no seals of officials of Khosekhem in the tomb of Khosekhemui. The problem of the 363 years will have to be studied. There is only a presumption that Mena might have started an epoch, but nothing to identify him with Hor-akhti. But there is a likely source for that name under Den, as *Semti*, the two groups of three hills, might readily be taken in later times to mean *akhti*, the two groups of the sun between two hills. This would closely accord with the dates given by the Egyptians ; Den began in 5383 B.C., so the 363rd year would be 5021 B.C., and this is the last year of Khosekhem who crushed the enemies, supposed to be the Set party.

A suggestion mentioned in ANCIENT EGYPT, 1920, p. 59, that a sphinx on the east bank faced that on the west, seemed worth examination. I therefore walked along the east side from Old Cairo to Ma'adi, searching for any rock line which might have been trimmed into a sphinx. There was only one ridge of rock along this bank, north of Basatin, projecting southward, and this was too wide to have ever been cut as a sphinx. A small settlement of late Roman and Arab times is on the east side of it. There is, then, no ground for the idea of a contra-sphinx.

W. M. F. P.

2. MODERN LOOM IN THE VILLAGE OF MAH

ANCIENT EGYPT.

TEXTS FROM THE HITTITE CAPITAL RELATING TO EGYPT.

THE Berlin Museum has recently published a number of fragmentary texts in cuneiform and the Babylonian language, which were discovered at Boghaz Keui (*Keilschrifturkunden aus Boghazköi*, Part III, 1922 ; copied by Weidner). The most interesting is part of a letter (No. 34) describing the visit of Khismi-sarma, the son of the Hittite king, to Egypt in the time of Rameses II or his immediate successor. The beginning and end are lost. The following is a translation of what remains :—

(1) " To the royal treasury (literally, place of the king) . . . .

(2) two envoys in . . . .

(3) Zidwalla did not have. [They have sent ?]

(4) to me the envoys of the king, and behold I am obedient.

(5) I have given (the money) for the journey of the (Egyptian) envoys ; this I will pay back

(6) to the treasury of the king ; let the royal treasuries pay (it)

(7) for the king's embassy. Now you say to me :

(8) ' Behold, when Khismi-sarma departed,

(9) he departed in the months appointed for departure,

(10) and since during the previous year he . . . ' "

The next two lines are too mutilated for translation.

(13) " Nakhkha (Nekht) of the domain of [the god (?) Was-] mua-Ria-

(14) Satep-na-Ria (User-maot-ra, Setep-ne-ra) in the domain of Amâna (Amon), and his prefect

(15) Lêya (Lui, Levi) of the domain of . . . [of] Ria-masesa = (Ra-messu)

(16) mâi-Amana in the domain of the god ; in all 3 officers ;

(17) and I have given (the money) for their journey to thee

(18) in the case of the envoys when sending the fine presents

(19) which they have taken to you. And they are with Khismi-sarma

(20) together with your envoys who have gone with him.

(21) And the royal envoys are protected by the commander of the cavalry

(22) Nakhkha of the domain of the horses, the officer of the king,

Obv. 1. along with the Hittite ambassador Kulaziti[s]

2. and the Hittite ambassador Zidwalla[s] ;

3. and they have allowed for their journey to you

4. on mission from the Hittite country 14 days which Kulaziti[s]

5. took from here to Egypt (or) 20 days

E

6. which Zidwalli[s] took from here
7. to Egypt as he was late.   This is what
8. they said.   (But) my envoys have taken
9. [so many days to] reach Egypt.
10. The king's ambassadors who were late . . . .
11. and . . . sa . . . za in the Hittite territory [and in Egyp]t
12. protects their road from the Hittite kingdom to assist
13. their journey to Egypt . . . . . month . . .
14. [and] year by year . . . . . .

15. He has given as follows for the journey of the son of the king of the
      Hittites, Khismi-sarma,
16. for the hire of all these ships . . . .
17. at the feet[1], and he has accomplished it according to command very
18. quickly and has manned numerous ships ; all the ships
19. for providing for their journey to Egypt [are ready]
20. to make [the voyage] . . . . . .
      . . . .

By way of supplement to this account of a Hittite embassy, I append a translation of an account of an embassy from Egypt to the Hittites given in the Hittite language by a Hittite king who is probably Mursilis II (*Keilschrifttexte aus Boghazköi*, V, p. 41, 1921).

1. " Now when my father (Subbi-luliuma ?) was in the city of Carchemish
2. then Lupakki and Hadad-zalma
3. into the land of Amka (the plain of Antioch) he sent ; so they went ;
4. the land of Amka they devastated ; the spoil of oxen and sheep back to
      my father
. they brought.   Afterwards the Egyptians of the overthrow of Amka
6. heard : they were terrified.
7. Then their ruler, namely Bib-khuru-riyas (Neb-khepru-ra)
8. just at that moment died ; now the queen of Egypt was Dakhamun . . ;
9. she sent an ambassador to my father :
10. she said thus to him : ' My husband is dead ;
11. I have no children ; your sons
12. are [said] to be grown up ; if to me
13. one of your sons you give, and if he will be my husband,
14. he will be a help ; send him accordingly
15. and thereafter I will make him my husband.   I send bridal gifts ' (?)
16. After my father had heard this
17. he summoned certain Hittites
[The next two lines and a half are destroyed.]
20. . . . . [to] Egypt
21. a secretary [. . . . by name], he despatched
22. enjoining (him) : ' A true report do you bring back,
23. why she has written the letter to me (and) as to the son of their ruler
24. what is become of him ; so to me a true
25. report do you bring back.'

---

[1] This is the literal translation.   What the idiom signifies is unknown to me.

26. When the secretary had returned from Egypt—
27. it was after this that my father captured the city of Carchemish ;
28. he had besieged it for 7 days
29. and on the 8th day he delivered battle one day
30. and then [he stormed ?] it on the 8th
31. and [9th] days . . .   and thereafter
32. captured the city . . . . .

44. An ambassador of the city (*sic*) of Egypt (Mizri), Khanis,
45. came to him from its ruler, and my father in return a secretary
46. sent to the land of Egypt who should thus
47. address him as head of the mission : ' The son of their lord
48. where is he ? me
49. she has deceived (?) ; my son to the kingship the general of the army
50. has not promoted.' To my father
51. the queen of Egypt thereupon thus
52. wrote back : ' What is this you say ?
53. ' She has deceived (?) me.' I, if
54. I had a son and if I my
55. [people] and my country . . . . ·
56. to another country I would have written.
57. But no one has had seed by me.
58. And now you say this to me : ' There is my
59. husband ' ; but he is dead ;
60. I have no son ; so I have taken a servant . . .
61. and to another country in this manner
62. I have not written : to you, however, I have written ; your sons
63. are said to be grown up ; so to me one
64. of your sons give, and he as my husband
65. in the land of Egypt shall be king.'
66. So my father was on his knees,
67. and then the lady soon fulfilled (her) words
68. and selected one of the sons."

The last line is written in Assyrian with the exception of one word—*ša mari kittan* (= Ass. *šapal*) *izbat*, literally " under the sons she took," which I suppose was a Hittite idiom signifying selection.

Bib-khuru-riyas must be Tut-onkh-amen Neb-kheperu-ra. But who was Da-kh-Amun . . .? The latter part of the name is illegible : the queen of Tut-onkh-amen was Onkh-s-pa-aten, altered to Oukh-s-amen. A form Ta-onkh-s-amen might yield Da-kh-amen.

The Hittite ambassador Kulazitis is mentioned in another fragmentary letter (*Keilschrifturkunden*, III, No. 67), from which we learn that the writer of No. 34 was probably an Egyptian doctor, Pa-Ria-ma-khû [Pa-ra-am-ăkhet] by name, who was resident in Asia Minor. Egyptian doctors were celebrated for their knowledge and skill, and were consequently in request in the civilised world of the ancient East. The fragment is as follows :—

(1) " . . . . . from here to the land of Egypt
(2) . . .   you have sent, and according to what I have sent

E 2

(3) . . . the presents which you have given to be taken
(4) [by] the hand of Kulaziti they have taken ; these presents
(5) which you have given to be taken by his hand
(6) you did not give your mind to (their) following after him.

---

(7) Thus now I summon the doctor who has written.[1]

---

(8) Pa-Ria-ma-hkû has carried out his journey to prepare[2]
(9) herbs for Kurunta the king of Tarkhuntas,[3] and he
(10) was in need of all kinds of medical plants until I sent (them) ;
(11) and when he will come to you and I recommend him
(12) to Kurunta the king of Tarkhuntas to prepare the herbs for him ;—
(13) and I summoned these two doctors who are with him ;
(14) and do you give (money) for their journey to Egypt ;—
(15) when the doctor Pa-Ria-ma-khû who has written shall reach him,
(16) day or night let them not detain [him] . . . . .

.   .   .   .

Keilschrifturkunden, III, 30, No. 66 :—
  1. " Thus *inśibya nib tawi* (the king of Upper and Lower Egypt, lord of
      the two lands), Was-mua-Ria. (User-maot-ra)
  2. Satep-na-Ria, son of the Sun-god, Ria-masesa-mai-Amana ;
  3. [Salutation ? of] the king of the land to the brother of the god Khâra
      whom Hadad loves.

---

  4. [To] Pudu-Khebe the great queen, the queen of the Hittites, he says :

---

  5. [Now] to the king there is peace ; to my houses there is peace ;
  6. [to the] queens there is peace ; to the royal children there is peace ;
  7. [to] my soldiers there is peace ; to my horses there is peace ;
  8. to [my] chariots there is peace ; and within all my lands
  9. may there be peace exceedingly !

---

 10. To thee the great [queen], the queen of the Hittites, may there be peace !
 11. To thy house may there be peace ; to thy children may there be peace ;
 12. to thy men may there be peace ; and within all thy lands
 13. may there be peace exceedingly !

---

 14. Thus now . . . . Ria-nakhta the royal ambassador
 15. along with the envoy[s ?] . . . [with] Biqasti have departed."

.   .   .   .

---

[1] Or " I, the doctor who has written, declare." The very faulty Assyrian in which the
letter is written, makes either translation possible ; but see line (13), where the same verb
is used.
[2] Literally " make."
[3] Tarkhuntas or Tarkhundas was in the neighbourhood of the later Kataonia.

The first line gives us the pronunciation of the Egyptian royal title, as well as that of the names of Ramses II; it may be added that it does not favour the Berlin system of transliteration. *Was-Mua* corresponds to ⌐∩⸝. Biqasti or Biqasta is mentioned in another letter from Ramses II to the Hittite king (*Keilschrifturkunden*, III, No. 69), where we read: " Now I have ordered (literally given) Biqasta to speak all the words which you (fem. !) have told him with his mouth in the presence of the king ; he has taken care (lit. given) that my sons should hear them all as the queen has enjoined. Behold ! these words which Biqasta has reported, what is the offence which I have committed against my brother ? And what is the offence which I have now committed against you (fem.) ? But the daughter [of the king] has declared : you have committed it ! I am safe and sound, and a brother of the king of the Hittites."

The use of the feminine in this fragment would indicate that this letter also was addressed to queen Pudu-khebe as well as to the Hittite king.

Keilschrifturkunden, III, No. 70 :—

 1. [Thus] Suta-khab-sadu (Set-heb-sed ?)
 2. [the . . .] of the great king, the king of Egypt.

---

 3. [To] Khattusili the great king
 4. [the king] of the Hittites he says :

---

 5. [To] you the great king, the king of the Hittites,
 6. O my [father], may there be peace, and to
 7. your [son]s may there [be peace], &c.
 9. . . . . the king of Egypt
 10. thy brother is well.

---

 11. Now the great king, the king of the Hittites, my father,
 12. has sent to me to enquire after
 13. the health of his son, and I
 14. am exceedingly pleased,
 15. since my father has sent to me
 16. to enquire after (his) health.

---

 17. The Sun-god and Hadad enquire after the health
 18. of the great king, the king of the Hittites, my father,
 19. and bestow the good fortune
 20. of health and the brotherhood of the great king,
 21. the king of Egypt, with the great king,
 22. the king of the Hittites, his brother, for ever and ever.

---

 23. And they give length of
 24. years to the great king, the king of Egypt,
 25. as well as years to Khattusili,
 26. the great king, the king of the Hittites, his brother.

---

27. And they (*i.e.* the kings) continue well in
28. splendid health, and they are brothers
29. in splendid brotherhood for ever and ever.

---

30. Now I have sent a present to my father
31. as a peace-offering (= birth-day gift) to my father
32. by the hand of Pa-rikh-nâwi [Pa-ari-khenu].

---

33. . . . . of the best gold, a lot of threads (?)
34. . . . . a full-grown ox with horns of white stone
35. a . . . . with horns of black stone . . . .
36. . . . . 3 shekels of the best gold.

The remaining list of presents is not sufficiently preserved for translation. The mutilated condition of the earlier part of text makes the relationship of the writer, who bears an Egyptian name, difficult to determine.

A. H. SAYCE.

[The astonishing letter of Dakhamen raises the question of the end of the Akhenaten family of daughters. So far as the data now go, they are exactly in accord with my *Tell el-Amarna* of 1894, and they give the following dates (and ages) :—

	Born.	Married.	Died.
Akhenaten	1395	(at 16) 1379	(30) 1365
Tadukhipa Nefertyti ..	about 1395	(16) 1379	
Nezem-mut, her sister ..	.. 1385	(53) 1332	
1. Mert-aten, mar. Smenkh-ka-ra ..	1377	(12) 1365	
2. Makt-aten	1375	not	before (10) 1365
3. Onkh-s-pa-aten (Dakhamen ?) ..	1373	by (20) 1353	alive (29) 1344
4. Nefer-neferu-aten	1371	mar. son of Burnaburiash	
5. Nefer-neferu-ra	1369 ⎱ disregarded in ⎰ (25)		
6. Setep-ne-ra	1367 ⎰ 1344 ⎱ (23)		

Tadukhipa was still alive long after the death of Amenhetep III, as four successive letters (IX to XII) were written from Mitanni referring to her ; and Nefertyti is associated with Amenhetep IV before abandoning Amen, so there is no reason to suppose that she is not the same as Tadukhipa. Nezem-mut, her sister, appears but little older than Mert-aten ; she was married at about 53 to Heremheb to legalize his position. Mert-aten was wife of Smenkhkara, after whose death she vanishes. Makt-aten was buried in her father's tomb, before him. A daughter was married to the son of Burnaburiash of Babylonia, and the fourth is the eldest possible. Of the last two there is no trace. They would be 25 and 23 at the death of Tut-onkh-amen ; probably married to some foreigner, who could not accede in Egypt.

Then we find the widow of Tut-onkh-amen (" living image of Amen ") named Onkh-s-amen, modified to Ta-onkh-ne-amen (" the life of Amen "), or Dakhamen, who was then 29, appealing to the Hittite king for a son of his to marry her and be king of Egypt. As her successors Ay and Ty were not of immediate royal descent, Ty being only nurse, this shows that Dakhamen was not unreasonable in wishing to imitate the earlier alliances of the Egyptian royalties with the Northern powers.—W. M. F. P.]

• HEDDLE-JACKS OF MIDDLE KINGDOM LOOMS.

IN ANCIENT EGYPT, 1921, page 97, there is an article by H. Ling Roth and G. M. Crowfoot on the model of spinners and weavers found by the Metropolitan Museum Egyptian Expedition in the tomb of Mehenkwetre' at Thebes. Toward the end of her remarks Mrs. Crowfoot notes that in the model " one very essential part of the Sudani loom is missing, the heddle-rod supports," and then makes the suggestion that " the curious wooden implements lying on either side of the (model) loom were used for this purpose," only to discard the idea because these objects seem to her " much more like tools used in the hand to adjust something." As no explanation along this line occurs to her, she finally republishes " a drawing of originals of similar implements from the University College collection in the hope of finding a solution."

It chances that independently of Mrs. Crowfoot I had arrived at the very solution which she discards, and believe that I have found ample confirmation of its correctness on the monuments and in the originals at University College (Fig. 1), and in still another original in the Cairo Museum shown to me by Mr. Quibell. Since the subject has been opened it seems worth while to clear up this one point in anticipation of any fuller discussion of these model looms.

The originals are wooden cylinders about a foot high, with a rounded, spoon-like, head above a notch in one side. In the model from the tomb of Mehenkwetre' (Fig. 2 and the photographs in ANCIENT EGYPT, 1921, frontispiece and p. 99) ; in another model in Cairo found by Quibell at Sakkara, and in the paintings from the tombs of Bakt. and Khety at Beni Hasan (Fig. 2), these objects are to be seen lying on the floor on either side of the loom not far from the ends of the heddle-rod. In all these cases the heddle-rod is lowered to form the counter-shed, but to form the shed (for the return of the shuttle through the warp) some appliance must be provided for raising the heddle-rod and the alternate warp threads leashed to it. In the fixed-heddle loom, which is still used across North Africa, up the Nile Basin and out to Madagascar, the heddle-rod is either suspended from an overhead frame, or is jacked up on supports such as those described by Mrs. Crowfoot from the Sudan, stones, baked clay pillars, Y-shaped sticks, or even a couple of pots. (See H. Ling Roth, *Royal Anthropological Society Journal*, 1917, Figs. 80 and 89A, and *Ancient Egyptian and Greek Looms, Bankfield Museum Notes*, 1913, Fig. 12). Since there was no overhead frame from which to suspend the heddle of the Middle Kingdom horizontal looms, some similar jacking support for the heddle-rod was absolutely necessary, and being an indispensable part of the contrivance, it must be shown in the models and the wall paintings. The short wooden cylinders lying at either end of the heddle-rods are the only objects invariably shown in the representations of these looms which could be put to this use, and I therefore feel that there should be no hesitation in calling them the heddle-rod jacks.

However, there is one essential difference between these jacks and the supports for the heddle-rods of the modern African looms already cited. The latter have heddle-rods permanently supported or fixed. Had the heddle-rods of the Middle Kingdom looms been fixed on the jacks, they would be so represented ; but, as a matter of fact, in most cases the rods are drawn or modelled as slacked down with the jacks lying prone beside them. This must be taken as a characteristic position in weaving, and the conclusion drawn that the Middle Kingdom loom had a movable heddle, which was not continuously jacked up.

To put these theories to a test, there seemed to me to be no more practical method than to make a working model of a loom, about 1 foot long (Fig. 2). As shown in the sketch, it is a perfectly practical machine. With the jacks removed from under the heddle-rod—as in the Mehenkwetre'.model and in the Bakt and Khety pictures—the counter-shed is formed, and the shuttle is passed from right to left. The heddle-rod is then raised by hand, first at one end and then at the other, and the jacks inserted. Evidently it is this operation of raising the heddle which is shown in the Khnum-hotep picture, and the sadly damaged Daga picture apparently shows the heddle supported on the jacks. The shed is now formed, and the shuttle given the return shot from left to right. The jacks are then knocked out, the counter-shed again formed, and the shuttle again shot, and so on.

The heddle-jacks thus have to be set up and knocked down for every two shots of the shuttle—a process which seems extremely laborious on the face of it, but which life-long practice probably made a lighter task for a skilful pair of ancient weavers than we should find it. Moreover, the jacks themselves are contrived to simplify the process as much as possible. The spoon-shaped top is expressly contrived to slip under the end of the rod when it lies close to the floor ; the rod end then slides into the notch ; a quick jerk is given, and the jack sits upright, firmly held on its broad base by the tension of the warp threads. To lower the heddle-rod a smart blow on either jack brings down the whole affair. A pair of tall, slender jacks with narrow waists, in University College (Fig. 1) seems to be designed to be pulled or knocked out by hand ; but the stouter ones in that collection, and the one in Cairo, show deep battering on the sides and marked rounding on the bottom, from long use in looms where the tension of the warp was so great that heavy blows were necessary to tip the jacks over on the earthen floors. This indeed seems to have been the usual thing, for in all three Beni Hasan pictures, and in the Mehenkwetre' model, the assistant weaver (the one who wields the beater-in) holds a stone in her hand to knock her jack down.

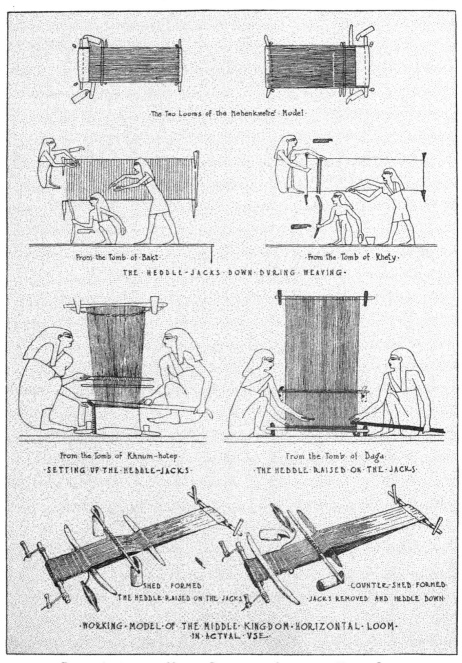

The Two Looms of the Nebenkwetref Model.

From the Tomb of Bakt.

From the Tomb of Khety.

THE HEDDLE-JACKS DOWN DURING WEAVING.

From the Tomb of Khnum-hotep.

SETTING UP THE HEDDLE-JACKS.

From the Tomb of Daga.

THE HEDDLE RAISED ON THE JACKS.

SHED FORMED
THE HEDDLE RAISED ON THE JACKS.

COUNTER-SHED FORMED
JACKS REMOVED AND HEDDLE DOWN.

WORKING MODEL OF THE MIDDLE KINGDOM HORIZONTAL LOOM.
IN ACTUAL USE.

FIG. 2. ANCIENT AND MODERN DRAWINGS OF LOOMS WITH HEDDLE-JACKS.

Whether or not there exists to-day a loom working on exactly this principle, I cannot say. However, the fixed-heddle loom of Libya and the Sudan—the zone of ancient Egypt's influence—appears to me to be the direct descendant of this Middle Kingdom loom. The jacks are now fixed, except when the fabric advances or is rolled up on the breast-beam, and the counter-shed is made by a complicated but rapid manipulation of shed-sticks, which is less laborious than handling the jacks. But the jacks remain, and the machine is that of the Middle Kingdom, except that it is operated in a slightly different way.

The available illustrations of Middle Kingdom looms are far from satisfactory. Only a very few tombs have preserved weaving scenes, and these are in bad preservation ; and they have been copied with scanty knowledge of the working of looms, and have rarely been reproduced in facsimile. In default of really intelligible copies of the Khnum-hotep weavers, Ling Roth (*Ancient Egyptian and Greek Looms*) has reproduced for comparison the copies by Cailliaud, Wilkinson, Rosellini, Lepsius, Newberry and an original drawing by N. de G. Davies. I have attempted to make a freehand composite sketch interpreting Davies' most recent copy from the older ones by Cailliaud (*Recherches sur les Arts et Métiers*), Rosellini (*Mon. civ.*, pl. xli) and Champollion (*Mons.*, pl. ccclxxxi bis). The Daga weavers are published only by Davies (*Five Theban Tombs*, pl. xxxvii), and are here redrawn with restorations none of which are important except the heddle-jacks, which I believe I can .ecognize in his copy. The weavers from the tomb of Baḳt are illustrated by Newberry (*Beni Hasan*, II, pl. iv) at a most inadequate scale—here enlarged freehand—while those from Khety are redrawn from Rosellini (pl. xli) and Champollion (pl. ccclxvi), with the jacks taken from Newberry (pl. xiii). Until fresh copies can be made from the monuments in the light of new technical knowledge, the student is warned to look upon these illustrations as makeshifts at the best. The diagrams of the Mehenkwetre' looms are from an illustration prepared by Mr. L. F. Hall for a future publication of the models by the Metropolitan Museum, and those of the working model are from a loom I have made and worked myself.

H. E. WINLOCK.

LOOM WEIGHTS IN EGYPT.

MR. WINLOCK'S discovery of a model weaving shop in the XIth dynasty tomb of Mehenkwetre' at Thebes has caused a great revival of interest in the subject of ancient Egyptian looms.[1]   Those in the model are horizontal ones, and so far bear out the evidence of tomb paintings that the looms of the Middle Kingdom were horizontal, and those of the Empire vertical.   In a country like Egypt, however, in which all artistic expression was bounded and restricted by convention, it is dangerous to generalise from the evidence of tomb models and paintings alone, and it is by no means safe to assume that vertical looms were unknown in the Middle Kingdom, or, as Mr. Ling Roth inclines to do,[2] that in the Empire they replaced horizontal looms as a result of Asiatic influence.   The simple form of loom represented in the model and in the tomb paintings could be used with equal facility in either position, and it would be more natural to suppose that under some circumstances a vertical adjustment would be found more practicable.   That is as may be.   In any case it is quite certain that the conventionalised tomb paintings are very far from giving us a complete picture of the knowledge of weaving that the artist must have had, for in none of them is there any suggestion of a weighted loom, and weighted looms the Egyptians certainly had.

Egyptologists have been strangely diffident about the loom weights that have been found in Egypt ; almost apologetic, as though the weights were objects that had no right to be there, and were for that reason to be ignored or explained away.[3] Why should we take up this attitude ?   We are all of us much too ready to assume that what we do not know cannot exist, and to affix a " foreign importation " label to anything that we do not much like the look of.   As a matter of fact, warp weights are by no means uncommon in Egypt.   I find them by the dozen in the ancient town of Lisht (Empire Period)—of mud, like the Kahun example, and also of stone— and there is no possible reason for doubt that they are Egyptian articles.   Samples of both types are shown in Fig. 1.

I. MUD AND STONE LOOM WEIGHTS, LISHT.

[1] See *Metropolitan Museum Bulletin*, December, 1920, Part II ; and the articles in ANCIENT EGYPT, 1921, IV, by Ling Roth and Crowfoot.

[2] " Studies in Primitive Looms," *R.A.I. Journal*, XLVIII, p. 141.

[3] As an example we may quote the mud warp weight from Kahun in the Manchester University Museum, which Dr. Hall decided " was probably found in the ruins of houses where Aegean pottery was found," and hence was " probably a temporary warp weight of these people, and not an Egyptian article." (Ling Roth, " Ancient Egyptian and Greek Looms," p. 17.)

The Egyptians must then have used weighted looms. The question is, what form did these looms take ? The most natural supposition would be that they belonged to the so-called ' Greek'" type, an upright loom with a single beam, the place of the second beam being taken by a series of hanging weights. There is another way, however, in which weights can be used, and one more easily adapted to the ordinary Egyptian two-beam looms. This is in Fig. 2 (frontispiece), which represents a loom in use to-day in the village of Maharraqa, close to the southern Lisht pyramid. It is a pit treadle loom, in which the warp threads, instead of being attached to the warp beam, are carried under a roller, then diagonally upwards to another roller, over which they are bunched and kept taut by means of heavy stone weights. The same principle is adopted in Syrian looms, but with a difference, the bunched warp threads in this case being carried back and suspended over the head of the weaver (see diagram in Ling Roth's *Ancient Egyptian and Greek Looms*, p. 39).

Now this is a much more practical form of loom than the upright " Greek " variety, and, as we said before, one much more likely to be adapted to the existing Egyptian type. The system of suspension weights would apply equally well to a simple form of loom, such as the ancient one must have been, and I think it more than likely that the weights which turn up in our excavations were so used. Indeed, it is quite possible that the modern loom is but a development from a form that has persisted in the district since ancient times. Such survivals are common enough, as every digger knows, and the excavation of the ancient town site of Lisht has furnished us with a number of other very striking examples.

A. C. MACE.

ON THE MEANING OF ⬡⬡.

IT has been assumed that the sign ⧖ in the group ⬡⬡, which occurs on several first dynasty objects (*R.T.* II, Pl. II, pp. 8–11), represents the *nebti* name of an early king. It seems more likely, however, that it is the archaic form of a queen's title, meaning consort (Sethe, *Beiträge* I, p. 32 ; Griffith in *R.T.* II, p. 48). Examples of this title are found in the titulary of queens in the Old Kingdom (Mariette, *Mastaba* 183, 225 ; De Rougé, *Inscriptions Hiéroglyphiques*, Pl. LXII and LXXVII) ; in the Middle Kingdom (De Rougé, *Inscriptions Hiéroglyphiques*, Pl. LXXV, *Tanis* II, Pl. XI, p. 171), and in the XVIIIth dynasty in that of Queen Aahmes (*Deir el-Bahri* II, Pl. XLVIII and XLIX).

In the Old Kingdom examples the word " consort " is written ⧖ ⬠ ⌣, whilst from the Middle Kingdom onwards the *w* is replaced by ⫴, in accordance with phonetic usage. It generally occurs in combination with the Horus title of the King, when it reads " consort of Horus." It may form part of a longer title, reading " companion (*Smert*) and consort of Horus." In the titulary of Queen Nefert (*Tanis* II, Pl. XI, p. 17), the word " consort " is combined with the vulture and uræus.

The writing of the word " consort " by the word sign only would be quite in keeping with ancient usage regarding the orthography of titles. The presence of the group ⬡⬡ after the name Neit-hotep on an ivory lid which was found at Abydos (*R.T.* II, Pl. II, p. 11) is strong evidence in support of the reading consort, as Neit-hotep was a queen. The two basket signs would then read *Nebti*, " the two goddesses," or Nebui, " the two lords." The latter reading is corroborated by two parallel phrases in the Pyramid of Unas, lines 38 and 39 (⫴ ⬚ ⬚ ~~~ ⬡ ⬡ ...... ⬚ ~~~ ⬚ " he has satisfied for thee the two lords, the two goddesses are satisfied with thee "). If this be the correct reading, " the two lords " would mean Horus and Set, and the two baskets be a variant of ⬚ ⬚ or of ⬚ ⬚ (*R.T.* I, Pl. V, 12 ; Pl. VI, 4, 8), and represent a King's title like the synonym ⬚ ⬚ (*R.T.* II, Pl. XXIII 191–200).

The reading " the two lords " gains further support from another Old Kingdom title of queens : ⬚ ⬚ ⬚ ⬚ " She who sees Horus and Set " (De Rougé, *Monuments . . . aux six premières dynasties*, p. 45), which appears to go back to the 1st dynasty (*R.T.* II, Pl. XXVII, 96, 128, 129, Sethe in *Mahâsna*, p. 23, and *Beiträge* I, p. 29, note 8).

The antiquity and persistence of a queen's title would not be surprising, since N. Maat. Hap, an early dynasty queen, bore the title ⬚ ⬚ ⬚ ⬚ ⬚ " She who says anything, it is done for her " (*R.T.* II, Pl. XXIV, 210, *Mahâsna*, Pl. X, 7), and this epithet occurs also in a later form (⬚ ⬚ ⬚ ⬚ ⬚ ⬚ ⬚ ⬚) in the titulary of Queen Aahmes (Deir el Bahri II, Pl. XLIX), and of Queen Mut-em-Uya, the consort of Thothmes IV (B.M., Registration No. 43, Exhibition No. 380).

L. B. ELLIS.

REVIEWS.

———•———

The Life and Times of Akhnaton. By ARTHUR WEIGALL. 1922. New and revised edition. 255 pp., 8vo. 12s. 6d. (Butterworth.)

Mr. Weigall has taken the place of an apostle of Atenism with much success. A preface describes the actual detail of work connected with the discovery of the king's burial. The conclusion is that the tomb in the valley of the kings was originally made for Queen Tyi ; that she was buried there ; that on the court abandoning Amarna, the body of Akhenaten was removed from his tomb in the desert there, and reburied in Tyi's tomb at Thebes. Later, when his memory was attacked by the priesthood, they removed Tyi from the tomb to bury her elsewhere, and left Akhenaten with his funeral furniture, including the alabaster canopic jars. Then in 1906 the tomb was discovered, with the sides of the great wooden funeral shrine of Tyi standing in the front of the chamber. Unhappily those who were responsible for managing the work (all now dead) ignored the means of preservation, and let this magnificent carving covered with gold foil go to pieces. The king's coffin, farther in, was better treated, and is now in good state in the Cairo Museum. The skull of the king, photographed in this volume, is set sloping backward ; it should be placed 10° more upright, for the true plane (of ear and base of eye) to be horizontal. This tilt gives a false idea of prognathism, and is a fault often seen in publishing skulls. When the true vertical outline is placed round this photograph, the drooping jaw of the sculptures is very marked. On comparing the skull with a normal form, the droop is seen to be due to the short distance between the ear and the plane of the face.

The work is divided into chapters dealing with the parentage of Akhenaten ; his birth and early years and the influences bearing on him ; his foundation of a new city ; his formulation of the religion ; the middle period of his reign ; the later period ; and the last years, ending with tracing the fall of his ideals. The translations give ground for much interpretation and application, with guesses and suppositions more or less likely, but within reach of a passable amount of imagination, needful to impress the self-satisfied British mind.

There are some matters which need more consideration. The ages of kings at their death are not quite so exactly fixed by the bones ; the family histories must also be taken into account, and probably Amenhetep III was 16 at his marriage, so that he could not be said to be " not yet in his 'teens," as on p. 27. In general, the ages of marriage are put needlessly early, unlike those in other periods. On p. 13 Ptah is assumed to be a dwarf god at Memphis, but he was of full height, and only a foreign form was dwarf, as a mixture with other deities.

Though mentioning the work done at Amarna in 1892, the author does not seem to know the publication of it in 1894, as he says that in 1910 " I was alone in my belief that Akhenaten was only thirty years of age at his death." That dating was fully stated as the basis of the chronology of his reign in 1894. Nor does he seem aware of the quantity of objects left by the successors of Akhenaten at Amarna, which contradict the shortening of the time between Akhenaten and Heremheb, for which there is no evidence in writing. Nor is there any hint of the fact that the artistic, ethical and religious revolution was fully described in 1894 from the archæological evidence only. The last thirty years has not altered, and has scarcely added to, the account of the history : in only one small detail is there any change to make in the long account of that period stated before the subject came into fashion. Later writing can only amplify that, by quoting texts which were not available earlier. The idea that Nefertyti was a daughter of Ay seems precluded by any hint of that relation when he describes her in his own tomb ; nor can the supposed title of " royal father-in-law " be accepted. Besides a few misprints, there is a slip on p. 64 describing an ivory figure as from Diospolis ; it is from Ballas, as described where it is published in *Prehistoric Egypt.* The only heart-scarab formula might be quoted, as a break with the past, from the scarab at University College, and another heart scarab of Akhenaten with a silver plate is in that collection ; there is also the Maudslay scarab with a gold plate. The last addition to the subject only appears in the present number of this *Journal,* the attempt of Onkhsenamen to bring a Hittite in as king of Egypt after Tutonkhamen's death. The various matters named here are but subordinate to the fluent and attractive account of the most extraordinary growth of ideas that is known in any decade of the world's history.

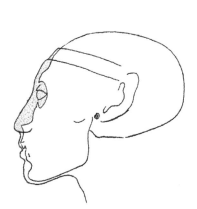 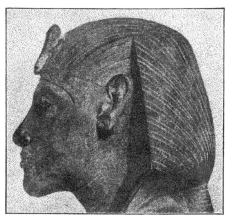

[We append here the authorities that we have for the portraiture of Akhenaten. The outer line on the left is the profile of the plaster death-mask, slightly worn on the lower part of the nose. The inner line is traced from the outline of the skull, described by Mr. Weigall. The portrait on the right is the best sculpture that we have of the king, from his alabaster statuette in the Louvre. The identity of the three is remarkably exact ; with a stereoscope the outlines and sculpture can be combined. This result conclusively settles the sources of the skull and the death-mask.—F. P.]

Les Frises d'objets des Sarcophages du Moyen Empire. By GUSTAVE JEQUIER.
4to, 363 pp. 857 figs. 1921. (Mem. Inst. Français d'Arch. Orientale, Cairo.)
85 frs.

This is a great work of archaeological research, which will long be a standard
of reference. The subject of the figures of objects represented on the interior of
coffins, as a substitute for models, or for the actual objects, has long been a
fascination, for the beauty of the drawings and the details. It was worthily
recorded by M. Lacau some years ago in his Cairo Catalogue of the Middle
Kingdom Sarcophagi, and he gave separate drawings of the objects classified.
Now M. Jequier has far exceeded that, and has taken the subject as a text, to be
discussed and illustrated by reference to the actual objects where such are known.
This is, in fact, a *corpus* of the archaeology of daily life.

The material is classified under Costume, Jewellery, Toilet, Sticks and Sceptres,
Weapons, Furniture, Food, Purification and Ritual. There is at the end a complete index of all the hieroglyphic words. Thus it is easy to find the way through
the mass of detail. The minute distinctions between different signs and varieties
are carefully observed and described. A few details may be here noted.

P. 32. The varieties of cloth are discussed, and twenty-four different names
are quoted. Some are from colours, as green and white ; others from places, ·
as Hermonthis and Hierakonpolis.

P. 49. The single large bead on the neck should be noted as the name-
bead which identified the wearer. (*Amulets*, No. 77.)

P. 50 and elsewhere the drop-shaped beads are never strung in line until the
XVIIIth dynasty.

P. 81. The sistrum was, in the XIIth dynasty, already furnished with
discs to rattle on a cross-bar, as at Beni Hasan.

P. 86. The *sma* sign appears distinctly human in the earliest representations,
applied to the union of king and queen (*R.T.* II, ii, 8–10), but it was afterwards
bowdlerised.

P. 120. It is difficult to accept Fig. 324 as a serviette. It seems to be
clearly a dress, with fringes on the neck, arms and legs. (*Riqqeh*, xxiii.)

P. 122. The identification of *suab* as soap is notable, also the cake of soap
on the washstand of Debhen in the IVth dynasty (L. D. II, xxxvi). The word
" that which cleans " seems obviously the origin of *sapo ;* yet the difficulty is
that the Romans attributed the invention of soap to the Gauls (Pliny, *N.H.*,
xxviii, 51), and Aretas states that the Greeks obtained it from the Romans.
Athenaeus (ix, 77) only refers to *smēma* for washing hands, and also to scented
earth, used as an absorbent. It may be that the name *suab* referred to crude
carbonate of soda used in Egypt for cleansing, and was transferred later to the
true soap of soda and fat, which was of European origin.

P. 141. The seven sacred unguents are fully discussed. The various types
of vases are figured, open-mouthed for stiff grease, and narrow-necked for oils.
The meaning of the names is discussed at length, but not much can be fixed
with certainty. The basis of several of the unguents was *men*, considered to be
a fat which took up the scents, with which it was mixed, much as oil of roses is
absorbed at present. The general use of this leads us to associate it with the
unguent which was the commonest in Egypt, equally in the prehistoric age, the
Ist and the XVIIIth dynasty, and which is believed to be palm oil brought from
the West Coast. The *hati ash* or " essence of pine " suggests that there was some

mode of distillation to separate turpentine or cedar oil. The latter easily separates, and condenses at ordinary temperatures, so that some simple heating and chilling would separate it readily. The free use of cedar oil for embalming shows that it was easily obtained. The *hati ent Tehenu* strongly suggests olive oil, from the " olive land " (ANCIENT EGYPT, 1915, p. 97) ; this must have been an oil very familiar to the Egyptian, from Libya and Crete, and would be almost certain to be used. Various other unguents and perfumes are also described from the early lists. The various eye-paints are mentioned.

P. 159. The variety of staffs are discriminated, the straight for walking, those curved below, the thinner staff of dignity, the forked staff, the crook of princely rule, the *mokes* like a disc-headed mace with a blade rising out of it carried by kings, lastly the divine sceptre of the *uas* or *zam*.

P. 181. The *oba* or *kherp* sceptre is described, but without referring its use to the head of a clan (ANCIENT EGYPT, 1921, p. 86). The *nehbet* was rather similar but rounded at the end. The flail was specially a divine emblem.

P. 203. The distinction of the disc and pear-shaped maces, as belonging to the first and second prehistoric age should have been noted. It must always be remembered that various objects remained in ceremonial use, long after they had disappeared from daily life. The disc mace, the harpoon, the dress below the breast with shoulder straps, were all fictitious survivals, like the Speaker's mace, the barrister's wig, or girls' college-gowns.

P. 296. The fans used by cooks, as at present in Egypt, to blow the charcoal fire, are represented ; it might be added that the models in copper are found in tombs of the VIth dynasty (*Diospolis*, XXV). The list of nine kinds of grain, and as many of fruit, is given in connection with the granaries.

P. 329. The object used in writing the name of Neit is not explained ; the proposal that it represents two bows in a case seems the most likely. The object termed a rammer is too short and wide for that purpose, and it evidently has something put over it, perhaps it is the wig stand. The object named perches (Fig. 848) seems to be a vertical rod, with two short pieces forming a triangle on one side, and a white disc halfway up (*Riqqeh*, xxiii). Looking at the way the Egyptian put guide-lines on his work, with a triangle on one side to mark that the measure was to the opposite edge (L. D. II, 1e ; *Medum*, viii), these seem to be survey posts for marking out ground, with the triangle to show that the opposite edge was the true line. The white discs might be for levelling marks. In such subjects there will long be fresh explanations to be considered, as many enigmas are before us. This fine classification of the objects of daily life will be an indispensable text book for this side of archaeology, useful for training students, and as a basis for fresh researches.

PERIODICALS.

———+———

Archives Suisses d'Anthropologie, 1919.

NAVILLE, E.—*Stèle funéraire du Musée de Bâle.* This is a round-topped stele, with a recess containing a mummiform figure of Să-setet, born of Săt-khati-ur. He appears to have been a grandson of Senusert I, whose figure is in a recess by the figure of Să-satet. See also the next stele.

Melanges de la Société Auxiliaire du Musée, Genève, 1922.

NAVILLE, E.—*Une stèle funéraire Égyptienne.* This stele was dedicated by Să-setet in the nineteenth year of Senusert III. It bears figures of Ameny, born of Săt-ameny, and his mother, Săt-ameny, born of Săt-sebek. This was the father of Să-setet, whose mother was Săt-khati-ur; also of twelve other members of the family. From the dates it seems most likely that he was a great-grandson of Senusert I, whom he claims as his ancestor. There is another stele of Să-setet dated in the first year of Amenemhet III (Louvre).

Annales du Service des Antiquités, XXI.

DARESSY, G.—*Sur une série de personnages mythologiques.* This is a series of hunters (?) of Mut, represented by partly animal figures. The word 𓂋 rendered " piqueur," seems difficult to define in its relation to the goddess ; it is read as *sheser.* The versions are on a lintel in Cairo Museum, on a slab from Sakha, and in one of the top chambers of Dendereh. The figures are (1) like Bes, holding two knives, or with the head of a crocodile. (2) Two bull-headed gods, joining hands. (3) Lion-headed god, standing on a serpent, or holding two knives. (4) Two lion-headed gods joining hands; or jackal monkey-headed gods. (5) Long serpent on which are four gods ; first human-headed, second jackal-headed, third disc-head, fourth hare-headed ; or two bull-headed gods joining hands, and a god holding a serpent. (6) Serpent with two pairs of wings, on which are two hare-headed gods, or bull-headed gods. (7) A Set-headed god, grasping a long serpent, on which is a similar god. The smaller variations and details should be studied in the plate if the foregoing outline leads to further comparisons. The resemblance to the Gnostic material is evident.

DARESSY, G.—*Le Dieu Hérôn sur les Monnaies du nome Diospolite.* In the Fayum several monuments show figures of the Thracian god Heron, which are similar to a figure on horseback on coins of the great Diospolis, or Thebes. There was Cohors ii Thracum at Thebes, about 200 A.D., and Cohors i Thracum at Hammamat, about 100 A.D., which may easily have been at Thebes.

GAUTHIER, HENRI.—*A travers la Basse-Égypte.* At Athribis (Benha) pieces of a limestone tomb have been found of a general Mentu-em-taui, of the XIXth Dynasty. At Tell Moqdam a tomb was opened with a broken limestone coffin in one chamber, and an intact granite coffin in another. It contained remains entirely rotted by water, but with a good amount of jewellery. The main piece is a pectoral with Khnum seated on a lotus flower, and Hathor and Maot as supporters ; a pair of bracelets, with applied figures of a scarab between winged uraei, several other pieces of gold work, and a heart scarab, of very short version, for the queen Ka-mo, supposed to be short for one of the Karomomo queens of the XXIInd Dynasty.

Various reliefs of funeral offerers, very graceful imitations of the Old Kingdom in the Saite age, have been found. " All of these monuments are preserved in the museum of Cairo," except one at Alexandria. It may be added that there is another piece at University College. The present illustration is of a new slab from Tell el Ferain (Buto) ; beside this the others are three from Memphis, three from Heliopolis, two from Bubastis, one from Sais, one from Athribis. A Sphinx of grey-green stone from Sais has cartouches partly defaced, of Psamthek I or II.

A statuette in black granite of Uazet has been found at Buto, confirming the identification of that place. It was dedicated by Peda-Her, born of Teda-Asar-unnefer.

A sandstone stele found at El Barada, near Qaliub, has a Ptolemy offering fields to Horus Khenti-khatu, lord of Athribis.

LEFEBVRE, GUSTAVE.—*Textes du tombeau de Petosiris*, Part III. The first is a long text beginning with usual desires, and then bewailing the untimely death of an infant, mourned by parents and family.

IV.—The usual request to passers-by to recite formulae for the dead is amplified, and enters on an argument for such help :—" Read the inscriptions, celebrate the rites in favour of my name, pronounce my name in pouring abundant libations, give me food for my mouth, provision for my lips. This will not tire your mouth to repeat, these are not riches which will fall from your hands. As one shall do, so shall one be done by ; it is a monument that is left behind one to say a good word. God himself shall requite one according to the way he behaves to my request ; whoever does well to me, so shall it be done to him ; he who praises my *ka*, shall have his *ka* praised ; he who does evil to me, so shall it be done to him ; because I am a devotee of God, who will grant that you shall be treated in the same way by those who shall come after you during all time to come. I have reached this tomb without having committed sin, without having incurred reproach from God."

ENGELBACH, R.—*Report of the Inspectorate of Upper Egypt*, 1920–21. At Karnak exchanges of land have been made, to expropriate householders. In the necropolis at Qurneh a map of all tombs and government property to scale 1/1000 is being made. More land exchanges are carried on here, to clear the tombs. In the Courts, punishments have been firmly given for not reporting the finding of antiquities, and for selling forgeries, and selling without a licence. The discoveries are :—

Lower part of seated figure of Sebek-hetep IV.

Scarab, *hypselogenia*, with *neferui kheper ka* in concentric circles.

Stele of Khuy, made by his son *ari nekhen* Her-nekht, born of Ates-senb, and his son Her-hetep, and the lady Oshă-senb.

Stele of Her-behudti-mes, son of Her-hetep, born of the priest Arer.

Stele of Her-her-khutef, son of Rames, and his wife Tuf.

Ushabti box of Pa-nef-em-dat-amen, and his wife Hent-neferu, adoring Horus-Ra seated (as Osiris) with the four genii on the lotus before him.

Part of black granite statuette of Humoy, keeper of the house of the divine wife.

Oukh-uas amulet of green glaze with names of Taharqa.

Limestone stele of youthful Khonsu.

Basalt base of statuette, formulae but no name.

Bronze legs for furniture, and simpula for dipping wine.

Limestone stele of Hat-iay.

Coptic ostrakon, letter, piously asking for attention to a flax crop.

MUNIER, HENRI.—*Manuscrits Coptes de Cheikh Abadéh*. These are various fragments of Psalms, Prophets and St. Mark ; Index of Sunday lessons ; fragment of Anaphora ; fragment of Matthew xxvii, 4–6, with variant.

Fasc. 2.

EDGAR, C. C.—*Selected Papyri from the Archives of Zenon*. This deals with the details of a debt running over fourteen years. It is complicated by repayments, stopped out of salary, with interest therefore continually changing, and the transfer of two female slaves. A matter of importance is that after a settlement the debt was considered to start *de novo*, and the interest would not amount to more than the capital, as Diodoros states. There are many details of the calendar, for which the text needs study.

ENGELBACH, R.—*Alphabetic Hymn in Coptic*. This is in four-line verses, each beginning with a successive letter of the alphabet, and the last line in each being the same, " He who was incarnate in the Virgin."

ENGELBACH, R.—*Fragment of the Gospel of St. Matthew in Coptic*. This is in Sahidic, from Matthew ix, 13, to x, 16.

ENGELBACH, R.—*Coptic Ostraka*. A letter, or memorandum, and twist patterns.

SCHIAPARELLI, E.—*La Missione Italiana a Ghebelein*. Three pages of various notes on the site, but no results of all the large cases of antiquities which were removed. " Riserbandomi dare di questi scavi più ampia e particolareggiata relazione," &c. ; but why not publish ? Let us hope that no more work will be tolerated till *all* the important things that have been removed to Turin are properly published.

DARESSY, G.—*La barque d'or du roi Kames*. The treasure of Aoh-hetep was found by natives, and only some months afterwards did Mariette obtain it. Hence there was no authority for the positions of the figures in the boats, except the material indications. In the boat with three gold figures, the soldier with an axe has been misplaced on the socket of the mast ; he should be in front of the man in the bows.

DARESSY, G.—*Sur une empreinte de Sceau.* This is a sealing from Deir El Bahri mummies, which Maspero did not explain. It is a variant of a title of an official, *Setm ne ta hat* (ne seten Ra-user-maot) Setep-ne-ra (em per Amen), the sections in parentheses being omitted. Thus the seal reads " Domestic of the house of Setep-ne-ra."

DARESSY, G.—*Fragments Héracléopolitains.* Stele of the ninth year of Pef-nef-da-bast, giving 50 setet of land ; doubtless the same king who dedicated the gold statuette of Hershaf there, named Ra-nefer-ka, Pef-da-bast, mes Bast. (*Ehnasya*, front, and p. 18.)

Upper part of a stele of the general Bak-ne-ptah. This general submitted Herakleopolis to the High Priest of Amen, Usarken, in the 39th year of Sheshenq III.

Upper part of a stele of Pa-da-bast, successor of Her-sā-ast.

Statue of black granite, about the XXXth Dynasty, of a governor of the south, over all the prophets of Herakleopolis, Sam-taui-tafnekht, son of the similar Onkh-sam-taui. No reason is stated why this should not be the Sam-taui-taf-nekht, well known early in the XXVIth Dynasty.

Statuette of schist of Oukh-thek-r, son of Pep, born of the priestess of Mut, Sedarbu.

LEFEBVRE, GUSTAVE.—*Textes du tombeau de Petosiris.* A younger brother recites all that he has done for the tomb of Petosiris, speeches of Zed-tehuti-auf-onkh, and of Seshu, his son. Some unusual protestations occur : " Good is the way of the man who obeys God ; happy is he whose heart strives to follow Him. I will tell you that which has happened to me, I will have you informed of the will of God, I will have you advance in the knowledge of His Spirit. If I have come to the eternal home, it is because I have done good upon earth, and my heart is fully on the ways of God, from my infancy to this day. All the night the Spirit of God is in my soul, and I rise in the morning to do that which He loves. I have done justice, I have detested wickedness. I have seen this (one) who lives, that in which He is pleased ; I have done the pure things which He loves ; I have not agreed with those who know not the Spirit of God, but I lean on those who act according to His will. I have not taken aught belonging to another, I have not done ill to anyone. Truly I have gained the gratitude of all my neighbours. All this have I done with the thought of reaching God after my death, and because I knew that the day would come of the masters of justice, when they would make the division in the Judgment. Happy is he who loves God, he shall come to his grave without sin." It looks here as if some of the Jewish settlements (which had been in Egypt some centuries when this was written) had spread the knowledge of the Psalms, and influenced the tone of Egyptian religion.

LEFEBVRE, GUSTAVE.—*Deux Inscriptions Grecques du Fayoum.* A dedication from Theadelphia is for Ptolemy and Cleopatra and their children ; " Phatres, son of Horus, dedicated the refectory and the altar of Heron the great god. Year 30. Pachons 8." This date proves it to be of Euergetes II and Cleopatra III, date June 3, 140 B.C. The god Heron appears again here. From Karanis is a lament in 18 lines of a girl of 20 who died unmarried.

Fasc. 3.

BARAIZE, ÉMILE. *Rapport sur les travaux exécutés à la grande Pyramide.*— The flow of visitors to the pyramids during the war led to an official wish to render the interior of Khufu's pyramid an easier show place. Accordingly the fragments of broken casing were removed from the north face to clear the way to Al Mamun's forced hole, which runs horizontal to the start of the ascending passage. Steps have been provided to divide the course-heights so as to walk up to it easily. The passage has been enlarged where needful. To rise to the ascending passage steps are provided. A wooden gangway is placed up the ramp, past the entrance to the Queen's Chamber, which is guarded at the end of the gallery floor. A wooden gangway is placed all up the gallery with a handrail ; steps up over the big granite step are provided. It was proposed to build up the old hollows in the entrance passage floor, into a tidy staircase ; but this seems to be omitted, and both entrance and exit are to be by the forced hole. Next the interior is to have electric lighting. The old interest of scrambling in and out, alone, and without even a light sometimes, has vanished. *Tourisme* triumphs, and every-thing is smoothed down to the capacities of those who do not think it worth any trouble. Handrails, iron cramps and steps, and wooden flooring, are a contradiction to a pyramid.

BARAIZE, ÉMILE.—*Rapport sur l'enlèvement et le transport du Sarcophage de la reine Hatchopsitsu.* It will be remembered that the natives found a tomb halfway up a cliff, screened by a projecting rock (ANCIENT EGYPT, 1917, 130) ; and Mr. Carter cleared it, and disclosed the second sarcophagus of Hatshepsut· This has now been removed to the Cairo Museum, a difficult task, as it was 175 feet above the floor of the valley, from which there was also a further descent. The weight is over a ton, but cut so thin that it could not withstand shocks. Access for the work was by a ladder, 65 feet high, secured at the top. The sarco-phagus was safely lowered this distance, and then moved by a light railway laid winding round the valley down to the floor. It was a difficult matter to remove it from such a position ; how about the people who succeeded in placing it there ? The two sarcophagi of the great queen now stand side by side in the Cairo Museum, one which she abandoned in this cliff tomb, the other which she placed in the royal valley—beautiful in colour, in the refinement of proportions, in the delicacy of low reliefs. The thought always recurs, in the Cairo Museum especially, is the world fit to assume responsibility for all these treasures of the past ; to ensure that fanaticism, violence, or greed will not extinguish them ; to guarantee them for some more thousands of years of existence ? Or is all this exposure the last stage ? Gold work is robbed from museums almost every year, and every-thing else runs some risk when exposed to the changes of an ever-shifting world— mostly ignorant, all selfish.

BARAIZE, ÉMILE.—*Rapport sur la découverte d'un tombeau de la XVIIIe dynastie.* In the same mountain as the previous tomb the natives had detected another cliff tomb. By successive ladders it was reached. It proved to have been entirely plundered anciently ; a scrap of gold foil, fragments of an alabaster vase, and a little pottery were all that was found. There must be somewhere another tomb of this date, from which the natives obtained the great find of XVIIIth Dynasty jewellery ; the only piece that has yet cleared the market is the massive gold statuette of Amen, which Lord Carnarvon exhibited at the recent

Exhibition in the Burlington Club. The rest is somewhere unknown ; if repression is too vigorous, the knowledge of it may die with the present owners, and the whole be lost. A fair policy of payment by the Government would save it, but legalism is too often against the interests of archaeology.

ENGELBACH, R.—*Notes of Inspection, April,* 1921. Work has been carried on—since completed—in clearing the quarry obelisk at Aswan.

From Edfu comes a scarab of Pepa (Shesha), with scroll borders.

A stele of a man who was a " royal son " of Dudumes, begotten by the " royal son," Sebek-hetep. This title implied royal descent of some generations back, as in the " royal sons of Ramessu," in the XXIInd Dynasty.

Stele of Amenemhat under Shabaka, with his wife Khikhiau.

Coptic iron fork, decorated, with two very long prongs.

A quantity of ushabtis of Ramessu VII were found in the government store at Luqsor, of the usual very coarse work in alabaster of that age, though none of the king were yet recorded, and it is not known where these were discovered.

Remains of a small temple of Domitian were observed behind the *markaz* buildings at Aswan.

GAUTHIER, HENRI.—*A travers la Basse-Égypte.* At Heliopolis, 125 yards from the station, toward the obelisk, a lintel of a tomb was found, which led to opening a series of small tombs, all swamped at high Nile. The largest chamber was for a divine father of Heliopolis, *kher-heb*, Rames. The jambs and lintels are in Cairo Museum. Only some common blue and green glazed beads were found.

At Terenuthis (Kom Abu Billu, 35 miles north-west of Cairo), the two great mounds are being rapidly worked out by *sebakhin*. Five steles have been found and sent to Alexandria. One is figured here, with a woman half reclining and holding a cup ; a table with offerings, amphora and sheaf of corn, below ; name Thaesis of Bekhenthos, and her son Asklas (for Asklepios). Date probably about 200 A.D. Other late steles from there are at Tanta ; those give the names Hippolenaios, son of Ptolemy, Tatitouôs, Eudemonis, Antemidoros, Theodosios, Tlaktôta, Ammonios and Arphbichis.

A much damaged triad of Ramessu II and two goddesses was found at Benha ; it was left in place as not worth transport.

HAKIM ABU SEIF.—*Une petite trouvaille à Karnak de modèles de sculpture.* A group of sculptors' trials were found by accident, on land which had been exchanged away to a native. It is said the best were quickly removed, but the guards came down on the remainder, seized them, and had the finders punished. This harshness is the sure way to make natives secrete all they can. The new law that all antiquities in private land belong to the State, will ensure their theft, destruction, or re-burial wherever possible. It is fatal to archaeology.

LEFEBVRE, GUSTAVE.—*Textes du tombeau de Petosiris.* In further addresses some phrases deserve notice. " Amenti is the dwelling of him who is without sin, happy is the man who reaches it. None can come there but he whose heart is true and does aright. There no distinction is between the poor and the rich, but only for him who is found without sin, when the balance and the weights are before the lord of eternity . . . to judge every man according to his deeds upon earth."

Petosiris then recounts how he managed the property of Thoth, during seven years of foreign rule, when there was trouble in the south and confusion in the north, and the temple was dismantled. This seems to have been a part of the eleven years of Persian misrule, 342–331 B.C. He then describes his labour and devotion in restoring the state and property of the temple, and his founding a temple of Ra in the temple garden. He built the house of the wives of the god in the interior of the temple, because it was ruined, and they had to live in the temple. He built the house of Nehemouat, and that of Hathor, in fine limestone. He enclosed and protected the temple precincts. He found the temple of Heqt in ruin from time immemorial ; the inundation swamped it. He called the scribe of the temple and gave him untold silver to restore it.

Zeitschrift für Aegyptische Sprache, Vol. LVI, 1920.

SPIEGELBERG, W.—*Ein Bruchstück des Bestattungsrituals der Apisstiere.* *Demot. Pap., Vienna*, 27.—Brugsch recognized this papyrus as an Osiris ritual or Osiris mystery. Spiegelberg shows that it is a book of ritual of the Osirianised Apis, written in a mixture of demotic and hieratic : the beginning and end are lost. The provenance is unknown ; by the writing it is undoubtedly from Lower Egypt ; Spiegelberg suggests the Serapeum of Memphis. The texts of the *recto* and *verso* are by two different hands ; both are Ptolemaic, about 250—100 B.C. The *recto* is easily legible ; the *verso* is written in a flowing hand which is illegible in places, and which is often only decipherable in that it occasionally contains a similar text to the *recto*. The scribe was most familiar with demotic, though, like all scribes, he also knew hieratic, which was still used in late times for all religious purposes. The papyrus contains instructions to certain priestly officials who were concerned with the mummification of the Apis, especially the *ḥri sšṯ* and the four *ḥriw ḥb*, who were priests of the cult of the dead. In this case, the *ḥri sšṯ* is manifestly the leader of the mummification, and Spiegelberg translates the term as Ritual Leader. Besides these are mentioned two " Little Friends " (𓈖𓏏𓁷𓁹𓏭𓏥) and the *wr iri*, the "Chief of Companions." Though the text in its present form is Ptolemaic, it apparently includes passages from a more ancient ritual. That it is not the final canonical form is proved by comparison of the texts of the *recto* and *verso* of the papyrus, which describe the same rites in different ways. Spiegelberg describes his translations as merely preliminary, intended to prepare the way for further work. The *recto* as it stands begins with the instruction that the Apis mummy is to be laid on a bed of sand, whilst a lament is to be made by the Ritual Leader and the four lector priests. The body is to be fastened to a board with metal rings and laid on a stand. Sarcophagus, shrines and boats are to be brought, and draped like the mummy. Then follows an exact description of the bandages for the head and extremities, which are to be prepared by the Ritual Leader and lector priests. Next comes a description of the bandaging and anointing of the mummy. A special priest is to direct the preparation of the skull, which is described in every detail, including the wrapping of the horns : he is to stuff the cranium (?) ; to remove four teeth ; to place wax, myrrh and incense in the head ; then to anoint, stuff, and bandage the mouth and face, then the eyes, nose and ears ; then to bandage the whole head. The bandaging of the head and breast follows ; the legs are to be stretched out as far as possible in order not to be bent. A lector is to stand in front of that part of the body which Spiegelberg supposes to be the abdominal cavity, to wash, stuff and bandage it. The embalmed mummy is then to be set up, after which follow further detailed instructions for bandaging. At the final bandaging the " fathers " and the priests (*hmw ntr*) raise a lament. The laying of the Apis mummy in the coffin and on the bier, is to take place near the Apis stable, and a *zed* pillar is to be fastened behind and in front of the sarcophagus. Then the corpse is to traverse the " Lake of the Kings," which is to be crossed from the west. Isis and Nephthys, Upuaut of Upper Egypt, Upuaut of Lower Egypt, Ra, Horus, Thoth and the Bed of Ptah are in front of the god, who faces south. During the crossing, nine papyrus rolls (which are named by their titles) are to be read aloud in the boat, including the " Glorification of the Drowned Osiris." Then follows the conveyance of the god to the place of embalming and the performance of the ceremony of Opening the Mouth. The *recto* as it stands ends with the enumeration by the priests of all the things they need in the embalming room, and of their purpose ; these include straw, byssus-cloth, jugs, vessels, mats, boats, sacred eyes, &c. " Horus metal " (*i.e.*, copper, perhaps copper instruments used in embalming) is frequently mentioned. The *verso* of the papyrus also contains directions for embalming part of the Apis ; the exact part is uncertain, as the term rendered above as " abdominal cavity " may mean " back of the head."

MÖLLER, GEORG.—*Zur Datierung literarischer Handschriften aus der ersten Hälfte des Neuen Reichs.*—By comparison with the dated papyri of the XVIIIth and early XIXth Dynasties, of which a short survey is given, Möller proceeds to determine the age of the following papyri :—(1) Cairo Hymn to Amen (Papyrus de Boulaq, ed. Mariette, No. 17 ; (2) London Medical Papyrus, Brit. Mus., No. 10059 ; (3) the so-called Astarte Papyrus of the Amherst Collection ; (4) Harris Papyrus 500 *recto* (love poems) ; (5) Harris Papyrus 500 *verso* (The Conquest of Joppa and the Tale of the Enchanted Prince). Four of the dated MSS. used by Erman in the palæographical section of his edition of the Western Papyrus, namely, the " Papyrus de Turin," Papyrus Boulaq 10, London Ostracon 5625 and London Ostrakon 5624, cannot be used for the palæography of the XVIIIth Dynasty, as they belong to Dynasties XX and XXI. The author protests against the error of dating a hieratic papyrus by general effect, and insists on the necessity for making a complete list of the signs and comparing them with the available dated material. He gives a selection of 31 signs, in three tables, from the five papyri in question, with references to his " Paläographie," and summarizes the means of recognizing papyri of the XVIIIth Dynasty and of the period up to the beginning of the reign of Rameses II.

Möller dates the Cairo Hymn to Amen to the middle of the XVIIIth Dynasty on the basis of the similarity of certain forms in the handwriting with those of the time of Amenhctep II (such as the form taken by ⳤ to avoid protrusion beyond the end of the line), and also of later forms, such as those of 𓅱 and ⳤ. Though the forms of 𓇋, 𓎛, 𓊪, 𓈖, 𓏏 and 𓆓 are those of the Ebers papyrus, this apparent discrepancy is explained by the assumption that the scribe was an old man who retained certain forms learnt in his youth which were antiquated when he wrote the text.

The London Medical Papyrus shows a later form of ⌐⌐ than do papyri of the period of Amenhetep III and Amenhetep IV, but it so closely agrees with them in other details that it must be placed as near them as possible. In it are thrice mentioned recipes which had proved efficacious in the time of Neb-Maat-Ra. The entry occurs twice as [hieroglyphs] and once as [hieroglyphs]. It is clear that Amenhetep III could not have been referred to thus in his own time, nor in that of his immediate successors, and Möller suggests that the disrespectful form of the second reference shows that the MSS. must have been written at a time when this king's race had waned, probably in the reign of Tut-anch-amen. On palæographical grounds, it is impossible to give the papyrus a later date. Similarly, the Astarte papyrus is near the London Medical papyrus in date, and cannot be much more recent. It probably belongs to the time of Horemheb.

The Harris papyrus 500 has certain signs in common with the handwritings of the time of Menepthah, Sapthah and Seti II, and others in common with those of the end of the XVIIIth Dynasty and the time of Seti I. The order of the signs [hieroglyph] for s₃, as in the *verso* of the Harris papyrus, is characteristic of these papyri of the first half of the N.K. That this papyrus comes palæographically between the Rollin papyrus of the time of Seti I and certain MSS. of the time of Menepthah and his successors is proved by the form of some of the signs, the actual form of writing being older than those of the dated MSS. of the second half of the reign of Rameses II. Möller would, therefore, place the older texts of the *recto* of the Harris papyrus 500 (love songs) at the end of the reign of Seti I or the beginning of the reign of Rameses II, and the texts of the *verso* (The Tale of the Conquest of Joppa and the Story of the Enchanted Prince) in the first half of the reign of the latter king. Amongst the wrongly dated papyri he includes the Millingen papyrus (Griffith, *Zeitschrift*, Vol. 34, pp. 36 and 37), which is undoubtedly contemporary with the Cairo Hymn.

SETHE, K.—*Die aegyptische Bezeichnungen für die Oasen und ihre Bewohner.*
—Sethe proposes a new reading w/ẖ₃.t for the word "oasis," which from the N.K. onwards is written [hieroglyphs] (with variants) and sometimes with the first consonant w, [hieroglyphs], etc. The reading w/ẖ₃.t for this word-sign would give a uniform word as a term for "oasis" throughout Egyptian history, the O.K. name for the Great Oasis being [hieroglyphs], and the Coptic word for "oasis" ⲟⲩⲁϩⲉ. From the way in which the word w/ẖ₃.t is used in N.K. texts, it seems likely that it was a general term for all the Oases of the Libyan desert and did not designate individual Oases.

The word w/ẖ₃t, which was the general term for oasis from the O.K. onwards, had a forerunner in the term [hieroglyphs], "field," which survived in the name for the Wad; Natrum, [hieroglyphs] "salt field," and in the name of its inhabitants [hieroglyphs], "field-dwellers."

SPIEGELBERG, W.—*Neue Schenkungstelen über Landstiften an Tempel.*—Five steles are described and figured which record the endowment of temples with land by private individuals. (1) A limestone stele (Strasbourg Institute of Egyptology, No. 1378) depicts Rameses I making an offering to Amen Ra of Pa-Bekhen. According to Brugsch, there was a series of places of this name (*p3b₂n*), all of which were in the Delta. The inscription of six lines relates to an endowment of 50 arura of land to the temple by the commander of the fort ; 21 arura seem to have been presented at his own charge, and the remainder at the charge of others, most of whose names have disappeared. (2) A limestone stele (Strasbourg Institute of Egyptology, No. 1588) records the dedication of five arura of land to Thoth by the scribe of a troop of Libyan mercenaries. The name and title of the benefactor (who is figured larger than the god) and the style of the inscription, which is mainly hieratic, point to the XXIInd dynasty. (3) The drawing of the third stele is based on a hand-copy made from three much-weathered fragments of a limestone stele which Spiegelberg saw in Cairo in 1905. Behind the goddess Sekhmet stands a youthful god with the Libyan name of *ḤwK3*. Approaching the two divinities is a man in a long tunic holding the 𓈖𓈖𓈖 sign, which means offerings of land, and accompanied by two smaller figures. The hieratic text (dated the eighth year of Shashanq) is much damaged, nevertheless Spiegelberg thinks he can detect the word *3ḥt* in the 3rd line. (4) A limestone stele, the squeeze of which was taken in Cairo in 1903, records a gift of land on the west of Sais to a temple, in the 23rd year of Psamtek I. Only the southern and eastern limits of the land are given. (5) A stele in the Cairo Museum (Recueil XVIII, 1896, p. 51) shows Neith with the *w3s* sceptre instead of the customary papyrus sceptre. In front of her is a male figure, possibly the king as the official donor, and behind her is a dwarf. Below is an incorrect inscription, mostly in hieratic, recording the gift of arable land, presumably to a temple of Neith, by a man of the Libyan name of *Iw3ḥ3n3*, " the dwarf of Neith."

ERMAN, ADOLF.—*Zusammenziehung zweier Worte in der Aussprache.*—The frequent occurrence of forms such as ⌐𓏧 for *dśśn* points to the improbability of such being caligraphical errors, and suggests rather the disappearance of one or two similar consonants in consequence of a slurring of two syllables in speech. Erman extends this explanation to another error in writing, which occurs in old texts and in those of the late N.K. This error consists in omitting one consonant in cases in which the last syllable of a word ends with the same consonant as the initial consonant of the next word. This explanation presupposes that the two words were run together in ordinary speech, and that there was no vowel sound after the last consonant of the first word ; for instance, ⊗ for ⊗ proves that the demonstrative was tacked on to the substantive, and that the feminine ending, even in old times, was something like -*at* and not -*atu*. Similarly *mdt* for *m mdt* " with ointment " shows that the preposition was joined to the substantive and was without a vowel ending. The objection that the scribe omitted the second consonant by mistake, thinking that he had already written it, disappears in the case of words with the same sound, but a different sign, such as the omission of *m* before ⌐, instances of which, however, are not frequent. Erman appends a tabulated list of examples of the omission of a consonant.

MÖLLER, GEORG.—*Das Amtsabzeichen des Oberrichters in der Spätzeit.*—Aelian (*Varia Historia*, XIV, 34) recounts that " from ancient times the judges in Egypt were priests. The oldest was their Chief. . . . Round his neck he wore an ornament of sapphire (= lapis lazuli) ; this decoration was called ' Truth.' " Diodorus states that this was put on before hearing cases, and was turned toward the successful party as a sign of the verdict. The picture of the goddess of Truth hanging from the neck of a Chief Justice is met with occasionally in inscriptions of the time of Ptolemy III Euergetes ; moreover, some statues of Chief Justices have been preserved showing the sign of office. The oldest known example (of the time of Necho) is in the Louvre ; there are two in Berlin of the time of Nectanebo and Ptolemy V Epiphanes respectively. Figures of the goddess of Truth, like those represented in the statues, are also in existence ; the Berlin Museum has three specimens, all made of lapis lazuli, and all with a loop at the back. A passage in the Gnomon of the Idios Logos, which Möller restores and renders as : " only the President (of the Court of Justice) is allowed to wear the sign of Justice," shows that this symbol was in use at least until the middle of the second century A.D.

RANKE, H.—*Keilschriftliches.*—The author supplements his work on cunei-form renderings of Egyptian names by suggesting that : (1) *Dûdu (Duddu)* =⁚ ⌒ 𓏤⌒𓏤, (2) *Anḫara* = 𓏌 ⧟ 𓏥, (3) *Manaḫpirja* (variant *Manaḫpija*) =⁚ 𓏐 𓎟 𓏺𓏺.

(1) On the assumption that *Twtw* is a Semitic name, there is no objection on phonetic grounds to the identification of Dûdu, the high Egyptian official (whose name occurs so frequently in the Tell el Amarna letters) with the high official of Amenhetep IV, called *Twtw*, who was buried at Tell el Amarna. His conclusion is confirmed by details in the letters and in the tomb inscriptions. *Dûdu* " sat before the king " ; Aziru promises him anything he desires if he will only intercede for him against the enemies who slander him at Court ; Aziru " fears the king and *Dûdu*. *Twtw* states that he " communicated the requests of the foreign ambassadors in the Palace, in that I was daily in the (house of the king ?), and I went out to them as the king's envoy, equipped with all his Majesty's commands."

(2) In the cuneiform titulary of Rameses II at Bogaskeui, the king is described as the god, the ruler of Heliopolis, the brother of *Anḫa.a.ra* . . . For his former translation of " brother of the god Horus," Ranke now substitutes " brother of *Anḫâra*, reading *an* as a syllabic sign instead of as the determinative for god. This reading would correspond very well phonetically with the N.K. vocalization of '*In Ḥr*, the only god who is ever termed " brother of the king " in hieroglyphic inscriptions (*cf.* Mariette, Abydos I, 6, 30, where the same king mentions his brother '*In Ḥr*).

(3) The variants *Manaḫpirja* and *Manaḫpija* each occur once in the Tell el Amarna letters as the name of an Egyptian king. The recipient of the letter in which King *Manaḫpija* is called " the father of his father " is generally taken to be Akhenaten ; consequently Thothmes IV should be *Manaḫpija*. Phonetically, this is impossible, as the *p* of *ḫprw* becomes an aleph in cuneiform. There remains only Thothmes III, but *Ra* in Middle Babylonian times was rendered as *riya*. Failing the supposition that the scribe in question omitted the sign *ri* by mistake

in two separate places, there remains only the assumption that the form is a rendering of an abbreviation of the name Men.Kheper.Ra, namely ⸗ 𓊹 𓏭𓏭, after the pattern of '*Imniï* for '*Imn-m-ḥȝt* (*Zeitschrift*. 42, 144). The occurrence of such an abbreviation in these two places only is explained by the fact that the passages in question are in a letter, and that the name does not form part of a formal address or titulary. On phonetic grounds this explanation is satisfactory, but the actual difficulty of regarding Thothmes III as " the father of his father " can only be overcome by assuming that the expression is used in the sense of " ancestor." This is a somewhat forced explanation, as the same expression used in the same sentence in connection with the writer himself must surely refer to his own grandfather.

MÖLLER, GEORG.—*Zu Herodoto aegyptischen Geschichten.*—Herodotus (II, 129 ff.) relates of Mycerinos that he built the third Pyramid ; that he was especially concerned with the administration of justice ; that he lived at Sais, or at least built there ; that he reigned not long before the Ethiopian domination ; and that he ruled for six years only.

[All this is explained by the interchange of two rolls, the restoration of which puts the history in perfect order. It is useless to find an elaborate explanation of only one of the errors resulting from the change.—F. P.]

(2) Spiegelberg derived ‘Ερμοτυβίες (Herod. II, 164 f.) from ⸗ 𓆱, 𓈖 𓃀 𓏭𓏭 " horsemen." Möller substitutes 𓄿 𓏤 𓏮 *dbȝ* " spear," for the second constituent of the word, according to which the term would mean spearmen, not cavalry.

(3) Μανερῶς (Herod. II, 79). A grave inscription (*Zeitschrift*, LV, p. 56) contains mention of a herdsman's lament on a reed flute for the god of vegetation. In a passage from Nymphis it is seen that the Manêros is a song of the country folk to Osiris, the god of vegetation. In the hieroglyphic text, the man who starts the lament is called 𓏤𓄿, ⳙⲁⲛⲉ⳯ⳣⲟⲧ, which would become in Greek Μανεῶς ; the *r* would then be introduced for euphony. In Μανερῶς Möller therefore recognizes the song of the cowherd, which was sung for Osiris, and which was accordingly also sung at burials, since the late Egyptians regarded all their dead as embodiments of Osiris.

SCHUBART, W.—*Rom und die Aegypter nach dem Gnomon des Idios Logos.*— The Idios Logos was a special office for dealing with irregular sources of revenue, such as fines and seizures. That the Romans attached great importance to it is proved by their placing a Roman noble at the head, who was of the same social rank as the Viceroy. He was frequently called simply the Idios Logos. The regulations for the Idios Logos were codified in a Gnomon. A new papyrus dating from about A.D. 150, of which the text only was recently published by Schubart, provides us for the first time with about 120 extracts from these Regulations. When Egypt became a Roman province, Augustus drew up a new Gnomon, which appeared as a Decree ; the introductory paragraph of the papyrus shows that the Decree was subsequently added to by other Emperors and functionaries. The papyrus is incomplete and scrappy, being obviously a compilation only, and in it imperial regulations are mixed with purely local ones ; nevertheless, it throws much light on the Roman administration of Egypt. The sections dealing with inter-marriage, and the inheritance rights of the offspring of mixed marriages, reveal the exclusion of the Egyptian from Roman citizenship ; whilst those relating to religious matters have added to our knowledge on certain points. In general, the children of a mixed marriage shared the nationality of the inferior partner (Egyptian) ; from the mitigating clauses relating to ignorance of status, it is clear that members of different grades of citizenship were indistinguishable in appearance and speech, so that differences which were originally national had become only political in course of time. Egyptian wives of discharged soldiers were not allowed to call themselves Roman for business purposes. If an Egyptian became a legionary unnoticed, he resumed his Egyptian status on discharge ; the same rule applied to naval service except in the case of an Egyptian who had served in the Misenum fleet. Evidently the Egyptian marriage customs had spread, as one clause forbids Romans to marry their sisters.

In spite of lack of clearness and completeness, the paragraphs relating to the priesthood show that the State wished to protect religion ; a clause, however, which empowers the state to appropriate "bequests for sacrifices to the dead if the persons to receive these bequests were no longer forthcoming," was probably precautionary. Young bulls were not to be sacrificed unless previously sealed by the priest. Priests were not allowed to have any calling other than the service of the gods, nor might they wear woollen clothing, nor have long hair. Certain priestly offices of high rank which were hereditary were to be reserved for the family, whilst those which might be sold were not to be sold at auction (see the sale of next presentations in England) ; in every sanctuary with a naos, there was to be a " prophet," who was to receive one-fifth of the revenues. The office of stolist was obtainable by purchase ; stolists could take the place of " prophets." Only the President (presumably of the ecclesiastical courts) might wear the symbol of Justice (see *ante*). Pastophores (the highest class of the lower grades of priests) were not allowed to call themselves priests, but they might seek lay posts. In Greek temples, the laity was allowed to take part in processions. " Prophets " were not allowed to partake of sacrificial meats, but this prohibition did not extend to the pastophores. Those who failed to send clothing for the apotheosis of the Apis or Theoris were fined. Those who buried the holy animals were not permitted to be " prophets," nor to carry a naos in the processions, nor to feed the holy animals.

STEINDORFF, W.—*Eine Statue der Frühzeit.*—The provenance of this statuette is probably the small cemetery at Abusir excavated by the Ernst von Siegelin expedition in 1909. It is now in Berlin. This small seated figure is carved in yellowish slaty limestone, and measures 42 cm. in height and 18 cm. across the shoulders. The condition is not good ; the right hand and the lower part of the body down to the feet are missing, also the eyes, which were inlaid, and the left side is badly damaged. The man is seated on a *ḥnd* stool, the four legs of which are joined by arched stays. The head is almost neckless ; the left hand lies closed on the chest. A long cloak passes from the left shoulder under the right arm, leaving the right shoulder bare. The skin and the cheek bones are prominent ; the eyebrows are modelled ; the face is beardless, with a small moustache ; the hair is parted in the middle and just covers the ears. The strands of hair are roughly chiselled in vertical lines ; the curly ends are indicated by horizontal strokes. The fingers and toes are but slightly indicated ; the body is not finely modelled. The style and treatment link this statue with other examples of archaic seated figures (London, Paris, Leyden, Berlin, Naples, and Cairo) ; Steindorff considers that it is the oldest of the series, and suggests the beginning of the IInd dynasty. It is the largest early example of a portrait figure with inlaid eyes. Unfortunately, there is no inscription.

MISCELLANEOUS.

1. WIESMANN, H.—In *A.Z.*, LIII, Wiesmann discussed the word ⲛⲉⲁⲧ ; he now points out that ⲛ is the definite article, and that the word is really ⲉⲁⲧ.

2. WIESMANN, H.—Rahlfs (*A.Z.*, XLIII) showed that the negative adverb ⲩ̄ⲛⲱⲡ is an emphatic imperative ; the absolute form, of which ⲩ̄ⲛⲡ̄ is the construct form ; in late Egyptian ⳨ ⟾, ⲩ̄ⲛⲱⲡ appears to take after it the preposition ⲉ- with the infinitive.

3. WIESMANN, H.—The derivation of ⲣ̄ⲧⲟⲟⲧⲉ was given by Spiegelberg (*Rec.*, XXIV) as from *ḥr dwʒ(.w)*, but later (*A.Z.*, LI) he suggested *ḥʒ-dwʒ(.w)*. Wiesmann considers the earlier one to be preferable.

4. WIESMANN, H.—According to Peyron and Stern the word ⲣ̄ⲟⲉⲓⲧⲉ *Garment*, is masculine, in distinction from ⲣ̄ⲟⲉⲓⲧⲉ *Hyaena*, which is feminine. Wiesmann now shows that it may be of either gender. He points out that the usually accepted derivation from 𓋴 𓅮 𓏎 is doubtful, and suggests that it was originally a feminine word, and to differentiate it from the feminine ⲣ̄ⲟⲉⲓⲧⲉ *Hyaena*, the gender was changed. Such changes of gender in Egyptian words and their Coptic derivatives are known.

5. MÖLLER, G.—A parallel case to that of Akhenaten is found in a later ruler of Egypt, also a religious reformer, namely El Ḥâkim ibn 'Azîz (A.D. 996–1021), who was under twelve years of age when his reign began. Though Möller does not wish to change the rendering of the name of ⟮𓇋𓏠𓇋𓁨⟯, which he states has become established in Germany as Echnaton, he suggests that it was probably pronounced 'Ôḫlatòn.

6. MÖLLER, G.—A small carved ivory reproduced from the second volume of Macalister's *Gezer* (p. 331, fig. 456) is not a pectoral but a portable sundial. Hitherto, sundials of this kind have not been known earlier than Ptolemaic times. Möller challenges Macalister's statement of a filling of green enamel, as real enamel was not known until later, and inlaid ivory is not common.

7. SPIEGELBERG, W.—The inscription on a damaged obelisk in the Borgia Museum at Velletri records its erection by a man with three names. Champollion correctly deciphered the last two as Sextius Africanus, without identifying the first name. Spiegelberg proves that this name is Titus. It is impossible to identify the Titus Sextius Africanus who erected the obelisk ; for during the first century B.C. and the first century A.D. there were several members of the same family who bore these three names.

NOTES AND NEWS.

ALL the world has been stirred by the great news of the discovery of a royal tomb by Mr. Carter, working for Lord Carnarvon ; a noble result after years of discouraging clearances which only showed blank rock. Here the archaeological facts may be recorded, so far as yet described. On November 5th, Mr. Carter found a step in the rock under the path leading to the tomb of Ramessu VI ; this is in the spur on the west side of the valley, immediately looking up the Hatshapsut ravine. This position proves that the burial, and the robbers' attack on it, took place before cutting the tomb of Ramessu VI. After Lord Carnarvon had arrived, the stairs were cleared. Broken pottery, flowers, and water skins lay about—the remains of the funeral, which could not be re-used after serving for the dead. At the first wall, a break in the plastering showed a thieves' hole, resealed by inspectors. After removing this, a passage was entered, in which was a broken box with names of Akhenaten and Smenkh-ka-ra. Then appeared another sealed door, with a thieves' hole, sealed up. Opening this, the first chamber was seen, containing three colossal gilt couches with heads of Bes, Hathor, and lions ; beds, carved, gilt and inlaid with coloured stones ; the four sides of a chariot, gilt and inlaid ; the throne with Tut·onkh·amen and Queen beneath the Aten rays, on the back, inlaid with turquoise, carnelian and lazuli of indescribable delicacy and grace ; the stool, with Asiatics for the feet to rest upon ; alabaster vases of intricate forms, as yet unknown ; sticks, with a gold head of an Asiatic, and one of filagree work ; gilt sandals ; a stool of ebony with ivory inlay and carved duck's feet ; gilt bronze musical instruments ; a box, inlaid, containing royal robes embroidered, with stones inserted, the most novel and interesting of all the objects ; a box containing emblems of the underworld ; a painted box with hunting scenes ; blue faience vases ; a dummy for royal robes and wig ; rolls of papyrus, which Dr. Gardiner will go out to edit ; great quantities of provisions, and wreaths.

In a second chamber there was a confused pile of chairs, boxes, statuettes, alabaster vases, and more gilt beds, piled up 5 feet high. Another doorway in the first chamber has the life-size wooden figures of Tut·onkh·amen, holding a golden stick and mace, standing on either side. This leads to a third chamber, but with the tell-tale thieves' hole in the corner. It is supposed that Tut·onkh·amen and perhaps other royalties are buried in this third chamber ; but it cannot be entered till a clearance is made. To handle such an enormous mass of delicate objects, Mr. Carter has been to Cairo to buy up cotton wool, wood, and preservatives, and Mr. Lucas, the Government chemist, will take part in the detail of dealing with this treasure. Where it can stand in the Cairo Museum is a puzzle. The museum is full now, and this prize will need a couple more halls to show it. Our felicitations to Lord Carnarvon for his enterprise, and congratulations to Mr. Carter for the result of his years of work, and to Mr. Callender who is with him, on having such a gorgeous experience.

Mr. and Mrs. Brunton, with M. Bach and Mr. Starkey, are at work for the British School at the great cemetery of Qow el Kebir.

Mr. Greenlees is with Mr. Fisher at Thebes.

The intention of the Egyptian Government to alter the law, and leave excavators without any claim on their discoveries, has called forth a united protest from all the British and American workers, who consider that it will bring the present course of excavation-to an end. Meanwhile a great prospect opens in Palestine, where the hill of Zion, the site of the palace and tombs of the Jewish monarchy, is to be open to excavation.

96

MOSAIC FROM SHELLAL, 560 A.D.

ANCIENT EGYPT.

THE SHELLAL MOSAIC.

DURING the war the Australian troops found a great mosaic pavement of a church which had been much cut up by Turkish trenches. This was between Beersheba and Khan Yunis; and it shows what prosperity existed down to the time of Justinian, in what is now a barren region incapable of supporting a population. As any dated example of mosaic is valuable, for comparison with other mosaics or decoration, it is here reproduced from the copy officially issued in Egypt. The broken border is here omitted, except an example at the top, in order to give the figures on a larger scale. There is a much more broken inscription also at the bottom. The top inscription reads: " This temple with spacious . . . was built by our most . . . and most pious George . . . in the year 622 according to . . ." It is supposed that this was according to the era of Gaza, the nearest city, with an era of 63 B.C., which was also usual in other Syrian cities. This date would be therefore equal to 560 A.D., or five years before the death of Justinian.

The fashion of placing subjects in circles is familiar at 330 A.D. in the mosaics of S. Costanza; but the development of flowing lines to form the circles comes from the vine pattern with leaf or grapes in the circle, as at S. Vitale, 546 A.D. The idea of placing animals in these circles is seen on the ivory throne of Maximian at Ravenna, 550 A.D. The Shellal mosaic has at the base one of the earliest groups of the vase between peacocks, which is not generally found till from two to four centuries later.

The mosaic was most carefully removed by the Australian troops, stored in Egypt during the war, and then removed to Australia. Beneath the inscription was found a burial, which was doubtless that of " our most pious George " who founded the church.

W. M. F. P.

G

AN OLD WORLD CUBIT IN AMERICA.

EVERY connection that can be traced between the civilisations of Asia and America is so important, for lighting up one of the greatest of historical questions, that it should be put on record, in hope of drawing out further information. The School of American Research at Santa Fé, New Mexico, has been exploring the remains in the Chaco Canyon, which was proclaimed a National Monument fifteen years ago. An account of the work, with many illustrations, is given in *Art and Archaeology* for September, 1922. The structures described by Mr. Edgar Hewett are built of naturally faced pieces of sandstone, like tiles, about 8 to 12 inches square and a couple of inches thick. They are laid with remarkable regularity to form walls with flat faces, which were covered with white plaster.

The principal class of remains are circular areas, with a bench about 3 feet high, around, and a wall behind that about 6 feet higher. Joining to this is a square chamber ; and around the circular wall is another beyond it, and the intervening space divided, by cross walls, into between eight and fourteen chambers. In the floor of the great area are two rectangular pits, in which had been a great burning ; they are about $3\frac{1}{2}$ feet deep. The great size, the regularity and also the fine finish show the importance and the care in construction of these works, and justify us in examining whether they were made by measurement.

On looking over the measurements that are given it is obvious that they indicate a unit of about 20·7 inches. This is not found by guessing, but by trying all simple ratios between the numbers on a slide rule, until a series of multiples is found which shall be in proportion to the quantities. Thus at Chattro Ketl—

	Inches.		
Diameter	750	÷ 36	20·8
Bench, wide	42	2	21
Post holes apart	312	15	20·8
Altar	61 or 62	3	20·5

At Aztec, San Judu River (36° 50′ N., 108° 5′ W.)—

Outside outer wall diameter	827	÷ 40	20·67
Inside outer wall diameter	786	38	20·68
Outside inner wall diameter	638	31	20·58
Inside inner wall diameter	*579·5	28	20·70
Inside lower bench	*495·5	24	20·65
Large chamber, wide	249	12	20·75
„ „ long	208	10	20·8
Post holes apart, over all..	290	14	20·71
„ „ „	283	14	20·21
„ „ „	310	15	20·67
„ „ „	308	15	20·53
Pits, long	*102	5	20·4
„ wide	* 42	2	21·0
Wide curved chamber	*124	6	20·67

In South-West Colorado—

Circular wall diameter	1,632	80	20·4

The starred measures are direct statements; others are measured from the plan in *Anthropological Papers* of the American Museum of Natural History, xxvi, Part 2, 1921.

Other dimensions are not detailed enough to give an accurate result.

Now from these it seems clear that the unit is about 20·68 inches by the most accurate measures. In the circle at Aztec it appears that the inside of the benches and the outer wall are the simple numbers of design (24, 25, 40), and the intermediate numbers result from 7, 3, 3 and 2 cubits for chambers and walls. This accords exactly to the well-known Egyptian cubit : 20·62 in the best early example, 20·65 in later cubit rods, 20·76 on the Roman Nilometers. Babylonia had a rather longer form, 20·88 for the cubit of Gudea's plotting scales, carved on the drawing-board that rests upon his knees in the Louvre statues. This was also the standard of Asia Minor, 20·6 to 20·9, mean of all 20·63. How could this reach New Mexico ? It was evidently Asiatic. We have evidence from weights of an Asiatic diffusion of a Babylonian original over India, China and Etruria. If the cubit similarly passed to China, it might thence reach North America. It has been already pointed out in this Journal (1916, p. 108) how the cross at Palenque (Southern Mexico) was in its detail of ornament derived from Italian crosses of about the eighth century, probably carried to China by the Nestorian mission. By the same route the Asiatic cubit may have passed over to the New World at some earlier period.

W. M. FLINDERS PETRIE.

WAS THE CONSTANTINOPLE OBELISK PART OF THE 108-CUBIT OBELISK OF HATSHEPSÔWET ?

WHILE studying the unfinished obelisk, now lying in a quarry at Aswan, which I excavated last season, I worked out, with a fair degree of accuracy, what internal strain due to bending would be set up when the obelisk, if completed, were supported at its centre of gravity. The dimensions of this obelisk are, in the rough :—

Overall length ..	..	..	..	..	41·75 metres.
Side of base ..	..	..	..	..	4·2 ,,
Base of pyramidion ..	..	..	..	2·5 ,,
Height of pyramidion ..	..	..	..˙	4·5 ,,

The total weight, when fine-dressed, would have been just over 1,100 tons (English).

The result of my calculations is that, if this obelisk were supported at its centre of gravity, the stress due to bending would have been 1,086 lbs. per sq. in. The maximum stress, or " modulus of rupture " for granite is given as 1,500 lbs. per sq. in. (It may be noted here that if the obelisk is supported at the base and the base of the pyramidion, the stress set up will be very nearly the same, the difference being in the plus or minus effect of the pyramidion in the moment formula.)

If an obelisk cannot endure the strain set up due to its own weight, an unevenness in the packing when it was being undercut in the quarry or the slightest concavity in the bed on which the rollers run (which seem to have been used), would result in the obelisk snapping across ; this applies even more in considering the question of its erection. I believe that a modification of the theory that the obelisk was let over the edge of an embankment is generally accepted. If this was the means employed, it is essential that the obelisk be rigid enough to resist breaking when supported at its centre of gravity. The theory that the obelisk was pulled and levered up while engaging in the notch on the pedestal is, to me, untenable for a 1,100-ton obelisk, however well it may have succeeded with the 35-ton obelisk of Seringapatam (Barber, *The Mechanical Triumphs of the Ancient Egyptians*). The standing obelisk of Queen Hatshepsôwet at Karnak never has engaged in the pedestal-notch, as the inner edge of the notch, unlike those of all other obelisks I know, is quite sharp, and the obelisk now stands several inches to a foot away from the notch (as it does not stand square on the pedestal).

Having reached the figure mentioned above, which leaves a very narrow margin considering the slight flaws unavoidable in very large granite blocks, it occurred to me that if the Constantinople obelisk is, as held by several authorities, merely the top of the 108-cubit obelisk mentioned in the well-known inscription of Thutiy as having been erected by Hatshepsôwet, it would suffer an even greater strain, if supported at its centre of gravity or ends, than would the Aswan Obelisk, had it been completed.

Turning to Petrie, *A History of Egypt*, xviith and xviiith dynasty, pp. 131, 132, we read, referring to the 108-cubit obelisk (L.D. iii, 27, 11) : " Taking the lighter obelisk, that of Hatshepsut, which weighs about 300 tons, if the thickness were increased proportionally to the length on 185 feet, it would imply a weight of over 2,000 tons. This is so obviously excessive (as the heaviest blocks yet known are the colossi of Ramessu II, 800 tons at the Ramesseum, and 900 tons at Tanis), that we cannot suppose that the thickness was proportionate to the height. Probably, therefore, the missing obelisks should be about the same width at the top as the other great obelisks, and wider at the base.

" The only obelisk that could fit this requirement is that of Constantinople. It is only the top of a broken obelisk ; but the inscription on the south face is exactly parallel to that on the west face of Hatshepsut's obelisk. If it continued like that, its height would come to about 120 feet ; but it may, of course, have been a longer inscription. If we suppose that it was 172 feet (or 100 cubits, leaving 13 feet for the pedestal), then, as the top is about 5 feet 6 inches wide (by photograph), and the broken end 7 feet wide, the base would have been 10 feet 2 inches wide, there being no perceptible entasis. As the Lateran obelisk is 9 feet 9 inches, this size of base would be very probable for a longer mass." The calculation of the stress set up in the proposed obelisk is as follows :—

If we allow 7 feet for the pyramidion, since we have no exact details of it, and since it affects the problem very little, we have a length of 165 feet or 2,000 inches, the side of the small end being 66 inches and that of the large end 122 inches.

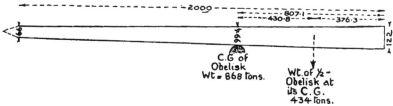

Centre of Gravity of the whole Obelisk.

The distance of the centre of gravity from the large end (D) of a truncated pyramid of length l, having sides to the thicker and thinner ends A and a respectively, is given by the formula :—

$$D = \frac{l}{4} \left\{ \frac{A^2 + 2Aa + 3a^2}{A^2 + Aa + a^2} \right\}.$$

Substituting the dimensions given above, we have :—

$$D = \frac{2000}{4} \left\{ \frac{(122)^2 + 2\,(122)\,(66) + 3\,(66)^2}{(122)^2 + (122)\,(66) + (66)^2} \right\} = 500 \left\{ \frac{14884 + 16104 + 13068}{14884 + 8052 + 4356} \right\}$$

$$= \frac{500 \times 44056}{27292} = 807 \cdot 12 \text{ inches.}$$

Width of Obelisk at its Centre of Gravity.

By proportion, this is equal to—

$$122 - \frac{807 \cdot 1}{2000} \text{ of } (122 - 66) = 99 \cdot 4 \text{ inches.}$$

Centre of Gravity of right-hand half of the Obelisk when supported at Centre of Gravity of Obelisk.

Here we have, in the formula quoted above,

$$l = 807 \cdot 1, \ A = 122 \text{ and } a = 99 \cdot 4.$$

G 3

Therefore the distance of the Centre of Gravity of the half-obelisk measured from the thicker end is :—

$$\frac{807 \cdot 1}{4} \left\{ \frac{(122)^2 + 2 \,(122)\,(99 \cdot 4) + 3\,(99 \cdot 4)^2}{(122)^2 + (122)\,(99 \cdot 4) + (99 \cdot 4)^2} \right\}$$

$$= \frac{807 \cdot 1}{4} \left\{ \frac{14884 + 24253 \cdot 6 + 29641 \cdot 08}{14884 + 12126 \cdot 8 + 9880 \cdot 36} \right\} = \frac{807 \cdot 1 \times 68778 \cdot 68}{4 \times 36891 \cdot 16}$$

$$= 376 \cdot 3 \text{ inches.}$$

The distance of the Centre of Gravity of the half-obelisk from the point of support will then be $807 \cdot 1 - 376 \cdot 3 = \underline{430 \cdot 8 \text{ inches.}}$

Weight of the Half-obelisk (W).

Calling $A =$ side at one end, and $a =$ side at other end, the volume is $A^2 + Aa + a^2 \times$ length $\div 3$, or $(99 \cdot 4^2 + 12127 + 122^2) \times 807 \cdot 1 \div 3$, which $\times$ weight per cubic inch (at 170 lbs. to cubic foot) $= 435 \cdot 9$ tons. The obelisk then, if of two similar halves, would weigh 872 tons.

Now (Stress due to bending) (Modulus of Section) = (Sum of moments on one side of support).

The modulus for a square sectioned beam is one-twelfth the cube of the side, or $\dfrac{(99 \cdot 4)^3}{12}$.

Substituting we have :—

$$S \times \frac{(99 \cdot 4)^3}{12} = \frac{(110 \cdot 7)^2 \times 807 \cdot 1 \times 170}{1728} \times 430 \cdot 8,$$

from which $S = \dfrac{(110 \cdot 7)^2 \times 807 \cdot 1 \times 170 \times 430 \cdot 8 \times 12}{(99 \cdot 4)^3 \times 1728} = 5{,}120$ lbs. per sq. in.

Thus it would not carry a third of its own weight if supported at the middle or the ends, as granite breaks at 1,500 lbs. per square inch. If the Egyptians could have handled and erected this obelisk, it would have been the greatest engineering feat which has come down to us.

With the exception of the obelisk of Hatshepsôwet at Karnak, which has rather a slight taper, there is no very great difference in the proportions of the large obelisks now known. Since the resistance to bending of beams *with the same relative dimensions* is proportional to their linear measurements, it follows that, with obelisks, there must be a limit to their possible length. Taking the sharpest known taper, this length is somewhere about 140 feet, though I doubt whether an obelisk of even that length could be erected unbroken, since granite is so rarely perfectly homogeneous.

The subject of the quarrying, transport and erection of obelisks is treated in detail in my volume *The Aswan Obelisk*, which is now in the press.

R. ENGELBACH.

[We may note here what would be the size of an obelisk 172 feet (or 100 cubits) long for it to carry its own weight. It would need to be about 36 feet square at the base, and 19 feet at the tip, and would weigh about 11,000 tons. It is evident that such a size and weight would be quite impossible; there must, therefore, be some other explanation of the boasted size of 108 cubits.—F. P.]

· THE RISE OF PRICES IN ROMAN EGYPT.

A VALUABLE collection of material relating to the course of prices in the Ptolemaic and Roman period in Egypt has been issued by Dr. Angelo Segrè, under the title *Circolazione Monetaria e prezzi nel mondo antico ed in particolare in Egitto* (Roma, Libraria di Cultura, 1922). Such a study has a special interest now that Europe is suffering from precisely similar troubles of depreciation of currency, and consequent rush of prices upward. The Roman world did not suffer the worst modern effects of that immoral course, as there were no permanent State loans nor paper debentures. Loans between individuals were only for short periods, and could be called in and readjusted without much loss. There was nothing like the entire confiscation of all the loan capital of the saving classes, such as has lately smitten Europe in the East, and partially in the West. The effects of that in wiping out the saving class, and deterring from saving, in Austria and Germany—to say nothing of Russia—will be a fatal injury to the stability of those peoples for generations to come. It is far worse in effect than the War which preceded it. Every stage of this terrible process of destruction in the Roman Empire has its practical interest for us, who are watching a similar dissolution. The depreciation and race between wages and prices sent up nominal prices to 5,000 and at last to 500,000 of their true value; in this crisis, labour ceased to be paid in cash, and payment was in corn; at last everything went on to a fixed pure gold basis, the same course which is beginning to be accepted in Europe.

For the examination of the true value of nominal money there is no better basis than wheat in the ancient world. In modern times it is complicated by importation from entirely different economic States; in the Roman world there was one general currency, and no wheat came from outside that. The production was under various conditions, and therefore was averaged; there was little difference of quality, and no variation of demand. Labour varied much more in quality, while slaves, animals, oil and wine varied greatly. The standard quantity of corn in Egypt was the artaba, equal to 0·8 bushel. We may first note how closely the true value of debased money was understood; the amount of silver was by no means obvious, yet it was known and the value reckoned accordingly. Taking a middle date for the main period, we find on the average that the price of the artaba was:—

B.C. 250	..	..	..	2 drachmae = 107 grains silver.
A.D. 100	..	..	..	8 dr. alloyed = 69
200	..	..	..	16 ,, ,, 63
600	..	..	..	1·4 (by gold) 70

The last is by gold value, taken as 14·4 × silver. This suggests that silver became rather scarcer, or more in demand for plate, between the early Ptolemaic and early Roman age; otherwise the silver value of corn was remarkably stable over many centuries of great political change. Comparing 70 grains of silver per artaba with modern values, it would be 530 grains per quarter; and on our usual price (before recent changes) of silver, 5s. per 480 grains, this would be 5s. 6d. a quarter, or about a tenth of the modern price of corn. Silver and gold therefore were about ten times more valuable than recently.

In looking at the prices of labour it is remarkable how uniform they remain when reduced to silver values. From 270 B.C., at 1 to 2 obols, the price slowly rises in relation to corn, and in corn values the rate is 1⅔ obols, in 100 A.D. The payment in corn at 338 A.D. is equal to 1⅓ obols, reckoned at the old rate of 2 drachmae of silver per artaba. In the seventh and eighth centuries the gold rate equals 1⅓ obols. So for eleven centuries the real silver value of a day's work was about 1½ obols. This seems very low ; but as we saw with corn, that precious metals were worth about 10 times the present amount, it is now equal to 2½ drachmae, or ⅓ of an ounce of silver—in last century values 1s. 8d. As the wages in Egypt were 5d. a day, or up to 10d. or 1s. before the war, it seems that the ancient 1½ obol had about double the purchasing power of even the higher modern wage in Egypt. Since the war the wage is about the ancient value, but prices are higher in proportion.

Wine followed a slightly different course, probably influenced by changes in the average of the quality recorded. It shows a slight fall from 300 to 100 B.C. and no distinct rise till about 150 A.D. At 300 the wine prices, like the corn, rushed upward. In the fourth century the gold values quoted are about those of the higher qualities of the Ptolemaic time. A very low price appears for soldiers' wine, which was probably little more than vinegar ; and by 690 rather a high price, suggesting that wine was scarce.

The price of slaves is naturally very variable, from 55 to 570 drachmae real value, average 250. This in equal modern values would be £20 to £240, averaging £100. Under Philadelphos little girls from Syria sold at £20 to £60, in modern corn values.

Among cattle, the ass was naturally of various quality, from 26 to 100 real drachmae of silver, average 53 ; or by corn values £7 to £28, average £15. This is about the modern price. Camels varied less in general, as might be expected, for there were no fancy prices ; from 60 to 200 drachmae, with an average of 140 ; or in modern corn values £17 to £56, average £39. For a horse the common price was 40 to 50 drachmae, but a very fine black Cappadocian was 1,100 ; in modern corn values £11 to £14, and £300 exceptional. The price of sheep was the same in Byzantine as in Ptolemaic time, about 8 drachmae, equivalent to £2. Hogs were about the same ; but goats were only 1 or 2 drachmae. All of the modern equivalents of these animal prices are in corn values much the same as at the present time.

In order to be able to show the whole course of prices over such an immense variation, the only way is to draw it on a logarithmic scale, as on this diagram : if it were all in proportion to the bottom part it would need to be some miles long. As far as about the second century A.D. the lines of price were drawn from the mean lines of diagrams of all the data ; beyond that, where the prices rise rapidly, the single data are spotted on this diagram and the lines drawn through them. The first. and obvious result is that the celebrated Edict of prices under Diocletian in 301, marked here as E, was not unfair or arbitrary ; it falls well into the line of actual values. The lines of wheat and wages keep close together through the E values. The oil and wine values of E may have been too low for the time, keeping to values of twenty years earlier, for the wage and wheat lines cannot have gone up vertically through all the E points. The E values are closely about the copper value of currency.

The real intention of the Edict is now explained. It was not a foolish attempt to stabilise prices by law ; Diocletian was too able an organiser and economist to do that. But coinage having come to mere copper, he tried to check the trade unions from making a nominal rise beyond copper values. The aim was to avoid artificial inflation by " money of account," and keep to real values of metal.

That this astounding rise of half a million, or a million, to 1 was not due

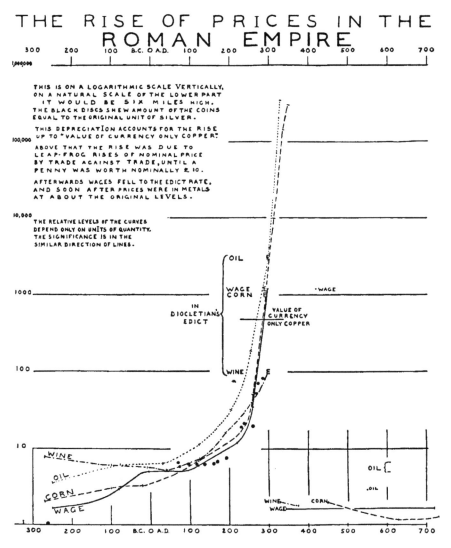

to proportionate scarcity is obvious, for in more disturbed and poorer ages the wheat and wage curves of 500–700 A.D. go back to the old silver values of the beginning. The slow decline in the late curve of wheat probably shows an exhaustion of gold, but wages seem level in that age. Wine was far cheaper, probably because all the finer kinds were extinct and only the sour wine was left, which was previously at this level for soldiers' rations.

On looking at the coinage, there does not seem any sufficient cause for such a change of values. The alterations were not so much in weight as in the amount of silver in the billon. The worst that this change can make is to reduce a nominally silver coin to a 480th of its value, when it arrives at plain copper. The changes in weight were very slight. The silver denarius ends in the fourth century A.D. at just the same weight as it was B.C. The follis does not decrease, nor its half. The Byzantine coinage, numbered 40, 20, 10, 5, 2, fluctuates, but does not diminish ; and it seems, by the weights, as if the 10 of that scale was the denarius, which had already been reduced to mere copper.

The worst examples of reduction of weight are outside of the system of Rome or Constantinople. Tetricus had a barbaric coinage in Gaul or Britain, which ran the half Antoninianus of 40 grains down from 35 to 10 grains. The Egyptians struck blank spangles of copper, which copied the 20-grain Byzantine copper with only 1 or 2 grains of metal. Yet even such reductions could not make more than a reduction to a twentieth of the value by weight, and there is no evidence of such a change imperially.

We are faced, therefore, with changes of value of perhaps 1,000 to 1, by change of metal and weight, but these cannot possibly explain a change of a million to 1 in nominal values. The only explanation of such changes seems to lie in a race of prices against wages, such as we experienced just after the War. In trying to avoid the general loss each union of wage-earners insisted on more pay (increasing the loss of all producers) ; in turn, production demanded a higher price. We ran perhaps to double in this race, and then saw it was hopeless. The Roman world seems to have run ceaselessly on this line, until prices and wages were a thousand times their value. This shows the terrible bondage of the trade unions, in which all labour was frozen ; without a rigid despotism over a trade it would have been impossible to force an arbitrary rise of wage above the level of other trades, and still more to force it so that metallic currency became of fictitious value in name, though not in purchasing power.

How could the currency bear it ? It never affected gold values of goods ; the gold solidus was worth 16 silver drachms, or 7,680 copper drachms, but was reckoned during the mad rise of nominal prices at 600,000 drachms, or 100 talents, and rose even higher. Thus, so far as gold was concerned, the rise was purely in " money of account." In mediaeval times various European nations traded entirely in " money of account," all the coins that were current having their fractional values, just as I have handled a dozen different currencies of irregular values for payments in " money of account " in Egypt. There is nothing improbable, therefore, in the whole trade for a century or two going on in the Roman world by money of account, incessantly driven higher by wages, by prices, by increased rating of the currency, on a fictitious basis. As a collateral matter, the dissolution of the third century must have closed a large amount of trade ; there was therefore an excess of small currency floating, and it tended to depreciate. This, however, was only a predisposing cause which started the system, as, in the finds of silver and billon coins buried later than Gallienus, there are very few coins before his time. There was an immense amount of burying of money during his reign, nearly half the groups that are found ending during his reign, and about a third of the groups start with the currency of his reign. Obviously all the old money of higher standard was either buried or melted up— one of the clearest cases of bad money driving out good.

Regarding the work of Segrè here noticed, it is a pity that so valuable a collection of material should have no list of the works quoted, nor any explanation of the abbreviations used for references. The students of papyri, such as Reil in his study of trades, forget that their sources and references are peculiar to their subject. There are also some arithmetical slips on p. 145 which suggest that a slide rule would be of value to the author. I have to thank Mr. Grafton Milne for many references, and the weights of his large collection of the Alexandrian mint, which he has most kindly supplied.

W. M. FLINDERS PETRIE.

[There has been a difficulty about the price of hiring slaves in the xviiith dynasty papyri (*Z.A.*, xliii, 31). The prices are expressed in rings, of which 12 were equal to 1 *deben*. This shows that the rings were a rather light shekel weight, 12 × 125 = 1,500 grains. All other values would be impossibly low if the day's wage was taken at literally a single day. It cannot mean so many days in a week over a long period, as 17 days is named ; but it might mean the hire of so many days' service in every month during a year. The result would be that a nominal day (= 12) was fixed at 2 shekels, so a single day would be ⅙th shekel, or just the 2 obols that it was in Ptolemaic silver. As certainly copper was far commoner in the xviiith dynasty than silver was under the Ptolemies, the rings cannot have been of copper. On this basis the other prices work out at : goat, 1 drachma ; cow, 12 ; bull, 16 ; female slave, 24 drachmae ; land at 4 drachmae an " acre " must be the hire for one cropping. Such prices are about half, or rather less than the Ptolemaic prices, but that would not be improbable.—W. M. F. P.]

DUALISM IN AFRICAN RELIGIONS.

It is possible to consult many works on comparative religion without being able to gain any ideas on African religions that are at once true and clear. Comparatively few works have appeared in which religious ideas, and more especially West African religious ideas, have received adequate notice. For the ordinary man African religion is characterized by the term " fetishism," one of the most indefinite and most ill-used expressions that it is possible to imagine. Properly speaking, fetishism is the doctrine of spirits embodied in material objects, and nothing corresponding to the popular idea of fetishism can be discovered in West Africa.

Owing perhaps to the dominance of this false notion of fetishism, African religions are often conceived of as homogeneous, though in point of fact there is as great diversity there as in other parts of the world. Mistaken etymologies have also been a source of misunderstanding, and for many years there has been current a myth that the word Tsui-goab, the name of the Hottentot god, means " Wounded Knee."

A year or two ago Dr. Struck unearthed an account of the Hottentots in a work published in 1700, de la Loubère's *Description du Royaume de Sham*, which had apparently been completely overlooked by bibliographers and descriptive writers alike. In this work are eight pages devoted to the "Hotantots," whose name appears to be derived from a word which they repeated in their dances. Regarding their religion, de la Loubère says : " I was told at first that they had no religion ; but I learnt later that, though they have neither priests nor temple, they do not fail at new and full moon to celebrate public festivals which represent their religious rites. I suspect that they are to some extent tinged with Manichaeism, for they recognize good and evil principles, whom they call ' captain of the height ' and ' captain of the deep.' The former, they say, is so good that there is no need to pray to him ; it is enough to let him go his own way, as he does nothing but good. But the ' captain of the deep ' is malevolent, and they have to pray to him to prevent him from causing mischief. That is what they say, but to all appearances they do not pray much."

Our principal authority for the Cape of Good Hope in the early eighteenth century is now recognized to be Peter Kolbe, and the above-cited account is in agreement with what he says. We may therefore assume that this dualism, which was rejected by Ratzel as a European misinterpretation, actually corresponds to the facts, the more so as in our own day Schultze has reported of the Nama of the Kalahari that they recognize a good (black) and an evil (red) god, precisely as do the Hamitic Masai and Nandi, north of the Equator. No reader of A. C. Hollis's accounts of the latter two tribes will be tempted to interpret his data as to dualism, as the result of European misinterpretation. We may therefore accept as accurate the older accounts of Hottentot religion.

Kolbe speaks of two gods—Touquo (perhaps a miswritten Tsui-goab), the evil god, and Gounia, the moon, the good god who gives honey, cattle and milk. There is little doubt but that they are identical with the pair mentioned by de la Loubère.

The Hottentots are completely isolated in South Africa, and there is some controversy as to their linguistic position. Meinhof has assigned them to the Hamitic family, and this near agreement in matters of religion adds force to the argument frȯm language.

Passing over the facts as to the Masai and Nandi, who are Hamites, not negroes, I turn to the area of the Lower Niger, a centre of the reincarnation creed, which I have, for other reasons, brought into relation with the Egyptian belief in the *ka* (*Jl. Eg. Arch.*, 1920, VI, 265–273). The Edo of Benin City believe that each man has two *ehi* (geniuses or doubles), one good, the other bad ; and precisely the same belief is found among the Ewe of Togoland, intimately related in language to the Edo, under whose domination they stood in the seventeenth century, as we learn from Romer. On the other side of the Edo are the Ibo, and in their reincarnation beliefs also we find the same dualism ; in the Asaba area each man is believed to have two *eṛi*, one good, the other bad. We know less of the beliefs of the Yoruba, who lie immediately to the west of the Edo ; it is therefore uncertain whether this feature reappears in their creed.

These facts would have perhaps little bearing upon dualism in religion were it not that among the Edo the dualism repeats itself in their dogmatic theology, so to speak. Their supreme god is Osa, probably a sky god ; the Edo proper, though not, so far as I recall, the surrounding tribes of the same stock, have duplicated Osa. They believe in Osalowa, Osa of the house, and Osaloha, Osa of the bush ; the latter is regarded as malevolent. Their names correspond to these given to the *ehi* and *eṛi*.

The Ewe creed is different, but there are points in it which lead to the conclusion that their beliefs have undergone great changes in a not very remote past; they have now a regular pantheon, by no means a characteristic of negro religion.

The Yoruba creed is in this feature similar, though the details differ. For this tribe we have really only one fundamental text, the account published in 1884 by Baudin, which Ellis issued again in his *Yoruba-speaking People* ten years later without a hint that it had appeared in print before. The Yoruba believe in a mischievous being, Esu, whom they have handed on to the Edo, their neighbours on the east. We have no account of the cult of Esu for the Yoruba, but in Benin I found that he had a priest and received sacrifices, though his ritual differed from that customary in the cult of other deities. The Ibo again offer sacrifice to Ago, a mischievous sprite of the same order.

So far, nothing has been said of the peoples of the Gold Coast, who share with the tribes already mentioned the reincarnation creed but do not, so far as we know, hold the view that the genius is double, both good and bad. Dualism is, however, found in their theology, for Sasabonsum, a deity of a red colour, is everywhere propitiated. It is a singular circumstance that the opposition between red god and black is repeated here.

For the rest of West Africa, partly, it may be, owing to our profound ignorance of the beliefs of many tribes, there is no evidence of dualism save among the Igara and the Kerikeri. The former, who are in language closely related to the Yoruba, worship a good god, Ojuosi, and an evil god, Opoku, according to Temple's *Notes on the Native Tribes*. The same work tells us that the gods of the Kerikeri are Dege (good) and Fifila (bad). It can be asserted with some definiteness that the Temne of Sierra Leone, though their creed included good and bad *krifi* or spirits, had no real dualistic element in their religion.

It has been pointed out already that in East and South Africa the creed of dualism (if we except some of the Nyasaland Bantu) is limited to tribes of Hamitic speech. It is, in this connection, by no means negligible that Yoruba (one of the dualistic tribes of the west) is also one that would be mentioned in any account of Hamitic influence as manifested in language.

It must, however, be admitted that the Yoruba, like the Ibo, have but a very attenuated dualism, so far as dogmatic theology goes. But if dualism is foreign to the negro mind, this is precisely what we should expect ; alien influences are assimilated or modified according to whether they find an echo in the native breed or not. Were it not for the dualistic features in the reincarnation beliefs it would perhaps be hardly worth while considering this side of negro religion at all.

When, however, we find dualism in a well-developed form in a creed which has, at least in part, a foreign element in it, it is worth while to put the question whether the situation is not best explained by supposing that the dualistic features in the reincarnation creed are not a reflection of a feature which came to them originally as a part of a religious creed, and did in fact obtain some small hold in native religion, but flourished unchecked in another field to which it was transplanted—that of human psychology.

It can hardly be accidental that dualism in religion is seen at its fullest development in Benin, where the type of house is wholly alien and absolutely unsuited to climatic conditions, though it does not fo'low that house form and creed were transmitted from the same area and in the same manner.

In putting together these few considerations I do not mean to commit myself to any theory of Egyptian origins ; but I wish to present the facts as one of the problems of African religion which, if they are not due to an internal development to which we should expect to find many parallels among other tribes, can best be accounted for by some influence from the Mediterranean area. It is easier to label elements of material culture with their date and country of origin ; but if we admit transmission in the one case we cannot well refuse to do so in the other, even though the identification of sources may prove difficult or impossible.

NORTHCOTE W. THOMAS.

[A possible relation in Lower Nigeria with the great dualism of Horus and Set in Egypt may be noticed in Eɟi the good and Esu the evil deity, at Asaba on the Niger, and Yoruba adjoining on the west.—F.P.]

ANCIENT EGYPTIAN MATHEMATICS.

CONSIDERING the fact that most of the mathematical learning of ancient times can be traced back to Egypt, it is certainly surprising that we have recovered so little in the way of papyri or other records dealing with the mathematics of Ancient Egypt.

With the exception of the so-called Rhind Papyrus and a few isolated examples of accounts and temple gifts, we have very little to work upon.

Apart from the Egyptian records, the earliest mathematical knowledge dates back to Thales, who in 600 B.C. himself visited Egypt. He wrote on eclipses, the heights of pyramids determined by the lengths of their shadows, the angles in a semicircle and similar problems.

Pythagoras studied in Egypt in the sixth century B.C. Plato spent 13 years at the University of On—Heliopolis—about 400 B.C., and two centuries later Euclid made a name for himself as professor at Alexandria.

The study of mathematics arose out of necessity. Arithmetic was essential for housekeeping, business and government. The need for geometry was of particular importance in a country such as Egypt, where boundaries of property were liable to be obliterated by a fluctuating river. It was essential to have some means of preserving the boundaries of fields and of re-measuring the land which the waters had altered. Herodotus (II, 109) tells us that geometry originated in this way. Diodorus also refers to the fact (I, 81).

The Rhind Mathematical Papyrus and the few other rather scrappy records are but isolated pieces of mathematical work.

The papyrus was copied about 1700 B.C. from an earlier work, dating back, perhaps, to 2000 B.C. It appears to be a handbook on the use of fractions for the agriculturalist, and gives tables and worked-out examples showing how to deal with problems such as the scribes of estates would meet with in their daily duties—the division of a number of loaves among a gang of men, the amount of grain required to fill a granary, and so on.

The first part deals with arithmetic and the use of fractions. Then follows the solution of certain equations, problems on division in unequal shares, and on volumes of granaries. The geometrical section concerns the areas of fields of various shapes. Then come the pyramid calculations and a number of problems of a practical nature.

From this work and the other meagre records we can glean some information as to the mathematical notions of the Egyptians.

From the first dynasty onwards, a decimal system of numeration was in use involving high numbers running into millions. There was a separate sign for unity and each multiple of ten up to a million. (See Fig. 1.)

Multiplication was effected by successive doublings, thus :—

" Calculate 9 to 6 times.

	.	9
	..	18
4		36

6   54 together."

Here the scribe had to multiply 9 by 6. On the left, he indicated by dots or figures the multiple of 9, written down · . As the work proceeded he watched these numbers and, ticking those which totalled 6, completed the addition on the right.[1]

Stroke		**1**
Hoop	∩	10
Cord	ℓ	100
Lotus Plant	⌇	1000
Finger	॥	10,000
Tadpole	⟋	100,000
God, "Heh"	⍦	1,000,000

1,234,567 was written thus :—

Each such sum, therefore, involved writing out part of the multiplication table. The Egyptian never seems to have tumbled to the fact that his work would have been simplified by tabulating the multiples or learning them by heart as we do.

Division was treated as a form of multiplication in the following way :—

" Multiply 7 to find 77.

*	.	7
*	..	14
4		28
8		56

11 together."

In this case, in dividing 77 by 7, the successive doublings bring the scribe to the number 56 : he then sees that 7, 14 and 56 add up to 77. Ticking 1, 2 and 8, he adds them to obtain the result, 11.

[1] In these examples, the ticks of the scribe are replaced by asterisks.

The fractional system was complicated since (with one exception considered later) only fractions with unity in the numerator were used in the working out of examples, thus :—

" Multiply 8 to find 19.

$$
\begin{array}{rcl}
\cdot & & 8 \\
\cdot\cdot & & 16 \\
\tfrac{1}{4} & & 2 \\
\tfrac{1}{8} & & 1 \\
\text{together} & & 2 \ \tfrac{1}{4} \ \tfrac{1}{8}.\text{''}
\end{array}
$$

Here the fractions $\tfrac{1}{4}$ $\tfrac{1}{8}$ are not added by reduction to a common denominator, but are written alongside the integral part of the result as shown.[1]

The fraction of smallest value occurring in the Rhind Papyrus is $\tfrac{1}{5133}$.

The Egyptian appears to have conceived of the fraction as the last part of the divided whole, thus :—$\tfrac{1}{6}$ was " the sixth part," " part 4," namely, the last and shaded portion of the diagram, Fig. 2. He could not work with " mixed fractions " such as $\tfrac{7}{15}$ or $\tfrac{3}{11}$. These conveyed no meaning to him.

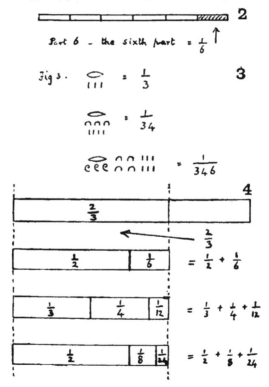

The exception mentioned above is $\tfrac{2}{3}$, which plays a large part in the mathematical work. The Egyptian could write down $\tfrac{2}{3}$ of any quantity without calculation. He may have had tables, but none have yet been discovered.

[1] In the following, when fractions are thus placed together, they are to be added.

Fractions were expressed by writing the symbols for the denominator under the consonantal sign " r," originally " the mouth," which came to have the meaning of " part." (See Fig. 3.)

As mentioned already (with the exception of $\frac{2}{3}$), the Egyptian could not deal with such fractions as $\frac{7}{8}$. He realized it was seven times $\frac{1}{8}$, but he preferred to express it as $\frac{1}{2}$ $\frac{1}{4}$ $\frac{1}{8}$. This brings us to a very important fact—that any fraction can be expressed as the sum of two or more fractions. This may be done in many different ways, *e.g.* :—

$$\frac{2}{3} = \frac{1}{2} + \frac{1}{6}$$
$$= \frac{1}{3} + \frac{1}{4} + \frac{1}{12}$$
$$= \frac{1}{2} + \frac{1}{8} + \frac{1}{24} \text{ and so on.}$$

This is illustrated graphically in Fig. 4.

The Egyptians knew of this and made great use of such " root-fractions." Tables of them have been found, and they existed down to Coptic times. Hero, the Greek mathematician, made use of them in the same way as the Egyptians.

A table in the papyrus gives the result of dividing 2 by odd numbers from 3 to 99, *e.g.* :—

$$\frac{2}{29} = \frac{1}{24} + \frac{1}{58} + \frac{1}{174} + \frac{1}{232}.$$

This fractional system held the Egyptian fast in its grip from the earliest period. There are, however, some indications that "mixed fractions" were dimly understood in a limited fashion, but even when their use had become common among the Greeks, the ordinary folk still held to the cumbrous methods illustrated above.

A little consideration will make it clear how these very cumbrous methods originated and were necessary in practical problems of division of food and other commodities.

Suppose that five loaves are to be divided equally among six people. The primitive method is as follows :—

(*a*) Divide each in half. Give half a loaf to each person. Two loaves remain.

(*b*) Divide these two loaves in quarters. Give one quarter to each person. Two quarters remain over.

(*c*) Divide each of these quarters in thirds. There are six parts, one for each person.

Thus each person has received $\frac{1}{2} + \frac{1}{4} + \frac{1}{12}$ of a loaf.[1] In Fig. 5 this is illustrated graphically and the shares of each of the six persons are numbered correspondingly.

The following is one of several examples from our Papyrus, and deals with the division of nine loaves among ten persons :—

" The making of nine loaves for ten persons. Do thou count it $\frac{2}{3}$, $\frac{1}{5}$, $\frac{1}{30}$, ten times."

Here the answer is given : the share of each is $\frac{2}{3}$, $\frac{1}{5}$, $\frac{1}{30}$—and the proof is set out as follows :—

" (*a*)			$\frac{2}{3}$	$\frac{1}{5}$	$\frac{1}{30}$
(*b*)	*	..	$1\frac{2}{3}$	$\frac{1}{10}$	$\frac{1}{30}$
(*c*)	*	4·	$3\frac{1}{2}$	$\frac{1}{10}$	
(*d*)	*	8	$7\frac{1}{5}$		
(*e*)	Together 9 loaves."				

[1] Professor Petrie points out that the proceeds of sale values are divided among crews of Scotch fishing boats, in precisely the same manner,

Line (*a*) is first multiplied by 2,

$$1\tfrac{1}{4} \quad \tfrac{2}{3} \quad \tfrac{1}{15}$$

but $\tfrac{2}{3} = \tfrac{1}{3} + \tfrac{1}{15}$ and $\tfrac{2}{15} = \tfrac{1}{10} + \tfrac{1}{30}$;

thus we get Line (*b*), which is multiplied by 2,

$$3\tfrac{1}{3} \quad \tfrac{1}{5} \quad \tfrac{1}{15}$$

but $\tfrac{1}{3} + \tfrac{1}{15} = \tfrac{2}{5}$ and $\tfrac{2}{5} = \tfrac{1}{3} + \tfrac{1}{10}$;

thus we have line (*c*), which is multiplied by 2, giving (*d*). Adding lines (*b*) and (*d*) we have

$$1\tfrac{2}{3} + \tfrac{1}{10} + \tfrac{1}{30} + 7 + \tfrac{1}{5} = 9 \text{ loaves.}$$

Other examples provide for double allowances of food for the chief officials.

The only example of a common rule deals with the multiplication of fractions :—

" Making of $\tfrac{2}{3}$ of a fraction, according as it is said to thee, what is $\tfrac{2}{3} \times \tfrac{1}{5}$. Make thou its double, its six times, that is its $\tfrac{2}{3}$."

Evidently the denominators, not the fractions, must be multiplied, thus :—

$$\tfrac{2}{3} \times \tfrac{1}{5} = \frac{1}{2 \cdot 5} + \frac{1}{6 \cdot 5} = \tfrac{1}{10} + \tfrac{1}{30}$$

The reason is obvious, since $\tfrac{2}{3} = \tfrac{1}{2} + \tfrac{1}{6}$.

The solution of simple equations of the form $y + \dfrac{y}{7} = 19$ was effected by the use of root-fractions, in the following way :—

To 7 is added its $\tfrac{1}{7}$ part. The result is 8. 19 is then divided by 8 (in Egyptian fashion), and the quotient $2 \tfrac{1}{4} \tfrac{1}{8}$ is multiplied by 7 to obtain the answer $16 \tfrac{1}{2} \tfrac{1}{8}$. The steps of the process correspond exactly to the modern solution :—

$$\frac{8\,y}{7} = 19$$

$$y = \frac{19}{8} \times 7$$

$$= 16\tfrac{5}{8}.$$

In some problems we get a glimpse of higher knowledge such as Arithmetical or Geometrical Progression. The following is an example :—

" Divide 100 loaves among five persons, $\tfrac{1}{7}$ of the shares of the first three being equal to the shares of the rest."

The " working out " shows that it is assumed that the shares are assumed to be in Arithmetical Progression.

" Proceed as follows. The difference is $5\tfrac{1}{2}$."

Then taking the share of the last person as unity, the scribe writes down the other shares. Finding that the sum is 60, he proceeds to increase each amount by $\tfrac{2}{3}$ and checks the results by adding to 100.

The question arises, how did he obtain the " common difference $5\tfrac{1}{2}$," which would in these days be found thus :—

With the usual notation,

$$(4d + a) + (3d + a) + (2d + a) = 7 (d + a + a)$$
$$\text{whence } d = 5\tfrac{1}{2}a.$$

Either tables were referred to, or use was made of a formula similar to the **modern one.**

Other examples of Arithmetical Progression occur in the papyrus.

In the Moscow Papyrus there is an example of a problem on the Volume of a Truncated Pyramid. This is of particular interest as it indicates a direct application of the modern formula :—

$$\text{Volume} = \frac{\text{height}}{3} \times (\text{sum of areas of top and base} + \sqrt{\text{product of areas}}).$$

The top and base are squares and the last term is obtained directly by multiplying the sides of top and base together.

This problem is not to be found in Euclid.

The Geometrical Section of the Rhind Papyrus is full of gross errors, due probably to the copyists, who often did not in the least understand what they were writing about.

However, it is clear that the Egyptians knew that the area of a rectangular field was to be obtained by multiplying the length by the breadth. In the case of the triangular field an error was introduced by taking the length of a slant side for what we now term the " perpendicular height."

An extremely interesting example is the earliest known attempt to " square the circle." A rough diagram shows a circle—which is evidently meant to be a circle of equal area. Inside is marked the diameter.

The working indicates that the area of the circle is $\frac{64}{81} \times (\text{diameter})^2$, and the following empirical rule was in use :—

" Subtract $\frac{1}{9}$ from the diameter and square the result."

This gives a value for π (ratio of circumference to diameter) of $3 \cdot 1605 \ldots$.

The Pyramid calculations indicate how the measurements of the pyramid slopes were reckoned. The quantity called the " *seqed* " gave a measure of the slope of the pyramid-face away from the vertical, and was equal to the number of spans displacement per cubit of height. A cubit was equal to 7 spans.

Thus in the case of a 4 : 3 pyramid (Fig. 6),

$$\text{the } seqed = \frac{21 \text{ spans}}{4 \text{ cubits}}$$

$$= 5\tfrac{1}{4}.$$

There are indications, too, that the Egyptians knew that if the sides of a triangle are proportional to 3, 4 and 5 (or to 20, 21 and 29) the triangle is right-angled.

One instance of Geometrical Progression occurs. The powers of 7 are set down in order up to the fifth power, and the sum is obtained by multiplication. A second calculation, however, starts with the number 2801, which is then multiplied by 2 and 4 in succession in Egyptian fashion to obtain 7×2801. This gives the same result as before.

With the usual notation,

$$s = \frac{1r - a}{r - a} = \frac{a(1 - 1)}{a - 1}, \text{ when } r = a \text{ as in this case,}$$

$$= 7 \times \frac{16806}{6} = 7 \times 2801.$$

Now by some means or other the Egyptian knew how to obtain the number 2801 in order to check his result.

It is necessary to emphasize again the fact that our knowledge is derived from isolated mathematical fragments. Of the really great mathematical minds among the ancient Egyptians we know nothing. Yet there must have been some who, like their Greek successors, studied the subject for its own sake and whose work gave so great an impetus to learning.

Speaking generally, the Egyptian appears to have regarded the subject from a strictly utilitarian standpoint in order to meet the needs of his everyday life.

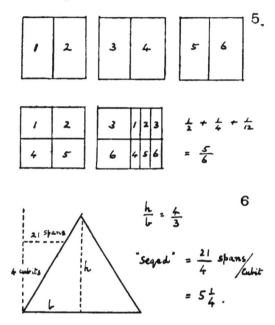

It is, however, not too much to hope that more complete papyri in the nature of mathematical textbooks may yet be discovered. Such works must have existed and Pythagoras alludes to them.

R. W. SLOLEY.

BIBLIOGRAPHY.

Eisenlohr, *Ein Mathematisches Handbuch der alten Aegypter.*
Griffith, " Notes on the Rhind Papyrus," *Soc. Bibl. Arch. Proc.*, Vol. 13, 14.
Borchardt, *Zeitschrift der Aegypt. Sprache*, Vol. xxxi, p. 9.
Touraeff, *Ancient Egypt*, 1917, p. 100.
Sethe, *Von Zahlen u. Zahlworten bei der alter Aegypter.*
Griffith, *Hieratic Papyri from Kahun and Gurob*, p. 15.

PERIODICALS.

Recueil de Travaux, XXXVIII, 3, 4.

MASPERO, C.—*Introduction à l'étude de la Phonétique Égyptienne* (resumed from 1917, p. 83, of this Journal). This deals first with the Greek equivalents of 𓇋. It is represented by A in a large number of words, as Amenti, Amen and its compounds, *anok*, Anup, Alexandros, Arsinoe and others. It appears as E in a few words; as H in others; as I in *iri*, Inaros, Imuthis, Isis; as O or U in Osiris, Onuris and On. In the xviiith dynasty is initial A as Amen, Assur, Arvad, Akhsaf, Apki; also as medial A in Amen Appa. The passage into O later is seen in Arunta (Syrian), becoming Orontes (Gr.); like the change in English of All into ôl as pronounced.

𓄿 in the xixth dynasty changes with 𓇋. Many words in Pyramid Texts beginning with 𓇋𓄿 begin with 𓇋 or with 𓄿 in later times. There is no example of initial 𓄿 in cuneiform renderings; in Greek it is regularly A. In medial positions it is always A, and does not change with 𓇋. It sometimes passes in Greek and Coptic into ε, η, ι, ου, ο, ω. In Greek names medial 𓄿 is *a*, ε, η. ο. The transfer to U is seen in 𓂝𓄿𓎸 KASHA = KUSHU, Assyrian. It passes into ο in Coptic.

𓂝 in early times changes with 𓇋𓄿; and this double vowel for the guttural is like writing Aali for Ali. In Coptic it is rendered by every one of the vowels. In Greek it is A, rarely E or O. In Semitic it is U or A (Assyrian). In Hebrew it is *'ayin*. The cuneiform always has A for terminal place, as in *riya* for 𓂝. The rendering of *'ayin* into Egyptian is 𓂝 or 𓂦 usually in the xviiith dynasty, but also 𓊖 as in Singara and Gaza (*Khazatu*, Assyr.), and as 𓇋𓇋 in Anab and 𓇋 in Anath, in which it varies between *'ayin* and *aleph* in the Phoenician.

The few instances of Semitic names in the xiith dynasty give 𓇋 as *aleph* in Absha (initial) and 'Amu-ansha (final). The conclusion is that it had the value A originally; and as the Latin A has become every other vowel in different words in French, and in English A has quite different values in father, man, what, all, leopard, name, so the original A passed into every other vowel by Coptic times, though it is more usually A than any other vowel. The proved change of A into O and U in proper names between the xviiith dynasty and Greek times confirms this. The group ⌡ 🦅 was to represent *'ayin*, like writing Aali for Ali. ⌡⌡ was ⌡ + ⌡, modifying it like English *ee* in *see*, *need, eel*. As initial it was partly a diphthong, but as medial and final it was usually a vowel, varying between E and I according to dialects.

This is the last paper that Maspero wrote, and there are not even notes to show what else he intended ; but it is of great value as a practical study of facts irrespective of theories. In face of these facts Akhenaten has now been spelt with E, I and O initial in Germany. The search for vocalisation is a vain quest for a permanent transliteration, and such is imperatively needed for Egyptian.

DARESSY, G.—*Un second exemplaire du décret de l'an XXIII de Ptolémée Épiphane.* The first example of this decree was published in *Rec.*, xxxiii, p. 1. The present example, found at Asfun, is in sandstone much worn away, and scarcely supplements the gaps in the previous copy. The name of the father of the canephoros of Arsinoe is corrected to Persomedos.

CHASSINAT, E.—*A propos d'un passage de la stèle No. 8438 du Musée de Berlin.* This stele records a building in Pharbaethos, of the 51st year of Psemthek I, by Paderpos, son of Padasmataui. The sense of the text has been disputed, and here it is proposed to read it, ' I built the' house (or temple) of Qed-nezes of the temple of Hermerti Osiris in Remehet" ', the word Qed-nezes being looked on as an epithet of Horus, like Qed-hou," constructor of the body " of Osiris, which again is like Khnum the modeller.

DÉVAUD, É.—*Un signe hiératique peu connu.* This is two parallel slanting strokes : these appear to be used for a duplication of the single-stroke sign of abbreviation, and may replace the eyebrows, jaws, uraei, lion heads, feathers, wings and other signs.

DÉVAUD, E.—*Le Conte du Naufrage.* A discussion of grammatical details of expression, which do not materially affect the sense.

CHASSINAT, E.—*Gaston Maspero.* This is a full picture of the activities of the great French master, by a devoted pupil who writes with a warm feeling of his sympathy and helpfulness.

Tome XXXIX.

NAVILLE, E.—*L'Auxiliare* ⬟. This is similar to English *do*, as beside being a simple infinitive it comes in such phrases as " do send me this book," or " the watching which I have to do." [Note also the English parallel " Where are you *making* for ? "] It has no form of past, present or future, which are all expressed by particles and auxiliaries. After a detailed discussion of many passages it is concluded that the auxiliary ⬟ expresses mainly the relation of time, as " when," the time in which an event happened or a matter was done.

JÉQUIER, G.—*Moulins funéraires.* The placing of corn-grinder stones in graves is here said to be frequent in prehistoric times ; but the references given are to a kitchen-midden of De Morgan, to xiiith dynasty pan-graves at Diospolis and one stone at Mahasna, apparently the only instance, as another stone there is merely a rough fragment. The millstones with servants grinding, in the ivth–xith dynasties, are not model stones for the dead to use. So it seems doubtful if there is a real prototype of the figures of the high priest of Memphis grinding corn before Ptah, except as a servant of Ptah. The two alabaster blocks with lion figures at the side, found at Memphis, called " libation tables " (Cairo, 63–64), are claimed as representing corn-grinder blocks. [Since this paper, similar blocks with lion figures were found, of the xixth dynasty, in a tomb at Sedment.] Another sloping block resting on two crouched lions is of the vth dynasty from Abusir.

Origine de la coiffure Nemes.—This paper agrees with Dr. Capart's view that the *nemes* is the cloth covering the wig.

Quelques passages de Sinouhit.—Some passages are here discussed, and the words *ua* and *mest-pet* are identified as the anthropoid coffin and the sarcophagus. The *kherp* sceptre had various other names, as *obá*, *hu*, *aáát* and *sekhem*.

DÉVAUD, E.—*Deux mots mal lus.* One hieratic sign is used for two words, ' baker" and a mineral, and has been supposed to be the nose, *khenti.* Here the evidence is given for the first sense " baker " to be the known word *retehti ;* and the second *seti* for the mineral, which was used as paint, and has been guessed to be green, red, yellow and clay by different translators. It was imported from Nubia and in jars, so M. Dévaud would render it " Nubian earth " ; and he adheres to the view that the ⌒⌀ sign is a bow.

SPELEERS, LOUIS.—*Un papyrus funéraire de basse époque.* This is a charm on a papyrus 8 by 7 inches, with one line on the back, visible when it is rolled up. It is one of the type of " writing that my name may flourish," or " endure " as is here proposed. The text consists of some ideas from common sources, developed according to the taste of the time. It reads : " Words spoken by ———— true voiced, born of Asgertet, true voiced, ' I am Ra at his rising, I am Atmu (at his setting), I am Osiris Khentamentet, the great god, lord of the East [read rather *Abdu*, Abydos]. Grant me your attention O ! guardians of the Duat, open to me (the gates of heaven and earth). Receive this good ———— O ! guardians of the hall of the two Maots who guard the (bull of the Duat). O ! Anubis in Ut, I am one of the guardians who watch for Osiris. Take pure water of Osiris, fresh water for thee, water from Elephantine, milk from Athribis . . . one brings to thee a jar full of drink offering. Receive fresh water of the temple of Ra . . . of Mehen. May thy *ba* go forth to follow the God. He will not reject thee from heaven or from earth . . . thou sittest as a prince unto the end. Thou art great ; thou shalt appear at Busiris, established is thy dwelling. . . . To thee (are given) the rays of the Sun, the pure flow of the jar of drink offering . . . in the midst of Dendera, thy flesh rejoiceth, thou art united to . . . thou art before the East. Receive for thee water from the altar of Thesduat at Heliopolis. (I am) the breath of Amen, and the water of the Nile. I am thus eternally.' " On the outside is written, " An effectual phylactery. May it remain on thy bones and rest on thy flesh, without being destroyed."

BLACKMAN, A. W.—*Sacramental ideas and usages in ancient Egypt.* At Heliopolis Ra was regarded as being purified by water before the sun rose, and the high-priest performed the washing of the image of Ra daily. The high-priest in prehistoric time " was of course the King of Heliopolis." Therefore the king had to be purified daily by priests acting as Horus and Thoth, otherwise Horus and Set. The pool from which the water was taken was identified with Nun, the primaeval ocean, from which the sun-god was born. [This suggests that the worship arose on the coast, where the sun was seen to rise over the Red Sea.] After that the king was purified by incense and natron mouth-wash. He was then robed and bore insignia. The same course of ceremony was applied to the Ra image. At the king's death the body was to be similarly prepared for its admission to the company of Ra.

In the Osiris system the dead god was likewise washed, and this revivified the corpse, which was otherwise stated to be revived by eating the eye of Horus. [But the passage of the Pyramid Texts quoted to show the washing, never mentions it, but is concerned with purification by disincarnation : " Unite to thee thy bones, take to thee thy head," after the skeleton had been dissevered and stripped. The different modes of purification must be carefully distinguished. Again in the xixth dynasty the same idea remained : " May Anubis attach for thee thy head to thy bones. Mayest thou be purified . . . in the presence of Horus and Set." Such passages should not be misquoted as referring to washing a corpse.]

Various examples are then illustrated of the lustration of a deceased person, figured in tombs. As these actors are funerary officials, and not gods, it implies that this indicates the actual purifying of the body, and not a moral purification by deities. This purification as applied to the dead Osiris is linked with the inundation covering the fertile land, which is the same as Osiris, as the god from whom vegetation springs up. Various other connections of ideas naturally arose, as that the water was from the pure caverns of the Nile, that it represented the vital fluid of Osiris, or that it was from the Pools of Life ; the Egyptian was capable of interminable permutation of ideas. The use of solar formulae in Osirian ceremony may suggest that the lustration is first solar ; but the priority of Ra or Osiris is a very complex subject, probably to be solved by their both being immemorial gods of different races coming from east and west.

CHASSINAT, E.—*Un type d'étalon monétaire sous l'ancien empire.* This deals with the well-known sale of a house in the ivth dynasty, published by M. Sottas. The house is valued at 10 ⬚ (), and was paid for by three pieces of goods valued at the same amount. This *shot* had been taken as a measure of cakes, from the usual word *shout*, cake. But examples are here quoted from the xviiith dynasty of values in ⬚, which is assumed to be the same unit, and translated " ring " *shot ;* and in one case 16 *shot* + 1 *deben* totals as 2 *deben* 4 ? *shot*, implying that 12 *shot* was equal to a *deben*. In any case, it was a standard of value. Here the subject is left : but we may ask why is this standard of 1/12th of a *deben* ? The *qedet* was well known as 1/10th of a *deben*, and therefore this is not likely to be another name for 1/10th. It looks like the leaf-shaped arrow-head, but that was unknown in metal in the ivth dynasty, and only approached in the xith ; and it is too heavy for a flint arrow-head, nor could that be made of regular weight. The 1/12th of a very heavy *deben* would be a light value for the Babylonian shekel ($152 \div 12 = 12.7$).

The phrase *em uzeb* is rendered by " in exchange " or " replacement," which would be a general term for barter, agreeing with *uzeb*, " to turn round." It was certainly usual in later times to state values of all kinds of goods in weights of copper, just as the Romans did before silver coin became usual. A list in the papyrus Mallet is quoted, also the supply of 50 *deben* of copper for the housekeeping at the Ramesseum, and we may add the list of values in the tomb robberies under Ramessu X, all stating weights of copper.

CHASSINAT, E.—*Sur quelques passages du* De Iside et Osiride *de Plutarque.* The statement that Horus was born " feeble in his legs " is traced to the form of the hieroglyph in the name ![glyph] . The fish, as an emblem of hatred, is the fish *betu*, and *betu*, to execrate or hate, has the fish determinative. The accusation by Set against the legitimacy of Horus is confirmed by passages where Isis states his posthumous conception. The story that Isis allowed Set to escape, Horus in wrath tore her royal head-dress off and Thoth replaced it by a bull's head, is found at length in the Sallier papyrus IV. The mutilation of Set by Horus, stated to be represented at Koptos, is a misunderstanding of the usual figure of Min. The pig is stated to have been unclean, but sacrificed and eaten at full moon because Set, chasing a pig by moonlight, found the coffin of Osiris. The sacrifice of a pig is named among offerings at Edfu.

CHASSINAT, E.—*Fragment des* Actes de l'Apa Nahroou. One leaf of parchment ; a fellow leaf is in Cairo Museum.

JÉQUIER, G.—*Le Monde à l'envers et le monde souterrain.* In the xcixth chapter of the Book of the Dead is described " that evil world where the stars fall upside down on their faces and know not how to raise themselves." While the astronomical scenes treat the invisible heaven like the visible, the commoner view was that some subterranean passage served to pass from west to east ; or an animal with two heads, double lion, double bull or double sphinx, which swallowed on the west and disgorged at the east. Lastly, the passage became divided into hours, with successive gates and monstrous guardians.

GUNN, BATTISCOMBE.—*The Egyptian for* " Short." The ignorance about the equivalents for many of the commonest ideas is remarked ; and it is proposed that the word ![glyph] is to be rendered as " short," as in several passages quoted it is in opposition to " long."

" *To have recourse to* " is proposed as the rendering of ![glyph] illustrated by several passages.

A note on the verb WRŠ proposes that it is not only " to spend the day time," but that it implies the whole time, and *szr* means similarly the whole night. The sense is that of continuous occupation.

CHASSINAT, E.—*Note sur deux scarabées.* A splendid scarab of lazuli, 4 inches long, is inscribed with *nesut da hetep* for the chief of the royal caravan Pedatnubt. Another scarab, 2 inches long, in schist, has eight columns of inscription naming tribute brought by the chiefs of Naharain to Tehutmes IV, who " smites the lands from Naharni to Kary," from north to south. This is interesting as the forerunner of the large historical scarabs of Amenhetep III.

TOURAIEFF, B.—*Les pertes récentes de l'orientalisme en Russie.* " Our unhappy land, where they destroy with so much zeal the acquisitions of civilization, has lost in the recent months many of its eminent orientalists. Nikolsky, Saleman, Radlöff, Wesselowsky, Chukowsky, de Lemm, are no more." To these we must now add the name of Turaieff himself, a victim since writing this dirge : " The death of the greater part of these scholars has been hastened by the terrible events which unfold themselves here." A short biography of Nikolsky and Oscar de Lemm is given.

SPELEERS, L.—*La stèle de Mai.* This Moiy was scribe of offerings to all the gods in the temple of Sety I at Abydos, son of a chief of archers, Bes, and Urmur. The stele shows Sety I receiving life from Osiris, with his chief son (*tep*) Rameses behind him bearing a feather fan, without a cartouche. This proves that the eldest son was already dead, and that Rameses was recognised as chief son in Sety's lifetime. The hymn to Osiris, in fourteen long columns, is completely set interlinear with the parallel copies I and II of the Middle Kingdom, III–V of New Kingdom and chap. 181 of the Book of the Dead, with a full translation. This will be the standard text for the future. There are also many notes and a statement of the position and functions of all the gods named, with references for every point, a very valuable key to authorities in mythology.

JÉQUIER, G.—*Le préfixe* 🦅 *dans les noms d'objets du Moyen Empire.* The conclusions are that most words beginning with *m* are compounds formed of a verbal or substantive radical, with preposition *m* in the usual sense of *for, in, of.* Some words with *men* are whole radicals. The preposition *m* may be compounded with the following letter in one sign, as in *men* and *mes.* Before a strong guttural, *k* or *q*, *m* is followed by *n* or *o* for euphony. The examples, for instance, are *m·onkht*, an amulet, " for life," *m·neferti* " for beauty," *men·qebyt* " for refreshing," *m·den·khes* " for (making) to cut the razor," the hone.

DÉVAUD, E.—*Étymologies Coptes.* A paper on thirty-eight Coptic words.

GAUTHIER, H.—*Les " Fils royaux de Kouch " et le personnel administratif de l'Éthiopie.* This paper completes the account of the Ethiopian viceroys given in the list by Dr. Reisner. The title " royal son " does not mean an actual son of the king, but is a title of the viceroy ; there are other " royal sons " of Nekhebt, Thinis, Amon, etc. The royal sons of Rameses are probably descendants. The viceroys were almost always in intimate contact with the king, before their acting as deputies. Their functions were solely civil, and not military. The names given are : Aohmes-să-Tayt, about 1570 B.C. ; his son Aohmes-Tura, 1555–1538 ; Sen, 1537–1486 ? ; Nehy, 1486–1449 ; Usersetet, 1449–1423 onward ; Amenhetep, 1423–1409 (or less at each end) ; Mermes, 1409 or earlier–1375 ? ; Tehutmes, 1375 ?–1350 ? ; Huy, 1350 ?–1335 ? ; Pasar I, 1335 ?–1325 ? ; Amenemapt, 1325 ?–1299 ? ; Any, 1299 ?–1297 ? ; Heq-nekhtu, 1297 ?–1280 ? ; Pasar II, 1280 ?–1262 ; Setau, 1262 or earlier–1237 or later ; Messuy, 1237 or later–1214 ; Sety, 1214–1209 ; Hera I, 1209–1180 ? ; Hera II, 1180 ?–1170 ? ; Pasar III, 1170 ?–1160 ? ; Un·ta·uat, 1160 ?–1155 ; Rameses-nekht, 1155–1130 ? ; Panehsi, 1130 ?–1110 ? ; Her hor, 1110 ?–1102 ; Pionkh, 1102–1080 ? ; Nesikhensu, 1020 ?–1006 ; Uasarken·onkh, about 850. Various other officials and lieutenants of Kush are discussed, for which the paper should be studied.

REVIEWS.

—•—

La Religion d'Israël. By RICHARD KREGLINGER. Sm. 8vo, 335 pp. 1922. (Bruxelles, Lamertin.)

This is another volume of the series which was noticed in this journal in 1920, p. 57. The first work dealt with principles admirably ; here, in the application of them to a very complex and debatable case, there is naturally much more scope for temperament. The author begins with the dating of the sources of the Old Testament ; he would place the final revision of the Hexateuch to the age of Malachi, while taking portions of it as being of the two or three generations after Solomon. These dates seem impossibly late, when we look at the general historical style. He agrees to the date of the earlier part of Isaiah, but what a gulf of style there is from that to the book of Samuel ; then again, what a gulf between that and the opening of Exodus ; again an immense difference between the business-like style of Exodus and the poetic style of Genesis. Can all these great changes be pushed through in two centuries of a uniform kingdom ? It looks far more like the five centuries back to Exodus, with large differences affecting the nation in the interval. There may have been small editing, but the bulk of the documents seem to require something very near their face value in dating. Again, if large changes were as late as after the return from exile, could they ever have been enforced on all the Jews who had been scattered in Egypt and elsewhere at the exile ? The accepted body of writings must be pre-exilic, except those which were new history, as Ezra and later works. In other respects Prof. Kreglinger sets his face against the extravagances of Cheyne and others, and keeps to a quiet and sane judgment.

The literary point of view seems to override the archaeology when we read, ' La critique biblique est essentialement littéraire ; elle recherche la date d'un texte; mais non point celle où les idées que ce texte exprime furent pour la première fois enseignées, verbalement ou par écrit." The archaeologist thinks of facts before the expression of them ; criticism must begin with the credibility of statements and their relation to known facts.

The various races and factors that enter into the complex formation of Israelite ideas are then discussed. There is the Troglodyte, as at Gezer, with his sacred caves (kept up still at the Haram and Bethlehem), the pig sacrifice, cave paintings as in Europe, and Neolithic work. Next the Canaanite Semites who burnt the dead and sacrificed the first-born. Here the author parts with the old view of their home being in Arabia, and recognizes the early Semite in North Syria and Babylonia, whence he spread to Assyria. This view, lately enforced by Prof. Clay, is strongly supported by the North Syrian invasion of Egypt in the VIIth dynasty. A remarkable detail of human sacrifice, at the foundation of building, is the burial of parts of bodies at Gezer ; similarly at the Labyrinth at Hawara, part of a man's body and a woman's body, cut in three, were found in the sand-bed beneath the corners of a building (*Labyrinth*, 33–4).

Next the Babylonian influence is considered, and the dynasty of Hammurabi is called Amorite. Tablets of his age name Yau-ilu, or Yahveh is god, centuries before Moses. The Babylonian Ishtar appeared as Ashtoreth in Palestine, and repelled some but attracted other Israelites. The Egyptian influence is first quoted in Sinai under Zeser, but it was as old as the Ist dynasty under Semerkhet. There are statements here which show the unfortunate habit of reading more in a text than is there : " La pratique de la circoncision dont les Israélites croyaient, peut-être à tort, que c'est en Egypte qu'ils l'avaient adoptée," with reference to Jos. v, 2. There is no such belief, only the statement that the generation which left Egypt had died off. Then the winged disc is said to ornament the high-priest's dress, with reference to Ex. xxviii ; there is no trace of any such ornament suggested. On p. 75 it is said that David set up a stone on the threshing-floor of Araunah, to connect this with the worship of sacred stones ; but it is really stated that he built an altar and sacrificed. On p. 87 the brazen serpent is said to have had prodigious powers in the rout of Amalek ; it is never alluded to in that account. Further, all the temples were guarded by a serpent ; there is no trace of that in Palestine. The facile statements, for which references are quoted, have no support in those references ; this " reading in " is too common a habit with biblical critics.

The references to Asher under Tehutmes III and Sety I ; to Samnu under Tehutmes III, and Samhuna under Amenhetep IV, as Simeon ; to the well-known Yakub-el and Yusef-el, are quoted as reasonable. Also the Khabiri and the Aperiu are both accepted as 'Abri, Hebrews, though one can imagine some hard things being said if anyone but a critic equated *'ain* and *cheth*. The account of Deborah is accepted, and not theorised away as has been the fashion. The usual word *shaqatz* for an abomination is read here as *tabu* ; but that distinct sense is not applicable in Ps. xxii, 24 : " For he (the Lord) hath not despised nor tabued the affliction of the afflicted " ; the simple " abominated " or " abhorred " is a far better rendering.

A proposal which is attractive is that there were four codes of different sanctuaries recorded. After the recognized code of Ex. xx. at Sinai there was the law attributed to the second tables, of which ten commands are in Ex. xxxiv, 14–26 ; there was the form of ten commands at Mount Pisgah, Deut. v, 6–21, which might belong to the sanctuary of Beth Peor beneath that ; and there was the code of 12 commands at Mount Shechem, connected with Baal-berith, the Lord of the Covenant.

There are many interesting suggestions under Magic, Mimetic rites, Vegetation rites, the Prophets and their functions as against mere ceremonial, the influence of Persian views of Dualism and the hierarchy of angels, and the function of intermediaries. There seems rather too mechanical a view of all these various parts, too German an air of analysis—a lack of the sympathetic realisation which is essential to anyone dealing with aspirations. In even the most mistaken devotion one may write of it from the worshipper's point of view, if it is to be really understood in its bearing on life, or its implications. One must be all things to all men if one is to understand their minds.

Die Plastik der Ägypter.—By HEDWIG FECHHEIMER. Sm. 4to. 59 pp., 168 pls. (Cassirer, Berlin.) 1920.

This popular book is of value to students as giving many large photographs

QUEEN OF GALLA TYPE.

of sculptures in Berlin which are not published or collected together elsewhere. We may note the remarkable sharp profile of Amenemhat III (53), the strange head (54–56) ; the queen with high cheek-bones and massive hair, like the Galla and El Kab sphinx type (57, 58). The group of Amarna heads (79–93) is welcome, pending a publication of the German excavations. The aspect of the profiles is greatly altered by the wrong positions given ; the facial slope has been sacrificed to keep the neck more upright : what the true position should be is proved by the Louvre bust (86) which places the brow and chin in a vertical plane. Some heads (as 83) are tilted up 18° skew. The same error is seen in the hawk head (45) repeated on the cover. The figure 115 is not from Medum ; by the name it is probably from Saqqara. The German is discreetly silent as to the price of the book, so as to get whatever he can.

On the Physical Effects of Consanguineous Marriages in the Royal Families of Ancient Egypt. By the late Sir M. A. RUFFER. 8vo, 46 pp., 27 figs. 1920. (" Proc. Royal Soc. Medicine," Vol. xii.)

This paper puts in shape the family histories of the XVIII-XIXth dynasty and the Ptolemies. The genealogy of the XVIIIth dynasty shows that each of six generations married a half-brother except Amenhetep I, who was a full brother ; and the last three married Syrian princesses, probably of Egyptian descent. Certainly these latter marriages did not improve the family vitality, and there is very little to show of any bad effects in the six related generations. In the XIXth dynasty there was closest in-breeding for three generations without any obvious ill effects. It is rather hard to write of Ramessu II as being completely bald ; he had a fair fringe of hair left when he died at 77 at least, or more probably 85. In the XXVth dynasty the Ethiopians followed half-sister marriage. In the Ptolemies full sister marriage was usual. The physical condition does not seem to have been much affected, but there seems to have been a moral deterioration, even for that bloodthirsty age. The main point which is pressed is that there was no deaf-mutism or congenital disease, which is usually attributed to such marriages. In modern times it may well be that certain weaknesses of structure tend to draw together, from unconscious sympathy and a sense of difference from the average world ; in short, the in-breeding is a result of the weakness, and not a cause of it. Nature does the right thing by pooling such stocks to their extermination.

NOTES AND NEWS.

The great event of recent weeks has been the opening of the tomb of Tut·onkh·amen. It will always occupy the first place in public imagination, as making the world familiar with the magnificence of the Egyptian monarchy. The existence of such kind of objects has hitherto only been imagined by those who were familiar with the monumental representations; now all the world will realise the sumptuous display of the "Great House." The art will also impress the public with the ability shown, though it will not surprise those who knew the fine work of the tomb of Yuaa, or the still finer style of earlier times. The taste shown in the alabaster vases, made in one with the stands, and over-loaded with elaborate handles, differs much from the simpler beauty and more graceful designs of previous epochs.

As for history, we cannot hope for much from a tomb, unless the king took with him a justification to the gods, like the great papyrus of Ramessu III. But a most interesting historical link is seen in the strange animal-headed couches. The cow-head couch has spotting inlaid on it of a trefoil form; this is foreign to Egypt, but is well-known in Mesopotamia, as on the couchant bull in the Louvre. The weird dog-head of another couch is also entirely un-Egyptian. Now, as Kallimasin, king of Babylonia, sent to Amenhetep III a couch of *ushu* wood, ivory and gold, with three couches and six thrones of *ushu* wood and gold, it is certain that there were Babylonian couches in the Theban palace; and this description of ivory and gold refers to the dog head with ivory teeth and tongue, while the other couches are of wood and gold only. Later than than Amenhetep III, Syria was too much disturbed, and Egyptian prestige in Mesopotamia was too slight, for such presents to be sent. They must be as old as Amenhetep III, and there seems no doubt that these are the very furniture described in the Amarna letter. In accordance with this, we find that each was constructed in four parts, with bronze jointing to fit together. Furniture made in Egypt is naturally all united in one, with fixed joints. But for a rough land journey of over a thousand miles, it was needful to make couches with separate sides, frame and base, in order to pack and transport them.

No doubt there was an imitation of Egyptian motives, as in the Hathor cow-heads, and the tails copied from lion couches. This only shows that they were made for presents to Egypt, and not that they were the work of foreigners in Egypt, because there would be no purpose in the elaborate bronze jointing, instead of solid joints. This detail would not be necessary if they were merely moved about the palace or put on a Nile boat. We see then, for the first time, court furniture of Babylon, and it will be of great interest to examine the technical details of the construction and compare it with Egyptian work. The short form of the couches shows that the Babylonian slept contracted, like the prehistoric people, while the Egyptian couches are all full length.

If some articles were thus of a previous generation, it is very likely that others were likewise old ; and the footstool, with nine foreigners under it, may well be that used by Amenhetep II as figured a century before.   On the death of Tut·onkh·amen, who was the last legitimate king of the great family, it seems that the palace furniture was largely buried with him, as there was no heir to inherit.

Of all the Egyptian work the most informing to us will be the dress and personal detail.   The colour weaving, the attachment of ornament, the construction of jewellery, will show much that is new to us.   The glove has astonished people, but, as Miss Murray observes, gloves are figured in scenes, both among offerings and also worn.

The immediately urgent matter is that all these things should be preserved in the dry air of Qurneh, and not taken to the winter fogs of riverside Cairo. A large new building must be provided in any case, as the Cairo Museum is far too full to take in properly all the objects which are piled up in four chambers of the tomb.   The obvious site is Qurneh, somewhere south of Deir el Bahri.   There a substantial museum should be built, without any upper floor, and entirely lighted from the north.   Then will come the question of the efficient publication of all this mass of objects.   The Egyptian Government should begin by an appropriation of £30,000 for the museum and £20,000 for publication.   They cannot grudge a few *per cent.* of the value of what has been found for them, if they get everything for nothing.   No one can hope that these things will last for another three thousand years ;   probably this sheen of gold will perish by ignorant greed within three hundred years.   A complete photographic and coloured reproduction of every object from various points of view, and with full diagrams of details, is the least that this generation owes to the past, which has guarded its treasure till now.

BRITISH SCHOOL OF ARCHAEOLOGY IN EGYPT.

Mr. Brunton and four students have been working steadily through the remains of the great cemetery at Qau-el-Kebir ; the site seems to have been largely exhausted by native, Italian and German workings, without any record or publication of the past discoveries.   A prehistoric cemetery will soon be examined, and there is much to do in copying tombs in that district.   This is the only British work in Egypt this winter.

Mr. Mackay is in Mesopotamia for Oxford and American work.   It is hoped that he will also clear up the history of the early civilisation in the Persian Gulf for the British School, in view of the possible connections with Egypt.

On behalf of our School also, application has been made to reserve an important site at Jerusalem.   These extensions of the British School work have been caused by the intended change in the Egyptian law of antiquities, by which the Government could take everything of interest or importance from an excavator.   All the British and American excavators have protested that such a change would probably stop excavation in Egypt.

PUBLIC LANTERN LECTURE OF BRITISH SCHOOL EXCAVATIONS. SEE PAGE 32.

ANCIENT EGYPT

1923. PART I.

CONTENTS.

EDITOR, PROF. FLINDERS PETRIE, F.R.S., F.B.A.

YEARLY, 7s. POST FREE.   QUARTERLY PART, 2s.

BRITISH SCHOOL OF ARCHAEOLOGY IN EGYPT.
MACMILLAN AND CO., LONDON AND NEW YORK;
AND
EGYPTIAN RESEARCH ACCOUNT,
CHICAGO.

ANCIENT EGYPT. Net price of each number from booksellers is 2s.

Subscriptions for the four quarterly parts, prepaid, post free, 7s., are received by Hon. Sec. "Ancient Egypt" (H. Flinders Petrie), University College, Gower Street, London, W.C. 1.

Books for review, papers offered for insertion, or news, should be addressed :—
Editor of "Ancient Egypt,"
University College, Gower Street, London, W.C. 1.

Subscriptions received in the United States by :—
Miss Helen Gardner, Art Institute, Michigan Boulevard,
Adams Street, Chicago, Ill.

1 ; 1 ALABASTER FIGURE OF MENKAURA. GIZEH.

ANCIENT EGYPT.

A PORTRAIT OF MENKAURA.

THIS remarkable figure, obtained some time ago for University College, London, is cut in white alabaster, highly polished. It shows a further stage of the idea of the great **Khofra** statue; there the king's head is shielded by the falcon's wings, spread out behind the head-dress; here the king is himself the falcon god, entirely human in front view, entirely bird-like at the back. How the figure was completed below is a difficulty; the lower part is gone, and the dealer had simply added plaster for a flat base. Was it seated or standing? It would seem more likely that the figure was seated, and the falcon's tail spread out on the seat behind, leaving the human legs to come forward unaffected. The

resemblance to the *bourgeois* face of Menkaura is obvious at first sight; and the development of the protecting falcon would accord with this representing the successor of Khofra. Further, on being asked about the source of it, the dealer at once said Gizeh, without apparently any idea of the portraiture. There can hardly be a question that it came from one of the two temples of Menkaura. We know of the dedication of falcon figures in the temple of Sneferu at Meydum (Petrie, *Medum*, xxix, and see xxxiv–v). This is a parallel figure of the king's *ba*, in its guise fit for the heavens.

A Portrait of Menkaura.

Another unique object of early date, obtained for University College, is a cylindrical measure with a loop handle, cut in dark green volcanic ash, or durite. It is fluted around the body, probably copied from a reed on a much enlarged scale. On either side of the handle it is inscribed. It is clearly a standard measure of the temple of Hor-behedet, and was stated by the seller to have come from Edfu. On it is a prayer to the hawk-sphinx, " Lord of Edfu give all life and health to the great god Hor . . . u." The finely simple and bold outline of the seated sphinx shows the early date, and it could hardly be assigned elsewhere than to the Old Kingdom. Evidently the Horus name is incomplete ; there has been a space left above the chick, apparently owing to indecision on the engraver's part. What names could be intended ? The first ending in *u* is *mezedu* Khufu. In the Vth and VIth dynasties most names end in *kho-u*. There is only room for one sign over the *u*, and only for a narrow sign possibly extending down before it.

Sekhem-kho-u Shepses-ka-ra, or *Onkh-kho-ra* Merenra would be possible. There does not seem to be room for *user*, *nefer*, or *neter* before the chick. If, however, any very common signs had been intended, it is difficult to see why the engraver was baulked, and waited for instruction. It is far more likely that it was the unusual sign *mezed*, which was not sufficiently explicit in the hieratic writing to make sure how it should be cut. It seems, then, probable that this is of Khufu, a part·of the general ordering and regulation of the country which was his great work.

The contents are 20·8 cubic inches ; this was the old Syrian unit, known later by the Greek name of kotula. It is reckoned in metrology as 21 c.i., the middle of the actual Egyptian examples that we have is 20·8, and in the tomb of Hesy of the IIIrd dynasty, the external volume of the measures figured averages 21·1 cubic inches, and, therefore, a little less internally.

. W. M. FLINDERS PETRIE.

THE MAGIC SKIN.

A CONTRIBUTION TO THE STUDY OF THE "TEKENU."

[The *Tekenu* is the figure of a man wrapped in a skin, which was drawn on a sledge at the funeral, as represented in the XIIth and XVIIIth dynasties. The discussion of the Egyptian examples will follow in the second part of this paper which here deals with the parallels which may serve to explain the rite.—F.P.]

THE true aim of archaeology is to put life into the dry bones of the facts revealed by excavation and research ; to reconstruct the skeletons of ancient customs and ceremonies from the bones of facts unearthed ; to clothe them with flesh, and so by comparing what we are with what we were, to enable us to appreciate at their true value the possessions, mental, spiritual, and material, which we have inherited, for the benefit of ourselves and posterity. Egyptology has unearthed many such skeletons of rite and ceremony, more or less complete, but the bodies had ceased to live ages before the religious practices had ceased to be performed, and one may well be pessimistic as to whether the ideas and beliefs that underlay them will ever be discovered. But, to use a medical simile, the body of the mass of facts that Egyptologists have at their disposal might well be tested to a greater extent than is yet being done with the serum derived from ethnological research, of which the Golden Bough is a notable example, so that the reactions may be noted, and more concrete knowledge gained thereby of the genera of ideas, beliefs and practices which lay behind. The mass of our ideas about the religion and ceremony of ancient Egypt are as lifeless and stiff as the sculptures and paintings which represent them on the walls of chapel and temple. We may be sure that the *Sa*, or magic fluid, imparted by the touch of priest, king, and god, and by magical implements, like the *ankh*, and *urhekau*, for example, was as real and vivid a reality to the ancient Egyptian as the " medicine " of the African witch-doctor of to-day, known in other verbal guises in various parts of the world as *mana, prana,* or *baraka.* " It implies some supersensual influence or power. It is not in itself personal, though it may dwell in persons as well as things. It lives in the song-words of a spell, it secures success in fighting . . . and benefits the one who can employ it in every walk of daily life. It has the range in idea of power, might, influence, and may include spirit energy of character and majesty . . . an immense reserve of potency pervading the world on which man may draw for good or ill. . . . The idea is clearly existent in Indian religious thought and many primitive African beliefs." Similarly : " On the West Coast of Africa [it is believed that] man has within him a kind of life power called *kra* : it existed before his birth . . . It will continue after his death . . . It is behind all the activities of nature . . . It operates in the storm wave, the lightning flash, the strength, cunning and lethal characters of lion, leopard, snake, and smallpox. The dead must be appeased with offerings lest he return and injure us . . . Primitive tribes set this energy working on their behalf by pantomimic dances to promote the growth and abundance of plant and animal."[1]

[1] Estlin Carpenter, *Comparative Religion* (Home University Library).

At the same time, it may well be true that quite early in Egyptian history, the glow of life had faded out of religious practices : that the rites performed by the tribe had become sacerdotal ceremonies, merely dramatic representations whose meaning was ill- or misunderstood, or even completely lost, the performances being regarded only as mysteries.

It is clear that in primitive society this life essence, *prana* let us call it, was supposed to imbue the sacred person of the totem, whether plant or animal, to which the tribe belonged. " The tribe was of animals as well as men ; the men kangaroos danced and leapt, not to imitate kangaroos, but for natural joy . . . that they were kangaroos, of the Kangaroo Tribe . . . As belief in magic declines, what was once intense desire issuing in the making or being a thing, becomes mere copying of it."[1]

Besides this engine-like " pumping up " of *prana* by the kinetic action of the tribal dance, it could be brought into the human body sacramentally on special occasions by the very materialistic and practical method of eating a *prana*-filled body : either the totem animal, or a member of the tribe specially devoted for the purpose. Similarly, it could be imparted to the fields for the benefit of the crops by scattering the chopped fragments or ashes of the burnt body upon them. When the idea of holiness and the concrete belief in the existence of gods materialised (gods still of a very human type), *prana* would similarly be transmitted to them, and the material body of the life devoted for the purpose would come to be regarded as a sacrifice in the ordinary sense of the word.

Now the *prana* with which the sacred body was imbued (the blood being the vehicle as the life stream) would, like the blood, be absorbed by the skin of the sacrifice. The skin so eminently adapted for dramatic usage in dance, rite and ceremony, would thus become an important adjunct to religious performances, and could be used to impart *prana* to the crops by hanging it on a tree or pole, typifying vegetation, or to superintend the growth of the corn as the corn spirit.[2]

The following are examples of rites performed with the skin as a vestment. At Hierapolis a worshipper knelt on the skin of a sacrificed sheep, drawing the sheep's head and trotters over his own head and shoulders. He prayed as a sheep to the goddess to accept his sacrifice of a sheep.[3] Similar, and even more striking in its significance, is a custom observed by Indian Moslem pilgrims at the largest mosque at Baghdad. In fulfilment of a vow on recovery from sickness, a man, stripped to the waist, has a lamb or kid slain over his head, so that the blood flows upon him. He is then wrapped in the skin. " How could the identification of the man with the kid be represented more graphically ? " is Frazer's[4] comment, and the identification is significant for the purposes of our subject in hand.

The following rite was performed by a Nubian woman at Sohag, Egypt, which the narrator learnt on enquiry was Egyptian. It is a form of the " Zar," and is performed in fulfilment of a vow to a saint in connection with a wish for health and prosperity. The woman, the vower, procures a brown or black ram

[1] Jane Harrison, *Ancient Art and Ritual* (Home University Library), pp. 30, 34, *seq.*

[2] Ainus practice with bear skin. Jane Harrison, *op. cit.*, p. 90. Prussian Slavs custom at harvest with goat skin. Frazer, *Golden Bough*, i, p. 18.

[3] Frazer, *Folklore in the Old Testament*, i, p. 414.

[4] Frazer, *op. cit.*, i, p. 427.

and feeds it 30 or 40 days. She is then purified with henna and cuts her nails. Henna is applied to the ram's brow against the evil eye. At dawn she and her female assistants, clad in white, bring the ram into a room. A fire is lit in the middle of the room, and, with the aid of her assistants, she rides round the fire eight or nine times, her bare body, apparently, in contact with the ram. As she rides she throws incense on the fire.

A man reputed for sanctity then enters, slays the ram, and goes out. The woman's feet are steeped in the blood, which is also smeared on her hands, brow, head, and breast. The assistants feast on the flesh, and the hoofs are tied to the woman's hair and are afterwards kept by her. Prior to the feast the woman lies on the blood-wet skin of the ram, which the slayer, entering again, had disembowelled and cut up. As she lies, the others cook the meat, and feast.[1]

The Hausas of Northern Nigeria, whose religious beliefs and practices are shown to have curious affinities with ancient Carthaginian cults, perform skin rites, of which the following are examples. At the sacrifice to the totem animal and its tree, a black bull or, failing that, a black he-goat, is killed, and the blood smeared on the tree, and led by a channel into a hole at the roots of the tree. The flesh is eaten and the head buried. The chief, who is also chief priest, and four other priests, don the hide in turn. They and the other worshippers dance round the tree, and eat the flesh.

In the worship of the snake totem, a black bull or he-goat was killed, and the blood spilt on the ground for the snake. The meat was eaten by the worshippers, and the priest-king or priestess danced round in the skin still wet with blood. Hag Ali, Tremearne's trusty informer, explained that the skin was worn in order to obtain *baraka* from it.

The king, when his strength fails, is killed and wrapped in the hide of a bull. His successor smears himself with the blood.[2] This is in the North. In other parts the slain (strangled) king is dragged to his grave in the body of a bull, which has been slain over the new king so that he is drenched with the blood.[3]

The practice in Ancient Egypt of killing a ram on the festival day of Ammon, and placing the skin on the statue of Ammon, may be fitly mentioned here (Herodotus ii, p. 42). There is reason to believe that the skin of a goat, the ægis of Pallas-Athene, was similarly placed on her statue, and Haj Ali's explanation applies to both cases.

Prana was similarly imparted to the new god-man in the terrible ancient Mexican ritual, after the killing and flaying of the man who had represented the godhead, and been previously and similarly imbued with the divine spirit.[4]

Similarly, priests dressed themselves in the skins of slaves, sacrificed to the Mexican god of fire, and were worshipped as the incarnate god.[5] These cases are all of the same category as the Hierapolis rite before-mentioned.

Examples have now been given of the use of the mystic skin to impart its powers to crops, men, statues of gods, and deified living men, and one can readily appreciate how, when men's thoughts turned to gods above them, they should have sent them *prana* to fortify and restore them by sacrifice of the *prana*-charged sacred creature, man or beast.

[1] Wakefield, *Cairo Scientific Journal*, V, Feb. 1911.
[2] Tremearne, *Ban of the Bori*, pp. 33–52.
[3] Tremearne, *Hausa Superstitions and Folklore*, p. 104.
[4] Frazer, *Golden Bough*, p. 220.
[5] Frazer, *loc. cit.*

The reason for stuffing the skin, and placing the animal in a plough or field of crops, or placing them about the tomb, is also clear enough. The spirit beast imparts his blessing to the fields or mystically ploughs it.

In Transylvania, at Ascensiontide, the village girls dress up the " Death "— a threshed-out sheaf of corn—as a girl, with a broom-stick for arms. The Death is stripped and thrown into the river by boys.

A girl dresses in the discarded clothes and they go through the village in procession, singing the hymn with which they had brought out the Death : " the girl is a resuscitated death."[1] We should rather say that the name Death was a misnomer, through confusion of the dummy victim with its fate. The rite seems closely allied with the Mexican practice above described, the dress playing the part of the skin.

A trace of a magic skin with powers of a diffused kind comes from an ancient Celtic source, the Mabinogion of Wales. In one of the tales, " The Dream of Rhonabwy," the hero enters a ruined hall, and finding rest impossible on the verminous and comfortless straw mattress, eventually lies down on the old yellow calf-skin before the smoking fire on the hearth, " a main privilege was it for anyone that should get upon that hide." There he has a series of wonderful prophetic dreams.

Examples will be next given where the virtue of the skin is of a less diffused kind. If the *prana* is absorbed by several persons at once this will naturally be regarded as a bond of brotherhood, or, rather, the skin could readily be employed with this object. A number of such rites are given by Frazer.[2] The Scythians made a covenant by treading upon the hide of a slaughtered ox. " They all become one with the animal and with one another : treading the hide is a substitute for wrapping a man completely in it." Pacts were similarly made by walking between the two halves of the body of an animal cut in two. The idea behind this appears to be brotherhood through ritual birth by passage through the body of the animal.

The following example of a ritual rebirth seems to be totemistic.

The Patagonian Indians sometimes, when a child is born, kill a cow or mare, cut open and remove the stomach, and lay the child in the still warm receptacle. The tribe feast on the rest of the animal. A variant of this custom is, to catch a mare or colt, hold it upright with lassoes, split the animal open, extracting the heart, and place the child in the cavity while the body is still quivering. " The motive is to ensure the child becoming a fine horseman in the future. It is a piece of sympathetic magic designed to endow the child with equine properties."[3]

Although it is not a skin rite, it is clearly legitimate to regard it as embodying the same category of ideas.

An analogous skin rite is performed, before circumcision, by the Kikuyu, who call it being born again, or born of a goat. A goat is killed and a circular piece of the skin is passed over one shoulder and under the arm of the child to be reborn. The other shoulder is similarly treated with the goat's stomach. The mother, or woman acting the part, sits on a hide with the child between her knees ; she and the child being bound about, together, with the guts. She groans

[1] Harrison, *op. cit.*, p. 60.
[2] *Folklore in the Old Testament*, Vol. I, part ii, chap. 1, pp. 391 *seq.*
[3] Frazer, *Folklore in the Old Testament*, i, p. 413.

as if in labour, the gut is cut by a woman as though it were the navel string, and the child imitates the cry of a new-born goat.

We can hardly be wrong in assuming that the use of the skin replaced the employment of the body, with all its unsavoury accompaniments, among races practising the skin rite as they became more refined ; the latter being besides a much handier way of performing it.

The strip of skin clearly takes the place of the whole hide in the following Galla custom. It is customary for childless couples to adopt children. The real parents relinquish all claim to the child. An ox is killed, the blood smeared on the child's brow, some of the fat is placed upon its neck, and its hands covered with portions of the skin.[1]

A further stage of the development of the rebirth rite, from which the sacrificial element is eliminated, is the form practised in India by persons of high rank as an expiation or cleansing from ceremonial impurity. The sufferer has to pass through the golden figure of a woman or cow as though in parturition.[2] Instead of a cow a vessel in the shape of a lotus (containing in the case reported a consecrated mixture of products from the sacred cow),[3] or a large pot representing the womb, is, or was, employed in India as an expiation for caste pollution (*cp.* note below), in which the person was sealed up for a prescribed time.[4] A tub filled with fat and water, in which a man sat with clenched fists, was similarly employed in India as a purification by simulated re-birth before he could return to his family after being given up as dead : that is, no doubt, after ghost-laying ceremonies had been performed against him in his absence.[5]

A large number of other re-birth performances, more or less graphic, are given by Frazer in this part of the work in question, one of which must be quoted in conclusion of this section, as the development *in excelsis* of the principle, since by means of it, in conjunction with certain sacrifices, a man was supposed thereby to become a god for the time being.[6]

After being sprinkled with water he feigned to be an embryo and was shut up in a hut (the womb). A white robe and black antelope skin typified the inner

---

[1] Frazer, *op. cit.*, ii, " Jacob and the kidskins," p. 6 *seq.* In this chapter Frazer discusses the affinities of the Kikuyu and the Gallas, regarding the similarity of their usages to those of the Semites. Arguments which go in the direction of indicating that elements of these tribes had their origin on the north-east coast of Africa (and, therefore, were near enough to Arabia to be influenced by Semitic customs, if not of similar origin to the Arabians)— such arguments apply equally to support the suggestion, that such customs may have been adopted from Egypt, or that they developed out of usages common to both, in the distant past.

[2] Frazer, *op. cit.*, ii, p. 35. It was performed by two Brahmins in the eighteenth century who had defiled themselves by going to England. The passing through the body of a colossal cow was performed as recently as 1894 by the Maharajah of Travancore, in accordance with custom, to attain high caste by rebirth : the family being by birth low caste (l.c.). *Cp.* Herodotos, ii, p. 129. Mycerinus' daughter entombed in the figure of a cow. The object, however, was rather that of the Galla and Kikuyu practice detailed above.

[3] Frazer, *op. cit.*, ii, p. 37. Used by Maharajah of Travancore in 1854.

[4] Frazer, *op. cit.*, p. 37. That the rite with the cow figure is a refinement of a practice similar to the Patagonian, Kikuyu, and Galla is rendered probable by the fact that for fancied or real pollution a child or man in North India is passed, or crawls to and fro, through a real cow's legs (p. 39).

[5] Frazer, *op. cit*, p. 31, where this interesting rite is given more fully. Rites of rebirth were celebrated in ancient Greece with the same object.

[6] Frazer, *op. cit.*, p. 32. It is called the *diksha* (v. also Moret, *Mystères*).

and outer membranes respectively, and a belt the navel-string. He kept his fists clenched, and if he moved it was because a child moved in the womb. " By these observances, besides . . . his natural body, he acquired a new and glorified body with superhuman powers . . . by new birth he became a god."

To summarise our conclusions. Rites are, or were, performed with the skins of animals with the objects of adapting, to human needs, the inherent vital magic force (which we call *prana*) which the animal possesses by virtue of its being a totem or else a sacred animal (probably the latter implies the former), or one specially devoted for sacrificial slaughter. *Prana* is immanent in all things, but the life principle is especially rich in it—a sacred or devoted life eminently so. The blood and skin are vehicles of it, especially convenient to manipulate and apply in any desired direction. Man can benefit the gods by supplying them with it through sacrifice, for the restoration of their energies. Through the skin worn on the body it may be of general benefit to the wearer ; it can imbue him with its own divine nature and power, or bind him in brotherhood through it to the persons who are in contact with it at the same time. It can impart its virtue to the spirit of a dead man by contact with the corpse. The benefits of regeneration and purification by virtue of the *prana* can be achieved by simulating physical birth from the body of a sacred animal, or the qualities of an animal can be imparted to a human being by simulated birth from it. This is done by employing the actual body of the animal, or a simulacrum of the animal, with appropriate rites and adjuncts, or a skin of the animal. The same end can be achieved by acting as an embryo in the womb, but, at this stage of development of the rite, the ritual is the potent element, and the same applies to the form of the rite in which a simulacrum of a body is used. At any rate, the materialistic utilisation of *prana* is not evident : if anything, this virtue is drawn down or attracted from the deity by the ritual. Lastly, the effect on a human soul of funerary ceremonial can be counteracted by a rite of rebirth, if the soul in question is, in fact, still in the flesh. Virtually, the man's body is dead and the ceremony is performed to benefit his soul. This is the nearest we get to rites of rebirth performed for the benefit of a deceased person, from the evidence above laid before the reader.

ERNEST THOMAS.

(To be continued.)

CUSTOMS AND SUPERSTITIONS OF THE EGYPTIANS[1] CONNECTED WITH PREGNANCY AND CHILD-BIRTH.

THE Egyptians are as a race eminently conservative. During a period of more than sixty centuries, the essential type has undergone but few changes. They still retain those distinctive traits of physiognomy, and peculiarities of manner and custom, which the united testimony of their monuments and the literature of the past reveal to us as characteristic of their ancestors.

Among the customs which have been handed down and preserved in this way few are more interesting than those which surround the birth of a child. These customs I believe to be identical with those which were observed in ancient times, and so have suffered no material change since the earliest days of Egypt's history, remaining unaltered among all the vicissitudes of fortune which the nation experienced in the course of so many centuries. Though we cannot always trace the origin of each particular custom, and explain the meaning of many practices and observances of to-day, we may safely attribute their obscurity and apparently meaningless character to the fact that they were a part of the primitive religion of the Ancient Egyptians, and have only become inexplicable since the religion itself became obsolete.

Following the natural order, then, I will deal first with pregnancy, giving a brief account of the system of hygiene and general treatment which is relied upon during this period ; and will then devote my attention in greater detail to the treatment adopted during confinement, which forms the main subject of my paper. I shall lay stress on the points which have an archaeological interest, and only mention in passing those of a purely medical consequence.

In those places in which the *harem* system is still duly observed in Egypt, or in the houses of the lower middle class, or in those of the country, the male physician has nothing at all to do with the pregnant woman. It is not until her life becomes positively endangered that the physician steps in to treat the case, and even this custom has only sprung up in quite recent times, with the spread of knowledge and increasing belief in the efficacy of medical science. In Cairo and the other towns there are many well-known accoucheurs who have earned a great deal of reputation and they find more than they can do ; but in the country, the old prejudices still dominate. Except when a serious case of this kind presents itself, the entire responsibility of the woman through the whole period is undertaken by the midwife. There are at present two orders of midwives. The first order are the graduates of the School of Nurses, and midwives attached to the Government School of Medicine. These are well educated and well taught. They are called *hakimahs,* feminine of *hakim,* which is the popular

---

[1] The subject of this article was first treated in 1904, and published in the *Records of the Egyptian Government School of Medicine,* Vol. ii. It was almost literally copied by a recent writer on the Copts. The present version of it is written from an antiquarian point of view and not from a medical one.

term of a medical man. It is a misnomer, because they are really no more than ordinary midwives. The second order of midwives are the traditional ones, that keep up the old state of things. They usually learn their art from their mothers, and old relatives, practise it on some women in their neighbourhood, and then, before they can be recognised by the Government, they pass a most perfunctory sort of examination in order to obtain a licence. They usually come from the lowest classes, and in the country, of both Upper and Lower Egypt, they reign supreme.

We hear of the midwives of Egypt in Exodus i, when they were asked by Pharaoh to kill all male children of the Israelites. The name given to them is in the Coptic version called ⲫⲉϧⲟⲩⲉⲥⲓⲟ, from the verb ⲑⲩⲉⲥⲓⲟ, to deliver. The common term in Arabic for the ordinary accoucheuse of the second order is داية, dâyah. The classical term is قابلة, qab¹l²h.

. . The Egyptians hold a strong belief about the changes which take place in the nervous system of the pregnant woman, and their effects upon the unborn child. The health and appearance of the coming offspring is thought to depend upon the objects with which the woman is brought into contact before delivery, especially during her first three months. The sight of a beautiful face, which has been habitually looked at by the woman, goes far to guarantee the birth of a comely child ; and any object for which the mother has shown a fondness before delivery tends to be reproduced in shape or form upon her child's body. A woman who had had a longing for apples during her first three months, and was unable to get them, was said to have given birth to a child with a growth of a reddish colour, not unlike an apple. In a second case, a woman who had trained an ape during her pregnancy, was said to have been delivered of a child of an ape-like appearance. A similar belief may perhaps be traced back amongst the Jewish nation by a reference to the similar occurrences recorded in Genesis xxx, 38, 40, 41, and xxxi, 10. Thus the custom has formulated the law that " all pregnant women should live comfortably, and should have what they long for." In this way has arisen the practice of giving to a woman any kind of food or drink that she demands during her period of pregnancy, in order to avoid the risk of reproducing the shape of the desired object upon her infant's body. I have known ladies of good position who during their whole period of pregnancy carried about with them the picture of a beautiful child, at which they were constantly looking, believing that this practice would ensure the reproduction of similar features in their own offspring. This belief is not a peculiarity of the Egyptian nation. Certain cases of barrenness among women are not attributed to any disease, or physical defect in the generative organs of the female ; hence it is considered absurd to consult a physician in such cases. The causes are to be sought elsewhere. Certain kinds of coins, particularly the ancient coins, whether Roman or Greek, in fact any gold jewel that is made of what they call Venetian gold, or 24 carat gold, if worn by a female on a visit to a friend in confinement are supposed to stop impregnation. The same effect is produced on the confined woman if the visitor should chance to see a funeral or dead body on her way to her friend's house, or have about her any old relic, as ancient Pharaonic amulets, or have been herself recently confined. In all these cases barrenness results. Such condition, when it arises, is not, of course, to be treated by ordinary human methods, but must be assailed by remedies of the same nature as the objects which caused it. Relics and coins similar to those which caused the mischief, if possible the same ones, must be taken and soaked in water for a certain length of time, usually twenty-four hours ; the infusion thus produced is to be drunk by the patient. If the cause were the sight of a funeral or a dead body, then the woman who has been thus affected by her friend has to visit the cemeteries or mortuaries and step across dead bodies or parts of corpses. They often request special permission to visit the dissecting rooms of the School of Medicine.

This superstition is called in Arabic مَشَاهْرَة, and a woman thus affected is spoken of as مِتْشَاهْرَة. The origin of this word is rather difficult to find out.

The word comes from شَهْر, a month, and, unless I am not much mistaken, must refer to the monthly periods of a woman. The whole superstition, in fact, is based on the idea that if a woman is losing face, another who is confined causes her the harm. The superstition is absolutely indigenous, and I have looked for it or any traces of it amongst the neighbouring nations of Syria, Palestine, or the Sudan, in vain. In the dictionaries of the Arabic language the word *meshahrah* does not possess this sense.

Charms and amulets are prescribed for the same reason by old women of experience, and are obediently worn by those who consult them. A pregnant woman may also be injured by the smell of any pungent substance, such as lime in process of slaking, carbolic acid, assafœtida, garlic roasted in butter, and so on. These same odours are supposed to be obnoxious to any open wound, and when infection takes place in any wound the cause is at once put down to the fact that the wound " has smelt."

Just as in the ancient times people were very curious to know the sex of the coming offspring, so do they nowadays adopt almost exactly the same methods as described in the ancient Medical papyri, such as Ebers Papyrus, the Berlin, the Magical Papyrus of London and Leyden, etc. The methods are so similar that I need not repeat them here.

As soon as the first pains of delivery are felt the midwife arrives, and brings with her the chair on which the pregnant woman is to sit while she is in labour. This chair is a sort of stool, with the seat hollowed out from the front in the form of a half-circle. Two upright rods are fixed, one at each corner of the front edge of the seat, and these act as supports for the woman to grasp when she bears down during the second stage of labour. These chairs are sometimes decorated, and they differ in their make according to the position of the family. Unfortunately, they are disappearing quickly in Cairo and other central towns in Egypt with the advance of modern methods of medicine, but in the country they are still very usual. This method of delivery is extremely ancient, and we find it adopted in exactly the same manner since at least the XVIIIth dynasty. It is common amongst many half-civilised people in Africa and elsewhere.[1]

The Egyptian monuments do not, unfortunately, speak of any ordinary cases of delivery, but of the miraculous ones there are many instances. In the story written in the Westcar papyrus[2] the birth of the first three kings of the Vth dynasty is described. Also in the series of inscriptions and pictures at Deir

---

[1] Larrey, *Description de l'Egypte*, Vol. xiii, p. 213.

[2] Erman, *Die Märchen des Papyrus Westcar*, Plate X, p. 7 ; Plate XI, l. 3, pp. 62–65 ; Maspero, *Contes populaires* (4th Ed.), p. 38.

El Bahri,[1] at Luxor,[2] which depict the birth of **Hatshopsitou** and Amenhotep III, both directly descended from Amon himself. Also certain pictures of the Late Period depict the birth of the Sun or other deities. From these documents one can gain the knowledge of certain data which are precise enough, and which enlighten us greatly about the ordinary methods of accouchements. The other data found in the Medical Papyri[3] and the Magical ones[4] contain a great deal for our instruction.

In the earliest times the chair had not yet, apparently, been in use. One can easily suspect this, as M. Jéquier says,[5] from the determinative of the words 〔hieroglyphs〕, that all signify " deliver, to give birth." The woman must have sat upon the ground on her feet and the helping women around her.

The use of the chair, however, must have been very early, and its development and evolution is described by M. Jéquier in the *Bulletin*, T. XIX, 1921, p. 39.

Apparently the word for this chair was 〔hieroglyphs〕, which was the most commonly used. There were other words, however, for it, viz.: 〔hieroglyphs〕. In Coptic it was called ⲧⲥⲟⲩⲓⲥⲓ, and, according to M. Jéquier, this word must come from an ancient word like *〔hieroglyphs〕, which has not yet been found. In Hebrew one finds the word אׇבְנׇיִם (sing אׇבֶן).[6]

As a rule the midwife never interferes with the progress of affairs, and leaves nature to accomplish its work. She simply sits squatting in front of her patient and invokes the aid of all the saints of which she knows, that they may intervene and facilitate the labour. يا ستى كهله انتعينا من دى الوحله " Y3 s̔tt̔y Kᵃḥlᵃʰ 3ntᵃʿyn3 m̔n dy 3l wᵃḥlᵃʰ." " O Lady Kahla, deliver us from this difficulty." While the patient is uttering cries and shrieks in the severity of her pains, all the members of her family sit round sympathising with her in her suffering. When the child is born the patient is transferred to her bed.

If the course of labour, however, be prolonged in any way, by weakness or any other cause, hot stimulant drugs are administered, which are mostly decoctions of cinnamon or crocus. So was it in the olden times, treatment was applied in the form of external application to the lower part of the abdomen or internally in the form of injections, or ovules to be introduced in the patient. All sorts of

---

[1] Naville, *Deir El Bahari*, Plates XLVI–LV.

[2] Gayet, *Le Temple de Luxor*, Plates LXVI–LXVII ; Champollion, *Monuments*, Plates CCCXL–CCCXLI ; Lepsius, *Denkmäler*, iii, Plates LXXIV–LXXV.

[3] Pap. Med. de Kahoun ; Griffith, *The Petrie Papyri*, Plates V, VI, pp. 7–11 ; Pap. Ebers, Plate XCIII, XCIV (*cf.* the translation of Joachim, Papyrus Ebers, pp. 169–173) ; Pap. Med., No. 3038 of Berlin, etc., see the *Bulletin de l'Institut Français*, T. XIX, 1921, p. 37 *seq.*

[4] Brugsch, *Recueil de Mon. Egyptien ;* Griffith, *The Petrie Papyri*, etc.

[5] *Bulletin, op. cit.*

[6] Exod. i, 16. The ordinary sense of this word is " potter's wheel." It might be cognate to אֶבֶן, " stone " (*v. Bulletin, op. cit.*). See also *Edinburgh Medical Journal*, 1908, September, by Sir Alexander Simpson.

material were used, viz. : salt, honey, onions, oil, incense, mint, wine, even pieces of tortoises and scarabs.[1] Hot drinks were also administered. Just as in olden times medicines and incantations were utilised for diseased breasts and milk, so nowadays the same means are also adopted.

As soon as the child is born the woman is placed in her bed and thus the first night is passed. In the morning the midwife proceeds to perform the operation of " opening the eyes." This is done by raising the child's eyelids and painting the eyelids with a solution of coal-tar قطران, and then sprinkling them with kohl. There are many kinds of kohl, but that used for children is made up by burning incense and almonds or nuts, and collecting the soot that is formed. The soot obtained in this way being very soft is employed as an eyepaint, the constant use of which is supposed to colour the eyes black.

On the third day the woman is subjected to special treatment. Leaves of bitter oranges, dried leaves of *Artemisia maritima santoninica* (Arabic شيح), the fruits of acacia, *Nilotica* (Ar. قرظ ، قرض), ϣⲟⲛⲧ Coptic, ⟨⟩ are boiled together in water, and a decoction is prepared therefrom ; with this are administered hot douches, hip baths, and stupes.

The next point to be considered is the diet. A puerperal woman is supposed to be abundantly fed for two purposes, firstly, to compensate for the loss of blood, etc., which she has sustained, and secondly, to fortify her system and assist the secretion of milk for the nourishment of her baby. However poor the woman may be, she has to provide herself with one chicken at least for each of the first three days of her confinement ; should she be better off, she is kept almost exclusively to a chicken diet during the first ten or twelve days. Wine is given to nearly every puerperal woman. Another very common but important article of diet is a sort of pudding made with bread cooked in treacle and the seeds of a very common indigenous plant named Helbah. It is the *Trigonella Foenum Graecum.* It is named in Coptic ⲛⲓⲁⲁⲓ,[2] and is supposed to be called[3] ⟨⟩ in ancient Egyptian. It belongs to the group of bitter stomachics, but is reputed to be a nervine tome restoring health to the exhausted patient. Another most important drug that is used is made from the powdered root of a certain plant known in Arabic by the name of مغاث, " Mugāt." The only name I could find to it in scientific language is the French *Grenadier Sauvage.* It is indigenous to Arabia, and is called in Classical Arabic القلقل . This is usually mixed with other drugs, when it is spoken of as مغاث ممحوج or "compound mughat." *Nigella sativa,* حبة البركة ، *Ceratonia siliqua caroube,* الخروب ، cinnamon, cloves, cardamoms, nutmeg, and various other drugs of the aromatic series are often mixed with it. The preparation is made as follows : a quantity of butter is first melted and some crushed nuts are roasted in it, *mughat* is then mixed with it, and the whole well cooked together; lastly, water is added, sweetened with sugar, and the mixture is then well shaken up and served in cups. Butter may be replaced

---

[1] *Papyrus Ebers,* Plate XCIV, L, pp. 4–22.

[2] *Kamal, Flore Pharaonique,* p. 61, قاموس النباتات ال فيروعنيفى .

[3] *Ibid.,* p. 61.

.with sesame oil or dispensed with altogether. It has the consistency of a jelly of a brownish-yellow colour, with a delicious aromatic odour and taste.

It may be noticed that this preparation is drunk not only by the confined woman, but also by all her visitors. " Mughat," as a decrepit old midwife informed me, " solidifies the liquefied bones of a puerperal woman." A decoction of hot caraway كراويه is also very commonly used.

A third preparation which is given to puerperal women is known as the *Hălăwăh Mefattaqah* حلاوةمفتقه , or the " composite sweets." It consists of the powdered extract of forty kinds of odoriferous plants, mostly of the species of the bitter stomachics. I shall make the study of these forty drugs the subject of a special paper. These are roasted in sesame oil (سيرج *sîrig*), treacle or honey is poured over them liberally, and the whole is eaten with the greatest relish. Women of experience have to be called in to prepare this dish, for it requires great skill to obtain the correct flavour which makes it so rich and delicious. When made with black treacle it is of a dark greenish-black colour and very thick, and of a rich and agreeable taste.

This *halawah* or electuary is usually eaten with a specially-made pastry called *kumagah* كُمَاجَه , which is made into round loaves about five inches in diameter, ornamented in the circumference, and painted over with a layer of honey and sesame. The dough is kneaded with butter (سَمَن) (or oil سيرج , if the patient be a Copt and the puerperum occur in a fasting season).

The *halawah* and *kumagah*[1] are usually distributed in small quantities to friends and near relatives, and are highly appreciated. Chicken, specially prepared with milk and flour (كشك), *kishk*[2] ·sauce, are also eaten. Before closing this part of the subject it may be mentioned that it is customary among the Copts to give to a confined woman large quantities of wine to drink, a stimulating treatment which may sometimes be most useful.

We now come to the seventh night after delivery, or the *Lĕlĕt-el Subûc*, ليلة السبوع . To call it the seventh night is really literally not true, because the fête is never really held on the seventh day, except very rarely. Most often it is adjourned to the tenth, fifteenth, or even to the fortieth day. Among the rich, especially those who have few children, this night is kept as a great festival ; a splendid banquet is served, musicians are hired, and the occasion resembles a wedding feast. But what chiefly concerns us is the treatment which the mother and babe receive at the hands of the midwife. The seventh night is the first occasion on which the child is given a bath, unless he be the offspring of syphilitic parents, in which case he is not touched with water until the end of his first year. The water in which the child is washed is not to be thrown away, but is kept in a glazed earthernware pot, ماجور اخضر . If the child is not washed, the pot

---

[1] This word does not exist in the Arabic dictionaries. It has an absolutely Coptic or Greek look about it, and may come from an original *ⲕⲟⲩⲟⲝⲉ, *ⲕⲟⲧⲩⲗⲗⲟⲅⲉ, or Κουμεγα ? ? I have never met with it.

[2] The plate, chicken with *kishk*, is so highly favoured that it goes as a saying, in speaking of a conceited person, that he thinks of himself as a " chicken with *kishk*," فرخة بكشك .

is filled with water in which a piece of soap is lathered. In the centre of the pot is placed an *abriq*, ابريق (a washing pot, a big copper vessel commonly used for washing the hands), if the infant is a boy, or a *qullah*,[1] قلة (the ordinary vessel for drinking water) if it be a girl. In either case the vessel in question is decorated with the usual insignia of the respective sexes. Thus the *abriq* is adorned with a tarbush and watch and chain, and the *qullah* with a headkerchief, earrings, and so on. Round the rim of the pot are stuck three candles,[2] which are lighted simultaneously. The parents and friends choose three names, and each candle stands for a name. At the end of the evening the candle which burns longest gives its name to the newborn child. This custom may be traced to an ancient Egyptian mythological origin. The seven Hat·hors[3] that were supposed to be present at the birth of children may be the origin of the seven candles.

On the same night the midwife provides herself with small quantities of corn and cereals of every kind, wheat, maize, peas, beans, lentils, and others, and places a portion of each, together with some nuts, in the pot. Another portion is stuffed into a small pillow, with the help of the instrument with which the cord is severed, and on this pillow the child must sleep until he has grown old enough to distinguish his own name. This is purely magical to protect the child from the evil spirits and to prevent his being exchanged by some evil spirit for a measly, feeble baby.[4] A third portion is tied up in a piece of cloth and placed under the pillow on which the mother rests her head.

In the morning of the eighth day the child is taken from his bed and placed in a large sieve (غربال), and shaken just as wheat is sifted in order to remove the dust and pebbles from it. (See *Ancient Egypt*, 1915, p. 88.) A large brass pestle and mortar are then placed by the child's head, and the midwife takes the pestle in her hand and makes with it a loud ringing sound as if she were crushing something in the mortar. As she makes this noise she mutters a sentence in the ear of the child : " Hear thy father's orders," says the midwife, wielding the pestle vigorously. " Follow thy mother's advice," she continues, and the mortar rings again under her blows. Then the mother is directed to step three times over her child as he lies in the sieve.

The *abriq* or *qullah* is next taken out of the pot, and the water found in the latter is sprinkled over the threshold of the room. Sometimes a boiled egg is placed in the pot and is given to the oldest person to eat. Each of the guests tries to snatch some of the nuts in the pot, giving in return a piece of money to the midwife, and places what she has captured in her purse for luck. A very interesting procession then follows. All the children in the house are gathered together, holding in their hands lighted candles. In front of the procession walks the midwife, holding the child to her bosom, and carrying a quantity of cereals and common salt in a piece of cloth. The procession starts from the room in

---

[1] The word قلة is the Coptic word ϪⲰⲗ, ⲕⲁⲁⲑ, Egyptian ⟨hieroglyph⟩ and has passed into Arabic unchanged.

[2] The original number of candles was seven, and in certain parts of the country it is still so ; but through Christian influence it has become three.

[3] Maspero, *Contes populaires Le Prince Prédestiné.*

[4] Marasmatic children, particularly those who are congenitally specific, are believed by a certain class of the population to have been changed by the spirits, مبدول.

which the birth took place. All the company chant in quaint Arabic the following rhyme :—

بدایاتك ورجلاتك حلقه زهــ من وداناتك

تغيش و ترنى ولاداتك

"With thy hands and thy feet, a golden ring in thine ears, mayst thou live and rear thy offspring." This hymn is, of course, addressed to the infant child. In this way the procession visits every room in the building, and the midwife sprinkles the grains in every room. When the round is completed the child is returned to the mother, and so ends the ceremony.

So far there is no difference in the adoption of these customs between Christians and Mohammedan Egyptians, and except for occasional mention of the names of saints, and the use of certain Christian names, one cannot tell the difference. There is no doubt whatever that the Mohammedans adopted those customs from the Copts.

Circumcision amongst the Copts in Upper Egypt is common, but never in Cairo or large cities. Amongst Mohammedans it is the rule.

Baptism follows on the twentieth day for boys and the fortieth for girls, according to the canons of the Church, but it is often delayed through negligence.

Dr. Geo. P. G. Sobhy,
Late Senior Assistant Professor of Anatomy,
School of Medicine ; Physician, Kasr El
Ainy Hospital ; Lecturer in Medicine, School
of Medicine.

REVIEWS.

———•———

[The following work by the great Czech scholar appeared at the beginning of the war, and was left unnoticed in England, but should be recorded.]

Das Getreide im alten Babylonien. By DR. FRIEDRICH HROZNÝ. Part I, pp. 216. 1914. (Vienna.)

Thanks to Dr. Hrozný's brilliant researches, our knowledge of cereal conditions in Babylonia has passed beyond guesswork. From Aramaic annotations on cuneiform tablets we knew, indeed, that the ideograms ŠE·BAR and ŠE·PAT, which occurred in later times, stood for barley. Such was the abyss of ignorance, however, that even an absurd suggestion found support that the ideogram GÚGAL might mean maize, though maize is known to be of American origin. This ignorance was all the more deplorable since ancient Babylonia has been considered by many to be the home of the cultivation of grain. The importance of agriculture in Babylonia is manifest from the mass of Babylonian records which are concerned with the revenue and expenditure of temples and palaces and with taxes and leases. Whilst silver was used as currency for purchases by the Babylonians, yet taxes, rents and wages were mainly paid in field produce, particularly in the older periods, hence the frequent mention of varieties of grain in cuneiform texts. (In this connection it is interesting to note that, in spite of statements to the contrary, the stage of pure commerce in kind cannot be confirmed by the cuneiform texts, as the oldest documents mention silver and copper as payment media.) The numerous finds of grain in Egyptian excavations have contributed most to the solution of the problem of what kinds of grain were cultivated in Egypt. In such departments of archaeology, Assyriology is far behind Egyptology, and even these finds date to the latest period, and have not been investigated botanically. The author appeals to all explorers to pay heed to the vegetable remains in graves, store-houses, clay bricks, etc., as being of equal importance with records and monuments. He also directs attention to the varieties now cultivated or growing wild in the Euphrates land, and quotes Glaser, who brought back some ears of grain from South Arabia, which enabled Kornicke to identify it as Emmer. Dr. Hrozný sets out to ascertain which kinds of grain were cultivated by the ancient Babylonians (Sumerians and Akkadians), and Assyrians, also the relative importance of these grains and their utilisation. Furthermore, he surveys the cereal conditions of the whole ancient East in connection with those of Babylonia, and discusses, with all due caution, the problem of the home of the varieties of grain from the Assyriological standpoint. The second portion of this (the first) volume concerns the numerous cereal products of Babylonia (flours, beers, etc.), the names of which have not been translated hitherto by those working on the inscriptions. The results of these researches are embodied in a glossary, in which for the time being, at any rate, numerous queries have to be inserted. There is also an appendix by Dr. Frimmel on the identification of seeds, and the chemico-botanical methods utilised in the examination of carbonised specimens. Dr. Hrozný's preliminary work was published in

B

the *Anzeiger der phil. hist. Klasse d. Kais. Akademie der Wissenschaften* (1909,
No. 6 ; 1910, Nos. 5 and 26), and his interpretations were accepted in the main
by his fellow experts. Confirmation of his conclusion that the ideogram GIG =
wheat was given by the Clay Inscription : Business Documents of Murashui
Sons, of Nippur, dated in the reign of Darius II (Univ. of Penns., *The Museum*,
Publ. of the Babyl. Section II/1, 1912), No. 69, where the ideogram *še* GIG·BA
(identical with GIG) is rendered in an Aramaic marginal note by the Aramaic (?)
word for wheat.

Dr. Hrozný shows that next in importance in Babylonia after barley was
ZIZ or ZIZ·A·AN, which he identifies with Emmer (*Triticum dicoccum* Schr.) by
the presence of the Akkadian (Semitic-Babylonian) annotation *kunâšu*, with
which he juxtaposes the Aramaic *kunnāthā*. Hitherto, *kunnāthā* has been
rendered as Spelt, but he shows that the true rendering is Emmer.

Emmer (*Triticum dicoccum* Schr.) is an ancient variety of wheat, now but
little cultivated. It differs from wheat (*Triticum vulgare*) in that the grains are
not freed from the glumes by threshing, but require a " dressing " process at the
mill before milling. It is still cultivated in Southern Germany, Switzerland,
Belgium, France, Spain, Italy, Southern Hungary, Serbia, Greece and Russia.
It was cultivated in Neolithic times in Europe, and by the Greeks and Romans ;
also cultivated in the ancient East, in Asia Minor, Persia, Egypt, Palestine
and Syria, Babylonia, Arabia and Abyssinia, but was unknown in ancient India
and China. The later supremacy of wheat may be explicable by ethnological
movements. Some remains of the once widely-spread culture of Emmer remain
in the East to this day. This variety is still cultivated in Abyssinia, Southern
Arabia, Luristan (Persia) and Egypt. In conjunction with the circumstance
that Spelt has not yet been proved with certainty in the East, the fact of the
present cultivation of Emmer shows that we are right in recognising the ancient
Eastern grain as Emmer, not Spelt. It is also very important that Aaronsohn,
the director of the Jewish Agricultural Experimental Station at Haifa, found wild
Emmer (*T. dicoccum* var. *dicoccoides* Asch. and Gr.) in Palestine and Syria,
generally in conjunction with wild barley.

In Egypt, three kinds of grain are mentioned throughout the entire literature
from the earliest times. Their identification is possible by means of the numerous
prehistoric finds and from the Coptic names. In the first place, barley was
cultivated. Hitherto, there is archaeological proof only of six-rowed barley and of

four-rowed barley. The Egyptians called barley 𓊪 ⌒, *at;* white, red, and

black barley were differentiated. *Šrt* (white and black), from which cakes and
also beer were prepared, also seems to be barley. As in Babylonia, the second
place in ancient Egyptian cereals was taken by Emmer (*T. dicoccum* Sehr. var.

tricoccum Schübl.). The old Egyptian name is 𓆸 ⌒ ⌒, *bdt*, Coptic ⲃⲓⲱⲧⲉ.

This word has been consistently translated as Spelt, but it should certainly be
rendered as Emmer, in view of the numerous archaeological finds of Emmer and
of the complete absence of Spelt. Herodotos proves the importance in Egypt
of ὄλυρα, or ζειά, which, according to archaeological finds, can only be
Emmer. White, red and black *bdt* were differentiated. In distinction to barley
the Upper Egyptian corn, Emmer was called Lower Egyptian corn. Schweinfurth

places the introduction of barley and Emmer into Egypt in the V–VIth millennium B.C., as Legrain found these grains with contracted burials at Silsileh without trace of copper or bronze. In addition, wheat has been found in Egyptian graves (*Triticum durum* Desf. and *Triticum turgidum* L.). The Egyptian name was

—●— 🐍 ⌒ ₒₒₒ , *swt*, Coptic coⲧo. Red and white *swt* were differentiated.

In Ptolemaic times ὄλυρα (Emmer) receded further and further into the background and, owing to Greek influence, its place was taken by πυρός, wheat. Wheat soon took up more than half of Egyptian cultivation ; in the second place came barley, κριθή to a far smaller extent, and last came ὄλυρα, Emmer. In Imperial Roman times, Emmer was practically suppressed ; the papyri and ostraca of this period only mention πυρός and κριθή. That Emmer was never wholly supplanted in Egypt is proved by the fact that it still occurs there, if but rarely only (var. *tricoccum* and var. *farrum* ?).

The Old Testament shows that the Hebrews cultivated principally wheat and barley ; both are named about equally often (30 times). A third grain of ancient Canaan was *kussèmeth*, which is named three times only. The LXX translates this word twice by ὄλυρα and once by ζέα. As these Greek words had always been translated as Spelt, *kussèmeth* was also translated in the same way. It has, however, been shown to be Emmer. The new identification rests on the Egyptian finds of Emmer, and on the ascertained fact that the ancient Egyptians cultivated Emmer, not Spelt. This meaning is confirmed by the important find of wild Emmer by Aaronsohn in Palestine and Syria (see above). One of the three passages in which Emmer is mentioned in the Old Testament gives valuable information on Babylonian grain, and furnishes a source for the grain conditions of the Babylonians other than the cuneiform texts. According to Ez. iv, 9, the prophet Ezekiel (who was led into captivity into Babylonia in the time of Nebuchadnezzar II, 604–561 B.C.) was enjoined by Jahveh to put wheat, barley, beans, lentils, millet and Emmer into a vessel and· make bread therefrom. From the rarity of the mention of Emmer in the Old Testament, it may be concluded that the Hebrews cultivated this grain to a slight extent only. The case may have been very different in still older times : the " Tale of Sinuhe " records that barley, *at*, and Emmer, *bdt*, grew in the fertile land of Yaa, which was somewhere in Palestine, and which Sinuhe received from the prince 'Ammienŝi.

The group of signs ZIZ·A·AN occurs in the name or ideogram of a month *araḫ* ZIZ·A·AN, which was the name of the eleventh month, corresponding approximately to February in New Babylonian times. The suggestion that *araḫ* ZIZ·A·AN means " Emmer month " is all the more likely as the ideogram of the following month araḫ ŠĒ KIN KUD, " harvest month," contains a grain sign (ŠE, corn, barley). It is strange that the Emmer month should precede the harvest month, as Emmer ripens later than barley (Exodus ix, 31 f) ; possibly the grain was harvested as green corn. Were other proofs wanting, the naming of a month after the grain would alone show the importance of Emmer in the Ancient East. In Egypt, also, a month was apparently called after Emmer : the month Tybi bore the name ⌷⌷ ⚍ ⌒ | , *ȝf. bdt.* Erman states that this word occurs once only, in the calendar of the Ebers Papyrus, as a popular name in place of the later Tybi, meaning probably, " the wheat swells," and certainly not " strength of wheat " (Brugsch).

Not only was Emmer the second most important grain in Egypt and Babylonia alike : in both countries it was called by the same name, which in all
probability originated in Babylonia. A strong Babylonian influence on Egyptian
agriculture is thus indicated. The Semitic rendering of ZIZ·A·AN was *bu-ṭu-
ut-tun*. Thus *buṭuttu* must also be Emmer or a product thereof. According
to another record, *buṭuttu* was prepared from ZIZ·A·AN (Emmer) by pounding,
so that it was probably a half-product between the grain and the flour, most
probably the grain freed from chaff. It is very important to find this Babylonian
name in the old Egyptian word *bdt*, Coptic вотє. The ancient Egyptian
d corresponds to the Semitic *d* and *t* ; the word may well have been pronounced
bōṭet, and would thus be completely identical with the Akkadian *buṭuttu*. Another
instance of the passage of a word from East to West, from Syria (Babylonia ?) to
Egypt, may be furnished by the possible derivation of the Egyptian word for
Emmer bread which, according to Herodotus, was prepared from ὄλυρα.
The name of this bread was ⌣▭⌣, *kršt* or *klst ;* it is not traceable
before the time of Seti I. It is tempting to derive it from the Babylonian
Aramaic *kunâšu-kunnâthâ* ; as the Egyptian *n* can correspond to the Semitic *l*,
the converse may also hold.

Dr. Hrozný proceeds to show that *kussèmeth*, the Hebrew name for Emmer, is
probably also of Babylonian origin (cf. *ku-su-um mi-id-di-tum*), and that the old
Aramaic שׁאת was probably derived from *šu'u*, an Assyrio-Babylonian name for
Emmer. From these derivations, the author concludes that Babylonia was the
centre of an ancient cultivation of Emmer, which radiated on all sides. And as
Aaronsohn (*vide supra*) found wild Emmer in Syria and Palestine, Dr. Hrozný
considers that one is forced to the conclusion that the cultivation of Emmer
originated in ancient Nearer Asia, especially in Babylonia. Emphasis must be
laid on the fact that Emmer was not cultivated in the eastern parts of Asia.
Since the wild form has not been found in Europe, this continent cannot be
considered the seat of the first cultivation of Emmer, and in company with the
whole Orient, Europe must be considered to be dependent on Babylonia for the
culture of the grain.

Emmer is mentioned in the earliest economic documents of Sumeria, which
are dated to about 3000 B.C. Schweinfurth places the introduction of barley
and Emmer into Egypt about 6000–5000 B.C. The Babylonian culture of Emmer
must be at least as ancient, if the Egyptians derived their name *bdt* from Babylonia. There is nothing difficult of acceptance in this theory, since the Sumerian
records of numerous kinds of flour, bread and malted beer show a high stage
in handling and utilising the grain, resulting from age-long experience.

The unity of the area of cultivation of Emmer in the Ancient East is shown
not only by the identity of ancient Eastern names for Emmer, but also by the
fact that Emmer was the second most important grain in the Ancient East,
particularly in Babylonia and Egypt, ranking next to barley. When wheat
took the first or second place, a foreign influence is usually recognisable, as in
Egypt, where Emmer was supplanted under the Greeks and Romans, and in
Babylonia under the Persian kings. A further proof of the similarity of agricultural conditions in the Ancient East is afforded by Dr. Frimmel's identification
of seed from excavations at Nippur as a many-rowed (four-rowed) barley of
primitive cultivation, and of seed from excavations at Gezer as wheat, probably
Triticum turgidum. Both these grains were cultivated in Egypt.

                                                        L. B. ELLIS.

Thoth the Hermes of Egypt. By PATRICK BOYLAN. 8vo, 215 pp. 1922. (Milford.) 10s. 6d.

This work is a valuable collection of all mentions of the god Thoth, grouped under his different connections and discussed as to their relations and bearing. The material of the Berlin dictionary has been used, with help from Erman and Junker. The purpose has been to distinguish and explain all the aspects and epithets of the god. The late texts have been freely used because they usually continue or reflect the views of early times. The various aspects of Thoth are classed under sixteen chapters, which seem to be fairly exhaustive of the material. Yet in all this completion there is a lack of new light or synthesis. One does not seem to see any further, or differently, to what was already accepted. There are many twinings around the conflicts of the gods, but no reference (except in a footnote) to the historical aspect of the conflicts as being those of the god's worshippers. Even the Horus and Set combat is never translated as the conquest of one tribe over the other.

The many diverse aspects and attributes of the gods is thought surprising (p. 82), but it was only the reflex of the extreme pluralism of officials, who might hold half-a-dozen high offices which seem quite incompatible. The season of November is referred to, as it is in the north, " when the trees shed their foliage, when Nature was visibly tending to decay," but the opposite is the case in Egypt. One sentence could only have been written in Ireland : " He (Set) is the brother of Osiris because the rivalry of brothers is the most obvious, and the most widely known." In the list of names compounded with that of Thoth, four in Lieblein's dictionary are omitted, and two others (*see* ANCIENT EGYPT, C. 170–1, D. 126). The ape is placed on the stand, not on the tongue of the balance (57). The firm of Holzhausen have done their work excellently, with only three small errata (pp. 22, 148, 212), and the Oxford Press seems to have a branch in Vienna. Why is there no index ? Altogether we must heartily welcome a new writer in the English (or Irish) field, who has given us a valuable book, and who we may hope will long increase in strength and production.

The Racial Origins of Jewish Types. By R. N. SALAMAN. 8vo. 22 pp., 12 plates. 1922. (Spottiswoode.)

This address to the Jewish Historical Society breaks new ground, and happily combines history and ethnology. With a biologist's training, Dr. Salaman views the mixed types as ancestral combinations ; and a wide range of practice here and in the East has made the varieties familiar to him. Even among the small and extremely exclusive tribe of Samaritans, though mostly dark and sallow, there are some blonde with red hair. The Hebrew origin, from Ur of the Chaldees, was in contact with the round-headed, aquiline Sumerians, here claimed as kin to Hittites, and the long, upright-headed Semite. The Hebrew stock is granted to be the Habiru, who were the Shasu or Bedawyn. The trek round by Haran was familiar to that people. The Aamu figured at Beni Hasan are mixed with the Habiru Bedawy type. The Amorites are accepted as a source of a fair type. The Hittite type is well known—short and thick-set, with large rounded heads, short necks, full, rather puffy faces, with a rounded wide nose ; others have a small mouth, refined lips and a sharper nose. The modern Armenian is the representative of the Hittite, with fair skin and dark hair and eyes. Though the earlier faces from Palestine are of Amorite type in 1500 B.C.

as far north as Damascus, by 1300 both Hittite and Amorite appear in North Syria ; and rather later three out of four people of Askelon are like Hittites. This agrees with the movement of the Hittites southward, which is recorded.

The Hebrews, then, were a Bedawy tribe settling among an Amorite and Hittite population. In Egypt the mixture would be with the Semitic Hyksos remains on the eastern border. The defeat of the Pulostau by Ramessu III threw them back on the Syrian coast to form Philistia. The total disappearance of the Philistines later in history shows that they were gradually absorbed in the Palestine population, though they left their name, much as the fair Franks have been absorbed by the Gauls. In Zechariah ix, 7, the mixed Philistine is described " as a governor in Judah." It seems agreed by all the evidence that the Philistine was a Cretan, and further, of a northern origin. This is taken to be the source of the fair " pseudo-Gentile " strain, which amounts to a fifth of the modern Jewish people. Though the Armenoid Hittite is the dominant type, yet the other survives, as in modern Greece the Armenoid type has overrun the old fair Heroic type. The summary, finally, is " that the Jews are sprung from an original Semitic Arabian stock, the Habiru (or Khabiri) ; that they freely mixed with the Amorites, the Hittites and the Philistines, and that of these three races, whilst the first is probably Semitic, the latter two are definitely non-Semitic. The Hittite possessed characters which dominated the others, and as a result the majority of Jews to-day present more or less completely the Hittite or Armenoid type." It might be added that the absorption of the Khazars and other tribes in the last two thousand years continues the same process. It is religion and not ancestry that defines the nation.

A History of Egypt from the Earliest Kings to the XVIth Dynasty.—By W. M. FLINDERS PETRIE. 8vo, 294 pp. 1923. (Methuen). 12s.

This new edition of the *History* has been entirely revised, to include all fresh material down to last autumn. The entirely new parts are in the viith–xth dynasties, where the Syrian dynasties and the Khety kings are put in order ; the latest arrangement of the xith dynasty ; and the grouping of the Sebekemsaf family as a southern dynasty contemporary with the earlier half of the xiiith dynasty in the north, with a fluctuating frontier between them. This last period was somewhat like that of the xxist dynasty, where the northern kings alone are in the lists, but contemporary with a dynasty of Theban kings. At the end are tables giving the complete hieroglyphic titles of every known king to the end of the xvith dynasty.

Historical Sites in Palestine. By Lieut.-Com. VICTOR L. TRUMPER. Sm. 8vo, 138 pp., 3 maps. 1921. 3s. 6d. (Nile Mission Press, 37, Sharia Manakh, Cairo.)

This handbook is modified from the short hand-lists of places that were supplied to the army when advancing over the country, to give them some idea of the history before them. Short statements of the events connected with each site are given, and 430 sites are identified. The places are grouped geographically, with a very full index. Some reference might be given to the various explorations of places, which would make visitors understand how much importance is attached to the sites. This well supplies the place of a handbook for any traveller who is not going expressly for the sites and history, for which he would need more detail.

L'Architecture, choix de documents. By JEAN CAPART. Sq. 8vo. 1922. (Vromant, Bruxelles.)

This is a very useful collection of 200 plates of architectural subjects from various works, mostly photographic. The facility for study is given by a full bibliography of works referring to the subjects, in 47 pages. Rather more than a quarter of the plates have appeared in Dr. Capart's *Art Egyptien*, of which this volume is one section, expanded to deal more completely with a particular branch. There are also complete references to the text of that work. One subject—a rose-lotus capital, pl. 194—should have been put to the Old Kingdom ; it was found beneath the level of Merenptah, and was doubtless re-used from much earlier work. The plates will be mainly of use for teaching in class ; but an analytic work, placing together all the examples of one feature at a time, is what is needed for advancing the study of the subject.

Les pastes cerámiques i els esmalts blaus de l'antic Egipte. By JOSEP LLORENS I ARTIGAS. 8vo, 57 pp. 1922. (Barcelona.)

This is the result of a mission sent to Paris to study the ancient faience, with a view to its modern reproduction in Spain. For us the value of it lies in the collection of analyses by various chemists. The base of the blue glaze is truly stated to be a siliceous paste, though the influence of a little iron in changing the glaze to green is not noticed. The body materials are :—

	Red pottery.	Hard pottery.	Glazed paste.				
Silica	52	56	81	88	91	90	94
Alumina	15	19	13	6	6	4	1½
Lime	24	5	3	3	..	2	1½
Iron and manganese	2	9	1	..	..	..	2
Soda	..	..	2	..	..	..	..
Magnesia	..	1	..	..	2	1	2
Carbonic acid	6	4	..	..	..	..	..
Water	1	6	..	..	..	1	..
Copper	..	..	..	3	..	2	..

The two including copper are mixed with the blue glaze. The absence of lead is noted, but lead is essential with iron for the Ptolemaic apple-green. The saline efflorescence seen on glazed ware is attributed to decomposition of the alkalis in the paste ; but the least acquaintance with Egyptian remains shows that it comes from salts in the soil, which are very difficult to remove. Several more analyses of the white paste are supplied, but they fall within the variations above noted. Unfortunately the dated specimens are none before the XXth dynasty. If the writer had come on from the Louvre to London, he could have studied the glazes back through the prehistoric, and been supplied with the complete studies of the production of the blue colour by Dr. Russell and Prof. Laurie, who are not even mentioned.

PERIODICALS.

Zeitschrift für Aegyptische Sprache, Vol. LVII, 1922.

SETHE, K., and colleagues.—*Die Sprüche für das Kennen der Seelen der heiligen Orte.* The whole paper (of which the first portion only is published in this number of the *Zeitschrift*) deals with those chapters of the Book of the Dead which were numbered by Lepsius 107–109, 111–116. These occur together, with a certain regularity, and are sufficiently uniform in title and ending to be called a complete group or collection of texts. In late versions, these chapters are separated only by Chapter 110, " The Fields of the Departed." Four stages of development may be distinguished in this group of chapters :—(1) no titles ; (2) non-funerary titles ; (3) funerary titles ; (4) the uniform title " knowledge of the souls of . . . ," and it is possible that the texts were not necessarily funerary in origin. The sequence of the texts was a fixed one in the Middle Kingdom, but varied later. The contents of these chapters are divisible into three groups : (1) texts concerning Heliopolis and Hermopolis, and dealing with the sun and the moon ; (2) texts relating to Buto and Hieraconpolis ; (3) texts concerning the East and the West. Several texts which appear independently in late versions of the Book of the Dead are only variants, and only occur in the first instance when the original texts are missing. The first group only (Chapters 115, 114, 116, and a chapter which disappeared in N.K. versions) is dealt with in this portion of the paper.

An interesting change is traceable in the title of Chapter 116. In Papyrus Ea of the XVIIIth dynasty, the title reads " Another chapter for knowing the souls of Hermopolis," though Chapter 114, of which it is a variant, is not included. Evidently this papyrus was based on a model which preserved Chapter 114. From XXIst dynasty onwards, the title changes to " Another chapter for knowing the souls of Heliopolis," presumably because in Ea it follows Chapter 115, which deals with *Heliopolis*. In XXIst dynasty, Chapter 114 is included with the correct title (Hermopolis) as an independent text at the end of the collection.

The general title of the collection of chapters reads : " To know what Thoth knows of preservatives," (2) " to know every sanctuary," (3) " to be a spirit in the underworld." There is a clear connection between *rḫ* of the first two sentences and the ". I know " which is common to all the chapters, and with which the speaker affirms his knowledge of the secrets, and which also lies at the root of the refrain " I know the souls of . . ." The sentences, however, contain nothing of a directly funerary nature unless it be *śdꜣw*, which is presumably *nomen actionis* of *swdꜣ*, " to preserve." The words *r pr nb* show that the title belongs to the whole collection, not to the following chapter only. It is conceivable that the title may have belonged to the collection before the texts concerning the East and the West were included, for these do not refer to a sanctuary, and were probably funerary in character from the outset. Like some of the other titles, this introductory title could be used equally well by a living as by a dead person. The *rḫ bꜣw* title of Chapter 115 is not preceded by an older title ; as the title of the first chapter of the collection, it may possibly have served as a model for the uniform re-naming of the other titles. The final refrain

" I know the souls of . . . " has no real connection with the text, unless b^3w be rendered by an abstract expression such as " mystery," " history," etc., in which case the explanatory sentence " these are Ra, Shu and Tefnut," must be secondary. Moreover, the word " souls " is expressed by the old form of the plural, namely, by a three-fold repetition of the word-sign for b^3, whereas the explanatory sentence definitely enumerates *three* gods. The inorganic nature of the first refrain is even clearer in the chapter which comes between Chapters 114 and 115. As the chapter deals with embalming, the three gods in this case are gods of the dead, namely, Osiris, Anubis and *Iśaś*. The first two are referred to in the text, and from the context cannot be included in the " Souls of the New Moon festival," of whom the visitor claims knowledge, and whom he addresses.

In Chapter 115, the deceased claims admission to the sanctuary of Heliopolis, because he is one of the " eldest " who may gaze on (*wn ḥr ḥr*) the sacred eye of the sun god. His object is to restore the damaged eye. He knows the mythological events to which certain institutions owe their origin : firstly, the injury to the sun by eclipse or clouding over, which is represented as a mutilation of the mouth of the sun god ; then the attempt of a serpent *Ḥtm* or *Imj-wḥ³·f* to contest with Ra the inheritance of Heliopolis. This attempt gave rise to three Heliopolitan cult institutions : the " Diminution " (⊙ 〗 ⌒×), the " Thirty " (Spears), and the " Brotherhood " festival. Then follows a meeting of the sun god with a creature called *Imj 'imsf* (" he who is in his bandages "), whom Ra outwitted in the form or with the help of a woman " with curls." For this reason, the High Priest of Heliopolis wears a " curl " or " plait " on his bald head, like a woman. He is called first " the pigtailed one," then " the bald one," and, finally, in his character of " heir " and " great one who sees his father," he received the title of *wr-m³.w*, which is usually translated as " great one of seers."

This chapter contains two references to injury to the mouth : ⊙〗×🦅 ↓↓↓〰⌒▭, " the decrease in the brotherhood festival " (possibly the feast of the sixth day, 〰⌒⧹⊙), and ⟵▫◁🦅⌒⸏⬚⊙〗⌒×▫🦆 ⭑▭, " his mouth was mutilated and so arose the decrease at the feast of the month." As the sun god's mouth suffered injury, the " decrease " must mean a solar eclipse, even though it is stated to occur regularly at a lunar festival ; in this case *'ibd*, which is usually the second day of the month, must be the day of the new moon. In another chapter, the injured part of the sun ($\frac{7}{10}$ of the disc) " belongs to him who counts the parts," *i.e.*, Thoth, who thus functions also in his character of moon god. It seems then that the Egyptians knew that the solar eclipse is caused by the moon. This chapter comes between Chapters 114 and 115 in Old Kingdom MSS., but disappears in the New Kingdom. Once again the deceased seeks admission to a sanctuary. He affirms that he understands healing or embalming, and is able to heal the injury which the eye of the sun suffered on the day of the new moon. The persons from whom he demands entry are " those who are at the New Moon Festival," or the " Souls of the New Moon Festival."

From the New Kingdom onwards there are two versions of the Middle Kingdom chapters dealing with a visit to the temple of Hermopolis, namely, Chapters 114 and 116. This chapter is obscure in certain important details.

Injury has been suffered by certain sacred things in the temple, including the eye of Horus, which Thoth had to find after Set had swallowed it. The speaker claims initiation into all these mysteries, moreover he comes as the emissary of the sun god to remedy the injuries and to hand over the eye of Horus to Thoth, who had " counted " it. One of the injuries is " the pushing of the feather into the shoulder of Osiris " ; the verb used in the Middle Kingdom is *twn*, determined by the horn. Sethe suggests a direct connection between this passage and the name of the twenty-seventh day of the moon, $\bigcirc$ ⩫ ⟍⟍ ☏, " the pushing of the horns." A further injury is referred to as the " shining of the red crown." After the remedy, the red crown is to be black, as if that were its natural colour. The third injury is the eating of the eye, which is evidently the eye of Horus from analogous passages elsewhere. Possibly the feather and the red crown represented other manifestations of the eye of Horus, which was susceptible of many transformations. The final words of the Middle Kingdom versions of Chapter 114 are : " I know the souls of Hermopolis, that which is small on the second day of the month " (*i.e.*, the new moon), " that which is big on the fifteenth day of the month " (*i.e.*, the full moon), " It is Thoth." In Chapter 116, two gods are added to make up the usual triad ; these are *št³ sy³*, " difficult of recognition," and *rḫ tm*, " Omniscient." It is possible that these names are epithets of the paraphrases of the moon given above. Chapter 116 is followed by a final clause affirming that knowledge of the chapter ensures against hunger and thirst ; it may refer to all the three chapters of the sub-group.

SCHARFF, ALEXANDER.—*Ein Rechnungsbuch des königlichen Hofes aus der 13. Dynastie.* Borchardt and Griffith have worked on this papyrus (Boulaq Papyrus, No. 18). It is dated to the XIIIth dynasty by the mention of a king Sebekhotep and of a Vizier, ⟨hieroglyphs⟩. The papyrus was found at Draʿ-abuʾn-Negga in 1860. The beginning and a large piece of the middle are missing ; the complete document was probably 7½ metres long. It consists of two hand-writings, of which the larger one only is dealt with in this article.

The scribe was called ⟨hieroglyphs⟩, and he bore the title ⟨hieroglyphs⟩. His office was at Thebes, where he kept the accounts of the rationing of the Court. These accounts cover periods extending from the twenty-sixth day of the second month of Inundation (Paophi) to the fourth day of the third month (Hathyr) of the same season, and from the sixteenth to the eighteenth day of the same month, in the third year of a King Sebekhotep. It is unfortunate that the daily balance sheets give the total issues without mentioning the number of persons supplied. The scribe received his orders either by word of mouth or in writing. The verbal instructions were transmitted by his chief, direct from the Cabinet ʿof the king, to the effect that " good things " are to be brought to N.N. The nature of the " good things " is not specified, so that presumably the scribe worked to standing instructions. The execution of the commission is entered by the words " done according to this order." The scribe made a copy of his written instructions ; his work consisted in reckoning out the respective shares to be issued by the three Administrations of Stores. Certain costly items, such as eye-paint, wine and honey, were, however, actually issued by the scribe himself, as the entries for these invariably begin with the words " taken from the sealed place." The regular daily receipts are called *ʿkw*, whilst the occasional revenues for issue on feast days, etc., are called *'inw.* The latter are tabulated in three columns : (1) amounts due ; (2) amounts actually received ; and (3) arrears. The daily balance sheets consist of a tabulation of receipts and issues ; the balance is carried forward to the next day, and correct working is indicated by the sign ⌡. The daily recipients are the royal family, the Court officials, and the servants. Among the royal recipients were the king's sisters (wives) and five " households " of king's sisters. Several high officials appear to have received supplies on special occasions only. About seventy persons " were led into the hall to eat " on each of the two festivals of Mentu, and extra stores were booked for these days. In fragments of the papyrus occurs the name of the town of Cusae, which seems to have been the northern boundary of the Theban kingdom in Hyksos times.

SPIEGELBERG, W.—*Ein historisches Datum aus der Zeit des Ptolemaios XI Alexandros.* A demotic stele (No. 110) from the Serapeum of Memphis bears a date at the end, which Spiegelberg translates as follows : " Written in the fifteenth year, which corresponds to the twelfth year, on the sixth of Mechir (?) of Queen Cleopatra and King Ptolemaios surnamed Alexandros, *when he was with the army at Pelusium.*" The words in italics need explanation. Spiegelberg is not sure of the reading of the place name ; it is undoubtedly identical with the town mentioned in Mag. Pap. I, which Griffith took to be ⲡⲉⲣⲉⲙⲟⲩⲛ = Pelusium. The double dating corresponds to 103–102 B.C., when Cleopatra undertook a campaign against her rebellious son Ptolemaios X, Soter II (Lathyros), which was nominally led by Ptolemaios Alexandros. According to Bouché Leclercq, Pelusium was the base of operations against Syria.

SPIEGELBERG, W.—*Horus als Arzt.* Diodoros (i, 25) relates that Horus practised medicine, like his mother. An unpublished ostracon in the Strasburg collection (H 111) takes this belief back to Ramesside times. Unfortunately the ostracon is not complete, but enough remains to show that the inscription consists of a series of statements extolling the healing effects of the *md.w* (spells) and *ḥkꜣ.w* (magic rites) of Horus.

GUNN, BATTISCOMBE.—" *Finger-Numbering* " *in the Pyramid Texts.* In Vol. liv of the *Zeitschrift*, Sethe discusses a rhyme for counting on the fingers which ends the " Spell for obtaining a ferry boat," which was published by Grapow from Middle Kingdom coffins. The initial sentences of the spell are nearly identical with the beginning of Pyr. Spell 359. Then follows the dialogue in which first *Mꜣ-ḥꜣ.f* and later *'Ḳn* delay the " magician " with objections and questions. To the last of these, namely : " This august god will say hast thou brought me a man who cannot number his fingers ? " the magician replies by repeating the rhyme in question.

Gunn points out that Pyr. Spell 359, which is also a spell for transportation by *Mꜣ-ḥꜣ.f*, contains an allusion to this matter. The passage in question ends with the words : " This Pepy is in charge (?) of the Eye of Horus which is his own ; this Pepy is going to the numbering of fingers." Gunn infers that there is to be a " numbering of fingers " on the other side of the water, in which the deceased king wishes to take part. The motive for the rite remains obscure. It seems to be closely connected with the eye of Horus.

[This may be connected with the quinary system of the assertions of innocence, which was probably learned on the fingers ; so the finger numbering may be the school name of the recital of the moral code as repudiation of sins.—F. P.]

WIESMANN, H.—*Die Determinative des sprechenden Mannes und der Buchrolle in den Pyramidentexten.* In the Pyramid texts, words have special determinatives; general determinatives are not used. Thus the sign of the man with his hand to his mouth (⦗𝅘𝅥𝅮⦘) and that of the papyrus roll (⊏⊐) have a more restricted use than in later times. A list is given of the words in which these determinatives occur and of the number of times they are used. The man with his hand to his mouth is the sign for eating, and occurs in some twenty words, of which nine designate food, or some process of eating. The use of this determinative may be explained by analogy, connection of ideas, or substitution for another human determinative, in all but five of the remaining words. The sign ⊏⊐ is used in thirty-four words; it originally designated a book or document and was used for words with these meanings, also for expressions which were usually conceived of as being written, and for legal or ceremonial expressions.

SETHE, K.—*Kurznamen auf j.* To the New Kingdom pet names ending in ⟨⟨, discussed in Vol. xliv of the *Zeitschrift*, Sethe now adds several examples from the Old Kingdom. According to ancient usage these end in ⟨. The suppressed element is usually the name of a god, king or K^3, and it would seem that the Egyptians termed the abbreviation " the beautiful name " in distinction to the " big name," as the full name was called. This agrees with the Old Kingdom custom of calling nicknames, such as ⟨, ⟨, ⟨, which have no etymological origin, by the term " beautiful name."

BISSING, F. W. VON — *Ein Kultbild des Hermes-Thot.* In the author's opinion, the fragment of sculpture dealt with in this article shows Greek influence. It is sculptured in finely-grained yellowish marble, and represents a cynocephalous ape squatting on a pillar and holding a roll in its paws. There is no trace of lettering on the roll. Including plinth, the height is 13½ inches. On the pillar is carved an ibis. The ape bears a disc on its head ; from the front of the disc springs an uraeus, with disc and horns. The back of the disc is touched, but not grasped by a carved human hand, which is proportionately large. Ape and ibis clearly point to Thoth ; the position of the hand leads Bissing to suppose that the figure to which it belonged was closely akin to the representations of Hermes-Thoth on coins of Roman times from Hermopolis-Eshmuneyn. These coins depict an erect human-headed figure, wearing the crown of an Egyptian god, and holding a crouching ape in the hand ; in front is an ibis. Representations of apes reading are extremely rare [see baboon reading, probably Middle Kingdom, Univ. Coll.] : it is doubtful if they occur in the New Kingdom, and they became popular only in Graeco-Roman times. Horapollo (i, 14) relates that there was an Egyptian variety of cynocephalous ape which knew its letters, and that apes which were brought to a temple were given writing materials by the priest to ascertain if they were of this variety. The three manifestations of the god are also found on a limestone tablet of the Roman period, which is divided into three registers. In the middle register, a cynocephalous ape is represented on an altar ; it is crowned with disc and crescent and it holds an object on which is perched an ibis. The ape is flanked by Thoth and Harpocrates. The bottom register is divided into three panels : the central one is occupied by a fully-dressed bearded man bound hand and foot ; in each side panel is a kneeling figure with its hand to its mouth. [A writing tablet in Univ. Coll. has all three forms painted on it, human‑Thoth, baboon, and ibis.]

MOGENSEN, MARIA.—*Ein altägyptischer Boxkampf.* A rare terra-cotta in the Egyptian collection of the Ny Carlsberg Glyptothek (Copenhagen) represents a boxing match between a cat and a mouse, witness the boxing gloves on the fore paws of both animals, whilst the hind paws show the claws. The bird above is explained as an eagle, waiting to award to the victor the palm of victory, which it holds in its claw. The terra-cotta probably dates to the first–second century A.D. It was found in Egypt, possibly near Memphis.

SPIEGELBERG, W.—*Der Stratege Pamenches.* A statue which was found at Denderah (published in *Ann. Serv.*, 1918) represents an official in Greek dress, wearing a wreath. His name and titles, which are given in demotic on the pedestal and in greater detail in hieroglyphs on the pillar, show him to be the *strategus Pn-mnḥ*, son of *Pꜣ-ꜥsm*. In the demotic, the father's name *Pꜣ-ꜥsm* (*ḥm*), " the falcon," is rendered by the Greek equivalent Ἱέραξ. Pamenches was *mr mšꜥ wr* = στρατηγός, in the Thebaid, of which the north and south boundaries are formed by Denderah and Philae respectively. He was also priest, and generally the high priest, in the temples of the gods who were worshipped in this region. From the style of the demotic, he might have lived in the first century B.C. or A.D. He is dated to the time of Augustus by an inscription in the quarries of Silsileh, and by his use of the title *šnjns* = συγγενής, which was apparently preserved only up to the beginning of the time of the Roman Emperors. To judge by the priesthood which he held, he was an Egyptian, in spite of his Greek attire.

Spiegelberg also gives a list of *strategi* known from Egyptian texts. Of these, the *strategus* Hierax mentioned on a Berlin ostracon of the 5th year B.C is probably identical with the father of Pamenches.

KEES, H.—*Ein alter Götterhymnus als Begleittext zur Opfertafel.* This religious text occurs on a stone slab which was found at Horbeyt, in the eastern Delta. Parallel texts are known ; these are connected with lists of offerings. The author considers that the text was a hymn, not an actual formula of offering, and belonged perhaps to the ⟨hieroglyphs⟩ which were recited at definite times. An instructive parallel is furnished by the similar use of extracts from the Pyramid Texts in two cases, in which the text under discussion is also used. Whereas these extracts are suitable for recitations accompanying offerings, this text contains one passage only which can be considered to have a direct connection with offerings, namely : " Behold, everything is completely brought to thee from the cultivated and inhabited places." In general, the orthography of the text is extremely ancient. Certain characteristics, such as the sparing use of determinatives, and the occurrence of certain ancient word signs, show that the orthography of the original text, on which the existing versions were based, corresponded with that of the Pyramid Texts. The introductory description is applicable to Nefertum, though this god is not directly named. Kees has no hesitation to making this identification, and considers that the introduction of the Horus myth is secondary. Among the other gods named is ꜥnti,ꜣ who functions here independently of Horus or Set, with whom he appears to be equated later.

KEES, H.—*Die Schlangensteine und ihre Beziehungen zu den Reichsheilig-tümern.* In the Pyramid Texts, the sign Ω accompanies the word *'itrty,* the name of the royal palaces or national temples of Upper and Lower Egypt. Two of these signs together form the word sign for *šnw·t.* Sethe recognised the mixed word sign Ω ▯ in an incompletely-preserved representation in the temple of Sahura of a god who cannot be identified. He also drew attention to a stele of the form Ω at Cairo, on which is a snake called " the good *'h'* snake of the house of Horus Khenti Khet." Kees maintains that the *šnw·t* was a building in front of which stood two steles shaped like the sign Ω, each of which bore a serpent as a protective deity. On a naos from Saft el Henna, such stones are called " gate-keepers," and there is some support for the view that such stones were placed at entrances for protection. There are also indications that the use of snake stones belongs to a religion older than the cult of Heliopolis. In old texts, Min was connected with the *šnw·t,* as well as Ra. The word *šnw·t* occurs in an Old Kingdom title *šmšw šnw·t,* which is usually rendered " Elder of the pillared hall."

(To be continued.)

Man. November, 1921.

New Light on the Early History of Bronze.—Prof. A. H. SAYCE. A tablet of Sargon of Akkad describes the size of the provinces of his kingdom, and their distance from the capital. The summing up is that his rule extended " from the lands of the setting sun to the lands of the rising sun, namely, to the Tin-land and Kaptara (Kaphtor or Krete) countries beyond the Upper sea (Mediterranean) and Dilmun and Magan (Dellim-Bushire and El Hassa), countries beyond the Lower Sea " (Persian Gulf). In another inscription of a later Sargon, governor in 2180 B.C., he stated that he had conquered Egypt, then under a Nubian dynasty ; this would fall in the confused age of the XVIth dynasty, when we know of a southern immigration from Nubian pottery at Esna, and also by the " pan-graves" at Hu and elsewhere. Another record which is earlier than Sargon of Akkad, states that " 5 minas of pure tin " had been received at Lagash. A Hittite text from Boghaz-keui mentions where various materials were obtained (places not yet identified) and " black iron of heaven from the sky, copper and bronze from the city of Alasiya and Mount Taggata."

Palestine Exploration Fund, Quarterly Statement. October, 1922.

The proposal that various bodies should join in the excavation of Ophel is here noticed. This region south of the temple area is considered to be the original hill of Zion, the site of the palace and tombs of the Jewish kings. It is much to be hoped that the Palestine Fund will be well supported in taking up a portion of this work. The whole direction will obviously have to be under the Department of Antiquities for Palestine, at least during the earlier stages of the work.

An account of the work of the University of Pennsylvania at Beisan records finding a basalt stele of Sety I.

Académie des Inscriptions. Comptes Rendus. Mai–Juin, 1922.

M. Virolleaud reported on May 8th finding in the contents of the sarcophagus at Byblos a small gold cartouche of Amenemhat III, the signs soldered on to a base plate, which fitted in a recess on the lid of an inscribed vase.

M. Naville drew attention in a letter to the resemblance of the obsidian vases with gold settings to those published in *Lahun I.*

On July 7th was reported the discovery of a second cartouche of Amenemhat III fitting a second vase of obsidian. Also of three bronze vases (? copper), one of which is a basin 17 inches wide.

In the same part are drawings of a slab lately found at Athens, of the fifth century B.C., on which a game of hockey is carved.

Bulletin of the Metropolitan Museum. New York. August, 1922.

This records an interesting group of objects which came from a tomb, but it is said not from Tell el Amarna. As usual with objects bought from natives, there is no assurance that the whole of them were found together. A double limestone ushabti for Khoemuast and his wife Mest gives the only personal name, and he is supposed to have been the owner of the tomb. There is a fine lotus flower goblet of alabaster, with the Aten cartouches, and those of Amenhetep IV and Nefertyti ; a heavy gold ring of Tut-onkh-amen shows that the group comes down to the latter part of his reign. There is a green faience globular vase with wide neck, bearing names of Akhenaten and queen in black inlay ; two ivory female figures have on one a lotus flower on the head, on the other a lily ; and there is a heart scarab, with the name left blank. The period assigned to the successors of Akhenaten in this paper seems impossibly short.

Museum of Fine Arts Bulletin. Boston. No. 114.

The Tomb of Dehuti-Nekht and his Wife.—The well-known tomb of Tehuti-nekht at Bersheh had been published, with a date of the 31st year of Senusert I, but owing to heavy falls of rock, the burial shaft had not been searched. The tomb had been plundered in Roman times, but no later attempt had been made until the Harvard expedition in 1915. On entering the chamber there were remains of two burials. One great cedar sarcophagus and coffin had the ends removed ; another had been separated as boards. Both sarcophagi and both coffins were inscribed for Tehuti-nekht. A mass of models of ships and servants lay ,piled between the great sarcophagus and the wall. The mummy lay on its left side, facing the doorway painted on the coffin. By the doorway is a scene of the noble seated before a table of offerings. The painting of funeral articles is of the standard type, but unusually fine in detail. The best of the models is of a procession bearing offerings ; a shaven priest leads, carrying a tall vase, three women with baskets and birds follow. There are also models of ploughing with a yoke of oxen, and of five men making bricks, bringing clay, mixing it, and pressing the bricks.

NOTES AND NEWS.

The lamented death of the Earl of Carnarvon has made a tragic break in the history of his and Mr. Carter's greatest success. The climate of Egypt prevents visitors realising the varied risks which easily beset those who are fatigued, and the strain of the last few months left little resistance to the familiar infections of the country. It is to be presumed that the responsibility for completing the clearance of the tomb of Tutankhamen will now rest on its owners, the Egyptian Government.

It is to be feared that the Government will remove all the contents of the tomb to Cairo, where they will inevitably deteriorate and slowly perish. An estimate of £36,000 has already been made for an extension of the present Cairo Museum, in its most undesirable situation. How it will be possible to transport the mass of the weighty shrines is one of the greatest difficulties. The side of the rock chamber will have to be entirely quarried away, and the shrine cut up into such sections as can be moved. Each side of the outer shrine will weigh nearly a ton, and could not be handled in anything like that mass without crushing the gilt gesso and the inlays ; it must be cut into many sections for removal. There will probably be over ten tons of such material to be removed in dealing with all the successive shrines. It will be a much slower and more expensive affair to build new halls at Cairo, and then shift the existing collection, and remodel the lighting of the present building for the new objects, than it would be to place a new building up at Deir el Bahri.

Mr. Mackay has been successful in finding an inscription of Samsuiluna, the successor of Khammurabi, identifying the site Tell Oheimer as Kish. As there were four supremacies of Kish before that, going back to the earliest times, we may hope for fresh insight on the earliest stages of Babylonian civilisation.

The Egyptian Government now announce that the law on antiquities will not be changed till 1925, so it will be possible to make arrangements for next season.

The British School has continued the clearance of the large cemetery of Qau el Kebir, begun in November. Mr. Brunton reports that a region containing tombs of all periods has now been reached, which was used from prehistoric to Roman times. The former German and Italian excavators have cleared most of the cemetery of this nome without attempting to issue any record of their work. This was mere plundering, and as bad ten years ago as it was a century before.

RECENT DISCOVERIES OF THE BRITISH SCHOOL IN EGYPT.

The Exhibition of Antiquities from Qua el Kebir will be held at University College, from July 2nd to 29th (evenings of 10th and 20th).

A public lecture, with lantern illustrations, will be given by W. M. Flinders Petrie, F.R.S., at University College, Gower Street, on Thursday, 17th May, at 2.30 p.m. Admission free, without ticket. This is the first of a guinea course of six lectures on Thursdays. The lecture will be repeated on Wednesday, 23rd, at 5 p.m., and Saturday, 26th, at 3 p.m. Admission free, without ticket.

ANCIENT EGYPT.

THE TOMB AT BYBLOS.

WE have noticed in past numbers the reports of a tomb of the XIIth dynasty, found last year by an accidental fall of the shore-cliff at Byblos, 20 miles North of Beyrut. The discovery has now been published fairly completely in the French journal *Syrie* (1922, pp. 273-306, with nine plates), which must be studied in detail by anyone dealing with the eastern Mediterranean archaeology. Here we can only give a few outlines of the forms which are most important in their bearing on Egyptian subjects.

The shape of the tomb is complicated. The burial chamber is rather irregular, 17 × 14 feet at the largest. About 3 feet has been walled off by rough stonework to support the roof, leaving it about 14 feet square. Opposite that wall is a filled up pit, the whole width of this chamber, made for lowering the sarcophagus. The access was in a third wall, by a bent and sloping passage, 47 × 66 inches at the smallest ; this is 44 feet long and was reached by a shallow pit from the surface. Accidentally a small circular chamber has broken through the side of the passage ; it is about 8½ feet across and had its own pit for access. This system is entirely native and not copied from Egypt.

The form of the limestone sarcophagus is likewise not due to Egyptian influence (Figs. 10, 11). The four large knobs on the top, for lifting the lid, are unlike anything in Egypt, as also is the curving of the top edges and of the lid to fit that. Happily, accurate measurements are given in the plate, though not repeated to show the variations in accuracy. These show considerable care in the proportions, and also the unit of measure. They are here reduced to inches, as being familiar to our sense of size.

Out length	..	111·14 ÷ 40	= 2·778 inches.
Out width	..	58·35 ÷ 21	= 2·778 ,,
In length	..	83·07 ÷ 30	= 2·769 ,,
In width	..	33·39 ÷ 12	= 2·782 ,,
Depth in	..	48·54 ÷ 17½	= 2·774 ,,
Depth out	..	66·18 ÷ 24	= 2·757 ,,

The deficiency in the last measure may be due to the bottom being invisible, and the measurement being only made from the ground. The mean of these, omitting the last, is 2·776, mean error ·004 ± ·002. This palm measure being multiplied by 12, 24 and 40, was probably a quarter of a foot of 11·10 ± ·01 inches.

Forty-six years ago, I published deductions from measures of monuments, with which we may compare this foot (*Inductive Metrology*).

Hauran	...	...	...	...	11·08 inches	=	·4362 metres.
Byblos, 1922 ...	...	...	...	11·10	,,	=	·4374	,,
Syria ...	...	...	...	...	11·13	,,	=	·4382	,,
Sardinia	...	...	...	...	11·14	,,	=	·4386	,,
Carthage	...	...	...	...	11·16	,,	=	·4394	,,
Asia Minor	...	...	...	...	11·17	,,	=	·4398	,,

These regions are all of Syria or the Phoenician Colonies, and this leaves then no doubt as to the true home of this foot.

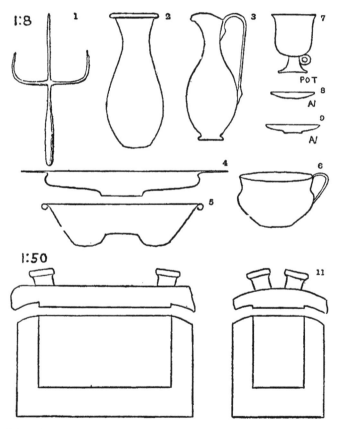

The lid of the sarcophagus was in place, and the gold dishes in it suffice to prove that it had never been opened. The contents of it are difficult to interpret. The place of the feet is shown by two silver sandals. With those were the jug, Fig. 3, the fluted silver vase, 17, a silver bowl with double spiral pattern inter-linked. Rather further up was a gold saucer, Fig. 8 ; and a falchion lay with the handle toward the feet. By the head end was the other gold dish, 10, and an obsidian ointment jar and lid, with gold mounting, like that found at Lahun, but with the name of Amenemhat III inlaid in the lid. Near this was a gold plating which had covered a wooden bracelet, a silver mirror and dish. The puzzle is that no skeleton was found. There were only some patches of broken bones, one patch on the sandals, and a patch in each corner of the head end. When such slight bones, as some of these are, had remained, it seems incredible that the massive limb bones could have entirely disappeared. Of these fragments of bone two were human, beside two teeth, others were of goat, ox, partridge and fish, apparently remains of food offerings.

In the chamber, outside of the sarcophagus, were ten large jars (Fig. 14), many plates, a copper vase (2) and three tridents (1), one of them inside a broken jar. There were also two large copper basins (4, 5), and a pot with handle (6). A most interesting pottery cup (7) was found lying on the floor, with the stem broken off. Some large copper rings with long stems, had evidently come from woodwork, probably 9 inches thick, indicating massive furniture. These lay together in one corner. It is also stated that some pieces of Roman glass were found in the chamber. There are strong suggestions that it had been entered and partly routed over, yet copper basins and vase were left behind, and no attempt was made upon the sarcophagus.

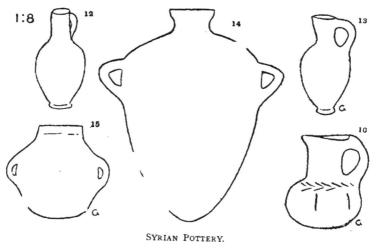

SYRIAN POTTERY.

Within the sarcophagus everything was covered with a thin layer of ashes (*cendres*) : " this was a black substance, brittle, shining in places, very damp, and bearing here and there the impression of woven stuff of more or less closeness." This layer was nowhere more than a couple of inches thick. From this description it seems that over linen there had been poured a layer of cedar resin, so often used in Egypt as a preservative : this perishes and falls into little blocks with glittering faces, by long exposure to damp. This layer makes the absence of a skeleton still more inexplicable.

We can now turn to consider the connections of the objects found. The date of the obsidian vase under Amenemhat III is beyond doubt, as it bears his name and closely resembles one of his in Egypt. That this was not an older object reburied is shown by the string of 102 amethyst beads and an amethyst scarab, as such are hardly ever found except in the XIIth dynasty, when the vein of amethyst was known.   Other Egyptian works are a gold uraeus, a heart amulet, a silver plate with part of a spread vulture embossed, ferrules with lotus flower pattern, a silver mirror, two alabaster vases, typical of the XIIth dynasty, and pieces of ivory and glaze panels from the sides of decayed caskets, like that of Lahun.   These inlays were blue and green glaze, but most have faded to white and yellow by the damp.

The Syrian objects are the important matter, as they give us for the first time many things exactly dated to the XIIth dynasty.   The peculiar sarcophagus has been noted (Figs. 10, 11).   A most interesting discovery is that of the jug and basin for washing hands, like the modern *abryq* and *tisht* (Figs. 3, 5).   The raised centre to the basin marks the purpose of it distinctly—as in present use.   It serves for the jug to stand on, to prevent it dripping when lifted up ; it marks distinctly that the use was for slight ablution by successive persons, the waste water lying round the central island.   No one would have credited these objects with half the age had they been found undated.   So far as we know, the Egyptian never used such till after the Arab conquest ; they show, like other things, the independent and superior civilisation of Syria.   The pottery cup (7) is again a Syrian invention, which later produced the lotus cup of the XVIIIth dynasty,

after the Syrian craftsmen were taken by Tehutmes III.   This also explains the source of clumsy forms of the cup with a foot, which are found during one or two dynasties, after the Syrian invasion of Egypt in the VIIth and VIIIth dynasties. The two golden platters or saucers (8, 9) are probably Syrian, as such are not found in Egypt.   The copper bowl with a handle (6), the tall jar (2) and the dish with a wide flat brim (4) are probably all Syrian.   The flesh hooks of copper (1) are not to be compared with heavy agricultural forks (*Tools and Weapons*, LXVII), but with the light flesh hooks of various forms (*Tools and Weapons*, LXXII, 61-5). The silver sandals seem to be probably Syrian, as the outline is rather straighter on the inner side than the Egyptian.   Such funeral copies in metal are, however, known in Egypt, as there is a pair in thin embossed copper in University College. The pottery is valuable as a starting point in dating.   The forms 12, 13 and 14 are from the tomb ; but 15, 16 are from the small circular tomb which broke into the passage, and might be either earlier or later.   The handles of 15 are found on foreign pottery in Egypt of the Ist dynasty.   The falchion is probably North Syrian or Asiatic.   The Cretan vases of silver are excellent examples, now fixed in relation to Egyptian history. The fluted vase with a spout carries on in metal the idea of the many stone vases with long spouts from Mochlos. Along with it lay a silver bowl with a double row of interlaced spirals, each centre having three branches. Such design lasted long, as it is also found on scarabs of Hatshepsut, and on a golden vase in the fourth tomb of the ring at Mykenae.

This tomb is thus a firm starting point for the dating of Syrian work, the definition of Syrian types, and the relations of Egypt, Syria, and Crete. Let us hope that this most important site of Byblos—temple and tomb—will be soon worked with full record and publication of all *groups* of objects, which alone can put the Syrian archaeology on a firm historical basis.

W. M. FLINDERS PETRIE.

NOTE SUR UNE TOMBE DÉCOUVERTE PRÈS DE CHEIKH-FADL PAR MONSIEUR FLINDERS PETRIE ET CONTENANT DES INSCRIPTIONS ARAMÉENNES.

LORS de sa campagne de fouilles 1921–22, à Bahnésa, M. Flinders Petrie découvrit—au cours d'une excursion sur la rive droite du Nil, et à 8 kilometres environ à l'E.N.E. de Cheikh-Fadl—un tombeau creusé au sommet de la montagne arabique dont les parvis portaient les restes d'importantes inscriptions peintes. Le savant anglais, avec sa maitrise ordinaire, reconnut de suite qu'il avait affaire à des textes araméens. Il voulut bien, avec un libéralisme auquel je suis heureux de rendre hommage, me demander de relever ces textes afin d'en entreprendre le déchiffrement. En mars 1922 je pus profiter de deux journées pour aller examiner les lieux et copier sommairement les inscriptions, mais je n'avais rien de ce qui aurait été nécessaire, pour établir une bonne copie. Le travail était rendu très-difficile par le manque d éclairage du tombeau et les ombres portées par les accidents des parois qui empêchaient de distinguer nettement les caractères subsistants. Je pus néanmoins me rendre compte de l'importance de la découverte de M. Flinders Petrie pour l'épigraphie araméenne. Je dus attendre décembre 1922 pour faire une nouvelle visite à Cheikh-Fadl en compagnie de M. Lacau, Directeur Général du Service des Antiquités, qui avait tenu à examiner lui-même la nouvelle découverte et qui—pour sauver ces textes à la science avant qu'ils n'aient été endommagés davantage par l'air ou les arabes du voisinage—avait amené avec lui M. Busutil, l'excellent photographe du Musée du Caire. En trois jours, nous pûmes cette fois avec les moyens appropriés—miroirs pour éclairer la tombe, plaques panchromatiques, écrans colorés à cause de la polychromie des peintures—obtenir de bonnes photographies de la presque totalité des textes[1] et prendre de nouvelles copies. C'est à l'aide des unes et des autres que je tente aujourd'hui de donner un aperçu, malheureusement bien incomplet, du contenu des inscriptions du tombeau de Cheikh-Fadl.

Ce tombeau s'ouvre face à l'est au sommet de la montagne. Il se compose d'un vestibule dont les parois ont été taillées à même la roche. Anciennement un toit fait de matériaux rapportés—peut-être soutenu par des colonnes du côté de la plaine—devait couvrir cette première salle et il est possible également qu'une rampe d'accés ait été ménagée en avant pour gravir la pente. Cette première partie du tombeau n'ayant pas été déblayée je ne saurais garantir l'exactitude de cette description. Étant donné l'importance que présenterait la découverte de nouvelles inscriptions, M. Lacau doit charger un inspecteur du service des antiquités de dégager entièrement ce vestibule. À la suite venait le tombeau proprement dit, une pièce rectangulaire d'environ 4 m. de large sur 5 m. de long et 2 m. de hauteur creusée dans le calcaire dont le plafond est constitué par la plateforme même du sommet de la montagne. Au fond, en retrait, une

---

[1] Par suite du manque de plaques, nous n'avons pu photographier les textes numérotés ci-après 1, 6, 7, 10, 14, 15 et 17.

niche béante aujourd'hui et qui devait être autrefois fermée par la *stèle-fausse-porte* qu'on retrouve dans les tombeaux congénères. Dans l'angle, sud-est de la tombe, s'ouvre un puits carré qui donne accès à trois (?) chambres que nous n'avons pu visiter. Ce tombeau se présente donc à nous avec les caractéristiques générales des monuments funéraires du Moyen Empire, et il est probable qu'il fût creusé à cette époque, mais il a été réutilisé au moins une fois beaucoup plus tard ; c'est la conclusion qu'on peut tirer de ce qui subsiste de la décoration. Cette décoration, fresques en teintes plates, qui orne les quatre parois, occupe un registre d'une hauteur de 0m.74 à compter du plafond. Au-dessous la roche qui n'a pas été *parée* laisse voir encore les traces de l'outil employé au creusement de l'hypogée.

Voici sommairement la description de ce que l'on peut *deviner* des peintures : sur la grande paroi (Sud) à droite de la porte, un bateau rouge à 21 (?) rameurs dans un double cadre de la même couleur, plus loin des personnages debouts, face à gauche, c'est-à-dire marchant vers la niche, dont les pieds seuls subsistent. Paroi du fond (Est), à droite de la niche, restes d'une barque (décoration primitive ? effacée ensuite ?) au-dessus personnages marchant vers la niche dont un a disparu. Même paroi à gauche de la niche, deux personnages debouts allant à droit : le premier à gauche, peint en bleu, conduit (?) un veau (?) rouge. Grande paroi à gauche de la porte (Nord), deux quadrupèdes (?) momifiés, disque et cornes en tête, encadrés de raies rouges, plus loin un épervier, plus loin encore des personnages face à droite tenant le sceptre ⌐.

C'est à peine si l'on peut saisir quelques linéaments de ces tableaux et dans ces conditions il devient impossible de préciser la date des figures d'après le style et la facture de ce qui subsiste. Au dire de M. Lacau le bateau à rames *pourrait* (??) dater du Moyen-Empire, le reste de la décoration serait plutôt saïte. Impossible également de préciser si les textes araméens, peints à l'encre rouge et très mal conservés qui coupent les figures, présentent un rapport quelconque avec elles. C'est cependant improbable.

Toute la partie supérieure du registre contenant les figures était peinte sur un banc de calcaire plus friable que le reste, elle a presque complètement disparu emportant avec elle le commencement des inscriptions. En outre, les textes qui subsistent sur les parties conservées ont été endommagés par le frottement du sable, martelés par endroits, et sont coupés dans toutes les directions par les *graffiti* postérieurs : un araméen, les autres grecs, coptes et arabes. Il est impossible de savoir à quelle hauteur se trouvait la première ligne des textes, et dans plusieurs cas on ne peut également déterminer avec certitude où commençaient et finissaient les lignes. Les difficultés de lecture se trouvent encore augmentées par les couleurs des dessins sous-jacents ; surtout quand ceux-ci sont également peints en rouge.

Je crois cependant pouvoir discerner 17 inscriptions différentes dont l'importance va d'un simple mot à neuf lignes conservées. Les textes ne paraissent pas toujours avoir été tracés par la même main. Partout cependant les mots étaient nettement séparés par des blancs. Pour passer plus facilement les inscriptions en revue, et les situer à leur place respective, je les ai numérotées de 1 à 17 sur le plan reproduit ici, d'après le relevé de M. Lacau. N'ayant pas noté les dimensions de chaque texte, j'indiquerai pour remédier à cette lacune provisoire le nombre approximatif de mots contenus dans une ligne moyenne de chaque texte.

PAROI (SUD).

No. 1. Sous le grand bateau à rames deux lignes comprenant quelques caractères seulement.

No. 2. Ce texte comprenait au moins 12 lignes (10 mots à la ligne). 9 d'entre elles sont encore susceptibles d'être déchiffrées dans les parties conservées. Je suis incapable, pour le moment, d'affirmer que nous possédions encore le commencement des lignes, mais il est certain que la fin manque.[1] Cette inscription parait se rapporter à l'ensevelissement du ou des propriétaires de la tombe, l. 8 :

$$\text{.....∘∘∘ שגיא לחי אנה רחם עמה אשׁכב אשׁבקנה אכל לא}$$

je ne peux l'abandonner, je reposerai avec lui (parce que) j'aime beaucoup Lehi (?). . .

On pourrait traduire aussi " j'aime beaucoup la vie " en prenant le ל comme préposition introduisant le complément. Sous réserve de la vocalisation du nom propre je préfère la première traduction parce que nous retrouvons ligne 3 :

$$\text{...אשׁכב עמה רחם אנה לחי שגיא ועלימא}$$

je reposerai avec lui (parce que) j'aime beaucoup Lehi (?) et le jeune homme . . .

et à un arrangement conclu avec des tiers à ce sujet :

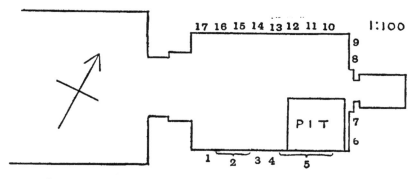

l. 6, לכמרן נתן(א), *je donnerai aux prêtres* (?), je crois reconnaître la mention du dieu שמש deux fois, ligne 9, et celle d'un nom divin composé avec le nom du dieu égyptien *Atoum* (?)

l. 5 $\text{....אתמנרן אלהא זי לה הן אנתן לה .....}$

ATMNRN son dieu. Si je lui donne.

Nos. 3 et 4 ne forment qu'un seul et même texte ; une grande lacune verticale coupe au milieu la partie conservée. On peut déchiffrer quelques lettres de 8 lignes ; il semble que nous possédions la fin des lignes ; tout le commencement manque. Ce texte est séparé du précédent par un espace où tout a disparu excepté deux lettres ...המ... Il ne saurait être question de le regarder comme représentant la fin des lignes du No. 2 parce que sa première ligne (dernière du texte) correspond comme position à la 6ème du précédent. Il était néanmoins la suite logique du No. 2, et devait contenir des clauses défensives contre les tiers

---

[1] Ici et plus loin je numéroterai les lignes en partant du bas dans l'ignorance où je suis du nombre de lignes manquantes.

qui voudraient éventuellement occuper le tombeau. C'est à quoi font allusion, je crois, les seuls mots pouvant se lire à la suite :

כל אנ[ש] יהוי תמה ‎•‎ · · ·

Tout homme (?) qui sera là.

No. 5. Le plus important de la série malheureusement dans un état lamentable. Restes d'au moins 11 lignes (12 mots à la ligne), dont 9 semblent susceptibles d'être déchiffrées avec de la patience. Les lignes de ce texte paraissent bien commencer immédiatement à gauche de la robe d'un personnage encore visible. Un large trait rouge vertical marque la fin des lignes de la première tranche du texte, la suite également incomplète par le haut est comprise entre ce trait rouge·et un second trait de même couleur qui lui est parallèle. De ce deuxième texte, 5 lignes (7 mots à la ligne) seulement peuvent être utilement étudiées. Je crois retrouver dans ce No. 5 les noms de פסמשך *Psamétique*, l. 9 et l. 8 deux fois, et de *Taharqa*, l. 6 deux fois, l. 5 une fois, appelé l. 6 :

תהרקא מלך כושיא (?) זי מלך תמה · · ·

Taharqa roi de Kouš (??) qui règne là-bas . . . .

Il faut remarquer que le nom de Tabarqa est écrit conformément à l'égyptien

⬭, תהרקא, forme déjà supposée par Oppert[1] comme type primitif de ce nom rendu dans la Bible תרהקה·

La lecture · · כושיא · · est très douteuse—sans parler de la forme insolite du mot—les deux premiers signes ne présentant qu'une tache informe. Il semble que le peintre avait commencé à écrire un מ, songeant sans doute à מצריא, puis qu'il s'est ravisé ne voulant pas donner à Tabarqa le titre de roi d'Egypte et de Néchao mentionné comme · · פרעה נכו] · ·

le Pharaon Néchao. Je complète ainsi le nom d'après le texte du numéro 8, voir plus loin.

D'après ce que je crois saisir—ceci sous les plus expresses réserves—le No. 5 relaterait certains évènements se plaçant à l'époque troublée des invasions assyriennes en Egypte. Il retracerait les démêlés de Psamétique I, de son père Néchao, et peut-être d'un autre prince avec Tabarqa. Un des morts ensevelis dans la tombe où un de ses ascendants aurait été mêlé à ces évènements comme partisan de Taharqa. La qualification de · · ·מראי· · · *mon seigneur* qu'il donne à Taharqa, l. 5, me semble l'établir. Je ne crois pas que le roi d'Assyrie ait été mentionné dans les parties du texte qui sont conservées et je suppose qu'à la l. 4 l'appellation · · ·מראי מלכא· · · *le roi mon seigneur* s'applique encore à Taharqa.

Entre la fin du No. 5 et l'angle peut-être y avait-il encore place pour un texte où rien ne subsiste.

PAROI (EST).

No. 6. Traces de quelques mots dont je n'ai qu'une copie et où je distingue seulement · · · אלהא אמר · · · *le dieu dit.*

No. 7, un seul mot · · · שמש · · ·

No. 8 devait contenir pour le moins 13 lignes (10 mots à la ligne), 7 sont conservées dont la fin se perd sur les pieds d'un personnage. J'y relève l. 7 · · · ענה ואמר · · · · *il parla et dit* l. 6 : · · · · תהרקא תמה · · ·

[1] *Mémoire sur les rapports de l'Egypte et de l'Assyrie*, dans *Ac. des Inscrip. et Belles-Lettres. Mémoires présentés par divers savants étrangers.* Tome VIII, 1ère partie, 1ère série, **page 625.**

Taharqa là-bas . . . l. 4 . . . לפרעה נכו . . . *au Pharaou Néchao* . . . ici nous avons encore affaire aux débris d'un texte historique.

No. 9, texte qui faisait probablement suite au précédent 7 lignes (7 mots à la ligne) reconnaissables, incomplet à droite. Je crois relever l. 5 mention d'une défaite des égyptiens · · · חבל מצרין · · · de l'envoi d'un message l. 4 שלח עליהם · · · et du Pharaon l. 1 פרעה.

PAROI (NORD).

No. 10, au moins 4 lignes dont on ne distingue presque plus rien, j'y ai cependant noté la présence du verbe שכב indiquant que ce texte avait un caractère funéraire.

No. 11, une ligne (4 mots à la ligne) incomplète à droite et peut-être aussi à gauche ; il y est question de sacrifices ?

l. 2 et 1

· · · ? מתעשתן אנחן · · מ · · תהרקא · · · ·

· · · · מן כמרן עבדן הם קרבא ·· · · · ·

. . . *nous pensons* . . . *Taharqa* . . . .

. . . *des prêtres qui font le sacrifice* . . .

No. 12, traces de 12 lignes très incomplètes ; il y était fait mention, je crois, des pénalités qui frapperaient ceux qui voudraient se faire enterrer dans la tombe et ensuite de certaines fêtes (?).

No. 13, 4 lignes (4 mots à la ligne) ; ce texte, bien que le commencement des lignes soit très—indistinct, paraît complet. J'y relève la mention כללה בשנת ווו וו . . . · · · "l'a terminé l'an V." Malheureusement de ce qui suit impossible de tirer un nom de roi. Le souverain n'était probablement pas indiqué.

No. 14.   Quelques signes tracés au travers d'un reste de peinture.

No. 15.   Un mot isolé entre un personnage et un objet indéterminé.

No. 16.   Restes d'une dizaine de lignes, 4 en haut et 6 en bas du panneau ; tout ce qui existait dans l'intervalle a disparu. Les deux textes paraissent avoir été tracés par deux mains différentes. Celui du bas se termine par לספרא זי כתב כתבא · · · · · · " au scribe qui a écrit (cette) inscription " . . . . Entre les deux textes un graffito araméen.

No. 17.   Restes de trois mots qui terminaient un texte.

* * *

Paléographiquement ces textes ne paraissent pas s'écarter de l'époque des papyrus araméens d'Éléphantine, ainsi qu'on pourra en juger par les quelques lignes reproduites ici.[1]

. . . . . ./ הוא בלעדיהם \ תה . . . . . .

. . . . ./ כען וימטאן בדי \הם . . . . .

. . . ./ אבדיהם י . . . . . ר\גו . . . . . .

←———————— robe ————→

[1] Elles appartiennent au début de l'inscription n° 12 et ont été choisies parceque c'est le seul passage où quelques caractères apparaissent entiers. Ils sont peints en rouge sur la robe verte d'un personnage et se transcrivent *matériellement* ainsi :

PHOTOGRAPH OF PRECEDING INSCRIPTION.

La mention de Taharqa, de Néchao et de Psamétique—si elle est confirmée—n'apporte pas nécessairement une contre-indication à ce diagnostic chronologique. Ainsi que je l'ai remarqué plus haut, le n° 5 relate vraisemblablement certains événements quelque peu antérieurs à l'époque où il a été écrit ; au moment où l'Egypte allait passer aux mains des Perses. Le récit nous faisant remonter jusqu'à Taharqa pourrait n'avoir qu'nn caractère d'histoire rétrospective rappelant les précédents d'une situation politique qui se serait établie plus tard.

Le tombeau aurait donc été réutilisé pour quelque fonctionnaire civil, militaire, voire religieux, de langue araméenne, dont l'inscription retracerait à grands traits le *curriculum*. Si réellement ce fonctionnaire, comme il semble, dépendait de Taharqa on pourrait songer à un ancien fonctionnaire assyrien qui aurait trahi son roi, Asarhaddon ou Assurbanipal, pour passer au service des maitres provisoires de l'Egypte. Cela fixerait approximativement la date des inscriptions entre le milieu du VIIème et la fin du VIème siècle avant J.-C. Toutes ces questions ne pourront avoir leurs réponses que lorsque les textes sommairement analysés ici auront été définitivement traduits. Ce travail demandera encore beaucoup de temps et plusieurs visites nouvelles à Cheikh-Fadl pour contrôler la vraisemblance des nombreuses hypothèses qui viennent à l'esprit.

NoËL GIRON.

THE BRITISH SCHOOL AT QAU.

THE work of our Society this year has been entirely at Qau-el-Kebir, a headland of the eastern cliffs, about thirty miles south of Asyut.   This was known to have been an important place, probably of the XIth dynasty, under a series of princes, who left large rock tombs.   As it was being continually plundered, it seemed desirable to finish what remained.   Unfortunately it has in recent times been largely worked by an Italian and by a German, neither of whom have published any account of their work ; the Italian plunder is of much artistic importance, yet it lies piled up in a case in Turin, useless at present to anyone. It was therefore rather a work of piety than promise, to follow after so much clearance had been made.

The oldest remains found were a collection of mineralised bones, mostly hippopotamus, but including portions of three human skulls, which, strange to say, had been gathered and piled in an ivory worker's store.   The reason is difficult to see, as they are very hard and almost unworkable.   The subject may have such importance that it will have to be studied on the spot next year, to find the natural source of these bones.   Small prehistoric cemeteries were found of the second period, which we hope to work further next year.   A fine group of vases from a tomb of the IInd dynasty were obtained, and many examples of the bright red polished pottery of the IVth dynasty, which has seldom been secured from recorded sites.   The historic interest begins with several tombs of the IVth–VIth dynasties, with characteristic alabaster vases.   With these are the stone amulets of parts of the body, deities, and animals, which are thus fixed to this period.   These amulets continued in use, rather rougher in work, and of ivory and green glaze, along with button badges, which were brought in by the Syrian immigrants, and were continued in use by the Syrian invaders of the VIIth and VIIIth dynasties.   With these were also the seals with geometrical figures of men, pyramidal seals with animals, and figures of lions and other beasts with geometrical designs on the base.   The whole of these varieties, which have been vaguely known hitherto, are now all tied together, and connected with the two Syrian dynasties.   Entirely distinct from this group there appears in the IXth dynasty a revival of the use of the scarab, but always with designs greatly degraded by repeated copying, showing that they are the successors of an earlier class of intelligible designs.   These agree with the scarabs of the same period which have been found at Harageh, Sedment, and elsewhere.   Thus the use of the scarab has been cleared up evidently as far back as the Old Kingdom.

The great rock tombs still need planning.   The architectural system is remarkable.   Large sloping causeways were made up to the entrance ; in the main tomb the causeway led to a large peristyle court levelled into the rock, like the forecourt of a temple.   In the axis a steep gangway of rock sloped up to the portico of the tomb above, cut across by a gap which may have needed bridging when the tomb was visited.   The tomb had two rows of columns in the portico, built out in advance of the rock chambers behind it.

On coming down to the XIXth dynasty the ivory worker's shop is the principal thing, providing a great number of simple pieces, and some of artistic interest. In late times the importance of the place continued ; a batch of 50 solidi of Constantius II, and several Coptic tombstones were found.

The outstanding discovery of the year is one of the earliest Coptic biblical manuscripts. It was a narrow book of nearly a hundred pages of papyrus, containing the gospel of St. John ; only a minor part is injured or missing. The handwriting is very regular, most like the Codex Vaticanus in the beginning, and more like the Codex Sinaiticus in the body of it. Thus it ranks in age with the earliest authorities for the text. It differs from the printed version of the Coptic ; and when the various readings shall have been collated, it will have much weight in settling which class of Greek readings was recognised by the Egyptians as the authority in the time of our earliest copies. This papyrus book has only one column on the narrow page. It had been evidently buried at a time of persecution, probably under the early Muslimin. It was doubled up twice across the hinge, tightly tied in a cloth, and buried in a jar in the ground, close to Roman graves.

All of this work was carried on by Mr. Brunton, aided by Mrs. Brunton, M. Bach, and Messrs. Frankfort and Starkey. I was prevented from going, owing to the necessity of finishing the publications of previous years. *Harageh* has been issued ; *Lahun II* is being printed ; *Sedment*, and the *Tombs of the Courtiers*, are ready for the press. When I was at Oxyrhynkhos in the previous season I found at Sheykh Fadl on the eastern desert a tomb of the Old Kingdom, much defaced, with Aramaic inscriptions. There are very few scholars who can deal with such material, and I asked M. Giron, of the French Embassy, to visit the tomb. He gave much attention to it, and M. Lacau had the inscriptions photographed. The first report on them is in this part, and is of great interest, as pointing to a Jewish settlement so far up in Egypt as early as the reign of Manasseh. Tirhaka is mentioned, showing that the family here went back to eighty years before the fall of Jerusalem. This proves that these people, and doubtless others, were passing freely through the Greek camp of Tahpanhes continually, and must have been familiar with Greek words and objects and thoughts in the time of the earlier prophets. Thus a strong light is thrown on the literary criticism of the prophetic books. M. Giron has preferred now to hand over all his copies and the photographs to Dr. Cowley, who has the greatest familiarity with the subject, and if any further results are possible, we shall be sure to reap them.

W. M. FLINDERS PETRIE.

THE MAGIC SKIN.

(Continued from page 8.)

WHEN we turn to consider the question of Skin Magic from the point of view of Ancient Egypt, little that is decisive can be discovered, although it is clear enough that skin rites were known and practised, the material is too elusive and enigmatic to interpret with certainty.

The most definite piece of evidence is the statement of a certain Wapwatua : " His Majesty allowed me to slay oxen in the temple of Osiris Khent Amenti in Abydos . . and I went forth over the hides there owing to the greatness of the favour with which His Majesty favoured me."[1]

Turning to the next source of evidence we are no longer on such sure ground. This is the body of references to the Mesqa in religious texts. Lefebure has made a valuable contribution to the subject in his discussion of this word.[2] His conclusion is that the Mesqa was originally the skin used in rites of rebirth, and that meska (mesek), mesken, mesqet, which occur fairly frequently in the Book of the Dead, and in tomb-chapel inscriptions occasionally, are cognate words which came to be applied to media and objects and places connected with ceremonial rebirth in more or less contingent degree. To traverse the Mesqa came to be a synonym for passing to the New Life ; the roads traversed, and the places reached, country, island, lake, mansion, city, sky, all came to be designated by words of this root with or without the appropriate termination or determinative ; at the same time these same names were used symbolically of the skin. This clearly opens a very wide field for diffuse and mystical theorising. A further flight of esoteric fancy represented the skin as the wings by which the dead reached the sky, or the Cow that bore them across the Sacred Lake.[3] Fantastic symbolism of this sort is characteristic of Ancient Egypt, and indeed all mystical philosophy, and there is no inherent difficulty in accepting Lefebure's results.[4]

The main hindrance is that the texts upon which so much depends, are so variously rendered by different translators. This applies especially to the Book of the Dead. Budge translates Mesqet as the chamber of torture, which is clearly the significance when the deceased prays that he may escape it.[5] One of

---

[1] Crum, *S.B.A.*, xvi, 133, translation of a Munich stela of the XIIth dynasty.

[2] *S.B.A.*, xv, 433.

[3] Sphinx, viii, 15.

[4] Crawford (*Thinking Black*, p. 457) mentions that among the Luba (W. Africa), in a certain village, he found he had a reputation for making the roaring in the mouth to cease. His fame for drawing teeth had preceded him. " Demon that roareth in the mouth " might well be a denizen of the Ancient Egyptian inferno from the Book of the Dead, and many apparently mystic names may have a similar matter-of-fact meaning. For example, ch. lviii. 4, " making the hair to stand on end is the name of the oars." If the lake is Osiris, spray may well be regarded as his hair : hence a suggested explanation of the name of the oars.

The products of the sub-consciousness of the savage and the civilized mystic would not unnaturally have the same family complexion.

[5] Naville, *B. of D.*, ch. XVII, accounts for the difference of meaning of the words by comparing the English words " hide," " skin," and " hiding," " beating."

these fundamental passages is chapter xvii, 126 following (Budge), and xvii, 79-81 (Pierret), which is accepted by Lefebure and Moret[1] as a reference to Anubis passing over the *Mesqa* skin for Osiris. Budge's translation reads "he who passes through the place of purification within the Mesqet is Anubis who is behind the chest which contains the inward parts of Osiris." The pertinent portion of Pierret's French rendering may be translated "I have traversed the liquid of purification in the place of rebirth . . . . this liquid of purification in the place of rebirth is Anubis who is behind the box containing the entrails of Osiris." The true meaning of this important text will be perhaps settled by the German version of the Book which is in process of publication.

The *mesqa* however is associated with an Ancient Egyptian rite which has every appearance of being a skin rite, namely, the *Tekenu.*

THE WAPRA SCENE. *See* next page.

This, as is well known since Maspero first quoted the name,[2] is the designation in many of the chapel tombs of the nobles at Thebes, and at El Kab, of an arresting object, roughly describable as pear-shaped, which is dragged by men upon a small sledge in the funeral procession. It is evidently a man, with a bull's hide about him. That it is a hide is proved, taking all the representations of it together, by the colour and markings. The walls of the chapels in the Theban necropolis are so often seriously damaged where the Tekenu sledge would have probably been—namely, near the ox-drawn hearse—that it is permissible to suppose that in the XVIIIth dynasty it played a significant part in the rites, and was represented pictorially in the majority of the larger chapels. The suggestion has been made that the frequency with which one part of the funerary pictures has been marked out for destruction, points to the work of a single objector, probably Akhenaton, and not to personal enmity to the deceased, as in Menna's

---

[1] Moret, *Mystères égyptiens.* This work is the most exhaustive that has been written on the subject : based mainly on Egyptological material, the classics, and Golden Bough. He argues that qeni, mest, shed (sed) seshed, shedt khen, khensu, are other names for skins of rebirth, local perhaps, other than the bull. If qeni is a hide, the meaning of mesqen seems clear.

[2] *Mission Archéologie française,* V. II, p. 435. Mentuherkhopeshef.

chapel, for instance. In either case the importance to the deceased of the part destroyed is emphasised by the act of erasure.

The earliest representation of the Tekenu known is that of Antefaker, Qurna (early XIIth dynasty). Sehetepabra[1] is also of Middle Empire date. With the single possible exception of Mentuherkhopeshef, it does not appear in chapels of the XIXth and later dynasties until the Saitic period, nor in the tombs of the Kings.[2]

But although the archaistic revival of the Saitic brought back Old and New Empire styles of tomb-chapel decoration, the lifeless disjointed manner in which the scenes are displayed are eloquent of ignorance of what they really represent, and there is no reason to suppose that the rites themselves were reintroduced in the old manner.[3] The inscription attached to the Tekenu scene throws no light on its significance, nor does the word itself yield any radical illuminating meaning.[4]

The following are the translations given to some of the best known examples :

a. [5]Antefaker (xi-xii) .. Dragging the Tekenu.

b. Sehetepabra (xii) .. To the West, to the West in peace to Osiris Lord of the place of Eternity.

c. Renni (xvii ? El Kab) Dragging the Kenu to this Khent Amenti.

d. Paheri (xviii El Kab) To the West, to the West, the place where thou art, the land of sweet life, I come (? he comes).[6]

The following are at Thebes, and of the XVIIIth dynasty :—

e. Nebamon .. .. Dragging the Tekenu to Khentamenti in peace with the people of Pe, Dep, and Hatehe.

f. Amenemhat .. Dragging the Tekenu by the people of Ked (?) and the Sa Serqet priest, *going forth and coming in four times* (?) by the northern nomes (?) (text corrupt).[7]

g. Mentuherkhopeshef, which is of peculiar importance for our subject, is considered separately later.

---

[1] Quibell, *Ramesseum.*

[2] The figure on the ox-legged bed in the Wapra scenes before the statue, is considered to be the Tekenu by Budge (*Book of Opening the Mouth*) and Moret (*op. cit.*) on rather insufficient evidence in view of Maspero's very convincing translation of the text, and the general nature of the Wapra rites (Maspero, *Revue de l'histoire des Religions*, 1887, p. 164).

[3] In Ramesside and later times the rites centred about the Tekenu Maspero suggests (Mentuh, *M.A.F.*) may be the theme of the curious vignette to ch. 168, *Book of Dead*, and stela C15 Louvre. Illustrated Moret, *op. cit.*, pp. 56 and 64. Ancient public rites naturally devolve into secret mystic cults.

[4] Moret translates an inscription in Renni as " he who passes under the skin is this imakhy Renni," whereas Griffith (Tylor, *Renni and Paheri*) takes the word " khensu " (skin according to Moret) in the usual sense of " travelling." A figure in a leopard's skin stands on the sledge and a man pours " water and milk " in front of it. A damaged part of the scene, however, appears to represent, as Moret remarks, a woman draping a man in a long garment in a shrine on the sledge. *See* Appendix.

[5] References to above chapels are : a. Davis, Antefaker. b. Quibell, Ramesseum. c. Tylor, Renni and Paheri. d. *idem.*, and Naville and Griffith, Ehnas and Paheri. f. Davis, and Gardiner, Amenemhat. g. Maspero, Mentuherkhopeshef, Missn. A. Français.

[6] Moret renders this : " land of renewal of life " (*uhem ankh*). But Tylor and Naville both copied it " *nozem ankh.*" Moret relies very largely on his rendering of these two texts.

[7] This text was restored by Gardiner from Menkheperaseneb which is of the same type but also damaged. The peoples mentioned in these texts appear to be denizens of a heavenly Delta whose living forbears accompanied Osiris on earth. For Sa Serqet, and the theory that the serqet-like object is a human skin, v. *op. cit.* under f. and Petrie, *Apries, Egyptian Res. Account.*

In Rekhmare the sledge-drawn Tekenu does not appear, but one may be sure it occupied its place on the surface which has been broken away.

Above we dealt only with the sledge-drawn Tekenu.[1] He is also shown in several chapels lying face downwards wrapped in his egg-shaped skin, on a bull-legged bed.[2] The same scene, without inscription, occurs in Sennofer, where a rope held by men, and the front of a sledge, alone remains of what was probably the sledge-drawn Tekenu. In Rekhmare the inscription reads " Bringing to the city of the skin (Meska with skin determinative) as a Tekenu one who lies under it in the pool of transformation." Here is another of the few tangible pieces of evidence that the Tekenu on the couch is engaged in a skin rite of some kind, as *Meska* here very clearly indicates.

The following are the usual concomitants in other chapels where it is shown more or less fragmentally and without inscription. Two men stand at either side of small twin-altars facing each other. One hand of each hangs next the edge of the altar nearest him : the other arm of each is raised above the altars towards his companion's. A double stream of blood (?) flows arch-wise under the raised arms over the outer edges of the altars. Next to them a man digs with a large scythe-shaped mattock. Behind him two men stand with their arms raised as over the altars, but these latter are replaced by two small obelisks. Beyond them again, a girl kneels towards the previous scenes at a small altar with pots containing wheat and " bread wrapped up " as superscriptions indicate : *bit* and *taou* respectively. Over her head is the legless carcass of a bull, which bears a general resemblance in shape to the Tekenu on the couch. Virey,[3] who has studied all the elaborate funerary scenes in detail, and puts upon them, in their entirety, a rather involved mystical interpretation, sees in the groups just described part of a symbolical representation of incidents in the story of Anpu and Bata (The Tale of Two Brothers). The blood of the bull into which Bata was changed became two persea trees, and these are represented by the obelisks. That the story conceals an ancient Osiris myth is undoubted : the Bitau (Bata) bull is a form of Osiris, " the bull ever born afresh."[4] The offering of the *bit taou* pots, the corn mixed with earth and spices for germination,[5] the bread representing the body ready to be resuscitated, fit suggestively into a mystical and magical resurrection drama-rite. The evidence is, however, on the whole inconclusive and the rest of the scenes which fill the wide wall space in the corridor of Rekhmare's chapel, in spite of names of officiants[6] and inscriptions, leave the uninitiated as unenlightened as before ; such was probably the intention. The fact that inscriptions occur without scenes, or attached to the wrong scene, and scenes are without inscriptions, and that in no two chapels are the scenes in

---

[1] Moret's reason for regarding the swathed figure as the Tekenu in the Neferonpet fragments (Capart Donation, Museum de Bruxelles) is not evident.

[2] There is an object in the Eastern Upper Gallery of Cairo Museum very much like an ox-hide rolled into a ball. It rests on a bed of similar form to the above.

[3] Virey, *Rekhmare, Mission du Caire,* V. 1.

[4] Anpu and Bitau were worshipped at Letoplis. Lefebure.

[5] Virey, *op. cit.* That this interpretation of the pots is correct is borne out by the Dendera inscriptions relative to the Osiris cult. Moret, *Revue de l'H. des Rel.,* 57, 87.

[6] In Mentuherkhopeshef at least twenty different officials take part, but their titles, as in Rekhmare throw no light on their actions or duties.

the same order, or are all the same scenes shown, render elucidation of the mystery of Egyptian funerary ritual at present impossible.

In the list of tomb-chapels from which material has been drawn for the purposes of this study Mentuherkhopeshef was reserved above for special consideration separately. The scenes have been carefully studied by Maspero and Davis. The difficulty of decipherment has been increased in recent years, as Dàvis found that the walls had suffered considerable damage since the artist whose drawings Maspero employed made his visit, and that his work is not to be relied upon in view of the errors which he (Davis) has discovered. There is no internal evidence of the date of this chapel. Maspero places it early XIXth from the resemblance of the style to that of Setil's tomb walls, and from the name " Tasuit " of his wife. Davis implicitly regards it as of early XVIIIth, from the style, and from the fact that the only other chapel containing remains of similar scenes is that of Amenemapt, of which sufficient remains to date it by a cartouche to Amenhotep II. It was only recently discovered, and Maspero would have had to weigh it against the evidence of the name Tasuit. This chapel presents many unique and remarkable features in connection with the Tekenu. He is shown leading the procession in front of the ox-drawn hearse. He is not clothed in the skin, and crouches on hands and knees on what appears to be the edge of the sledge ; *i.e.*, the sledge is drawn on edge. This has been interpreted to mean that he is lying on his side. In front of the oxen is a shrine containing a ram and a large zad emblem.[1] Over the Tekenu is written " Come drag the Tekenu that he may depart to his city." His sledge is drawn by men in the usual way. Another inscription at this stage reads, " M. coming to see the Tekenu being brought (dragged ?) and the ointments conducted to the mountain top (?)." These ointments or oils are on a sledge between him and the oxen. On another part of the wall, over the Tekenu, still on the sledge, is read, " M. coming in peace to see the dragging of the Tekenu on his sledge." " The Tekenu enters " is above a walking figure in front of M., and " the Tekenu sets out " over a sledge drawn by men as before. In front of the four men who drag it is a feature, on which the bad state of the wall, and the doubtful accuracy of the artist above mentioned, cast some doubt. The latter represented it as a large skin, held up by a man, with the work Meska[2] written over it. A tail remains, however, and does a good deal to restore confidence. In fact it can hardly be doubted that it was as shown in the drawing reproduced by Maspero. At this stage then it would appear the Tekenu was wrapped in the skin, and then set out again in the manner more commonly represented ; having reached the city for which he had departed, in the skin.[3]

---

[1] Griffith (Mendes) considers that the straight horned ram really represents a goat, classical writers being unanimous that the goat was the sacred animal of Mendes. Durst (*Lortet, Gaillard Faune Mommifère*, p. 107) thinks that the goat replaced the straight-horned ram in the New Empire in the Mendes cult. Lortet's opinion is that the ancient writers confused the straight-horned ram and goat, and that the former only replaced the ram in Ptolemaic times. The fact that the goat was sacred to Dionysos whose cult is traced to Egypt, as well as the bull, weighs in favour of Durst and Griffith. But there is apparently no other evidence that the goat was sacred to Osiris as well as the bull. As god of herds as well as agriculture, one would expect to find it.

[2] Meska written with the ka sign suggests that the skin was a regenerator of the spirit.

[3] In adjoining registers there is a picture of a man flaying a bull. Another man holds the horns of an animal's head, to which is attached the hide. This is clear from the inscription " putting a *skin* behind him." Davis translates " em sa ef " as " behind him." Perhaps " on his back " is a possible rendering :—with reference to the Tekenu ?

No useful purpose would be served by describing the scenes on the two upper registers,[1] in which now and then we get details reminding us of some of the more stereotyped ceremonies seen in Rekhmare and elsewhere. Men digging with the large mattocks before described and several large holes (represented as circles) in two of which are bulls, several slaughtered cattle, and goats evidently being driven to the slaughter constitute their subject.[2]

In the lowest register, however, below the *Meska* skin, is the scene for which this chapel is famous. Two men kneel facing one another. About their necks, or rather across their necks, are short ropes, the ends of which are held by four men, two to each kneeling figure. Here is evidently a scene of real or mock strangling. Over the heads of the standing men is the *sekhem* sign of power. The kneelers are " Nubian Anu," and above each of them is a crenelated cartouche containing the double sign *kes* or *keres* ; each cartouche being supported by two small kneeling figures. To the right of the group two figures lie extended : " laid aside " or " laid on their side." Beyond them again is a pit containing a sledge, towards which two men are bearing the object in question. To the left of the group is a fire-encircled pit containing the word " Tekenu," above signs representing the hair, heart, haunch and hide of a bull ; the hide following and perhaps forming a word-group with the word " Tekenu."

The above scene is well known as a unique representation of human sacrifice, or a ceremony which is the survival of it. Moret considers it an actual sacrifice and of the Tekenu, Maspero and Davis consider it very probably the real thing, but not proven ; but the latter leans to the side of the mock ceremony more than the former. Davis considers the crenelated cartouches containing the word *qeresui* or *qasui* (*qasi*) to be the name of the place the Anu came from. Maspero inclines to the view that they are destined to be " swathed " and therefore for death in the rite. That the word in the crenelated cartouche is not necessarily a " city name " is shown by the form of a pit containing " black hair " besides which a man is digging with a large mattock ; which is of identical shape.

There is a clue perhaps to the reason why such a barbarous practice—of which, however, Egypt with all its high civilisation was not entirely guiltless— should have been introduced into Egyptian funerary ritual and proudly recorded for posterity in this way. One of M.'s titles was " King's Son " ; another " Fan Bearer on the King's right hand." He was also Governor of the Southern Nomes. King's Son Governor of the Southern Lands was the best known title of the Governors of Kush in the XVIIIth dynasty. But King's Son, Fan Bearer, etc., was also the title of some of the Governors.[3]

Reisner's excavations at Kerma in the S. Sudan showed that Hepzefa of Assiut, Governor of Kush in the XIIth dynasty, was buried at Kerma in a

---

[1] The walls are divided into three registers, partitioned off by vertical lines.

[2] In connection with the pits, goats, and slaughtered bulls, the following is of interest described by Tremearne (*Ban of the Bori*, 33) which is the continuation of the sacrifice of bull and goat, and skin dance (*v.* above):—On the 4th day another bull was sacrificed and the 7th day, midnight, a he-goat ; every part of this except the flesh being buried in the hole made for the bull's blood. The worshippers washed their hands over the hole. (The magic influence was not to be brought into the house.)

[3] *v.* Gauthier, Fils r. de K, *Receuil des Trav.*, xxxix, p. 179 *seq.*, criticising length of rule of Reisner's list. (Reisner, *Sudan Notes and Records*, I, iv, 231.) Davis calls M., Viceroy of Kush, but gives no reason for so doing. His name does not occur in Reisner's or Gauthier's list.

tumulus in which was discovered upwards of 350 human skeletons grouped about the body on its couch and in the passages.[1] A similar custom appears to have been perpetuated in the Sudan until as late as 1350 A.D.[2]

It is a plausible reason at any rate to account for the unusual scenes, in spite of the legend " the Prince coming to see the procedure practised in Kenemt." This is the name both of Kharga Oasis and Diospolis Parva in the Delta, as well, apparently, as a spiritual region like Dep, Pe, and the rest.

Was he Governor of Kharga, and did such practices prevail there also ? In any case, whether the *Qasi* are human sacrifices or not, there is no reason to imagine that they and the Tekenu are the same, or subject to the same treatment.[3] This is the opinion of both Maspero and Davis. Nevertheless the Tekenu is, on the strength of the Qasi reliefs, spoken of by a number of writers as a supposed or possible human sacrifice.

It is not certain in what order the registers should be read. It may be that the Tekenu's hide is burned in the pit with the hair of the bull, and that the procession in which his sledge precedes the ox-drawn hearse,[4] which is the bottom register of all, is the representation of the final stage of the journey to the mountain chapel, and that M.'s Tekenu goes to it skinless ; having completed the ceremonies at the chapel in the plain below designed for these rites. On the other hand, the remains of the hide of the bull from which the Tekenu's skin was taken, together with the other portions of the animal, may have been burnt in the pit ; the designation " Tekenu " applying to the remainder of the hide, or perhaps to the animal which supplied the hide for him. The suggestion is often made that at the last moment the bull is substituted as a victim for the Tekenu. But, as Davis notes, there is nothing in the inscriptions in other chapels to suggest that there is an element of sacrifice at all about the Tekenu. He usually accompanies the hearse-sledge, preceded by dancers to perhaps the cry of the legend " to the West, to the West, the land of sweet life." The concluding words in Paheri, " I come " or " he comes," might, of course, be taken in a sinister sense, but the tomb may be meant. Moreover, the inscription, which is similar to one often written over the ox-drawn coffin, may, in Paheri, be an instance of a legend written to serve instead of a scene, for the coffin sledge and ox-team are not shown, no doubt on account of the small dimensions of the chapel.

To summarise : the following is a suggested explanation of the rôle of the Tekenu, based upon examples of skin and analogous rites quoted from various sources above.

There is clear evidence that the skin played its part in Egypt as a vehicle of magic power, which a human body could absorb by contact with it. The rôle of the Tekenu was to come out of the skin as he lay on the couch. He possibly

---

[1] Reisner, *op. cit.*, Vol. I, ii, 68.

[2] Baker, *Ismailia*, Vol. II, 205, quotes the Arab historian Ibn Batuta, whose informant was an eyewitness of the burial of a chieftain, at which many servants and some 30 notables were buried with him ; he himself had been selected for the honour but had been able to buy himself off.

[3] In Amenemhat the funeral cortège with bull-drawn hearse is depicted in the bottom register with the Tekenu above it. In Mentuherkhopeshef Antefaker (and probably) Rekhmare, both are (were) in the bottom register. In Anena, Tekenu is in bottom register, cortège not shown. In Horemheb, Nebamon, Ramose, Renni, cortège and Tekenu are in topmost register.

[4] The chief argument against the identity is the obvious one that there are *two Qasi.*

played the part of Anubis who seems to have performed a similar rite for the dead Osiris.[1] By contact with a sacrificial bull-hide, the Tekenu is the Bull : the Bitau Bull and when he emerges he is born, like an embryo issuing from the womb, as the bull.[2]

This idea is a natural development from a complex of ideas depending on an implicit belief in the real, almost material potency of the skin ; analogous to the development which resulted in a ceremony like the Indian *diksha* described above : the skin represents a kind of uterus, like the Indian antelope skin. The *prana* of this Bitan Bull—the spiritual counterpart of which is brought into being by the acts of the Tekenu thereafter—and all the rites associated with him, react on behalf of the deceased, who himself is thus enabled to revive in his new environment by " sympathetic action." The blood of the bull whose hide covers the Tekenu also plays its part in the drama and causes the persea trees to spring up.[3] The bull is dead but the potent *prana* of his skin can materialise a spirit bull, incarnated temporarily or when required for the purpose of the drama, in the Tekenu, who lives and moves and acts : the blood plays its own and equally important part. " Transformation " or " becoming " (kheper) as a function of the skin (the bed or skin being the lake where the Tekenu lies) is thus intelligible.

In the XVIIIth dynasty another striking rebirth or resurrection rite was employed, perhaps simultaneously with the Tekenu, as an extra reinforcement of power. This is the corn-growing practice, a development no doubt of the other corn-germinating rites, practised in the Osiris temple ritual, which almost certainly forms the subject of pot-offering scenes and other pictures which are met with on the tomb-chapel walls. This is the Osiris corn figure, formed by seed grown in an earth-covered figure of Osiris drawn on canvas, or in other ways. Corn was grown from seed-filled models of Osiris in mud and spices[4] to promote the crops. By an easy transition of ideas, familiar to us from St. Paul's allegory, the life-giving principle was transferred from vegetable life to human life. Each individual seed was a corpse, capable by the magic of water and soil of producing life : the seedling is born out of the grain. When once the close parallel with human life and death seized men's minds it is easy to understand why the vegetative rite should have superseded the animal ; the latter being relegated to an esoteric mystery sublimated so as to be hardly recognisable.[5]

Why is not the Tekenu shown in the funerary scenes in the tombs of the Kings ? A plausible answer is, that the King was Osirified in life and therefore there was no need for the funerary rite. A good deal of evidence has been

---

[1] In tomb chapel 54 Qurna, there is a picture of Anubis being dragged on a small sledge by men, with a chest which is perhaps the chest of oils which generally accompany the Tekenu. Anubis's head also appears above the destroyed area over the small sledge referred to previously as probably the Tekenu's.

[2] The mes root in mesqa is significant. For discussions of other manifestations of the part played by emblems of the concomitants of birth in A.E. ritual, *vide* Blackman, *J.E.A.*, iii, 235, and Seligmann and Murray in *Man*, XI, 11, 97, also Moret, *op. cit.*

[3] For other possible indications of Bitau elements in the ritual, *v.* Davis, *Fine Theb. Tombs*, p. 16, models of the bull, fish emblem, olive tree representing the persea flower, or reed-crowned men representing the soul-flower. These are at present unique scenes occurring in Mentuh. and Amenemapt only.

[4] Fraser, *Adonis, Attis, Osiris*, 321, 324 *seq.* Moret, *Revue de l'Hist. des Rel.*, lvii, 87.

[5] Moret, *Mystères*, pp. 56 and 65.

established to show that the Sed festival was fundamentally a rite of Osirification.[1] In the scenes representing the King, from Den onwards, he is always shown in the tight-fitting shroud of Osiris, holding the flail. Now on the North Wall of the Birth House of the temple of Amenhotep III at Luxor, there is, almost certainly, among the almost defaced sculptures. a representation of the Tekenu lying on a sledge, entirely wrapped in the skin.[2] On the East wall the Sed festival scenes are displayed.[3] The King follows the sledge with a long rod held horizontally, directed towards the Tekenu. He is probably about to strike him, but the action does not necessarily imply violence. Purification is a much more likely object.[4] Campbell regards this scene as referring to " ceremonies required to be performed to ensure the new birth celebrated on the East wall." The scene does not suggest two consecutive acts : namely, that the King himself is in the skin. It is more likely that the rebirth rite is being performed by deputy ; an interesting link in that case with the similar rite performed for the dead.[5]

Frazer, in support of the theories he advances to explain the customs and rites he deals with in the *Golden Bough*, justifies his appeal to analogous rites in other parts of the world in support of his explanations by an argument which with the change of a word applies fittingly to this study. " The positive and indubitable evidence of the prevalence of rites in ·one part of the world, may reasonably be allowed to strengthen the probability of their prevalence in places for which the evidence is less full and trustworthy."

E. S. Thomas.

---

[1] Moret, *Mystères*, 73 *seq.*, 188 *seq.*   C. Campbell, *Miraculous Birth*, 79. Petrie, *Apries*. Murray, *Man*, xiv, 2, 12. The last two writers would contend that the Sed festival took place when the Crown Prince took up the regency with his ageing father, and that the Osirification replaced the killing of the King. The drama would be completed by the burial of a statue of the King. The large Osiris statue of Mentuhetep IV (?) from the hill-tomb behind the Mentuhetep temple at Deir el Bahri, has been referred to in this connection by Professor Petrie.

[2] Campbell, *Miraculous Birth*, 73.

[3] Gayet (*Luxor Temple, M.A.F.*) thinks the object on the sledge is the trussed Bitau bull. But Campbell could find no trace of the requisite bodily features.

[4] *cp.* Frazer, *G.B.*, ii, pp. 215, 216, 233, for examples of ceremonial " striking " to dispel bad influences ; to make healthy, and to purify generally, living things and inanimate objects.

[5] Campbell says that at Soleb the King and his *Ka* are dragged into the Hall of Eating wrapped in skins, on sledges, but I have not been able to find the scene on the plate of the publication of Soleb temple. If this is so, a Tekenu rite would appear to have persisted in temple ritual long after it ceased to figure in funerary ritual : *i.e.*, after, roughly speaking, the end of the XVIIIth dynasty.

APPENDIX.

The following are passages in the Book of the Dead (Budge) in which the word Tekenu occurs, with the exception of No. 5.

(1) 58.2. Separate thou from him head from head when thou *goest into* the divine Mesqen chamber.

(2) 64.6. Hail ye two hawks who are perched upon your resting places who hearken to the things said by him who *guides* the bier *to* the hidden place who lead along Ra.

(3) 64.11. Make thou thy roads glad for me and make broad for me thy paths when I shall set out from earth for life in the celestial regions. I am one of those about *to enter in.* (Addressed to Ra.)

(4) 64.27. *I have come* as the envoy of my Lord of Lords . . . . from Sekhem to Anu to make known to the Bennu bird there concerning the events of the Duat.

(5) 72.7. I know also the name of the mighty god before whose nose ye set your celestial food and his name is Tekem. When he opens up his path in the Eastern heaven . . . . . . may he carry me along with him. . . . . . Let not the Mesqet make an end of me . . . . let not your doors be shut in my face because my cakes are in the city of Pe and my ale in the city of Dep, and there in the celestial mansions of heaven which . . . . Tem has established let my hands lay hold on the wheat and barley. . . . .

(6) 78.3. Let not him that would do me harm *draw nigh* unto me.

(7) 100.11. If this be done for the deceased he *shall go forth into* the boat of Ra . . . . . every day.

(8) 125.4. . . . my protector (?) *advanced to* me and his face was covered and he fell upon the hidden things.

(9) 149. VIII. 4. *The 8th Aat.* The name of the god therein is Qahahetep and he guards it gladly so that none may *enter.* I am the Ennur bird . . . IX . . . . and I have brought the possessions of the earth to the god Tem.

(10) 149. IX. 6. *The 9th Aat.* He has made the city so that he may dwell therein at will, and none can *enter* in except on the day of great transformations.

(11) 149. XIII. 6. The gods and the khus though they wish to *enter* into them cannot do so.

(12) 169.13. Thou shall keep away from thee death so that it shall not *come nigh* thee.

The word Tekenu ⏥ (also spelt thekenu, kenu ⏥, ⏥), is rendered *approach* in the dictionaries, and is, as will have been seen, translated in this sense by Budge in the above passages ; transitively in No. 2.

In 6, 7 and 12, this seems the obvious meaning ; 9, 10 and 11 perhaps also. In 1, 2 and 8 the obscurity of the text seems to suggest that the word may be used in another hidden sense. No. 1 is especially interesting, as the word taken is immediately followed by the " skin " word Mesqen, and Lefebure (*S.B.A.*, *loc. cit.*) has drawn attention to it as a reference to the Tekenu. Nos. 2 and 4 are from one of the oldest chapters of the Book, and are sufficiently obscure to make it probable that the true sense has not yet been discovered.

In 6 out of the 11 passages above quoted there are references to Sun gods or their emblems, the hawk and the bennu bird.

Tekem is mentioned nowhere in the Book except in the passage quoted under No. 5, and is clearly a name of a Sun god. Is it possible that the final syllable was *nu*? It will be noticed that the Mesqet is referred in the context, as well as the inhabitants of Dep and Pe who accompany the deceased's ox-drawn hearse, with the Tekenu, according to some inscriptions, as we have seen (*v.* pp. 14 and 20). Tem is also mentioned, the old sledge-drawn Sun god. The sledge-drawn Tekenu would thus be a solar rebirth ceremony.

Two derivations of the word Tekenu have been suggested ; both of sinister import : viz., Maspero's (Mentukh, *M.A.F.*) *tek*, to cut up, and *nu* formative and Lefebvre's Tektenu Libyans (*Sphinx*, 8, 5).

WAS AFRIES OF ROYAL BLOOD?

THE XXVIth dynasty consisted of the following kings (Petrie, *A History of Egypt*, Vol. III, p. 325) :—

						B.C.
Psamtek I	..	..	..	..	54	664–610
Nekan	..	..	..	..	16	610–594
Psamtek II	..	..	..	..	5	594–589
Uahabrā (Apries)	..	..	..	..	19	589–570
Aāhmes ..	..	..	..	..	44	570–526
Psamtek III	..	..	..	..	1	526–525

It has long been accepted on the authority of Herodotus that Nekan, Psamtek II, and Uahabrā (Apries) were the son, grandson and great-grandson respectively of Psamtek I ; and more recently the evidence of the Second Adoption Stele has been regarded as establishing conclusively that Apries was the son of Psamtek II. It will therefore be convenient before putting forward the grounds on which this view may be doubted, to consider what the evidence really amounts to. The Second Adoption Stele informs us that Psamtek II died in his viith year on the 23rd of the 1st month, and that " thereupon his son (𓅭) Apries rose up in his place." The question is whether the word here translated " son " implies physical relationship, as has been assumed. There is well-known evidence that it does not always do so, but into this we need not enter, since the stele goes on to say that Nitocris died on iv.12.4. of Apries, and her daughter (𓅭) Ānkhnesneferabrā carried out all the ceremonial of the burial.[1] Now the two Adoption Stelae have demonstrated, what had been conjectured before their discovery, that the succession to the Theban principality was kept up by adoption. Ānkhnesneferabrā (daughter of Psamtek II and Takhuat) was the *adopted* daughter of Nitocris, just as the latter (daughter of Psamtek I and Mehitenusekhit) was the adopted daughter of Shepenapt. We thus see that the mere use of the words which we customarily translate by " son " and " daughter " does not compel us to believe in a blood relationship if there is sufficient evidence to displace the normal meaning.

The primary ground for not accepting the ordinary meaning in this case is that the hypothesis of adoption enables us to explain an anomaly, which it is believed has never been satisfactorily accounted for ; viz., that Uahabrā, the throne name of Psamtek I, is the *personal* name of his supposed great-grandson Apries. No parallel case occurred in the whole course of Egyptian history, and surely we are entitled to look for some very unusual cause to account for it. The learned Dr. Hincks, of Dublin, discussed the problem as far back as 1855,

---

[1] Gauthier, *Livre des Rois*, Vol. IV, pp. 94, 105.

and came to the conclusion that Apries received his name because he was born in the reign of Psamtek I.[1] It is almost certain that this was so ; but Dr. Hincks did not explain why this particular prince was given the throne name of the reigning monarch when others were not. A personal name was often repeated within the same dynasty, and a throne name might be repeated after a long interval in a different dynasty ; but there is only the one instance of a king's throne name becoming a later king's personal name. Why ? All kings must, except in periods of chaos, have been born in somebody's reign ; and it was therefore clearly the rule that princes of the blood were not named in the way so common among the nobility. This is precisely the rule that would be expected to prevail, if only as a matter of convenience. We are therefore forced to one of two conclusions : that the rule was departed from in this one instance only, or that Apries was the son of some high officer, who named him, after the manner of his class, in honour of the reigning Pharaoh. It is submitted that the latter conclusion is by far the more probable.

The circumstances of the times and of the persons are consistent with our hypothesis. Egypt, no longer dominating the neighbouring nations, was in danger from more than one quarter ; and there is every probability that Psamtek II left no son of sufficient age to take command in the field. This seems to result from what we know of his daughter Ānkhnesneferabrā. She was alive in the short reign of Psamtek III,[2] some 70 years after her adoption by Nitocris in the first year of her father's reign, and may of course have lived longer. Assuming her to be 80 years old at this time, she would have been 10 years old at her father's accession, and therefore about 15 to 16 at his death.[3] It is quite possible that any son he may have had was even younger, and there was not likely to be a son very much older. What more natural than to provide by adoption, or even by pretended adoption, for the succession of a king capable of commanding the national forces ? It will be seen from the list of the dynasty that anyone of suitable age to discharge this office must have been born in the latter part of the reign of Psamtek I ; and, other things being equal, such believers in omens as the Egyptians were would be likely to give the preference to one who bore a royal name. Finally, if Apries, having no claim by descent, were chosen for military reasons, his overthrow by Aāhmes, when he had been found incapable, would be regarded with far less disfavour than a revolt against one who had succeeded to the crown in ordinary course.

And there is a yet further confirmation. Not only does the name of Apries suggest that he was not of royal birth ; not only do the circumstances existing at the death of Psamtek II render an adoption highly probable ; but there has been fortunately preserved to us a record of a man who fulfils in the most striking manner all the requirements of the situation. A very interesting

[1] *Transactions*, Royal Irish Academy, Vol. XXII, pp. 432-3.

[2] *Annales du Service*, Vol. VI, p. 131.

[3] Although Psamtek II lived into his seventh year (dying on the 23rd day), he had probably not reigned much longer than five full years. Prof. Breasted has argued (*Ancient Records*, Vol. IV, p. 502) that the adoption of his daughter by Nitocris was a political device that would probably be carried out as early as possible in the reign. If this be so, Psamtek would have come to the throne not long before the eleventh month, his daughter having arrived at Thebes from Saïs on i.11.29. With this agrees the earliest known date of the reign, i.11.9, when the Apis was installed which was born on xvi.2.7. of Nekau, doubtless in the same calendar year.

find of bronzes at Mitrahiny (the site of the ancient Memphis) described by M. Daressy[1] includes a plaque greatly injured but still in large part legible. The first register shows Psamtek II presenting an offering of incense to certain divinities, while in the second register 𓉹𓄿𓏤 ⊙𓊪𓋴𓏤𓂝𓎛𓀠𓀾 𓅢𓏤 𓉹𓄿𓏤 𓈖𓅷𓄿𓂋𓏤𓋴𓈖𓀠𓂝 " the General Uahabrā-aāqenen, son of the General Psamtek-aāneit deceased," stands in adoration before an altar bearing offerings to Amen, Mut, Khensu, Mentu, and Tum. We thus learn the following facts :—

(1) Uahabrā-aāqenen was a general, and the son of a general. He did not bear the military title associated with other offices : it was his *only* title. We may therefore conclude that he was of military stock, and that he, like his father before him, made soldiering the serious business of his life.

(2) He was living and holding high office in the reign of Psamtek II. It is important to observe that the plaque is not at all of a funerary character. It was one of eight objects in the same find, all clearly dedicated in a temple as a means of securing the divine favour for living persons.

(3) The general Psamtek-aāneit was born in the earlier part of the reign of Psamtek I and received the king's personal name. When his son Uahabrā was born in the later part of the reign, this son was given the king's throne name. This hypothesis alone will fit the facts.

If it be permissible to look for the future king outside the royal family, no other candidate for the position so eligible as this one is ever likely to be found.

F. W. READ.

[1] *Annales du Service,* Vol. III, p. 139, and Plate II, Fig. 1.

THE OBELISKS OF PYLON VII AT KARNAK.

AN article has appeared in the *Annales du Service*, Vol. XXII, p. 245, by M. M. Pillet, Director of Works for Karnak, in which he carefully estimates the height of the two large obelisks which stood before the pylon which we know as Pylon VII. He arrives at 51 metres for the height of these obelisks by calculation, which he cuts down to some 46 metres as the probable height. To me, this seems an over-estimate.

Let us set out the problem, much as the scribe Ḥori in ancient times put them to the scribe Amenemôpet :—Before Pylon VII we have the base of an obelisk of unknown taper and height. The obelisk dates to Tuthmôsis III. Find the height.

M. Pillet tackles it in this way (I translate from page 245) : " The obelisk must have been much larger than the standing obelisk of Hatshepsôwet. Actually, the south side of its base, which is still intact, measures 3·17 metres, while the mean of the sides of the base of that of Hatshepsôwet measures 2·44 metres and that of Tuthmôsis I 2·107 metres only. The difference of heights of the obelisks of Hatshepsôwet and Tuthmôsis I is, in round numbers, 10 metres (29·50 metres and 19·60 metres), that of their bases 0·34 metre *or 34 millimetres per metre* (difference in height ?). Applying these figures to the obelisk of Tuthmôsis III, which measures at its base 724 millimetres more than that of Hatshepsôwet, one finds 51·77 metres for the total height."

Generalised, this is equivalent to saying that, if the difference in the height of two obelisks of very different taper[1] correspond to a certain difference of base measurement, then the difference in height between another obelisk of unknown taper and the larger of the two known obelisks is proportional to the difference in their bases !

The height, on this assumption, appears to have been calculated as follows :—

> A base difference of 34 millimetres corresponds to a difference in height of 1 metre.
> Therefore 724 millimetres will correspond to a difference of $\frac{724}{34}$ or 21·3 metres.

Hatshepsôwet's obelisk is 29·50 metres high, therefore Tuthmôsis III's obelisk must be 29·50 + 21·3 = 50·8 metres.

Have we any other obelisk of the same date having a base large enough to make a useful comparison with that of Pylon VII ? That now known as the Lateran Obelisk has a base of 2·87 metres.[2] Let us apply the above calculation to this obelisk, assuming that its height is to be determined from its base-measurement ; here the difference in base measurements is 430 millimetres, so that its height will be $\frac{430}{34}$ or 12·65 metres higher than the obelisk of Hatshepsôwet, making a total height of 42·15 metres. But its height is 32·15 metres only.

[1] By taper I mean the number of units of height required before the obelisk decreases one unit in width.
[2] Gorringe, *Egyptian Obelisks*, p. 145.

On the obelisk of Aswan there is the outline for a smaller obelisk, which it was proposed to extract when the original scheme proved to be impossible owing to the granite being flawed (see my *Aswan Obelisk*, p. 8). The base of this is almost of identically the same size as that of the obelisk before Pylon VII ; moreover, the width just below the pyramidion is 2·02, while that of Pylon VII is found, from a fragment, to be 2·08 a trifle lower down the shaft, yet this obelisk is only 32·10 metres high.

The late M. G. Legrain's calculation of the height of this obelisk is correct only if it is assumed that its taper was the same as that of Hatshepsôwet, and that it was *similar*[1] to it in Euclid's sense. This assumption was not justifiable, as the Queen's obelisk tapers 1 in 42·8, which is far less than any other known obelisks, whose mean taper is about 1 in 28. , Legrain estimated the length of the obelisk at 37·77 metres,[2] which M. Pillet comments on as being an under-estimate.

As I have pointed out in *The Aswan Obelisk*, p. 42, all known obelisks could have been supported at any point in their length without breaking owing to the stress set up internally due to their own weight, and in ANCIENT EGYPT, 1922, Part IV, I show that, if the upper part of an obelisk now at Constantinople formed part of the problematical 108-cubit (56·7-metre) obelisk mentioned in the inscription of Thutiy,[3] then the stress set up, if supported at its centre of gravity, would be far in excess of the ultimate breaking stress of granite.[4] In other words, it would do what a ship often does in an ice bank, and that is break in two. If we assume that, in the adventures of an obelisk between its quarrying and its erection, it never was liable to be supported for an instant at its centre or its ends, then we must look upon obelisks as evidence, not of clever engineering, but of magic.

Taking M. Pillet's most conservative estimate of 46 metres for the height, let us assume the top and bottom bases to be 2·08 and 3·2 metres (that is a slightly stronger obelisk than that which he assumes was erected) and find what stress is set up when the obelisk is supported at its centre of gravity. I will not give this extremely wearisome calculation at length ; a similar one is given in full in the volume on the Aswan Obelisk on page 42. The stress which would be set up in the 46-metre obelisk would be more than 1950 pounds[5] per square inch. Granite, if free from flaws, breaks at 1500 pounds[6] per square inch.

It will be seen from the above remarks that (*a*) mathematically, (*b*) by comparisons with known examples, and (*c*) mechanically, the calculations given in M. Pillet's article might be questioned.

Though obelisks seem to have no very definite relation between base and height as was the case of pyramids, where the height is about equal to the radius of a circle having a circumference equal to the circuit of the base, yet all obelisks, about which I have notes, have their height between 9 and 11 times the length of the base, with the sole exception of Hatshepsôwet's obelisk of which the height factor is 12·3.

---

[1] It should be noted that obelisks having the same taper are not necessarily *similar* to (that is scale-models of) one another ; further obelisks, whose upper portions are identically equal, cannot be similar unless the obelisks are of equal length.

[2] Legrain, *Annales du Service*, Vol. V, p. 12.

[3] Breasted, *Ancient Records*, II, p. 156.

[4] 2,560 pounds per square inch (180 kg. per square cm.).

[5] 137 kg. per square centimetre.

[6] 105 kg. per square centimetre.

When M. Pillet informed me that he estimated the height as over 45 metres, I pointed out on my plan of the Aswan Obelisk the outline of the reduced scheme, and its close resemblance to the Lateran Obelisk and the base of the obelisk of Pylon VII. It may be that his proofs had been passed before his statements could be amended.

R. ENGELBACH.

[The simplest point of view is that most obelisks have a height which is between 9 and 11 times the base. The obelisk of Tahutmes III, at Karnak, was probably therefore between 28·5 and 35 metres, 94 and 115 feet, high ; so it need not have exceeded the Lateran Obelisk.—F. P.]

[Correction to ANCIENT EGYPT, 1922, p. 102.

I have been checking the calculations in my article on the Constantinople Obelisk, which appeared in ANCIENT EGYPT, as I have long suspected that an error had somehow crept in, since the figure of 5120 lbs./sq. in. seems so very excessive. I find that, by a slip, I have calculated the stress-formula using the Moment of Inertia instead of the Modulus of Section, which is *one-sixth* the cube of the depth of the obelisk and not, as written, *one-twelfth* the cube. This makes the stress set up exactly one half of that given, namely, 2560 pounds per square inch.

This error does not occur in my volume on the Aswan Obelisk, and I am quite unable to account for my lapse. Fortunately, the error does not in any way affect my argument that the Constantinople Obelisk is not part of the 108-cubit obelisk of Thutiy.

R. ENGELBACH.]

REVIEWS.

Egyptian Art.—By JEAN CAPART; translated by W. R. DAWSON. 1923. Large 8vo. 129 pp., 64 pls. (Allen and Unwin.) 16s.

This work is introductory to the general study of Egyptian Art, explaining what should be the common stock of knowledge before entering on the details of monuments. The country, its historic setting, the growth of the art, and the various elements of the architecture are each set out. All this is excellent for the beginner, and worth noting by the student who knows more. There are some points in which it would have been well if the translator had asked for more precision. It must be very confounding to a beginner to find early works spoken of as debased imitations of later designs (p. 53) ; or prehistoric drawing as a crude rendering of one of the usual figures of late times (p. 53) ; or the prehistoric knife handle of Gebel Arak described as " imitating the productions of a more accomplished art." Considering that nothing in Egypt before or for centuries after that carving is in the least comparable with its beauty, and that the motives are certainly of foreign origin, the whole treatment of it seems misleading. Regarding the use of bronze, it is certainly not common in the Middle Kingdom, and probably the use of metal statues is as old as Khosekhemui (p. 95). It is rather awkward to say that the Nile soil is incapable of compression, in reality it moves up and down some inches at every inundation. It is misleading to say that there was any " proposal " to add another Sothaic period to the history ; it always was recognised by the Egyptians, and the only proposal is that of Berlin to cut it out, and shorten the history. Whether right or wrong in that scheme, at least the source of the difference should be fairly stated. The translator has hardly followed the subject, or there would not be " trenches " for divisions of a period (p. 46), or stoneware (p. 50), or enamel (p. 60), or brick arches upholding masonry (p. 91). More references to English publications might be given, " Royal Tombs " and " Prehistoric Egypt " are not in the extensive bibliography. The plates unfortunately have no link with the text, either by position, or reference on the plates or in the text ; these matters need proper editing to make the work intelligible as a whole. With some revision of such detail, and of other minor errata, the manner would correspond with the excellent matter here laid before the public.

The Glory of the Pharaohs.—By ARTHUR WEIGALL. 1923. 8vo. 286 pp., 16 pls. (Butterworth.) 15s.

This is an interesting and amusing series of sketches, or essays, out of the author's full experiences in Egypt ; but the title must surely be due to the publisher, as there is little about Pharaohs, and nothing about their glory. In the first paper the right note is struck about the necessity of knowing the country, if one is to understand the past or the present of the people. Mr. Weigall's indignation has been stirred by the removal of antiquities from Egypt ; but it is the injury to things which remain there which is reprehensible. Whatever stays in Egypt waits to be destroyed, by the dealer, or the engineer, or the stonemason, or the lime burner, or the fanatic, or the small boy with a big stone. The heart-rending thing is to see the destruction going on, and know that it will always go on, Egyptians being Egyptians. When anything can be removed to safety without damage, it had better be at the North Pole or the Equator than be left in Egypt. There is a reference to the "immediate purchase" of the letters from Tell Amarna ; would that it had been immediate, for they were ground about in a sack on donkey back, and waited for months to find a purchaser. It is not personal greed that wishes to see things removed. Rather should every portable valuable go to Arizona than be left in a country where no native cares for it except to sell, and where it may be exposed any year to a fanatical mob which will delight in destroying an image and would be urged to do so by its leaders.

An essay on the preservation of antiquities is occupied with the analogy between Futurists and Prussians ; the real enemies to preservation are utter ignorance which has no interests, and mad fanaticism. Till those can be cured, at home and abroad, all antiquities have a short life when they are visible.

In the " Morality of Excavation," the constant destruction going on in Egypt is rightly pointed out as the only alternative to clearing out and removing things by trained hands. It is useless to sentimentalise over leaving the dead as they were laid, when to leave them is to ensure their destruction by their descendants. The conscientious course is to observe, record, and preserve everything that can be of importance. Even here there are plain limitations, or the world would not contain the books that would be written. The sieve needful is a full knowledge of what is known and published already, thus sifting out the new material that is wanted, from the much larger mass of repetitions of familiar things. For this reason, a beginner's notes are of little value ; for, if complete, the new facts are lost in the common mass ; if incomplete, it is generally the essential matter that is missed. It needs years of experience to know what to neglect, in order to give hours and days to the things that have never been seen before, and from which every scrap of knowledge must be extracted.

The Temperament of the Ancient Egyptians is well illustrated, and a true sketch of conditions of work is in the chapter on excavations. Two chapters are given to a permanently valuable record of the opening of the tombs of Tyi, Akhenaten, and Horemheb. The " Nubian Highway " and " The Alabaster Quarries " recount interesting exploration in the deserts. Some amusing native letters are quoted, showing the real working of the mind, as well as the pathetic attempts at writing English, which are much better than almost any Englishman's Arabic letters. Two gems are not given here : the plaguey hanger-on who tries to recommend himself by saying proudly, " My name is The Limit " ; and the hydraulic ram which was put into Arabic by an engineer, and then re-translated as " A watery sheep." Such are enough to cure one of venturing on a foreign language ; how innocent, and how impossible, are such attempts. Other chapters are also worth having ; and we may thank the author for so truly dwelling on the value of the consciousness of the historic past as an ethical background for present action..·

The Exodus in the Light of Archaeology.—By J. S. GRIFFITHS. 1923. Sm. 8vo, 79 pp. (Robert Scott.) 2s. 6d.

This is a well-packed book, written with insight and thought. The position regarding the historic details is reasonable, and after setting that out fully, the various other views are stated, and the reasons for and against them. It is as good and as impartial a statement of the historical position as could be found, and it deserves the widest circulation.

TYPES OF SCARABS BEFORE THE XIIth DYNASTY.

ANCIENT EGYPT.

TYPES OF EARLY SCARABS.

DURING the last few years several early cemeteries have been searched, and scarabs found in some of the graves. Owing to these scarabs not being as common as those of the XVIIIth dynasty, a belief had arisen that there were no scarabs before the XIIth dynasty, though even the advocates of that belief admitted that there were possible exceptions. So far, however, there has not been any general statement as to what were the types and appearance of the scarabs before the XIIth dynasty. To make them more familiar, then, we have grouped together the scarabs from Abydos (1), Qau marked Q, Sedment marked S, and Harageh marked H.

The kind of evidence as to the age of these scarabs is the essential matter. That from Abydos (No. 1) was placed between the arm and chest of a contracted burial, packed in a small box, buried within the square of graves of Zet. Contracted burials are unknown after the VIth, or perhaps the Vth, dynasty ; that this was not accidentally contracted is seen by the small box-coffin used. Were it not for the scarab the burial would have been assumed to be coeval with all the other contracted burials of the Ist dynasty. It does not seem possible to place this later than the VIth dynasty in any case. The examples from Qau were with pottery of about the IXth dynasty and earlier, and without any of the objects so well known in the XIIth dynasty. Those from Sedment were with pottery of the IXth dynasty, in the hundreds of burials of that age which have no trace of the XIth or XIIth dynasty objects. Those from Harageh are likewise from burials whose whole character is of that same age. In these three sites we are dealing with extensive cemeteries of a uniform character, quite different from that of later times. Beside these there was a single grave with pottery of the IXth–Xth dynasty at Kafr Ammar, with a well-designed scroll scarab, and another (see *Heliopolis and Kafr Ammar*, XXVI, 2, 3, and XXVII, 1, 5, 19, 22, 24, 26, p. 32, tomb 509), but as this was a single isolated case there is less certainty about it. There are also the eight scarabs found at Ehnasya with burials earlier than the temple. That temple was destroyed, and rebuilt by the XIXth dynasty, so it could hardly be other than of the XIIth dynasty, of which many pieces of sculpture were re-used in the XIXth dynasty. The burials are almost certainly, therefore, before the XIIth dynasty ; but as the evidence is indirect, these eight scarabs are not quoted here as types.

Regarding the types, the scarab upon 1 and 2 is of the same style and the form of head is identical. The Abydos example, 1, is the most degraded, and implies a considerable period of transition from a true form ; yet this cannot be

E

put after the VIth dynasty. The lion and lizard, 3, and the men upon 4, are much like the figures upon the buttons, which are of the VIth–VIIIth dynasties.

The scrolls show what a variety was developed before the Middle Kingdom. There is the simple symmetric scroll on each side, 6, cut on a large calcite scarab, much worn. There is also the skew scrolls, 7, on a long beetle, with narrow pointed elytra. The two pairs of spirals 8–10 seem to have been admired, as they are found both at Sedment and at Qau ; large scarabs of this type are also known. 11 and 12 are placed together as found in one tomb ; the form of linked spirals in 11 is that on the scarab of Zedkara of the Vth dynasty, and as there is no question that this type is as early as the IXth or Xth dynasty, the king's name in the Vth can hardly be further disputed (P.S.C. 5.8.4). The large scarab 13 is cleanly cut in dark green jasper ; it belonged to a burial of Haur.em-sekhti, which had an early form of cartonnage mask with separate beads painted on it ; this burial was wrecked, and another put over it which cannot be as late as the XIIth dynasty. It is probable that this scarab belongs to the VIIIth or early IXth dynasty.

The group 14–17 were found together, and they link to two others found together, 18–19. This group of lotus is very usual on scarabs, but is rare at Kahun among the sealings of the XIIth dynasty ; it is probable, therefore, that most of this type are early. 20–21 are ovoid backs, not scarabs ; they will carry with them a good many more such patterns.

· A very coarse style of degraded types is from 22 to 28, connected with the style of the geometrical figures of men. They evidently have a long history of degradation lying before this stage was reached. 25 is figured in side view to show the characteristic form of a high scarab raised up on the legs. This form is peculiar to the IXth dynasty scarabs at Qau.

29 is placed here as it has the two *neb* signs, which belong to the group 30–34. This idea of the double lordship over Upper and Lower Egypt was favoured in the IXth dynasty ; but it is notable that the crown is always that of Lower Egypt. On 33 it looks like a degradation of the vulture and uraeus on the *neb* signs.

From these scarabs we now know the types and style of the IXth and Xth dynasties ; from the Kahun sealings we know the work of the latter part of the XIIth dynasty ; and from the Hyksos graves we know the later styles—so it should be possible now to classify scarabs according to period.

FLINDERS PETRIE.

TRACES OF A *KA*-BELIEF IN MODERN EGYPT AND OLD ARABIA.

PROF. C. G. SELIGMAN, in his paper on the survival in Modern Egypt of a *ka*-belief,[1] has collected a considerable number of examples from various informants, but my own researches among a good many Egyptians of the simpler kind, carried on in the first half of 1914, met with little result, although I questioned several old men whom I had previously found well stocked with folklore. It would seem that the belief is dying out, though so long as it is held by demon-expellers such as the one figuring later in this paper, it will survive, however faintly.

The cases found were two. An aged native of Heluan believed that a spirit- "sister" (*ukht*) follows men and women through their lives : she is quite distinct from the immortal soul (*ruh*) ; she goes with the person to the tomb, but what happened to her after that he did not know. She has generally no direct influence on a man's character or actions, but has one peculiar quality—that if he gives way to a violent temper she is evilly affected and gives power to local *ginns* to materialise and work mischief on the man.

The second account was obtained at Nezlet Batran, a village near the Gizeh Pyramids, famous for a sacred acacia-grove. There I heard of a wise-man, a seer, living in the village, whose chief business, as usually in Egypt, was to reveal hidden things ; but he had won special fame as an exorciser of evil spirits. At his house I found people gathered from all parts of the country, even far in the south.

When pursuing his wizardry he was himself possessed of a guiding spirit, not always the same, sometimes male, sometimes female (*sheikh* or *sheikhet*), but he seems to have changed them seldom, a single one attending him for long periods. His voice changed as the spirit spoke through him ; he practised a kind of ventriloquism. A visit to an Italian spiritualist, an itinerant professional, in Cairo, had caused him to adopt the hackneyed curtain and tambourine, to him a new and desirable fashion ; previously, we learnt, he set up for professional use a kind of small canvas tabernacle[2] in the courtyard of his house, or, if visiting, his host's.

Among his recent deeds of exorcism was one of special interest, the subject being the *ka* (*ukht*). A young man became subject to the attacks of a hostile spirit, causing him to fall down and roll about, shrieking and tearing at his clothes. He was brought to the wise-man, who, on enquiring of the spirit about its nature, learnt that it was no ordinary demon, but the patient's spirit-"sister." She told the exorciser that the young man "walked about waving his long hanging sleeve and turning his head from side to side "—acts which denoted excessive vanity and so enraged her that she resolved, if he did not amend, to kill him. The wise-man undertook the cure, with such success that the patient became his faithful follower and a promising candidate for seerdom: his master also had begun his career after a series of fits.

The "sister," it was explained, was born with every man, and accompanied him, walking underground, in all his ways, even to the tomb, but what befell her then was not known. As in all the cases reported, a clear distinction was made between the *ukht* (or *qarinet*) and the attendant spirits, good and bad, the " guardian " and the " tempter," who are also named *qarin*. To orthodox Muslims these are religious realities, attested by a *hadîth* (saying of the prophet Mohammed, handed down by tradition) and not to be confounded with the vague " sister "-spirit or any other.

The descriptions given above resemble, as far as they go, those related by Prof. Seligman, but my informants did not use the word *qarineh*, although its meaning, a " female companion " (fem. of *qarin*), makes it appropriate. *Ukht* is probably preferred, to prevent confusion with the demon *qarineh* known and feared in every Egyptian family, ever prowling to snatch away new-born children, sometimes leaving changelings in their place, the equivalent of the Babylonian *Labartu*[3] or the later Jewish *Lilith*,[4] and probably derived from the child-snatching demon feared by the ancient Egyptians.[5]

The ancient Egyptian idea of the *ka* underwent in the course of ages many developments and even sophistications, some of them early in history, but it probably kept among the illiterate subject classes, especially the peasants, its original simplicity as a protective genius, attached through life to man and welcoming him in the Elysian Fields.

The modern *ukht* has a different character ; she is a guardian no longer in the old material sense, but morally, protecting her ward against his evil self, ready to go to the murderous lengths for a long time practised by saviours of souls in mediæval Europe. Yet, with all this, some of Prof. Seligman's reports show a kindly, reverent feeling towards the sprite—exhibited, for example, in the ejaculation of bystanders when a person stumbles : " God's name on thee and thy sister."

Between the *ka* and the *ukht* Islamic doctrine has intervened. In the Qorân the word *qarin* appears three times in the sense of " accompanying demon " —not ' angel.'" The texts are :—

1. Ch. 41, v. 24.—" And we bound to them companions (*qarin*) and they painted [falsely] for them the present and the future."

2. Ch. 43, v. 35.—" Whosoever withdraws from the admonition of the Merciful, we chain a devil (*shaitân*) to him and he shall be his inseparable companion (*qarin*) ; they (the devils) shall turn them from the way, yet they (the men) shall imagine themselves to be rightly directed, until, when (the erring man) appears before us [at the Day of Judgment], he shall say [unto the devil] ' . . . oh, how wretched a companion art thou ! ' "

3. Ch. 50, v. 22.—This text refers to the Day of Judgment, when " the sentient worlds " ('*alamîn*) are brought to trial (Qorân, ch. 31, v. 27), this term including spirit-beings, angels, ginns and demons, as well as the " sons of Adam."

   " And his companion (*qarin*) shall say : ' Our Lord, I did not cause his excesses, but he was wandering afar.' "

The *qarin* is here shown as trying to throw the guilt of his own actions on the man to whom he is bound, but the Lord cuts short the wrangling and punishes both delinquents.[6]

Lastly, commentators[7] on the above passages lay it down that the devil (*shaitân*) who is " made companion " (*maqroon*) of a man never leaves him.[8]

It is clear from these texts that the God of Islam, of his own volition, couples demons to men as part of his discipline. Orthodox Muslims are bound by these texts and the authoritative exegesis of them, yet the bonds have not proved strong enough, at least among the illiterates, to destroy older ideas of a favouring genius, though they have materially altered them, robbing the ancient spirit of his material protective quality.

II. ARABIA.

Thus far we have dealt with Egypt, and now turn to Early Arabia.

The root of the word *qarin* conveys the idea of " a pair " (one of its derivatives, for example, is *qarn*, " a horn "), and *qarin* is an adjectival form denoting the quality of being one of a pair.

That the prophet Mohammed should have attached to this word a deliberately invented idea of an accompanying spirit is very improbable. On the contrary, it is likely that he found such an idea already existing under the name of *qarin* and adapted it to the object of his mission—moral discipline—by making the *qarin* a devil (*shaitân*).

This inference is strengthened by another meaning of *qarin*, or *qarineh*, as well as the cognate *qarîna*, " immaterial self." This is not an early concept, the fruit of primitive imaginings, but belongs to a comparatively late period, that of philosophical reasoning. There must have been an earlier denotation of the term *qarin*, within the category of the immaterial—namely, an immaterial, or spiritual, " companion." It is likely, too, that the old companion-spirit was of a protective nature, and that when the prophet, in his *hadîth*, added a good *qarin* to the evil one announced in the Qorân, he simply reverted to an older tradition of a guardian spirit.

In one way the *ukht*, as described to me, corresponds closely to the indefinite personal " god " of the Babylonians—" My god who walks by my side."[9] Dr. Langdon, in his contribution to Dr. Blackman's paper on " The Pharaoh's Placenta,"[10] gives many incantation texts referring to this personal " god " and says : " The fundamental concept of personality in Sumerian and Babylonian religion is a sort of dualism, a person and a super-person. ' A man and his god ' form a unity which under normal conditions always exists."

Thus the early Arabians found a *ka*-belief held on one side of them by their Semitic congeners, and on the other by their Egyptian neighbours ; that they should share it, even if in a differing form, would be but natural.

One cannot, of course, claim more than that the existence of a kind of *ka*-belief among the early Arabs is suggested by their use of the word *qarin* and is in itself probable. It is possible, doubtless, that the Semitic conception of guardian-spirits is of independent origin, having no connection with the *ka*-belief of Ancient Egypt, and that the Arabian belief is merely a phase of the former. It is, further, possible that Semitic beliefs in the matter influenced those of Egypt before the rise of Islam, in the later periods of penetration ; an example of this may be seen in the domains of magic, on comparing the Harris Hieratic Papyrus of the 20th Dynasty (edited by Chabas) with the Magic Demotic Papyrus of the third century A.D. (edited by Griffith and Thompson), so full of strange, un-Egyptian demons, exactly like those invoked by the modern ink-magicians of Egypt.

These and similar questions I have put aside ; my object has been to put on record things observed likely to be useful to students of such matters.

G. D. HORNBLOWER.

NOTES.

[1] *Essays and Studies presented to Wm. Ridgeway on his Sixtieth Birthday,* Cambridge University Press, 1913.

[2] The use of the special tabernacle is worthy of note ; it seems to point to a pre-Islamic time when some kinds of spirits would require an abode. We may compare the practice of a mediæval African people of the same race as the Early Egyptians, the Beja, who in the days of Makrizi were not yet converted to Islam and of whom he relates that each family had a priest (*cp.* the early Hebrews, Judges, xvii, 5 ff.) who set up a tent of skins in which he consulted " the spirit " (*v.* Prof. C. G. Seligman, *J.R. Anthr. Inst.,* Vol. XLIII, p. 661).

[3] *v.* F. Thureau-Dangin, " Rituel et Amulettes contre Labartu," in the *Revue d'Assyriologie,* Vol. XVIII, No. IV, Paris, 1921, and R. Campbell Thompson, *Semitic Magic,* p. 41.

[4] *v.* J. E. Hanauer, *Folklore of the Holy Land,* London, 1907, pp. 266 and 322 ff.

Some of the features reported to Prof. Seligman show, I think, traces of confusion, very natural, with a demon *qarina.*

[5] *v.* Breasted, *Development of Religion and Thought in Ancient Egypt,* p. 291.

[6] In sect. iv of Sale's *Preliminary Discourse* to his translation of the Koran he describes a popular belief of Muslims about the Judgment Day—derived from late Jewish—that the guilty, using all possible pleas for exculpation, will cast the blame of their evil deeds on anyone they can, and thus the " soul " and " body " will mutually attack each other but will both be condemned as were the blind man and the lame in the parable—also of Jewish origin—who, set to guard an orchard, combined to steal the fruit, the lame riding the blind.

[7] The principal authorities consulted were *Tabari, Tag-ul-'Arûs, El Qamûs, Lissan-ul-'Arab, Mishkwet-ul Masabîh,* and originals referred to by them.

[8] Some commentators hold that the demon bound to a man is a *ginn.* Even in early Islamic times there is confusion between *shaitân, ginn* and *qarîn.*

[9] Quoted by Prof. Elliot Smith in *The Evolution of the Dragon,* p. 214, from Dr. Langdon, " A Ritual Atonement for a Babylonian King," in the *Museum Journal, University of Pennsylvania,* Vol. VIII, No. 1.

Sale, in his description of the Early Arabian divination by arrows (*Prel. Disc.,* sect. v, p. 90, of Tegg's undated 8vo edition), relates that the arrows kept in the temples were marked with the phrases " My Lord hath commanded me " or " forbidden me." This suggests a god for the person of the oracle-seeker, recalling Mesopotamian beliefs. (The Babylonians, as we learn from Ezek. 21[21], used similar divinations.)

[10] *Journal of Egyptian Archaeology,* Vol. III, part iv, p. 239.

THE SUPPORTS OF THE PYLON FLAGSTAVES.

THE device by which the gigantic wooden flagstaves, always placed before the pylons, were held secure, has, I believe, never been satisfactorily explained, though several contemporary sculptures and paintings of these flagstaves have come down to us.

In Luxor Temple we have a contemporary sculpture of the pylon of Ramesses II, and in the procession of Tutankhamûn, in the same temple, there are two views of the pylon of Amenophis III, which was then the front pylon of Karnak Temple. In Karnak Temple King Herihor gives a sculpture of a pylon with eight flagstaves, probably representing that of the Khonsu Temple, before his successor Paynozem remade it on apparently a smaller scale. Tombs 16 and 19 at Qurneh both have paintings of pylons dated to about Ramesses II and Sety I respectively, though I am not at all sure as to which pylons they are intended to

PYLON OF EDFU, WITH GROOVES FOR FLAGSTAVES.
TWO HOLES ABOVE EACH HELD THE SUPPORTS.

be. The flagstaves, some of which must have weighed over 5 tons, were formerly believed to have been of cypress or cedar ; Loret, however, in the *Annales du Service*, Vol. XVI, pp. 33-51, has brought a good deal of evidence to show that they were of Cilician Fir (*Abies Cilicica*), though, to my mind, he lays too much stress on the colour as given in the ancient paintings. In some cases, as Tutankhamûn's sculpture in Luxor and Herihor's at Karnak, the flagstaves are trees with the branches merely lopped off, and not smoothed in any way, whereas in Ramesses II's sculpture and in the presentation scene of Tuthmôsis III behind the sanctuary at Karnak the flagstaves are shown perfectly smooth.

E 4

Figs. 1 to 5 show the various indications which have come down to us from ancient times of the method by which the flagstaves were supported; they are all reduced to the same scale. They are from the following sites :—

Fig. 1, Herihor's sculpture, probably of the previous pylon of the temple of Khonsu. (Karnak.)

Fig. 2, Tutankhamûn's sculpture of the pylon of Amenophis III at Karnak. (Luxor Temple.)

Fig. 3, Ramesses II's sculpture of his own pylon at Luxor. (Luxor Temple.)

Fig. 4, Unknown pylon from tomb of Amenmôse. (No. 19, El-Qurneh.)

Fig. 5, Unknown pylon from tomb of Pinehas. (No. 16, El-Qurneh.)

No. 16 is dated to Ramesses II, and No. 19 is probably of the time of Ramesses I–Sety I.

Before we can say that we have explained the curious form of the supports, we must not only account for every line in the most detailed picture known, but we must account for every fact observed in the pylons themselves; further, we must show that it is a natural and simple method of attachment (for the Egyptian was, above all, practical, apart from his religion) or that it perpetuates some feature in the reed-and-mud buildings from which the pylons are derived. The latter possibility may be ruled out at once, as if such a reed building ever had flagstaves of proportional height to those associated with the pylons, they would not need upper supports at all, but would be simply fixed in the ground.

Let us examine the ports in the pylons in which the supports were held. We are struck with their great size—generally slightly over a yard square—and with the fact that in no pylon is there any trace of the ancient supports. The inference is that either the ports contained material which was of value to later generations, or that they contained something which has perished in the course of ages. In the unfinished pylon at Karnak the ports are empty, like all the others which we know to have been furnished with flagstaves. It may be added that the ports do not necessarily coincide with the interior chambers of the pylons, so that the supports cannot have been removed in order to obtain more light, as one might well imagine from an examination of Edfû pylon.

Let us consider the support shown in Fig. 1, as being the most detailed. Taking its outline only, it is seen that it, like most of the others, is just about the size of the ports in the pylons, and appears to be rectangular. This immediately suggests a cantilever of considerable size projecting from the port. The part of the support which holds back the flagstaff, which we will call the clip, is only of half the depth of the entire support. Taking the lower half, it is seen that the flagstaff is in no way hidden, strongly suggesting a semicircular groove in the end of the cantilever.

As to the material of the cantilever, apart from the clips, it seems almost certain that it was wood, since that would readily account for the fact of its disappearance from the ports in the pylon, having been either used as fuel or having rotted away. Had the cantilevers been of stone, which is perfectly feasible mechanically, we should expect to see them, at any rate in the rough, in the unfinished pylon of Karnak; it would involve an unnecessary expenditure of labour, and be a difficult matter to haul a block, weighing at least three tons, up the face of the pylon after the constructional ramps had been removed.

Whether the cantilever was of one piece or not, matters little, so long as each piece was of full depth. In the Luxor pylon the cantilevers would only have to project about 6 feet, and in the upper supports of the Edfû Temple they might have had to project 10 feet, which is well within the powers of any wood of 2 feet depth.

As to the holding-back device, the most simple means nowadays would be to use a thick metal band round the cantilever and flagstaff, but it is obvious that this is not the method used by the Egyptians, as vertical pegs are about the one method by which such bands could *not* be attached (Fig. 1). The Egyptians

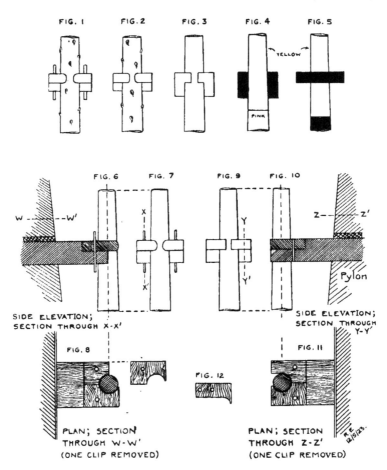

did not like using heavy masses of copper, unless it was in a place which made a good show, and where plating was out of the question. It seems that they did not like covering the entire flagstaff with the clips ; possibly the idea was, in the earlier examples, to show clearly that such flagstaves were of one piece— a matter of pride in the case of flagstaves and obelisks. A straight fir of 30 to 50 yards high took a great deal of finding, besides being a most unmanageable thing to transport, and, in a two-support pylon, it would have been fairly simple to make the holding-back clips conceal a joint. I admit this appears rather far-fetched, particularly as, at any rate in Ramesside times, they appear to have had the bad taste to plate the masts with electrum. The fact remains, however, that the clips do not conceal the wood completely. Fig. 5 shows supports which might be metal bands round the cantilever, but I place little reliance on this, as the whole painting is very carelessly done. In Figs. 4 and 5 the supports are coloured black, which is the normal colour of the parts of the flagstaff which are not painted or plated.

One of the most simple and natural methods of holding back the masts is by clips of wood resting on the cantilever, which is " halved " to receive them, the clips being pegged or skewered down. Figs. 6 to 8 show the details of a support of this description, which gives a front view exactly like that of Herihor's sculpture. Whether there were two skewers on each side of the masts cannot be determined, as only one would show from the front. If there were only one, the clip would have to have the form shown in Fig. 8 ; if, on the other hand, there were two, a more simple design, such as Fig. 12, would answer the purpose.

In Figs. 6 to 8 it is seen that the recess in the end of the cantilever is a semi-circle, and that the clips project in front of it, thus making the line between the clips and cantilever show clearly, especially if there is a top light. If the ends of the cantilever are brought out as far as the ends of the clips, the division line will hardly show at all (Figs. 9 to 11), especially if the supports are metal-plated, giving a front view like that of the pylon of Ramesses II at Luxor.

In ancient records the flagstaves are nearly always described as being either wrought with electrum or copper or having electrum tops. An examination of the paintings of these flagstaves in tombs 16 and 19 at El-Qurneh shows them to have been parti-coloured. In tomb 19 they are painted in alternate bands of pink and yellow, and in tomb 16 in bands of black and yellow. The tops are in all cases yellow. To our minds, this indiscriminate plating or painting is most unpleasing, and one might well doubt if the Egyptians could have been guilty of it. It seems, however, that we must accept the artists' version, at least in this matter, as the general aspect of the pylons and flagstaves must have been familiar to every one, though the details of the flagstaff supports may well have been unnoticed. In the case of the tombs of El-Qurneh the artist was working some distance away from a pylon, while in the temple sculptures he was close to it and could thus render the details faithfully.

The colouring of the flagstaves was not done only if they were smooth ; one of those shown in tomb 16 clearly shows that the branches had only been lopped off, yet it is painted like the others. In the sculptures no trace of paint remains except in Herihor's at Karnak, where the supports, and possibly the masts, are green. The reason for this colour is not clear to me.

In tomb 16 one of the pylons has no streamers on the masts ; can it be that they were only so decorated during festivals ?

R. ENGELBACH.

PITHOM AND RAAMSES.

IN a series of articles contributed by him to the *Journal of Egyptian Archaeology* for 1918 (Vol. V) under the title of "The Delta Residence of the Ramessides," Dr. Alan H. Gardiner brings together a vast quantity of learned and valuable observation which has an intimate bearing on an interesting period of Hebrew history. His own standpoint in the matter is indicated on p. 261 : "So far as the Biblical city of Raamses-Rameses is concerned, the plan of this essay has been less to solve the problem than to provide the material for its solution. An estimate of the historical value of the Exodus narrative obviously lies outside the province of the Egyptologist ; nor, indeed, can our quest be so extended as to include an exhaustive revision of the geography of the Exodus-route in the light of the Egyptian sources. Nevertheless, the conclusions here reached do seem to provide a basis for further deductions. These will be suggested in a tentative way, and it will remain for Biblical students to reject or to confirm them." Biblical students can best show their gratitude for Dr. Gardiner's work by discussing and using it freely, and it is with a view to this that the following remarks are offered.

We begin by considering his views as to the position of Pithom. Since Professor Naville's excavations at Maskhûteh this has been generally recognised as the site of the Biblical Pithom, the Greek and Latin Hero, Ero, Erocastra or Heroonpolis. On this Dr. Gardiner writes : "Now it cannot be denied that the evidence for the identification of Pithom-Heroonpolis with Maskhûteh provided by Prof. Naville's excavations there is very formidable, seeing that they yielded not only hieroglyphic inscriptions mentioning Pithom, but also Latin inscriptions mentioning Ero" (p. 268). He, however, argues against this, and tries to show that the true site of Pithom is Tell-er-Retabeh, 8½ miles to the west. His main reliance is on a milestone found at Maskhûteh bearing the inscription "Ab Ero in Clusma M VIIII." This he interprets as meaning "Nine miles on the road from Ero to Clysma" (Suez). Mommsen, however, was of opinion that this milestone was no longer in its oriignal position.[1] The point has been definitely decided by the excavation of Retabeh, as Mr. J. S. Griffiths has pointed out in his recent book on the Exodus.[2] "The work of the first winter has shown that, so far from being a Roman camp, this is the oldest site known East of Bubastis and that it has not had any Roman occupation," writes Prof. Petrie.[3] It follows that it cannot possibly be Erocastra, and the milestone is therefore not *in situ.* This leaves Naville's identification of Pithom with Maskhûteh in a stronger position than ever.

It is, however, not merely in the case of Pithom that Dr. Gardiner's work sheds light on the biblical narrative. Other and greater gains result from our knowledge of the biblical Raamses. In order that full use may be made of his work it is necessary to test it by another method. He has collected all the occurrences of the name Pi-Ra'messe, house of Ramesses, the well-known Delta residence of the Ramessides, and other names that resemble it. Assuming rather

---

[1] "Repertus videlicet non suo loco, sed postea ad castrum ædificandum adhibitus." *Corpus Inscriptionum Latinarum,* Vol. III, Suppl. I, p. 1,214.

[2] *The Exodus in the Light of Archaeology,* p. 79.

[3] *Hyksos and Israelite Cities,* p. 28.

than proving that there was only one royal residence in the Eastern Delta, he
has then drawn certain inferences from the materials he has collected. It is
proposed to check these by examining first whether there was only one such
residence. Dr. Gardiner states his case thus : " Either Raamses-Rameses of
the Bible is the Residence-city of the Ramessides near Pelusium, or else it is a
town unknown to the Egyptian monuments, the existence of which is merely
postulated " (p. 261).   It will be submitted that the Egyptian monuments know
of another town.

From the texts cited by Dr. Gardiner it appears that Pi-Ra'messe was
described as being " *betwixt Zahi and Egypt* ".and as " *the forefront of every land,
the end of Egypt.*"   Thàt Pi-Ra'messe was a seaport, whether actually beside the
sea or some little distance inland beside the river-mouth, is shown by the words
" *the harbourage of thy ships' troops* " ; " its ships fare forth and return to port "
(p. 252).   With this in mind let the following document (Papyrus Anastasi V)
of the reign of Meneptah's successor, Sety II, be considered. Dr. Gardiner's
translation is quoted as being the most recent known to me :—

" I was despatched from the Courts of the Royal Palace on the ninth day of
the third month of summer, at eventide, in quest of those two servants. I
reached the enclosure-wall of Theku (*i.e.*, Tell el-Maskhûteh in the Wâdy Tûmîlât)
on the tenth day of the third month of summer, where they told me that they had
said in the South[1] that they (the slaves) had passed on the tenth (sic ?) day of
the third month of summer.   And [when I] reached the fortress (*scil.* of Theku),
they told me that the groom (?) had come from the desert [to say] that they
had passed the north wall of the Migdol of Sety-Meneptah-(is) beloved-like-Seth."[2]

Dr. Gardiner places this Migdol at Tell el-Her near Pelusium. That he is in
error appears clearly from a glance at the map.   The idea that fugitive slaves
went from Pelusium to Maskhûteh, some 43 miles to the south-west, on the
way to Tell el-Her, some 6 or 7 miles away from their starting-point, is obviously
impossible,[3] as also the view that the groom coming from the neighbouring desert
could have reported what had happened at this distance.

While a portion of the document is obscure, certain inferences can be drawn
from the parts of it that are clear :—(1) There was a royal palace situate at the
distance of only one stage from Maskhûteh, for the narrator arrived at the latter
on the morrow of leaving the palace.   (2) Persons seeking to go from that palace
to a point beyond the Egyptian frontier would pass through or near Maskhûteh
in, at any rate, some cases.   There is no possibility of equating this palace with
Pi-Ra'messe, having regard to the relative positions of the sea and Maskhûteh
and the impossibility of calling the situation of the palace the end of Egypt.

It is thus certain that there were at least two royal residences in the Eastern
Delta.[4]

---

[1] Dr. Gardiner points out in a footnote that the meaning is not clear.

[2] *Jl. of Eg. Arch.*, Vol. VI, 1920, p. 109.

[3] Presumably the *Migdol* of Sety Meneptah is identical with the fortress of Meneptah
of Pap Anastasi VI : " we have finished causing the Beduin tribes of Edom to pass the
fortress of Meneptah belonging to Theku towards the pools of Pithom [of] Meneptah belonging
to Theku, in order to feed themselves and to feed their flocks " (p. 268), and the Migdol
of Ex. xiv, 2.

[4] Professor Petrie suggests the following further point.   Seeing how Rameses II put
his name on monuments, it seems probable that he called many cities after himself, like the
Roman cities from London to Cilicia called *Augusta*.

Retabeh lies at the exact spot that would best suit this document. It was a store city of Rameses II. One inscription has been found there referring to a palace. Prof. Petrie writes as follows :—

" To the left are two pieces, which must be from the pylon gateway, being on so much larger a scale than the temple front. They bear part of the titles of Atmu, ' lord of Succoth,' and of the king ' Ramessu, living eternally.' Next is a column of inscription, ' Adorations to thy *ka.* . . .' Then comes a piece of a door-jamb from a tomb, which was re-used for stone in the town." It reads, according to Mr. Griffith, " Chief archer, keeper of the foreigners of Syria in Succoth, *keeper of the Residency in Succoth*, USER·MAAT·NEKHTU." Ta·nuter here probably refers to Syria, as in some other cases, and not to its principal meaning of Arabia. That there were foreigners here is important, as showing that this was a city of foreign settlement.[1]

There can be no doubt whatever of the exact correspondence of these Egypto-logical facts, so far as they go, with the data of Ex. xii, 37, and Nu. xxxiii, 3–6, according to which the Children of Israel journeyed from Rameses and pitched in Succoth.

So far, then, the Egyptian and Hebrew evidence makes it clear that there was a royal residence in or near Theku which cannot be identified with Pi-Ra'messe. What light does this throw on the collection of passages which Dr. Gardiner refers to the latter ? In most of his citations there can be no doubt what place is meant, but in some of them the balance of probability seems to be against Pi-Ra'messe. His No. 34 (p. 197) is a clear instance of this : " The letter preserved in *Pap. Anastasi VIII* goes a step further, writing the name of the city with the *prenomen* of Ramesses II and without the preceding qualification ' House-of ' (l. 44). The writer makes allusion to a ship ' *which is going to the town of Usimarĕ'-setpenrĕ' with the s'rt-wool* (?),' but there is nothing to indicate where the town was situated. What makes it difficult to recognise the Delta residence in this place-name is the fact that '*House-of-Ramesses-Beloved-of-Amūn*,' *i.e.*, Pi-Ra'messe normally written, is mentioned in l. 27 in the sentence ' *I will spend from the second month of inundation, day 8 to day 10, there* (*i.e.*, in Memphis), *and then we will set forth to Pi-Ra'messe, if we live.*' " Once we know that there was another royal residence in the Delta which seems to have been known in Hebrew as Raamses without the Pi, the probability arises that the town to which the wool was going should not be identified with Pi-Ra'messe. The same comment applies to his (35), " Yet another reference to Pi-Ra'messe may be contained in *Anastasi VIII* in the sentence ' *As to the s'rt-wool* (?) *of the god which is in Tomb* (?)-*of Ramesses-Beloved-of-Amūn on the bank of ' The-Waters-of-the-Sun,' as whose freight shall it be given ?* ' The word *ḥr* elsewhere means ' tomb ' ; but the tomb of Ramesses II was at Thebes, and not on the arm of the Nile known as ' The-Waters-of-the-Sun.' Some mistake or unusual word may here be concealed, and ' Tomb (?)-of-Ramesses ' may possibly be a variant name of the Delta capital. This is the more likely since the ship bound for ' *the town of Usimarĕ'-setpenrĕ'* carried the same commodity (s'rt-wool) as is here apparently mentioned as stored in ' *Tomb* (?)-*of-Ramesses.*' " Again he only succeeds in identifying his (36) with Pi-Ra'messe by forcing.

HAROLD M. WIENER.

[1] Petrie, *op. cit.*, p. 71 (my italics).

CURRENT FALLACIES ABOUT HISTORY.

THE fanciful resemblance of clouds to other objects, on which Hamlet plays, the visions of angels with drawn swords in the sky, or the bloody spears and lances of the red aurora, are the popular forms of that habit of fallacy which clings still to those who have not the knowledge and growth of discrimination to keep it in check.

The simplest and lowest form of this primitive frame of mind is seeing faces in the fire, or shapes of animals and men in natural stones. The face is the most familar object of close examination, hence it is the type to which anything unexplained is compared. The first dynasty Egyptian collected baboon-like flints and placed them in his temple ; they are the link between the fetish stone of the savage and the art of the sculptor. In recent years several men have collected flints which suggest human or animal forms ; they may also have been so regarded anciently, but only the proof of artificial trimming could certify that belief.

One of the commonest causes of these fallacies is insufficient experience, which does not give enough ground for comparison. For long ages, Jewish history was the only glimpse of pre-classical times. There was no wider experience, and hence everything in the dark was brought into the Jewish illumination. Since then, Egypt became the familiar boundary of thought, and many writers—some even now—try to explain everything by Egyptian comparisons. Then an ample chance of fallacy came to hand in the Atlantis myth, and anything would be attributed to a supposed civilisation of which nothing was known. Because Hebrew was the only Oriental script familiar in England, we had the Sinaitic inscriptions read by it, and the "one primæval language" fallacy not a century ago.

Akin to this is the fallacy of fluent declamation. ·By the time an assertion, whether in advertisements or popular books, has been repeated confidently, and often enough, it becomes a popular axiom. "In a thousand and one details of our common civilisation the originality of Ancient Egypt is revealed." It would be difficult to prove a hundredth of this assertion. "Egypt has been displaying the full story of the coming of copper, complete in every detail and circumstance, written in a simple and convincing fashion that he who runs may read." Yet the story is probably elsewhere in a land of copper ores. Or we read of "Egyptians who died abroad when exploiting foreign sources of wealth," while there is no evidence that any Egyptian exploited wealth abroad, or died in such an adventure. A common source of fallacy is a lack of familiarity with details, and a lack of training of the eye in discrimination. Almost anyone going abroad at first regards all foreigners as alike. It is only when the variety of character is learned that it is possible to see the differences, beneath the broad dissimilarity of the people from what is already known. In the same way a literary friend, who is not artistic, remarked on the similarity of Mexican and Egyptian figures as indicating some connection. To my eyes there is no similarity, the Egyptian is so familiar that the Mexican appears different at every point. We see books quoting American buildings as evidence of Egyptian origin, where there is no real resemblance. It is commonly said that early races drew animals perfectly, but could not draw men. We know the men better than we know the animals, but a cow's opinion might be opposite to ours as to the perfection of animal drawing. A lack of seeing details is the base of the claim that the Egyptians originated the calendar ; but we inherit the Babylonian calendar and Zodiac, with which the Egyptian constellations have hardly anything in common. The mere fact of a calendar of months is common to most races.

There is often the fallacy of noting a resemblance in a part and then claiming that it refers to the whole ; like Fluellen's " M " in Monmouth and Macedon. This lies at the base of sympathetic magic ; colour your arrows red and they will spill blood ; eat yellow food and you will get jaundice ; or wear a *Dentalium* shell for easy teething. So we read also of fallacies of resemblance ; because the Egyptians had ships we are assured that they originated ship-building ; yet other people's ships were entirely different from those of Egypt, and obviously arose from different ideas. Because metal tools cut we read, therefore, they gave the Egyptians " mastery over the hardest materials " ; but granite was worked by stone hammers and emery, and no copper chisel would be of the least use upon it. Copper is said to have been valued as resembling gold ; yet copper is found in use for practical purposes long before any gold is found in Egypt. We are told that green malachite " was compared to the green Nile which made the land of Egypt green and fertile." But there never was a green Nile, which is persistently brown. The *uaz ur* is the green Mediterranean Sea, which certainly does not produce fertility. Another writer describes Egyptian furniture as being made of bamboo, which is totally unknown there ; much like an artist putting cactus hedges and maize from America into pictures of ancient Palestine.

There is another fallacy about resemblance, which dominates anthropology seriously. A particular appearance of skull, often only a vague impression about it, is taken as evidence of the diffusion of a race all over the world. Now the sane view of modern students is that skull form is dominated by conditions of life, quality of food and stress of grinding, even by the need of sucking the mares as the nourishment of the grassland nomads. Wherever similar conditions prevail, a similarity of form will therefore tend to arise. The conditions of any country usually remain similar, and hence the country subdues the invaders to its own type, as now Americans and Australians are being subdued. The mutability of the skull form is seen by the very exclusive Jewish race being assimilated to the type of each country where it is found. No doubt anthropologists resent this fact, as depriving them of a cherished criterion ; but no one has ever proved racial continuity of the type of skull for centuries in different conditions, and there are strong instances to the contrary.

A similar fallacy is the notion that all races were maintained pure until the beginning of history, and we read protests against supposing that there was any serious invasion of Egypt in prehistoric ages. This view is ludicrous when we look at written history. See the whirlwind of races driving about the world. Goths from Scania, round by the Black Sea, across Europe, through Spain, and settling in Africa. Arabs swamping North Africa, up through Spain, and barely checked at Poictiers from swamping Europe. As far back as we can see, these changes have always been going on ; and the less of settled civilisation there is, the more readily will such flux of races take place. Egypt has had a large immigration every five hundred years during known history, and we cannot credit less movement in wilder ages before that. The similarity of type in different ages is due to the climate and country, as history proves to us ; it has nothing to do with purity of race.

Another kind of fallacy arises from not regarding the possibilities of a case, owing to antecedent causes. We have been assured that agriculture arose in Egypt ; yet the names of corn came from Mesopotamia, and the corn is wild in North Syria and Asia. It must have been cultivated first in its native sources before it would be introduced into Egypt. Again, linen is said to be first woven in Egypt. But the flax plant is native in cold countries, flourishing now most in Russia, as formerly among the Scythians, who cannot have cultivated it, being nomads ; it is exotic in Egypt, and the use of it must have been discovered elsewhere before it would be introduced there. Then, copper is claimed to have been first wrought in Egypt. Now the earliest copper there is a pin used to fasten the sheepskin of the very earliest prehistoric folk, and it seems likely that it was brought in with the pottery peculiar to their culture from Algeria. There is no period known of using malachite before the use of copper, and copper would doubtless be first wrought where the ore was discovered, and not in Egypt. We even read that megaliths were erected by men searching for gold and pearls ; yet they are mostly found here far remote from either gold or pearls, and the ludicrous explanation has been given that the gold of the Wiltshire streams had been exhausted. Not a grain of gold could ever be found in a chalk stream. We are told that carpentry began in Egypt, a country so destitute of suitable wood that it always had to be imported ; such would be the last country to start using material which it had not got. The rise of carpentry is natural in a forest land, and among people who developed tools more readily than the Egyptians.

Another antecedent cause is the natural order of development as seen in other countries. We have been told that the use of irrigation led to the recognition of " the powers of the king who conferred this elixir of life upon the community " ; " and out of pondering upon these new revelations there emerged . . . . primitive religion and magic." Thus it is said that the order is (1) irrigation, (2) kingship, and (3) religion and magic. The obvious order of social development is just the contrary of what is stated ; tribes have magic without kingship (Australia), and kingship without irrigation or cultivation (Scythia). Another instance of reversing the obvious order is stating that it is certain " that Elam and Sumer derived their culture from Egypt." On the contrary, there is much that is Sumerian in early Egypt, but nothing that is Egyptian in Sumer. The Arak knife-handle shows unmistakably an Elamite source of myths for people invading Egypt ; and also an art far in advance of anything that the Egyptian was doing at the time when he made the rippled flint blade of that knife. The priority of civilisation in Elam and Sumer is assured. All of these matters are examples of disregarding the antecedent causes.

Another fallacy that is often seen is the assumption that if a view is possible its truth is proved, without seeking if other views are equally possible, or more so. It is possible that Queen Tyi was of Egyptian parentage ; it is possible that some Roman municipalities survived in Britain ; it is possible that Mary Queen of Scots did not conspire against her husband or Elizabeth. But none of these possibilities prove that there is not a greater probability against such views.

A favourite mode of argument—especially with Biblical critics—is to assume the truth of one proposition, and then proceed to demonstrate something else that rests upon the first assumption. We have been assured that there were no good scarabs before the XIth dynasty, without any proofs ; and that therefore all earlier kings' scarabs were not contemporary work. The first proposition has now been swept away by discoveries, and so the deduction from it vanishes.

Similarly a difficulty in some view is often taken as evidence that it cannot be true. The only real argument lies in the absence of any better explanation. There are difficulties, no doubt, in every system of Egyptian chronology that has been adopted ; but the question is, where is the least difficulty ? A view may be reckoned as having only 40 *per cent.* probability, but if nothing else can be credited with over 20 *per cent.*, the 40 *per cent.* view must hold the field. In historical work, without the possibility of experiment, and usually with imperfect material, we have to take results on the ground of relative probability, without usually reaching the certainties of an experimental science.

It is often assumed, notwithstanding the defects of our information, that no other source for a thing is possible than that known to us. Jade was assumed to be solely Asiatic till it was found in Switzerland. All sources of material are only probabilities, and some fresh source may come to light ; such reasoning on probabilities may be worth something, but it is not conclusive.

Another fallacy to be avoided is the forming of theories about unknown periods which will not work when applied to known periods. An elaborate theory about the derivation of the years of dynasties in the Hyksos age was supposed to prove that they were fictitious. But just the same reasoning could with better grounds be applied to the well-known period of the XXIInd–XXVIIth dynasties, where the duplication of one from another is nevertheless impossible. Theories should be applied to known cases, whenever they can be, before using them to deal with the unknown.

A flagrant instance of this fallacy is the assumption that changes in art are proportionate to time, hence that a similarity in style shows a nearness of period. Apply this to known history. The works of the Roman age in its decline in the third century are so closely copied in the sixteenth century that it is even a dispute as to which age some sculptures belonged. Anyone a few thousand years hence, where the less substantial mediæval work has largely disappeared, will be ready to believe that there was but a century between the decline and the renaissance, between the burghers commemorated by Roman tombstones on the Moselle and those figured by Dürer. This is not only due to copying, it is national taste, which survives all that is thrust upon it. An argument which is bankrupted by historic facts cannot guide us anywhere in the unknown. The truth is, that style is only changed by the dominant influence of a much higher art, and even that is sooner or later thrown off when the intruders are subdued by the country. All such intrusive changes are very rapid, and then fade imperceptibly. Hence the variations in style may be fifty times quicker at one time than at another, and they have no relation to the period elapsed.

The reliance on similarity of names has prevailed from the earliest times. The Egyptian was always trusting to a parallel word or name as proof of connection. This abuse of philology was usual down to recent times ; but one clear case serves to warn us off the shoals. The similarity of name and of status of Minos of Crete, Mena of Egypt, and Manu of India was held to prove that they were all forms of our wide-spread myth, which therefore underlay all those

F

cultures. Now that the period of Mena has been found to be solid history, with much civilisation before it, the mythical theory vanishes ; for Manu is certainly a more recent personage than the rise of Knossian civilisation.

A curious perversion in the literary criticism is the habit of reading into a passage something of which there is no trace. It is a mental failure probably due to strong prepossession. Thus, a recent writer has stated that the Israelites believed that they adopted circumcision in Egypt ; the winged disc is said to have been placed on the high-priest's dress ; the altar built on the threshing floor is said to be a sacred stone ; the brazen serpent is said to have been effective in the rout of Amalek. Now all of these connections are entirely figments of modern prepossession, and have no trace of reality in the source. Similar material prepossessions are seen when we are told that " so-called steatopygous dolls . . . were not intended to portray racial characters, nor were they representations of . . . steatopygy. They are simply models of the cowrie-shell . . . anthropomorphized as the Great Mother." Yet they are as entirely human as could be made, without the smallest trace of the form of a shell ; it would be nearer the mark to call them representations of King Charles's head. It is said that the Egyptians " taught the Syrians the value of metal weapons." As the Syrians were far ahead of the Egyptians in the forms and design of their weapons, which have no resemblance to those of Egypt, the teaching, if any, was in the other direction. It is also said that " it is now known that the disturbed condition in which many Proto-Egyptian graves were found is evidence . . . of the handiwork of the prehistoric grave-robber." Yet no attempt is made to show how the unfleshing of the body, reversal of bones, and severance of the head, found within the complete bandages in undisturbed burials, could be due to robbers ; while the recorded Egyptian traditions of such treatment, and the modern African customs, can leave no possible doubt on the matter. We must always be on guard against accepting statements from writers who show this habit of assertion regardless of facts, owing to mental prepossession. For this reason we should also avoid trusting for our facts to second or third hand sources. " A" may declare that " B " has proved something needed for "A's" argument ; but "A" must quote the facts, not "B's" authority, for the result. Unless the basic facts are clearly set out, we have to trust to the judgment of other writers, while we are entirely in the dark as to their logic or their prepossessions. Opinions should never be quoted, except as an interpretation of stated facts, or as showing a change in a writer's position.

We must also beware of applying any principle more widely than it can be proved. We can prove descent of some items of culture from one land to another ; that does not prove that all culture was so transmitted to all lands. We can prove independent invention, as for instance the jewelled tubular drill and the facing plate in the IVth dynasty, entirely forgotten and unknown when re-invented in the last century by engineers. But that does not prove that there never was transmission. As a general principle it is safest to draw the line between these opposite positions, by taking purely artistic treatment, when it cannot arise from utility, as a proof of connection, that is, of connection by transmission, or by unconscious revival of national taste, such as the late Celtic ornament under Louis XV. Where utility leads to a process or a device or a form, there it is as likely to arise from independent invention as from transmission.

Lastly, we may note the fallacies of numerical coincidences. This is a special jungle haunted by cranks. In the more obscure regions of it they disregard the meaning of the numbers. " The circuit of the Chapter House internally appears to be 192 feet ; and 192·84, beside being the diameter of the sphere of the Zodiac, taking the sun's distance at 10, is the numerical value of the name Mariam " (*The Canon*, 236). Here are the number of English feet, the arbitrary distance of a celestial sphere on an arbitrary basis, and the plunge into the Kabbala, all placed in relation together. Not only was the alphabetic order of the Syrian alphabet taken as a number system (started about 1,000 B.C.), but the number values of each letter of a word were added together as a total number of the word. Then, by a higher flight, that total number could be decomposed into other numbers and letters, and so one word was proved equal to another. Although we may resolutely bar such aberrations, yet in reasonable study we must beware of many traps. Recently there was a dispute whether proportions of the pyramid of Khufu were based on the area of the face being equal to that of the height squared, or some of the many properties which were really identical with this ; all of these being statements of the same form, the only question is which of them has analogy to any other coincidence elsewhere. The only safe test for the reality of intentional connections is their being part of a system. Thus the proportion of a radius to a circle, in the height and circuit of Khufu's pyramid, is supported by a similar proportion in the King's chamber and in the sarcophagus ; and this being practically laid out as 7 : 44 is proved by Khufu's pyramid being 7 and 44 times a unit of 40 cubits, and Snefru's pyramid 7 and 44 times a unit of 25 cubits, for height and circuit.

Beside such coincidences there is a large field of geometrical hypotheses about buildings ; theorists are fond of drawing triangles and rectangles all over a plan or section, but when one looks into the detail they seldom really coincide with the structure, and often seem purely arbitrary.

Our business in life is to learn our own ignorance ; to realise how many pitfalls there are, owing to the small extent our knowledge covers, and the many fallacies to which our reasoning is liable.

As two important questions have been touched on here, it may be well to conclude by stating them clearly apart. The priority of Sumer and Elam in civilization before Egypt is shown by the continuous history of those countries. Reckoning this backward, the result is that the IIIrd dynasty of Kish is equivalent to the Ist dynasty of Egypt (see *Cambridge Ancient History*, on the short chronology, or both may be earlier on the long chronology). In detail, the cylinder seals appear in the period next before Urnina, between the IIIrd and IVth dynasty of Kish ; and these are equated with the cylinder seals of eastern style at the beginning of the Ist dynasty in Egypt, when copper became common. When we reach this period, " we are in the same realistic and decadent state of art (in Sumer) as in Elam . . . The Sumerian civilization has its roots in the remote age of a glorious art, and we first meet this people in a decadent stage." (C.A.H. 376.) Here Sumer had, then, a great civilization in the past, before the first dynasty of Egypt. With this agrees the magnificent knife handle from Gebel Arak, showing the highest art linked with Mesopotamian motives and Elamite climate, yet dated by the rippled flint blade into the second prehistoric age of low art in Egypt. There can be no question, by the continuous history and by the contemporary art, that Sumer was a whole age ahead of Egyptian development.

The other important matter to observe is the extreme independence of the culture of each country. A few imported objects might pass from one land to another, invaluable as evidence of trade and date, but with little or no influence. In Crete the imports had no trace of effect on the sculpture, architecture or painting. In Syria, although it was a parade ground of Egypt for centuries, there is no trace of Egyptian influence, except in things made by Egyptians. In Babylonia no trace of Egyptian influence has been found. In the reverse direction, the Sumerian invaders of the Ist dynasty brought cylinder seals and other things with them, which were sooner or later all thrown off by the Egyptians, in spite of a mixture of race. Syria had developed the most perfect forms of tools by the period of the XIIth dynasty, yet the Egyptian went on refusing to use a haft to his axe or hammer, or to strengthen his tools by ribbing, until Egypt was swamped by Greece. The " Oriental Mirage " has died away in the study of European archaeology, and it is generally recognised that each land had an independent style and development of its own, and threw off extraneous borrowings sooner or later. There is no high road, by some universal source or synthesis, in history, any more than in language or in art.

FLINDERS PETRIE.

REVIEWS.

Die Literatur der Aegypter.—By ADOLF ERMAN. Leipzig. 1923.

This book has been written in order to give the general reader a knowledge of the literature of ancient Egypt. It is difficult for anyone, except those who are actually studying the subject, to know where to obtain translations, which are usually published only in learned tomes or in specialist journals. Here, however, Prof. Erman has gathered together specimens of the principal literary texts from the Old Kingdom to the Late Period. The religious hymns comprise extracts from the Pyramid Texts and hymns to various deities, including Akhenaten's hymn. Then there are stories, instructions, love-songs, folk-songs and triumph-songs. All these are translated flowingly and make a distinct addition to the literature of any country. As the translations are by one of the great masters of ancient Egyptian, they can be relied upon absolutely. It is to be hoped that the volume may be translated into English, that the general reader in England may also enjoy the literature of ancient Egypt. M. A. M.

The Coptic Theotokia.—By DE LACY O'LEARY, D.D. (Luzac & Co.) 1923. Price 10s. 6d.

Dr. O'Leary has published the hymns to the Virgin known as Theotokia. He points out, however that the Theotokia being always sung the word is now practically used to mean a choir-book, but it really corresponds with the Parvum Officium B.V. Mariæ of the Latin Church. In his careful introduction Dr. O'Leary gives details of the use of the Theotokia in monasteries and in non-monastic churches, and discusses the traditions as to the authorship of the hymns. The Theotokia for each day of the week are then given ; the codex used is the Vatican Cod. Copt. XXXVIII, and to every day there are appendices of ⲟⲡⲩⲉⲛⲓⲁ and other additional matter. In this way the book is invaluable for Coptic and liturgical scholars. Dr. O'Leary has very wisely not attempted to simplify (?) his originals by altering the spelling and dividing the words, but has copied the originals exactly with the mis-spellings where they occur. For students who wish to work on MS. this is the only method ; the German system of dividing up the words and correcting orthographical errors is required only by beginners. M. A. M.

Egypt and the Old Testament.—By T. ERIC PEET. 8vo. 236 pp. 5s. (University Press of Liverpool.) 1922.

It is to be regretted that the valuable constructive work which the author wrote on Italy, fourteen years ago, has been succeeded by a devotion to the barren field of destructive criticism. This obsession of the Biblical critics depends on verbal questions rather than matters of fact, and is too often accompanied by facile misstatement. To give some ground for telescoping Egyptian dynasties, while not a word is said about the proofs that they were successive, we are told that the Babylonian IInd dynasty ruled " in the Country of the Sea, and may therefore for chronological purposes be eliminated from the king-lists " (p. 45) ; yet on p. 52 it is said that it partly overlapped the Ist dynasty, while in reality it was the sole dynasty for nearly half the time, yet it is to be " eliminated." Why this should overrule the regular system of Egypt is not evident. On p. 98 the marriage of Joseph into the family of a priest of Ra is " a later colouring," because " All that we know of the Hyksos occupation of Egypt . . . makes such an admission very difficult." What we do know is that Apepa II favoured the Egyptian worship by making columns and gates of copper, to adorn the temple at Bubastis. Priests were then by no means out of fashion. It is said that the Biblical narrative states that Pharaoh was drowned ; no such statement appears in the narrative.

The main subject is that of the Exodus, and in this theories (of Dr. Gardiner) regardless of the physical facts are accepted as an authority. The Roman station of Heroon is agreed to have been Pithom, in the Wady Tumilat ; and there is no Roman station in that Wady except Tell el-Maskhuta, where the stone of Ero Castra was found. It is absurd to seek to place it at Tell Retabeh, where there is no trace of Roman occupation. At Tell Retabeh is a large granite stele of Rameses, stating that he "built in the cities upon which is his name," and this would be pointless if his name was not on this city, where he did build extensively. It is impossible, therefore, to assert that " there is probably no city called after Rameses in this district " and " not a particle of evidence " for such a name here. The city of Raamses is proposed to be placed, along with Avaris, at Pelusium. Yet Avaris is stated by Josephus to have been upon the Bubastite channel, which implies that it was south of Bubastis, and certainly not at the Pelusiac mouth. Also the only monument known from Avaris was found re-used in Cairo, implying that the city was within reach of Cairo stone-hunters. The indications agree to its having been at the great Hyksos camp of Tell el-Yehudiyeh. No such camp is known at Pelusium.

The Exodus route is, then, proposed to start from Pelusium and go to Kadesh, beginning in the middle of the narrative of Numbers and entirely neglecting Exodus. But really there is no contradiction as to the route ; in Num. i, Israel is in the wilderness, again in Num. ix, in the second year of the Exodus. In Num. x they left Sinai and came to the wilderness of Paran, where was Kadesh (Num. xiii). It is quite a gratuitous disregard of the narrative to begin in the middle of it, and there is no incongruity between Exodus and Numbers. An attempt is made by the J. E. P. process (generally discredited by the much earlier versions) to assert that the J narrative records a direct march from Egypt to Kadesh. It must be by some marvellous internal consciousness that this is evolved ; for in every one of these stages between Egypt and Kadesh Yahveh is named, both in the Heb. and LXX, as also in the detailed route described in Exodus. It is an insult to a consistent narrative to state that " the Israelites leave Egypt and march direct across to Kadesh." Moreover, such a march would be impossible for a large company, as it is many days across a waterless desert.

In the later history many pages are spent inconclusively over the possibility of Solomon's queen being a daughter of Shishak. Fortunately, we can settle this by relative dates only. The war with Rehoboam was just before the

XXIst year of Shishak, as the stone for his triumph scene was then being quarried. If XXth of Shishak = Vth of Rehoboam, Ist of Shishak = XXVth of Solomon. But Solomon was married before the temple was finished in his XIth year (I.K. 3, 1), and therefore 14 years before the end of the 35 years' reign of Pasebkhanu. It is impossible, therefore, that " Pharaoh's daughter " could be other than that of Pasebkhanu, being married about the middle of his long reign.

In many other cases gratuitous difficulties are raised for which there is no ground. The site of the temple of Onias is disputed ; but if the 180 stadia were taken according to the Greek measure of that very variable unit, the site would fall on Heliopolis, and Josephus could not have failed to describe it as being at a place which he knew well. There is therefore no ground for not accepting the Egyptian stadium, which thus places the site of Onias at Tell el-Yehudiyeh. The celebration of the Passover there is disputed, as being abstractly unlikely ; but the facts are that the Jews celebrate the Passover wherever they are, in Egypt or any other country ; and the ovens found, and the leg-bones in them, exactly agree to the Passover ceremony.

There does not seem to be a single case of the results which are disputed in this book being discredited ; on the contrary, the statements made here are sometimes seriously in error.

Catalogue of Textiles from Egypt. Vol. III.—By A. F. KENDRICK. 8vo, 107 pp., 32 pls. 5s. (*Victoria and Albert Museum.*)

This is a welcome completion of the Catalogue from South Kensington, dealing with what are considered distinctively Coptic textiles. The illustrations are excellent, on blocks with a very fine grain (250) which permits of magnifying the details. The remarkable feature is the entire absence of the cross, and the prevalence of the Oriental motives. This suggests the influence of the Persian rule in Egypt, 616-626 A.D. ; and the hunting scenes, horsemen, pairs of birds and trees, may well be placed after this Eastern penetration. One explanation might be modified ; No. 780 seems to represent the Annunciation and the visit of Mary to Elizabeth. It is well that Mr. Gaselee is to discuss the Coptic inscriptions, as they are scarcely noticed here.

The Edwin Smith Papyrus.—By J. H. BREASTED. 8vo, 45 pp. (*Recueil . . . à la Mémoire de Jean-François Champollion.*)

In this Paper Professor Breasted enters on the details of the first ownership of the Papyrus Ebers by Edwin Smith, and describes another medical papyrus now known by his name, which belongs to the New York Historical Society. This papyrus is 15 feet long and 13 inches high. The signs are compared with dated examples, and it is concluded that it is of the XVIIth dynasty or earlier. The subject is medical, like the Ebers Papyrus ; the system is to state the title, examination, diagnosis, verdict and treatment. The method of the work is strictly medical, without resort to magic, and it shows a regular order, beginning at the top of the head and proceeding downward.

The Prophets of Israel.—By HAROLD M. WIENER. Sm. 8vo. 196 pp. (Robt. Scott.) 1923.

This is a vigorous and careful study of the prophetic writings, with the view to the direct fulfilment of the prophecies in the centuries between the exile and the Roman Age. The canon that all " prophetic " description must be after the event is justly disregarded here, as it is disproved by the printed prophecies of Savonarola, which were closely fulfilled thirty years after his death (Blass, *Philology of the Gospels*, 41). Various explanations may be given, but real prediction is a fact. The treatment of the documents is with a reasonable view of the uncertain elements in the matter, of misunderstandings, corruptions of text and other difficulties. The separate detail cannot be dealt with here, but we may note that the early spread of the Jews in different countries is stated, as in Damascus (I.K. xx, 34), and the various lands of Isa. xi, 11. This agrees with the Jewish settlement far up in Egypt under Manasseh. The perversity of modern critics in making difficulties where there is a perfectly plain course is well exposed, on pp. 77, 127. All through the work the contemporary Assyrian and Babylonian records are fully quoted in comparison with the prophecies. This book should be carefully read by anyone concerned with later Jewish history or the prophetic writings.

The Aswan Obelisk. By R. ENGELBACH. 4to, 57 pp., 8 pls. 1922. (*Service des Antiquités.*)

This work records a careful study of the unfinished obelisk lying in the quarry at Aswan, and of the questions involved in the transport and erection of obelisks. The obelisk was encumbered with blocks fallen from above, and much clearance was needed to expose it. The length is 137 feet, much larger than any erected obelisk; the base is 13 feet 9 inches, and the estimated weight 1,168 tons. Such was the intended monument, which would have eclipsed all others; but flaws in the granite were found, and these needed testing, by cutting away the face to see if the flaw ran deep. Step by step the grandiose plan had to be reduced, and the several outlines drawn on the top surface show how the scheme was whittled down to less than half the weight, 105 feet long and 10 feet 4 inches wide. Allowing for the finishing of the sides, this would have been closely equal to the Lateran obelisk, if it had been completed.

The method of detaching such immense masses was not by wedges or chiselling, but by pounding away the granite to form a great trench along the whole length, and so isolate the block from the main rock. For the working down of a flat surface before starting the excavation, burning was largely used, to weaken the granite so that it could be crushed with less difficulty. This would explain the crumbly masses of crystals, which are not reduced to powder, found on the sites where blocks have been dressed, as at Lahun.

Wedging was used on lesser masses, from the IVth dynasty onward, as may be seen on the roof blocks of Menkaura. Whether wooden wedges wetted were used or metal wedges with side plates ("feathers") is left an open question. The absence of any trace of copper stain on the sides of the wedge holes favours the idea of wooden wedges, which were swelled by wetting. The "black granite hammer*" with handles (Cairo), which is here suggested for driving wedges, is ike a basalt block with handles (Univ. Coll.), which is supposed to have been a weight.

The mode of pounding out the trench in the granite produced a series of scoop hollows along the side and hollows in the floor. Large balls of dolerite abound in the quarry working, and were evidently used as hammer-stones. They vary between 8 and 13 inches diameter, weighing from 9 to 15 (? 40) pounds. The wear is not spread all over, but on a few parts of the balls, which points to their being fixed on the ends of rammers. This would probably be managed by having a hide strap, with a hole rather less in size than the ball. There were four pounding spaces to each worker, taken in rotation ; this would allow for a boy squatting below to sweep out the dust from the work on to the next space. It is estimated from present experiments that the trench would require seven months of work. Each working area, of four spaces, has a register marked in red above it, showing what depth had been removed ; these marks average 2·7 inches apart ; as the rate of work is estimated at ·8 inch per day over the whole working area, the register would be marked up every three or four days. As the lines of register are in groups of 10 marks, this suggests marking every three days, and starting a fresh line each month.

The removal of the obelisk from the bed is a more difficult task. The use of wetted wedges along the base would be risky, for if the strain were greater at one end than at the other the mass would break across rather than rend the whole length. The author prefers the notion of hand pounding ; yet this would be a gigantic work, far more difficult than cutting the side trenches : (1) because the blow would be sideways, and not assisted by gravity as when vertical ; (2) because there would not be width enough to work readily ; (3) because soon the work would be far in under the mass, and difficult to reach, as it would be over 6 feet inward from each side. Perhaps the most practical way would be to side-cut a groove about a foot square and pack this with baulks of timber wedged in tight. Then, by wetting, the force of swelling such a mass along the whole length might suffice to split off the obelisk. Unfortunately the beds of other masses have been dressed away for further work ; if a bed could be found left intact, the question might be solved. Lifting the obelisk out of its hollow is another problem ; the use of levering seems to require an impossible number of men ; the method of ramming in sand is slow but certain, and should be considered. It is said that two natives in last century raised a sarcophagus from a deep pit in a few months by ramming sand.

The difficulties in erecting obelisks have never been fully accounted for. Not only has the weight to be raised, as a colossus can be, by dragging up a long embankment, but the main trouble is in handling such a mass when nearly upright. The obelisk of Hatsheput has jumped a foot out of place, and flawed off one corner by pressure. The improved proposal of the author is that a brick box was built up to half the height of the obelisk and filled with sand ; the obelisk was dragged up until the butt rested on the sand, which was then extracted through a passage below, thus gradually lowering the butt and bringing the obelisk nearly upright, when it could be finally pulled into place by cables. This seems quite feasible, and works well in model ; it agrees with the Egyptian methods of banking up brick staging in building a pylon, and filling up a hall with earth as the walls rose, so as to have a wide working platform. There is nothing easier and safer in Egypt than massive earthwork and brickwork. Placing and removing such materials cost nothing, as the people could do it during the inundation, when everyone was idle. This book will always remain a standard one on the subject of obelisks.

" *And in the tomb were found.*"—By TERENCE GRAY. 8vo, 236 pp., 11 pls. 1923. (*Heffer.*)

Mr. Gray continues to work in the vein which he opened by his previous book. It is a difficult style for a writer to follow, as our age differs from all others in its conciseness and lack of form ; the speeches and sermons of even a century or two ago seem to us insufferably lengthy. Hence the Oriental prolixity of the Egyptian can scarcely be made palatable in modern shape. The incidents of the four scenes of different periods that are here constructed are all true to the country and conditions, and are very deftly woven together ; that of Khufu seems the most successful of them. In the " Graph of Egyptian History " the form of the curves of change are too symmetric ; really the rise is always very rapid, and the descent gradual, as in the curves in *Revolutions of Civilisation*, p. 85, of which the author does not seem to be aware. The highest point of the XIIth dynasty was under Senusert I, not II ; also Piankhy was quite as high in work as Psamtek.

The Oldest Letters in the World.—By Mrs. SYDNEY BRISTOWE. 8vo, 96 pp., 1923. 5s. (*Allen and Unwin.*)

This is another sketch of the Amarna letters, which are by no means as old as those of the XIIth dynasty. The authoress deals very freely with the historic materials, ascribing to " the Egyptian priests " " the fabulous story of Queen Hatshepsut " ; " Hatshepsut's coronation is taken verbatim from the account of Amenhetep III's coronation." " My perhaps startling theory is that the Ramesside kings were only priestly inventions . . . and that the name Rameses was only a copy of that of the city Rameses." The bodies of Yuya and Tuyu " are those of Amenhotep [III] and Queen Teia." We also read of " exquisite wreaths found in Hyksos tombs in Egypt." When further the Khabiri are said to be certainly Hebrews (though named centuries before Abram), and all Conder's renderings are preferred, our readers will hardly care to enter on such a mass of misunderstandings.

Revue Biblique, Oct., 1922.

LEFEBVRE, G.—-The parallels are set out between the biblical expressions and the passages in the tomb of Petosiris, which have been noted in *Anc. Eg.*, 1922, pp. 83, 85, 87. It is suggested that editors of biblical books may have known Egyptian writings in the Persian period. The evidence that Jews were probably in Egypt as early as Taharqa points to Egyptians having been open to knowing Jewish writings before the rigidity of the religion after the Captivity.

PERIODICALS.

—•—

Zeitschrift für Aegyptische Sprache, Vol. LVII, Pt. I, 1923.

(*Continued from* ANCIENT EGYPT, *p.* 30.)

MISCELLANEOUS.

BISSING, FR. W. VON.—*Die angebliche älteste* Darstellung der " Lebensbinde." Jéquier's conclusion (*P.S.B.A.*, 1917, p. 87) that this symbol goes back to remote archaic times is based on an unreliable publication. The essentials in his essay in *Bull. de l'Inst. Français* (1914) are to be found in an earlier publication by von Bissing on ancient Egyptian knot amulets, as is also the proof that the

♀ sign occurs in Ist dynasty texts. [See Den, in *R.T.*, II, xix, 149.]

SETHE, K.—*Der Lautwert von* 🦅. The sound of this sign is ⅓ not *'i³h.* This is proved by a correct reading of Pyr. 480 *d* (W. 590), and by several passages in Middle Kingdom mortuary texts.

Mśn·w " Harpunierer " (*A.Z.* 54, 50). A further proof of this reading is given by *L.D.*, II, 149 *g*, ' ... ...' 🏹🪶♀ ⌒ ⌒," " overseer of the harpooners on the water-courses," also by seal impressions in *R.T.*, II, vii, 5,6. One of these scenes shows king Usaphais struggling with a hippopotamus ; in this he is called 〰. In the other scene, the king is harpooning the animal, and he is called " harpooner," the curious sign after the *ś* obviously corresponding to the harpoon implement ⇌, with which the word is frequently written later.

Ein Missbrauch des Qualitativs im Koptischen.—The Coptic qualitative, which is derived from the Egyptian pseudoparticiple, should only be used in sentences which have the form of Praesens I or II (Stern, *Copt. Gr.*, § 349). Sethe quotes instances of its use with its own peculiar meaning of " to be in the state " with other tenses in place of the infinitive, ᴜɴᴛϥ-ⲥⲱⲧⲩ " *er kann nicht hören.*"— Sethe quotes four passages from the Pistis Sophia to illustrate this use of the expression " he cannot hear," literally " he has not hearing " (*i.e.*, " the possibility of hearing ").

ⲉⲝⲟ.—Sethe combats Rösch's assertion that ⲉⲝⲟ is the Achmimic equivalent of the Sahidic ⲉⲩϫⲉ, " when," and suggests the rendering " nevertheless."

Zu den Märtyrerakten des Apa Schnube (ⲩⲙⲟⲧⲃⲟ).—Sethe elucidates two obscure passages in this publication. (1) In the account of wounds inflicted on a virgin martyr, he (the Governor) " sent for ⲓⲓⲓⲓⲡⲉ, salt and boiling vinegar, and they were mixed together and poured over her." ⲛⲓⲛⲣⲉ is obviously " pepper." (2) The second passage mentions " Kameepolis which is Bubastis." Sethe recognises in this the name of a town compounded with πόλις, a Roman substitution for a native name, such as Kainepolis (Kene), " new town " near Koptos. He suggests that Kameepolis may represent Kainepolis.

DÉVAUD, E.—ⲟⲃⳉⲉ (*Sah.*). This word (Egyptian, *'ibḥ*, " tooth ") has hitherto been classed as a plural masculine noun. It is really a feminine noun, of which the singular and plural are the same, and it belongs to the same category as ⲣⲟⲩⲡⲉ, " year." Thus it cannot derive directly from $\left(\!\!\!\left.\right\vert\right.\!\!\!\! \square \!\!\!\! \frac{\square}{\square} \!\!\!\!=$, but must come from an ancient Egyptian word of the form *'ibḥ·t*, which may have been a popular parallel form of *'ibḥ*.

SPIEGELBERG, W.—*Die ägyptische Gottheit der " Gotteskraft."* . The abstract idea of " power," " strength," expressed by the word *nḥt*, has long been known from demotic texts as a conception of divinity. The most important passages are in the Setne Romance (I, Kh.). A plural form *n'nḥt·w* is also known. Both forms are known in personal names ; the singular is only recorded in one name, probably denoting " the (servant) of the divine power." The Greek transcriptions show that ⌐ is not to be read, but is a sort of determinative placed before the word *nḥt*. This word appears to denote an abstract divinity, and is one of the fourteen attributes (*k'·w*) of Ra. This abstract conception of " power " or " powers " is always regarded as a personal god, as is shown by the hieroglyphic rendering ⌐⌐𓏥 of the demotic name. In several passages of the Setne Romance, the " divine power " is apparently a water-spirit. This connection with water occurs in the oldest mention, namely, in the " Tale of the Doomed Prince," in which *w'n nḥt* is the guardian of a crocodile. Hitherto this personage has been considered to be a giant, in spite of the determinative of a divinity, but Spiegelberg regards it as a river god. The god can thus be traced to the XIXth dynasty, to which period the name *Ns n³ nḥt·w* also belongs.

SPIEGELBERG, W.—*Das wahre Motiv des Zugunsten der Prinzessin Nes-Chons erlassenen Dekretes des Gottes Amon.* Amon was expected to provide a blessed Hereafter for the royal line of the XXIst dynasty. There is a deification decree for two members of this dynasty, Pi-notem and his wife Nesi-Chons. The decree for the wife pays particular attention to the earthly welfare of the widower ; Amon undertakes therein that the dead wife shall bring good and not evil to him and his. The husband is doubtless responsible for the purport of the wife's decree. Having thereby assured for himself a long and happy life on earth and protection from the evil influence of his wife's spirit, he need only be concerned in his own decree for happiness in the life to come.

SETHE, K.—*Miszelle.* 𓅭 *für* " *und*," " *mit*." 𓅭 occurs for the preposition " with," " and " (presumably the old Egyptian *ḥn'*), in an inscription of the time of Philippos Arrhidaïos. Sethe points out several passages in which Daressy (*Ann. du Serv.*, 18, 19) ·missed this meaning.

Vol. LVIII, Pt. I, 1923.

SETHE, K.—*Die Sprüche für das Kennen der Seelen der Zeiligen Orte.* The first part of this paper was published in *Zeitschrift*, LVII (see *A.E.*, 1923, i). The current portion deals with Chap. 112, which forms one of the group of texts concerning Buto and Hieraconpolis. It is connected with Chap. 113 by a joint postscript, which has more bearing on Chap. 112 though it follows Chap. 113.

Chapter 112 is composed of four parts which had no connection originally :— (1) the question why Buto was given to Horus, and the answer that it was reparation for the injury to the eye ; (2) the reason for the impurity of the oryx antelope and of the pig (typhonic animals) and of the taboo on pork ; (3) the division of the children of Horus between Buto and Hieraconpolis ; and (4) an invocation of the gods of the Underworld, borrowed from the Pyramid Texts and added in the N.K.

The injury to the eye forms the connecting link between (1) and (2). Whilst his eye is still suffering from the wound inflicted by Set, Horus is told by Ra to look at a black stroke (presumably on a white ground). He " sees it all white " (*i.e.*, the bad eye does not see the stroke) " and so arose the oryx antelope " (*m₃ ḥd* = " seen white "), which was the animal emblem of the 16th U.E. nome. Horus is then told by Ra to look at a larger object, namely, a black pig. His eye " rages," being as it was at the first blow that Set gave him, Set having attacked him in the form of a black pig. And so arose the abhorrence of the pig for the sake of Horus. As is usual, cause and effect are confused, the choice of animal being the natural consequence of the fact that the pig was unclean. The first object on which Horus is told to look is written as a stroke : Sethe suggests that the remarkable writing of the word *km*, " black " in Pyr. 227*a*, 228*b* and 252*b* may be explained thus, and may supply the reading for the ideogram in this text.

The part dealing with the children of Horus begins abruptly with their names, and must be an interpolation from a tale in which they are mentioned. This text must have been comparatively late, as it conforms to the triad nature of the " souls." The " children's " parentage is given ; their father is Horus the elder. The addition of the epithet must be to explain the anomaly that Isis is their mother, and Sethe considers that the whole distinction of an " elder " Horus rests elsewhere also on similar grounds, namely, to cloak contradictions in divine genealogies. It is clear from the text that the Horus who asks for the company of the " children " in Buto and Hieraconpolis is their father, and is the same Horus whose injured eye is the theme of the earlier parts of the text.

Precedence is given to Buto in several ways : the chapter on Buto precedes that on Hieraconpolis, and Horus names Buto first in his demand for two " children " in each town. Moreover, Imsty and Hapy, who are always named first, are assigned to Buto, whilst the jackal-headed god and the falcon-headed god are given to Hieraconpolis. The customary representations of the souls of Buto and of Hieraconpolis show them with falcon heads and jackal heads respectively, in conformity with the old conception of their identity with the " worshippers of Horus," so that the allocation must have been made at a time when their form and sequence were completely settled.

SETHE, K.—*Die aegyptische Berechnung der Schwangendauerschaft.* Owing to the difference in calendar, the Greeks reckoned the period of pregnancy as ten months, the Egyptians as nine. Numerous examples from Greek and Roman literature are given by Fritzsche in his short *Exeg. Handb. zu den Apokryphen* 6, 138. The Coptic translation (ed. *Lagarde*) renders the words by ū-ulltū-GBOT, "ten months long"; in the London MS. published by Thompson, the original ullt has been erased and emended by +IC, "nine." The Egyptian reckoning occurs also in II Maccab. VII, 27, whereas IV Maccab. XVI, 7 gives it as ten months. [The Greeks obviously reckoned by moons, as do the modern Hindus, whereas the Egyptians reckoned by the calendar month.]

SPIEGELBERG, W.—*Bemerkungen zu den hieratischen Amphoreninschriften des Ramesseums.* The author gives the results he has obtained from the inscriptions published in "Hieratic Ostraca and Papyri" (Egyptian Research Account, extra vol., 1898), and adds some new material. A list is given of the geographical names found on wine jars, and also a list of names of head vintners. Spiegelberg is unable to decide the meaning of the words $\odot$ followed by a numeral, which frequently come after the word "wine"; the circular sign is to be read $\odot$, and means a day of the month. Maspero's translation, "wine for three days," cannot hold, as the amphoræ are the same size, and the number of days varies between three and twenty-five. Spiegelberg suggests "wine of the *x*th day," on the assumption that the amphoræ were docketed at the vineyard before despatch (*cf. sbt* = "transport" or the like on oil jars in Tell-El-Amarna, XXIII, 32, 33, 37, 38). From his survey of material from the Ramesseum, Spiegelberg explains the inscriptions as follows:—they denote vintages from vineyards in the Delta (mainly near Pelusium) which belonged to the Ramesseum. The date does not contain the king's name, but must refer to the reign of Rameses II; witness the high figures 57 and 58. After the date follows the name of the brand and of the vineyard, with the frequent comment that the vineyard belonged to the temple of Rameses II. At the end comes the name of the head vintner (*ḥry Kmy·w*).

ASSELBERG, HENRI.—*Ein merkwürdiges Relief Amenophis' IV im Louvre-Museum.* The fragment, which is here reproduced in photograph, was first published by Prisse (*Monuments*, pl. 10, 1). It measures 130 × 60 cm. It was found in the 10th pylon of the big temple at Karnak, and had formerly belonged to an Aten temple of Horemheb. King Amenhotep IV is shown at either side offering incense to the disc, of which only a small arc remains. Above him are his cartouches, and above these are fragments of other cartouches, presumably of the Aten. Behind each figure is a long vertical line; behind the line on the left side is the name of Queen Nefertiti. The carving is in sunk relief. Seventeen rays proceed from the disc: the outermost on each side offers the hieroglyphs of a million *ḥbsd* festivals to the King; the others hold the ♀ and ⌐ signs alternately. The representations of the King are characteristic of the old style, and do not show the marked peculiarities of later portraits of Akhenaten. Nevertheless the mouth, nose and chin are quite different from those of Amenhotep III, and show that the figures represent Akhenaten himself and are not merely portraits of Amenhotep III with his son's name added.

SETHE, K.—*Zur Jahresrechnung des Neuen Reichs.* In the IVth and Vth dynasties, in the M.K. and in Ptolemaic times alike, the regnal years coincided with the calendar years. The last year of a king ran from his last New Year's day (1st Thoth, óf old called 1st day of 1st month of Inundation) to the day of his death, and together with the first year of his successor made but one calendar year, so that the first and last years of a reign are only fractions of a true year. There seem to be some exceptions to this rule in the N.K., in which the regnal years are counted from the date of accession and not from the 1st of Thoth. According to Sethe, these exceptions cannot be explained away ; he considers that a new custom arose after the Hyksos dominion and lasted at least until the end of the N.K.

SETHE, K.—*Zu den Sachmet-Statuen Amenophis' III.* In this article Sethe furnishes some corrections and amplifications to the lists published by Newberry and Gauthier of the Sekhmet statues erected by Amenhotep III in Thebes.

SETHE, K.—*Die hieroglyphe des Auges und das Wort i̯rr·t " Weintraube."* From the N.K. onwards the sign ⬡ occurs in the word i̯rr·t, " vine," " grapes " $\left(\begin{smallmatrix} \end{smallmatrix} \right.$, etc.$\left.\right)$, and from the M.K. onwards it takes the place of *r* in the word *irt·t*, " milk " $\left(\begin{smallmatrix} \end{smallmatrix}\right)$. Loret concluded that the group ⬡ in the first word must read *irr*, a view which is strengthened by the absence of *r* in the second word. He believed that he had settled the question of the reading of the old writings of the verb stem ⬡ " to do," where the forms in which gemination is to be expected are generally written ⬡, and would thus read *irr*. Sethe cannot agree with Loret's conclusions, which do not explain the frequent N.K. variant $\left|\begin{smallmatrix} \end{smallmatrix}\right.$, nor a IIIrd dynasty form $\left|\begin{smallmatrix} \end{smallmatrix}\right.$. Sethe holds that the remarkable M.K. writing $\left|\begin{smallmatrix} \end{smallmatrix}\right.$ clearly shows that the word is connected with the stem *i̯rr*, and has no etymological connection with the word ⬡, " eye," from which the eye sign in the word " to do " derived its sound *ir*. The substitution of the stem sign ⬡ *i̯rr* (*i̯r*) for *r* in the word *i̯rr·t* is inexplicable, but seems to have a parallel in the substitution of the two-consonant sign ⬡ *ir* in *irt·t*, " milk." Equally inexplicable is the vocalisation of the Coptic forms of the word *i̯rr·t* (ⲉⲗⲟⲟⲗⲉ, etc.), which show the existence of a vanished consonant between the two *l*'s.

SPIEGELBERG, W.—*Die Empörung des Hohenpriesters Amenhotpe unter Ramses IX.* An unpublished papyrus of Rameses IX in the British Museum mentions the rebellion of a high priest of Amon. It has been always tempting to identify this unknown rebel with the Amenhotep who is known to have lived under Rameses IX. This guess is confirmed by Spiegelberg's correction of a passage in Peet's translation of the Mayer A papyrus.

ALT, ALBRECHT.—*Zwei Vermutungen zur Geschichte des Sinuhe.* The words in which *Wḏꜣ Ḥr rśn·t* (*uza·hor·res·neit*), head physician and high priest of Neith of Sais, describes his official journey from Elam to Egypt in early Persian times, suggest to the writer of the article the influence of Sinuhe's description of his wanderings to Byblos. The word *ḫꜣst* is used in both passages for the regions traversed. It is obvious that at both periods the term must have been purely geographical, and could not apply to cultural conditions.

Though the term *ḥḳꜣ* had a wide application in the M.K., Alt considers that the words *ḥḳꜣ·w ḫꜣs·wt* are used as the name of a tribe in B 97–99. This passage would thus contain the first mention of the Hyksos.

SPIEGELBERG, W.—*Gipsproben aus Tell el Amarna mit hieratischen Aufschriften.* Two small lumps of plaster (gypsum) about 45 mm. high are in all probability test pieces. Each has a round flat surface (68 mm. and 72 mm. diameter respectively) which bears an inscription in XVIIIth dynasty hieratic. The inscriptions give the day of the month without the year and the words ' *Ḳd* (⌂ 𓅓 𓇋 𓅓 °₁₁₁), from Akhetaten." The words gypsum and *Ḳd* have probably the same etymology. *Ḳd* is probably a loan word from Akkad. *gaṣṣu*, Latin gypsum. As the word is not known in Egypt before the N.K. and is spelt in " syllabic " writing, it is to be regarded as a Babylonian word.

Miscellaneous.

SETHE, K.—*Noch einmal zu den Worten n-nk tm am Anfang von Totb. 17.* Further examples are given of the meaning " to me belong " for *n-nk* and of " Lord of All " for *nb tm.*

SETHE, K.—*Ramses II als " erster Prophet des Amun."* A relief from the great hypostyle of the temple of Karnak shows Rameses II acting as, and bearing the title of, " first prophet of Amon." This scene presumably represents the great festival at Luxor which was held in the first year of the King's reign, in which he took part in person. At that time the office of high priest was vacant (*Zeitschrift*, 44, 30 *ff.*).

SETHE, K.—ⲙⲉϣⲁⲕ " *vielleicht* " *und die Zugehörigen Formen.* Erman derived ⲙⲉϣⲁⲕ, the Coptic-sahidic expression for " perhaps," from N.E. 𓂡𓂝𓎟𓎡 " thou knowest not " (*Zeitschrift*, 32, 128). The phrase cannot properly be used to a woman, nor to more than one person. In the instances known to Sethe the addressee is nearly always masculine. He quotes an example of a corresponding feminine form ⲙⲉϣⲁⲣ in the Sahidic version of the history of Saint Theodorus (*Munier, Ann. du Serv.*, 19, 228 *ff.*).

SPIEGELBERG, W.—*Die Etymologie von* ⲍⲟⲩⲍⲉ, " *Fehlgeburt.*" Spiegelberg brings forward evidence for the derivation of ⲍⲟⲩⲍⲉ, " miscarriage," from 𓃭𓏤𓅓𓉐, *Why ḫ·t.*

SPIEGELBERG, W.—*Ein Priestertitel des Hathorkults.* A priest of Hathor is given the titles 𓊹𓊪𓏲𓋹 and 𓀭𓊹𓊪𓏲𓋴𓇋 on two fragments in the Strasburg collection, presumably from Deir-el-Bahari. Thus ꜥs (" the elder " ?) was a title of a priest of Hathor, who is here called the " golden." These passages supply the translation of an inscription on a fragment figured in Naville's XIth Dyn. Temple at Deir-el-Bahari, III, plate 9B : " . . . her ꜥs priest, he being satisfied, I am an ꜥs priest, I speak to the golden one (= Hathor).".

L. B. ELLIS.

ANCIENT EGYPT.

THE BRANCH ON PREHISTORIC SHIPS.

In Ancient Egypt, Part I, 1914, page 33, Professor Petrie enumerates the reasons for interpreting the well-known paintings on prehistoric pottery as ships and not towns. In two of the figures accompanying the text, the boats (as they are without any reasonable doubt) have a single frond or a pair of palm fronds in the bow; in one figure, a leafy branch (or bunch of small date-palm fronds or a dôm palm leaf) bends over a small cabin amidships.

Both these are referred to in the text, as probably shelters from the glare or heat of the sun; but a single frond, or a pair of fronds, stuck high and upright in the bow of a boat would hardly afford a shelter worth resorting to, and another explanation perhaps fits it better.

Sir H. Johnston (*George Grenfell and the Congo*, II, p. 958), speaking of the boats of the primitive Bube people of Fernando Po, says: "On the extremity of the prow is fastened a kind of flagstaff, the top of which is decorated with a bunch of feathers. Bauman states that this can become the mast of a primitive sail." He continues: "It may resemble what the present writer has seen in the estuary of the Cameroons River, where the canoes are more or less propelled by a huge raphia frond being fastened like mast and sail in one, and serving the purposes of a sail." The figure accompanying is a rough copy of the author's sketch (reversed), and the resemblance to the Egyptian form is obvious.

E. S. Thomas.

EARLY HITTITE RECORDS.

THE Egyptians and the Hittites were so intimately connected in the age of the New Empire that Hittite ancient history is no longer out of place in ANCIENT EGYPT. Indeed it is by no means improbable that future discovery will indicate earlier relations between the two peoples than the time of the XVIIIth and XIXth dynasties ; M. Montet's recent discoveries at Jebêl show that as far back as the IVth dynasty the Egyptians had established themselves on the coast of Canaan, and had a colony in a port which was in maritime relation to the coast of Asia Minor, while we now know that the copper, lead and silver mines of the Taurus were worked by Babylonian firms as far back as the period of the IIIrd dynasty of Ur (B.C. 2400). It was from Cappadocia that Babylonia and Syria were at that time supplied with their bronze, and the geometric buttons which characterise the Syrian VIIth and VIIIth dynasties in Egypt point to Cilicia as their source.

To render the present position clear, it is well to state the following names of Hittite kings, which can now be put in historical order. The family descent is broken where a bar is placed.

Pamba, conquered by Naram-sin.

Biyustis, contemporary of Anittas.

Dudkhaliyas I, the Tidal of Gen. xiv, 9.

Labarnas, queen Tawannannas.
Khattusilis I.
Mursilis I, q. Kharabsilis ; conquered the dynasty of Khammurabi, 1926 B.C.
Bimbiras.

Khantilis, q. Waliannis.
Bisenis (or Kassenis).

Zidantas, q. Iyayas.
Ammunas.
Zurus (short reign).

Titiyas (short reign).
Khuzziyas, q. Summiris.
Telibinus, q. Istapariyas.
Mursilis II.

Dudkhaliyas II.
Khattusilis II.
Subbiluliumas (son), wrote to Akhenaten, 1383 B.C.
Arnuwandas I (son).
Mursilis III (brother).
Muwatallis, or Mutallis (son) ; war with Ramessu II, 1292 B.C.
Urkhi-Tessub (son).
Khattusilis III (uncle) ; treaty with Ramessu II, 1280 B.C.
Dudkhaliyas III (son).
Arnuwandas II (son).
Dudkhaliyas IV (son).

The Hittite cuneiform texts recently published by Dr. Forrer (*Die Boghaz-köi—Texte im Umschrift : Geschichtliche Texte aus dem alten Chattireich*, II, 1 ; Leipzig, 1922) throw new and unexpected light upon the early history of Asia Minor. As no translations of them have yet appeared, readers of ANCIENT EGYPT will probably be interested in the following extracts. At present, indeed, nothing more than extracts can be attempted ; the Hittite language is still in process of decipherment, and most of the texts are so mutilated that in many passages only a word here and there is intelligible.

The earliest texts are translations into Hittite of the campaigns of Sargon of Akkad and Naram-Sin (B.C. 2750) in Asia Minor. The Assyrian version of the campaign of Sargon, which was found by the German excavators in the house of the Hittite ambassador at Tel el-Amarna, was translated by myself in the *Proceedings of the Society of Biblical Archaeology*, December, 1915, and since then by Dr. Weidner in *Boghazköi-Studien*, VI (1922). It had been written by a Hittite, not by a Babylonian, though doubtless a Babylonian original lay behind it. But some Hittite writer who was acquainted with Assyrian had extracted from this original the history of the campaign in Asia Minor and put it into " Hittite " Assyrian, which was not exactly the Assyrian of the Babylonian scribes.

The beginning of the Naram-Sin text is lost ; then we have :—

" Then the temples of Ellil which are in the city (of Babylon ?) [I restored] :

" And I at that time against all the enemy lands made war.

" Mana-ila king of the Western coast (?), Bunana-ila king of Pakki   .   .

" Lapana-ila king of Ullini, . . innipa-ila king of   .   .   .

" Pamba king of the Hittites (Khatti), Khutuni king of Kanes, Nur-[Dagan king of Buruskhanda],

" Akwaruwas king of the Amorites, Tissenki king of Parasi   .   .   .

" Madakina king of Armani, Izkibbu king of the Amanus mountains, Tess[inki king of   .   .   .],

" Ur-Larag king of Larag, Ur-banda king of Nikki   .   .   .

" Ilsunaîl king of Dur, Tisbinki king of Kursaura (Garsaura)."

" Altogether 17 kings who formed an alliance, I overthrew them."

" I entrusted the soldiery to a Kharrian and offered libations of sweet wine."

Kanes was the modern Kara Eyuk, 18 kilometres north-east of Kaisariyeh, which in the time of the IIIrd dynasty of Ur became an Assyro-Babylonian settlement. Nur-Dagan had been the antagonist of Sargon, whose campaign in Asia Minor had been directed against his capital Buruskhanda or Barsukhanda, and from whence he had brought back vines,. roses. figs and other trees to Babylonia. The name of the city occurs frequently in the cuneiform tablets of Kara Eyuk, postal and commercial intercourse between the two cities of Kanes (or Ganis) and Buruskhanda being frequent and active.

The Kharrians (or Murrians, as the name may also be read, perhaps with better reason) spoke the Mitannian language and were of the Mitannian race. They were of Asianic origin, but at an early period occupied the northern part of Mesopotamia, which they called Mitanna, " the land of Midas," after the name of their leader, as well as the later Assyria.

The alliance which was formed against Naram-Sin is interesting since it embraced Babylonian cities (Larak or Larancha, and Dur) as well as northern Syria and eastern Asia Minor, and so proves the intimate connection that existed between all parts of Western Asia in the third millennium before our era (*cf.* Gen. xiv). Dur is the modern Salihiyeh on the Euphrates, which the recent excavations of M. Cumont have shown was the Europos of Greek geography.

A fragment of the second column of the tablet recounts the tribute received by Naram-Sin and includes " talents of silver," " talents of copper " and " lapis lazuli " which were brought to the city of Akkad.

On the reverse of the tablet is a paragraph referring to a war with some enemy whose name is lost but who was presumably of Asianic origin. It reads : " In the first campaign 190,000 soldiers I led ; they defeated him. On the second occasion 120,000 soldiers I led ; then they defeated him. The third time 60,000 soldiers I led ; then they defeated him."

The fragment of another tablet (No. 5) relating to Naram-Sin mentions the Sa-gaz or Khabiri. They were the mercenaries who served as the body-guard of the king ; inscriptions of Rim-Sin, the contemporary of Khammurabi, refer to them in Babylonia, and at Boghaz-Keui, where they were called Khâbiriyas, there were 1,200 of them, 600 of them keeping guard on one side of the palace of " the god," *i.e.*, the king, and 600 on the other side (*Hittite Texts from the British Museum*, 32, 37). *Khabiri* in Assyrian meant " companions " or " auxiliaries," the word having been borrowed from " Amorite " or West Semitic, and it resembled the names under which the free lances of mediaeval Europe were known. Heber the Kenite may have been one of them, and I am inclined to think that they were the prototypes of the Greek Kabeiri. Their communal god was called Khabiru, " the Companion." In one inscription mention is made of 3,000 Khabiri. Along with the Khabiri, but apparently of less consequence, another body of mercenaries called Lulakhi is also enumerated. The Khabiri of the Tel el-Amarna tablets must have been Hittite bands.[1]

The fall of the Amorite dynasty of Khammurabi, in Babylonia, was brought about by the invasion of the country by the Hittites about B.C. 1900, during the reign of its last king, Samsu-ditana. We now learn from the Boghaz Keui tablets that the Hittite leader was Mursilis I, the son of Khattusilis I. A later king, Telibinus (whose name signifies " Son of Telis "), gives us the following information on the subject (No. 23) :—

" Thus (speaks) the Lord Telibinus the great king : Originally Labarnas was the great king ; then his sons, his brothers and his priests, family and soldiers were mustered. But the territory was small. From hence he went to war and with his arms conquered the enemy's country.

" So he annexed territory and extended his dominions. He made them subject as far as the sea. Afterwards he returned from the campaign, but his sons and whoever wished went from hence to the (new) country.

" Now the lands they governed were those of the cities Khubisna (the Greek Kybistra), Tuwanuwa (Tyana), Nenassa (also written Ninassa), Landa, Zallara, Parsukhanda[2] and Lûsna ; the great fortresses were entrusted (to them).

[1] Lydian tradition related that Akiamos, king of Lydia, campaigned in Syria, and that his general, Askalos, founded Ashkelon, where the Lydian Mopsos, or Moxos, flung the goddess " Derketo " (Istar) into the sacred lake. Already in the time of Rim-Sin, or Erim-Aku, Ti'dal—the cuneiform Tudkhula and Tudkhaliyas, " Spear-holder "—king of " Nations " (the Babylonian Umman-Manda, or " Nations " of Asia Minor)—accompanied the army of Babylonia and Elam in its campaign against Southern Palestine (Gen. xiv).

[2] Miswritten Massukhanda. The Hittite scribes confound characters which closely resemble one another—*par* (or *bar*) and *mas*, *ma* and *ku*, *um*, *dub* and *ab*, *uk*, *ar* and *sum*, &c.

"Afterwards Khattusilis became king; then his sons, his brothers, his priests and his relatives and his soldiers were mustered; from hence he went to war and with his arms conquered the enemy's country. So he annexed territory and extended his dominions. He made them subject as far as the sea. When he returned from his campaign his sons and whoever wished went from hence to the (new) country and to their hands the chief fortresses were entrusted.

"When for the second time the slaves of the king's sons made sedition, they took possession (?) of their houses and . . . their masters; so they caused bloodshed.

"When Mursilis became king of Khattusas (Boghaz Keui) then his sons, his brothers, the priests and his relatives and his soldiers were mustered, and he invaded the land of the enemy in arms and extended his territory: he made them subject as far as the sea.

"He marched to Khalpa (Aleppo) and captured Khalpa. The abundant spoil of Khalpa he carried to Khattusas. After that he marched to Babylon; he captured Babylon and overthrew the Kharrians (of Mitanni); the abundant spoil of Babylon he gave to Khattusas. Now Khantilis was cupbearer; after this he took Kharabsilis, the wife of Mursilis, as a wife (after slaying Mursilis).

"And Zidantas was . . .; he took . . . the daughter of Khantilis as a wife. Now Zidantas plotted with Khantilis; evil words they [uttered] and they murdered Mursilis and shed blood.

"So Khantilis was supreme."

Here the tablet is broken, a few words only being decipherable: "soldiers," "he marched," "territory," "the cities of Khurpanas (Herpa) and Carchemish."

Then we read :—

"And when Khantilis descended upon the city of Tegarama (Togarmah) he spoke as follows: ' This have I done, since Zidanta . . .'"

Here again the tablet is broken and the paragraph ends with the words: "then the gods avenged the blood of Mursilis." It seems that they brought the Kharrians upon "the land of the Hittites."

"The queen of the city of Sukzia" next appears upon the scene. We are told that " she died," being murdered along with " his " (not " her ") sons. This is followed by a paragraph of which the first half only of the lines remain :—

"When Khantilis the queen of Sukzia . . .
"afterwards he avenged; whoever murders . . .
"the chief of the palace officials delivered a message; then . .
"they were mustered; they the city of Tegarama . . ."

The following paragraphs are intact :—

"And when Khantilis became old he retired as a god (*i.e.*, abdicated). Then Zidantas murdered Bisenis (or Kassenis), son of Khantilis, along with his sons; his principal servants he (also) slew.

"So Zidantas became king; then the gods avenged the blood of Bisenis; the gods made Ammunas his son his enemy and he murdered his father Zidantas.

"And Ammunas became king; then the gods avenged the blood of his father Zidantas by [denying] to his hand wheat, wine, oxen and sheep."

Here follows another break. Then we read :—

"The lands were hostile to him . . . the soldiers of Adania (Adana), Arzawa, Sallapa (perhaps identical with Zalpa), Barduwata and Akhkhula (probably the Greek Anchiale) came hither on a campaign, but the attempt had no success, and when Ammunas became a god (*i.e,.* died) Zûrus, the captain of the bodyguard of spearmen in those days, who was his own son, delivered Takharwailis to the Gold-stick,[1] whereupon Titiyas killed the whole brood together with their children.

"And he delivered Tarukhsus to the ..-man ; then he murdered Khantilis with his sons. So Khuzziyas became king and Telibinus took Istapariyas as his first wife. Then Khuzziyas murdered the others and published the statement : ' Telibinus has made away with them ! '

"His 5 brothers, he has assigned houses to them ; let them go and inhabit them ; so let them eat and drink ; but none (of them) must do evil ; should I learn (that evil were done) for the evil they have done to me I will destroy them.'

"When I, Telibinus, had ascended the throne of my father, I made an expedition against the city of Khassuwas (' the royal city '), the city of Khassuwas I conquered. While my soldiers were at the city of Zizzilibbis, they wrought destruction on the city of Zizzilibbis.

"Later on I, the king, came to the city of Lawazzantiyas (Laviansênê ?) : Lakhkhas was my enemy ; he had sent instructions to (?) Lawazzantiyas ; the gods gave him (*or* it ?) into my hands, and first of all the head of the agri-cultural bureau (?) Tessub . . ., [the head of the . . .] Karruwas, the head of the . . . Inaras, the chief cupbearer Killas, [the . . .] Tessub-mimmas, the chief scribe Zinwaselis and Lillis [all] great men to Tanûis the scribe, the spearman, gave . . ."

Telibinus now furnishes further details of his reign, and after a long break enumerates the cities over which he held rule. Fragments of two lists remain, one naming the cities north of south-eastern Cilicia, the other the cities of Syria. Among the first are included : Sukzias ; Asur-nas, "the city of Asur," which implies an Assyrian settlement ; Samukha, north of Boghaz Keui (occupied by the Kharrians) ; and the Mountain of the city Barsukhandas (or Buruskhanda), near the river Khulayas (the Pyramus, the modern Jihun which may preserve a reminiscence of the old name). Then follows a list of " the 34 cities " of Syria annexed by the Hittite king, of which only the last few names are left. These are : Kuwannas ; then three lost names ; Lakhkhurumas ; two lost names ; Kharakharas (the Assyrian Qarqar, Hebrew Aroer) ; Mallitaskurias ; one name lost ; Kharsuwas ; Tipilas ; Kursa . . . ; one lost name ; Suwanzuwannas ; Tamlutas ; Bikumias ; Dammaskhunas (Damascus) ; one name lost ; Khalip-passuwas (Aleppo) ; Kalasummiyas ; one lost name.

The mention of Damascus is important ; it is the earliest reference to the city yet found in the cuneiform inscriptions and shows that Hittite sovereignty extended as far south as the northern border of Palestine. There is no difficulty, therefore, in understanding how Hittite settlers could have found their way to Hebron in the time of Abraham.

We learn from an inscription of Mursilis II, the son of Telibinus (K.T.B.K. IV, No. 4), that Tegarama, or Togarmah, lay on the road between Carchemish and Harran. From the same inscription we also learn that Telibinus had made his son, to whom he had given the Semitic name Malik-Arakh (" a king is the Moon-god "), the vassal kinglet of Carchemish. Mursilis afterwards confirmed the son of the latter in the kingship of the city, and further made Rimi-malik, another son of Telibinus, kinglet of Aleppo.

---

[1] A high official who seems to have superintended the gendarmerie. His should probably be entitled " Gold-lance " rather than " Gold-stick."

Khantilis has left a fragmentary inscription (No. 20) in which we read :—

" After Khattusilis the king his son Mursilis became king, and he was a premier king. When he had invaded the lands of the enemy he handed over all the lands to Khattusas, and so he enriched Khattusas.

" Then he marched to Aleppo and afterwards avenged the blood of his father (who had apparently been killed there) when Khattusilis went to survey (lit. mark out) the kingdom of Aleppo. Mursilis made the country of Aleppo responsible and conquered all the lands of the Kharrians.

" All its wealth he seized. This he carried to Khattusas. Then he marched to Babylon and captured the city of Babylon."

Here the tablet is broken. The next intelligible fragment is :—

" Now the fortresses of the land of the Hittites (Khatti) no one had previously built, but now all the fortresses of the country I Khantilis have built and the city of Khattusas I Khantilis have built, and this tablet [according to] the words of the stela [have written]. . . ."

The " building " must have been a restoration or extension of the city. It will be noticed that Aleppo was " in the lands of the Kharrians " (or Murrians) of Mitanni. Many years ago I pointed out that Aleppo and the neighbouring Dunip must have been Mitannian, since in the Tel el-Amarna correspondence the letter of the people of Dunip (KNUDZTON, 59.) contains the Mitannian words *naprillan* and *ammati* ' elders.'" Moreover, the names of Dunip (Tennib) and Khalip (Aleppo) which stood on the river Khal terminate in the Mitannian suffix -*p*.

The kings and many of the queens were regarded as incarnations of the Sun-god and were deified after death. Their images were erected in the temples and stated offerings made to them. In this way we have learnt the names of a considerable number of early rulers. Thus a broken tablet (No. 24) describes the offerings of food and drink made to " 44 (former) kings " of which the following names remain :—

Alluwamnas and queen Kharabsilis, Khantilis, Zidantas and queen Iyayas, Khuzziyas and queen Summiris, Tudkhaliyas (Tid'al) and queen Nigalmatis, Arnuwandas (I) ; Telibinus, Malku-Arakh " king of Carchemish," queen Wallannis, Zidanzas, Mûwatallis (Mutallis I) and Ammunas.

In another list we have : Khattusilis (?) and queen Kassulauiyas, Kantuzzilis and queen Wallannis, Taki-malik and Asmi-malik, Telibinus " the High-priest," Malik-Arakh, " king of Carchemish." In another list Asmi-malik is stated to be the son of Arnuwandas.

Mutallis (K.T.B.K. No. 4) states that after confirming . . . .-malik, the son of Malik-Arakh, in the kingdom of Carchemish, " I made Rimi-malik the son of Telibinus king in the country of Aleppo, and caused the country of Aleppo to swear obedience to him. Then I set in order the country of Carchemish, and marched out of the country of Carchemish and came to the country of Tegarama. Afterwards I arrived at the city of Tegarama. Nuwanzas, the overseer of the wine-cellars, and all the officers in the city of Tegarama came to me ; they dissuaded me from marching to the city of Khayasas since the year was too advanced, and the officers said to me : ' The year is too advanced, so, our lord, do not go to Khayasas.' Accordingly I did not march to Khayasas, but went to the city of Kharran. The army flocked to me in the city of Kharran, for I had ordered the army to come there."

Yet another list gives us ; Pu-malik the son of Tudkhaliyas, Pawâkhtelmakh, Bimbiras, Ammunas, Khantilis and Alluwamnas, and in various fragments we find : (1) queen Tawannannas and Labarnas, queen Kattusis and Mursilis (I), Bimbiras ; (2) Kantusilis and queen Wallannis, followed by Taki-malik and Asmu-malik ; (3) Telibinus and queen Istapariyas, Alluwamnas and queen Kharabsilis, followed by Khantilis, while elsewhere the queens Dâdu-khepa and Khinti.. are coupled with Subbi-luliuma, the founder of the later empire.

Altogether I have recovered the names of the following kings from the various ritual texts :—

Khate-binns (*Hittite Texts in British Museum*, 42, No. 58) ; Wâlizanisûs, Takhbiltanus, Walizilis, queen Titi-ûttis, Wâsinzilis and Wakhsis the Kharrian, Ninnassarus, Yaliyas, Telibinus ; Mezzullas of Arinua ; Khasamnilis "the swordsman" ; Khasawanzas, Sâuwaskhilas, Khilassiyas ; Zibarwas of Pâlâ (north-west of the Gulf of Antioch), Kalumziburis, Ilaliyantas ; Ziliburiyas, Takasûkh, Sulinkattis ; Zidkhariyas, Karzis, Khabantaliyas ; Argapas, Alkhisuwas ; Kattiskhabis ; Siwattis, Kuwansas ; Kantuzzilis ; Uriyadus ; Zakhbunas ; Tuskhapadus ; Kurusiyantis, Makhni.., Khuwatassis ; Khantidasus ; Khebemalik ; Tessub-GUR. To these must be added those of the Labarnas dynasty : Khattusilis I, Mursilis I, Khantilis, Zidantas, Ammunas, Khuzziyas and Telibinus. Telibinus came from Turmitta (Thermodon ?), north of Boghaz Keui, and founded a new dynasty (*Keilschrifturkunden aus Boghazköi*, iv, 1). The names between semi-colons belong to same group and with the exception of the Semitic Khebemalik, which is compounded, however, with the name of the Kharrian Sungoddess, are all Proto-Hittite, a language in which *kattis* signified " king " and *-zilis* " son of."

We must also add to the list the name of Biyustis, a contemporary of Anittas, son of Bitkhanas, king of Kussar, who seems to have lived not long after the time of Naram-Sin. Anittas tells us (B.K.T., II, i, p. 9) :—

" All the country from the city of Zalpu to the sea [I conquered]. Formerly Ukhnas king of Zalpu had taken my god (Khalmasuittum) from the city of Nêsas to Zalpu, but afterwards I, Anittas, the great king, took back my god from Zalpu to Nêsas, and carried Khuzziyas king of Zalpu alive to Nêsas. Now the city of Khattusas Bi[yustis..]ed ; I annexed it. He subsequently surrendered it. My god Khalmasuittum took it away : I captured it by night by *agreement* (?), and defined its boundaries.

" Whatever king shall come after me, do you inhabit the city of Khattusas : may Tessub of heaven bless him."

Zalpu, or Zalba, is often mentioned in the Cappadocian tablets of Kanis (Kara Eyuk), and is coupled with Aleppo, Pâlâ, Parsukhuntas and Ussû (Issos) in K.T.B.K., IV, p. 71.

A. H. SAYCE.

THE CAVE OF MACPELAH.

THE magnificent work lately issued by Père Vincent and Captain Mackay on *Hebron, le Haram el Khalil*, sets out fully the labours of these workers in 256 pp. 4to, with an album of 28 plates (Paris, Leroux). The production is a credit to the patronage of the Académie des Inscriptions. The former plans are set out, successive alterations of the building are discussed, with the help of eighty-six photographs and detailed drawings in the text, and the records are all quoted at length and compared with the actual site by Père Vincent. Capt. Mackay's plan is most careful in its detail of variations and irregularities, and, happily, is fully supplied with the measurements. The drawings of the pilastered outer wall give some idea of the nobility of its appearance (Fig. 1), and no point of interest seems to have been omitted. We must congratulate Père Vincent on such a monumental work, mainly from his own drawings.

The centre of interest, however, is in the original history of the Mu-kafaleh, or double cave (as named by the LXX), which underlies this great Herodian monument. The subterranean parts were strictly prohibited to the explorers; they were not even allowed inside the Arab cenotaphs on the surface, so our main interest yet remains to be satisfied when the fanaticism of the present population may be less insistent. As the conclusions stated in this work depend on an erroneous reckoning of the mediaeval measures, we here reconsider the subject.

To understand the history of the Haram we must begin with the subterranean parts, which were the whole cause of the superstructure. For the chambers and cave now hidden, the only material information is in the careful account of the examination in 1119 A.D. by the monks, which was written up in 1136 by a visitor from the testimony of two who had taken part in the work. This statement is fully published, in the Latin and French translation in the present work, together with every other fragment about the place recorded by pilgrims or historians. The essential parts of the account are that a monk resting by the cenotaph of Isaac found a wind blowing up between the paving slabs. This doubtless came in from the small opening in the outer wall below, where the Jews are permitted now to pray. This led to raising the paving, and finding a pit 11 cubits (7·6 metres, 25 feet) deep ; in this account all levels will be quoted as beneath the floor of the Haram area. This measurement raises the question of what was the length of the cubit. Happily, this is fixed in the same document by stating the height of the Haram wall at 18 cubits, limiting it to between ·67 and ·95 metres, or 26½ and 37 inches, according to whether the back or the front was measured. This is further fixed by the breadth being stated as 49 cubits ; this fixes the cubit at ·695 metres, or 27·3 inches. In the present work these data have been neglected, and the cubit has been assumed as half a metre ; it was really the modern *pic*.

The description of the pit as being near the tomb of Isaac leaves no doubt that it is beneath the mediaeval canopy (I) at the S.E. end of the church (Fig. 2) where paving slabs are secured by iron cramps. The pit was large enough to place in it a double flight of stone stairs in later times. There was no apparent exit from the pit, but by striking the wall a hollow was found, and, breaking away the stone, a passage was opened 11 cubits high (7·6 metres, 25 feet), 17 cubits

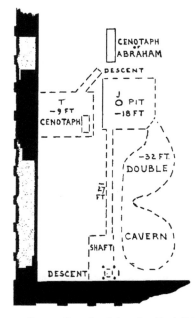

long (11·8 metres, 38 feet), and 1 cubit wide ; the stones were like those of the Haram wall. This led to nothing, but by striking the wall a further hollow was found, and they broke into a chamber like a basilica but rounded, probably referring to a vaulted or domed roof. This was large enough to hold 30 persons and was of very fine work. Near the entrance to this hall an inserted stone was found, which closed a natural cave. In this cave bones were found, and an entrance to a second cave, where were also bones and 15 pottery jars full of bones.

To connect this with the visible parts is difficult. There are two clues, perhaps equally wrong. The description of a very narrow and high passage and fine building suggests that it ran along the inner side of the Haram wall ; that length cannot be along the S.E. end, but must be along the S.W. side. The other clue is that it led to the vault under the other canopy (J). The length recorded would then imply that the first entrance chamber was nearly as long as the vault under (J) ; also that this vault was the "basilica." As it is estimated (by view through an opening at the top) as being over 30 square metres area, that would be fairly in accord with its holding thirty people. Taking either view, it is impossible to suppose that the caverns described as opening near the end of the passage could be on the N.W. of the vault. They must lie off the E. corner of the vault, where some kind of closure was detected in viewing it from above. The floor of the cavern is said to be 14 cubits (9·7 metres, 32 feet) under the floor. This would be 2 metres under the level of the lowest part of the front wall, and probably 6 metres from the surface of the rock at the part indicated. The finely built passage may be the masking wall closing the naturally open front of the cavern. This position of the caverns would make it quite likely that the altar of the Byzantine church was over the inner cavern, thus consecrating it by the relics beneath. This custom seems to have been as early in the Eastern as in the Western church. It will be seen then that, in any case, the description of the cavern as being entered near the end of the passage puts it quite out of the possibility of being near the N.W. end of the Haram. The cavern indicated in plan and section at pp. 63 and 155 of this volume would be

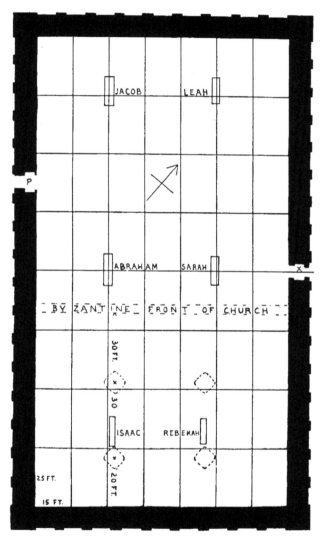

unlikely. It is double the size of an existing cavern, and would therefore have naturally a much more vaulted roof, while there is nothing to suggest so large a space.

A limit to the arrangements is given by the chamber (T) visited by Capt. Meinertzhagen, from the cenotaph of Abraham. The passage opened off the S. side of the cenotaph ; it must be longer than in his sketch, and the chamber lower, in order to be beneath the floor. I have reconciled it by supposing a passage 9 feet long, descending 9 feet, and leaving a foot or two for flooring over the chamber. The size of the chamber here would only just lie between the vault (ɟ) and the front wall. It precludes' any deeper chamber, like vault (ɟ), being in this position. The chamber was evidently intended to contain a subterranean cenotaph ; perhaps to withdraw attention from the actual caverns below.

The passage described by the monks was a planned mode of access, from the time of the original building. Whether the careful blocking by concealed stones was due to the builders, or was inserted by the Byzantines, we cannot yet say. Certainly the caverns were carefully concealed, and not intended to be visited.

Now we turn to the visible constructions (*see* Fig. 3). It is evident that the disposition of the cenotaphs can have no exact relation to natural caverns ; they are too regular, and they do not accord with the record of the place of the caverns The crossing lines here drawn over the whole area are placed to show the proportions of the arrangement. It appears probable that the Isaac and Rebekah cenotaphs have been slightly displaced, from a position symmetric with those of Jacob and Leah, by the requirements of the position of columns for the Byzantine church, which were almost certainly in the position of columns of the present church ; these may partly be the original columns with altered capitals. It is clear that the space between the cenotaphs of Abraham and Sarah is to the space beyond them, as 3 : 2 ; this divides the breadth into 7. Lengthways the Jacob and Leah cenotaphs are at a quarter of the distance from the end to the middle, thus dividing the length into 8. Now these spaces are in simple relation to each other ; the length is $8 \times 25 = 200$ Jewish feet, the breadth $7 \times 15 = 105$ Jewish feet, of $10 \cdot 6$ or $10 \cdot 7$ inches. This is the half of the 6-palm cubit, the commonest Jewish measure. The walls are 10 feet thick. A surprise comes, however, when the outside measures are taken, which conform to the Roman foot ; it is 200 Roman feet long, 115 feet wide, walls 9 feet, buttresses 4 feet, and bays 7 feet. The dimensions inside and outside cannot all fit the same standard ; it is Roman to the outer world, Jewish at heart, a type of Herod himself. The design is based on the fact that the Jewish and Roman feet could be worked together on a ratio of $10 : 11$ in length, or $11 \cdot 5 : 12 \cdot 5$ in the breadth, or $9 : 10$ in the wall thickness. There is a little cooking in fitting the pilaster and bays on the Roman fort, as the corners ought to be 10 feet on the ends and 9 feet on the sides, yet they were made equal.

How was this grand structure entered ? That the cenotaphs (but not the shrines over them) are parts of the original design is shown by their relation to the inner dimensions. They would hardly have been erected unless to be visited, and they imply some access to the enclosure. The N.E. entrance is exactly in the middle of the side, but it is stated to be clearly a forced hole ; moreover, one would expect that the cenotaphs of the men would be near the entrance and the women behind them. On the S.W. side there is the opening P, which is thus described, " A spacious bay (P) in the old western wall, placed between two pilasters, has not any rigorous symmetry." On the contrary, when we revert to the original scheme of the interior this bay is seen to be exactly between the northern and the middle tombs ; it leads evenly into the wide space between them It is really $\cdot 20$ metres too near the northern end, agreeing to the slightly lesser size of the northern cenotaphs. This position is too precise to be accidental, it clearly belongs to the original design. It is entirely covered by the added building against the side of the Haram, called the tomb of Joseph. How this entrance was reached from outside cannot be settled ; whatever existed in front of it was swept away at the building of the shrine. In the section (p. 23), there is marked the " probable place of the primitive door," on the ground level, in the lower chamber which supports the shrine of Joseph ; but there does not appear to be any authority for this, and it belongs to a scheme of western caverns for which there does not seem to be any reason.

We thus arrive at the idea that the old entrance of the caverns was masked by a wall, a passage ran along the front from the south to the north, there entering a chamber (J) from which the caverns had an artificial entrance. Over all this a large area was laid out, within a grand enclosure, 194 feet long by 111 feet wide, the wall of which was 30 feet high inside and 55 feet high on the front. This seems undoubtedly to have been one of the constructions of the magnificent Herod. It was closely like his work at Jerusalem, and also like the great tank at Hebron, which is not mentioned in the new account. The mode of access was by a door in the high front about 30 feet from the ground. It may have been reached by a ladder or moveable scaffold ; but if there were a permanent entry it must have been all cleared away in making the new shrine. This shrine of Joseph already existed in 1047, when it is said that there was no entry. Yet there is a record that the E. door was made in 918 A.D. Probably it was made when the Joseph shrine covered the earlier entrance ; and blocked up again before the visit of 1047.

The great internal change was when a wall was placed across the interior, and nearly half of it converted into a church. The date of this is not fixed, but it was in existence by 570 A.D. It may have been one of the Constantinian foundations, like the basilica at Bethlehem. It was divided by a balustrade into two portions, for Jews and Christians. This recognition of Jews continued for a century after Constantine, as in rather a different degree it is seen in 430 A.D. by the mosaics of the Church of the Circumcision and Church of the Gentiles in St. Sabina at Rome.

A remarkable detail of this church is that the spacing of it is on the same Jewish foot as the lay-out of the whole interior. From the S.E. end to the nearest pillar centre is 20 Jewish feet, thence to the next is 30, and on to the wall is 30 feet more.

During the century after the Arab conquest the shrines were built over the cenotaphs. Those of Abraham and Jacob, octagonal ; of Sarah and Leah, hexagonal. The reason for the smaller square shrines of Isaac and Rebekah was doubtless that, as the church had been converted into a mosque, it was desired to avoid blocking it up by such large buildings as the other shrines.

The Crusading kingdom remodelled the church, with slightly pointed arches. The date is not recorded within this period of 1100 to 1187 ; but probably it was in the earlier part. After Saladin's re-conquest the mosque was emphasized by cutting a *mihrab* in 1332, and as late as 1755 there were porticoes built on two sides of the inner court. Changes are still being made, such as the columns of the Arab tribune (p. 16) being converted into an internal portico along the entrance wall. There is also an evidently modern feature in a gallery running round the nave, at the spring of the roof arches, supported on iron brackets let into the wall, and with a light iron grille front.

So far this splendid building is safe ; we may hope that some day the later accretions may be removed, and let it stand out as the paternal focus of the Jewish race, which alone has any right in the tombs of their patriarchs.

Photographs are given of the lower part of a large building, about a mile N. of Hebron, known as Ramet el Khallil, and it is attributed to Roman work. Certainly it is not Herodian, as there is none of the usual drafting of the joints. The dressing of the blocks is with long strokes of a single-pointed pick ; whereas Roman work is dressed by the claw-tool, or comb-pick, which is first seen at the Parthenon, and is a mark of Roman age in the East. The later lining blocks of the megalith building of Ramet are dressed with a comb-pick, and have remains of inscriptions of the IIIrd century A.D. The great door was 9 feet wide, with sloping sides. It seems impossible to assign this work to the Roman age, and it ought to be easy to clear in and around it and seek for evidence of its history. Some day it will be seized on as a holy place, and then be made inaccessible to research.

FLINDERS PETRIE.

REGNAL YEARS AND CALENDAR YEARS IN EGYPT.

WHEN Mariette made his wonderful discovery of the Serapeum at Memphis and brought to light the steles of the Apis bulls, it was at once perceived that the new material was of enormous importance for the later chronology of the Egyptian kings, and especially for that of the XXVIth dynasty. It is well known that these documents, by giving the dates of birth and death of the bulls expressed in regnal years, together with the length of life of the animals, enable us to calculate, within very close limits, the lengths of the various reigns. About this there was never any room for difference of opinion ; but it has been claimed by two recent historians of Ancient Egypt— Prof. Petrie and Prof. Breasted—that the data also prove that the regnal years and the calendar years were assimilated ; that is to say, year 2 commenced on the New Year's Day following the king's accession and not on the anniversary of the accession as with a true regnal year. It is hoped to show in this paper that the information conveyed by the Apis steles and by somewhat similar inscriptions referring to the lives of men cannot be made to yield any such conclusion, though the assumption is very probably in accordance with the fact.

It will be convenient first of all to set out for reference in tabular form the data contained in the Apis steles to the end of the XXVIth dynasty.

IN THE XXVITH DYNASTY.

Dealing first with the XXVIth dynasty, we find the view to be here examined expressed by Prof. Petrie thus : " The absence of odd months and days for the lengths of reign (except irregularities)[1] shows that the dates

[1] The irregularities referred to by Prof. Petrie are those resulting from some scribes counting and others not counting the epagomenal days included in the broken period after the last complete year, and also from some omitting and some including the day of birth in the length of life.

Apis.	Date of Birth.				Date of Installation.				Age at Installation. Days.	Date of Death.				Date of Burial.				Age at Death.		
	King	Y.	M.	D.	King	Y.	M.	D.		King	Y.	M.	D.	King	Y.	M.	D.	Y.	M.	D.
30	Sheshenq III (II in Gauthier)	28			Sheshenq III (II in Gauthier)	28	2	1						Panay	2	6	1	(25)		
33	Sheshenq IV	11			Sheshenq IV	12	8	4						Sheshenq IV	37	3	27	(25)		
37	Taharqa	26	6	19	Taharqa	26	8	9		Psamtek I	20	12	20	Psamtek I	21	2	25	21		
39	Psamtek I	53	2	7	Psamtek I	54	3	12	268	Nekau	16	2	6	Nekau	16	4	16	16	7	6
40	Nekau	16	1	7	Psamtek II	1	11	9	272	Apries	12	8	12	Apries	12	10	21	17	5	
41	Aāhmes	5			Aāhmes	5	10	18	281	Aāhmes	23	7	6	Aāhmes	23	9	15	18		6

All the figures in the Table are taken from the Apis steles except the ages at installation, which are calculated (see post).

The months in the dates have, for convenience, been indicated by numbers. For instance, "Psamtek II 1.11.9," means the ninth day of Epiphi in the king's first year, when he had probably reigned no more than a few days; not a period of one year, eleven months, and nine days.

The numbers assigned to the Apises are those given by Mariette in Le Sérapéum de Memphis. The ages in loops are fixed by length of reigns.

The Bibliography will be found in Gauthier, Le Livre des Rois d'Égypte, Vol. III, pp. 363, 370, 373-4 ; Vol. IV, pp. 34, 69-118.

are in fixed months of the year, and that the years were counted from New Year's Day."[1]

Prof. Breasted shows us in detail how this result is arrived at. Referring to Apis 39, he writes :—

" This stela furnishes the data for computing the exact length of Psamtik I's reign. Having lived sixteen years seven months and seventeen days, this Apis died in the sixteenth year of Necho, on the sixth of the second month. The bulk of his life fell in the reign of Necho, and he was only one year, six months, and eleven days old at the accession of Necho.[2] This period of his life thus coincided with the last year, six months and eleven days of Necho's predecessor, Psamtik I. Now, the Apis was born in the fifty-third year of Psamtik I, on the nineteenth of the sixth month ; hence the total length of Psamtik I's reign was the sum of

$$52 \text{ years, } 5 \text{ months, } 19 \text{ days}$$
$$\text{and } \quad 1 \quad ,, \quad 6 \quad ,, \quad 11 \quad ,,$$
$$\text{or} \quad 54 \text{ years, } 0 \text{ months, } 0 \text{ days.}$$

" This would indicate that Psamtik ruled an even number of complete years, but we cannot suppose that Psamtik I died on the last day of the year ; it is evident that he died in the fifty-fifth year of his reign, and that the fraction of that incomplete year was, after his death, included in the first year of his successor Necho. It is thus clear that the years of the king's reign in the XXVIth dynasty began on New Year's Day."[3]

The result of the calculation comes out so neatly at exactly 54 years, without any odd months or days, that the reader is apt at first to assume that the conclusion drawn from it is correct ; but in truth there is no connection at all between the arithmetical result arrived at, and the fact which it is supposed to prove. Let us imagine for a moment that the figures which Prof. Breasted discusses belonged to the XVIIIth instead of to the XXVIth dynasty. The figures being the same, and the same method being applied to them, the result must be the same ; in other words, we can prove that " the years of the king's reign in the [Eighteenth] dynasty began on New Year's Day." Neither Prof. Breasted nor anyone else would admit this to be true, seeing that we have the clearest evidence that the years of the king at that time were true regnal years, exactly like the years of our English kings. Wherein does the fallacy lie ? Clearly in the failure to observe that from the nineteenth of the sixth month in one year to the sixth of the second month in some other year *must* be a period of a certain number of years plus seven months and seventeen days.[4] The method of counting the king's years has not the smallest bearing on the matter. For the argument to be valid it would be necessary to have a system

---

[1] *A History of Egypt*, Vol. III, p. 339.

[2] Prof. Breasted does not say how this figure is reached, and an explanation may make the argument more easy to follow. When the bull died on 16.2.6 of Necho, the king had reigned (assuming an assimilated year) 15 years, 1 month, and 6 days ; and this being deducted from the 16 years, 7 months, and 17 days of the bull's life leaves 1 year, 6 months and 11 days. Similarly, when he was born on 53.6.19 of Psamtek I, the king had reigned 52 years, 5 months, and 19 days.

[3] *Ancient Records*, Vol. IV, p. 497.

[4] The bull really lived five days longer, the scribe not having counted the epagomenal days.

of "regnal months" running with the regnal year. Needless to say, the complications arising out of a regnal year distinct from the calendar year were not rendered still more troublesome by the use of "regnal months." The 1st January of the thirteenth year of George V means the 1st January, 1923, not the first day of King George's thirteenth year. Similarly in Egypt, the first of the first month meant the first day of the *calendar* year, no matter where it might happen to fall in the regnal year. Therefore the only possible difference in calculating a period of time by the calendar year and by the regnal year is in the number of *years*.

The argument may be further illustrated by a consideration of the famous Obelisk Inscription of Queen Hatshepsut.[1] In this we are told that the work on the obelisk occupied from the first of the sixth month in the fifteenth year to the thirtieth of the twelfth month in the sixteenth year, "making seven months." From this statement we see that the work was proceeding during the last seven months of a calendar year ; and, as these seven months were divided between two regnal years, it is clear that the queen used a true regnal year commencing at some time between the second of the sixth month and the thirtieth of the twelfth month (both inclusive). It should be noted, however, that, while the fact of the regnal year changing within this period proves that it was not assimilated to the calendar year, the fact that it did not change within these seven months would not have proved that it was. Since there are many other days on which it might have changed besides New Year's Day, the assimilation would be a possibility merely. Let us suppose now that we had the text as it stands, but with the omission of the statement that the time occupied was seven months. There would then be two possible views (and two only). Either the whole period was comprised within one calendar year, and therefore amounted to seven months ; or it commenced in one calendar year and finished in the next, and therefore amounted to *one year* and seven months. To state the conclusion as a general proposition, if we are dealing with dates expressed in regnal years, and do not know when the regnal year commenced, we *may* be a year wrong in our estimate of the time between any two days, but we shall not be wrong as to the odd months and days.

It by no means follows, however, from the foregoing argument that the regnal years of the XXVIth dynasty were *not* assimilated to the calendar years, and there is a very great probability that they *were*. Indeed, if there had been evidence for the period similar to that for the XVIIIth and XIXth dynasties, the argument we have criticised could hardly have been put forward at all. We proceed, then, to a consideration of the chronological data in detail.

(1) Apis 37 died on 20.12.20, and was buried on 21.2.25 of Psamtek I. There being a regular interval of seventy days between the death and burial of an Apis, we know that the second date must have been in the *calendar* year immediately following the death. Therefore the regnal year changed between 12.20 and 2.25.

(2) Apis 41 was born on 5.1.7 and installed on 5.10.18 of Aāhmes. These dates, being necessarily in the same calendar year, prove that the regnal year did not change between 1.7 and 10.18, and therefore must have changed between 10.19 and 1.6 (both inclusive).

(3) Psamtek III must have had a very short reign (six months according to Manetho), and yet the only dated document of his time is of the fifth month

[1] Gauthier, *Livre des Rois*, Vol. II, p. 238.

H

of the *second* year.[1] The obvious explanation is that he came to the throne late in the calendar year, and commenced to count his second year from the following New Year's Day.

(4) A difficulty is introduced by the stele of the third year of Aāhmes, recounting his conflict with the dethroned Apries.[2] Line 1 of this document commences with the date 3.10 (without day), while line 14 commences with the date 3.3.8. If, as has been hitherto assumed, the second date is later in time than the first, the regnal year could not have changed between 10.19 and 1.6, as it must have done according to the evidence cited in (2). It has been proposed to explain the contradiction by supposing that the assimilation of the regnal and calendar years was adopted by the people for practical convenience, but was not followed in state records. This seems to be altogether too modern a view. From the Egyptian standpoint, it is likely that the Apis steles were just as much state documents as the stele of the year 3.[3] It may be suggested that the real solution is that the date 3.10 is that of the making of the stele, and therefore *followed* 3.3.8. The fact that no day is specified strongly supports this view, as the making of a stele could not well be attributed to any precise day.[4] The famous Piankhy stele commences with a date that contains no day, and later has specific dates, exactly like the stele under discussion; and various opinions have been held as to the significance of the first date.[5] Doubtless in both cases the opening date is that of the making of the stele.

In the XXIInd to XXVth Dynasties.

Unfortunately, the Apis steles do not give us the same amount of information for the period preceding the XXVIth dynasty, but what there is tends to show that the system of counting by true regnal years continued to the end of the XXVth dynasty. A reference to the table above shows that Apis 39 was installed at the age of 268 days, Apis 40 at 272 days, and Apis 41 at 281 days, an average age of 275 days.[6] We do not know the age at which the first three Apises in the table were installed, but we may reasonably suppose that it was somewhere near the 275 days indicated by the later information. If this be so, the Apis installed on 28.2.1 of Sheshenq III was born about 28.5.1 ; and that installed on 26.8.9 of Taharqa was born about 26.11.9.[7] As, therefore, in both cases the animal must have been born in the calendar year before the installation, while birth and installation were in the same regnal year, the latter was not assimilated to the calendar year.

[1] Gauthier, *loc. cit.*, Vol. IV, p. 131.

[2] Gauthier, *loc. cit.*, Vol. IV., p. 114.

[3] It will be seen later that there is good ground for believing that the assimilation came in with the XXVIth dynasty, and therefore almost certainly by royal authority.

[4] It has been contended that when a month is written without specifying a day, the *first* day of the month is meant. This may be true in some cases, but is hardly likely to be so always.

[5] Gauthier, *Livre des Rois*, Vol. IV, p. 2.

[6] In the case of Apises 39 and 40 the age *might* have been one year more ; for Apis 41 only can we be certain of the exact interval between birth and installation. It is sufficient for the argument that the bulls were *not less* than the ages given above.

[7] Apis 33 was born in the regnal year preceding his installation, which is consistent with either system of reckoning the regnal years.

To sum up, the Apis steles afford no conclusive evidence for either period. But, as the whole of the data for the XXVIth dynasty (with one easily explicable exception) are at the least consistent with an assimilated regnal year, while the data for the preceding period are apparently inconsistent with it, we may conclude that the assimilated year was introduced by Psamtek I.

F. W. READ.

REVIEW.

Academie des Inscriptions. Comptes Rendus, 1923, Mars-Avril.

Fouilles de Byblos.—A little sketch plan is given of the temple site as far as uncovered. The entrance was between two columns 7 feet apart. Before them are on one side the bases of three seated figures, and on the other side the base of a statue. Entering a hall, there is on one hand a large oval tank, 23 by 20 feet ; on the other side is a space with remains of statuary. So far there is no dating for these remains.

A site a hundred feet away is that of the so-called Phoenician temple. Here two columns are 15 feet apart. Under the pavement was a jar in the ground in the line of the axis between the columns ; it was half full of beads of carnelian, crystal, glaze, bronze, silver and gold, which formed collars. On one bead is " Life of Ra " in hieroglyphics. Many rings were found with bezels of carnelian, crystal, bronze, bone and soft stone ; more than a hundred scarabs were also set, cut in carnelian, crystal and bone. There were eight diadems, one silver and seven bronze, bands with bosses. A hundred clothes-pins, with a hole through the middle to tie them on (*Tools and Weapons*, lxii, N 14–18), aecompanied a hundred rings of wire, 2 to 4 inches across, which it is supposed served to pull clothing through before pinning it. A disc of gold is ornamented with filigrain work, in circles and crescents. There were also a silver cup, two cups and two vases of bronze, and many statuettes in stone, bone and bronze (? copper). Three small cylinders of stone are engraved in Cypriote style. A small plaque has hieroglyphs of the " sealer of Horus of the south and north " (Horus and Set). There were also two other foundation deposits, with vases of Pepy I, a vase of Pepy II in the form of a baboon with young, " discs of offerings " in alabaster and breccia, blue paste figure of baboon, quartz gaming pieces, a little gold sistrum, a copper chisel, votive axes of polished stone and flint knives. All of these should be published as soon as possible, for, being grouped in three deposits, they are of similar age and any one will serve to date the rest. It is a discovery which may be the foundation of Syrian archaeology if it is properly utilised. Above the pavement were many fragments of Egyptian sculpture, a head in basalt, the point of an obelisk, a cartouche of Usarkon and other fragments. The whole work seems to be carried on in a slow and insufficient manner, and the account is vague and without any dating by style or precise statement of character.

H 2

NOTES AND NEWS.

THE work of the British School at Qau will be continued this winter, especially the search for the source of the most ancient human remains which were found last season. The cemetery where the oldest Coptic MS. of St. John's Gospel was found will be completely explored, and the prehistoric cemeteries to the north will be worked in the hope of finding more of the strange group of ripple pottery and its associated styles. For this there will be a large party of workers. Mr. and Mrs. Brunton, M. Bach and Mr. Starkey have left already ; the Director leaves at once, with Mr. Greenlees, Lieutenant Wheeler, and Mr. Yeivin ; Mrs. Benson is also taking up work at the camp ; Miss Caton Thompson comes as a student of the School, after her work at Cambridge, to deal with the palaeolithic remains. Lady Petrie is detained in London, but will continue working for the increased support required for these excavations.

The papyrus of the Gospel of St. John has been completely opened, photographed and mounted. It will be placed in the collection of the British and Foreign Bible Society, in Queen Victoria Street ; in return for this a donation has been given which will provide for the complete publication of full-sized photograph of the 84 pages, transcription in Coptic type, and discussion of the results. As it is not only the oldest Biblical Coptic MS., but is older than any Greek MS. of the Gospel except the Vaticanus, it will be of great textual value. The fine writing of it shows that it was carefully transcribed. We are most fortunate to have enlisted the help of Sir Herbert Thompson to edit and discuss the text. The volume will be issued as the second volume of this year to all regular subscribers of two guineas.

The scale of work of the School involves heavy expense for travelling—about £700 yearly—owing to the great rise of fares. This, and collateral expenses, are all needful before the cost of excavating and transport can be dealt with. It is only by an increase of subscribers for the volumes of publications that such heavy costs can be met.

At the Tombs of the Kings, Mr. Carter, Mr. Mace, and their assistants are dealing with the very difficult problems of managing the vast treasure house of Tutankhamen.

Mr. Griffith and Mr. Newton are at Tell el Amarna, to carry on the excavations of the Egypt Exploration Society.

All Europeans in the Egyptian Government service are to leave by 1926, and therefore the English Inspectors will retire, and the monuments be left entirely to native protection. The recent letters of Sir Martin Conway in *The Times* are not reassuring as to the future of the treasures of Egypt.

The Palestine Exploration Fund has undertaken important work at Jerusalem, clearing part of Mount Ophel, south of the Temple area. Prof. Macalister and Mr. Duncan are carrying on the excavations.

The work at Kish is progressing under Captain Mackay.

In the review, p. 87, of Mr. Kendrick's Catalogue, No. 780 should be stated as correctly described, but two blocks were transposed by the printer.

INDEX.

Supplied in the last part of every fourth year.

1920 marked as E, 1921 as F, 1922 as G, 1923 as H.

(1918, 1919 suspended during the War.)

Letters are used for clearness along with the page numbers.
All entries are to be understood as referring to Egypt.
Books and articles are referred to by subject, and not *verbatim*.
This index will serve for the foreign periodicals, 1920-1923, as every ancient name is entered.
1914 Part I is out of print and cannot be supplied.

Lightning Source UK Ltd.
Milton Keynes UK
UKHW021805240419
341549UK00012B/218/P